SAMS *Teach Yourself*

Internet and Web Basics

All in One

Ned Snell
Bob Temple
T. Michael Clark

SAMS *201 West 103rd St., Indianapolis, Indiana, 46290 USA*

Sams Teach Yourself Internet and Web Basics All in One

Copyright © 2003 by Sams Publishing

International Standard Book Number: 0-672-32533-0

Library of Congress Catalog Card Number: 2003102938

Printed in the United States of America

First Printing: May 2003

06   05   04   03   4   3   2

Trademarks

Warning and Disclaimer

Bulk Sales

Sams Publishing offers excellent discounts on this book when ordered in quantity for bulk purchases or special sales. For more information, please contact:

U.S. Corporate and Government Sales
1-800-382-3419
corpsales@pearsontechgroup.com

For sales outside of the U.S., please contact:

International Sales
+1-317-581-3793
international@pearsontechgroup.com

ACQUISITIONS EDITOR
Betsy Brown

DEVELOPMENT EDITORS
Lorna Gentry
Damon Jordan

MANAGING EDITOR
Charlotte Clapp

PROJECT EDITOR
Tonya Simpson

INDEXER
Heather McNeil

PROOFREADER
Suzanne Thomas

TEAM COORDINATOR
Vanessa Evans

DESIGNER
Gary Adair

PAGE LAYOUT
Kelly Maish

Contents at a Glance

Introduction   1

PART I Internet Basics   **3**

Chapter 1   What Is the Internet and What Can You Do There?   5

2   What Hardware and Software Do You Need?   19

3   Getting Connected to the Internet   35

4   Basic Browsing   57

5   Sending and Receiving Email   79

6   Chatting and Instant Messenger   103

7   Participating in Newsgroups and Mailing Lists   121

8   Using Internet Explorer 6   151

9   Using Netscape Navigator 6   169

10   Using AOL 6   185

11   Plug-In and Add-On Programs   199

12   Searching   213

13   Downloading Programs and Files   245

14   Enjoying Safe Family Fun and Games   263

15   Buying and Selling on the Net   279

16   Going Wireless   293

PART II Using a Free Web-Authoring Program   **305**

Chapter 17   Understanding Web Authoring   307

18   Getting Started with a Web Authoring Program   323

19   Choosing a Title, Text Colors, and Other Page Basics   335

20   Adding, Editing, and Formatting Text   345

21   Formatting Text   365

22   Organizing Text with Tables and Rules   381

23   Making Links   403

24   Using Links to Build a Web Site   433

25   Adding Pictures (and Picture Backgrounds)   445

26   Editing HTML   461

	27	Dividing a Page into Frames	477
	28	Designing Fill-in-the-Blanks Forms	489
	29	Putting Multiple Links in One Picture	501
	30	Publishing Your Page	511
	31	Developing Your Authoring Skills	531

Part III Creating Your Own Web Graphics with Paint Shop Pro 541

Chapter 32	Paint Shop Pro Basics, Tools, and Preferences	543
	33	Opening, Saving, and Printing Files	569
	34	Creating Your First Image	579
	35	Creating and Working with Selections	593
	36	Working with Deformations	607
	37	Drawing Tools and Techniques	617
	38	Painting Tools and Techniques	631
	39	Creating Cool Text Effects	647
	40	Applying Filters	665
	41	Retouching Your Images	679
	42	Preparing Your Graphics for the Web	693
	43	Buttons and Seamless Tiles	719
	44	Animation	733
	45	Advanced Animation	745
		Index	751

Contents

Introduction   **1**

Who We Wrote This Thing For 1

How This Book Is Organized 1

Things You Would Probably Figure Out by Yourself 2

    Instructions, Tips, and Terms 2

One More Thing… 2

PART I Internet Basics   **3**

CHAPTER 1 What Is the Internet and What Can You Do There?   **5**

Understanding the Net (Easy Version) 6

    A Little History Lesson 7

    What It Became 8

Making the Net Work: Clients and Servers 9

What Can You Do Through the Net? 10

    Browse the Web 10

    Exchange Messages 15

    Have a Discussion 16

    Chat 17

Summary 17

CHAPTER 2 What Hardware and Software Do You Need?   **19**

Modems—Wherein the Lack of Speed Kills 19

Choosing a Computer 22

    A PC for the Internet 24

    A Mac for the Internet 25

    Internet Appliances 26

    Other Internet Options 28

Getting Internet Software 30

    What Do You Need? 30

    Where Can You Get It? 31

    About the Suites: Microsoft Internet Explorer and Netscape 32

Summary 33

CHAPTER 3 Getting Connected to the Internet   **35**

Types of Internet Accounts 35

    Dial-Up Accounts 36

    Cable Internet and DSL (Broadband)? 36

    Email-Only Accounts 40

Who Can I Get Dial-up Access From? 40

    Commercial Online Services 41

    Internet Service Providers (ISPs) 44

    Free Internet! 45

    Finding a Local ISP 46

How Do I Choose a Dial-up Internet Plan? 47

Getting Connected 49

    Number, Username, and Password 49

    Using Supplied Software 50

    Why Use a Signup Program? 51

    Running a Typical Signup Program 51

Using the Connection Wizard on Your Own 52

    Running the Connection Wizard 54

    Connecting at Last 54

Summary 55

CHAPTER 4 Basic Browsing   **57**

About Your "Home Page" 58

Understanding Web Page Addresses 59

    Anatomy of a Web Address 61

Going Straight to Any Web Address 63

    Entering and Editing URLs 64

Basic Jumping Around 67

    Finding and Using Links 68

    Using Navigation Buttons: Back, Forward, Home, and Stop 69

Fussing with Frames 76

Summary 77

CHAPTER 5 Sending and Receiving Email   **79**

Types of Email Programs 80

Understanding Email Addresses 80

Setting Up Your Email Program 81

    Configuring Email 83

Getting Around in Your Email Program 84

    Choosing a Folder 85

    Displaying a Message 85

Composing and Sending a Message 87

    Writing Your Message 87

    Sending a Message 90

Receiving Messages 92

Replying and Forwarding 93

Using an Address Book 95
    Adding to Your Address Book 96
    Addressing a Message from the Address Book 97
Attaching Files to Email Messages 97
Using the Web for Email 100
Summary 102

CHAPTER 6 Chatting and Instant Messenger   103

Understanding Internet Chatting 104
Chatting Through Your Browser 105
    Finding Sites with Chat Rooms 105
    Chatting at Yahoo! 105
    The Chat Window 107
Chatting in AOL 109
    Using the People Connection 109
    Moving to Another Room 111
Using Microsoft Chat 112
Joining a Chat Room 113
    Choosing an Identity 114
    Entering a Room 116
What Is Instant Messenger? 118
    Sending "Instant" Messages 118
Summary 119

CHAPTER 7 Participating in Newsgroups and Mailing Lists   121

Getting Started with Newsgroups 121
    Configuring Your Newsreader 123
    Downloading the Newsgroups List 124
    Finding and Subscribing to Newsgroups 125
Reading Newsgroup Messages 129
Composing and Replying to Messages 130
The Basics of Mailing Lists 132
Working with Mailing Lists 132
    Subscribing to a Mailing List 133
    Composing the Subscription Message 134
    Reading the Welcome Message 135
    Contributing to a Mailing List 137
Online Communication Tips and Tricks 137
    Observing Proper Netiquette 138
    Adding Personality with Smileys and Shorthand 140
    Stopping Junk Email (Spam) 142
Summary 149

CHAPTER 8   Using Internet Explorer 6   **151**

Why Choose Internet Explorer? 151

Where and How to Get Internet Explorer 152

    Downloading the Latest Version 153

    Starting Up Internet Explorer 157

Features of Internet Explorer 158

    Basic Features of Explorer 6.0 158

    Using the Explorer Bar 160

    Working with Favorite Place 163

Setting Your Internet Options 165

    General Options 165

    Content Options 166

Summary 167

CHAPTER 9   Using Netscape Navigator 6   **169**

Why Choose Netscape Navigator? 170

Where and How to Get Netscape Navigator 170

    Download the Latest Version 170

    Starting Up Netscape Navigator 174

Features of Netscape Navigator 175

    Basic Features of Netscape 175

    Working with My Sidebar 176

    Changing Your Theme 179

Working with the Preferences 180

Working with Bookmarks 182

    Putting Bookmarks in Your Personal Toolbar 182

    Removing Bookmarks from the Personal Toolbar 184

Summary 184

CHAPTER 10   Using AOL 6   **185**

Understanding AOL 186

    Why Should I Choose AOL? 186

    Why Shouldn't I Choose AOL? 187

Taking a Quick Tour of AOL 188

    The Welcome Screen 188

    The Channels 189

    Getting Places, Saving Places 193

Where Can I Get the AOL Software? 194

Summary 197

CHAPTER 11   Plug-In and Add-On Programs   **199**

Understanding Plug-Ins, Java, and Other Programs in Pages 200

    Finding Plug-Ins and Helpers 201

    Installing and Using Plug-Ins and Helpers 202

Playing Audio and Video 203
    Playing Downloaded Audio or Video Files 204
    Playing "Streaming" Files 206
    Taking Advantage of Media Options in Internet Explorer 209
    Where Can I Get Streaming Audio/Video? 209
Downloading and Playing CD-Quality Music (MP3 Files) 210
    Getting MP3 Files 210
    Playing MP3 Files 211
Summary 212

CHAPTER 12 Searching   **213**

What's a Search Site? 213
Can I Really Search the Whole Web? 215
Where Are the Major Search Sites? 217
Simple Searching by Clicking Categories 218
    Why Use Categories Instead of a Search Term? 219
    Using a Directory 219
Understanding Searches 223
Phrasing a Simple Search 225
Phrasing a Serious Search 229
    Using Multiple Words in a Search Term 230
    Using Operators to Control Searches 231
    Conducting a Super Search 233
About Site Searches 233
Finding People 234
    Finding the People-Finding Sites 234
    Using People-Finders Through Your Email Program 238
    Finding People in America Online 239
    Other Folk-Finding Tips 241
Summary 243

CHAPTER 13 Downloading Programs and Files   **245**

What's Downloading, Anyhow? 246
    Click a Link, Get a File 246
    How Long Does Downloading Take? 247
Choosing Files You Can Use 251
    The Two File Types: Program and Data 251
    Common Data File Types on the Net 252
Finding Sites That Help You Find Files 253
    All-Purpose Shareware Sites 254
    Commercial Software Sites 258
Working with Zip Files 259

Watching Out for Viruses 260

Downloading Files in AOL 261

Summary 262

CHAPTER 14 Enjoying Safe Family Fun and Games   **263**

Choosing a Family Starting Point 264

Important Family Safety Steps 265

    Supervise! 265

    Don't Defeat Passwords 266

    Be Extra Careful with Broadband 266

    Resist Chat 267

Online Rules for Kids 268

Resources for Parents 268

Censoring Web Content 269

    Getting a Safe-Surfing Program 270

    Using Internet Explorer's Built-In Content Advisor 270

Using AOL's Parental Controls 275

Summary 277

CHAPTER 15 Buying and Selling on the Net   **279**

Shopping 'Til You Drop 279

    Using Accounts and Shopping Baskets 282

    Buying Stocks and Such 286

    Investment Starting Points 287

Finding All the Sites Online That Sell What You Want 288

Buying and Selling Through Online Auctions 289

    How Online Auction Houses Work 290

    Bidding Tips 291

    Selling Tips 291

    Using a Payment Service 292

Summary 292

CHAPTER 16 Going Wireless   **293**

What Is Wireless Internet/Email? 294

Real-Time Versus Synched 294

Hardware to Get You Going 296

    Wireless for Your Laptop 296

    Internet/Email into Your Cell Phone or Pager 297

    Handheld Computers 299

    Wireless Email Devices 301

    Phone/PDA Combination 301

Summary 303

PART II Using a Free Web-Authoring Program   305

CHAPTER 17 Understanding Web Authoring   307

Anatomy of a Web Page 308
    Parts You See 308
    Parts You Don't See 310
How a Web Page Works 312
Pictures, Sound, and Other Media 316
Extensions: Love 'Em!, Hate 'Em! 317
Ways to Organize a Web Site 318
Summary 322

CHAPTER 18 Getting Started with a Web Authoring Program   323

Opening Composer 324
Exploring the Composer Toolbars 325
Starting a New Web Page 327
Saving and Naming Web Page Files 327
Editing Pages You've Saved 329
Checking Out Your New Page in a Web Browser 331
Printing Pages 333
Summary 333

CHAPTER 19 Choosing a Title, Text Colors, and Other Page Basics 335

About Page Properties 336
Choosing an Effective Page Title 336
Helping Search Pages Catalog Your Page 339
Choosing Custom Colors for a Whole Page 340
Summary 344

CHAPTER 20 Adding, Editing, and Formatting Text   345

Understanding Paragraphs and Their Properties 346
Understanding What Each Paragraph Property Does 346
    Normal 346
    Headings (1–6) 347
    Address 348
    Formatted 348
Entering Text and Assigning Properties 350
    Entering Paragraphs by Typing 350
    Typing Symbols and Special Characters 350
    Copying Text from Another Document 351
    Assigning Paragraph Properties to Existing Text 354

Aligning and Indenting Text 357
    Aligning Paragraphs 357
    Indenting Paragraphs 359
    Adding Blank Line Spaces in a Page 359
Editing Your Text 360
    Highlighting Text 360
    Replacing Selected Text 360
    Deleting Selected Text 361
    Copying or Moving Selected Text 361
    Undoing Edits ("Goofs") 361
Checking Your Spelling 361
Tips for Good Text Design 363
Summary 363

CHAPTER 21 Formatting Text   **365**

Working with Lists 366
    Creating Basic Lists 367
    Changing the Look of a List 369
Dressing Up Text with Character Properties 372
    Choosing Fonts 373
    Choosing a Size for Text 374
    Making Text Bold, Italic, or Underlined 375
    Choosing the Color of Text 378
Summary 380

CHAPTER 22 Organizing Text with Tables and Rules   **381**

About Horizontal Lines 382
About Tables 385
    Table Basics 387
    Filling in the Table 389
    Editing and Formatting Tables 390
    Adding a Caption 394
    Creating Column and Row Headings 395
    Working with Rows, Columns, and Cells 395
    Turning Table-Type Text to a Table 398
    Using a Big Table to Control Page Layout 399
Summary 401

CHAPTER 23 Making Links   **403**

What's in a Link? 404
What's Linkable? 405
Web Pages 406
Anchors in Pages 406

Local Files 407
    Relative Pathnames 407
    Absolute Pathnames 409
    Other Internet Services 409
Creating New Links 413
Creating a Signature (Linking to Email) 416
Copying Links from Other Pages 418
Checking That Links Lead Where They're Supposed To 421
Editing Links 421
Delinking Text 422
Understanding Targets 423
Creating Targets in a Page 425
Deleting Targets 426
Linking to Targets 426
    Linking to a Target in the Same Page 427
    Linking to Targets in Other Pages Online 427
Creating Links that Download Files 429
Summary 431

CHAPTER 24 Using Links to Build a Web Site   **433**

The Basic Act: Linking One Page to Another 434
Linking from One Page to a Target in Another 436
Site-Design Tips 437
    Building a Multipage Linear Site 438
    Tips for Multipage Linear Site Design 439
    Working with One-Page Linear Pages 439
    Tips for One-Page Linear Design 440
    Making a Web-Style Site 441
    Tips for Web-Style Design 441
    Making a Hierarchical Site 442
    Tips for Hierarchical Design 443
Summary 444

CHAPTER 25 Adding Pictures (and Picture Backgrounds)   **445**

Inserting a GIF or JPEG Image in Composer 446
Using the Same Image Multiple Times 448
Deleting an Image 448
Choosing an Image's Size and Other Properties 448
    Changing the Dimensions (Size and Shape) of an Image 449
    Controlling Alignment 450
    Controlling Spacing and Borders 453
    Entering Alternative Text 454
Entering Images in Table Cells 454

Inserting Fancy Bullets and Rules 455
Using an Image as a Link 456
Adding a Picture Background 457
Summary 460

CHAPTER 26   Editing HTML   **461**

Reading an HTML File 462
Viewing the HTML Source Code of a Document 465
Using Composer to Insert an HTML Tag 466
Adding Attributes with the Composer Advanced Edit Buttons 466
Editing an HTML Source File Directly 467
About HTML Assistant Pro 468
Editing Composer Pages in HTML Assistant Pro 470
Using HTML Assistant Pro to Add Sound and Video to Your Web Pages 471
     Creating a Times Square-Style Animated Marquee 472
     Inserting an Inline Video Clip 473
Summary 475

CHAPTER 27   Dividing a Page into Frames   **477**

What Does It Take to Make a Frames Page? 478
     The Frame Definition Page 479
     The Frame Content 479
Using HTML Assistant Pro to Create a Frames Page 480
Creating Frames in HTML 483
Specifying the Frame in Which a Linked Page Opens 486
     Naming the Frames 486
     Making Links Point to Frame Names 486
Accommodating the Frame-Intolerant 487
Summary 488

CHAPTER 28   Designing Fill-in-the-Blanks Forms   **489**

Understanding Forms 490
Creating the Visible Form 491
     Building a Fast, Easy Form with a Template 491
     Adding Form Fields 496
     Customizing Fields 497
Summary 499

CHAPTER 29   Putting Multiple Links in One Picture   **501**

About Imagemaps 502
Server-Side Versus Client-Side 503
Choosing (or Creating) Images Suited for Imagemapping 504
Creating an Imagemap 505
Summary 509

CHAPTER 30 Publishing Your Page   **511**

About Web Servers 511

How Much Space Do I Need? 515

Preparing to Publish 516

Publishing from Composer 517

Viewing Your Page Through the Internet 519

Testing and Maintaining Your Page Online 519

Testing Your Pages 519

Evaluating Your Page's Ergonomics 528

Updating Your Page 529

Summary 530

CHAPTER 31 Developing Your Authoring Skills   **531**

Getting Your Own Domain (Your Own Dot-Com) 531

Advancing to New Authoring Tools and Techniques 535

Microsoft FrontPage 535

Macromedia Dreamweaver 537

The Future of Web Authoring: XHTML 537

How to Grow as a Web Author 539

Observe 539

Dissect 539

Summary 539

PART III Creating Your Own Web Graphics with Paint Shop Pro   541

CHAPTER 32 Paint Shop Pro Basics, Tools, and Preferences   **543**

Overview of New Features 544

Using Online Help 546

Overview of the Paint Shop Pro Interface 547

The Standard Toolbar 549

Other Toolbars 551

The Toolbox 551

The Arrow Tool 551

The Zoom Tool 552

The Deformation Tool 552

The Crop Tool 553

The Mover Tool 553

The Selection Tool 554

The Freehand Tool 554

The Magic Wand Tool 554

The Dropper Tool 555

The Paint Brush 555

The Clone Brush 555
The Color Replacer 555
The Retouch Tool 556
Scratch Remover 556
The Eraser Tool 556
The Picture Tube 556
The Airbrush Tool 556
The Flood Fill Tool 556
The Text Tool 557
The Draw Tool 557
The Preset Shapes Tool 557
The Object Selector Tool 557
The Menus 558
The File Menu 558
The Edit Menu 558
The View Menu 559
The Image Menu 559
The Effects Menu 560
The Colors Menu 560
The Layers Menu 560
The Objects Menu 560
The Selections Menu 560
The Masks Menu 560
The Window Menu 561
The Help Menu 561
Using the Palettes 561
The Color Palette 562
The Tool Options Palette 562
The Layer Palette 563
The Tool Palette 564
The Overview Window 564
Setting Preferences 564
General Program Preferences 565
CMYK Conversion Preferences 565
File Format Preferences 566
File Format Associations 566
File Locations Preferences 566
Color Management Preferences 567
Monitor Gamma Adjustments 567
Autosave Settings 568
Summary 568

CHAPTER 33 Opening, Saving, and Printing Files   **569**

Opening a File 569
    Opening a New File 569
    Opening an Existing File 570
    Browsing for an Existing File 571
Importing Files 572
Saving Files 573
Exporting Files 573
Printing Basics 574
Multi-Image Printing 576
Summary 577

CHAPTER 34 Creating Your First Image   **579**

Issues to Consider Before Constructing an Image 579
    Choosing an Image Size 580
    Choosing an Image Type 580
Creating a Simple Image 582
    Using the Preset Shapes Tool 582
    Avoiding Aliased Images 584
    Using Brush Tips 586
Editing a Simple Image 587
Fixing Errors 591
Summary 592

CHAPTER 35 Creating and Working with Selections   **593**

Using the Selection Tools 593
    The Selection Tool 594
    The Freehand Tool 594
    The Magic Wand Tool 598
Editing Selections 600
    Adding to a Selection 600
    Subtracting from a Selection 601
    Expanding and Contracting a Selection 603
    Growing a Selection 603
    Selecting Similar Areas 604
    Loading and Saving Selections 604
Summary 605

CHAPTER 36 Working with Deformations   **607**

Using the Deformation Tool 607
    Rotating Text 610
    Using the Perspective, Shear, and Distort Options 611
    Adding a Shadow Effect 614
Summary 616

CHAPTER 37 Drawing Tools and Techniques   **617**

The Drawing Tools and Their Options 617

Drawing Shapes 619

Drawing Lines 624

  The Single Line Tool 624

  The Bézier Curve Line Tool 627

Summary 629

CHAPTER 38 Painting Tools and Techniques   **631**

Painting and Drawing with the Paint Brush Tool 631

  Using the Tool Controls 632

  Custom Brush Tips 635

  Using Patterns and Textures 636

Using the Airbrush Tool 637

Using the Flood Fill Tool 638

  Filling an Area with a Solid Color 638

  Filling with a Gradient 639

  Creating and Editing Multicolored Gradients 639

  Filling with a Pattern 643

Learning the Mysteries of the Clone Brush Tool 644

Summary 645

CHAPTER 39 Creating Cool Text Effects   **647**

Using the Text Tool 647

Creating Wooden Textured Text 649

Creating Chrome Text 652

Adding a Drop Shadow 654

Adding a Glow to Your Text 657

Creating Text on a Path 658

Vector Text 661

Summary 663

CHAPTER 40 Applying Filters   **665**

Why Filters? 666

Where You Can Get Plug-ins 666

Using Built-In Filters 667

  Buttonize Filter 667

  Chisel Filter 668

  Cutout Filter 668

  Drop Shadow Filter 669

  Filter Effects with Layer Blending Mode Variations 671

Using Third-Party Filters 672

  Installing Plug-ins 672

  Alien Skin's Eye Candy 673

Auto F/X's Photo/Graphic Edges 674
Flaming Pear's BladePro 675
Other Plug-ins 677
Summary 677

CHAPTER 41   Retouching Your Images   679

Using the Retouching Tools 679
Fixing the Brightness and Contrast 680
Removing Dust Marks and Scratches 681
Using the Unsharp Mask Filter 684
Retouching to Remove Portions of an Image 686
Summary 691

CHAPTER 42   Preparing Your Graphics for the Web   693

Working with File Formats 694
GIFs 695
GIFs: The Good, the Bad, and the Ugly 695
Transparent GIFs 696
Saving Transparent GIFs with Paint Shop Pro 698
JPGs 700
Did You Lose Something? 701
Why Use JPG? 704
Adjusting the Compression Factor on a JPG Image 704
Removing Artifacts from a JPG Image 705
GIF or JPG? 706
Adjusting Color Depth 707
8-Bit Color 707
16-Bit Color 707
24-Bit Color 707
Using Palettes 708
Problems with Limited Palettes 708
How to Build or Select a Palette 708
Exact Palette 709
Adaptive Palette 710
Web Palette 710
Loading a Palette 711
Previewing Your Images in SmartSaver 711
Understanding Dithering 712
Understanding Anti-aliasing 714
Aliasing 714
Anti-aliasing 716
Summary 718

CHAPTER 43 Buttons and Seamless Tiles   **719**

   Creating Buttons 719
      Ordinary Buttons 720
      More Elaborate Buttons 720
      Complex 3D Textured Buttons 722
      Using the Buttonize Effect 725
   Creating Seamless Tiles 726
      The Basics of Seamless Tiles 726
      Creating Seamless Tiles with Paint Shop Pro 728
      Using the Convert to Seamless Pattern Option 730
   Summary 732

CHAPTER 44 Animation   **733**

   Animation Concepts 733
   Why Use Animation? 734
   Building an Animation 734
      Creating Your First Animation 735
      Saving and Previewing an Animation in Your Web Browser 738
      Editing Your First Animation 739
      Using the Mover Tool to Edit the Animation 740
   Using Transitions 741
   Creating Text Effects 743
   Summary 743

CHAPTER 45 Advanced Animation   **745**

   Using Layers and Masks in Animation 745
      Putting Your Own Spin on the World 746
      Creating the Animation 748
      Spreading Your Wings 749
   Summary 749

   Index   **751**

Lead Author

NED AVERILL-SNELL has been making technology make sense since 1986, when he began writing beginner's documentation for one of the world's largest software companies. After writing manuals and training materials for several major technology companies, Snell switched sides and became a computer journalist, serving as a writer and editor for two national magazines, *Edge* and *Art & Design News*.

A freelance writer since 1991, Snell has written more than two dozen computer books and hundreds of articles. Between books, Snell works as a professional actor in regional theater, commercials, and industrial films.

Contributors

BOB TEMPLE is the owner and president of Red Line Editorial, Inc., an editorial services and content services provider. He is a contributing author of *Sams Teach Yourself the Internet in 24 Hours, 2002 Edition*, and has written five other books on Internet-related topics, including three others for Sams Publishing. In addition, he is the author of 18 children's non-fiction books.

T. MICHAEL CLARK is an award-winning graphic artist who owns and operates GrafX Design, a popular Web site that features online tutorials for Paint Shop Pro, Photoshop, CorelDraw, and more. He is a moderator and member of i/us, the site for visual professionals, and is the author of *Sams Teach Yourself Paint Shop Pro 7 in 24 Hours*.

We Want to Hear from You!

As the reader of this book, *you* are our most important critic and commentator. We value your opinion and want to know what we're doing right, what we could do better, what areas you'd like to see us publish in, and any other words of wisdom you're willing to pass our way.

You can email or write me directly to let me know what you did or didn't like about this book—as well as what we can do to make our books stronger.

Please note that I cannot help you with technical problems related to the topic of this book, and that due to the high volume of mail I receive, I might not be able to reply to every message.

When you write, please be sure to include this book's title and author as well as your name and phone or email address. I will carefully review your comments and share them with the author and editors who worked on the book.

Email: consumer@samspublishing.com
Mail: Mark Taber
           Associate Publisher
           Sams Publishing
           201 West 103rd Street
           Indianapolis, IN 46290 USA

Reader Services

For more information about this book or others from Sams Publishing, visit our Web site at www.samspublishing.com. Type the ISBN (excluding hyphens) or the title of the book in the Search box to find the book you're looking for.

Introduction

Welcome to *Sams Teach Yourself Internet and Web Basics All in One*, the book that gets you into and all around the Internet and Web authoring all in one volume.

Who We Wrote This Thing For

We've designed this book for people who:

- Are new to the Internet
- Want to create great-looking Web pages without having to get a computer science degree
- Want to personalize their Web pages with beautiful, custom graphics and animations
- Don't appreciate being treated like imbeciles

By the way, being new to the Internet doesn't mean you're an idiot or dummy. You just have other priorities. Good for you.

You do not need to know a thing about the Internet, Web authoring, computer networks, or any of that stuff to get started with this book. However, you do need to know your way around your own computer. With a basic, everyday ability to operate your computer, you're ready to begin. We'll take you the rest of the way.

How This Book Is Organized

This book is divided into three parts:

- Part I, "Internet Basics," introduces you to the Net and the many different things you can do there—Web browsing, email, chat…the works.
- Part II, "Using a Free Web-Authoring Program," introduces you to creating your own Web pages and sites, and publishing them online. You'll do it with a free, easy-to-use program called Netscape Composer.
- Part III, "Creating Your Own Web Graphics with Paint Shop Pro," shows how you can create your own pictures—and even animations!—with the popular and powerful graphics program Paint Shop Pro. You can use the pictures you create in the Web pages you'll design in Parts II and IV, or anywhere else you need slick, professional-looking graphics.

Things You Would Probably Figure Out by Yourself

There's a long tradition in computer books of using the introduction to explain the little tip boxes and other page elements that are absolutely self-explanatory to any reader over the age of six. Just call us "Keeper of the Flame."

Instructions, Tips, and Terms

Here and there, we use step-by-step instructions to show you exactly how to do something. We will always explain how to do that thing in the text that precedes the steps, so feel free to skip the steps when you want to. However, anytime you feel like you don't completely understand something, do the steps, and you'll probably get the picture before you're done. Sometimes we learn only by doing.

You'll also see three different kinds of handy advice set off in boxes:

A Tip box points out a faster, easier way to do something, or a cooler way. These boxes are completely optional.

A Note box pops out an important consideration or interesting tidbit related to the topic at hand. They're optional, too, but always worth reading. (Otherwise, we wouldn't interrupt.)

A Caution box alerts you to actions and situations where something bad could happen, like accidentally deleting an important file. Because there's very little you can do with this book that's in any way dangerous (except dropping it on your toe), you'll see very few Cautions. So when you see 'em, take 'em seriously.

One More Thing...

Actually, no more things. Dive in. The water's fine. And don't forget: Have fun!

Part I
Internet Basics

Chapter   1   What Is the Internet and What Can You Do There?

2   What Hardware and Software Do You Need?

3   Getting Connected to the Internet

4   Basic Browsing

5   Sending and Receiving Email

6   Chatting and Instant Messenger

7   Participating in Newsgroups and Mailing Lists

8   Using Internet Explorer 6

9   Using Netscape Navigator 6

10   Using AOL 6

11   Plug-In and Add-On Programs

12   Searching

13   Downloading Programs and Files

14   Enjoying Safe Family Fun and Games

15   Buying and Selling on the Net

16   Going Wireless

CHAPTER 1

What Is the Internet and What Can You Do There?

You probably think you already know what the Internet is. And you're probably 90 percent right, for all practical purposes. But by developing just a little better understanding of what the Net's all about, you'll find learning to use it much easier.

You don't need to know exactly how the Net works to use it, any more than you need to know the mechanics of an engine to drive a car. This chapter is not about the tiny, techie details of how the Net works. Rather, this chapter is designed to give you some helpful background—and perhaps dispel a few myths and misconceptions—so you can jump confidently into the stuff coming up in later chapters.

If some of the information in this chapter seems a little—shall we say—elementary, I'm sorry. But it's a good idea to have a basic understanding of the Internet before you jump headlong into it. So if I cover some things that you already know, well, then you're ahead of the game!

Understanding the Net (Easy Version)

No doubt you've heard of a computer network, a group of computers that are wired together so that they can communicate with one another. When computers are hooked together in a network, users of those computers can send each other messages and share computer files and programs.

Computer networks today can be as small as two PCs hooked together in an office. They can be as big as thousands of computers of all different types spread all over the world and connected to one another not just by wires, but through telephone lines and even through the air via satellite.

To build a really big network, you build lots of little networks and then hook the networks to each other, creating an internetwork. That's all the Internet really is: the world's largest internetwork (hence its name). In homes, businesses, schools, and government offices all over the world, millions of computers of all different types—PCs, Macintoshes, big corporate mainframes, and others—are connected together in networks, and those networks are connected to one another to form the Internet. Because everything's connected, any computer on the Internet can communicate with any other computer on the Internet (see Figure 1.1).

FIGURE 1.1

The Internet is a global internetwork, a huge collection of computers and networks interconnected so they can exchange information.

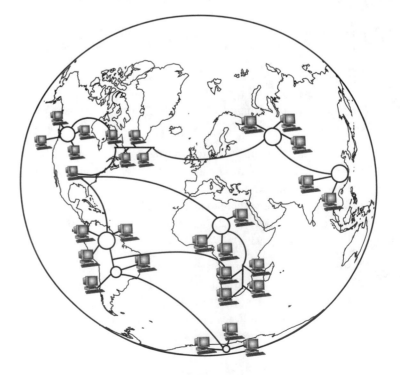

A Little History Lesson

The successful launch of Sputnik by the Soviets in 1957 might have triggered the space race, but it also helped bring about the Internet (although somewhat indirectly). In part because of Sputnik, the Advanced Research Projects Agency (ARPA) was formed as part of the U.S. Department of Defense, also in 1957.

Among other things, ARPA created research centers at a number of universities across the country. It soon became clear that these research centers needed to be able to communicate with each other through some type of infrastructure. The first four sites to be connected were at the University of California-Los Angeles (UCLA), the Stanford Research Institute, the University of California-Santa Barbara (UCSB), and the University of Utah.

Because this first network was military-oriented, the distribution of information through it was highly secretive. A system of splitting data into tiny "packets" that took different routes to the same destination was developed to make it more difficult to "eavesdrop" on these transmissions. It is this method of "packet switching" that allows the Internet to function as it does today: Large numbers of computers can go down, and data can still be transferred.

By 1969, new research into networking was being conducted. Standard systems of networking were needed in order for computers to be able to communicate with each other. Over time, a system known as TCP/IP was developed; it became the standard protocol for internetworking in 1982.

> TCP/IP is an abbreviation for the Internet's fundamental communications system. It stands for Transmission Control Protocol/Internet Protocol, but you don't need to know that unless you think it will impress your friends. (Pronounce it "tee see pee eye pee," and say it real fast.)

Because all these internetworks communicated in the same way, they could communicate with one another, too. The government, defense contractors, and scientists often needed to communicate with one another and share information, so they hooked all of their computers and networks into one big TCP/IP internetwork. And that fat internetwork was the infant Internet.

When you use a computer that's connected to the Internet, you can communicate with any other computer on the Internet.

But that doesn't mean you can access *everything* that's stored on the other computers. Obviously, the government, university, and corporate computers on the Net have the capability to make certain kinds of information on their computers accessible through the Internet and to restrict access to other information so that only authorized people can see it.

Similarly, when you're on the Net, any other computer on the Net can communicate with yours. However, that does not mean that someone can reach through the Net into your computer and steal your résumé and recipes.

What It Became

The first great thing about the Internet's design is that it's open to all types of computers. Virtually any computer—from a palmtop PC to a supercomputer—can be equipped with TCP/IP so it can get on the Net. And even when a computer doesn't use TCP/IP, it can access information on the Net using other technologies, "back doors" to the Net, so to speak.

The other important thing about the Net is that it allows the use of a wide range of communications media—ways computers can communicate. The "wires" that interconnect the millions of computers on the Internet include the wires that hook together the small networks in offices, private data lines, local telephone lines, national telephone networks (which carry signals via wire, microwave, and satellite), and international telephone carriers.

It is this wide range of hardware and communications options, and the universal availability of TCP/IP, that has enabled the Internet to grow so large so quickly. That's also why you can get online from your home or office, right through the same telephone line you use to call out for pizza. Heck, you can even get online from the neighborhood park using wireless technology. It's a crazy world.

When your computer has a live, open connection to the Internet, you and your computer are said to be *online*. When the Internet connection is closed, you're *offline*.

Making the Net Work: Clients and Servers

The key to doing anything on the Net is understanding two little words: "client" and "server." Figure 1.2 illustrates the relationship between clients and servers.

FIGURE 1.2

From your computer, you use a set of client programs, each of which accesses a different type of server computer on the Net.

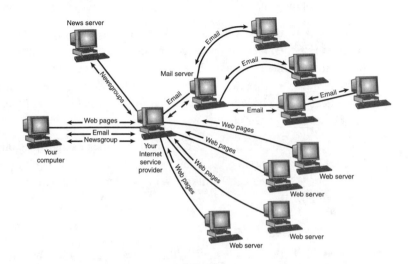

Most of the information you will access through the Internet is stored on computers called *servers*. A server can be any type of computer; what makes it a server is the role it plays: It stores information for use by clients.

A client is a computer—or, more accurately, a particular computer program—that knows how to communicate with a particular type of server to use the information stored on that server (or to put information there). For example, when you surf the Web, you use a client program called a Web browser to communicate with a computer where Web pages are stored—a Web server.

In general, each type of Internet activity involves a different type of client and server: To use the Web, you need a Web client program to communicate with Web servers. To use email, you need an email client program to communicate with email servers.

This client/server business shows what the Internet really is—just a communications medium, a virtual wire through which computers communicate. It's the different kinds of clients and servers—not the Net itself—that enable you to perform various activities. And because new kinds of clients and servers can be invented, new types of activities can be added to the Internet at any time.

What Can You Do Through the Net?

I've known people who have gone out and bought a PC, signed up for an Internet account, and then called me to say, "Okay, so I'm on the Internet. Now what am I supposed to do there?"

That's backward. I think the marketers and the press have pushed so hard that some folks simply think they must be on the Net, without knowing why, sort of the way everybody thinks they need a cell phone. But unless there's something on the Net you want or need to use, you don't need the Net. You shouldn't buy a rice steamer unless you like rice. You don't need a cell phone if you never leave the house. Don't let Madison Avenue and Microsoft push you around.

So, here's a good place to get a feel for what you can actually do on the Net. If nothing here looks like something you want to do, please give this book to a friend or to your local library. You can check out the Net again in a year or two, to see whether it offers anything new.

Browse the Web

It's very likely that your interest in the Internet was sparked by the World Wide Web, even if you don't know it. When you see news stories about the Internet showing someone looking at a cool, colorful screen full of things to see and do, that person is looking at the World Wide Web, most commonly referred to as "the Web" or occasionally as "WWW."

The term "the Web" is used so often by the media to describe and illustrate the Internet, many folks think the Web is the Internet. But it's not; it's just a part of the Net, or rather one of many Internet-based activities. The Web gets the most attention because it's the fastest-growing, easiest-to-use part of the Net.

All those funky-looking Internet addresses you see in ads today—www.pepsi.com and so forth—are the addresses you need to visit those companies on the Web. With an Internet connection and a Web browser on your computer, you can type an address to visit a particular Web site and read the Web pages stored there. (Figure 1.3 shows a Web page, viewed through a Web browser.)

Figure 1.3

Seen through a Web browser, a Web page is a file of information stored on a Web server.

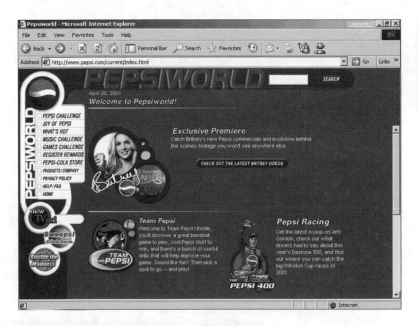

Web site and *Web page*. These terms are used flexibly, but, in general, a Web site is a particular Web server, or a part of a Web server, where a collection of Web pages about a particular organization or subject is stored.

When you use your Web browser to contact a Web site, the information on the server is displayed on your computer screen. The particular screenful of information you view is described as one Web page.

For example, the site shown in Figure 1.3 is one Web page from www.pepsi.com. All the pages that Pepsi has put up for you to see make up Pepsi's Web site.

By browsing the Web, you can do a staggering number of different things, including all the activities described in the following sections—and much, much more.

Visit Companies, Governments, Museums, Schools...

Just about any large organization has its own Web site these days. Many smaller organizations have their own sites, too, or are covered in pages stored on others' sites. You can visit these sites to learn more about products you want to buy, school or government policies, and much more.

For example, I belong to an HMO for medical coverage. I can visit my HMO's Web site to find and choose a new doctor, review policy restrictions, and much more. I can do this any day, any time, without waiting on hold for the "next available operator."

Just as easily, I can check out tax rules or order forms on the Internal Revenue Service Web site. Or view paintings in museums all over the world. Or find out when the next Parent's Night is at the local elementary school.

Read the News

CNN has its own Web site (see Figure 1.4), as do the *New York Times*, the *Wall Street Journal*, and dozens of other media outlets, ranging from major print magazines and fly-by-night rags spreading rumors, to small sites featuring news about any imaginable topic. You'll also find a number of great news sources that have no print or broadcast counter-part—they're exclusive to the Web.

FIGURE 1.4

CNN is among the up-to-the-minute news sources available on the Web.

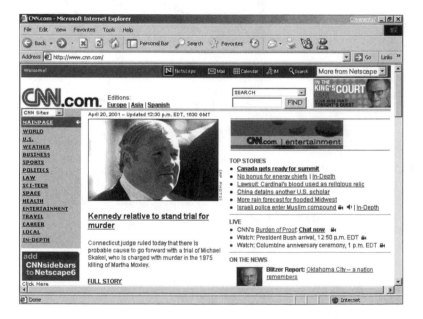

Whatever kind of news you dig, you can find it on the Web. And often, the news online is more up-to-the-minute than any print counterpart because unlike broadcast news, you can look at it any time you find convenient. Best of all, after you read a news story on the Web, no one ever says, "Thanks for that report, Carla. What a terrible tragedy."

1

Explore Libraries

Increasingly, libraries large and small are making their catalogs available online. That means I can find out which of the dozen libraries I use has the book I need, without spending a day driving to each. Some libraries even let you borrow online; you choose a book from the catalog of a library across the state, and in a few days you can pick it up at a library closer to you, or right from your mailbox.

Often, entire collections of works, scholarly papers, entire texts of books, research works, and more are available through libraries online.

Read

Books are published on the Web, including classics (Shakespeare, Dickens) and new works. You can read them right on your screen, or print them out to read later on the bus. (Please don't read while you drive. I hate that.) The Web has even initiated its own kind of literature, collaborative fiction, in which visitors to a Web site can read—and contribute to—a story in progress.

Get Software

Because computer software can travel through the Internet, you can actually get software right through the Web and use it on your PC. Some of the software is free; some isn't. But it's all there, whenever you need it—no box, no disc, no pushy guy at the electronics store saying, "Ya want a cell phone with that? Huh? C'mon!"

Shop

One of the fastest-growing, and perhaps most controversial, Web activities is shopping (see Figure 1.5). Right on the Web, you can browse an online catalog, choose merchandise, type in a credit card number and shipping address, and receive your merchandise in a few days, postage paid. Besides merchandise, you can buy just about anything else on the Web: stocks, legal services, you name it. Everything but surgery, and I'm sure that's only a matter of time. One of the hottest trends in online shopping continues to be the online auction house, a Web site where you can bid on all kinds of items, new and old, from odds and ends to objets d'art.

The controversy arises from the fact that sending your credit card number and other private information through the Internet exposes you to abuse of that information by anyone clever enough to cull it from the din of Web traffic. But that risk factor is rapidly shrinking as the Web develops improved security. And while shopping from your PC, you can't get mugged in the mall parking lot.

FIGURE 1.5
*Shopping may be the
fastest-growing online
activity.*

Watch TV and Listen to CD-Quality Music and Radio Broadcasts

Through your Internet connection, you can actually watch live TV broadcasts and listen to radio programs. The sound and picture quality won't be as good as you get from a real TV or radio (unless you have a "broadband" Internet connection—see Chapter 3, "Getting Connected to the Internet"). But the Net gives you access to programs you can't get on your own TV or radio, such as shows not offered in your area or special programs broadcast only to the Internet. With music, however, there's no compromise. Right from the Internet, you can copy high-quality music files that you can listen to anytime, even when you're not on the Internet.

> You can not only listen to CD-quality music online, but also buy it by downloading it to your computer and playing it there, or copying it to a portable player. See Chapter 11, "Plug-In and Add-On Programs."

Play Games, Get a College Degree, Waste Time...

Have I left anything out? There's too much on the Web to cover succinctly. But I hope you get the idea. The Web is where it's at. In fact, there are many folks on the Internet who use the Web and nothing else to get and disperse information. But those folks are missing out.... Read on.

Oooops. There's one more thing you can do on the Web: publish. Just as you can access any Web server, you can publish your own Web pages on a Web server, so that anyone on the Internet with a Web browser can read them.

You can publish Web pages to promote your business or cause, to tell others about a project or hobby that's your passion, or just to let the world know you're you. You'll learn how in Part II, "Using a Free Web-Authoring Program."

Exchange Messages

Email, in case you didn't know, is a message sent as an electronic file from one computer to another. Using Internet email, you can type a message on your computer and send it to anyone else on the Internet (see Figure 1.6).

FIGURE 1.6

Email is a great way to keep in contact with people, especially those who live far away.

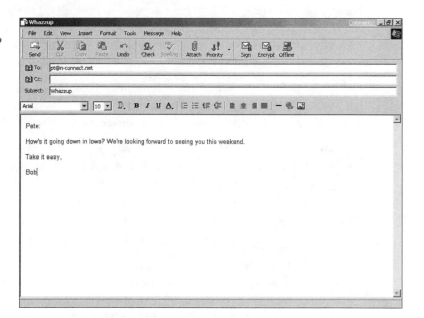

Each user on the Internet has a unique email address; if your email address is suzyq@ netknow.com, you're the only person in the world with that email address. (Isn't that nice?) So if anyone, anywhere in the world, sends a message to that address, it reaches you and you alone. As mentioned earlier, to use email, you need an email client program, which interacts with the email servers that store and send email around the world.

Email is great for simple messages, but these days, it can do more. You can attach computer files to email messages to send them to others, broadcast a message to two or a hundred recipients at once, and even create cool, colorful messages with graphics and sound.

> Most email is sent and received through a program called an email client. But some folks send and receive email directly from a Web page, using their Web browsers. Still others can send and receive Internet email through their digital cell phones, pagers, and palmtop computers. You'll learn how to use all kinds of email in this book.

Have a Discussion

Using your email program, you can join mailing lists related to topics that interest you. Members of a mailing list automatically receive news and other information—in the form of email messages—related to the list's topic. Often, members can send their own news and comments to the list, and those messages are passed on to all members.

One of the Internet's principal discussion venues is the newsgroup, a sort of public bulletin board. There are thousands of newsgroups, each centering on a particular topic—everything from music to politics, from addiction recovery to TV shows.

Visitors to a newsgroup post messages that any other visitor can read. When reading a message, any visitor can quickly compose and post a reply to that message, to add information to the message, or to argue with it (usually to argue—you know how folks are). As the replies are followed by replies to the replies, a sort of free-form discussion evolves.

> You might have heard that you can pick up a lot of unreliable information on the Internet, and, indeed, that's true. As when absorbing information from any communications medium—print, broadcast, Internet, water cooler, back fence—you must always consider the source, and take much of what you learn with a grain of salt.
>
> You must also trust that, just as the Internet offers a forum to nutballs with axes to grind, it also offers an incredible wealth of authoritative, accurate information that's often difficult to find elsewhere. It's just like TV: You can watch *CNN*, or you can watch *Hard Copy*. If you choose the latter, you can't blame the TV for misinforming you.

1

Chat

Exchanging messages through email and newsgroups is great, but it's not very interactive. You type a message, send it, and wait hours or days for a reply. Sometimes, you want to communicate in a more immediate, interactive, "live" way. That's where Internet Relay Chat—a.k.a. "IRC" or just "Chat"—comes in.

Using chat client programs, folks from all over the world contact chat servers and join one another in live discussions. Each discussion takes place in a separate chat "room" or "channel" reserved for discussion of a particular topic. The discussion is carried out through a series of typed messages; each participant types his or her contributions, and anything anyone in the room types shows up on the screen of everyone else in the room.

In addition to chat, there are other ways to have a live conversation over the Internet.

You can also have live text and voice chats through any of several different "instant messaging" programs that enable you to not only chat, but also find out which of your friends are currently online and up for a gab session. You'll learn about instant messaging in Chapter 6, "Chatting and Instant Messenger."

Summary

The Internet is a huge, and growing, internetwork that nobody really planned but that happened anyway. Your job is not really to understand it, but to enjoy it and to use it in whatever way you find valuable or entertaining.

The value and entertainment are stored all over the world on a vast array of servers; to tap the benefits of the Net, you deploy a family of client programs that know how to talk to the servers. In a way, most of this book is really about choosing and using client programs to make the most of the Internet's servers.

CHAPTER 2

What Hardware and Software Do You Need?

Got a computer made within the last 10 years? Then odds are you can get it onto the Internet. The power of your hardware doesn't have that much to do with whether you can get on the Net. But it has everything to do with what you can do there.

In this chapter, you'll discover the hardware required to use the Internet and explore the available options and the pros and cons of each. After you've settled on a computer, you'll need to know which client programs and other software your Net travels will demand.

Modems—Wherein the Lack of Speed Kills

There are ways to connect to the Internet without a modem, which you'll discover more fully in Chapter 3, "Getting Connected to the Internet." But odds are that you will start out with a modem and phone line for your Internet connection, so you must consider the capabilities of your modem in choosing or upgrading your computer for Internet access.

A modem is a device that enables two computers to communicate with one another through phone lines. Using a modem (installed inside, or connected to, your computer), you can communicate through a regular phone line with the modem at your Internet provider. That's the main way (although not the only way) you connect to the Net. Other, newer options include cable Internet.

If you will use one of the new, high-speed "broadband" Internet connections, such as DSL or cable Internet, you will not need a traditional modem; each of these technologies requires a special communications interface (see Chapter 3). However, nearly all new PCs include a fax/modem, and even if you use broadband for Internet, you may want the modem, too, for such activities as PC faxing.

It doesn't really matter what brand of modem you buy, or whether it's an internal modem (plugged inside your computer's case), an external one (outside the computer, connected to it by a cable), or even one on a PC card inserted in a notebook PC. What does matter is the modem's rated speed. That speed is usually expressed in kilobits per second (kbps, often further abbreviated to simply "K").

The higher the number of kbps (or K), the faster the modem. And the faster your modem is, the more quickly Web pages will appear on your screen, which makes Web surfing more fun and productive. A number of other Internet activities—especially such things that involve audio or video—will also run more quickly and smoothly over a faster modem.

On some modem packages, you might see the speed expressed in bits per second (bps). For example, a 56K modem may also be described as a 56,000 bps modem, though 56K is the more common usage.

Most modems for use with regular telephone lines are rated at one of the following speeds:

- 28,800 bps (28.8K)
- 33,600 bps (33.6K)
- 56,000 bps (56K)

The minimum modem speed for Internet cruising (including Web browsing) is 28.8K, although at that speed, you'll be very frustrated by the length of time it takes pages to appear. Most experts deem a 28.8K connection unacceptably slow. Modems rated at 56K are affordable (almost all new PCs and Macs come equipped with a 56K modem), and almost always your best option.

A 56K modem is capable of sending data at 56K, but almost never does. Noise in the phone line and other limiting factors keep actual speed down to around 53K or even lower. No matter—that's still a whole lot snappier than what you'll see through a 33.6K or 28.8K modem.

And under current telecommunications law, 56K modems can only send information to the Internet at 56K; they *receive* information at a maximum rate of 53K, even on the clearest line.

It's important to keep in mind that a faster modem does not always deliver vastly superior performance. A number of factors—such as the reliability and noise level in your phone line, the speed supported by your Internet provider, and the responsiveness of the servers you contact—can cause 33.6K and 56K modems to perform no better than a 28.8K modem much of the time. In some areas, the equipment installed by the local phone company might not even support Internet connections any faster than 28K or so. Using a 33.6K modem or 56K modem through these lines won't hurt anything, but the performance you'll see will not be any better than what you'd get through a 28.8K modem. (Little by little, local phone companies are upgrading their lines to support faster access.)

Finally, although it's the most important factor, connection speed is not the only thing that governs the apparent speed with which things spring onto your screen. If it takes your computer a long time to process and display the information it receives through the Net, you'll see some delays that have nothing to do with the speed of your modem or phone lines or Internet provider. A fast computer is almost as important as a fast modem—it's a team effort.

Choosing a Computer

I've told you that almost any computer—even an older one—can be used to get on the Internet, and that's true. But to take full advantage of what the Internet offers, you need a top-of-the-line computer, or pretty close to it.

You see, some Internet tasks, such as email, demand little processing power from a computer and don't require a really fast Internet connection; they're neither processor-intensive nor communications-intensive. However, the main thing most newcomers to the Net want is access to the Web, and browsing the Web is just about the most processor-intensive, communications-intensive thing a computer can do.

To take full advantage of the Web, a computer must be able to display and play the multimedia content—graphics, animation, video, and sound—that's increasingly built in to Web pages. Such tasks require a fast processor and plenty of memory. In fact, a Web browser capable of supporting this multimedia is about the most demanding application you can put on a PC or Mac, requiring more processing power and memory than any word processor or spreadsheet on the market.

In addition to the multimedia, more and more Web pages feature programs (more about that later) that enable all sorts of advanced Web activities (see Figure 2.1). To run the programs in Web pages, your computer must use a fast 32-bit processor (such as a Pentium or better) and operating system (such as Windows 98/Me, 2000, or XP), which have been available in PCs and Macs for only the last few years. As a rule, a PC that cannot run Windows 95 or higher, and a Mac that cannot run System 7.5 or higher, cannot run Java programs or the browsers that support the programs.

Java is a programming language specially designed for use in computer networks, such as the Internet. On the Web, programmers add Java programs to Web pages to enable the page to do stuff it couldn't do otherwise, such as collect and process order information for an online store or make images dance around the page. Java makes the Web more powerful and interactive, but also more complex and demanding.

What about notebooks and other portable computers? No problem. Notebook PCs, Mac notebooks, and other portables make perfectly good Internet computers, as long as they meet the same general requirements (processor, modem speed, and so on) that a desktop computer must meet, as described later in this chapter.

Note, however, that a portable computer always costs much more than a desktop computer with the same specifications. Also, some portables with otherwise acceptable specifications might have screens that are too small for comfortable Web browsing; any screen that measures less than 12 inches diagonally is probably too small, unless you have really, really, really good glasses.

Any size screen is fine, however, for email and other text-based, off-the-Web Internet activities. That's especially handy when you use a handheld PC or "palmtop" computer to access the Net on the go.

2

FIGURE 2.1

To enjoy the multimedia and Java content built in to many Web pages today, you need a powerful, well-equipped computer and a fast modem.

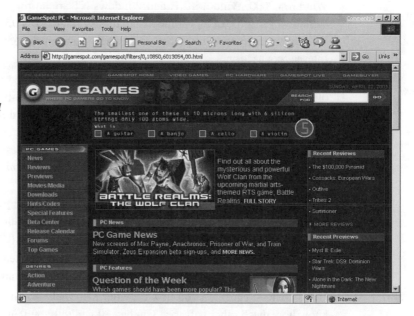

Finally, newer, more powerful computers are required to run the newest, most advanced operating systems, such as Windows XP on the PC or OS X on the Macintosh. These operating systems have been designed with the Internet in mind, making setting up your computer for the Net much quicker and easier.

Again, you can get a lot out of the Internet on a less capable computer—you just won't see or hear what your computer can't handle. But the bottom line is this: Most of the exciting innovations on the Internet, now and in the future, are designed for use by the newest, most powerful computers. So if you're shopping, aim high. And if you're standing pat now with an older machine, forge ahead with the understanding that your Internet experience is not going to be all that it might be.

A PC for the Internet

To make the most of today's Internet, the minimum reasonable PC would be equipped as follows:

- **Processor**—A Pentium processor (or Pentium equivalent, such as the Celeron, AMD K6, or Athlon) is recommended for its capability to support the preferred operating systems listed next; look for a Pentium rated at 500MHz or faster (even 1GHz processors are very affordable now). The latest Pentium version is Pentium 4.

- **Operating System**—Windows 95, Windows 98/Me (Millennium Edition), Windows 2000, Windows XP, and Windows NT are all fine choices. On all these Windows versions, except some installations of Windows 95, you'll find a built-in Web browser (Internet Explorer) and an easy-to-use program for setting up your Internet connection.

- **Display**—The ideal display for Web browsing is configured to run at 800×600 resolution and 16,000 colors (also known as high color, or 16-bit color). Higher-color modes, such as 24-bit color (millions of colors; often called *true color*), are fine, but little online requires those modes. Web designers are increasingly moving to a 1024×768 resolution, but most Web pages today are still designed to look their best when displayed at 800×600. If the prices are similar, you might want to look at a 1024×768 display.

- **Memory**—If you're running Windows Me or XP, at least 128MB of RAM is recommended to support Windows and a browser. A reasonable minimum for older versions of Windows, such as Windows 98, would be 64MB. The software package's box may indicate a lower minimum, but experience teaches us that the minimum is almost always insufficient for decent performance and reliability.

- **Hard Disk**—I can't tell you how big your hard disk should be, because I don't know how much other software you have. I can tell you that, after you've set up all of your Internet software, your hard disk should be at least 50% empty. Windows Web browsers need lots of free disk space for temporary data storage; when they don't have enough, performance and reliability suffer.

- **CD-ROM Drive**—A CD-ROM drive is not required for any Internet activity. However, you might need one to install the Internet software you need to get started, if you acquire that software on CD. For installing software, the speed of the CD-ROM drive is unimportant; any drive will do. Every new computer comes with a CD-ROM drive, anyway.

- **Other Peripherals**—There's plenty of fun sound and music online these days, and to hear it you'll need a sound card and speakers (or headphones) installed in your PC and configured in Windows. If you plan to create your own Web pages, a scanner or digital camera is a useful addition.

A Mac for the Internet

To make the most of today's Internet, the minimum reasonable Macintosh system would be equipped as follows:

- **Processor**—A PowerPC-based Mac (such as the iMac) is recommended. Anything older than that won't support today's Web browsing.

- **Operating System**—OS9 or OS X is recommended. They have a built-in, easy-to-use routine for setting up your Internet connection; built-in Java processing; and a complete set of Internet-client programs.

- **Display**—The ideal display for Web browsing is configured to run at 800×600 resolution and 16,000 colors (also known as *high-color* or *16-bit color*). Higher-color modes, such as 24-bit color (millions of colors; often called true color), are fine, but little online requires those modes. A resolution of 640×480 is an acceptable alternative, but most Web pages are designed to look their best when displayed at 800×600.

- **Memory**—Consider 64MB the workable minimum for Web browsing on any Mac.

- **Hard Disk**—Should be large enough to leave at least 25% free space after you have installed all your software.

- **CD-ROM Drive**—A CD-ROM drive is not required for any Internet activity. However, you might need one to install the Internet software you need to get started, if you acquire that software on CD. For installing software, the speed of the CD-ROM drive is unimportant; any drive will do.

- **Other Peripherals**—If you want to make a long-distance phone call through the Internet or have a voice conference, you'll need a microphone hooked to your Mac, and for videoconferencing, you'll need a Mac-compatible video camera. If you plan to create your own Web pages, a scanner or digital camera can be handy.

If you're considering a Mac for the Net and have high-speed Internet service available via your cable TV supplier (see Chapter 3), I should point out that most new Macs—including that cute little fruit-colored iMac—come equipped with the communications hardware required for using a cable

> modem. Most PCs do not include this hardware, which you must then pur-
> chase (or rent from the cable company). However, more and more PC manu-
> facturers are including Ethernet cards preinstalled, which allow for
> high-speed Internet access.

Internet Appliances

Over the last couple years, a whole new category of computer device has emerged, sometimes called a Net appliance, or Internet appliance.

Essentially a PC stripped down to the components required for Net surfing, a Net appliance is generally less expensive than a full-blown PC, and smaller and more stylish than
most PCs, as well. Most often, Net appliances have flat LCD screens (like those used in
notebook PCs) and are designed for those who want to use the Internet but do not need a
computer for any other purpose.

Their affordability made them quickly popular. While some models were available for
less than $200, others can be had for free at this writing, as long as you agree to a three-
year connection package with the Microsoft Network. Like most technologies, this market was quick to develop. Some of the major players, however, have also been quick to
pull out.

One of the first companies to offer an Internet appliance, Netpliance, still offers its "i-
opener" but has announced a new direction for the company. And 3Com, maker of the
popular Palm handheld devices, announced the demise of its Audrey device in the first
quarter of 2001.

There are still some good options out there, however, and they are worthy of consideration if you xwant a computer to use on the Internet but do not need to use that computer
for any other reason, such as word processing. Some folks who have full-blown computers may purchase Net appliances so they can have a second Internet machine in a bed-
room or the kitchen. (It's a pretty inexpensive machine for the kids to use for games or
homework research while another child can use a "real" computer to write a paper.)

Besides being incapable of taking on non-Internet computer tasks, a Net appliance may
prove difficult or impossible to upgrade as Internet technology evolves and may limit the
range of client software you may use, as well.

Compaq's iPaqs

Compaq offers two different iPaq models, retailing for around $500 at this writing. Both
can be significantly reduced through various rebates, including the aforementioned MSN
Internet access agreement.

Both come with a monitor and a wireless keyboard (see Figure 2.2). The more-expensive model offers a space-saving flat-panel monitor, but it is a markedly smaller screen than the cheaper, bulkier unit.

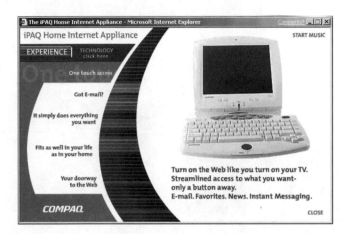

These machines allow you Internet access at the touch of a button, and have enough expandability to include a port for a printer, for example. So it's plenty powerful enough for handling your emailing, shopping, or general surfing needs.

MailStation

If email is your primary reason for wanting connectivity, then MailStation is a good option for you. For $99 (at this writing) plus a $9.95/month connection fee, you get a keyboard attached to a tiny LCD screen (see Figure 2.3). It basically resembles a hand-held device, such as a Palm, with a keyboard attached. This is the absolute bare minimum in Internet connectivity, but for many people, it's all they need.

Who does the MailStation unit fit? Well, think about Grandma. Maybe she lives on the other side of the country or maybe she winters in Florida. The thought of a full-blown computer intimidates her. With MailStation, she can take the unit with her to her winter home, plug her phone into it and be corresponding with the grandkids before you know it.

What You'll Miss with an Internet Appliance

Internet appliances like those previously mentioned are great for people with specific needs: You're on a tight budget, you just want email, you want a cheap second machine, and so on. But there are major drawbacks for people who have other computing needs.

FIGURE 2.3

MailStation allows quick access to email in a tiny package.

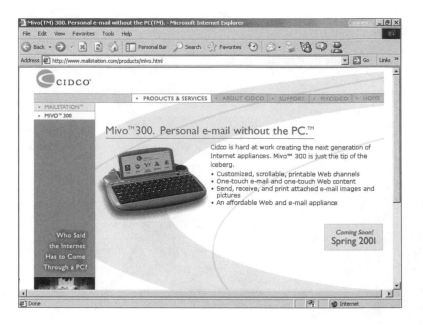

We all know a person or two who had a computer eat a file somewhere along the lines and has decided they have no place in their lives. Then the email arrives with an attached picture of the new niece or nephew. Sure, you can view it on the appliance, and even forward it to other family members. But when you decide you want to put your little one's photo out to friends, well, you're out of luck.

The key factor missing is that you can't manipulate files on an appliance. There's no saving, editing, copying, or anything. You can't install new software and it's difficult to upgrade to the latest technologies. It won't be long and the Internet will outpace your equipment.

They do make a nice second machine, because they are inexpensive and can offload some of the demand for screen time in a one-computer family. But before you buy one as your only Internet connectivity, be sure that what you're getting is all you'll need for a while.

Other Internet Options

The overwhelming majority of folks just getting online now are doing so through their own, personal Mac or PC, at home or at work. That's the main scenario, and that's where much of this book's focus will rest.

However, I should point out that there are many, many folks online who are not using PCs or Macs or are not even using their own computers or signing up with an Internet provider. Here are a few ideas for getting online without buying a computer:

- **School or Company Computer**—If the company you work for or school you attend has an Internet account, you might be permitted to use the organization's computers to explore the Net (usually within strict guidelines). Locate and speak to a person called the network administrator or system administrator; he or she holds the keys to the computer system and is responsible for telling you whether you may use the system and how and when you're permitted to use it.

- **Public Library**—Many public libraries have Internet terminals set up for use by patrons. You may use these terminals to do quick research on the Web or news-groups. As a rule, you cannot use them for email, because you won't have your own email address, and library machines are never equipped for chat. Even if they were, it's not polite to hog a library PC (as many evil people do) for a long, chatty Internet session.

- **Cyber Café**—In all cool cities, you can find cyber cafés, coffeehouses equipped with Internet-connected computers so patrons can hang out, eat, drink, and surf (see Figure 2.4). Some cyber cafés will let you have an email address, so you can send and receive email. Still, there might not always be a computer available when you need one, and you could probably afford your own computer with what you'll spend on Hawaiian Mocha and scones.

FIGURE 2.4

The Web page of a cyber café.

- **Copy Shop**—Many full-service print/copy shops, such as Kinko's, also offer Internet terminals for rent at reasonable rates.

In general, the compromises you must make to enjoy these alternatives makes them poor long-term substitutes for having your very own computer and Internet account. However, these are great ways to get a taste of the Net and reap some of its benefits, if you're still trying to make up your mind about the Internet or are still saving up for that new computer.

Getting Internet Software

Getting Internet software is like borrowing money: It's only difficult when you really need it. If you already have money (or Internet software), getting more is easy. So the trick is getting started.

You see, once you go online, you can search for, find, and download all the software you want, some of it for free, most at least cheap. You'll learn all about downloading software in Chapter 13, "Downloading Programs and Files."

> *Downloading* means copying a file—through a network—from another computer to your own. When you get software online, you copy that software from a server somewhere, through the Internet, to your computer and store it on your hard disk.

What Do You Need?

To figure out what Internet software you need to get started, you must begin by looking at what your computer already has. Recall from Chapter 1, "What Is the Internet and What Can You Do There?" that you need two types of software:

- Communications software, which establishes the connection between your computer and your Internet provider.
- Client programs for the activities you want to perform through the Net: a Web browser for the Web, an email program for email, a newsreader for newsgroups, and so on.

Table 2.1 shows what software each popular operating system (PC and Mac) includes.

TABLE 2.1 Required Internet Software Each System Features or Lacks

Computer Type	Operating System	Internet Software Included	You Still Need
PC	Windows 98/NT/2000/ME/XP	Communications software, plus clients for Web browsing, email, newsgroups, and more.	None
	Windows 95	Communications software.	Client software. (A few clients are included, such as email, Telnet, and FTP, but these are not designed as beginner's clients, and no Web browser is included.)
Mac	OS8, OS9, OS X	Communications software, plus clients for Web browsing, email, newsgroups, and more.	None

You needn't feel that you have to get all of your client software right away. At first, all you'll really want or need is your Web browser and an email program.

You won't need client software other than your Web browser and an email program until we get into more advanced topics, like creating your own Web pages. If you want to, you can simply set yourself up for Web browsing now, and forget about all the other software until you need it. You'll learn more about each of the other clients—including how to get some of the more popular options—in the chapters in which those clients are introduced.

Where Can You Get It?

The best place to get your start-up Internet software is from your Internet provider (which you learn to select in Chapter 3).

Why? Well, again, once you're online, you can easily acquire any software you want. All you need from your startup software is a way to begin. Whatever your Internet provider offers is usually given free of charge, and may include an easy-to-use setup routine, specially designed for your Internet provider.

You'll often see "free" Internet software offered as a "bonus" by Internet providers and PC sellers, and bound into the backs of computer books. Although this stuff can help you get started, and is therefore worth considering, it's a mistake to think it's as valuable as it's touted to be. Certainly, it's rarely valuable enough to be the main reason you choose a particular provider, PC, or book.

Much of the software you get this way is outdated, or is "trial" software, which you might have to pay for if you use it for longer than a month or two. Often, the trial software has key features removed or disabled, to get you to pay for the full version. And even when the software truly is free, it's almost always stuff you could also download for free, for yourself, from the Web, often in a more up-to-date version.

As an alternative to using the software your provider supplies, you can walk into a software store and buy commercial Internet software right off the shelf. Most prepackaged Internet software is inexpensive ($5 to $50), and often comes with setup programs to conveniently sign you up with one or more Internet providers. Be careful, though, not to pick up a box that is designed to sign you up with one (and only one) Internet provider, unless it happens to be the one you already plan to use.

About the Suites: Microsoft Internet Explorer and Netscape

In just the past few years, the two major suppliers of Web browsing software—Microsoft and America Online (Netscape)—have recognized that it's confusing for Internet users to have to go out and pick separate programs for each Internet activity.

Don't confuse America Online, the online service, with America Online, the company that markets the Netscape browser. It's the same company, but two different enterprises.

The first America Online, or AOL, is a commercial online service that offers Internet access among other activities. If you are an AOL subscriber, you can use either browser—Netscape or Internet Explorer—to explore the Web.

A few years ago, America Online, the company, purchased the company named Netscape, and now owns Netscape, the browser. But you can use the Netscape browser with any Internet supplier—you are not restricted to AOL just because America Online owns Netscape.

Confused yet?

So both Microsoft and America Online (Netscape) have developed "Internet suites," bundles that include a whole family of Internet programs that install together and work together well. Within each suite, you can jump from one program to any other simply by clicking a button or choosing from a menu. For example, you can conveniently jump from cruising the Web to checking your email to opening a newsgroup, all with a few clicks.

Both suites include a Web browser, email program, and newsgroup reader. Both also include a Web authoring tool for creating your own Web pages. You can buy either suite on CD at any software store, or order the CD directly from the developer. You may also be able to get a copy from your Internet provider. And, of course, once you're online, you can download the latest version of either program.

In this book, we've devoted an entire chapter to each of the browsers, plus another chapter devoted solely to the America Online service.

Summary

The window through which you view something frames and colors that thing, affecting your entire perception of it. Look at a landscape through a big, clean window, and then again through a small, dirty, distorted window, and you experience two very different yards.

A person who visits the Net through a slow, tired PC and modem or through inferior software does not perceive the same world that someone else sees through a capable PC and snappy software. When you choose your computer and software, you are defining the character of your Internet experience to come.

CHAPTER 3

Getting Connected to the Internet

If you have a mailing address, you probably know about Internet providers because they're the people who keep cramming free signup CD-ROMs and disks in your mailbox (creasing your National Geographic!) and begging you to join. Heck, you don't even need an address—you get free signup disks today in magazines, cereal boxes, and bundled along with any new computer.

The provider you pull out of your cereal box might be a perfectly good choice, but it's not the only choice—not by a long shot. In this chapter, you'll discover the full range of different ways to get signed up for the Internet, so you can choose the provider that best matches your needs and bank account. You'll also learn the basics of making that connection, so we can get you on your way.

Types of Internet Accounts

When you sign up with—subscribe to—an Internet service, you get what's called an *Internet account*.

With an Internet account, you get the right to use the provider's Internet service, your very own email address (so you can send and receive email), and all the other information you need to set up your computer for accessing the Internet through the service. From most providers, you also might get any communications or client software you need, as discussed in the previous chapter.

Dial-Up Accounts

Most Internet accounts are called "dial-up" accounts because you use them by "dialing up" the Internet provider through your modem and telephone line. These are sometimes also described as "IP" accounts because they require your computer to communicate through TCP/IP (see Chapter 1, "What Is the Internet and What Can You Do There?"). Dial-up IP accounts are the principal, general-purpose accounts offered by most Internet providers.

Dial-up accounts generally come as what's called a PPP account. With a PPP account, you have access to the full range of Internet activities, and you can use any client programs you want to.

An account with an online service such as America Online is also a "dial-up" account, but it's not the same thing as a regular Internet PPP or SLIP account. An online service account requires a different kind of communications software (supplied by the service) for accessing the service and its non-Internet content.

When you access the Internet through an online service, the service may temporarily switch you over to a PPP account, or it may funnel you to the Internet using a different communications scenario.

This is why online services often limit you to one or two different Web browsers and other clients, instead of letting you choose the one you want. Any client software used through the service must be specially configured for the service's unique communications system.

Cable Internet and DSL (Broadband)?

In the last few years, a new category of personal Internet account has emerged, sometimes described as broadband because it sends and receives information so much faster than a regular dial-up account—as if the information were moving through a nice, fat, "broad" pipe instead of a slow, skinny pipe.

Depending on what's available to you, you have your choice between two different kinds of broadband Internet access, described in the next sections: Cable Internet and DSL.

(There are other broadband options, used mostly in business environments, but these two are the popular options for personal users.)

The two options are different from each other, but have seven characteristics in common:

- They are much, much faster than a 56K dial-up account.

- Their speed enables them to carry Internet activities that are simply impractical over a dial-up connection, such as watching a movie online, high-quality videoconferencing, or using a computer somewhere out on the Net as a storage facility for your own files or backups.

- They allow you to use your phone line for telephone calls, faxing, or anything else while you are online.

- They can be set up so that you are always online. You don't have to do anything to get online each time you use the Net (as you must with a dial-up account); you just sit down and get to business.

- They are more expensive, on a monthly basis.

- They require more expensive communications hardware for your computer, rather than relying on the inexpensive modems included in nearly all computers today.

- Once you're online, actually using a broadband account—opening Web pages, exchanging email, and so on—takes the same steps you use on a regular dial-up account, the steps described throughout this book.

Broadband services are not yet available everywhere. Many neighborhoods today cannot get any type of broadband service, even though they might have regular phone and cable service. The hardware in local phone and cable systems must be upgraded to support broadband Internet. Phone and cable companies are furiously making these upgrades to begin selling broadband service, but it will still take a few years to get broadband availability to everyone.

However, as more and more neighborhoods gain access to both broadband technologies, the monthly cost should drop as the phone and cable companies compete for those customers.

Cable Internet

Supplied by your local cable TV company, cable Internet enters your house through the same cable that TV signals travel through. Cable Internet can support speeds up to 4,096K—more than 70 times as fast as a 56K dial-up connection. Figure 3.1 shows a Web site describing Road Runner, a cable Internet service offered by Time Warner Cable in some (but not all) of the neighborhoods it serves.

FIGURE 3.1

*The Web site of Road
Runner, a cable
Internet service offered
by Time Warner Cable
to some of its sub-
scribers.*

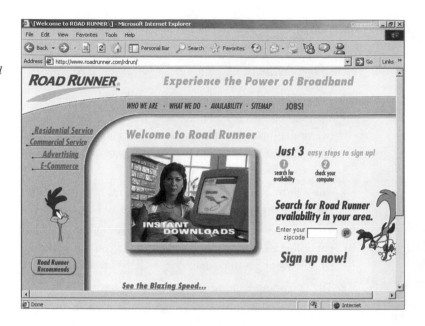

FIGURE 3.1

*The Web site of Road
Runner, a cable
Internet service offered
by Time Warner Cable
to some of its sub-
scribers.*

To use cable Internet, you must have

- A cable Internet account, offered only by the cable TV company that serves your neighborhood.

- A cable modem installed in, or connected to, your PC. A cable modem is not really a modem, but a specialized network adapter. You can usually rent your cable modem from the cable company, which also makes it easy for the cable company to set up your computer for you. You can also purchase cable modems, which run more than $100—but, before buying, be sure to talk first to your cable company to determine the specific hardware required.

- An Ethernet card installed in your computer (or other network adapter). This allows the modem to talk to your computer. Many computer manufacturers are now preinstalling Ethernet cards in their computers.

At this writing, a cable Internet account costs from about $40 to $50 per month—twice the cost of a regular dial-up account. To learn whether cable Internet is available at your home, call your cable TV company.

There are two potential minuses to cable Internet that are worth considering before you take the plunge.

First, the "always-on" nature of a cable Internet connection has been found to make computers using cable connections somewhat more vulnerable to computer hackers than those on regular dial-up lines. You can protect yourself from hackers with a "personal firewall" program such as Black Ice or ZoneAlarm. And, as with any Internet connection, users of a cable Internet connection need to use a good anti-virus program.

Second, cable Internet connections have been shown to become dramatically slower when many people within a neighborhood are using cable Internet simultaneously. At such times, cable would still remain much faster than a dial-up connection, but you might be disappointed by the times when you felt you were not getting all the speed you paid for.

3

DSL

Used through your regular phone line, a Digital Subscriber Line (DSL; also known by various other abbreviations such as ADSL or xDSL) account is supplied by, or in cooperation with, your local telephone company. The fastest broadband option, DSL can support speeds up to 7,270K.

Oddly, DSL can be faster than cable Internet when you are receiving information—such as opening a Web site or video clip—but it is usually slower than cable when you are sending information, such as sending email. For most folks, these speed distinctions are academic; either broadband option is fast enough to deliver the full broadband benefit.

Note that although DSL uses your regular phone line, it transforms that line into a carrier of multiple services; with DSL, you can use the Internet and talk on the phone at the same time.

Like cable Internet, DSL requires a special modem, typically called a DSL modem, which can cost substantially more than a cable modem. The monthly cost of a DSL account, however, is roughly the same as for a cable Internet account, around $40–$50.

To find out whether you can get DSL where you live, contact your local phone company, or contact an Internet service provider that serves your neighborhood and offers DSL service. (See "Internet Service Providers (ISPs)," later in this chapter.)

If you already have access to the Internet through a library computer or other option, you can look up DSL suppliers online at `http://www.dslmarketplace.com/`.

Email-Only Accounts

With an email-only account, you get full access to Internet email, and nothing else—no Web, no newsgroups, no chat, no shoes, no shirt, no service. You will have access to mailing lists, however, which enable you to get through email much of the same discussion content you'd see in newsgroups.

Email accounts can be run from the lowliest of computers and cost next to nothing. In fact, a few companies now offer you an email account free of charge, in exchange for the right to send you targeted advertisements.

Who Can I Get Dial-up Access From?

You can get your Internet account from any of three main sources:

- A national Internet service provider (ISP)
- A local ISP, one that's headquartered in your city or town
- A commercial online service, such as AOL or CompuServe

Each of these options is explained next.

Whatever service you choose as your provider, be sure the company offers a dial-up telephone number for connecting to the Internet that is a local call from your PC's location. Otherwise, you'll end up paying long-distance fees to the phone company in addition to whatever your provider charges for Internet access.

In most cities, finding local access numbers is no problem—any local ISP, national ISP, or online service will have a local number you can use. In some suburbs and many rural areas, finding a local number gets more difficult. Often, your best bet in such circumstances is to find a local ISP (discussed later in this chapter), or to see whether your local telephone company offers Internet access. (Many do.)

Some services offer a toll-free number (an 800 or 888 number) that you can use to access the service when the ISP provides no local number. But that number is rarely truly "toll-free." The ISP almost always charges a higher rate for using the service through the 800 or 888 number, kicking the toll back to you.

Commercial Online Services

You've no doubt heard of at least one of the major online services, such as America Online (AOL; see Figure 3.2) or CompuServe (CSi). These services promote themselves as Internet providers, and they are—but with a difference.

FIGURE 3.2

Online services such as America Online (AOL) offer Internet access as well as other services available only to their own subscribers.

In addition to Internet access, these services also offer unique activities and content not accessible to the rest of the Internet community. These services have their own chat rooms, newsgroup-like message boards (usually called "forums"), online stores, and reference sources that only subscribers to the service can use. Setup for an online service is usually very easy: You install the free software the company provides, follow the onscreen instructions, and you're connected.

The principal drawback to online services is flexibility. You often cannot choose and use any client software you want; you must use a single client environment supplied by the service, or one program from among a limited set of options. When new, enhanced releases of client programs come out, ISP users can install and use them right away, whereas most online service users must wait until the online service publishes its customized version.

On the plus side, for Web browsing, most online services do supply a version of either Navigator, Internet Explorer, or both (specially customized for compatibility with the service), making the look and feel of the Web through an online service essentially identical to that of an ISP.

Another beef about online services is capacity. When America Online introduced more attractive pricing a few years ago, it picked up far more subscribers than it was prepared to serve. The result was that subscribers often got busy signals when they tried to connect, and could not get through to the overburdened system for hours. A few times, the system crashed altogether.

This is a legitimate complaint, as are the reports that the online services sometimes tend to supply slow, unreliable Internet access. But to be completely fair, many ISPs also get overloaded, and may be burdened by busy signals and poor performance, too.

Whomever you choose, you must be prepared for the possibility you'll get fed up and switch. You can't expect any provider to be perfect. But the possibility of losing subscribers is the only incentive for providers to continually improve.

Also, try to avoid signing long-term contracts with providers; these deals can cause you great pain if the provider fails to give the level of service you expect.

Online services used to be dramatically more expensive than ISPs. Lately, they've adopted pricing policies that are generally competitive with the local and national ISPs, although you can still usually get a slightly better deal from a regular ISP than from any online service. For example, America Online offers a respectable flat rate of around $20 per month; if you shop around, you can get a flat rate from an ISP for as little as $15.

One final thought: In their advertising, the online services often tout their ease-of-use. That claim refers exclusively to how easy it is to use the service's non-Internet content from its own client software, not to ease-of-use on the Internet. For all practical purposes, using the Internet is the same—no harder nor easier—no matter which online service or ISP you choose.

America Online (AOL)

Voice Number: 800-827-6364

America Online is the biggest of the online services (and also, therefore, the single largest Internet provider in the world), largely because of aggressive marketing and the initial convenience of setting up an account from a CD-ROM that came in junk mail. The non-Internet content is indeed the easiest to use of all services. AOL's Internet access, however, is notoriously slow, and busy signals continue to be a problem. AOL offers a wide range of pricing plans, including a flat rate, an annual rate, and several different pay-as-you-go plans. (America Online is covered in detail in Chapter 10, "Using AOL 6.")

CompuServe (CSi)

Voice Number: 800-848-8199

CompuServe (see Figure 3.3) wasn't the first online service, but it's the oldest still in operation, and it was once the undisputed king. That legacy leaves CompuServe with an unbeatable range of local access numbers. CompuServe is owned by America Online but still operates as an independent service.

FIGURE 3.3

The Web home page of CompuServe, an online service.

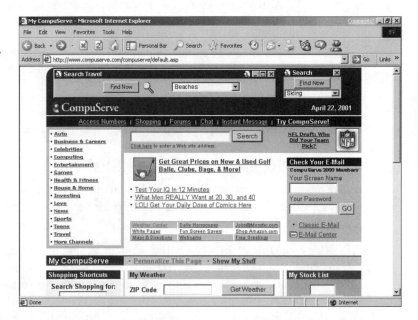

Functionally, CompuServe is similar to America Online in most respects, and it still offers some non-Internet content, exclusively to its own subscribers. Its reputation for providing fast and reliable Internet service is somewhat better than America Online's; its reputation for non-Internet ease-of-use, slightly worse. However, CompuServe can support almost any computer in the world, whereas AOL is essentially limited to popular personals: PCs and Macs.

Microsoft Network (MSN)

Voice Number: 800-FREE-MSN

Microsoft Network started out in 1995 as a service very much like AOL, as the first foray in Bill Gates' ongoing effort to own the Internet. (I guess for some people, having billions of dollars just doesn't seem like enough power.) MSN has since evolved away from the online service model, to the point where it is now more or less a regular national (actually international) ISP, although it still supplies some content accessible only to its subscribers. MSN offers true PPP access, so you can use any browser you want to. (Although, not surprisingly, MSN works best through Microsoft's own browser, Internet Explorer.) The service offers a variety of reasonable flat-rate and pay-as-you-go plans.

> All the online services, and most ISPs (described next), provide setup software for their service on a disk or CD. This software is required for the online services, but often is optional for an ISP.
>
> Even when it's optional, I strongly recommend getting any signup software your provider offers. The software leads you step-by-step through setting up your PC for the particular provider, and makes setting up your computer properly a no-brainer. As soon as you've selected a provider, call the provider to request the software and instructions for your computer type.

Internet Service Providers (ISPs)

Unlike an online service, an Internet service provider, or ISP, does not offer its subscribers special content that's not accessible to the rest of the Net. You get Internet access, period.

ISPs offer greater flexibility than online services, providing dial-up IP, shell, and email accounts (and often DSL, as well). Through IP accounts, they can enable you to use virtually any client software you want and to add or change that software whenever you feel like it. ISPs also might offer more attractive rates and better service than the online services, although that's not always the case.

There are many large, national ISPs that provide local access numbers all over the United States (and often across North America). Table 3.1 lists a few of the major national ISPs and their voice telephone numbers, so you can call to learn more about the service and also find out whether the service offers a local access number in your area. Just in case you have access to the Net through a computer at school, work, or the local library, the table also shows the address of a Web page where you can learn more about each service.

TABLE 3.1 A More-or-Less Random Selection of National ISPs

Company	Voice Number	Web Page Address
Earthlink	800-395-8425	www.earthlink.net
AT&T WorldNet	800-967-5363	www.att.com/worldnet
Prodigy	800-213-0992	www.prodigy.com
US Internet	888-873-4959	www.usinternet.com

Free Internet!

You might have heard that you can get a completely free Internet account, and that's a fact. In exchange for the right to show you a steady stream of advertising whenever you are online, some companies supply you with free access to the most popular Internet activities: the Web and email.

Free Internet services abounded a year or so ago, but like so many dotcom businesses, these companies fell on hard times and began to charge for access. One of those that still offers free access, NetZero (see Figure 3.4), only allows 40 hours per month for free. It also now offers a low-cost unlimited-access service with no banner ads to clog up your screen.

FIGURE 3.4

Although it still offers free access at this writing, even NetZero is offering a for-pay service.

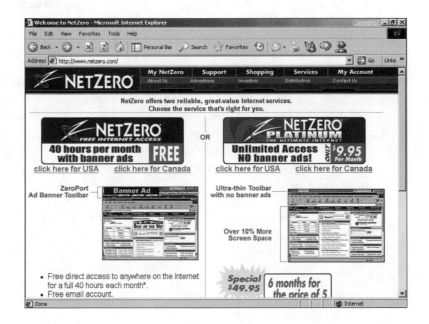

3

There are a few others still out there, and it's a great idea, and worth a try. The benefit is obvious: You'll have an extra $20 a month for sandwiches. Here's the potential downside:

- At this writing, the free accounts are somewhat notorious for poor performance and a complete lack of customer service.
- It's difficult to sign up for these accounts unless you are already online and already know how to use the Web, because signing up requires access to the company's Web site. So they make a nice money-saver for those who already know their way around, but may befuddle newcomers to the Internet.
- The ads may grow tiresome.
- You may prefer the features and flexibility of using a real email program instead of the Web-based email the free accounts require.

Finding a Local ISP

Besides the national ISPs, there are thousands of local ISPs in cities and towns all over the United States and Canada. Typically, a local ISP cannot offer access numbers beyond a small, local service area of a few cities, towns, or counties. But it can provide reliable Internet access, personal service, and often the best rates you can get. If you're having a problem, it can be a terrific help to be able to stop by your Internet provider's office and chat face-to-face. Local providers also play a vital role in keeping the big national providers honest; the continual reduction of rates by the big providers was spurred in large part by competition from even lower-priced local ISPs.

Unlike online services and national ISPs, local ISPs don't have the marketing muscle to advertise heavily or send out free disks. That's what makes them harder to find, but it's also why they're often cheaper. Finding a local ISP is getting easier all the time. Friends, coworkers, and local computer newsletters are all good sources for finding a local ISP. You can also check the Yellow Pages for ISPs: Look first under Internet, and then try Computers—Internet Services. The folks at your nearest computer store might also know of a good local ISP or two.

If you have access to the Internet (through a friend's computer, your job, a local library, or cyber café), you can search online for an ISP. A Web site called the List (see Figure 3.5) at `thelist.internet.com` is one of several that lists hundreds of ISPs in the United States and in many other countries.

FIGURE 3.5

Using somebody else's Internet account or an Internet terminal at your local library, you can visit the List to find a local ISP.

How Do I Choose a Dial-up Internet Plan?

Of all the options that are available to you, a dial-up account is still the most popular type of home Internet connection, by a long shot. So, how do you go about picking a dial-up provider and plan?

Beats me. If there were one reliable way to choose the best Internet provider, we would all be using the same one. But different people have different priorities: For some, it's price. For others, it's a range of access numbers; for others, it's speed. Some people have a particular need to use content that's available only through a particular online service; most people don't. You have to check out how each of your available ISP options addresses your own priorities.

Obviously, if you have friends who use the Internet, find out which services they use, and ask whether they're happy. It's always a good idea to use a friend's Internet account to test the service the friend uses, and to explore your other options. Magazine reviews can help, but they rarely cover more than the online services and the largest national ISPs. To judge a local ISP, you need to listen to the word of mouth.

For what it's worth, here's a quick look at a few things to consider:

Stressed out over making a choice? Relax, and remember that—unless you agree to a long-term deal—you can always quit and try another service if your first choice disappoints you.

The only caveat to switching services is that your email address changes any time you switch. But many services will forward your email to your new service for a few months after you quit, and you can always get in touch with all your email partners and let them know your new address.

Of course, switching services also provides an excellent opportunity to not tell some folks your new email address, if those folks have been getting on your e-nerves.

- **Plans and Rates**—Most providers offer a range of different pricing plans. The kinds of plans you'll see most often, however, are unlimited access (or flat rate) and pay-as-you-go. Flat-rate plans are the most common, because they allow unlimited access for a flat monthly fee. Pay-as-you-go plans charge a low base rate for a small number of hours (such as $10 for the first 20 hours), then an hourly rate after that. I generally recommend that new users first choose a flat rate plan with no long-term commitment, and to keep track of their monthly hours for six months or so. If you do that, you'll know whether you're getting your money's worth at the flat rate or whether you should switch to a per-hour plan.

- **Billing Options**—Most providers will bill your monthly charges automatically to any major credit card. Some local ISPs can bill you by mail, and some others can actually add your monthly Internet charges to your regular monthly telephone bill (itemized separately from your calls to Grandma, of course). All other things being equal, you may lean toward the provider that will bill you in the way that's most convenient for you.

- **Access Numbers**—Obviously, you want a provider that offers a local access number in the area where your computer resides. But what if you need to use your account from both home and work, using two different computers or bringing a portable back and forth? Does the provider offer local access numbers that work from both locations? What if you want to be able to use the Internet when you travel? Does the provider offer local access everywhere you and your computer might go?

- **Software**—The online services require that you use a software package they supply for setting up your connection, using their non-Internet content, and often for using the Internet, too. Most ISPs can also supply you with any communications or client software you require, although using the ISP's software package is optional. If you need software to get started, you may want to consider what each ISP offers as a software bundle.

- **Web Server Space**—If you think you might want to publish your own Web pages you'll need space on a Web server to do so. Many ISPs and most online services offer an amount of Web server space free to all customers; others charge an additional monthly fee.

- **Newsgroup Access**—You'll learn all about newsgroups in Chapter 7, "Participating in Newsgroups and Mailing Lists." For now, just be aware that there are tens of thousands of newsgroups, and that not all providers give you access to all of them. Some exclude "racy" ones, while others only offer those specifically requested by users.

Getting Connected

So you've chosen an ISP for dial-up access to the Internet. Whether that's an online service like AOL or a local or national ISP, your next step is to actually connect to them.

In most cases, the company you've chosen is going to make this as easy as possible for you. They'll either supply you with the software you need—which is often preinstalled on your computer, if you choose a national service—or they'll give you some type of brochure that walks you through the process, step-by-step.

Because the provider usually takes care of that type of thing and there are so many different ways of getting started, we're not going to spend much time on that type of stuff here. Instead, we'll just concentrate on the basics—things that you'll need to understand regardless of which provider you use.

Number, Username, and Password

No matter how you set up your account and computer, you'll wind up with three pieces of information that are essential to getting online:

- **Local access number**—The telephone number your modem dials to connect to your Internet provider.

> In this section, we're talking about a typical dial-up connection. If you've chosen AOL, or cable or DSL, your setup will be different. Some dial-up providers handle things differently, too. You'd be smart to get setup instructions straight from you provider, to make sure you do it right.

- **Username**—To prevent just anybody from using its service, your Internet provider requires each subscriber to use a unique name, called a username (or sometimes user name, user ID, or userID), to connect.

3

- **Password**—To prevent an unauthorized user from using another's username to sneak into the system, each subscriber must also have his or her own secret password.

Entering your username and password to go online is called *logging on* (or sometimes *logging in* or *signing in*) and the name used to describe that activity is *logon* (or *login*, or *sign-in*). If you use a signup program to set up your Internet account and computer as described next, you'll choose your username and password while running the program. If you set up your computer without a signup disk (as described later in this chapter), you'll choose a username and password while on the phone with your provider to open your account.

Every user of a particular Internet provider must have a different username. If you choose a large provider, there's a good chance that your first choice of username is already taken by another subscriber. In such cases, your provider will instruct you to choose another username, or to append a number to the name to make it unique. For example, if the provider already has a user named CameronDiaz, you can be CameronDiaz2.

There are rules regarding what you can and cannot use for your username and password.

The rules vary by provider but, in general, your username and password must each be a single word (no spaces or punctuation) of five or more letters and/or numerals. Nonsense words, such as FunnyDad or MonkeyMary, are fine as usernames. For a password, avoid using easy-to-guess items such as your birthday or kids' names. Total nonsense—such as xkah667a—makes the most effective password, as long as you can remember it.

Your username often doubles as the first part of your email address; if your username is Stinky, your email address might be something like Stinky@serveco.com. Before choosing a username, consider whether you also like it as an email address, which your friends and associates will see and use.

Some systems are case-sensitive; that is, they pay attention to the pattern of upper- and lowercase letters. On a case-sensitive system, if your username is SallyBu, you must type SallyBu to log on—sallybu, SALLYBU, or sallyBU won't work.

Using Supplied Software

As I pointed out earlier, a special signup program is required for each online service provider, and many ISPs can also supply you with a signup program for your computer. I highly recommend using signup programs whenever they're available, even when they're optional. You can get free signup disks by mail from the providers, just by calling them on the telephone. Also, signup programs often come preinstalled on new computers, and in computer magazines and junk mail. If you choose to go with a local ISP, you can usually pick up a signup CD or disks just by stopping by the provider's office.

Why Use a Signup Program?

Why? Well, first, the signup programs kill two birds at once: They sign you up with a provider and configure your computer to access that provider. The program automatically takes care of all the communications configuration required in your computer, some of which can be tricky for inexperienced computer users.

> Depending on the provider you select, the signup program might or might not set up all your client software.
>
> After completing any signup program, you'll be able to connect to the Internet and use your Web browser to explore the Web. However, in some cases, your email, news, and other programs might require a little further setup before you can use them. You'll learn about configuring each type of client software in the chapter that covers it.

Running a Typical Signup Program

Before running a signup program, be sure your modem is connected to a telephone line, because the signup software usually dials the provider at least once during the signup process. Also, be sure you have a major credit card handy; you'll need to enter its number and expiration date to set up payment.

> Signup programs are almost always designed to set up credit card payments for your Internet service. If you do not want to pay by credit card, you might not be able to use the signup program. (Actually, you might not even be able to use a particular provider; some accept payment solely by credit card.)
>
> Call your selected provider to ask about payment terms. If the provider accepts other payment methods, but its signup program handles only credit cards, you can establish your account over the telephone, and then set up your computer without a signup disk, as described later in this chapter.

You'll find instructions for starting the program on a page or card that accompanies it, or printed right on the CD or disk.

After you start the program, just follow its lead. The program will prompt you to type in your name, address, phone number, and credit card information, and to choose a logon username and password, email address, and email password. The program may also present you with a list of payment plans from which to choose (see Figure 3.6).

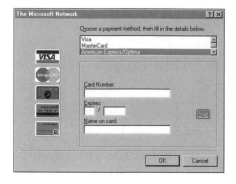

When you choose each of the following during signup, be sure to jot it down for later reference:

- Your logon username and password.
- Your email address.
- Your email password. Sometimes different from your logon password, this is used to retrieve email others have sent to you.
- The telephone number of your provider's customer service and/or technical support departments.

Once or twice during the signup process, the program uses your modem to contact the provider. It does this to verify your payment information, find the best local access number for you, check that your selected username is not already taken, and ultimately to send all the information it collected to the provider to open your account.

When the program closes, your computer and account are ready to go online and explore.

Using the Connection Wizard on Your Own

Setting up your computer without a signup program is a little more difficult, but well within anybody's capabilities. Often your ISP will provide you with all the instructions you need on a brochure or instruction sheet.

> The instructions in this section are for setting up dial-up IP accounts, the most popular type.

When you don't use a signup disk, you must set up your account with your selected Internet provider over the telephone first, and then configure your computer. While setting up your account, your provider will tell you all of the communications settings required for the service, and will work with you to select your local access number, username, and password.

It's important that you make careful notes of everything your provider tells you. You'll use all of that information when setting up. In addition to your access number and logon username and password, you'll probably come out of the conversation with the following information:

- One or more IP *addresses*—a string of numbers separated by periods—required for communicating with the provider.

> More and more Internet providers are set up so that they automatically assign you an IP address whenever you connect to the Internet. This makes it unnecessary to know the IP addresses.

- The addresses of the provider's email and news servers. You'll need these addresses to configure your email program and newsreader. server addresses may be described as SMTP and POP3 servers, and news servers may be described as NNTP servers. You don't need to know what the abbreviations mean; just know that if your provider mentions an NNTP server, he's talking about a news server.
- Your own email address, the one others can use to send email to you.
- Your email username and password, required for retrieving email people have sent to you. These may be different from your logon username and password.
- The telephone number and hours of the provider's customer service or technical support departments.
- Any other special communications steps or settings the particular provider requires.

No matter how you go about it, setting up your computer for the Internet is a simple matter of entering this information in your communications software. Once that's done, you can go online.

Running the Connection Wizard

Short of using a signup program, the next easiest way to set up an ISP account on a PC running Windows 95, 98, Me, or XP is to set up Internet Explorer and run its Connection Wizard. Internet Explorer is included in every copy of Windows 98, Me, and XP, and is often included with Windows 95.

If your computer is new, you might have the latest version of Internet Explorer already installed: version 6.0. Even if you're using IE5 or IE5.5, however, the Connection Wizard is essentially the same.

The Connection Wizard leads you through each step of the process, prompting you for all the required information, such as IP addresses. That's almost as easy as using a signup disk, except that the Connection Wizard doesn't sign you up with your ISP—you must take care of that first—and it prompts you for your IP address and other setup information, which a signup program can supply for itself.

To launch the Connection Wizard, simply right-click the Internet Explorer icon on your desktop, choose the Connections tab, and click the Setup button. You'll see a screen like in Figure 3.7. From there, you follow the prompts, filling in the appropriate information. The wizard walks you through the process quite succinctly.

FIGURE 3.7

The Connection Wizard offers easy-to-follow instructions for getting connected to your ISP.

Connecting at Last

When it's done, you'll end up with an icon on your desktop for your connection to your provider. When you want to connect to use the Internet, just double-click that icon. You'll get a dialog box (see Figure 3.8) with your username already included. Just type your password, click Connect, and off you go. Now, you're ready to browse the Web, a topic that (conveniently enough) is covered in the next chapter!

FIGURE 3.8

After opening your connection program, you supply your password to log on to the Internet.

3

Summary

Well, I'd say you've had just about enough prelude and general fooling around by now. In these first three chapters, you've learned what the Internet is, what hardware and software you need to get on the Internet, how to find and choose your Internet provider, and how to get connected.

That's all the preparation you need—it's time to start browsing. You'll do that in Chapter 4, "Basic Browsing."

CHAPTER 4

Basic Browsing

Whew. You've made it through the first three chapters, which are full of all the necessary—yet occasionally mundane—details that provide the background of Internet usage. Alas, you can now rest assured that the remainder of this book will be nothing but fun, fun, fun!

Well, that might be stretching it a bit. But the fact of the matter is that with this chapter, you begin to get into the meat of why you wanted to get on the Internet in the first place—browsing the World Wide Web. The Web is one of the two biggest reasons that the average Joe hops online; the other is email (which is covered in Chapter 5, "Sending and Receiving Email").

Over the last six years, the Web has blossomed—okay, make that *exploded*. In this one chapter, you'll pick up the basics of getting all around the Web. We'll cover the things that work roughly the same regardless of what browser or ISP you're using. We'll cover specific information on each browser, plus America Online, in Chapters 8 through 10.

About Your "Home Page"

Most Web browsers are configured to go automatically to a particular Web page as soon as you open them and connect to the Internet. This page is generally referred to as the browser's "home page."

Home page. A Web page a browser is configured to go to automatically when you open it, to provide a starting point for your Web travels. It's also sometimes called the "startup page." But remembering that the page is "home" is important, as you'll learn later in this chapter.

Note that "home page" has two meanings in Web parlance: It also describes a Web page that serves as the main information resource for a particular person or organization. For example, www.toyota.com may be described as Toyota's "home page."

For example, if you get Internet Explorer directly from Microsoft, it opens at the Microsoft Network's home page at www.msn.com (see Figure 4.1). If you get Netscape Navigator directly from Netscape, it opens automatically to a similar startup page at Netscape.

FIGURE 4.1

Your browser goes automatically to its home page. The home page might have been selected by the browser maker or by your Internet provider.

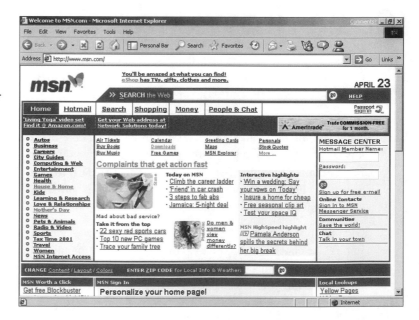

However, if you get your software from your Internet provider, your browser might have been reconfigured with a new home page, one that's set up by your provider as a starting point for its subscribers. This home page also serves as a source of news and information about the provider and its services.

A few specific Web sites are used as home pages by a very high proportion of Web users because these pages offer a convenient set of links to the things many folks like to do as soon as they go online: Search for something, check out the latest news, weather, or sports scores, or other common activities.

Some folks call these sites *Web portals* because they function as an everyday point of entry to the Web. Popular portals include such search pages as Yahoo!, Excite, and Lycos, and other sites such as Netscape's Netcenter.

You don't have to do anything with your home page. You can just ignore it, and jump from it to anywhere on the Web you want. But some home pages provide valuable resources, especially for newcomers.

Often, you'll find a great selection of *links* on your home page to other fun or useful pages. If your home page happens to be one set up by your local ISP, the page might even contain local news, weather, and links to other pages with information about your community. Now and then, before striking out onto the Web, be sure to give your home page a glance to check out what it has to offer.

A *link* is an object in a Web page that you can activate to jump to another page or another part of the page you're on. Links can appear onscreen as a block of text or as a picture or graphic. In most browsers, you go where the link leads simply by pointing to it with your mouse and clicking it. See "Basic Jumping Around," later in this chapter.

4

Understanding Web Page Addresses

Using the Web is easy—that's why it's so popular. But if there's one thing about Web surfing that trips up newcomers, it's using Web page addresses effectively. So here and now, I'll set you straight on Web page addresses so that you can leap online with confidence.

For the most part, you'll deal with only two kinds of addresses for most Internet activities:

- **Email addresses**—These are easy to spot because they always contain an "at" symbol (). You'll learn all about email addresses in Chapter 5.

- **Web addresses**—These never contain an @ symbol. Web page addresses are expressed as a series of letters separated by periods (.) and sometimes forward slashes (/), for example, `www.microsoft.com/index/contents.htm`. A Web address is sometimes referred to as a *URL*.

> A *URL* (Uniform Resource Locator) is the official name for the address format you use when telling a Web browser where to take you. (You can pronounce it "you-are-el" or "earl.")

Although most URLs are Web page addresses, other types of URLs may be used in a Web browser for accessing other types of Internet resources. You'll learn about Web page URLs in this chapter, and about other types later in this book.

If you keep your eyes open, you'll see Web page and site addresses everywhere these days. By typing an address in your Web browser (as you learn to do shortly), you can go straight to that page, the page the address "points to." Just to give you a taste of the possibilities, and to get you accustomed to the look and feel of a Web site address, Table 4.1 shows the addresses of some fun and/or interesting Web sites.

> As Table 4.1 shows, many addresses begin with the letters "www." But not all do, so don't assume.

TABLE 4.1   A Few Out of the Millions of Fun and Interesting Web Sites

Address	Description
www.cnn.com	Cable News Network (CNN)
www.ebay.com	eBay, an online auction house
www.epicurious.com	A trove of recipes
www.scifi.com	The SciFi Channel
www.carprices.com	A site where you can learn all about buying a new or used auto
www.uncf.org	The United Negro College Fund
www.rockhall.com	Cleveland's Rock & Roll Hall of Fame Museum
www.un.org	The United Nations
www.nyse.com	The New York Stock Exchange

TABLE 4.1 continued

Address	Description
college-solutions.com	A guide to choosing a college
www.sleepnet.com	Help for insomniacs
www.nasa.gov	The space agency's site
www.adn.com	The Anchorage, Alaska, Daily News
www.twinsmagazine.com	Advice for parents of multiples
imdb.com	The Internet Movie Database, everything about every film ever made
www.amazon.com	Amazon.com, a popular online bookshop
www.nhl.com	The National Hockey League

Anatomy of a Web Address

The address of a Web site is made up of several different parts. Each part is separated from those that follow it by a single, forward slash (/).

The first part of the address—everything up to the first single slash—is the Internet address of a Web server. Everything following that first slash is a directory path and/or filename of a particular page on the server. For example, consider the following fictitious URL:

www.dairyqueen.com/icecream/sundaes/fudge.htm

The filename of the actual Web page is fudge.htm. (Web page files often use a filename extension of .htm or .html.) That file is stored in a directory or folder called sundaes, which is itself stored in the icecream directory. These directories are stored on a Web server whose Internet address is www.dairyqueen.com.

Sometimes, an address will show just a server address, and no Web page filename. That's okay—many Web servers are set up to show a particular file to anyone who accesses the server (or a particular server directory) without specifying a Web page filename.

For example, if you go to the address of Microsoft's Web server, www.microsoft.com, the server automatically shows you an all-purpose Web page you can use for finding and jumping to other Microsoft pages. Such pages are often referred to as "top" or "index" pages, and often even use index.htm as their filename. The extension at the end of a file-name (such as .htm) will vary based on the program that created it. You'll see lots of .cfm, .jsp, and .asp extensions along with the .htm and .html ones.

4

Technically, every Web page address begins with `http://` or `https://`, particularly when described as a URL, the technical designation for the address format you use when working in a Web browser.

But the latest releases of Netscape Navigator and Internet Explorer no longer require you to type that first part. For example, using either of those browsers, you can surf to the URL `http://www.mcp.com` just by typing

`www.mcp.com`

(In fact, you don't even need to type the `www` part—if it's required, these browsers will fill it in for you.) Because of this change, Web page addresses often appear in advertising, books, and magazines with the `http://` part left off.

If you use a browser other than the Big Two, or older versions of the Big Two, however, you probably have to include the `http://` part when typing URLs in your browser. For example, to go to `www.pepsi.com`, you would type

`http://www.pepsi.com`

1. Connect to the Internet and open your Web browser. After a few moments, your home page (whatever it may be) appears (see Figure 4.2).

FIGURE 4.2

Step 1: Open your browser to your home page.

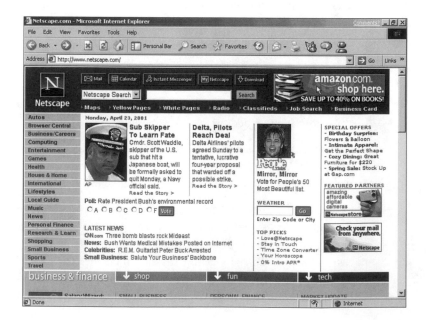

2. Examine your browser's toolbar area. The address you see there is the address of your home page (see Figure 4.3).

Address of home page

Toolbar area

FIGURE 4.3

Step 2: Find the address of your home page.

3. Make a mental note of the spot where you saw the home page address. That's where you'll always see the address of whatever page you're currently viewing. That's usually also the place where you'll type addresses to navigate the Web, as described next.

Going Straight to Any Web Address

Before you can jump to a page by entering its address, you must find the place in your browser provided for typing addresses. The term used to describe this area varies from browser to browser, but to keep things simple, I'll just call it the *address box*. Figure 4.4 shows the toolbar area of Internet Explorer, with the address box containing an address.

Address box showing URL of current page

FIGURE 4.4

In most graphical browsers, you'll see an address box in the toolbar area where you type an address to go to a particular Web page or site.

4

In both Internet Explorer and Netscape Navigator, you'll see the address box as a long text box somewhere in the toolbar area, showing the address of the page you're currently viewing. If you don't see it, the toolbar that contains the address box might be switched off.

To switch on the toolbar that contains the address box:

- In Internet Explorer, choose View, Toolbars, and make sure a check mark appears next to Address Bar in the menu that appears. If not, click Address Bar. If you still don't see an address box, try dragging each toolbar to the bottom of the stack, so that all toolbars are visible, and none overlap.

- In Netscape, choose View, Show, Location Toolbar. If you still don't see it, it's there, but collapsed so it's not visible. Click at the far-left end of each line in the toolbar area, and it should appear.

If you use a browser other than the Big Two (Internet Explorer or Netscape Navigator), you might see an address box in the toolbar area or at the bottom of the browser window. In some browsers, you might have to choose a menu item to display a dialog that contains the address box. Look for a menu item with a name like "Enter URL" or "Jump to New Location."

Entering and Editing URLs

After you've found the address box, you can go to a particular address by typing the address you want to visit in the box and pressing Enter. When the address box is in a toolbar, you usually must click in it first, then type the address, and press Enter.

Before you type an address in the address box, the address of the current page already appears there. In most Windows and Mac browsers, if you click once in the address box, the whole address there is highlighted, meaning that whatever you type next will replace that address.

If you click twice in the address box, the edit cursor appears there so that you can edit the address. That's a handy feature when you discover that you made a typo when first entering the address.

Note that when you type an address to go somewhere, your starting point doesn't matter—you can be at your home page or on any other page.

When typing the address, be careful of the following:

- Spell and punctuate the address exactly as shown, and do not use any spaces.

- Match the exact pattern of upper- and lowercase letters you see. Some Web servers are case-sensitive, and will not show you the page if you don't get the capitalization in the address just right.

- Some addresses end in a final slash (/), and some don't. But servers can be quirky about slashes, and many print sources where you see addresses listed mistakenly omit a required final slash, or add one that doesn't belong. Always type the address exactly as shown. But if that doesn't work, and the address appears not to end in a filename, try adding or removing the final slash.

- If you do not use a recent version of Internet Explorer or Netscape Navigator, you might be required to include the `http://` prefix at the beginning of the URL. For example, when you see an address listed as `www.discover.com`, you must enter it in your address box as

```
http://www.discover.com
```

What happens if you type an address wrong? Nothing bad—you just don't go where you want to go. Usually, your browser displays an error message, reporting that the browser could not find the address you requested. Check that you spelled, punctuated, and capitalized the address correctly. If you discover a mistake, edit (or retype) the address and press Enter to try again.

Note that Web servers and their pages are not permanent. From time to time, an address will fail not because you made a mistake, but just because the page or server to which it points is no longer online, either temporarily (because of a system glitch) or permanently.

Honest, I'm not shilling for Sams Publishing here, even though Sams publishes this book. It's just that Web pages come and go. Most Web site URLs for large organizations work fine for years. But addresses can change, and Web pages and sites do disappear from time to time.

I want to give you a reliable set of steps, and I know that the Sams Web site will still be around when you read this.

1. Connect to the Internet and open your Web browser (see Figure 4.5).

FIGURE 4.5

Step 1: Open your Web browser.

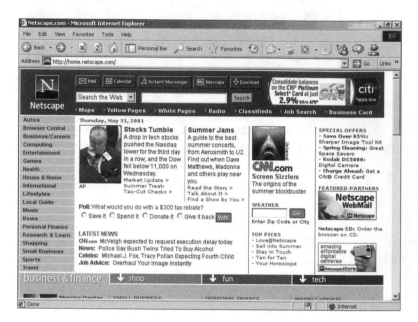

2. Find the address box, and click in it once.

3. Type the URL (see Figure 4.6)

   www.samspublishing.com

   (If you are using an older browser, you may have to add the http:// prefix.)

FIGURE 4.6

Step 3: Type in the URL http://www. samspublishing.com.

4. Press Enter. Sams's Web site appears (see Figure 4.7).

FIGURE 4.7

Step 4: Press Enter to see the Sams Publishing Web site.

Basic Jumping Around

I've shown you first how to move about the Web by entering an address, in part so you could discover along the way a number of important concepts that will help you navigate successfully.

Now I must show you that many—even most—of the times you jump from page to page, you won't type an address. All you'll do is click a link or button.

Sorry to show the hard way before the easy ones, but you must understand that you're not always going to find a link that takes you exactly where you want to go. URLs are like cars—they take you directly to a particular place. Links are like the bus: They often take you just to the right neighborhood.

Here is as good a place as any to point out that some Web pages take a long time to appear, even if you have a fast modem and Internet connection. If some pages do seem terribly slow, don't worry that there's something wrong with your computer, modem, or connection. The problem is probably that the page you're accessing is very complex.

You see, each time you display a particular Web page, the whole page must travel through the Internet to your computer to appear on your screen. A page that's mostly text appears quickly, because text pages contain little data, and thus travel quickly through the Net. Pictures, multimedia, and Java programs balloon the number and size of the files that make up the Web page, and thus take much longer to appear.

Reclicking the link to a page over and over again is only going to slow down the process, and may cause your computer to freeze.

Finding and Using Links

Activating a link in most browsers is simple: Point to the link and click it; your browser takes you wherever the link leads.

Most links lead to another Web page, or to another part of a long Web page you're viewing. However, links can do much more. For example, some links, when activated, may start the download of a software file (see Chapter 13, "Downloading Programs and Files") or play a multimedia file.

It's not using links that can be tricky, but finding them in Web pages that aren't designed well enough to make the links obvious. Links appear in a Web page in any of three ways:

- **As text**—You'll notice text in Web pages that appears to be formatted differently from the rest. The formatting differs depending upon your browser, but text that serves as a link is usually underlined (see Figure 4.8) and displayed in a different color than any other text in the page.

FIGURE 4.8

Often, links are indicated by underlined text.

- **As pictures**—Any picture you see in a Web page may be a link. For example, a company logo may be a link leading to a page containing information about that company.

- **As imagemaps**—An imagemap is a single picture that contains not just one link, but several. Clicking on different parts of the picture activates different links (see Figure 4.9).

FIGURE 4.9

Each part of this imagemap is a different link. In this case, clicking on any of the signs these people are holding will take you to a different page.

Text links are usually easy to spot because of their color and underlining (refer to Figure 4.8). Picture and imagemap links can be harder to spot at a glance.

But most browsers provide a simple way to determine what is and is not a link. Whenever the mouse pointer is on a link, it changes from the regular pointer to a special pointer that always indicates links.

Using Navigation Buttons: Back, Forward, Home, and Stop

In most browsers for Windows and the Mac, you'll see a whole raft of toolbar buttons, many of which you'll examine as this book progresses. But by far, the most important are the Big Four: Back, Forward, Home, and Stop (see Figure 4.10). These buttons help you move easily back and forth among any pages you've already visited in the current online session, and to conveniently deal with the unexpected.

Back   Stop

FIGURE 4.10

*The main toolbars in
Internet Explorer
(shown here) and
Netscape Navigator
prominently feature
the invaluable Back,
Forward, Stop, and
Home buttons.*

Forward   Home

For example, when exploring a particular Web site, you often begin at a sort of "top" page that branches out to others. After branching out a few steps from the top to explore particular pages, you'll often want to work your way back to the top again, to start off in a new direction. The Big Four buttons make that kind of Web navigation simple and typing-free.

Here's how you can use each of these buttons:

- *Back* retraces your steps, taking you one step backward in your browsing each time you click it. For example, if you move from Page A to Page B, clicking the Back button takes you back to A. If you go from A to B to C, pressing Back twice returns you to A. When you reach the first page you visited in the current online session, the Back button is disabled; there's nowhere left to go back to.

- *Forward* reverses the action of Back. If you've used Back to go backward from Page B to A, Forward takes you forward to B. If you click Back three times—going from D to C to B to A—clicking Forward three times takes you to D again. When you reach the page on which Back was first clicked, the Forward button is disabled because you can only move Forward to pages you've come "Back" from.

- *Home* takes you from anywhere on the Web directly to the page configured in your browser as "home," described at the start of this chapter. Going Home is a great way to reorient yourself if you lose your way and need to get back to a reliable starting point.

- *Stop* immediately stops whatever the browser is doing. If you click Stop while a page is materializing on your screen, the browser stops getting the page from the server, leaves the half-finished page on your screen, and awaits your next instruction.

Back, Forward, and Home do not care how you got where you are. In other words, no matter what techniques you've used to browse through a series of pages—entering URLs, clicking links, using buttons, or any combination of these—Back takes you back through them, Forward undoes Back, and Home takes you home.

Back and Stop are particularly useful for undoing mistakes. For example, if you click on a link that downloads a file, and while the file is downloading you decide you don't want it, you can click Stop to halt the download but stay on the current page. Click Back to halt the download and return to the preceding page.

1. Go to the ESPN Web site at espn.go.com, find any interesting-looking link, and click it (see Figure 4.11).

FIGURE 4.11
Step 1: Go to espn.go.com *and click on a link.*

2. A new page opens, the one the link you clicked points to (see Figure 4.12). Click Back to return to the top ESPN page.
3. Click another link on the top ESPN page (see Figure 4.13). On the page that appears, find and click yet another link (see Figure 4.14). (If you see no links, click Back to return to the top ESPN page, and try another route.)

Back button

FIGURE 4.12

Step 2: Click the Back button.

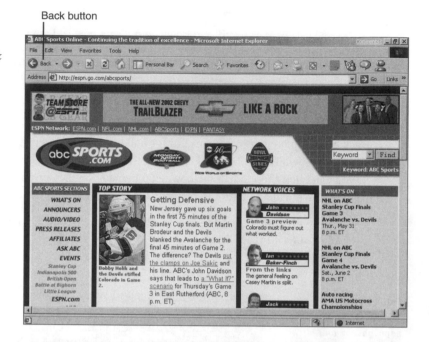

FIGURE 4.13

Step 3: Click on another link.

Another link ─

FIGURE 4.14
Step 3: Click on yet another link.

Yet another link ——

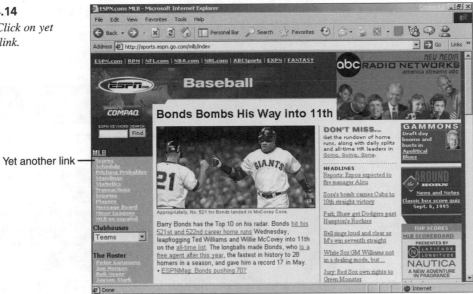

4. Click Back twice (see Figure 4.15) to return to the top ESPN page.

4

Back button

FIGURE 4.15
Step 4: Click Back twice.

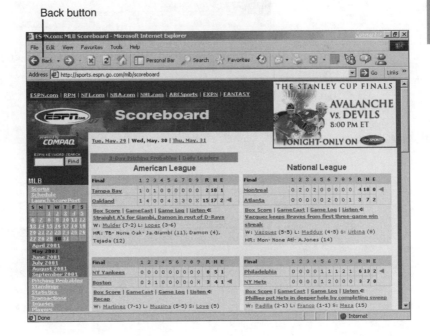

5. Click Forward twice. You go ahead to where you just came back from (see Figure 4.16).

Forward button

FIGURE **4.16**

Step 5: Click Forward twice.

6. Try a new URL: Enter www.akc.org for the American Kennel Club (see Figure 4.17).

FIGURE **4.17**

Step 6: Enter a new URL.

7. From the AKC page (see Figure 4.18), click Back once. You return to a page at ESPN.

8. Click home, and you'll return to your home page, as you see in Figure 4.19.

FIGURE 4.18

Step 7: Click Back once.

FIGURE 4.19

Step 8: Click home.

4

Fussing with Frames

You'll find that some pages are split into frames, two or more separate panes (see Figure 4.20).

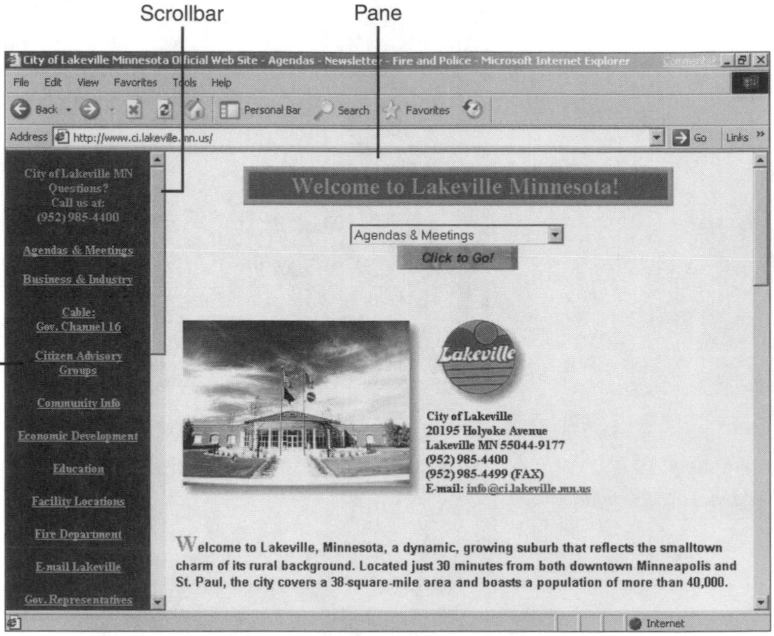

FIGURE 4.20

A frames page can show two or more separate documents at once, each in its own pane.

In effect, each pane in a frames page contains its own, separate little Web page. That enables each pane to operate independently of the others; for example, clicking a link in one pane can change the contents of another.

Some folks get all boxed up by frames, but using a frames-based page doesn't have to be tricky. Just remember the following tips:

- All links within panes are active all the time.
- Some panes have their own scrollbars. When you see scrollbars on a pane, use them to scroll more of the pane's contents into view. If you want to use your keyboard's Up and Down arrows to scroll within a pane, you need to click within the appropriate pane first.

- While you're on a frames page, the Back and Forward buttons take you back and forth among the panes you've used in the current frames page, not among pages. Sometimes, it can be tough to use Back to "back out" of a frames page to the page you saw before it; at such times, it's often easier to enter a new URL or click Home to break free of the frames, and then go from there.

- Some pages use "borderless" frames, and so do not appear at first glance to be frames pages. But after a little experience, you'll quickly learn to identify any frames page when it appears, even when the frames are implemented subtly.

> Internet Explorer, Netscape Navigator, and a few other major browsers support frames, but some others do not. For this reason, many frames pages are preceded by a non-frames page that provides two links: One for displaying a frames page, and another for displaying the same content in a no-frames version.
>
> If your browser can't handle frames—or if your browser can handle them but you can't—just choose the no-frames version. Life's too short.

Summary

That's all there is to basic browsing. Just by entering URLs, clicking links, and using buttons like Back and Home, you can explore near and far. Little bumps like frames add a little complexity to the mix, but nothing you can't handle.

4

CHAPTER 5

Sending and Receiving Email

Web browsing is the hottest Internet activity, but email might be the most widely used and most productive one.

Using Internet email—which has become such an everyday fixture that many people now call it plain "mail"—you can easily exchange messages with anyone else on the Internet. An email message typically reaches its addressee within seconds (or at most, within an hour or so), even on the opposite side of the globe. It's faster than paper mail, easier than faxing, and sometimes just plain fun.

It's so easy, in fact, that I know people who haven't written a dozen paper letters in a decade but who write email daily. It's a great way to keep up with friends and communicate with business contacts. In fact, there are some business people so tied to their email that if you contact them in any way other than email, you might not get an answer.

Types of Email Programs

Email can be as complicated as basic as you want it to be. There are a wide variety of different email programs—some that you have to buy as part of a huge suite of applications, some you get automatically with a browser, and some you can use right over the Web, without installing anything.

Making matters more confusing is the fact that both Microsoft and Netscape, the two companies who hold all the cards when it comes to using the Web, offer a wide variety of choices. Both offer a free program as part of their browser suite, but both also offer free Web-based email (Microsoft has Hotmail, Netscape has Netscape Webmail). Web-based email allows you to read messages right off a Web page, just like you are browsing. It is covered later in this chapter.

This chapter can't possibly cover all the options for email; it's designed to cover the most commonly used features. After you're comfortable with those, we figure, you'll be ready to pick up your program's little nuances on your own.

Understanding Email Addresses

The only piece of information you need to send email to someone is that person's Internet email address. An email address is easy to spot: It always has that "at" symbol (@) in the middle of it. For example, you know at a glance that

`sammy@fishbait.com`

is an email address. In most email addresses, everything following the @ symbol is the domain address of a company, Internet service provider, educational institution, or other organization. The part before the @ is the name (or user ID) of a particular employee or user. For example, the addresses

`SallyP@genco.com`

`mikey@genco.com`

`Manager_of_Sales@genco.com`

obviously belong to three different people, all of whom work for the same company or use the same Internet service provider (whatever Genco is).

Each online service has its own domain, too: For example, America Online's is `aol.com`, and Microsoft Network's is `msn.com`. So you can tell that the email address

`neddyboy@aol.com`

is that of the America Online user named `neddyboy`.

Online service users usually can omit the @ symbol and anything that follows it when sending to other users on the same service. For example, suppose you want to send email to

`allieoop@aol.com`

If you use a regular Internet ISP or any online service other than America Online (`aol.com`), you would use the address as shown. However, if you use America Online, you can address the message simply to

`allieoop`

Setting Up Your Email Program

There are many different email programs out there. Internet suites such as Internet Explorer and Netscape Communicator include an email program—but you must take care when installing these programs not to optionally omit the email component of the suite. Choosing the "full" installation option when setting up a suite ensures that you include all the suite's client programs.

In the suites, the email programs are called

- **Messenger, in Netscape Communicator**—You can open Messenger from within the Navigator browser by choosing Communicator, Messenger (see Figure 5.1).

FIGURE 5.1

Netscape Messenger, the email program that's included in the Netscape Communicator suite.

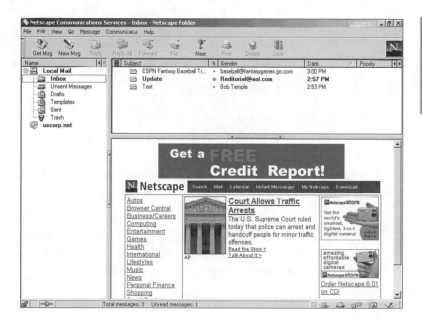

5

- **Outlook Express, in Internet Explorer**—You can open Outlook Express from within the Internet Explorer browser by clicking the Mail button on the toolbar and choosing Read Mail from the menu that appears (see Figure 5.2).

FIGURE 5.2

Outlook Express, the email program that's included with Microsoft Internet Explorer.

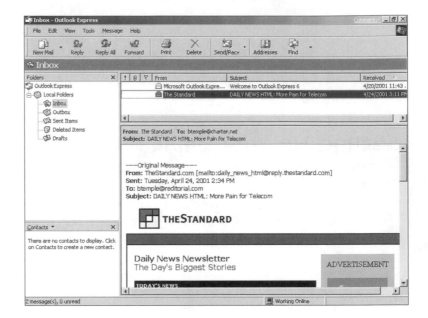

Don't confuse the free Microsoft email program Outlook Express with another Microsoft program, Outlook (no "Express"). Like Outlook Express, Outlook is an email program. But Outlook also does many other things Outlook Express does not do, such as personal scheduling and contact management. And, of course, Outlook is not free. Most people who use Outlook buy it as a part of Microsoft's Office suite.

If you don't already have an email program, you can jump ahead and apply the file-finding techniques from Chapter 13, "Downloading Programs and Files," to search for one, or check out the Tucows directory of Internet software at www.tucows.com.

Among the links you'll likely find in any search for email programs are links to various versions of a program called Eudora, one of the most popular email programs outside of the suites. If you simply want to go straight to learning about and downloading Eudora, visit the site of Eudora's maker at www.eudora.com.

If you use an online service, such as America Online or CompuServe, you might not be able to easily choose just any email program you want to use; you might be required to use the online service interface—the tool you use for accessing the service's non-Internet content—to send and receive email.

However, using an online service interface for email is similar to using an Internet email program, as described in this chapter. And from the online service interface, you can send email both to others on your service and to anyone on the Internet.

You need not configure email, as described next, for an online service. Email configuration is handled automatically when you sign up for the service and install its software.

Configuring Email

After installing an email program, you need to configure it before you can use it. All email programs have a configuration dialog of some kind (or a series of dialog boxes) in which you can enter the information required for exchanging email. You'll find the configuration dialogs

- In Netscape Messenger, by choosing Edit, Preferences to open the Preferences dialog box. In the list of Categories, choose Mail & Newsgroups. Complete the configuration settings in the Mail & Newsgroups category's Identity and Mail Servers subcategories (see Figure 5.3).

- For Outlook Express, by completing the Mail dialogs of the Windows Internet Connection Wizard (see Chapter 3, "Getting Connected to the Internet"). If you open Outlook Express without having configured it first, the Connection Wizard opens automatically to collect configuration information from you.

5

FIGURE 5.3

In Netscape Messenger, configure email settings in the Mail & Newsgroups category of the Preferences dialog box.

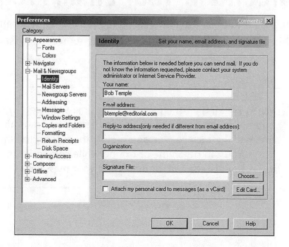

The automated setup routines supplied with programs such as Netscape Communicator and Internet Explorer not only set up your browser and Internet connection, but can optionally collect the information required to configure their email components (Messenger and Outlook Express). If you open Messenger or Outlook Express without first having configured them, a dialog opens automatically, prompting for the configuration information.

The configuration dialog boxes for most email programs require most or all of the following information, all of which your Internet service provider will tell you:

- Your full name. (Okay, so you don't need your ISP to tell you this one.)

- Your full email address. (Some configuration dialog boxes make you indicate the two parts of your address separately: the username—the part of the email address preceding the @ symbol—and your domain—the part of the email address following the @ symbol.)

- The address of your service provider's outgoing mail server, sometimes called the SMTP server.

- The address of your service provider's incoming mail server, sometimes called the POP3 server (some ISPs use another type of server called IMAP4). The POP3 address is sometimes (but not always) identical to the SMTP address.

Also, to ensure that no one but you gets your email, most ISPs require you to choose and use an email password. Some email programs let you enter that password in the configuration dialog box so you needn't type a password each time you check your email.

Getting Around in Your Email Program

Before jumping right into sending and receiving messages, it's a good idea to learn how to get around in your email program, move among its folders (lists of messages), and display messages you select from a folder.

When working with email, the only time you need to be connected to the Internet is when you actually send messages—transmit them to the Internet—or receive messages—copy them from the Internet to your computer. You can be online or offline while composing messages, reading messages you've received, or managing your messages.

Choosing a Folder

Netscape Messenger and Outlook Express divide their messaging activities into a family of folders. In each folder, you see a list of messages you can display or work with in other ways. The folders are

- **Inbox**—The Inbox folder lists messages you have received.
- **Outbox (called Unsent Messages in Messenger)**—The Outbox folder lists messages you have composed but saved to be sent later.
- **Sent**—The Sent folder lists copies of all messages you've sent, for your reference.
- **Deleted (called Trash in Messenger)**—The Deleted folder lists messages you've deleted from any other folder.

> Outlook Express and Messenger both handle two different jobs: email and newsgroups. Each therefore has folders not only for email, but also for newsgroups. Before performing an email activity in one of these programs, always be sure first that you're in an email-related folder, such as Inbox, and not a newsgroup folder.
>
> You'll learn about using newsgroups in Chapter 7, "Participating in Newsgroups and Mailing Lists."

To switch among folders in either Outlook Express or Messenger, click a folder name in the panel along the left side of the window (see Figure 5.4).

Displaying a Message

From the list displayed by each folder, you can display any message. You do this in either of two ways (the steps are the same in both Outlook Express and Messenger):

- Single-click the message in the list to display it in the preview pane (see Figure 5.5) in the bottom of the window.
- Double-click the message in the list to display it in its own message window (see Figure 5.6).

In general, the preview pane is best when you're simply scanning messages and need to move quickly from one to the next. Use a full message window to read a long message, or to read a message you will reply to or forward (as described later in this chapter).

5

FIGURE 5.4
Select a folder to choose the messages you want to work with.

Folders ——

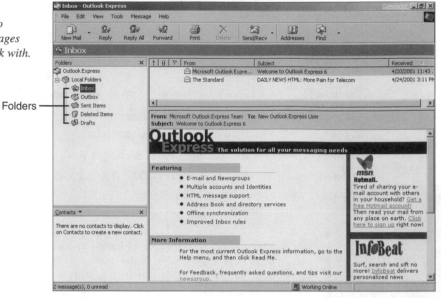

FIGURE 5.5
Single-click a message in a folder to display the message in the preview pane.

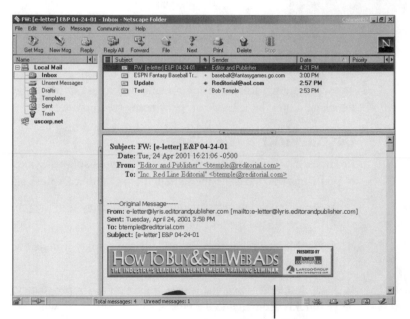

Preview Pane

Message window

FIGURE 5.6
Double-click a message in a folder to display the message in a message window.

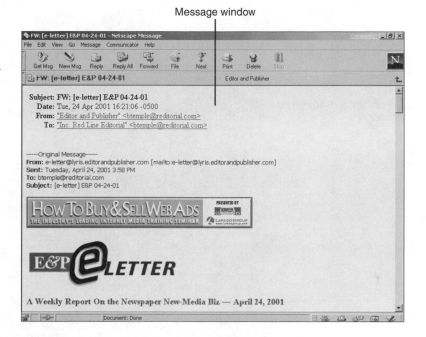

Composing and Sending a Message

When you have something to say, and the email address of someone to whom you want to say it, you're ready to go.

Writing Your Message

In most email programs, you compose your message in a window that's very much like a word processing program, with a special form at the top for filling in the address and subject information—the message's *header*. Below the form for the header, you type your message text in the large space provided for the message body.

The *body* of a message is the text, which you compose in the large pane of the message window. The address information you type—including your recipient's email address and the subject of the message—is called the *header* of the message.

The following steps show how to compose a simple email message. Following these steps, the next section describes how you can send that message.

1. Click the New Mail button (see Figure 5.7).

New Mail button

FIGURE 5.7

FIGURE 5.7
*Step 1: Click the New
Mail button in Outlook
Express.*

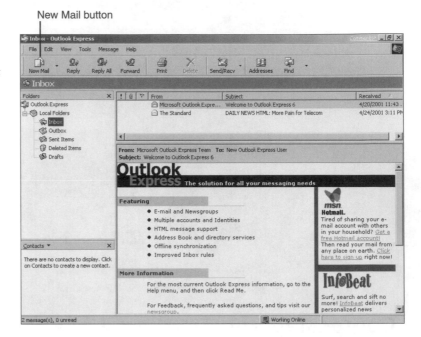

2. In the To line (near the top of the window), type the email address of the person to
    whom you want to send a message (see Figure 5.8).

FIGURE 5.8
*Step 2: Type in the
recipient's email
address.*

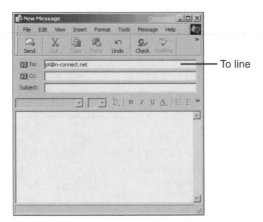

To line

3. Click in the Subject line, and type a concise, meaningful subject for your message
    (see Figure 5.9). (The subject appears in the message list of the recipient, to
    explain the purpose of your message.)

FIGURE 5.9

Step 3: Type in a subject for the message.

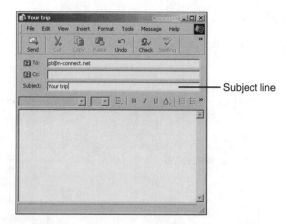

Subject line

4. Click in the large panel of the new message window and type your message, just as you would in a word processor (see Figure 5.10).

FIGURE 5.10

Step 4: Type in your message.

5

It used to be that email programs automatically created text-only messages, because many email readers weren't configured to display HTML messages. The latest versions of both Outlook Express and Netscape Messenger allow you to create messages in HTML format.

What does this mean to you? Simply put, it allows you to format the text, using bold, italics, different fonts, and so on, so the message can have a personal touch. Be aware, however, that some of those who receive your messages might still be using email clients that don't allow them to display HTML messages.

Here's how to compose a new message in Netscape Messenger:

1. Click the New Msg button (see Figure 5.11).

New Message button

FIGURE 5.11

Step 1: Click the New Msg button in Netscape Messenger.

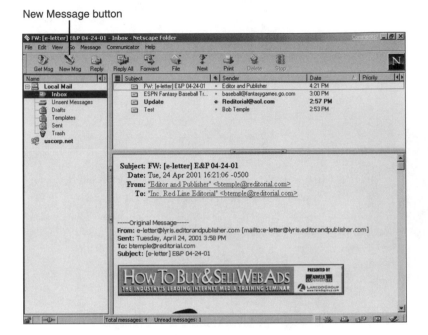

2. Follow steps 2, 3, and 4 of the preceding example for composing a message.

> You can send one message to multiple recipients in several different ways. For example, you can "cc" (carbon copy) your email to recipients other than your primary addressee(s). To do this, just enter their email addresses into the CC: field of the New Message window.

Sending a Message

After the header (To and Subject) and body (what you have to say) of the message are complete, you send your message on its way. In most programs, you do so simply by clicking a button labeled Send in the toolbar of the window in which you composed the message.

What happens immediately after you click Send depends upon a number of different factors:

- The email program you use
- Whether you're online or off
- How your program is configured

The message can be sent immediately out through the Internet to its intended recipient. If you're offline when you click Send, your email program can automatically connect you to the Internet to send the message. Otherwise, you must connect before sending.

However, instead of sending your message the instant you click Send, your email program can send the message to your Outbox (or Unsent Messages) folder, to wait. After clicking Send, you can open your Outbox or Unsent Messages folder to see whether the message is there (see Figure 5.12).

FIGURE 5.12

In some programs, messages are sent to wait in the Outbox or Unsent Messages folder, and then finally go out to their recipients at a later time.

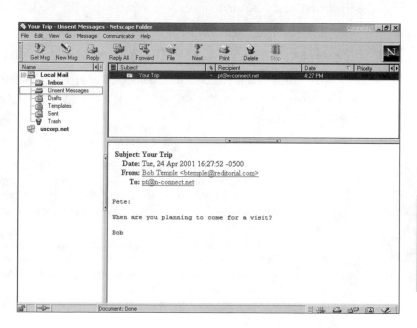

Why does this happen? Well, actually it's pretty smart. This Outbox scenario enables you to do all your email composing offline, saving as many messages as you want in your Outbox folder. Then, when you're all done, you can send all the messages in one step.

Here's how to send waiting messages:

- In Outlook Express, click the Send/Recv button (it might be labeled "Send/Receive" in your copy) to send all messages in the Outbox folder.
- In Netscape Messenger, click the Get Msg button (short for Get Messages) to send all messages in the Unsent Messages folder.

If you are offline when you click the Send/Recv (Send/Receive) or Get Msg button, Outlook Express and Messenger connect you to the Internet automatically (or prompt you to do so) to send your messages.

> The Send/Recv and Get Msg buttons not only send all waiting messages, but also receive any new messages sent to you.

Receiving Messages

When others send messages to you, those messages go to your service provider's mail server, and wait there until you choose to receive messages. To receive messages

- In Messenger, click the Get Msg button on the toolbar.
- In Outlook Express, click the Send/Recv (or Send/Receive) button on the toolbar.

If you are offline when you click the Send/Recv or Get Msg button, Outlook Express and Messenger connect you to the Internet automatically (or prompt you to do so) to retrieve your new messages.

> As I mentioned earlier, your ISP provides you with a special password you use only when receiving email (you don't need it to send email). When you click the button to receive mail, a dialog box might appear to prompt for your password. Just type your password and press Enter to continue receiving email.
>
> In the configuration dialog boxes of some email programs, you can type your email password; this enables the email program to automatically enter your password for you when you receive messages, saving you a step. This feature is handy, but should be used only if your computer is located where no one else might try to retrieve and read your email if you leave your desk while connected to the Internet.

Your email program contacts your ISP and checks for any new messages addressed to you. If there are none, the words "No new messages on server" appear in the status bar at the bottom of the window. If there are new messages, the messages are copied to your PC and stored in your Inbox folder, where you can read them any time, online or off.

In the message lists displayed by most email programs, the messages you have not yet read appear in bold (see Figure 5.13).

FIGURE 5.13

Messages listed in the Inbox in bold type are those you have not read yet.

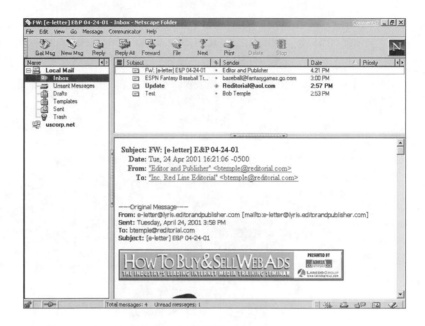

Messages you receive can contain computer viruses, particularly (but not exclusively) when those messages have files attached to them or they come to you from strangers. The best way to protect yourself from these files is to have a good anti-virus protection program installed on your computer; keep it updated to protect against newer viruses; never open an email or attachment from someone you don't know. Two of the top anti-virus programs are Norton AntiVirus (www.norton.com) and McAfee VirusScan (www.mcafee.com).

5

Replying and Forwarding

Most email programs provide you with two easy ways to create new messages by using other messages you have received: *reply* and *forward*.

Replying means sending a message back to someone from whom you have received a message, to respond to that message. *Forwarding* is passing a copy of a message you've received to a third party, either because you want to share the message's content with the third party or because you believe that, although the message was originally sent to you, the third party is a more appropriate recipient for it.

To reply or forward, you always begin by opening the original message. From the message window's toolbar, you then click a button or menu item with a label like one of the following (see Figure 5.14):

- **Reply**—Reply creates a reply to the person who sent you the message.

FIGURE 5.14

The Reply, Reply All, and Forward buttons offer different ways of responding to messages you've received.

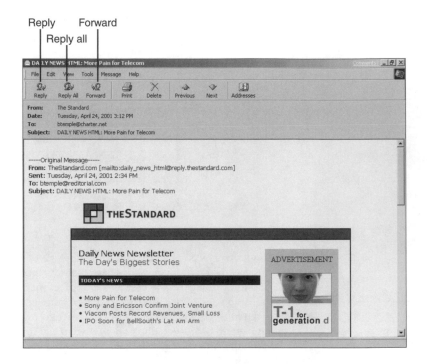

- **Reply All**—Reply All creates a reply to the person who sent you the message and to everyone else in the email's recipient list.
- **Forward**—Forward creates a new message containing the entire text of the original message, ready for you to forward.

Whichever button you click, a new message window opens. In the body of the message, a complete quote of the original message appears (see Figure 5.15).

A *quote* is all or a portion of a message you've received included in a reply to indicate what you're replying to, or included in a forward to carry the message you're forwarding.

FIGURE 5.15

A reply or a forward includes a quote from the original message.

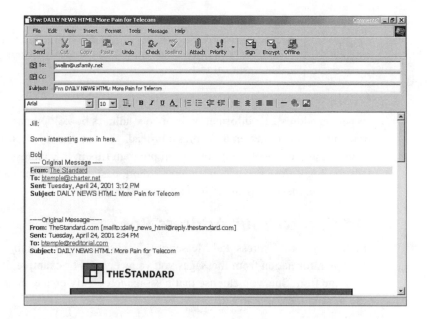

You can edit the quote, cutting out any parts that aren't relevant and inserting your own comments above, below, or within the quote.

In the message window of a reply, the To line is automatically filled in for you, with the address of the person from whom you received the message (or multiple addresses, if you chose Reply All). The Subject line is filled in with the original message's subject, preceded by Re:, to indicate that your message is a reply to a message using that subject. To complete the reply, all you have to do is type your comments above, below, or within the quote, and then click Send.

In the message window of a forward, the To line is empty, so you can enter the address of the person to whom you want to forward the message. (As with any message, you can enter multiple To recipients, and Cc recipients as well.) The Subject line is filled in with the original message's subject, preceded by FW: (forward). To complete the forward, address the message, type your comments above, below, or within the quote, and then click Send.

Using an Address Book

Most folks find that there's a steady list of others to whom they email often. Keeping track of those all-important names and addresses, and using them, is easier when you use your email program's *address book*.

5

> An *address book* is a directory you create, containing the names, email addresses, and often other information (mailing address, phone, notes) about your contacts.

When an addressee's information is in your address book, you needn't type—or even remember—his or her email address. Instead, you can simply choose the person's name from the address book, and your email program fills in the address for you. Some address books also support *nicknames*—short, easy-to-remember names you type in the To line of a message instead of the full email address.

Adding to Your Address Book

In both Outlook Express and Messenger, the easiest way to add to your address book is to copy information from messages you've received. For example, if you've received a message from Sue, you can use that message to quickly create an address card you can use to send messages to Sue.

To create a new address book entry from a message, begin by displaying the message in its own window. Next...

- In Netscape Messenger, from the message window's menu bar, choose Message, Add Sender to Address Book. A New Card dialog box opens (see Figure 5.16). Be sure the name and email address boxes on the Name tab have been filled in, and complete any of the other, optional boxes you want. Click OK to save the new entry.

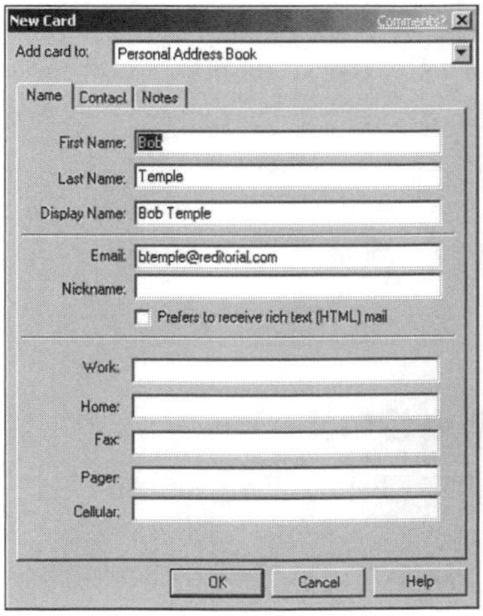

FIGURE 5.16

When you use a message you have received to add someone to your address book, that person's name and email address are entered for you, automatically.

- In Outlook Express, from the message window's menu bar, choose Tools, Add Sender to Address Book. Make sure the name and email address boxes on the Name tab have been filled in, and complete any of the other, optional boxes and tabs you want. Click OK to save the new entry.

To create an address book entry from scratch (without beginning from a message you've received):

- In Outlook Express, choose Tools, Address Book, click the New button, and then choose New Contact from the menu that appears.
- In Netscape Messenger, choose Communicator, Address Book, and then click the New Card button.

Addressing a Message from the Address Book

To use an address book entry to address a message (in Netscape Messenger or Outlook Express), begin by opening the new message window as usual. Then open the address book list:

- In Netscape Messenger, by choosing Communicator, Address Book.
- In Outlook Express, by clicking the little icon in the To line that looks like an open address book.

In the list, click the name of an addressee, and click the To button to add the addressee to the To line.

When you are finished choosing recipients, click OK to close the address book, and complete the Subject line and body of your message.

5

Attaching Files to Email Messages

Once new Internet users get the hang of using their Web browsers and email programs, nothing causes more frustration than file attachments.

An *attachment* is a file (any type—a picture file, word processing document, anything) that's attached to an email message so that it travels along with the message. The person who receives the message can detach the file from the message and use it.

The following example shows how to attach a file to an email message in Outlook Express. You'll send that message to yourself, so you can also learn how to detach and use a file attachment you receive. Note that the steps are similar in Netscape Messenger.

In Chapter 13, you will learn about the risk of catching a computer virus from programs and other files you download from the Internet. Well, you can pick up a virus just as easily from an email attachment.

If you're like most people, most email attachments you receive come from people you know, so you may think that those files are safe. But what if your friend is just passing on a file they received from someone else, maybe a stranger? That's one way email viruses spread; innocent, well-meaning people catch them and spread them around.

You can use most major virus protection programs, such as Norton AntiVirus and McAfee VirusScan, to check email attachments for viruses. Just save the attachment as a file separate from the message (as described in step 5 of the following example); then scan the file for viruses.

DO NOT open the file (by double-clicking its file icon or right-clicking it and choosing Open or Run) until after you have scanned it for viruses and determined that it's safe.

To attach a file to an email message:

1. Compose and address your message (to yourself) as you normally would. Then click the Attach button (see Figure 5.17).

FIGURE 5.17

Step 1: Click the Attach button in a new message.

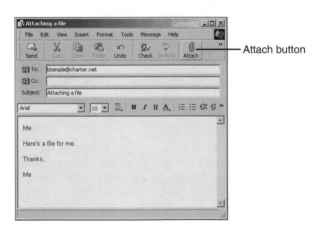

Attach button

2. Use the dialog box to navigate to and select the file to attach, and then click the dialog box's Attach button (see Figure 5.18).

FIGURE 5.18

Step 2: Find the file, and then click the Attach button.

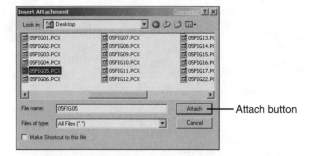

Attach button

3. Send the message (see Figure 5.19). If you do not immediately receive it, click Send/Recv again to receive the message.

FIGURE 5.19

Step 3: Send the message.

5

 Step 4 shows how to open a file attachment directly from the message, which is okay because you know the source of the file (you). But as a rule, unless you're very confident about the source of a file attachment, you should skip step 4, and instead do step 5 to separate the file from the message. Then you can use your virus-scanning software to check the file for viruses before you open it.

4. In the header of the received message, you'll see an icon and a filename representing the attached file. To view the file, double-click the icon (see Figure 5.20).

FIGURE 5.20

Step 4: To read the attachment in the received message, double-click the file's icon.

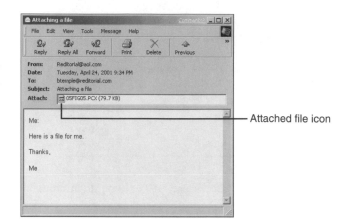

———— Attached file icon

5. If you want to save the file separately from the message (for use later), right-click the icon, and choose Save As (see Figure 5.21).

FIGURE 5.21

Step 5: To save the file, right-click and choose Save As.

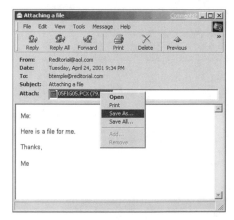

Using the Web for Email

Increasingly, people are using Web-based email to communicate. Web-based email allows a user to send and receive messages directly from a Web page, rather than opening a separate email program.

The advantages of this type of email are twofold: You can access your email and send and receive messages from any computer connected to the Internet, so it's great for travelers; and typically, the email account is free.

They are available all over the Web; Yahoo! and Hotmail, the Microsoft Network's Webmail offering, are the two biggest. But lots of sites offer free email as a way to increase visitors to their site. The more people sign up for it, the more people visit the site, the more people see the ads on the site, the more the site owner can charge for the ads. Free enterprise is a wonderful thing!

Heck, even the Major League Baseball site (www.majorleaguebaseball.com) offers free email to its users.

The primary drawback, however, is that these aren't full-featured email programs. Handling attachments to email is more difficult, if it's available at all. Saving emails is harder, too. And typically, you can't use an address book.

> After you've been on the Web a while, you will encounter some sites that want you to "register" with them in order to be able to use certain features. Although registering is often free, you usually have to supply an email address, so they can send you "special offers" and the like. Many people sign up for one of these free email accounts simply so they have an alternate email address to give to these sites. That way, your regular email account will receive less junk mail.

5

There is a combination of regular email and Web-based email that's a wonderful thing, however. Some ISPs offer a Web-based mail client to their regular members, so you can access your email if you're away from your regular computer.

America Online is one of these. AOL members can read their email from anywhere in the world, simply by logging on to the AOL site at www.aol.com. You simply sign in with your screen name and password, click the Check Your Mail! button, and you'll be able to read your messages. You can also reply, forward, or create new mail messages, right from the site (see Figure 5.22).

Each message appears as a highlighted and underlined link. Clicking on the link opens the message. It's pretty simple.

FIGURE 5.22

America Online offers a Web-based email option so its members can access their email from anywhere in the world.

Summary

Wow! You learned a lot this chapter. As you saw, the hardest part about email is getting yourself set up for it. Composing, sending, and receiving messages is a breeze, and techniques that can make you even more productive—such as using an Outbox or Address Book—are also pretty easy, and always optional.

CHAPTER 6

Chatting and Instant Messenger

Feel the need to reach out and touch someone, live and (almost) in person? Chat puts you online in a live conversation with other Internet users anywhere in the world.

And whereas chatting used to require a high degree of technical understanding, that's no longer the case. It used to require downloading a software program—a chat client—and installing it on your computer. Now, however, more and more people simply chat using their browser, through one of hundreds of sites that offer it.

Instant messaging is another way of reaching out and touching someone. What began as an America Online–only exercise is now available to anyone on the Web.

You might as well know that a substantial amount of chat traffic on the Internet is dedicated to sex chats of various persuasions and fetishes. There are many sex chat rooms, and sex-chat–oriented chatters often wander into non–sex-oriented rooms looking for new friends.

If that's okay with you, have fun. Live and let live, I always say, especially between consenting adults. But if you have an aversion to such stuff, tread carefully in chat. If you have a severe aversion to it, it's best to stay out of chat altogether.

And regardless of your own interests, I strongly advise against permitting children to use chat, especially unsupervised. My warning isn't about sex, but about safety. You'll find more about kids and chat in Chapter 14, "Enjoying Safe Family Fun and Games."

Understanding Internet Chatting

You might have heard people refer to chatting on the Internet as being in a "chat room." Well, you don't have to go into a special room in your house that you designate only for these chats. Chats are divided by subject matter, and the term *chat room* really refers to the subject area you have entered on the Internet.

Room is an appropriate word to use, however, because it's very much like being in a room full of people, all talking about the same subject. Everything you "say" by typing it into your computer can be "heard" by everybody else in the room—they will see your words appear on their computer screen. That can be a very small group of people, or dozens.

Thousands of different chats are under way at once, each in its own chat room. When you join a chat, you enter a room, and from then on you see only the conversation that's taking place in that room.

A *chat room* is a space where a single conversation is taking place. In Internet chat parlance, a chat room is sometimes known as a *channel*. This can be a confusing term, however, because it has several other meanings on the Internet. Stick with chat room.

In most chat rooms (or channels), the conversation is focused on a given subject area. In a singles chat room, participants chat about stuff singles like to talk about. In a geology chat, people generally talk about rocks and earthquakes.

When you're in a chat room, everything that everyone else in the same room types appears on your screen. Each participant's statements are labeled with a nickname to identify who's talking. Those participating in a chat (known as *members*) choose their own nicknames and rarely share their real names. In a chat, you can be whoever you want to be, and so can everyone else.

> Your *nickname*, which you choose yourself, is how you're known to others in a chat. Your nickname appears on every statement you make so everyone knows who's talking.

Chatting Through Your Browser

Chatting through your browser is the simplest way to get involved in chatting online. For that reason, it's also the most commonly used type of chat online.

All kinds of sites offer chats for their users. Big portals such as Yahoo! offer chats on a wide variety of topics. Specialized sites also offer chats for their users. Heck, even the Weather Channel (www.weather.com) offers chats. Hot enough for ya?

There are really two different kinds of chats. There are open chats that can involve anyone and everyone from around the globe, all talking about a particular subject of interest. These are sometimes moderated by someone whose job it is to keep the discussion clean and on-topic. The other kind of chat is a celebrity chat, in which a particular person appears in a chat room at a specified time to answer questions. For example, a local TV news crew might have its anchorperson online in a chat room for an hour one night a week to talk with viewers.

Finding Sites with Chat Rooms

It's not very difficult to find sites that offer chats for their users. Simply go to any site that interests you, and look around for a chat button. Some sites will call it "interact" or "forums" or the like, but it's often there if you want to find it. The chances are pretty good that the site you've been visiting all along has a chat area, and you didn't even know it.

Chatting at Yahoo!

If you're really interested in chatting, however, a great place to start is at the Yahoo! site or that of another major portal. These sites will typically offer chat rooms on a wide variety of subjects, giving you the opportunity to get chatting and change "rooms" easily.

6

We'll use Yahoo! as our example of a portal with good chat capabilities. They make it pretty easy to get started, too. All you have to do is sign up, choosing an ID and a password, provide some other basic information, and you're ready to go. To get started, go to the chat area at Yahoo! (`chat.yahoo.com`), and click on the Sign Up for Yahoo! Chat! Link (see Figure 6.1).

FIGURE 6.1

Signing up for chatting on Yahoo! is quick and easy.

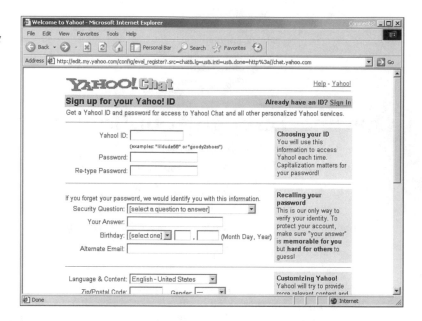

 The hardest part of signing up for Yahoo! or any other popular service is picking a username (or ID) that hasn't already been chosen. Because signing up for Yahoo! chat also registers you for a free Yahoo! email address, you're in the mix with the millions who have already joined. So you may end up with an ID that's a little nonsensical.

Signing up takes only a minute (after you've found an ID that's not already in use). Once your information has been accepted, click on the Complete Room List button to get an idea of what's out there in terms of chat.

Yahoo! chats are broken into categories, and each category contains several different rooms. For example, under the Music category, you'll find chats on subjects ranging from Britney Spears to jazz (see Figure 6.2).

FIGURE 6.2

Yahoo! chat offers a wide variety of rooms from which to choose.

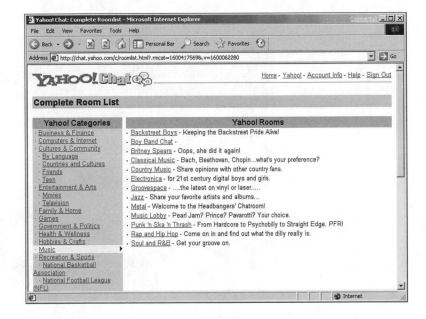

After you've found a subject that interests you, just click its link to enter the room. Now, it's time to chat!

The Chat Window

Before you can be a successful chatter, you need to know the ins and outs of the chat room itself. Yahoo! is a good example, because its chat rooms appear much like those at many other sites.

After you've entered a chat, you'll see the chat window (see Figure 6.3). It's divided neatly into different frames, and each has its purpose.

The biggest pane in the window, in the upper left, is the viewing pane. This is where all the messages appear, including those that you write. Below that, you will see some formatting buttons that allow you to change the way your text appears, and the Chat: pane. This is where you will type any messages you write in the chat. Type it out, click the Send button, and they'll appear in the viewing pane, for you and all the others in the room to see.

Speaking of the others, they are listed in the member list pane, at the upper right. The list is by ID.

6

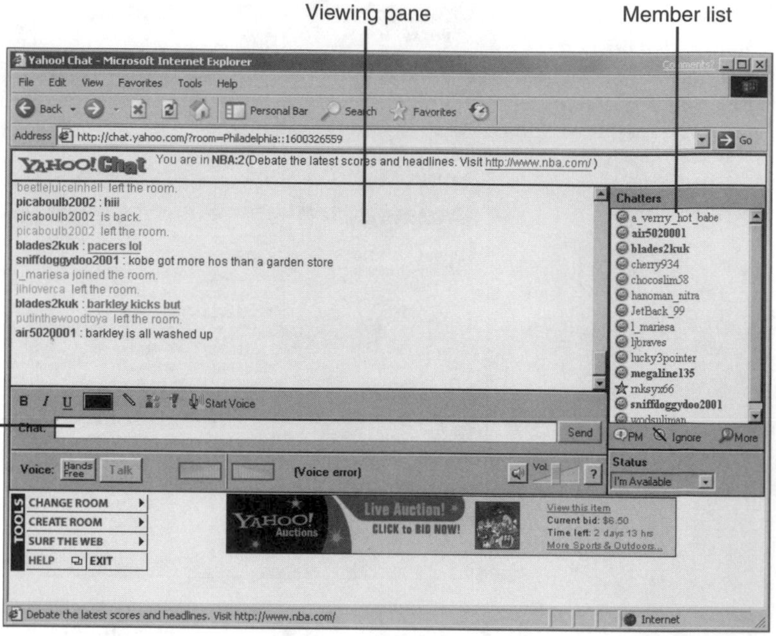

FIGURE 6.3

The Yahoo! chat window is similar to those of many other chats.

At the very bottom, you'll see some tools. There are also other special tricks you can do, as well:

- **Create Room**—You can create your own chat room if you wish. This is great if you want to have a private chat with a group of people, say for business purposes. Or, if you want to have the entire extended family all in one place to announce a baby on the way! You can set up your own chat room, make it password-protected so the ordinary Joes can't enter, and then set a time for the chat and give the appropriate people the room name and password.

- **PM**—Under the member list, you see the PM button. Use this to send a private message to someone in the chat room. Just highlight their name, click PM, and type your message to them.

- **Ignore**—If there's one person in the room who really bugs you, highlight their ID and click Ignore. You will no longer see any messages posted by that person.

- **Voice**—If your computer is properly equipped, you can participate in a voice chat by clicking the Start Voice button. You need a good sound card, speakers, and a microphone to participate.

Chatting in AOL

America Online's chats are one of the service's most popular features. Chat rooms are all over AOL. You'll find chat rooms in forums to discuss just about any topic the service offers.

Just choose a channel from the list on the left side of your AOL screen and you'll be able to find chats within that area of interest. For example, take the Parenting channel. If you click on the Parenting button, you'll find a special "Moms" area inside. Go there, and you'll find a Chat Now button. Click it, and you'll have a wide range of chatting options (see Figure 6.4—everything from a special chat for disabled moms to chats about dealing with teenagers (good luck), and so on.

FIGURE 6.4
AOL's chats are specialized by topic, so you can meet with people of similar interests.

Using the People Connection

As many chat rooms as there are in the Channel forums, you'll find many more in the People Connection. The People Connection is abuzz with chat 24 hours a day, seven days a week. These are different than the chats in the various channels.

Chat rooms are so popular that there's a Chat button on the Welcome window that greets you when you sign on. You can click that or select People Connection from the People menu on the toolbar—either way, you'll go to the People Connection.

When you click the Chat button, you move into the People Connection screen. There are many options here; choose Chat Now, and you're dropped into a lobby chat room in Town Square (see Figure 6.5). Town Square is the generic chat category online—there are others (you'll see them in a moment). A lobby is just that: a waiting room where you can chat or move on to a room with a more defined topic of conversation.

6

FIGURE 6.5

Your basic chat room—
this one's a lobby.

At any given moment, there can be hundreds of lobbies in the People Connection. They are all given a number—the one shown in Figure 6.5 is Lobby 75.

On the right side of the chat window is a list of the people who are in the lobby with you (your screen name is there, too). You can find out a little something about the folks in your room by seeing if they have a Member Profile. To read a Member Profile, double-click a screen name from the room list, and then click Get Profile on the dialog box that appears.

> Just like in Yahoo! chat, if someone is getting on your nerves in a chat room and you wish they would just shut up, you can shut them up—as far as you're concerned at least. The same Info dialog box that lets you read another member's profile also has a little check box labeled Ignore Member. Click it so that it's checked, and nothing that person says will appear on your screen. You're ignoring him; perhaps he'll lose interest and go away.

When you first start out in a chat room, it's a good idea to sit and read the chat scrolling up your screen. It gives you a notion of what's being talked about, who's doing the talking, and whether you want to join in. If you want to participate in a lobby chat, simply type what you want to say in the text box at the bottom of the window and then press Enter (or click Send). Your chat appears in the chat window, and you can carry on a conversation.

If there isn't much going on in the lobby, you might want to move to a room with a more specific chat theme.

Moving to Another Room

To see a list of the currently active chat rooms in the People Connection, click the Find a Chat button at the bottom-right side of the chat window. A list of categories and chat rooms appears in the Find a Chat dialog box, as shown in Figure 6.6.

FIGURE 6.6

Find a Chat helps you find rooms of interest.

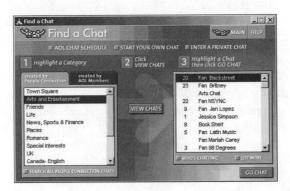

In the Find a Chat dialog box, you'll see a list of room categories in the box on the left side of the screen. When you highlight a category name and click the View Chats button in the middle of the window, the list box on the right of the screen shows all the rooms that are available for that specific category. At peak chatting hours, you might need to click the List More button a couple of times to see all the chat rooms in a given category.

To enter a room, double-click its name in the list. You can also peek in and see who's chatting in a room. Click on the room's name in the list and then click the Who's Chatting button. A list of the members in the room appears, much like the room list in an actual chat room. You can use it to see who's around before you drop in for a chat.

You might notice that the categories list on the left side of the Find a Chat window has two tabs. The second tab reveals the same category list as the first tab, but the chat rooms listed in the right side are instead those that have been created by AOL members, not AOL staff. The list looks, and works, exactly the same as the one shown previously in Figure 6.6, but the rooms have all been created by AOL members.

You can create your own chat room from the list of Member Chats by clicking the Start Your Own Chat button (top middle of the Find a Chat window).

6

These member-created rooms can be much wilder and woollier than the AOL sanctioned rooms—consider that a warning, or a piece of advice, depending on your mood.

Using Microsoft Chat

Another type of chat involves downloading and using a chat client software program.
These programs used Internet Relay Chat, or IRC, to conduct their chats. There are many
such programs, but one of the best is Microsoft Chat—it's free, and it's a little bit
unusual in that it makes the chat look like a comic strip.

If you don't have Microsoft Chat, you can download it free from the Tucows software
directory at www.tucows.com or directly from Microsoft at www.microsoft.com.

Like any chat program, Microsoft Chat—henceforth to be known simply as Chat with a
capital C—lets you communicate with chat servers. You can view the list of chat rooms,
join a chat room, read what everyone says in the chat room, and make your own contributions to the discussion. What's different about Chat is the way it displays the conversation.

Most chat clients show the text of the conversation a line at a time and label each line
with the speaker's nickname.

Chat, however, can display the conversation as text or as a comic strip, using little cartoon characters to represent members and showing their words in cartoon word balloons
(see Figure 6.7). The folks at Microsoft think this approach makes chatting feel more
human, more fun. In its first versions, Chat was actually named Microsoft Comic Chat.

A *balloon* is the little bubble you see in comics in which the words or
thoughts of a character appears.

FIGURE 6.7

*Microsoft Chat can
make a chat session
look like a comic strip,
with a different cartoon
character for each par-
ticipant.*

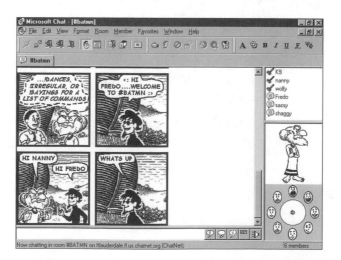

It's important to understand that most folks you'll end up chatting with probably won't use Microsoft Chat. Many will use ordinary text chat clients; they'll see your statements labeled with your nickname but won't see your comic character.

On your display, Chat converts all statements in a chat—even those made by users of text-only clients—into comics. Other Chat users in the same room appear as their chosen cartoon characters. For users of other chat clients, Chat automatically assigns and shows unused characters.

Joining a Chat Room

It's time to hit a server and see it for real. On the way, though, you'll perform some automatic configuration that Chat needs to operate properly.

> Before you open Chat, you can be online or off. If you're offline when you begin, Chat connects to the Internet automatically. Also, your browser need not be open for you to use Chat, although it won't hurt anything if it is open.

To start a chat and display the chat rooms list:

1. Open Microsoft Chat. In Windows, you do so by choosing Programs, Microsoft Chat.
2. Select the Show All Available Chat Rooms option, and then click OK to connect to the chat server listed in the dialog (see Figure 6.8).

FIGURE 6.8

Step 2: Select Show All Available Chat Rooms, and then click OK.

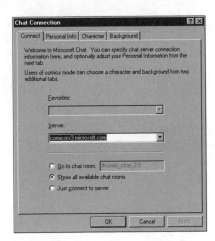

6

3. A message appears. This message differs by server, but typically it contains any special rules or instructions for the server, plus any disclaimers in which the server operator reminds you that he's not responsible for what people say there.

4. A list of all chat rooms available on the server appears (see Figure 6.9). You are now connected to a chat server and are ready to chat—except that, as a new user, you have not yet selected a nickname and a comic character, as described next.

FIGURE 6.9

Step 4: A list of available chat rooms appears.

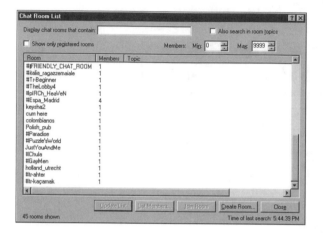

Choosing an Identity

Before you can join in a chat, you must create a nickname. And because of Chat's unique presentation style, you must choose a comic character, too. In addition, you can select a background that appears behind the characters in each panel of the comic, as you see it on your screen.

After you choose a nickname, character, and background, Chat remembers them for future sessions. You do not need to choose them again unless you want to change them.

Choose View, Options to open the Options dialog box, and choose the Personal Info tab if it is not already selected (see Figure 6.10).

Click in the Nickname box and type a nickname for yourself. Your nickname should be one word with no spaces or punctuation, and it should also be unusual enough that another member hasn't chosen the same nickname. (If you attempt to enter a room where someone is already using the same nickname as you, Chat prompts you to change your nickname before entering.)

FIGURE 6.10

The Personal Info tab allows you to set your preferences.

 On the Personal Info tab, you can enter other information besides your nickname, such as your real name and email address. Think carefully before doing so, however. Any information you supply here can be seen by other members whose clients (like Chat) can display member profiles. If you want to keep your anonymity, enter your nickname and nothing else.

To choose the character you would like to use for your likeness, click the Character tab and click a name in the Character column (see Figure 6.11). The Preview column shows what the selected character looks like—what you will look like to other Chat users if you stick with that character.

FIGURE 6.11

Select a character for your likeness.

6

When you're choosing a character in the Character tab, you can click the faces in the Emotion Wheel (beneath the character preview) to see what the character will look like when you apply a given emotion to it when making a statement. You'll learn about choosing emotions later in this chapter.

You can also specify a background to use by clicking the Background tab and selecting one.

Entering a Room

To enter a chat room, you select a room from the chat room list. Figure 6.12 shows the list of chats available on the server. Each server has its own list, and the lists change often.

FIGURE 6.12

To enter any room in the list, double-click its name.

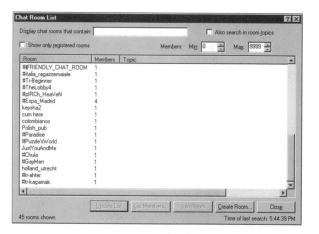

The chat room list reappears after you finish selecting your identity, but you can open the chat room list anytime you're connected to the server by clicking the Chat Room List button on Chat's toolbar.

In the list, the name of each room begins with a pound sign (#). The name of the room is followed by the number of members currently in the room, and sometimes also by a description of the conversation that usually takes place there.

When you first arrive in a room, you might not see any comic panels right away. The server shows you only what's been said since you entered the room. After you enter, statements begin appearing one by one as members make them.

Now that you're in a room, you can just lurk or listen in on the conversation, or you can contribute to it by sending your statements for all the others to see. Note that you are not obligated to add anything to the conversation. In fact, just lurking in a chat room is a great way to learn more about chats before diving in.

When you're ready to contribute your comments to the chat, just type them in as you did in the browser-based chats we discussed earlier.

While you're typing and editing your statements in the Compose pane, no one sees them but you. A statement is sent to the chat only when you press Enter. This gives you a chance to choose your words carefully and correct typos before committing your statement to the chat.

After you press Enter, those in the room who are using regular chat clients see your statement labeled with your nickname, so they know you said it. Those in the room who are using Microsoft Chat see your chosen comic character speaking the words in a say balloon, the type that surrounds words that comic characters say aloud.

You can format your words by picking a special balloon from the right side of the Compose pane. The balloons allow you to indicate you are thinking (bubbles) or whispering (dotted outline). You can also have your character express emotions by picking the appropriate face from the Emotion Wheel in the lower-right corner.

There are lots of other chat clients out there. If you want to look for others, you can always check the Tucows directory at www.tucows.com.

6

Because some members in the room might not be using Chat and therefore can't see expressions, be sure your words alone carry your meaning.

What Is Instant Messenger?

Instant messaging is a lot like chat, with a few key differences. One, most instant messages are sent to or received from people you know. Two, the conversations are just between you and one other person.

America Online members automatically get AOL's Instant Messenger and can use it within the service. If you know another person's screen name, you can use Instant Messenger to check to see if they are online. If they are, you can type them a quick message, and it automatically pops up on their screen.

Those who don't have AOL can still use Instant Messenger. You can download it from the Netscape Web site (www.netscape.com). It's a quick download, and it walks you through the steps of setting it up.

Sending "Instant" Messages

Instant Messenger lets you see, from among a list you set up yourself (a "Buddy List"), which of your friends are online at the same time you are (see Figure 6.13). You can exchange typed messages with those friends—but unlike email, those messages show up instantly. The moment you send a message to a friend who's online, he or she sees it, and vice versa. So you can carry on a live, interactive conversation, much like chat.

FIGURE 6.13

AOL Instant Messenger lets you exchange live messages with friends who are online at the same time you are— even if neither of you uses AOL.

The easiest way to sign up for Instant Messenger is to install Netscape Communicator. From Navigator's menu bar, choose Communicator, AOL Instant Messenger Service, and then follow the prompts to sign up.

Note that AOL Instant Messenger is not the only such service available. Another is Yahoo! Messenger, which you can learn about at `messenger.yahoo.com`. Internet Explorer offers a similar instant messaging system, called MSN Messenger. There are other instant message systems, but these are the main ones, and they are all free and fun.

> You might think it's cool that you can know whether or not a friend is online by using your Buddy List. However, that means others can know if you're online as well. If you want to limit who knows you're online and who can contact you, open the My IM menu and select Edit Options, Edit Preferences. Then click the Privacy tab, and you can create a more private setup for yourself.

Summary

Chat and instant messages are fun, as long as you stay among people whose reasons for chatting are the same as yours. Like a carnival or circus, chat is an entertaining place with a seedy underbelly and should be enjoyed with caution. But if you're careful, you can have safe, interactive fun with chat and instant messages.

6

CHAPTER 7

Participating in Newsgroups and Mailing Lists

Now that you've gotten started with email and chat, it's time to look at a couple of other ways of communicating: newsgroups and mailing lists. They both share aspects of emailing and chatting, but they work in different ways. And they both offer great ways to get involved with a subject that interests you, or to just have fun.

Getting Started with Newsgroups

When you know how to an email program, you know 90 percent of what you need to know to use newsgroups. Reading a message, composing a new message, and replying are all very similar in an email program and a news-reader.

Where a newsreader differs is that it retrieves messages from and posts messages to Internet newsgroups, sometimes known as discussion groups or, collectively, as Usenet. The newsgroups and their messages are stored on a family of servers called *news servers* or *NNTP servers*.

> Sending a message to a newsgroup is known as *posting*, because you're publishing the message in a public forum, just as if you had "posted" a paper note on a bulletin board.

Your ISP or online service has a news server that you are authorized to use for reading and contributing to newsgroups. Access to one news server is all you need; the messages sent to any news server on the Internet are automatically copied—at regular intervals—to all news servers.

On any news server, you can open any newsgroup and read any current message posted to that newsgroup, no matter which news server the message was originally posted to. That's why a newsgroup on an ISP's server in New York has messages from folks in Canada, California, and the U.K.

Before you can open newsgroups and display their messages, you must configure your newsreader to contact your ISP's news server, and you must download the complete list of newsgroups from the server.

> In general, all news servers carry the same newsgroups and current messages—but not exactly.
>
> First, a few ISPs or online services do not carry all newsgroups, omitting those they deem potentially offensive to their customers, such as sex-oriented groups. A few ISPs carry only newsgroups specifically requested by their subscribers, instead of all of the thousands of groups out there. And some ISP's servers carry special newsgroups of local interest that are not copied to other news servers.
>
> Beyond those differences, note that it takes a day or so for a message posted to one server to be copied to all the others. At any given time, a new message might be on some servers, but not yet on others.
>
> Finally, no news server keeps messages forever. After a set number of days, a newsgroup message is automatically deleted from the server. Each server has its own schedule for removing these old—*expired*—messages, so a message that's been deleted from one server might remain on others.

Configuring Your Newsreader

As with other types of Internet programs, there are many different newsreaders out there. In the Big Two Internet suites, the programs are the same ones you use for email: Netscape Messenger and Outlook Express. You just have to switch these programs from email mode to newsgroup mode.

There are a number of good newsreader programs available on the market. If you have the Microsoft Office suite, you could use Microsoft Outlook as a newsreader. Forte, Inc., offers two good newsreader products, a freeware program called Free Agent, and a commercial program called Agent. You can check them out at www.forteinc.com.

To switch either program to newsgroup mode, you simply click your news server's name near the bottom of the folder list (see Figure 7.1). Observe that choosing the server changes the toolbar buttons and menu choices from those used for email to those you need for newsgroups.

FIGURE 7.1

To use Outlook Express (shown here) or Netscape Messenger for newsgroup activities, click your news server's name in the folder list.

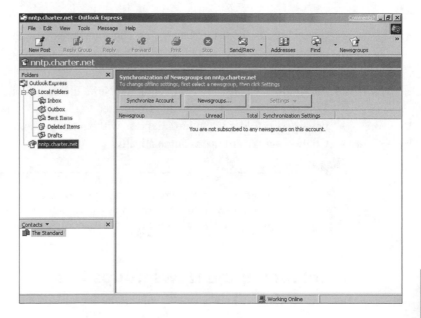

7

You can open Outlook Express directly in newsgroup mode from Internet Explorer by clicking the Mail button on IE's toolbar, and then choosing Read News from the menu that appears. You can open Netscape Messenger directly in newsgroup mode by choosing Communicator, Newsgroups from within any Communicator component (such as Navigator).

If you use an online service, such as America Online or CompuServe, you might not be able to choose your own newsreader; you might be required to use the online service interface—the tool you use for accessing the service's non-Internet content. However, this will still allow you to access the newsgroups on the Internet just like another newsreader would.

All newsreaders have a configuration dialog box in which you enter the information required for communicating with your ISP's news server. That dialog box always requires the address of your ISP's news server. If your newsreader is not part of a suite (and thus cannot copy configuration information from the email component), the configuration dialog box also requires your email address and full name.

You'll find the configuration dialog box

- For Netscape Messenger by choosing Edit, Preferences to open the Preferences dialog box. In the list of Categories, choose Mail & Newsgroups. Complete the configuration settings in the Mail & Newsgroups category's Newsgroup Servers subcategory.

- For Outlook Express by completing the News dialog boxes of the Connection Wizard (see Chapter 3, "Getting Connected to the Internet"). If you choose your news server folder in Outlook Express without having configured first, the Internet Connection Wizard opens automatically.

Instead of using the Internet Connection Wizard, you can configure newsgroup access in Outlook Express by choosing Tools, Accounts, and then clicking the Add button on the Internet Accounts dialog box.

Downloading the Newsgroups List

After your newsreader knows how to contact the server, you must download the complete list of newsgroups, which usually takes just a few minutes. If you open some newsreaders (including Netscape Messenger and Outlook Express) without first having downloaded the list, a prompt appears, asking whether you want to download the list.

If your newsreader does not prompt you, find a button or menu item for downloading the list by doing one of the following:

- In Netscape Messenger, make sure you are in newsgroup mode by clicking the name of your news server or choosing Communicator, Newsgroups. Choose File, Subscribe and, on the dialog box that appears, click the Refresh List button.

- In Outlook Express, click the name of your news server, and then click the Newsgroups button. On the dialog box that appears, click Reset List.

The list of newsgroups changes periodically, adding new groups and removing others. Netscape Messenger, Outlook Express, and some other newsreaders detect automatically when the list changes, and display a prompt asking whether you want to update your list.

If your newsreader does not detect changes in the list, it's smart to redownload the full list once a month or so, to keep current.

Finding and Subscribing to Newsgroups

Once the list has been downloaded to your computer, you can find and subscribe to any newsgroups you want. While exploring Web pages devoted to topics that interest you, you'll probably come across the names of related newsgroups. But newsgroups are easy to find, with or without a Web page's help.

Unlike mailing lists, you are not required to subscribe to a newsgroup in order to use it. All subscribing really does is add the group to an easy-access list in your newsreader, to make visiting it convenient.

Most people have a small list of groups they visit often, so subscribing makes sense. But in most newsreaders, you can pick a newsgroup out of the full list, or enter the group's name in a dialog box, to open the list without subscribing.

Newsgroups are perhaps the one Internet activity where names are a reliable indicator of content. Newsgroups are organized under a system of names and categories. The leftmost portion of the name shows the top-level category in which the group sits; each portion further to the right more narrowly determines the subject of the group.

7

For example, the top-level category rec contains recreational newsgroups, those dedicated to a recreational—rather than professional—discussion of their topics. So the hypo-
thetical newsgroup name

rec.sports.basketball.womens

indicates that the discussion focuses on a recreational interest in women's basketball.
There are thousands of rec groups, many rec.sports groups, several rec.sports.
basketball groups, and just one rec.sports.basketball.womens newsgroup. See how it
works?

Some of the other major top-level categories include the following:

- alt—Alternative newsgroups, those in which the most freewheeling conversations
  are accepted
- biz—Business newsgroups and ads
- comp—Computer-related newsgroups
- k12—Education-related groups
- misc—Miscellaneous
- sci—Science-related groups

To choose, subscribe to, and open groups in Outlook Express:

1. Connect to the Internet, open Outlook Express, and click the news server's name in
   the left-hand column (see Figure 7.2).

FIGURE 7.2

*Step 1: Click on the
news server's name in
the left-hand column of
Outlook Express.*

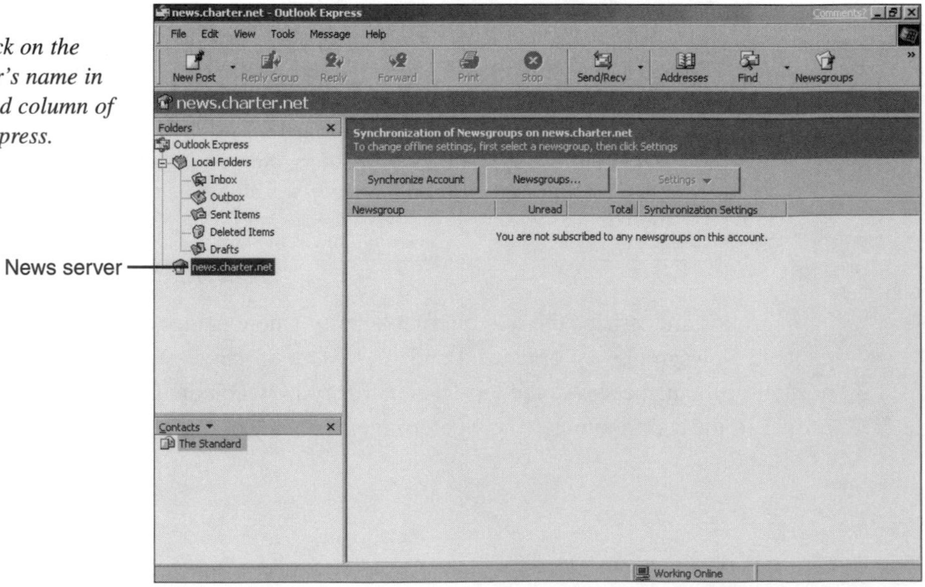

News server

> If you are using Netscape as your newsreader, the steps are very similar. To get started, open the Communicator menu and select Newsgroups.

2. Click the Newsgroups button to open the list of newsgroups available to you (see Figure 7.3).

FIGURE 7.3

Step 2: Click the Newsgroups button to open the list.

3. In the All tab, display the group's name in the Newsgroup box (see Figure 7.4). There are several ways to do this:

   - If you know the exact name of the group you want to subscribe to, type the name in the box.

   - Use the list to scroll to the group name, then click it. In the list, the groups are presented alphabetically.

   - Enter a search word or phrase in the box and click OK to search for newsgroups of a particular topic.

FIGURE 7.4

Step 3: Display the group's name in the Newsgroup box.

7

4. When the name of the group you want to subscribe to is highlighted, click the Subscribe button, and then click OK (see Figure 7.5). The newsgroup's name appears under your news server's name, and in the bigger list of newsgroups on your screen.

FIGURE 7.5

Step 4: The subscribed newsgroup appears in your list.

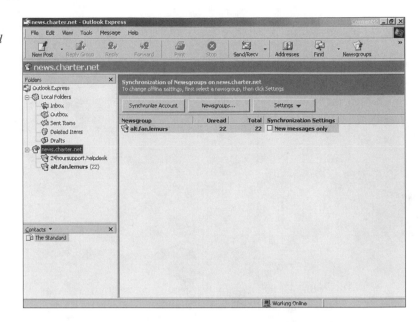

5. To open a newsgroup, click its name in the list (see Figure 7.6).

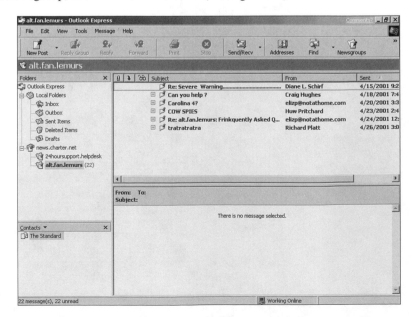

Reading Newsgroup Messages

Once you open and display a newsgroup's message list, reading messages is just like reading email messages in an email program. Single-click an item in the list to display it in the preview pane (as shown in Figure 7.7), or double-click it to display the message in its own window.

FIGURE 7.7

You can organize your newsgroup message list by thread, to better follow the flow of individual conversations.

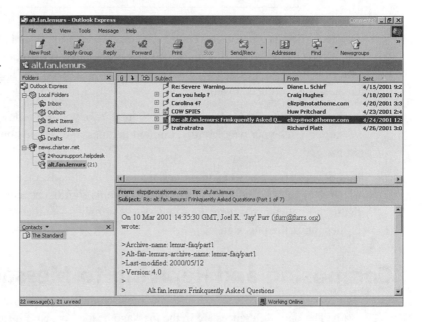

The message lists you see in an email program generally show messages that have been copied to your computer. But in most newsreaders, the messages in the list you see when you open a newsgroup are not on your computer; they're on the news server.

All that's been copied to your computer are the message headers, to make up the list. When you display any particular message, that message is then copied to your computer. Because the messages aren't copied until you request them, you must stay online while working with newsgroups.

Some newsreaders—including Netscape Messenger and Outlook Express—support *offline news reading*. You can configure them to automatically download messages from newsgroups so you can read them later, offline.

7

The tricky part about reading news messages is organizing the list in a way that works for you. Most newsreaders let you arrange the messages in myriad ways: alphabetically by subject, by author, by date, and so on. (The options for sorting the message list in

Netscape Messenger, Outlook Express, and most other Windows and Mac newsreaders appear on the View menu.) But the most useful sorting is by *thread*.

In a newsgroup, a *thread* is one particular conversation—a message and all replies to that message (and replies to those replies, and so on).

In effect, threads group messages by subject. Two messages can have the same subject but not the same thread, if neither is a reply to the other (or a reply to a reply to the other). If you sort messages by thread, and then by subject, you'll get all threads on a given subject grouped together.

When you sort messages by thread (see Figure 7.7), you can follow the flow of the conversation, click your way in order, through the messages to see how the discussion has progressed.

In most newsreaders, when messages are sorted by threads, the replies to a message do not appear automatically in the list; instead, a plus sign (+) appears next to the message's listing, to indicate that there are submessages—replies—to that message. To display the replies, click the plus sign.

Composing and Replying to Messages

You compose and reply to messages in a newsreader exactly as you do in an email program. The only differences are in the message header, because instead of addressing a message to a person, you're addressing it to a newsgroup.

The only other important difference between sending email and newsgroup messages is the terminology you see applied on buttons and menu items:

- In email, you click Send to send a message; in a newsreader, it's either Send or Post.
- In email, you click Reply to reply to a message; in a newsreader, it's either Reply or Respond.

The easiest way to deal with that difference is to start in the right place. For example, when you want to compose a new message (not a reply) and post it to a newsgroup, begin by opening that newsgroup, and then clicking your newsreader's button for composing a new message. (It's New Msg in Netscape Messenger, New Post in Outlook Express.) When the message window opens, you'll see that it's preaddressed to the currently open newsgroup.

> When you first join a newsgroup, it's a good idea to "lurk" for a while before posting. Lurking is the act of reading other people's posts and just "getting the lay of the land" before jumping in head-first.

When replying, open the message to which you want to reply, and then click the Reply (or Respond) button on the message window in which that message appears. In the message window that opens, the message is preaddressed to the appropriate newsgroup, the subject line is correctly phrased to add the reply to the same thread as the original message, and the original message is quoted in the message area (see Figure 7.8). Just add your comments, and edit the quote as necessary.

FIGURE 7.8

Start a new message or reply while viewing the message list of a newsgroup, and that message is preaddressed to the open newsgroup.

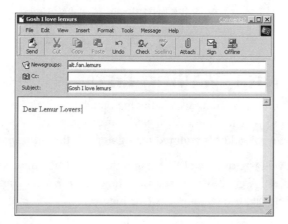

After completing a new message or reply, send the message by clicking the button or menu item labeled Send or Post.

> When you choose to reply, most newsreaders provide the option of replying to the newsgroup or sending an email reply directly to the author of the message you're replying to. The email option is handy when your reply is really intended only for the author, not the whole group.

7

The Basics of Mailing Lists

A mailing list is much like a newsgroup in that you subscribe to a list based on its topic. The primary difference is that instead of visiting the newsgroup and reading messages of your choice, a mailing list will automatically send every post to the group to your email address.

For a mailing list to work, someone has to handle its management and administration: mostly signing up new members and removing members who have asked to be removed.

In a few mailing lists, that administrative task is handled by a real person. However, most mailing lists are managed not by a person, but by a *list server*. Sometimes, the mailing lists managed by people are called *manual* mailing lists, to distinguish them from the lists automated by list servers.

> A *list server* is a program that automatically manages a mailing list. Actually, there are several different programs that manage mailing lists, including Listserv, Listproc, and Majordomo. They are often grouped generically under the term "listserv."

Working with Mailing Lists

The first step in using mailing lists is finding one that interests you. When visiting Web pages devoted to your favorite topics, you'll often see mention of related mailing lists, along with the email address required for signing up: the *subscription address*.

You can also visit any of several Web pages that help folks find mailing lists related to a particular subject. A good first stop is Liszt (www.Liszt.com), a search tool dedicated to helping you find and use mailing lists (see Figure 7.9).

You can browse through Liszt's categories to find a list, or use its search engine to find lists related to a search term you enter.

Besides Liszt, other good places to find mailing lists (and instructions for using them) include the following:

- The list of Publicly Accessible Mailing Lists at http://paml.net/
- The List of Lists, at catalog.com/vivian/interest-group-search.html
- Yahoo!'s directory at www.yahoo.com/Computers_and_Internet/Internet/ Mailing_Lists/

FIGURE 7.9

Use Liszt to browse for a mailing list or search for one.

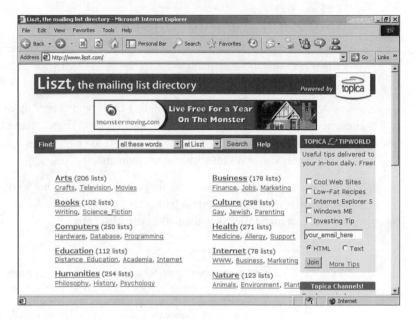

Subscribing to a Mailing List

To use any mailing list, you need to know two different email addresses:

- The address of the person, or program, that manages the list. This address might be called the "management" or "subscription" address.

- The list address, an email address to which you send all your contributions to the list, the comments or questions you want all others in the list to see.

Sorry, sorry… Hate to break into an easy topic like mailing lists with a big fat Caution. But I really want to alert you to the one major mailing list mistake: Mixing up the list address with the management address, and vice versa.

If you accidentally send your list contributions to the management address, the others on the list won't see them. And if you send management commands to the list address, those commands will not be carried out. Worse, the message containing those commands might show up in the mailing list of everyone in the list, which won't win you any friends.

Never forget: Contributions to the discussion go to the list address, commands for managing your subscription go to that other address (subscription, management, whatever), which is usually the same one you used to subscribe.

7

Composing the Subscription Message

When you're ready to sign up, you send to the subscription address a simple email message that contains the command required to subscribe. Unfortunately, the command differs from list to list.

Most references to mailing lists—including those you'll turn up in the directories described earlier—include subscription instructions. Those instructions typically tell you the command you must send, and also where in the email message—the Subject line or the message body—you must type that command.

Command instructions use a syntax diagram to tell you what to type. Even manually managed lists generally require a particular command syntax, although they're more forgiving of command mistakes than automated lists are.

> A *syntax diagram* shows what you must type to properly phrase a command to control a computer program, such as a listserv. In a syntax diagram, the exact words you must type are shown in normal type, while any parts of the command you must add are surrounded by brackets or shown in italics.

For example, to phrase the command indicated by the syntax diagram

```
subscribe lastname firstname
```

or

```
subscribe [lastname] [firstname]
```

I would type

```
subscribe Snell Ned
```

Notice that I replace any portions in italics or brackets with the information indicated, and that I do not type the brackets.

To subscribe to a list, read the instructions to find the following:

- The syntax diagram for subscribing
- The part of the message where the command should be typed (either the Subject line or body)
- The subscription address

Compose an email message containing only the command indicated by the instructions, and send it to the subscription address. Figure 7.10 shows a typical subscription message in which the command appears in the message body.

FIGURE 7.10

You subscribe to a mailing list by typing a subscription command in an email message and sending it to the list's subscription address.

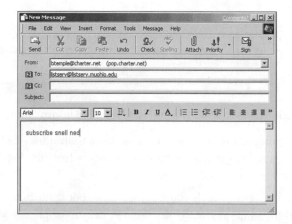

When composing your message, don't type anything the instructions don't ask for. If the instructions tell you to put the command in the message's Subject line, leave the message body blank. If the command belongs in the message body, leave the Subject line blank, and put nothing but the command in the body. (Many lists don't care whether you follow this rule, but because you can't predict which lists *do* care, it's best to follow the rule always.)

Because many automated list management programs manage more than one list, the subscription command syntax often includes the name of the list, so the program knows which list you're subscribing to, for example:

subscribe listname firstname lastname

Reading the Welcome Message

Shortly after you send your subscription message, you'll receive a reply message from the list. An automated list might reply within a minute or two. After sending a subscription message to an automated list, stay online, wait a few minutes, and then check your email—the reply will probably be there. (Some automated and manual lists might take a day or more to reply, so be patient, and don't resend the subscription message if you don't receive an immediate reply.)

If you did not phrase your subscription message properly, the reply reiterates the subscription command syntax and usually includes instructions. You must compose and send another subscription message, carefully following any instructions in the reply.

7

Always, always, always read and save the Welcome message, if for no other reason than that it contains the instructions for *unsubscribing*—quitting— the mailing list if you choose to do so later.

The Welcome message contains lots of very valuable information, particularly:

- A syntax diagram for phrasing the command to unsubscribe. If and when you decide you no longer want to receive messages from the list, you'll need to send this command to the subscription address.

- The list address to which you must send all your contributions, and the management address (that is usually the same as the subscription address, but not always).

- Syntax for other commands you can use to manage the way messages come to you. For example, many lists let you send a command to temporarily pause—stop sending you messages—if you go on vacation or want messages paused for any other reason.

- Any other rules or policies all members of the list are required to observe. These typically include the basic rules of netiquette (covered later in this chapter).

Sometimes, the Welcome message includes instructions to send a reply to the Welcome, to confirm your subscription. In such cases, you're not officially subscribed until you send a reply as instructed.

Always read and save the Welcome message, so you can refer to it when you need to know a command or policy or want to unsubscribe. If your email program lets you organize your messages in folders, create a special folder for Welcome messages (or a folder for each list you subscribe to), so they're easy to find and you don't accidentally delete them when cleaning up your Inbox. You might also want to print the Welcome message and file it.

Shortly after you receive the Welcome message (and reply to it, if so instructed), you'll begin receiving email messages from the list. How many and how often depends on the list, but it's not unusual to receive a dozen or more messages per day. Read anything that looks interesting; ignore (or delete) the rest.

Some mailing lists are purely informational. They're designed not as a discussion forum, but to keep you abreast of news and developments in a particular company or other organization.

Usually, such lists don't have list addresses to which you can contribute. It's a one-way conversation; you just subscribe, and then read whatever shows up.

Mailing lists can send dozens of messages a day, which can clutter up your Inbox and make it hard to find other messages. If your email program supports a facility called *filtering*, you can set up a separate folder where all messages from the list are stored automatically as soon as they're received, leaving your Inbox for other mail.

Contributing to a Mailing List

You are not required to contribute to a mailing list. Many people simply read and enjoy the messages they receive, and never add their own comments or questions.

If you do feel inspired to contribute, just send a message to the list address. If the contribution is related to a previous message, use your email program's Reply feature to reply to the group. In the reply, include a quote of any portion of the original message that's relevant to your comment or question.

When using Reply to send a message to a mailing list, always double-check the To: line in your message to be sure that it shows the correct list address. Many lists are configured so that when you click Reply, the message is addressed not to the list, but to the individual sender of the message. In such cases, you'll want to type the actual list address in the To: line (or choose that address from your Inbox).

Online Communication Tips and Tricks

Internet communication is very simple to understand and to use. But a few key mistakes can cause you lots of trouble—that is, if you're not careful.

A different form of etiquette is followed on the Internet. It's called *netiquette*, and if you don't understand the basic principles of it, you run the risk of offending people, or worse.

And, after you've opened yourself up to Internet communication, the chances that you'll receive unwanted mail are pretty good. Just like all those credit card solicitations you get in your mailbox at home, the Internet can fill up your email box pretty quickly with unwanted offers for this or that.

7

Observing Proper Netiquette

How you communicate with private friends in email is between you and your friends. But after you begin contributing to discussion groups—mailing lists and newsgroups—you're participating in a public forum, and have an obligation to follow a code of conduct that keeps the conversation pleasant and productive for all.

> *Netiquette* is the unofficial online code of conduct. It boils down to the Golden Rule: Do unto others. As you gain experience, you'll begin to notice things others do that bug you, such as quoting too much or writing sloppily. Obviously, those are the things you must remember not to do yourself.

Here are the basics of being a good cyber-citizen, particularly in discussion groups. Note that none of this stuff is law; if you skip a rule, the cyber-police will not show up at your door. (Although there are a few strictly managed lists that will kick you out if you break certain rules—another reason to read and follow the Welcome message!) Like all forms of courtesy, netiquette is often not strictly required, but always highly recommended.

- **Don't shout**—SOME FOLKS LIKE TO TYPE ALL MESSAGES ONLY IN CAP-ITAL LETTERS, and some others overuse capital letters FOR EMPHASIS! On the Internet, capitalizing letters means you are SHOUTING. Capitalize like you would in a typed letter, and use your word choices and phrasing for emphasis, saving the all-caps trick for rare, EXTREME EMPHASIS.

- **Stay on topic**—Nothing is more aggravating than subscribing to a list and then receiving all sorts of messages that veer off on tangents. If your message does not pertain directly to the discussion group's stated topic, don't send it.

- **Keep current**—Newcomers to a list or group, or folks who only drop in occasionally, tend to ask questions that have already been asked and answered a dozen times, which annoys the regulars. Keep up with the conversation so you know what's going on. Read the FAQ, if one is available.

> A *FAQ* is a Frequently Asked Questions file that contains a general list of common questions and answers pertaining to a particular list, newsgroup, Web page, or other topic.

By reading FAQs (pronounced "faks" so that computer book authors can make stupid puns with "fax"), you can quickly bring yourself up to speed on the background information shared by others in the group.

When a FAQ is available for a mailing list, you'll find instructions for obtaining the FAQ in the Welcome message.

- **Don't use sarcastic language**—It's very difficult to communicate sarcasm effectively in a written message. Often, exaggerated messages intended as sarcasm are taken literally by those who read them, and confusion or arguments ensue.

- **Keep personal discussions personal**—Before sending any message, ask yourself, "Would this message interest the whole list, or is it really a personal message to just one member?" If the message is really for one person, you can find that person's email address in the header information quoted in all list and newsgroup messages, and send your comment or question directly to that person, in private.

> Avoid small, conversational contributions that add little information. For example, if someone posts a message with a great idea in it, don't send a reply to the group just to say "Great idea!" No one wants to go to the trouble of receiving and opening a message with so little to say.

- **Don't over-quote**—When replying, cut quotes down to just what's necessary to show what you're replying to. When a series of replies builds up and nobody cuts the quotes, each message can be pages long even if it contains only one new sentence. Try to leave enough information so that a newcomer to the conversation can tell what's being discussed, but cut everything else.

- **Write and spell well**—In the name of speed and efficiency, some folks boil their msg.s down to a grp. of abbrev.'s &/or shorthnd, or write toooo quikly and slopppilly. Do your readers the courtesy of writing whole words and complete sentences, and fix mistakes before you send.

- **Neither flame nor counter-flame**—A *flame* is an angry tirade or attack in a message, the kind that flares when a debate grows into a spat. No matter how hot the argument gets, try to keep your cool. When flamed personally, don't rise to the bait: Flame wars only escalate, and no one ever wins.

  Some folks flame others for breaches of netiquette, but that's hypocritical. Take responsibility for your own online behavior, and let others worry about theirs.

- **Fit in**—Usually, I'm no fan of conformity. But every mailing list and newsgroup has its own, insular culture. After reading messages for a while, you'll pick up a sense of the general technical level of the group, whether they're experts or novices (or both) on the topic at hand, the overall tone, catch phrases, vocabulary, and so on.

7

By all means, be yourself—any group needs fresh ideas, new personalities. But try to be yourself within the style and culture of the group, to ensure that you can be understood by all.

Adding Personality with Smileys and Shorthand

Over the years, a system of symbols and shorthand has developed to enable folks to be more expressive in their messages: *Smileys* and *shorthand*. You'll see both used online often, in discussion groups and in email.

> Although I show you smileys and shorthand next, I'm doing so mainly to help you understand them in messages you receive. Except for the occasional, simple smiley face, I don't recommend using these in your contributions to discussion groups.
>
> There are many newcomers online today who don't know smileys or shorthand, so if you use these, many of your readers won't understand you. Try to put all your meaning in your words, so everybody gets the message.

Smileys

Smileys are used to communicate the tone of a message, to add an emotional inflection. (In fact, smileys are sometimes called *emoticons*—emotional icons.) They're little pictures, usually of faces, that are built out of text characters.

To see the picture, you tilt your head to the left. For example, tilt your head to the left (or tilt this book to the right) while looking at the smiley below, which is made up of three characters: a colon, a dash, and a close parenthesis:

:-)

Looks like a little smiling face, doesn't it? Folks follow a statement with this smiley to indicate that the statement is a joke, or is made facetiously (see Figure 7.11).

There are many different smileys, some so obscure that only the real Net jocks use or understand them. But you're likely only to see the basics, including the basic smile shown earlier and also

:-(Frown

;-)   Wink

:-0   Surprise

8-)   Smile with glasses or bug-eyed

:'-(　Crying

:-D　Laughing

FIGURE 7.11

Using emoticons allows you to add a little personality to your messages.

Some folks omit the nose from their smileys; for example:

:) ;) :0

Shorthand

Shorthand abbreviations are used to carry a common phrase efficiently, to save space and typing. Some of these are commonly used offline, every day, such as ASAP (as soon as possible). Another shorthand expression used commonly online is IMO (in my opinion) and its cousin, IMHO (in my humble opinion). Figure 7.12 shows an example.

FIGURE 7.12

Shorthand allows you to communicate more succinctly.

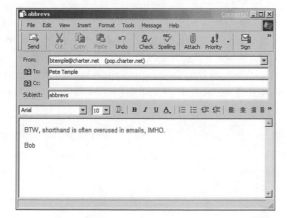

7

Other popular shorthand expressions include the following:

BTW—By the way

B4—Before

FWIW—For what it's worth

IBTD—I beg to differ

IOW—In other words

LOL—Laughing out loud (generally used to declare that a statement is laughable)

OTOH—On the other hand

ROTFL—Rolling on the floor laughing (generally used to declare that a statement is extremely laughable)

Stopping Junk Email (Spam)

Within a few weeks after you begin using the Internet, you'll make an unpleasant discovery: The same sort of take-no-prisoners direct marketing types who telemarket you at suppertime and stuff offers in your mailbox have found you online. Over time, you'll see an ever-increasing number of ads, offers, chain letters, pyramid schemes, and other such scams in your Inbox. This mountain of unwanted crapola is collectively known as *spam*.

> *Spam* is unsolicited email sent out to a large group of strangers for purposes of advertising products and services, promoting political causes, or making mischief. (Senders of spam are called *spammers*.) The name might derive from the fact that the messages multiply the way the word "spam" does in an old Monty Python skit, but the term's origin is unconfirmed.

It's easy and cheap for an advertiser to automatically crank out an email ad to thousands—millions, even—of Internet users all at once. These messages often have subject lines designed to entice you into reading the message (FREE $$$) or to trick you into doing so (MESSAGE FROM AN OLD FRIEND). As the Internet population has grown, so has the spam problem.

The next few pages offer advice for dealing with the spam problem.

I should say right up front that nothing today can prevent or eliminate spam altogether—the problem is too pervasive. But by following the advice in this chapter, you can reduce spam to a tolerable amount. Until and unless it's outlawed, spam will remain as sure a fact of life as death, taxes, and tele-marketing.

How They Get You

The more widely known your email address is, the more spam you'll get—it's that sim-ple. So a logical first step in stopping spam is being very careful about how and when you reveal your email address.

Unfortunately, you cannot fully enjoy the Internet while keeping your email address a secret. Many online activities, such as shopping or posting to newsgroups, create an online record of your email address. In fact, anytime you send email, an unscrupulous spammer might harvest your address by intercepting messages on their way across the Net.

Still, you can effectively reduce the extent to which your address is known by making some smart surfing choices. In particular, be careful about

- **Forms**—Be very careful how and when you fill out online forms or surveys. A growing number of Web sites request that you complete a form to "register" in order to use the site; the form data is almost always used for marketing, and often for spam. On any site where you might complete a form, look for a link to a pri-vacy policy; some Web sites promise in that policy not to spam you or to sell your information to spammers.

Some folks use a secondary email address—such as a Web-based email address—on all forms and other activities that are not part of their personal communications. That way, any spam resulting from filling in forms goes to the secondary address, where it's easier to ignore.

You still need to check messages on the secondary address from time to time, in case you do get a legitimate message there, and to clean out old messages. But at least you can minimize the day-to-day spam intrusion.

7

- **Newsgroup postings**—When you post to a newsgroup, a spammer can easily learn two things about you: your email address, and that you're interested in the news-group's topic.

That's valuable direct marketing information; if you post a message to a newsgroup about a particular kind of product, you can expect to receive spam trying to sell you such a product. If you post to a sex-related newsgroup, you will soon receive spam selling phone sex or other sex-related stuff. You can read newsgroup messages anonymously—but when you post, you reveal your address. So watch where you post.

> Again, all the suggestions offered here are ways to reduce spam—nothing yet can truly eliminate it. So even if you never visit a sex-related newsgroup and never, ever post to one, you probably will receive spam from sex-related advertisers from time to time.
>
> It's not your fault; receiving such messages does not necessarily mean that you did something to bring it on yourself. It's just that the merchants of sex and the merchants of get-rich-quick schemes are the two most aggressive kinds of spammers, and they spam anyone—and everyone—they can find.

- **Cookies**—Cookies are files on your computer stored there by a Web site, such as an online store, to record information about you that the page can access next time you visit. Unfortunately, the cookies on your computer—which might contain your email address and other personal data—might be read not only by the servers that put them there, but by other servers you visit, who might use that information for spam.

- **Mailing lists**—When you subscribe to mailing lists, your name, email address (and your interest in the list's topic) are recorded in a database that might be accessed and copied very easily by a spammer, particularly if the list is managed by an automated program. (Some mailing lists let you keep your address private; read the list's Welcome message for information about a CONCEAL command.)

A newsgroup covering the same topic is a safer choice, as long as you don't post to it. If you contribute to the discussion, the mailing list is still less spam-risky than the newsgroup.

> Stopping spam is a little trickier for users of online services than for users of ISPs. The online services derive some of their revenue from advertisers, for providing access to you. So they're not too keen on letting you block those ads.
>
> Experts on AOL and spam advise users to avoid posting messages on AOL's forums, and to use Internet newsgroups instead. Despite the spam exposure risk in newsgroups, AOL's forums are notoriously harvested by spammers.

Report 'Em!

The people who run Internet servers are generally described as system administrators (*sysadmins*) or as system operators (*sysops*). These folks usually hate spam as much as you do, because it dramatically increases the traffic on their servers, taking up room needed for legitimate communications. There are two times you should contact sysops about spam:

- If you do not want to receive spam, always let the sysop of your Internet provider know how you feel. He or she might be able to take steps to minimize (but not eliminate) spam to your account. You can email your sysop by sending a message to the technical support address for your account.

- You can report spammers to the sysops of their Internet providers, who might then cancel their accounts or issue a warning. To address the message, take the part of the spammer's email address following the `@` symbol, and put `system@` or `sysop@` or `support@` in front of it. For example, if you get spam from `jerko@serv.com`, address messages to

  `support@serv.com`

  `system@serv.com`

  `sysop@serv.com`

  reporting that the user named Jerko is sending spam. This technique won't work all the time, because spammers are savvy about hiding their real server names. But it's a start.

In Newsgroups, Spoof 'Em!

Ultimately, having to restrain yourself from posting to newsgroups can severely hamper your ability to enjoy the Net. Here's a technique that some folks use to post to newsgroups while foiling spammer's efforts to cull their addresses: *spoofing*.

> *Spoofing*, also known as *munging*, is the practice of scrambling your return email address in newsgroup postings just enough so that if it's harvested by one of the programs spammers use, the resulting spam will never reach you (it'll be sent to the spoofed address, not your real one).

A properly spoofed email address fools the automated harvesting programs that spammers use, but enables real folks on the group to still send you messages. For example, suppose your address is

`shirley@aol.com`

7

You can use your newsreader's configuration dialog boxes to change the Reply to address to

shirleytake_out_this_part@aol.com

If you use a signature at the bottom of your messages to identify yourself, change the address there, too. You can even add a note to your signature telling readers of your postings how to decode your address to send you email. The programs spammers use aren't smart enough to decode the address or read the note.

To spoof your newsgroup return address in Outlook Express, choose Tools, Accounts from the menu bar. On the dialog box that appears, click the News tab, and then click Properties. In the box labeled Email Address, type the spoofed address (see Figure 7.13).

FIGURE 7.13

Use this dialog box in Outlook Express to spoof your return address on newsgroup postings.

Spoofing your newsgroup return address in Netscape Mail is not recommended, because doing so also spoofs your return address on your email messages. That makes it difficult for people to make legitimate replies to your email messages.

At the time of this writing, spoofing works pretty well. But inevitably, spammers will smarten up their harvesting programs so that they recognize and decode spoofed addresses. Spoofing is only one step in reducing spam; you still need to do the other stuff described here, too.

Never Reply! Never! *Never!*

Many spam include "removal" instructions, telling you that if you reply to the message and include the words "REMOVE ME" or a similar phrase in the subject line, you'll receive no further messages.

In some cases, doing so might work. But in many cases, the "REMOVE ME" bit is actually a trick intended to make you verify your email address, so that the spammer knows he has a live one. In such cases, following the removal instructions won't remove you from the spammer's list, and might even increase the amount of spam you get.

Some folks also try to stop spam by sending angry replies to spammers. This approach never works. Often, the "From" line in the spam is left empty, or filled with a dummy or spoofed email address, so a reply won't even reach the real spammer. When angry replies do reach spammers, spammers ignore them. (They know full well that they are bothering some folks. They don't care. If they must annoy a million people in order to make a sale or two or three, they're happy with that.)

The moral? Never do anything an unsolicited email tells you to do, even if the instruction claims to be for your benefit. Never.

Filter 'Em Out!

If you can't stop the spam from coming, your next best bet is to avoid having to look at it. A variety of programs and techniques *filter* your incoming email to remove unwanted messages.

> *Filters* are settings in your email program (or a special utility) that automatically delete or move messages under specified circumstances. For example, if there's a person whose messages you never want to read, you can configure a filter so that all messages from that person's email address are deleted automatically upon receipt; you'll get them, but they'll be gone before you ever see them.

Filters cannot completely remove spam. In order to set up filters to delete all spam messages, you'd have to know the address of every spammer. No complete master list of spammers exists (new folks start spamming every day, and slippery spammers change addresses often), but you can pick up lists of many of the worst offenders, and then import or manually copy the lists into your email program so you can create filters to block messages from them.

Use the following URLs to learn about and download lists of spammers for filtering:

- The BadMail from Spam List: `www.webeasy.com/w2/spam/`
- The Network Abuse Clearinghouse: `www.abuse.net/`
- The Blacklist of Internet Advertisers: `www-math.uni-paderborn.de/%7Eaxel/BL/#list`

7

> You can pick up utilities that combine a filtering system with a spammers database, for fast and easy configuration of anti-spam filters. Check out Spambuster at www.contactplus.com, and Spameater Pro at www.hms.com/spameater.htm.

Finding Filters in Your Email Program

Most full-featured email programs have their own built-in filtering systems you can apply to manage incoming mail and, to a limited extent, control spam.

If you don't have a list of spammers, or if creating filters for a long list is too difficult, you can deal with spam by creating filters for your legitimate contacts.

It works like this: If you have a steady group of people you communicate with regularly, create a filter that automatically stores all messages from those people in a separate folder. When you receive email, all the important messages are automatically stored in the folder, while all of the spam stays in your Inbox, where you can ignore it. (You'll still want to scan your Inbox from time to time to check for legitimate messages from folks you haven't added to your filters.)

You can find the filters dialog boxes

- In Messenger by choosing Edit, Message Filters.
- In Outlook Express by choosing Tools, Message Rules.

> In Outlook Express, you can choose Tools, Message Rules, Mail to open a dialog box in which you can set up all sorts of rules for how incoming messages are handled (see Figure 7.14). But when all you want to do is prevent certain senders from sending you email, just choose Tools, Message Rules, Blocked Senders List, click Add, and type the address of the person from whom you will no longer accept email.

The Last Resort: Move

When all else fails, if you're still getting too much junk mail, there's one reliable (albeit temporary) solution: Change ISPs, or ask your current ISP to change your email address.

When you change your email address, spam directed to your old address can't reach you. (Be sure to inform all your legitimate email partners of your new address, and instruct your old ISP not to forward email to your new address.) If your address has found its way into lots of spam databases, you can get a clean start this way.

FIGURE 7.14

Email programs use filters (which Outlook Express, shown here, calls Rules) to automatically deal with certain incoming messages in whatever way you choose.

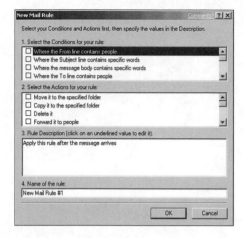

Changing your email address is an extreme measure, especially if you have been using your address for important purposes, be it business or otherwise. No matter how diligent you are in informing your contacts about the move, some won't notice and you'll miss others. This action should be reserved for only the most severe circumstances.

Eventually, spammers will find you. But if you start clean with a new address, and then diligently apply the steps you learned in this chapter, you might be able to keep the spammers at bay for a time.

Summary

Newsgroups and mailing lists are both great ways to keep up with a subject that's of interest to you. You can jump in and participate and, better yet, unsubscribe any time you want. Take some time to subscribe to one or two mailing lists and a few newsgroups, just for fun.

And now that you know how to stop spam, use emoticons, observe netiquette, and so on, you know even more than you really have to. Doesn't that make you feel special?

7

CHAPTER **8**

Using Internet Explorer 6

We've already spent a fair amount of time talking about browsing and Web communications, and you've seen a lot of figures that include screens from Microsoft Internet Explorer.

There might be a part of you wondering why those screens don't look exactly like the screens you see on your computer. That's an easy one—you're probably using a different version of Explorer than I am.

In this chapter, we'll take a look at the Explorer program. We'll cover its features and offer some tricks and tips for using the program. After all, if you're going to be using the Internet, you might as well get accustomed to the software through which you'll view it. (Netscape Navigator is covered in Chapter 9.)

Why Choose Internet Explorer?

A better question than the above might be, "Why not?" Internet Explorer is, along with Netscape Navigator, one of the two most-often used Web browsers. That alone isn't reason to pick it as your browser of choice, of course. What that brings along with it is, however.

Depending on where you stand on Microsoft in general, the company is either a behemoth trying to devour the computing world in general (and online communications in particular), or a forward-thinking, revolutionary, and creative genius, forever pushing the envelope of new technology to improve our lives.

Maybe both.

At any rate, say what you want about Microsoft. The fact is the company is big enough and smart enough to continually offer updates to its software, constantly improve it, and back it up. So there are some good reasons to choose Explorer.

Beyond that is the program itself. Explorer is a full-featured browser with some great new additions in its latest version, 6.0. It's also free, which doesn't hurt matters.

Where and How to Get Internet Explorer

How's this for some good news: You probably already have Internet Explorer. How do I know? Two reasons. First, if you're running a Windows-based computer, virtually all versions of Windows in recent history came with a version of Explorer included. You may not know you have it, but chances are you do. Second, we did some Web browsing back in Chapter 4, and unless you cheated and were reading without using your computer, you must've been using a browser. Chances were good it was Explorer.

Regardless, the chances are also good that you don't have the latest and greatest version of Explorer. How do I know that? Well, Microsoft—like most software manufacturers—is constantly updating its software. These updates often add a new feature, but even more often they fix a little glitch or two that's been found in the works somewhere. Gotta get rid of those gremlins!

So, even if you bought your computer yesterday, and it came with a pre-installed version of Explorer 6.0, Microsoft might have come out with version 6.0.1 or 6.0.2 by now. Heck, depending on when you bought this book, Microsoft might even be on 6.2!

All those little numbers in the version of a software program might not mean that much to you, but they can be important. Let's say you're using version 6.0.1, for example. Any time the first number (in this case, the 6) changes, that means the software has undergone a remake that is fairly significant. Usually, this will mean a new look to the software, its buttons, icons, and so on. The second number reflects changes to the software that might offer improvements or new features, but not changing the basic way it functions. When the third number changes, it usually means that the updated version has fixed some bugs.

So, for example, if you are using Explorer version 5.5 (the last revision
before 6.0 came out), you'll notice a new look to the software when you
download version 6.0.

Downloading the Latest Version

There's one great way to make sure you the latest version of Explorer: Go to the
Microsoft Web site and download the latest version available. It doesn't take long, is easy
to accomplish, and guarantees you're up to date.

Chapter 13, "Downloading Programs and Files," gives a more detailed look
at downloading. Consider the following tutorial a little preview to that
chapter.

So, let's give it a try! Here's how to download and install the latest version of Internet
Explorer:

1. Open your browser and go to the Microsoft Web site at www.microsoft.com. From
   the menu across the top of the page, click Downloads, and then click Download
   Center (see Figure 8.1).

FIGURE 8.1

*Step 1: Click on the
Download Center link
from Microsoft's home
page.*

2. Using the pull-down menus on the Download Center page, select the most recent version of Internet Explorer (the one with the highest number) and your operating system. Leave the Show Results For box set at "Most Recent." Click Find It, and the page will display a list of the most recent versions of this software (see Figure 8.2).

FIGURE 8.2

Step 2: Display the most recent versions of Internet Explorer.

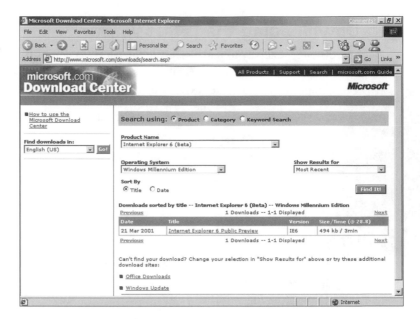

 Because Explorer 6.0 wasn't yet released to the public at the time of this writing, you see the word "Beta" in parentheses in the Product Name field in Figure 8.2. This was a public preview version of the software that was available prior to the official launch. You should be aware that "beta" software can be unstable and can cause problems with your computer. By the time you read this, version 6.0 will have been released, so you shouldn't see that word when you download.

3. Click the link to the latest version of the software that is not a "beta" version. On the screen that appears, select your language (I'm guessing it's English) from the drop-down menu, and click the Download Now button (see Figure 8.3).

FIGURE 8.3

Step 3: Choose your language and click Download Now.

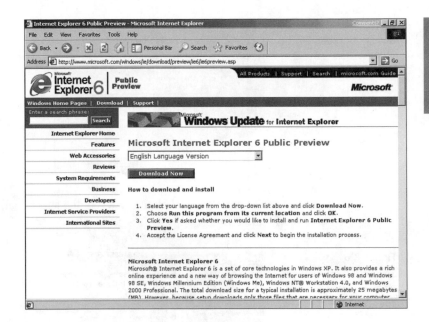

4. Click the button to "Run this program from its current location," and then click OK (see Figure 8.4).

FIGURE 8.4

Step 4: Select "Run this program from its current location."

5. After a brief download of setup files, a Security Warning appears. Click the Yes button (see Figure 8.5).

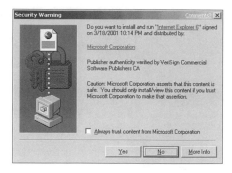

FIGURE 8.5
Step 5: Click the Yes button.

6. Read the license agreement, click the "I accept the agreement" button, and click Next (see Figure 8.6).

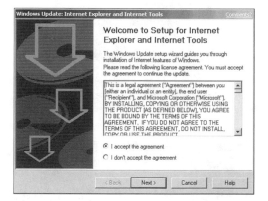

FIGURE 8.6
Step 6: Accept the license agreement, and click Next.

7. The program name appears, and you click Next again. The program begins to download and install automatically (see Figure 8.7).

FIGURE 8.7
Step 7: The program downloads and installs automatically.

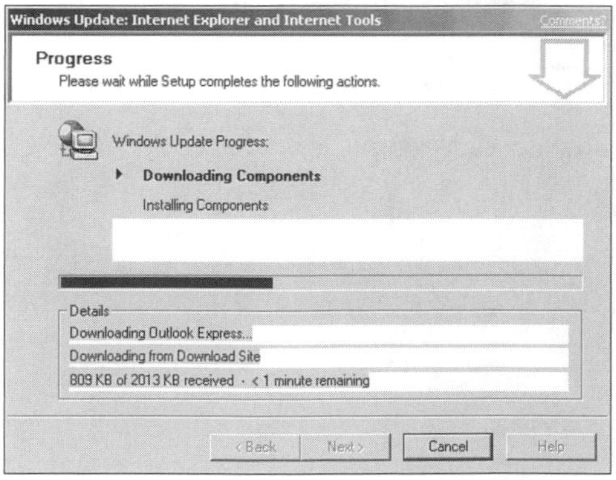

8. When the install is complete, you will be asked to restart your computer. Do so, and you're ready to go!

> Depending on the speed of your connection, this download/install can take anywhere from about 15 minutes (on a DSL or cable connection) to more than an hour (on a 56K). Be patient; it's worth the wait.

Starting Up Internet Explorer

Now that you've downloaded the latest version of Explorer and restarted your computer, all that's left is to connect to the Internet, start up Explorer, and off you go.

During the install process, Explorer probably created an icon on your desktop that you can simply double-click to launch the program. If not, just click on the Start button, and choose Internet Explorer from your list of programs.

As discussed in Chapter 4, Explorer opens automatically to its predetermined home page, www.msn.com (see Figure 8.8). You can change that home page to any page you like (covered later in this chapter).

FIGURE 8.8

Explorer opens automatically to the Microsoft Network's home page.

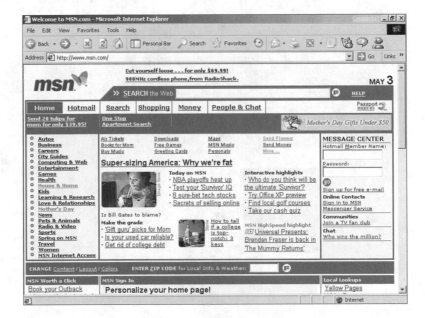

Features of Internet Explorer

Whether you're familiar with past versions of Internet Explorer or not, you'll find a lot to like about version 6.0. But before we delve too deeply into the advancements that have been made for 6.0, let's look at some of the basic features of the software that have been available in older versions (and continue in 6.0).

Basic Features of Explorer 6.0

Because of Microsoft's position on the cutting edge of Internet technology, Internet Explorer has always been able to display pages that contain advanced programming. Microsoft continues to keep pace with new advancements in software design (if not making those advancements themselves).

There's not enough space here to go over all the many features of the software, but I'll do my best to highlight some of the ones that are most likely to come into play for you. Some of these are discussed in greater detail later in this chapter.

- **IntelliSense**—Explorer senses the direction you're heading in many different ways and helps you get there faster. For example, if you're typing in the address of a site you've visited before, Explorer fills in the rest of the address and opens a History window for you to choose other possible options (see Figure 8.9).

IntelliSense options

FIGURE 8.9

As soon as you start typing an address, Explorer offers options based on your browsing history.

- **AutoSearch**—There are lots of ways to conduct a Search in Explorer. You can click the Search button, open the Search bar from the View menu, or simply type in a search word or phrase directly into the Address box. (Searching is covered in detail in Chapter 12, "Searching.")

- **Related Links**—No matter what site you visit, Explorer is ready to offer you some options for other sites just like it. On the Tools menu, just select Show Related Links, and the links appear in the Explorer bar to the left of the main browser window (see Figure 8.10). This window, called Search Companion, also gives you valuable info about the site you're seeing, such as an address and phone number.

Related links

FIGURE 8.10
Related Links offers users options for other content similar to what they are viewing.

- **One-click Email, Printing**—Buttons to print the page or to quickly open Outlook Express for email are available on the main toolbar. Many Web pages don't print out like they appear onscreen, however, so Explorer offers a Print Preview option from the File menu that allows you to see how the page will print before you waste the paper.

There are many more features available in Explorer, and some of them are discussed throughout the rest of this chapter.

Using the Explorer Bar

One of the many things you'll notice is the Explorer bar. Although it's not visible when you first start up the program, you might soon find that it's a valuable part of your surfing experience. It displays on the left side of the browser window, taking up as much as half the screen if you expand it.

Best of all, the information it presents is up to you. To get to the Explorer bar, open the View menu, select Explorer bar, and here are your options:

- **Personal Bar**—This feature, new for version 6.0 allows you to use the left portion of the browser window to display personal information (see Figure 8.11). You can use the Search feature at the top, display news and weather from your area in the middle, and use the bottom portion to play and/or manage media files. The first time you use the Personal Bar, you can enter your ZIP code and the symbols of your favorite stocks and your personal information will be displayed.

The three choices on the Personal Bar—news, search, and media—can also be used to fill up the entire Personal Bar if you select them individually as options from the Explorer bar menu.

FIGURE 8.11

The Personal Bar offers you the ability to display information you choose in Explorer.

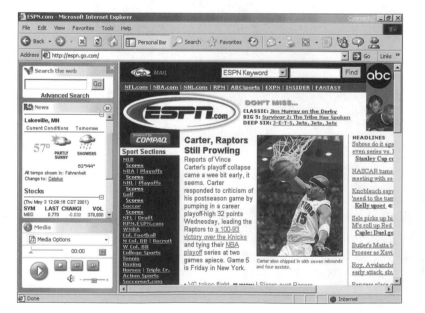

- **Search**—The Search Companion displays in a couple of different circumstances. If you choose Search from the Explorer bar menu, you can type a question into the Search box and use it to search the Internet or your own hard drive.

- **Contacts**—This is a handy feature to have on your screen while surfing the Web. You can create a list of Contacts that you regularly interact with (see Figure 8.12), and by double-clicking on a name, a New Message window opens with the contact's email address included, so you can send them a quick email.

FIGURE 8.12

Viewing your Contacts in the Explorer Bar allows you to send off a quick email.

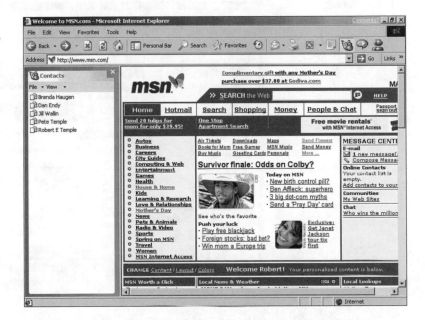

- **Favorites**—Your Favorite Places are the Web sites you have stored for quick access later (there's more information on Favorite Places in the next section of this chapter). You can display them in the Explorer bar, too, so you can jump to them quickly.

- **History**—As you travel around the Web, Explorer keeps a little record of your travels for you called History. This is a useful feature in that it allows you to return to these sites more quickly, even if it's been a few days since you last used your computer. Sites you've visited are stored in History for 20 days by default.

- **Folders**—You can use the Explorer bar to display folders on your computer, so you can access them quickly.

Customizing the Personal Bar

The center panel of the three in the Personal Bar displays the News view by default. However, you can change that so your Personal Bar is, shall we say, more personal. The two right-pointing arrows in that center panel lead to a list of Explorer bar options that you can display in that panel (see Figure 8.13). Simply select the one you would like to display from the list.

FIGURE 8.13

The Personal Bar can be customized to show other views.

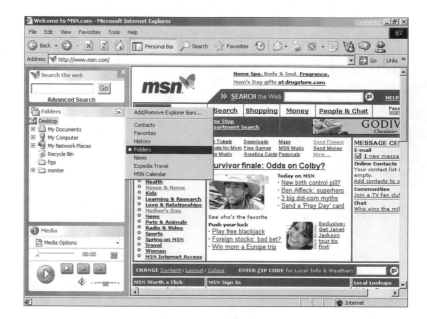

Adding/Removing Explorer Bars

Another option on the list of Explorer bars you can display in the center panel is Add/Remove Explorer Bars. There are a number of different bars that can be added for services offered over the Internet, and more are expected.

You can get travel information from Expedia, or you can use the MSN Calendar to display your appointments for the day. Simply click the Add/Remove Explorer Bars option, and then click "Add new Explorer Bar" to get a list of options.

They load quickly, and you can change your display to show them almost immediately (see Figure 8.14).

8

FIGURE 8.14

Displaying Expedia in the Personal Bar allows quick access to flight and other travel information.

Working with Favorite Place

As you travel around the Web, you're going to find a lot of sites that you like. In some cases, you'll know right away that you're going to want to return. In others, you might find yourself going back to the site a few times before you realize it's one of your favorites.

Explorer makes it easy for you to return to those places over and over again, by allowing you to add them to a list called—cleverly enough—Favorite Places.

It's very simple to use, and it's a great resource. It eliminates the need to remember the URL of the sites you like to go to. Even better, you're not just limited to home pages for your Favorite Places list. If you've found some obscure page deep within a Web site, you can add it to your list. Then, you'll be able to return to it with one click, instead of going to a home page and navigating your way back to your favorite spot. It's a little like leaving a bookmark in the book—in fact, in Netscape Navigator, they're called Bookmarks.

Adding a page to your Favorites list is extremely easy. All you have to do is go to the exact page you want to jump back to. Then, open the Favorites menu and select Add to Favorites (if you've displayed your Favorites in the Explorer bar, you can just click the Add button there). The Add Favorite window opens, as you see in Figure 8.15.

FIGURE 8.15

Adding a page to your Favorites list makes it easy to get back there.

A name is provided for the Favorite, but you can change it to whatever you want by clicking in the box and typing. Then click OK, and the next time you open your Favorites list, it will be there.

To go back to that page next time, just select it from your Favorites list.

You might notice the "Make Available Offline" check box in Figure 8.15. This feature allows you to view this site even if you are not connected to the Internet.

That list will grow pretty long, pretty quickly, and you'll need to pare it down some. You can create folders for Favorites by category, delete those that have fallen out of favor (excuse the pun), move your Favorites into different folders, and rename them by using the Organize Favorites option from the Favorites menu (see Figure 8.16).

FIGURE 8.16

Organizing your Favorites makes your list cleaner and easier to use.

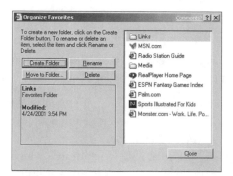

Creating folders is easy—click the Create Folders button—and you can move Favorites by dragging and dropping them on folders or by highlighting them and clicking the Move to Folder button. Take a few minutes every couple of weeks to clean up this list; if it's not organized well, you won't save much time by using it!

Setting Your Internet Options

Every piece of software known to man these days comes with a complete set of options. These options, depending on your perspective, either make using the program easier or make it a complex web that is beyond human comprehension. Your call.

Explorer's options are viewable by opening the Tools menu and selecting Internet Options. You'll find a myriad of possibilities here; for our purposes, we'll concentrate on the General and Content tabs.

General Options

On the General tab (see Figure 8.17), you'll find basic options settings, as you might expect. The top panel allows you to select a new home page (the page that appears when you first start Explorer). The Use Blank button opens a blank page, and the Use Current button allows you to select whatever page is currently displayed on your browser. The Use Default button sets it back to Explorer's default page, www.msn.com.

FIGURE 8.17

The General tab allows you to change basic settings.

As you surf, a variety of files get saved on your computer. These Temporary Internet Files can, over time, take up a lot of room on your hard drive. From time to time, you may want to delete the files and cookies that are consuming your hard drive. It'll make some pages load slower when you visit them the next time, but it will also remove pages from your hard drive that you never intend to visit again. The Settings button allows you to determine exactly how much room on your drive can be consumed by these files.

Your History is also kept as you surf, and you can specify in the bottom panel how many days worth of sites you want kept on your computer. The Clear History button will completely clear out your surfing trail.

You can use the buttons along the bottom to specify colors, fonts, languages, and accessibility options as well.

Content Options

The Content tab offers one major feature for parents: the ability to limit what can be seen over the Internet using Explorer.

The Content Advisor (see Figure 8.18), as it's called, comes disabled by default. But any parent whose child might spend time on this computer without supervision should probably enable at least some of these controls.

FIGURE 8.18

The Content Advisor allows you to set boundaries for objectionable content.

Using a sliding scale, you can select from a four-point scale the level of language, nudity, sex, and violence you will permit on this computer. Setting the levels low allows little or no potentially dangerous content; setting them higher allows more content; not setting them at all allows a free-for-all.

Not to put on the Ward Cleaver hat here, but I strongly urge parents to set these controls if their children are going to spend any time online unsupervised. I'm not saying you have naughty kids; it's just very easy to stumble onto objectionable content on the Internet. One link leads to another, and another, and before you know it, little Jimmy's at a porn site. Or, it can be more direct—a youngster looking for information on the White House for a research paper might type in www.whitehouse.com, which is a porn site. The one for the president's residence is www.whitehouse.gov.

Summary

8

Internet Explorer is one of the two best options for you to use when browsing the Web. Netscape Navigator, covered in the next chapter, is the other. I recommend you go through both chapters and have the latest version of both browsers on your computer. Then you can use them both, and decide for yourself!

Chapter 9

Using Netscape Navigator 6

So, you've learned all about Internet Explorer in the last chapter, and now you're ready to really jump into the Internet and take off, right? Hold on a minute there, pardner.

There's another choice. Netscape, which is now under the umbrella of America Online, offers its Navigator browser as Explorer's chief rival. Navigator has undergone a recent facelift, adding new features and taking on a new look. It's just as functional as ever, if not more, and it's every bit as good a browser choice as Microsoft Internet Explorer.

So, take the time to walk through the Netscape browser with me, and you'll have both of them to try out for a while. Then, you can make your own choice.

Why Choose Netscape Navigator?

In the last chapter, this section indicated that one of the reasons to pick Internet Explorer was that it was from Microsoft. That means it's backed by the largest software company in the world, and that carries with it a certain degree of clout.

So, why choose Navigator? Well, that's a funny one. Navigator has just as many features as Explorer. The two programs mirror each other in a number of ways, with similar features that are called by different names.

To be frank, one reason that some people choose to go with Navigator is that Explorer is produced by Microsoft. There is a sizable faction out there that believes that Bill Gates and his boys have gotten a little too big for their britches (the U.S. government included), and that using Navigator, in some way, helps prevent Microsoft's stronghold on the consumer software industry.

But there are much better reasons to pick Navigator than that. Like Explorer, Navigator has added features that make it more customizable for the user. In fact, Netscape has gone a step farther than Microsoft in allowing users to set up user profiles, so that different people using Navigator on the same computer can automatically view the browser the way they want to, without having to reset a bunch of preferences.

In the rest of this chapter, you will learn about many of Navigator's options and features.

Where and How to Get Netscape Navigator

Like Explorer, you might already have a copy of Navigator on your computer. Navigator isn't as widely preinstalled as Explorer, but the chances are still pretty good, especially if you've purchased your computer within the last year or so.

But like we discussed last chapter, it's also very likely that you don't have the latest version of the browser on your computer. Netscape can take care of that for you by allowing you a free download of the software from its Web site.

Download the Latest Version

Even if you're pretty sure that you have the most recent version of Netscape Navigator on your computer, it can't hurt to check. Besides, if you do have the latest and greatest Navigator, the Netscape Web site will sense that and tell you not to download another one. Pretty cool, huh?

So, using your old, antiquated version of Navigator (or Explorer if you don't have Navigator on your computer at all), log on to the Netscape site at home.netscape.com, and we'll get started.

Download and Install the Latest Version of Netscape Navigator

1. At the Netscape home page, click on the Download button on the top of the page. This opens the main download page (see Figure 9.1). As you can see, you can also use this area to order a free CD, but let's download instead. Click on the Netscape Browsers link.

FIGURE 9.1

Step 1: Go to the Netscape download page.

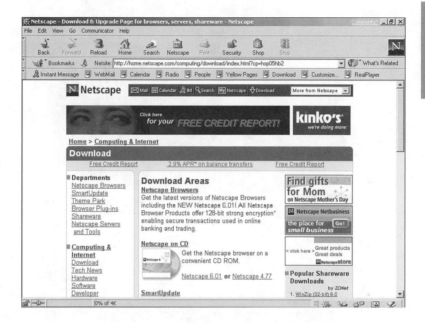

Whenever you plan to download or install anything you'll need to make sure you have sufficient disk space available for the files. Most installation programs perform a check for you before installing files. It will let you know how much room the files will take up, and how much space you have available.

To suite or not to suite? At the time of this writing, there were two different browser versions available for Netscape. If you download the entire Netscape Communicator suite, it comes with Netscape Messenger for email, Composer for creating Web pages, and Navigator. But at this writing, the Communicator suite was in version 4.77, as was the version of Navigator that came with it. You could also download Navigator 6.01, which offers Netscape Mail (instead of Messenger). Netscape Mail now supports multiple email addresses, but Messenger is a more full-featured email program. For purposes of this chapter, we'll be using the latest version of Navigator, 6.02, because it offers more features and functionality as a browser.

2. This page shows you the version of the browser you are now using (see
   Figure 9.2). Click the Download button under the name of the latest version of
   the Navigator browser (not the Communicator suite).

FIGURE 9.2

*Step 2: Click on the
Download button.*

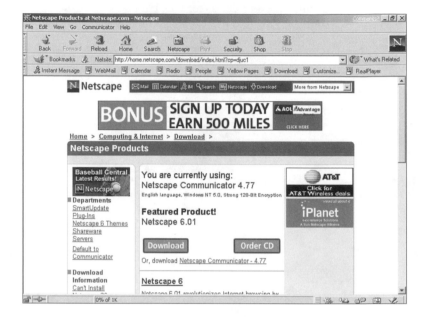

3. Choose a location for the file you are going to download (see Figure 9.3). The
   Desktop is a convenient location, because the file will be easy to find later.

FIGURE 9.3

*Step 3: Choose a loca-
tion for the file.*

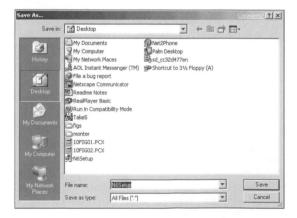

4. When the file is done downloading (it is a relatively small file), double-click its
   icon on your desktop. This launches the Netscape Setup program (see Figure 9.4).

FIGURE 9.4

Step 4: Launch the Setup program.

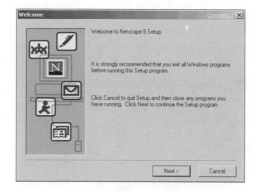

5. Click the Next button, read the license agreement, and click the Accept button (see Figure 9.5).

FIGURE 9.5

Step 5: Read the license agreement and click Accept.

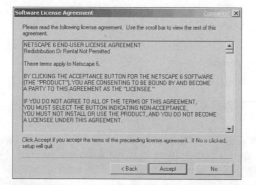

6. Choose the Recommended installation, and click the Next button (see Figure 9.6). Netscape asks you where you want to download the program from; I recommend leaving this setting at Default. Click Next. On the Start Install screen, click Install.

FIGURE 9.6

Step 6: Select the Recommended installation.

9

7. The program begins to install on your computer (see Figure 9.7). This may take a few minutes (or longer, depending on the speed of your connection). When it's completed, you'll have a Netscape 6 icon on your desktop.

FIGURE 9.7

Step 7: The program begins to install on your computer.

Starting Up Netscape Navigator

A simple double-click on the icon you now have on your desktop will launch the Navigator program. By default, Navigator opens to the Netscape home page at home.netscape.com (see Figure 9.8). You'll learn later in this chapter how to change that home page to one of your choosing, if you want.

FIGURE 9.8

Navigator opens to the Netscape home page by default.

You might be asked to activate a screen name the first time you launch Netscape. If so, follow the onscreen prompts to do so; it won't cost you anything.

Version 6.01 of Navigator has a completely new look over previous versions of the program. As a result, some of the basic buttons have been moved.

As you can see from Figure 9.8, the Back, Forward, Reload, and Stop buttons are all in their usual locations. The Home button, however, has been moved to the Personal Bar, a toolbar that you can customize (discussed later in this chapter). Meanwhile, the Search button has been moved to the right of the address box.

9

Features of Netscape Navigator

Netscape (like Microsoft) is working to make everything on the Internet more personal. Customizable this, customizable that. The goal is to make you feel more at home, and to allow you to set up things so that when you return next time, it's just the way you left it.

One of the biggest complaints of newcomers to the Internet is that it is such a vast wonderland, the difficulty in finding the information they are looking for makes it seem more like a vast wasteland. Netscape has attempted to boil everything down for you, so you can get where you want to go in fewer clicks.

Basic Features of Netscape

The basic functionality of Netscape is very similar to Microsoft Internet Explorer. Let's take a few minutes to look at some of the basic features that make up Navigator.

- **Task Toolbar**—Along the bottom of the screen, there's a Task toolbar in the lower-left corner, giving you access to Mail, Instant Messenger, Composer, and Address Book.

- **Advanced Search**—There's a reason that Search button is to the right of the address box. You can use the address box as a search tool, by entering any search word or phrase directly into the box and clicking Search. Click on the Search button when the Address box is empty, and it brings you to the search page on Netscape's site.

- **Quick Access to Netscape Pages**—At the bottom of the screen, near the center, you see menus for Business, Tech, Fun and Interact. These menus offer one-click access to specific areas within the Netscape site. So, for example, if you wanted to check on the latest news from Hollywood, you would open the Fun menu and select Movies (see Figure 9.9).

My Netscape   Search

FIGURE 9.9

You get quick access to Netscape content from the toolbar at the bottom of the screen.

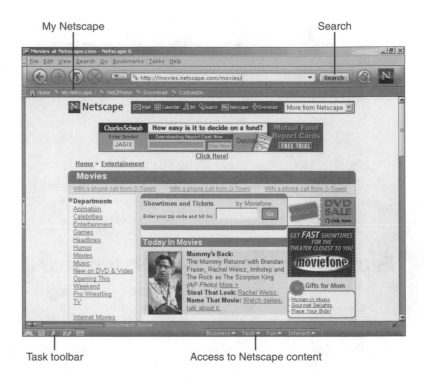

Task toolbar   Access to Netscape content

- **My Netscape**—The button leads you to a personalized home page. The first time you visit, you are asked for your ZIP code and birth date. Enter it, and you're on your way. On the My Netscape page (see Figure 9.10), you can choose the types of content you would like to appear, how you want the layout to look, and other settings. The ZIP code is used to provide local news and info.

Working with My Sidebar

Explorer had the Explorer bar on the left side of its browser window, Netscape Navigator offers My Sidebar. If you haven't seen it yet, it's because it's hidden. And cleverly, too.

Along the left side of the default browser window, you'll notice a little button with a couple of arrows. That's where your Sidebar is hiding. Just a single click on that button, and the Sidebar appears (see Figure 9.11). It's very similar to the Explorer bar, but it offers some additional functionality.

FIGURE 9.10
My Netscape allows you to customize a home page.

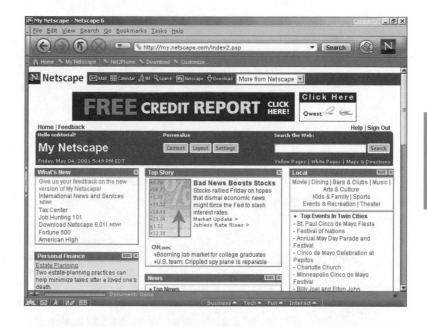

FIGURE 9.11
Navigator's Sidebar offers a variety of information at a glance.

Click to show/hide
My Sidebar

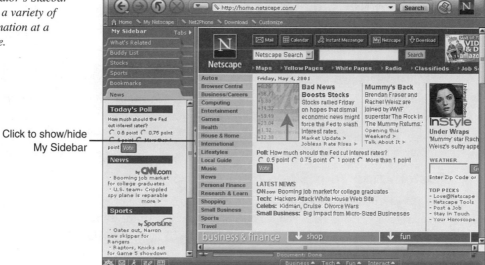

Lots of people don't like these frames that run down the left side of their pages, because the frames force the image of the Web page they are viewing off the right side of the screen. That can be annoying, but Sidebar has such great features and it's so easy to quickly tuck it away, it's a great option to use in Navigator. And if you don't like it, you can always close it by clicking the same button you used to open it.

By default, the tabs that appear are Search, What's Related, Buddy List, Stocks, News, and Today's Tips. A quick click on any of the tabs will reveal its content. For example, What's Related will show you links to other Web sites that have content similar to the site you are currently viewing.

The Buddy List tab needs to be customized with your Instant Messenger screen name and password the first time you use it. After that, it brings instant messaging to within a single click, any time you're using Navigator.

You can make Sidebar fill up to half of your screen if you want by dragging the right-hand border over to the center of the screen. But this pushes your browser window further to the right.

Changing the Sidebar Tabs

What if you don't like the choices that Netscape gives you for tabs? Now you don't think they would leave you high and dry for choices, do you?

Of course not.

Right at the top of the My Sidebar tabs is a button called Tabs. Click it, and you'll display a list of tabs the Netscape has provided for you (see Figure 9.12). The ones that are checked are the ones currently displayed. Clicking on a checked name will deselect it; clicking on an unchecked name will select it.

Customizing Your Sidebar

Still haven't had enough of the Sidebar, eh? Well, Netscape offers more options for you. If you refer to Figure 9.12, you'll notice that at the top of the Tabs menu, there's an option called Customize Sidebar. Click it, and you'll see the window that appears in Figure 9.13.

In the right pane, you'll see a list of the tabs that are currently available to you from Netscape. In the left pane, you'll have a list of other possible tabs you can add to your browser. Just highlight the name of the tab, and you can get a preview of it by clicking the Preview button. When you're ready to implement it, click Add.

FIGURE 9.12

Netscape offers different tabs for you to choose from.

9

FIGURE 9.13

You can customize your Sidebar with tabs developed by non-Netscape providers.

Also, in the lower-left corner, there's a Find More Tabs button. Click there, and you'll be taken to a Web site that will include tabs from all kinds of different sources. There are literally hundreds available, with more being offered all the time.

Changing Your Theme

Navigator offers the latest in browser customization, an option called Themes. It allows you to change the entire look and feel of the Navigator program, including such basic things as the Back and Forward buttons.

These different options can be created by Web developers anywhere—in fact, Netscape had a contest to encourage designers to create more Themes. Two Themes are offered in Navigator: Classic, which looks like older versions of Navigator; and Modern, which is what you've seen in the figures in this chapter. The Modern Theme is also the default Theme for Navigator 6. The Themes created by outsiders can be downloaded from the Netscape Web site at `home.netscape.com/themes/index.html` (see Figure 9.14).

FIGURE 9.14

Themes change the look and feel of the entire Navigator program.

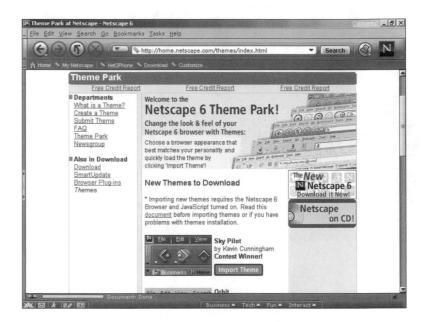

Just click the Import Theme button next to the Theme(s) of your choice, and it will download. Navigator automatically changes to the new Theme immediately. You can change it back by selecting Preferences from the Edit menu. In the window that appears, highlight Themes, and then highlight the name of the Theme you would like to use (more on Preferences in the next section).

Working with the Preferences

Preferences in Navigator are like Internet Options in Explorer. You can use them to set and change all manner of settings within the program. You can alter how the program displays information, captures information, the length of the history of Web sites you've visited, and more.

To open the Preferences window, open the Edit menu and select Preferences (see Figure 9.15).

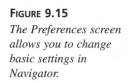

FIGURE 9.15

The Preferences screen allows you to change basic settings in Navigator.

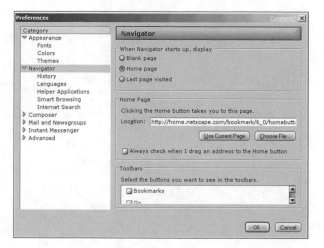

9

On the right side of the Preferences screen, you can select the page you want for your home page (middle pane) and a different page (if you want) to appear each time you start Navigator. For example, a lot of people want to pick up their surfing where they last left off, and you can do that by selecting "Last page visited" in the top pane of the Preferences window. In the bottom pane, you can select the items you want to appear in your toolbars.

Here's a look at some of the other features you can alter using Preferences:

- **Internet Search**—You'll learn more searching in Chapter 12, "Searching." Suffice it to say, there are a lot of options for search sites on the Internet. You've no doubt heard of or used Yahoo!, Lycos, and many others. Netscape offers its own search tools, but it also realizes you might want to use a different site. By clicking Internet Search (under the Navigator menu in Preferences), you can tell Navigator which site you want to use for your searches (see Figure 9.16).

- **Instant Messenger**—Instant Messenger is integrated into Netscape Mail. So much so, in fact, that when you open an email from someone who is an Instant Messenger user and is currently online, a little Instant Messenger icon shows up next to their email address. You can enable or disable this function in the Instant Messenger menu in Preferences.

- **Collecting Addresses**—One of the least fun things about emailing is entering all those email addresses into an address book. Netscape allows you to automatically save email addresses from incoming and outgoing emails in a special address book called Collected Addresses. Then, if you want, you can easily drag them into your regular address book. This option is enabled by default; you can disable it in the Address Books window in the Mail and Newsgroups menu in Preferences.

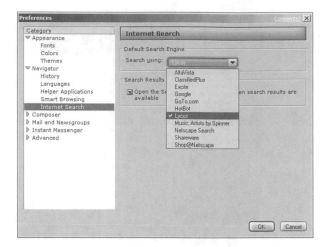

FIGURE 9.16
*Navigator allows you
to choose your default
search site.*

Working with Bookmarks

Bookmarks are a great way to keep your favorite sites handy all the time. Netscape makes bookmarking sites easy, and offers a couple of ways for you to have one-click access to those bookmarked sites.

There are a couple of different ways to bookmark a site in Navigator. One is the old-fashioned way: Go to a site you like, open the Bookmarks menu and select Add Current Page. Without hesitation, the page jumps into your Bookmarks list.

Earlier in this chapter, you learned how to add a tab to your Sidebar. One of the tabs that you can add is Bookmarks. After you've added it, if you have that tab displayed on your Sidebar, you can drag the address of the site you're visiting (by grabbing the icon to the left of the address) onto the Sidebar, and it will drop into your Bookmarks list automatically.

Putting Bookmarks in Your Personal Toolbar

Okay now, try not to get confused. We know there's a Personal Bar in Explorer, but this is different. In Navigator, the Personal Toolbar is that thin bar that runs right above the top of the browser's main window; it includes the Home and My Netscape buttons (see Figure 9.17).

You can add your most important Bookmarks to this toolbar. To do so, open the Bookmarks menu and select Manage Bookmarks (see Figure 9.18). Now, simply drag any bookmark you have into the Personal Toolbar folder area, place it in the order you want it to appear, and release it.

Personal toolbar

FIGURE 9.17

The Personal Toolbar can be personalized in Netscape.

9

When you close the Manage Bookmarks window, your Personal Toolbar will contain any of the bookmarks you put there. Now, the next time you want to go to that page, it's literally one click away!

FIGURE 9.18

You can add bookmarks to your Personal Toolbar.

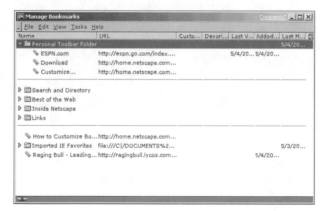

Removing Bookmarks from the Personal Toolbar

Okay, so that site you used to visit all the time just doesn't do it for you anymore. And it's just taking up space on the Personal Toolbar. You can remove it just as easily as you put it there in the first place.

Just go back to the Manage Bookmarks window. There, you can either drag the offending bookmark to the bottom pane, thus relegating it to a spot among the "regular" bookmarks, or you can highlight and press your delete key, thus getting rid of it altogether.

Summary

Netscape Navigator is an outstanding browser that offers all the basic functionality of Microsoft Internet Explorer, plus some extra bells and whistles. Now that you've seen both programs, you can take the time to try them both out and see which one best fits your style.

CHAPTER 10

Using AOL 6

You can hardly turn on the television anymore without hearing something about America Online. If it's not a commercial for the service itself, then you'll hear it mentioned at the end of a commercial for something else, such as, "Visit us at www.microsoft.com; AOL keyword 'Microsoft.'"

AOL was once a part of a three-way national online service war with CompuServe and Prodigy. Today, however, AOL is the undisputed king. It seems like a hundred years ago when AOL struck the key blow in that war when it offered unlimited access to its customers for $19.99/month. Before that, all the services were offering "packages" such as 40 hours for this price, with additional charges for additional hours.

When AOL made its bold move, it walked out on a dangerous ledge. At first, customers signed up in droves, only to encounter busy signals when they dialed in because AOL wasn't ready to handle the demand created by the success of their new pricing structure. For a while, it appear AOL's own success would doom it to failure.

But largely, its members stuck with the service. Those who left were likely to return after the connection problems were solved. Today, Virginia-based AOL is the largest Internet service provider in the world. But it's more than an ISP, too.

AOL offers content—lots of it—that only its members can see. And, members get full access to the Internet as well, making AOL the largest ISP in the world.

In this chapter, we'll give you an introductory look at AOL 6.0, the latest version of the software, and the services that AOL offers, so you can decide whether AOL is right for you.

In the preceding chapters, you learned about the two primary browsers, Internet Explorer and Netscape Navigator. In both cases, I walked you through downloading the latest version of the software and then its features.

AOL is different because it's not just a browser. AOL offers its own content, and it requires a subscription (typically in the low $20s per month). As a result, this chapter will be presented backward from the previous two. First, we'll look at the features and advantages of AOL. Then, if you're interested in signing up, you can read about where to get the software and how to sign up.

Understanding AOL

It's a question I get asked all the time: What's the difference between AOL and the Internet? It's a good question, too. The truth is that by using AOL, you get everything that the Internet has to offer, plus content that is only available to AOL members. After all, you can get to the Internet using AOL and browse any site in the world. Plus, you have access to AOL content: channels, chat rooms, email, instant messages, a calendar feature, forums, shopping, and so on.

AOL is a little pricier than many local ISPs would charge. But you do get more for the money, too.

Why Should I Choose AOL?

So the question then becomes, "Why should I choose AOL?" Here's a quick look at some of the top reasons:

- **People**—AOL's slogan, "20 million people can't be wrong," says it all. Many people you know (or many kids your children know) are using AOL. Joining gives you quick access to them through Instant Messenger, email, chat, and so on.

- **Ease**—AOL makes it simple. Getting the software is easy, as is logging on and setting up your account. After you've done that, your Internet access, email, and everything else is all ready to go for you. That's why tons of first-time Internet users gravitate toward AOL to get themselves online.

- **Content**—AOL's content is divided into 20 different areas of interest, which AOL calls Channels. Channel topics range from Women to Sports to Shopping to Personal Finance to Kids Only to Health to Games. Some are serious, some are just for fun, some offer a little of both. But they all are packed with content.

- **Worldwide access**—This one's often overlooked. AOL makes it easy to log on to someone else's computer somewhere else in the world and still get on to your account. This allows you to access your own email (you can also access from AOL's Web site) and do everything just as you would at home.

- **Multiple Users, One Account**—AOL allows up to seven screen names on one account. This means that you and your spouse, plus little Billy, Johnny, Pookie, Muffin, and The Beav can all have your own email accounts.

- **Parental Controls**—This is perhaps the biggest reason (along with "multiple users") that AOL is so popular with families. Although there are other ways to limit what your kids see on the Internet, AOL's Parental Controls allow you many options for setting what each child, based on age, can see. So, have 8-year-old Muffin's settings at a more restrictive level than 16-year-old Billy's and make sure Muffin doesn't know anyone else's password, and Muffin won't see any naughty stuff.

Why Shouldn't I Choose AOL?

This one's a little tougher, because AOL does have a lot to offer. Here's why some people stay away:

- **It's for Beginners**—Some "serious" Internet users, especially business people, don't want an @aol.com email address because they wrongly believe it is an indication they are novices. The truth is, a lot of these "serious" types have their business account and keep an AOL account as well for personal reasons, and for its worldwide access. However, do know that the perception that "AOL is for beginners" is very much alive, but AOL offers plenty for new and experienced users.

- **Email Compression**—AOL compresses automatically any emails that have multiple attachments. This can make them difficult to open and use for non-AOL members. Not a big problem, really, but something to consider if you send or receive lots of attachments.

10

- **Advertising**—Having a captive audience of 20 million does come with its draw-backs, including lots of advertising. Every time you sign on to AOL, you'll get a pop-up ad before you ever hear the friendly, "Welcome!" or the ubiquitous "You've Got Mail!" The ads, though, can be limited through your preferences.

- **Junk Mail**—If you're an AOL member, you're going to get a fair amount of junk mail.

Taking a Quick Tour of AOL

AOL has a lot more to offer than can be covered in one chapter of this book. If you decide to become an AOL subscriber, I strongly recommend that you pick up a Sams book on using AOL.

Let's take some time, however, to take a quick look around the service to see what it offers.

Remember now, AOL also allows you full access to the Internet, so you can get everything that's on the Web, too. This section just covers the stuff that's only available to AOL members.

The Welcome Screen

When you first log on to AOL, you're greeted by a warm, "Welcome!" (assuming you have a sound card and speakers in your system). The Welcome screen (see Figure 10.1) appears.

FIGURE 10.1

AOL's Welcome screen offers quick access to AOL features.

Here you'll find quick access to lots of great AOL content, including:

- **You've Got Mail**—If the little mailbox icon shows a letter sticking out and the words, "You've Got Mail," well, you've got mail. If you don't, it shows a closed mailbox and the words, "Mail Center." A double-click gets you to your mailbox either way.

- **You've Got Pictures**—A relatively new service that allows you to drop off your film at a participating processing center, check a box on the envelope and, for a small fee, be able to access your pictures online through AOL.

- **My Calendar**—AOL's calendar service allows you to input your personal (or professional) schedule and be able to track it from any computer with AOL installed on it.

- **My Places**—A customizable list similar to Favorite Places or Bookmarks. You can choose what appears in the list and have one-click access to those features.

The Channels

AOL's Channels are the foundation upon which the service is built. You can get access to any area of AOL through the Channels.

The Channels list appears down the left side of the screen when you log on to AOL (see Figure 10.2). The list gives you easy access to AOL's 20 different content areas. To visit a channel, just click on its name and a new window pops into the middle of the screen, opening that channel (see Figure 10.3).

FIGURE 10.2

Click on Entertainment in the Channels list ...

One of the nicer features of AOL 6 is that when you switch between channels, the rest of the channel options remain on the left side of the window. Only the content area changes, leaving you with access to all the other channels. To get back to the Welcome screen, simply click the Welcome bar at the top of the Channels list.

Let's take a brief look at some of the channels and what they offer.

Entertainment

The Entertainment channelshown in Figure 10.3, provides information on all things entertaining—from music and musicians to movies, television, and books. Every day, you'll find a couple of entertainment items in the spotlight (see the Today's Top Features area), as well as buttons for the channel's main departments.

The Entertainment channel departments are Movies, Music, Television, Celebrities, Books & Arts, Photos, and Fun and Games. Each covers what the name implies.

Speaking of clicking and going, go ahead and explore the Entertainment channel. Don't be shy—click a department button or check out one of the Top Features. Poke around and have some fun. It is the Entertainment channel, after all. Pick a topic that interests you and go nuts.

The Welcome screen can't be closed. You can minimize it, but you can't close it. Don't let it throw you.

Kids Only

AOL is a great place for kids—there's lots for them to see and do, and there are other kids online with whom they can share their thoughts and ideas. The Kids Only channel (shown in Figure 10.4) is like a mini-AOL that preteen kids have all to themselves.

The Kids Only channel is a collection of fun, entertainment, and education just for kids. Your children can chat with some online friends, play a game, or even get help with their homework.

FIGURE 10.4

Kids Only—it really is just for kids.

As you saw with the Entertainment channel's main screen, the Kids Only screen gives you a few highlights of what's going on online for kids today, plus buttons with which you can access the Kids Only departments.

The departments include the following:

- **News and Sports**—Profiles of athletes, up-to-date stories, and news from a kid's point of view.
- **Art Studio**—Kids get an opportunity to draw, write, and create.
- **Clubs**—There are clubs for everything from cartoons to movies for kids to join.
- **TV, Movies, and Music**—Keep up with Britney Spears, the latest Disney offerings, and more.
- **Games**—This department is fairly self-explanatory.
- **Homework Help**—Help from real teachers no less.

At the bottom of the Kids Only channel's main window, you also see a chat button that leads you to the Kids Only chat areas.

Personal Finance

After the kids are done playing and learning on America Online, you might want to hop online yourself to see whether you can send them to college someday…yikes!

The main Personal Finance screen offers all manner of financial resources, including the latest market reports, stock quotes, mutual fund information, stock and insurance brokers, banking, and a vast array of advice and financial services (see Figure 10.5). In the My

10

Portfolios area, you can build a portfolio of investments for yourself and track their
progress. You can also get the latest Business News or do some research on companies in
the Stocks area.

FIGURE 10.5

*The Personal Finance
channel allows you to
keep up with the mar-
kets and monitor your
portfolio.*

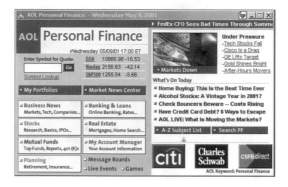

Computer Center

The Computer Center channel, shown in Figure 10.6, is a Mecca for computer lovers, but
is also a good resource for newbies. It's the source of all sorts of computer news, information, and even software. Whether you're an old hand with computers or just learning
your way around one, the Computer Center channel has something for you.

FIGURE 10.6

*The Computer Center
Channel has software
and information for
new and experienced
computer users.*

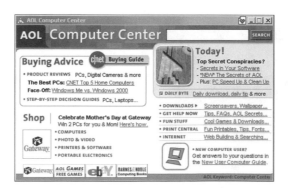

A *newbie* is slang for someone who is new to the Internet, America Online,
or any online service.

As with the other channels we've seen so far, the Computer Center main screen features
a breakdown of the channel's departments as well as highlights of popular areas. The

departments include Downloads (where you can search for and copy to your computer actual software you can use), Get Help Now, Fun Stuff, Print Central, and Internet.

News

A lot is happening in the world, but most people have little time to keep up with it—unless there's some major calamity or hot news topic, the electronic media reduce everything to eight-second sound bites. If you want news with a little more depth, you can find it on AOL. Nearly every channel offers a News button or index: entertainment news, software news, kids' news, Internet news, weather news…you get the idea.

An entire News channel is also available, shown in Figure 10.7, which you can flip through rather like a newspaper.

FIGURE 10.7
AOL News acts a little like your local newspaper.

From the News main window, you can access the hour's headlines and news by department: Nation, Business News, World, Health News, Entertainment News, Family News, Life, Weather, Sports, Photos, and Local.

Getting Places, Saving Places

AOL offers a quick way to get from place to place, called *keywords*. Almost all the places you can go within the service are identified by a keyword. If you know the keyword, or can hazard a guess, you can type in the word and go directly to that area.

To do this, just click the Keyword button near the upper-right corner of the AOL screen. A Keyword box appears, as you see in Figure 10.8.

FIGURE 10.8
Enter your keyword, and jump right to that area within AOL.

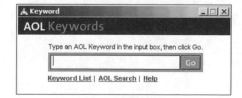

Several keywords work for each area. For example, if you type in the word "genealogy," you go right to the genealogy section within AOL. You would also get there by typing in the word "genealogy."

After you've found places you like within AOL, there are a couple of ways you can bookmark them. AOL's My Favorites allows you to keep a list of bookmarks—just like Internet Explorer or Netscape Navigator—for Web pages. But you can also mark favorite areas within the AOL services, giving you quick access to them. As stated earlier in this chapter, your My Places area on the Welcome screen can also be customized with your most-used places and sites.

Where Can I Get the AOL Software?

If you haven't received a free copy of the AOL software by now, you're the one person they missed. AOL routinely sends out free CDs with its software. Sometimes it's stuck in a magazine, sometimes with your newspaper, sometimes it comes on its own.

However, if you didn't have a computer before or weren't interested in AOL when you got it, the chances are good you tossed it in the trash (or made a drink coaster out of it). So, what do you do now?

Well, almost every computer retailer, especially the electronics superstores, offer the AOL software for free (they sometimes charge a penny) on CD. You can also get it at libraries and other major stores, like Wal-Mart or Target.

You can also get it online, direct from AOL. If you're interested in signing up for the AOL service, take the following example and download the latest version of the AOL software.

In the following exercise, you will download the latest version of AOL. All this does is load the software on your computer. You are not required to sign up yet. So completing this exercise won't hurt a bit!

1. Using Internet Explorer or Netscape Navigator, go to the AOL Web site at www.aol.com (see Figure 10.9). Click on the Try AOL 6.0 button (the version number might have changed between this writing and your visit to the site).

2. On the download page (see Figure 10.10), click the Download Now button.

FIGURE 10.9

Step 1: Go to the AOL Web site and click the Try AOL button.

FIGURE 10.10

Step 2: Click the Download Now button.

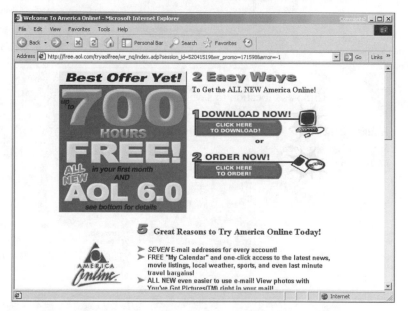

3. Click the download button that is appropriate for your operating system (see Figure 10.11).

Some versions of AOL might not operate properly on some versions of Windows, so be sure you're choosing the right one.

FIGURE 10.11

Step 3: Click the download button for your system.

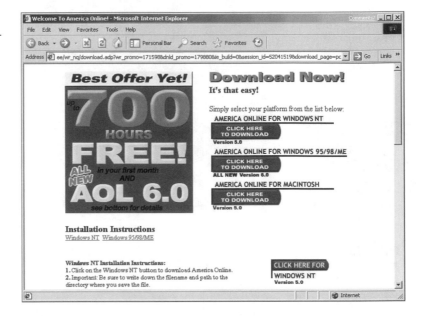

4. Choose a location to save the download file (see Figure 10.12).

FIGURE 10.12

Step 4: Choose a location for the file.

5. The file begins to download to the location you specified (see Figure 10.13).

FIGURE **10.13**
Step 5: The file down-loads.

After the file has completed its download, all you need to do is decide whether you are ready to sign up to be an AOL member. If you are ready to give it a try, just double-click the icon for the file (from the location where you saved it), and the AOL setup program will launch (see Figure 10.14).

AOL does a great job of walking you through the process of registering and getting started. The hardest part of the process is deciding on a screen name. Because there are already millions of members, a lot of screen names are taken!

10

FIGURE **10.14**
The AOL setup pro-gram walks you through the process of signing up and getting into the service.

Summary

America Online is full of great content and features, and it also gives you access to the full Internet. It's a great choice as an ISP for both novices and experienced Internet types. And, it's easy to use!

CHAPTER **11**

Plug-In and Add-On Programs

It might have happened to you already—surfing around the Internet, you come across a link that looks particularly promising. You click it, and a screen pops up telling you that in order to run this or see or hear or use it, you must have a program that is not currently installed on your computer.

"Would you like to download it now?"

You might, and you might not. That's up to you. But the fact of the matter is, as the Web develops and becomes more interactive and more multimedia-oriented, you're going to need more of these programs.

These additional programs function with your browser to allow you to view certain types of files, hear music, view video, have a conference call, and so on.

Your PC is not really your TV yet. But it's getting there. Already, you can watch live or recorded video through the Internet and listen to live radio broadcasts and CD-quality recorded music, too.

Your ability to do that depends on your browser. Good, up-to-date browsers come equipped to play most of the multimedia content on the Web (sometimes with a little help from programs built in to the Windows or Macintosh operating systems). Good browsers are also *extensible*; that is, they can be refitted to deal with new file types and Internet services as they come along. New stuff always does come along, all because petulant teenage geniuses keep inventing new multimedia formats (like CD-quality music files) and putting 'em online.

Taking advantage of today's hottest multimedia—and tomorrow's—requires an understanding of the accessory programs—often called *plug-ins*, *players*, or *helper programs*—that endow your browser with new powers. In this chapter, you discover not only how to fit your browser to play the coolest online multimedia, but also how to make your browser play anything even newer and cooler that may come along.

You'll hear a lot about "downloading" files in this chapter. If you're not already familiar with downloading files, fear not: You'll learn all about it in Chapter 13, "Downloading Programs and Files."

In the meantime, you might find that you can figure it out on your own. Simply put, to download a file, you click a link (you already know how to do that!), and then do whatever your browser tells you to do.

Understanding Plug-Ins, Java, and Other Programs in Pages

Up-to-date versions of Internet Explorer and Netscape Navigator come pre-equipped to play most (but not all) of the stuff you'll encounter online. So the most important step in preparing to play multimedia is making sure you have the latest version of your browser, so it supports native play of those file types.

When a browser has the built-in capability to play a particular kind of file, the browser is said to include *native* support for that file type. Anything the browser can do without help from another program is native; any capability in which the browser must call on another program (such as those in this chapter) is *non-native*.

As part of being extensible, Netscape Navigator and Internet Explorer can, in effect, be reprogrammed through the Web to acquire new capabilities. This happens chiefly through four types of program files:

- **Plug-ins**—A plug-in is a program that implants itself in the browser to add a new capability. Usually, after you install a plug-in, that new capability appears to be a native, built-in part of the browser, as if it had always been there.

- **Helper programs**—A helper program is a separate program that the browser opens automatically to deal with a particular type of file. For example, when you play a video file from within Internet Explorer in Windows, the browser typically opens up the Windows Media Player—a separate program—to show you the file.

> In practice, there's often not a whole lot of difference between a helper and a plug-in. In fact, the terms are often used interchangeably (and therefore incorrectly). The main difference is that a plug-in is generally more tightly integrated with the browser and usually can't play if the browser is closed. A true helper is self-contained—it can be opened as needed by the browser, but can also be used when the browser is closed.

- **Applets and scripts (Java, JavaScript)**—Both Big Two browsers can run program code delivered to them from servers—in effect, little programs that run once and then go away. This code—sometimes described as a script (when in JavaScript) or an applet (Java)—is used increasingly to enable advanced multimedia and other cool, interactive stuff on Web pages.

- **ActiveX controls**—An ActiveX control is a file of program code that teaches the browser how to do new things.

11

In general, you don't have to do anything special to take advantage of scripts, applets, or ActiveX; they're delivered to the browser automatically by Web sites. You just have to make sure that you use the most up-to-date version of Internet Explorer or Netscape Navigator, and you'll be all set.

Most other capabilities are delivered today through plug-ins (or plug-in–like helpers). Although plug-ins are occasionally delivered automatically, more often than not you must deliberately download and install a particular plug-in to enjoy whatever it does.

Finding Plug-Ins and Helpers

Usually when you come across a Web site or a file that requires a particular plug-in or other program, it's accompanied by a link for downloading the plug-in.

In fact, when you first enter the site, a message may appear on your screen informing you that a particular program is required and giving you a link for downloading it. On some sites requiring a specific program you do not have, your browser may show you a message telling you about the program. Often, that message includes a button you can click to get the program right away (see Figure 11.1).

FIGURE 11.1

Sometimes, when you enter a site that requires a particular plug-in or other program, you'll see a message that provides a handy way to go get the program you need.

Occasionally, though, the site doesn't help you get the right program, and you have to go hunting for it.

Fortunately, several excellent indexes are devoted to these programs. The logical first stop is Netscape, where a full directory of plug-ins is maintained, along with links to the latest, coolest ones to come out (see Figure 11.2). You can reach Netscape's Plug-Ins index at `home.netscape.com/plugins/`.

The simplest way to find out what file types your computer is already equipped to play is to simply try files as you find them. If, when attempting to play a particular file type, you see a message telling you that your computer or browser doesn't know what to do with that file, you need to find and install a player program for that file type. Before trying any files, however, make sure you have an up-to-date virus protection program installed and operating on your computer.

Installing and Using Plug-Ins and Helpers

Because these programs can come from any software publisher, no single method exists for installing them. Typically, though, you have to run some sort of installation program and then specify the directory in which your Web browser is installed.

When you come across a link to a plug-in or helper program a site requires, carefully read any instructions you see, click the link, and follow any prompts that appear.

After you install the program, you really needn't think about it any more. Any time you initiate an action in your browser that requires the plug-in or other program, it springs into action automatically. For example, if you've installed a plug-in that plays a particular kind of audio file, any time you click a link for that type of file, the plug-in kicks in to play it.

FIGURE 11.2
Netscape offers a terrific directory of plug-ins.

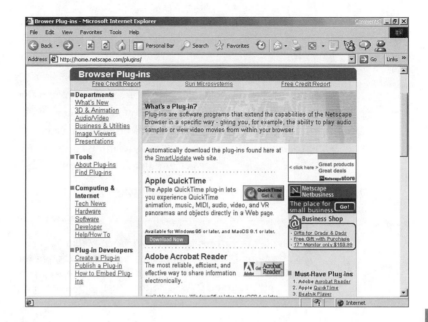

If you keep up with the latest release of your browser, you might not come across many occasions when you need to add anything to it, and you can deal with the rare situations one by one, as they arise.

Still, there are a few enhancements you're likely to need fairly soon. One is RealPlayer, described later in this chapter. Two more are the programs for playing two types of advanced media online: Flash (which enables you to see certain kinds of animation in Web pages) and Shockwave (which enables you to use certain advanced interactive features in some Web pages). Players for both Flash and Shockwave are available for download free from Macromedia (www.macromedia.com), although sites containing Flash and Shockwave content nearly always include an easy-to-find link for downloading the necessary programs.

Internet Explorer (versions 5 and higher) comes with a built-in Flash player, so you might not need a plug-in for Flash. However, the types of content these kinds of plug-ins play are constantly being updated, necessitating upgraded players.

11

Playing Audio and Video

Audio and video come in many different file types online. But all audio and video can be divided into two basic types:

- **Download and play**—These audio and video file types—including sounds in .WAV, .AU, .MID, and .MP3 formats and video clips in .AVI, .MOV, .QT, and .MPG formats—are generally downloaded to your computer and then played. After they are downloaded, these files play anytime, whether you're online or off.

- **Streaming**—Streaming audio and video begin to play a few moments after the audio or video data begins arriving at your computer; in other words, while you're watching or listening to a few seconds of audio or video, the next few seconds are being transmitted to your computer. Streaming is essential for live broadcasts, but is also used to give you faster gratification with some non-live audio and video.

In the next two sections, you'll learn about playing each type.

Besides the aforementioned Windows Media Player and the about-to-be-mentioned RealPlayer, another important program for playing video clips is the QuickTime player. Available both as a Netscape plug-in and as a separate helper program, it equips a computer to play video clips stored in .MOV and .QT formats, of which there are many online.

This free player is not quite as critical as the two I just mentioned, though. All Macintoshes include native support for QuickTime files (they can play them without a separate player program), and some Windows systems already have a QuickTime player installed that browsers will automatically use as a helper. (Recent versions of Windows Media Player play QuickTime, and on older systems, a QuickTime player has usually been installed at some time or other by a multimedia CD-ROM program that featured QuickTime video.) If you have a Macintosh, or if your PC already has a player, Internet Explorer or Netscape Navigator will probably use the existing player to play MOV files.

If you have trouble playing .MOV video, however, get the player at www.apple.com/quicktime/.

Playing Downloaded Audio or Video Files

If you have a computer equipped with the latest operating system (Windows 98/Me/2000/XP on a PC or OS8/OS9/OS X on a Macintosh) and an up-to-date version of Internet Explorer or Netscape Navigator, you will find that you already have everything you need to play all the common video and audio file types (non-streaming) you can download from the Web.

When you click a link that downloads an audio or video file, a dialog box generally appears (see Figure 11.3), asking whether you want to save the file on disk or open it as soon as it finishes downloading.

FIGURE 11.3
When downloading a media file, you can choose to save it (for later play) or open it (play it as soon as it finishes downloading).

• Choose Save to save the file on disk, so you can play it later (online or offline). A regular Save dialog box opens, just as it does when you download any file. On that dialog box, you choose a location where the file will be stored. After downloading, you can play the file at any time by going to the folder or directory you chose to store the file in and double-clicking the file's icon.

• Choose Open to play the file as soon as it finishes downloading, so you can watch it right away and you don't have to fiddle with choosing where the file will be stored.

When you play a file (whether online or off), your computer automatically uses whatever program it has that's registered (assigned) to play that type of file. For example, in Windows, nearly all audio and video file types play in the Windows Media Player program (see Figure 11.4). (The version of Windows Media Player you have may differ, depending on which version of Windows you run and how long ago you got it.)

Observe that Windows Media Player has buttons that look like the buttons on a VCR or tape recorder. You use these buttons the same way you would on those devices: The Play button plays the file, Stop stops play, Fast-Forward skips ahead, and so on.

Whether or not you have Windows Media Player already depends on your version of Windows. Windows ME, 2000, and Windows XP include it. But early shipments of Windows 98 did not include an up-to-date version of the Windows Media Player. On top of that, the Media Player is updated and improved from time to time.

No matter which Windows version you use, the best way to ensure that you always have the latest player is to use Windows's Update feature. Just click the Start button and then choose Windows Update; Windows contacts Microsoft through your Internet connection to see whether there are any

11

updates available for your version (including Media Player upgrades and other enhancements).

If updates are available, you will be presented with the option to easily download and install them (free), right then and there.

FIGURE 11.4

Programs that play audio and video files typically show buttons that mimic the functions of similar buttons on a VCR or tape recorder (Play, Stop, and so on).

The latest version of Windows Media Player, version 8, acts not only as a player, but also as a sort of media-specific browser. As Figure 11.4 shows, buttons along the left side of the window offer access to a Media Guide (a Web page, displayed within Windows Media Player, that offers links for playing the hottest music video, film clips, and more), a Media Library of stuff you have downloaded and saved, and more.

Playing "Streaming" Files

Streaming audio and video is the fastest-growing type of multimedia content on the Internet. It enables you not only to enjoy various multimedia programs designed for delivery through the Internet, but also to experience broadcast TV and radio programs from all over the world—programs you could not otherwise see or hear without first jumping on a plane to the places where these programs are actually broadcast.

Streaming media is audio or video (or both together) that begins to play on your computer before it has been completely downloaded. The main use of streaming audio and video is to present live Web broadcasts of audio or video content or to reduce your wait when playing a very large audio or video file.

Windows Media Player plays most popular streaming audio and video types currently in use, so if you have Windows 98 or newer, you might not need another program for streaming audio/video.

But if you have another type of system, you'll need a player program to play streaming audio and video. And even if you do have Windows Media Player, it never hurts to pick up another streaming audio/video player (as long as it's free). In either case, the best choice is RealPlayer, at www.real.com. RealPlayer is available in a free, scaled-down version and also in a version you pay for—RealPlayer Plus. It's also available in a "Real Entertainment Center" suite that includes other tools, such as Real Download, a program for making downloads of any type of file more convenient. But for playing streaming audio and video online, all you really need is the free RealPlayer.

RealPlayer enables you to play streaming video and audio feeds from television and radio broadcasts to news updates to live music. The RealPlayer home page (see Figure 11.5) also provides links to fun places where you can try out RealPlayer.

FIGURE 11.5
Download RealPlayer to play streaming audio and video from the Web.

11

After you have a streaming audio/video player properly installed, it opens automatically anytime you click a link in a Web page that opens one of the streaming audio or video file types for which the player is built (see Figure 11.6). Like regular audio/video play programs, streaming audio/video players feature the familiar VCR buttons (Play, Fast Forward, and so on) for controlling playback.

FIGURE 11.6

Like Windows Media Player, RealPlayer plays streaming audio/video.

Windows Media Player and RealPlayer both play most of the common streaming media file types online. But there are special "Real" files that play only through RealPlayer. Many people use both programs to be sure that they can play anything they come across.

Note that when you install either RealPlayer or Windows Media Player, the program may automatically set itself up as the default media player—the program that opens automatically when you click a link to a media file online. For example, if you already have Windows Media Player and you install RealPlayer, the next time you open a media file, you'll see RealPlayer.

If this happens and you would prefer to have your old player remain the default, no problem.... The next time you open the displaced player, it will display a note asking whether you would like to make it the default player again. Check the check box provided, and you have your old default player back.

Taking Advantage of Media Options in Internet Explorer

In Internet Explorer 6's Personal Bar, you can display a Media pane, which puts buttons for playing radio broadcasts and controlling the volume within easy reach (see Figure 11.7). Note that broadcasts you open and control through the Personal Bar are ones you could also play from RealPlayer—it doesn't give you access to anything special but rather makes accessing the regular stuff easier.

FIGURE 11.7

Internet Explorer's Personal Bar can make accessing and controlling live Web radio broadcasts more convenient.

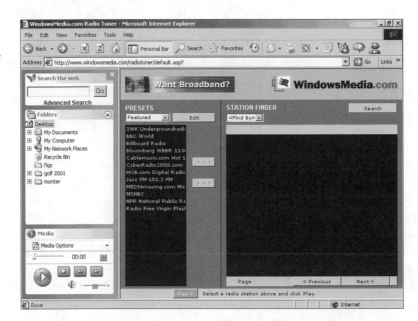

To open the Personal Bar, just click the Personal Bar icon from the toolbar at the top of Internet Explorer. By opening the Media Options menu, you can explore other possibilities available to you, including a list of radio stations from which you can choose.

Where Can I Get Streaming Audio/Video?

You'll come across it all over the Web in sites devoted to other subjects, but the following are a few good starting points for getting to some of the good stuff:

- **RealGuide** (www.realguide.com)—One-stop access to lots of great sites with streaming content
- **Film.com** (www.film.com; see Figure 11.8)—Film clips and movie trailers
- **Cinemapop.com** (www.cinemapop.com)—Free, streaming full-length movies through the Internet

- **CSPAN** (www.cspan.org)—Live Congressional action
- **Emusic** (www.emusic.com)—Live (and prerecorded) streaming music programming

FIGURE 11.8

Film.com offers streaming film clips.

Downloading and Playing CD-Quality Music (MP3 Files)

Although most audio and video you can get online is pretty small and scratchy, one file format online supplies top-quality sound: MP3. MP3 files, which have the filename extension .MP3, are downloadable files containing CD-quality music or other high-quality audio.

Getting MP3 Files

Downloading MP3 files is like downloading any other type of file; you typically click a link in a Web page and then wait for the file to download to your computer. After the file is on your computer, you can play it anytime, even offline. A typical MP3 file containing one pop song is between 3MB and 4MB; over a 56K connection, it typically takes no more than about 15 minutes to get the file.

Of course, the trick with MP3 files isn't downloading them—it's finding the exact song you want to hear from among the thousands available online. To help with that, there are MP3 search pages, which you use just like regular search pages, but which are specifically designed to find MP3 files online when you supply all or part of the song's title or the artist's name. Check out music.lycos.com (see Figure 11.9). Using the Search box at the top of the page, you can search for MP3s by clicking the MP3 radio button.

FIGURE 11.9

There are MP3 search engines that help you find exactly the song you want to hear.

 There are lots of sites with MP3 files and players, but a good place to start with MP3 is (you guessed it) www.mp3.com.

Playing MP3 Files

If you use Windows and have a recent version of Windows Media Player, you'll find that it plays MP3 files you've downloaded from the Web. Otherwise, you'll need to pick up an MP3 player to hear MP3 files. Good shareware and freeware players are available all over the Web; the following are a few sites to check out for good players:

- Sonique (see Figure 11.10) at sonique.lycos.com
- Winamp at www.winamp.com
- Macamp (for Macintosh) at www.macamp.net

FIGURE 11.10
Sonique is one of many great freeware and shareware MP3 players available online.

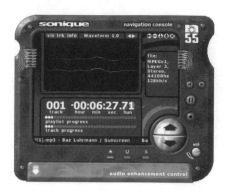

 Most MP3 players not only play MP3 files, but also serve as all-purpose sound players playing other sound file formats (such as .WMA) and also audio CDs in your CD-ROM drive.

Summary

If you have the latest version of Netscape Navigator or Internet Explorer, your browser comes equipped to do so much that you'll rarely come across a situation in which it needs enhancement. Still, no matter how fast developers enhance their browsers, the new file types and programs stay one step ahead. Knowing how to deal with plug-ins and helper programs ensures that you don't get left behind when something new and wonderful hits the Web.

CHAPTER 12

Searching

There's just too much on the Web. It's like having a TV set with a billion channels; you could click the remote until your thumb fell off and still never find the *Law & Order* reruns.

Fortunately, a number of search sites on the Web help you find exactly what you're looking for, anywhere on the Web, and even beyond the Web in other Internet arenas. In this chapter, you'll discover what searching the Web is all about, and discover a simple but effective searching method: cruising categories. You'll also learn how to use search terms and how to phrase them carefully to produce precisely the results you need.

What's a Search Site?

Put simply, a search site—which you may also see variously described as a *search page*, *search tool*, or *search service*—is a Web page where you can conduct a search of the Web. Such pages have been set up by a variety of companies that offer you free Web searching and support the service, at least in part, through the advertising you'll see prominently displayed there. Figure 12.1 shows a popular search site, Excite.

The term *search engine* is sometimes used to describe a search site. But this term more accurately describes the program a search site uses, behind the scenes, to perform searches. When you hear someone refer casually to a "search engine," just remember that they probably mean "search site."

FIGURE 12.1

Excite, a popular search site.

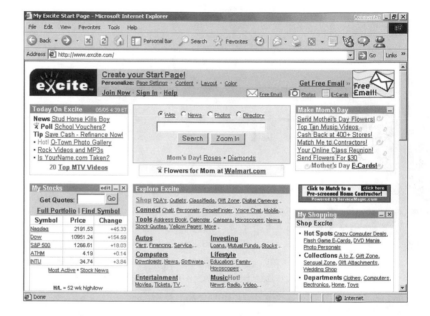

No matter which search site you use, and no matter how you use it, what you get from a search site is a page of links, each pointing to a page the search site thinks might match what you're looking for. When using a search site, your job is to provide that tool with enough information about what you're searching for, so that the resulting "hit list" (see Figure 12.2) contains lots of good matches for you to explore.

FIGURE 12.2

*Search sites show you
list of links—a "hit
list"—of Web pages
and other resources
that match what you
told the search site you
were looking for.*

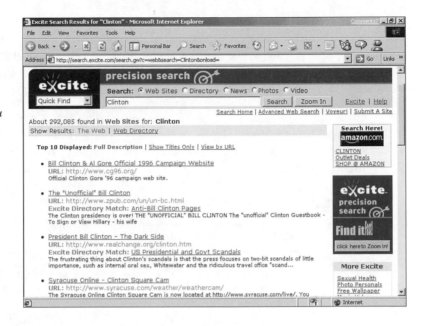

Can I Really Search the Whole Web?

Well, yes and no…. (Don't you *hate* that answer?)

Although using the various search sites works similarly, each has its own unique search methods. But, more important, each has its own unique set of files—a *database*—upon which all searches are based.

You see, no search site actually goes out and searches the entire Web when you ask it to. A search site searches its own index of information about the Web—its database. The more complete and accurate that database is, the more successful your searches are likely to be.

The database for a search site is created in either (or both) of two ways:

- **Manually**—Folks who've created Web pages, or who've discovered pages they want the world to know about, fill in a form on the search site's Web site to add new pages (and their descriptions) to the database. If the search site's editors deem the site to be worthy of inclusion, it gets added.

12

- **Through a crawler (or spider, or worm)**—All these creepy-crawly names describe programs that systematically contact Web servers (at regular intervals), scan the contents of the server, and add information about the contents of the server to the database. (They "crawl" around the Web, like spiders—get it?) It takes the crawler a month or so to complete each of its information-gathering tours of the Web.

If a search site's database has been created by a crawler, the tool tends to deliver results that are more complete and up-to-date, whereas manually built databases tend to contain more meaningful categorization and more useful descriptive information. Also, most search sites with crawler-built databases do not offer you a way to search by browsing through categories—a valuable technique you'll pick up later in this chapter. All search sites, however, support the main search method: entering a search term.

A *search term* is a word or phrase you type in a text box on a search site's main page, to tell the search site the type of information you're looking for. You learn all about search terms later in this chapter.

Because search sites search a database and not the actual Web, they sometimes deliver results that are out of date. You might click a link that a search site delivered to you and find that the page to which it points no longer exists. That happens when a page has been moved or deleted since the last time the search site's database was updated.

When this happens, it's no big whoop. Just click Back to go back to the list of results, and try another link.

How sites are ranked within their categories also varies from search site to search site. Some will simply list sites in alphabetical order. Some sell higher placement for a price, and then list the rest in alphabetical order. Some display results based on the likelihood that the site matches your search term. One site, Google, uses a unique page-ranking system that examines the Internet's elaborate system of links to determine a site's "value" based on the number of other sites that link to it.

Despite differences and strengths and weaknesses among the available tools, the bottom line is this: Any of the major search sites might locate a page or pages that meet your needs, or it might not. If you can't find what you want through one tool, try another. Because each tool has its own database, and each tool applies a different technical method for searching its database, no two search sites turn up exactly the same results for any given topic.

Where Are the Major Search Sites?

There are about a dozen, general-purpose search sites out there, and many, many more specialized search sites.

Table 13.1 lists the major players. You can visit any search site by entering its URL.

TABLE 13.1   The Top Search Sites

Tool	URL
Yahoo!	www.yahoo.com
Excite	www.excite.com
AltaVista	www.altavista.com
Lycos	www.lycos.com
Google	www.google.com
WebCrawler	www.webcrawler.com
Ask Jeeves	www.askjeeves.com
GoTo	www.goto.com

Note that a few of the search sites listed in Table 13.1 are also Web portals, pages that are popular as home pages because they provide easy access to searching, news, and other popular services. Two other popular portals not only offer searches, but actually let you use several different popular search sites, all from the portal page. These are

- Netscape: home.netscape.com
- MSN: msn.com

For example, right from the Netscape portal, you can submit a search term to Netscape's own search engine, or to Infoseek, AltaVista, and other popular search sites (see Figure 12.3).

12

There's a confusion about search sites, created by some ISPs and browser sellers. In part to simplify their sales pitch for novices, these folks sometimes tout their products as "featuring all the best search sites," or words to that effect. That implies that a search site is a feature in a browser, or a service provided by an ISP.

That claim is, oh, what's the word... hooey. A search site is a Web page, and anyone with a browser can use it. Browsers sometimes include features that can make accessing search sites easier, but no browser has a real built-in search engine, and no ISP can claim ownership of any of the important search sites.

FIGURE 12.3

Some Web portals, such as the Netscape portal shown here, provide one-stop access to multiple searches.

Before beginning to use search sites, take a peek at a few from the list in Table 13.1. While visiting these pages, watch for helpful links that point to

- Instructions for using the search site, often called Help
- A text box near the top of the page, which is where you would type a search term
- Links to categories you can browse
- Reviews and ratings of recommended pages
- "Cool Sites"—a regularly updated, random list of links to especially fun or useful pages you might want to visit just for kicks
- Other search engines

Simple Searching by Clicking Categories

These days, all the major search sites accept search terms. But a few also supply a directory of categories, an index of sorts, that you can browse to locate links to pages related to a particular topic. Tools that feature such directories include Yahoo!, Excite, and Infoseek.

Directory browsing is something of a sideline for other search sites, but it's the bread and butter of Yahoo!. When you want to search in this way, Yahoo! is almost always your best starting point.

Why Use Categories Instead of a Search Term?

When you're first becoming familiar with the Web, forgoing the search engines and clicking through a directory's categories is not only an effective way to find stuff but also a great way to become more familiar with what's available on the Web. As you browse through categories, you inevitably discover detours to interesting topics and pages that you didn't set out to find. Exploring directories is an important part of learning how the Web works and what's on it.

Also, the broader your topic of interest, the more useful categories are. When you use a search term to find information related to a broad topic (cars, dogs, music, plants), the search site typically delivers to you a bewildering list containing hundreds or thousands of pages. Some of these pages will meet your needs, but many will be pages that merely mention the topic rather than being about the topic.

Some links that a search term delivers will match the term, but not your intentions; a search on "plant" will likely turn up not only botany and houseplant pages, but others about power plants, Robert Plant, and maybe the Plantagenet family of European lore. Categories, on the other hand, help you limit the results of your search to the right ballpark.

Using a Directory

Everything in a directory is a link; to find something in a directory, you follow those links in an organized way.

You begin by clicking a broad category heading to display a list of related subcategories (see Figure 12.4). Click a subcategory heading, and you display its list of sub-subcategories.

You continue in this fashion, drilling down through the directory structure (usually through only two to five levels), until you eventually arrive at a targeted list of links to pages related to a particular topic. You can explore those page links one by one, and after finishing with each, use your Back button to return to the search site's list and try another link.

Here's how to explore categories:

1. Go to Yahoo! at www.yahoo.com (see Figure 12.5).

2. In the list of categories, click Entertainment (see Figure 12.6).

3. In the list of subcategories that appears, click Amusement and Theme Parks (see Figure 12.7)

12

FIGURE 12.4

A subcategory list in Yahoo!.

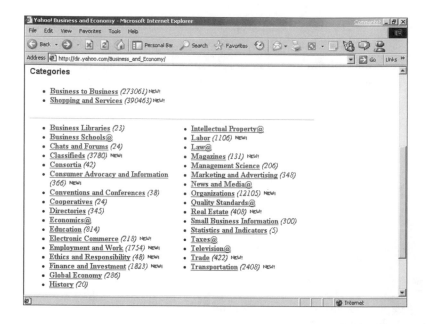

FIGURE 12.5

Step 1: Go to Yahoo!.

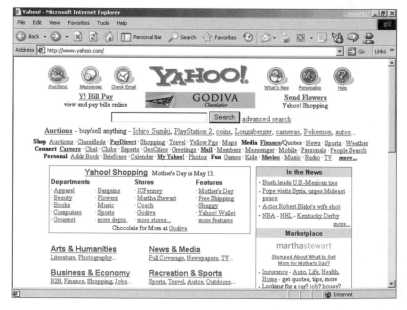

Categories

FIGURE 12.6

Step 2: Click Entertainment.

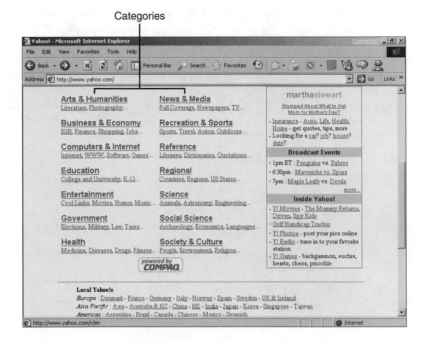

Subcategories

FIGURE 12.7

Step 3: Click Amusement and Theme Parks.

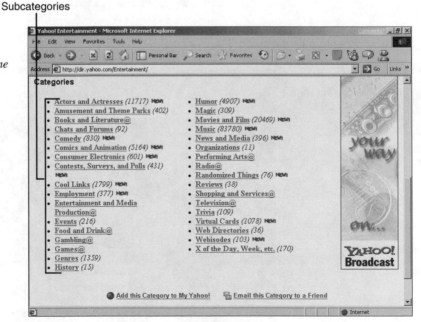

12

4. Scroll down to reveal links leading to pages about amusement parks. You can click one of the preceding subcategories to see more options, or visit one of the following pages (see Figure 12.8).

FIGURE 12.8
Step 4: Choose a sub-category or visit a site.

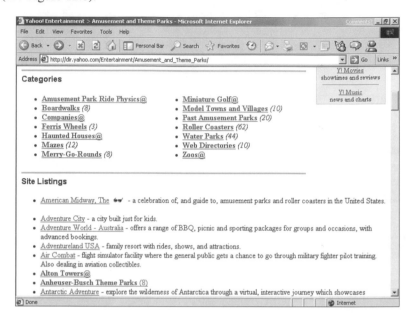

5. If you choose a site, such as Adventureland USA, you'll get to that home page (see Figure 12.9).

FIGURE 12.9
Step 5: Visit a site, like Adventureland USA.

6. Click Back until you return to the top Yahoo! page. Observe that you can try any path or page and then back out by as many levels as you want to so that you can try a different path.

7. Explore on your own, clicking down through the directory and then back up again with Back.

Understanding Searches

Each of the search tools described thus far, and just about any other you might encounter on the Web, has a text box featured prominently near the top of its main page (see Figure 12.10). That text box is where you will type your search terms. Adjacent to the box, there's always a submit button, almost always labeled "Search."

FIGURE 12.10

The text box you see on all search tool pages is where you type a search term.

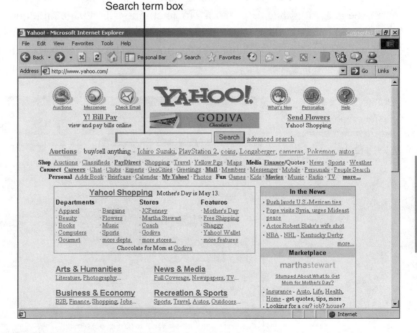

Search term box

Typing a search term in a text box and then clicking the submit button to send the term to the search tool is known as *submitting a search term*. Such searches are sometimes also described as *keyword searches*, because the search term serves as a key to finding matching pages.

When you submit a search term, the search tool searches through its database of information about pages, locating any entries that contain the same combination of characters in your search term. Although the contents of the various search tool databases differ, the record for each page typically contains the page's URL, title, a brief description, and a group of keywords intended to describe the page's contents. If your search term matches anything in that record, the search tool considers the page a match.

After searching the whole database (which takes only a moment or two), the search tool displays a list of links to all the pages it determined were matches: a *hit list*.

> A *hit list* is a list of links, produced by a search engine in response to a search term you have entered. Each link is a "hit": a page that contains a match for your search term.

Each hit in the list is a link (see Figure 12.11). You can scroll through the hit list, reading the page titles and descriptions, to determine which page might best serve your needs, and then click the link to that page to go there. If the page turns out to be a near miss, you can use your Back button to return to the hit list and try a different page, or start over with a new search.

FIGURE 12.11

Excite organizes the hit list from best matches to worst.

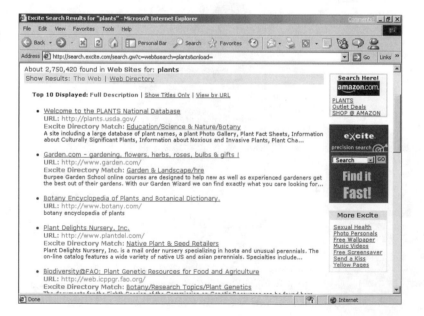

A hit list may show no hits at all, or it may have hundreds. Zero hits are a problem, but hundreds or even thousands of hits really aren't. Remember, most search engines put the best hits at the top of the list, so even if your hit list has thousands of links, the links you want most likely will appear somewhere within the top 20 or so.

Regardless of the number of hits, if you don't see what you want somewhere in the first 30 to 50 links, you probably need to start over with a new search term. And if your first search turned up hundreds of hits, use a more specific term in your second try.

Some tools organize the hit list in smart ways, attempting to put the best matches at the top of the list so you see them first, and weaker matches lower in the list.

For example, suppose you use *Godzilla* as your search term. A particular search tool would tend to put at the top of the hit list all pages that use the word "Godzilla" in their titles or URLs because those are the pages most likely to be all about Godzilla. Matches to keywords or the page's description come lower in the list, because these might be pages that simply mention Godzilla, but aren't really about Godzilla. Even lower in the list, a tool might show links to "partial" matches, pages to which only part of the search term, such as those containing the word "God" or the partial word "zilla."

Phrasing a Simple Search

You can get awfully artful and creative with search terms. But 9 times out of 10, you needn't get too fancy about searching. You go to the search site, type a simple word or phrase in the text box, click the submit button, and wait a few moments for the hit list to show up.

If the list shows links that look like they hold what you're after, try 'em. If not, try another search term.

You can use multiple words in a search term; for example, someone's full name (*Michael Moriarty*) or another multi-word term (*two-term presidents*). But when you use multiple words, some special considerations apply. See "Phrasing a Serious Search," later in this chapter.

12

Here are a few basic tips for improving your search success:

- **Use the simplest form of a word**—The search term *Terrier* will match references to both "Terrier" and "Terriers." However, the term *Terriers* may fail to match pages using only "Terrier." Some search sites are smart enough to account for this, but some aren't. So try to use the simplest word form that's still specific to what you want.

- **Use common capitalization**—Some search sites don't care about capitalization, but some do. So it's always a good habit to capitalize words as they would most often be printed, using initial capitals on names and other proper nouns, and all lowercase letters for other words. Be careful to observe goofy computer-era capitalizations, such as AppleTalk or FrontPage.

- **Be as specific as possible**—If it's the German shepherd you want to know about, use that as your search term, not *dog*, which will produce too many hits, many unrelated to German shepherds. If the most specific term doesn't get what you want, then try less specific terms; if *German shepherd* fails, go ahead and try *dog*. You might find a generic page about dogs, on which there's a link to information about German shepherds.

- **Try partial words**—Always try full words first. But if they're not working out, you can use a partial word. If you want to match both "puppies" and "puppy," you can try *pup* as a search term, which matches both.

 When you use a search term in Yahoo! (www.yahoo.com), the hit list typically shows not only pages, but Yahoo! categories related to the search term. You can try one of the pages, or start exploring related category headings from the head start the search provides.

Try a simple search:

1. Go to AltaVista at www.altavista.com (see Figure 12.12).
2. Click the search term box, and type *DaVinci* for a search term (see Figure 12.13).

FIGURE **12.12**
*Step 1: Go to
AltaVista.*

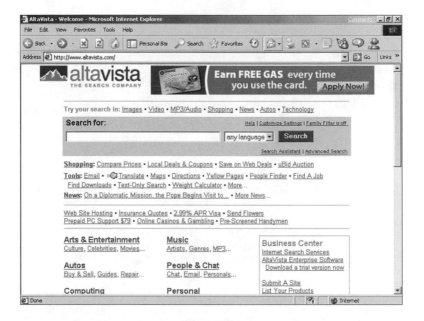

FIGURE **12.12**
*Step 1: Go to
AltaVista.*

FIGURE **12.13**
*Step 2: Type DaVinci
into the search
term box.*

12

3. Click the submit button, labeled Search, to reveal the hit list (see Figure 12.14).

FIGURE 12.14

Step 3: Click the Search button to reveal the hit list.

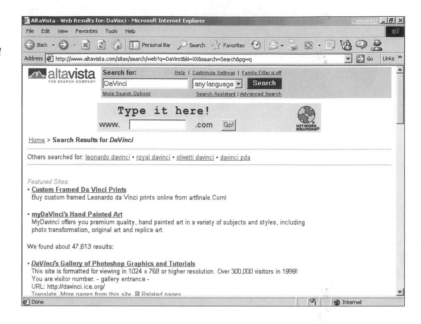

4. Click any link in the hit list, to see where it leads (see Figure 12.15).

FIGURE 12.15

Step 4: Try a link to see where it leads.

5. Click Back to return to the hit list. Scroll to the bottom of the page, and observe that there are links for moving ahead to more pages of the hit list (see Figure 12.16).

FIGURE **12.16**
Step 6: Scroll down to the bottom of the page.

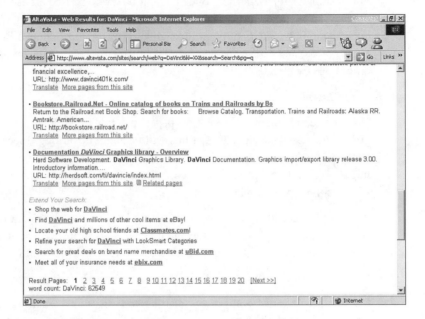

Observe that the search term box appears on every page of the hit list. You can start a new search at any time, from any page of the hit list, by entering a new search term.

Some search sites display the search term box only on the top page; to start a new search in those, just click Back until you return to the top page.

12

Phrasing a Serious Search

Sometimes, in order to phrase a very specific search, you need multiple words. And when you use multiple words, you might need to use operators to control the way a search site works with those words.

In mathematics, an *operator* is a word or symbol used to specify the action in an equation, such as plus or minus. Operators are used in search terms to express a logical equation of sorts that tightly controls how a search engine handles the term.

Using Multiple Words in a Search Term

In a search you can use as many words as you need in order to make the term specific.

For example, suppose I want to learn about boxer dogs. I could use the search term *boxer*. Although that term might turn up some hits about boxer dogs, those hits may be buried among hundreds of other links about prizefighters, China's Boxer rebellion, Tony Danza (actor and ex-boxer), and people named Boxer. So to make my search more specific, I use two words:

boxer dog

Now the search engine will look for pages that contain both "boxer" and "dog," which greatly increases the chances that hits will be about boxer dogs, because most pages about all those other "boxers" I mentioned earlier will not also be about "dogs." I still might see a link to a page about George Foreman's dog, if he has one. But the hit list will be a lot closer to what I want.

If my hit list is still cluttered with the wrong kind of pages, I might remember that a boxer is a breed of dog, so a page about boxer dogs probably also uses the term "breed" prominently. So I might try a third term to further narrow the hit list:

boxer dog breed

Get the idea? Now, if you get too specific, you might accidentally omit a few pages you want—there might be boxer dog pages that don't use "breed" anywhere that would show up in a search database. So it's best to start off with a happy medium (a term that's specific but not overly restrictive), see what you get, and then try subsequent searches using more or less specific terms, depending on what's in the hit list.

A few search engines support *natural language queries*. In a natural language query, you can phrase your search term as you might naturally phrase a question; for example, you might use the search term *Who was the artist Leonardo da Vinci*, and the search site applies sophisticated technology to determine what you're asking.

Natural language queries are a good idea, and they're worth experimenting with. But in my experience, their results are usually not as good as you would probably get with a really smartly phrased search term.

Using Operators to Control Searches

Whenever you use multiple words, you're using operators, even if you don't know it. Operators are words you use between the words in a multi-word search term to further define exactly how the search site will handle your term. Using operators in this way is sometimes described as *Boolean logic*. There are three basic operators used in searching:

- **And**—When you use *and* between words in a search term, you tell the search engine to find only those pages that contain both of the words—pages that contain only one or the other are not included in the hit list.

- **Or**—When you use *or* between words in a search term, you tell the search engine to find all pages that contain *either* of the words—all pages that contain either word alone, or both words, are included in the hit list.

- **Not**—When you use *not* between words in a search term, you tell the search engine to find all pages that contain the word before not, and then to remove from the hit list any that also contain the word following not.

Table 13.2 illustrates how *and*, *or*, and *not* affect a search site's use of a term.

TABLE 13.2 How Operators Work in Search Terms

Search Term	What a Search Tool Matches
Dodge and pickup	Only pages containing both "Dodge" and "pickup."
Dodge or pickup	All pages containing either "Dodge" or "pickup," or both words.
Dodge not pickup	All pages that contain "Dodge" but do not also contain "pickup." (This gets all the Dodge pages, and then eliminates any about pickups.)
Dodge and pickup and models	Pages that contain all three words.
Dodge or pickup or models	Pages that contain any of the three words.
Dodge not Chrysler	Pages that contain "Dodge" but do not also contain "Chrysler." (This gets all the Dodge pages, and then eliminates any that also mention Chrysler.)

Before using operators in search terms, check out the options or instructions area of the search site you intend to use (see Figure 12.17). Most search sites support *and*, *or*, and *not*, but some have their own little quirks about how you must go about it. For example, Excite and AltaVista prefer that you insert a plus sign (+) at the beginning of a word rather than precede it with *and*.

12

FIGURE 12.17

Click the Advanced Search link near Yahoo!'s search term box to learn how Yahoo! supports operators and other advanced search techniques.

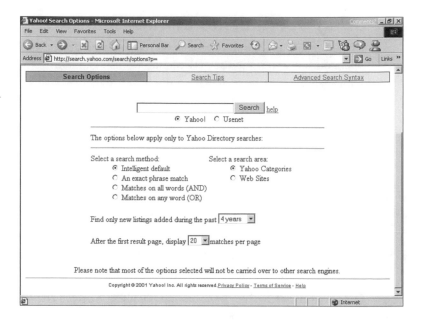

Another powerful way to use multiple words is to do an *exact phrase match*, which most search sites support. In an exact phrase match, you surround the multi-word term with quotes to instruct the search to match only pages that show the same words as the term, in the same order.

For example, suppose you want to know about the film *Roman Holiday*. A search on *Roman Holiday* will probably match any page that uses both of those words anywhere, in any order, together or separately. That'll still get you some good hits, but a lot of bad ones, too. A search on "Roman Holiday" (in quotes) matches only pages that use the exact phrase Roman Holiday, so the hit list will be much better targeted to what you want.

When you use multiple words and don't include operators, most search engines assume you mean to put "and" between words. (See, you are using operators, even if you don't know it.)

For example, if you use the term *candy corn*, most search engines assume you mean "candy *and* corn" and match only pages that contain both words.

Some engines will apply *and* first, and then use *or*. The "and" hits go to the top of the hit list, and the "or" hits go to the bottom, as lower-rated hits.

Conducting a Super Search

In high school, they warned you that you'd need algebra one day. If you ignored that warning (like I did), then you've forgotten all of that stuffabout grouping parts of equations in parentheses.

If you remember algebra, then note that you can apply those techniques for super searches. For example, suppose you wanted to find pages about pro boxers (the kind that hit each other). You would need a hit list that matched all pages with *boxer* or *prizefighter*, but eliminated any that matched *dog* (to weed out the boxer dog pages). You could do that with either of the following algebraic terms:

(boxer or prizefighter) not dog

(boxer not dog) or prizefighter

If you can apply these techniques, drop your old math teacher a note of thanks for a job well done.

About Site Searches

The major search sites mentioned in this chapter are for finding information that may reside anywhere on the Web. Because they have that enormous job to do, they can't always find everything that's on a particular server.

However, large Web sites often provide their own search tools, just for finding stuff on that site alone. For example, Microsoft's Web site is huge, encompassing thousands of pages. So Microsoft supplies a search tool (you can open it from a SEARCH link atop most pages) just for finding stuff at Microsoft. Even fairly small sites may have their own search tools; Figure 12.18 shows one for *Discover* magazine.

You use a site's search tool just as you would any search site, by entering a search term. Many such search tools even support multi-word searches and operators—but always check the instructions accompanying the search tool to find out whether it supports fancy searches.

12

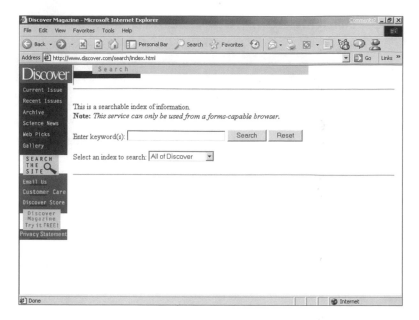

FIGURE 12.18

Discover *magazine supplies its own search tool just for finding stuff on its site.*

Finding People

Using mainly the search techniques you've already picked up in this chapter, you can find people on the Internet—or rather, the email addresses, mailing addresses, or telephone numbers through which particular people can be reached.

This people-finding power is one of the Internet's most valuable and controversial capabilities. Applied properly, it can aid research, locate missing persons, track down deadbeats delinquent in their child support payments, reunite old friends, and even help adult adoptees find their birth parents, if they so desire. When abused, this capability aids stalkers and overaggressive direct marketers. Unfortunately, as is always the case with freedom of information, there's no practical way to preserve the benefit of this capability without also enabling its abuse.

Finding the People-Finding Sites

As with all types of search tools, every people-finder on the Web draws from a different database of names and contact information. Note that these tools don't find only people who have Internet accounts; they search public telephone directories, and thus can show you addresses and telephone numbers of people who wouldn't know the Internet if it snuck up and bit 'em.

In this section, we'll cover people-finding methods and sites that are free on the Internet. There are a number of people finders that charge a fee. These can be useful for finding long-lost relatives or classmates, but they aren't necessarily better than the searching you do yourself. Do some research before paying for such a people-finding service.

For any particular name, a search using one tool may turn up no hits, while a search with a different tool may hit pay dirt. It's important to know where several different search tools are, so that if one tool fails, you can try another. Figure 12.19 shows a typical people-finder page.

If there's a possibility the person you seek has his or her own home page on the Web, using a special people-finding tool may not be necessary. It's usually a good idea to first perform an ordinary search with a tool like AltaVista or Excite, using the person's name (plus maybe the city or town they live in, to help narrow the search) as your search term.

Such a search will likely turn up that person's home page, if they have one (along with any references to other folks who have the same name, of course). If you visit the home page, you'll likely find contact information on it.

FIGURE 12.19

InfoSpace is one of several handy people-finders on the Web.

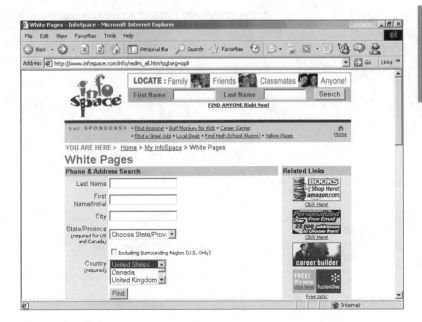

12

You use these tools like any other search tool: Enter as much as you know about the person—name, city, and so on—and the tool finds matches in its database. But that database contains only contact information, so your search won't turn up all sorts of references that have nothing to do with contacting someone.

Some of the better people-finders include the following:

- Yahoo!'s People Search, at `people.yahoo.com`
- Excite's Email Lookup (for email addresses), at
  `www.excite.com/reference/email_lookup/email`
- Bigfoot, at `www.Bigfoot.com`
- InfoSpace, at `www.infospace.com`

> Depending on the people-finder you use and the options you choose, you may find a person's mailing address, phone number, or email address (or all three). There's also a chance, of course, that you'll find no matches.

Because you're probably already familiar with Yahoo!, Yahoo!'s People Search is a great first place to try finding someone.

1. Go to Yahoo!'s People Search at `people.yahoo.com` (see Figure 12.20).

FIGURE 12.20

Step 1: Go to Yahoo!'s People Search site.

2. Fill in the boxes in the Telephone Search form: First Name, Last Name, City, and so on, and then click the button labeled Search (see Figure 12.21).

FIGURE 12.21

Step 2: Fill in the Telephone Search form and click Search.

3. On the list of matching names (not shown), click Back to return to the People Search page.

4. Now fill in the boxes under Email Search, and click the Search button (see Figure 12.22).

5. Just for fun, click Back to try another Email Search, but this time, leave some boxes empty, to see how these tools will show you more names to choose from when you don't have complete information about a person (see Figure 12.23).

If you found yourself in your Yahoo! searches, you might be wondering, "How did my phone number, email address, or other information get on the Web?"

Most of the information in the search tool databases—including names, addresses, and phone numbers—comes from public telephone records. By agreeing to have your name, address, and phone number listed in the phone book, you've agreed to make it public, so there's nothing to prevent it from winding up in a Web database. Some databases may also obtain records from other online databases (such as your ISP's user directory), or even from online forms you've submitted from Web pages.

12

So even if you have an unlisted telephone number (which phone companies call "unpublished"), a record about you may find its way into a database from another source. That's just one reason you must be careful about how and when you enter information about yourself in an online form.

FIGURE 12.22

Step 4: Fill in the Email Search form and click Search.

Using People-Finders Through Your Email Program

There is a family of people-finding directories, known collectively as *LDAP directories*, that are specifically and solely for finding email addresses, both in North America and worldwide.

LDAP (Lightweight Directory Access Protocol) is a standard followed by some people-finders so that a single dialog box in an email program can be used to search LDAP directories.

Some LDAP directories, such as the aforementioned Bigfoot (www.Bigfoot.com) are accessible through a Web page. But these and several other LDAPs may also be accessed from within some email programs. This enables you to search for an email address from within your email program—which is, after all, the place you need email addresses.

FIGURE 12.23

Step 5: Try it again leaving some boxes empty.

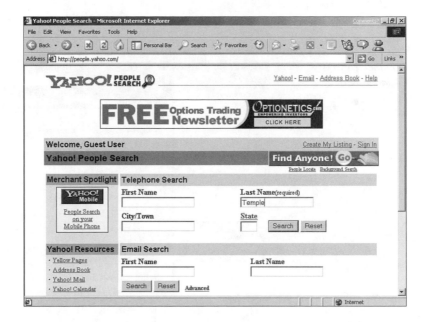

The two email programs included in the big two Internet suites both support LDAP searches, from within their *address book*, a utility that helps you keep track of email addresses.

Searching an LDAP directory from within your email program is just like using a people-finder on the Web: You fill in a name and other information in a form. The only difference is in getting to that form. Instead of opening a Web page, you go online, open your email program, and navigate to the LDAP search form.

For example, in Outlook Express, click the Find button and choose People (see Figure 12.24). A search dialog opens. Use the top list in the dialog to choose the LDAP directory to search, fill in the other boxes in the dialog, and then click Find Now.

Finding People in America Online

America Online members have an advantage when looking for others on the service—because America Online controls the database, it's easy to search.

However, the individual members are the ones who fill out their member profiles in AOL. So, the likelihood of your finding the person you're looking for depends directly on how well that particular member filled out their profile. Many people fill their profiles with jokes, making a serious attempt to find them unlikely to be successful (perhaps that's the point of the jokes!).

12

FIGURE 12.24

Searching an LDAP directory from within Outlook Express's Address Book.

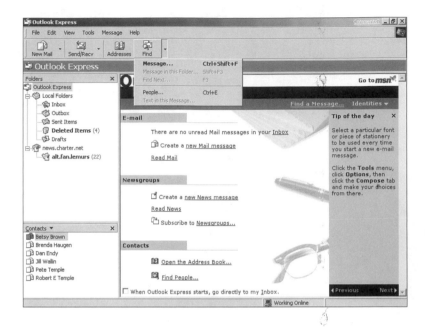

Another problem, of course, is the possibility that the person is not a member of AOL at all. If that's the case, you're just as well off to search using an LDAP directory over the Web.

There several different ways to find people through (and on) America Online. In addition, there are ways you can learn about people if you know their screen name but nothing else. Here are the options:

- **People Directory**—This allows you to search the AOL member directory through either a Quick Search or an Advanced Search (see Figure 12.25). You can search for specific things in a person's profile, such as a city of residence, or you can search by name. To access this feature, open the People menu and select People Directory.

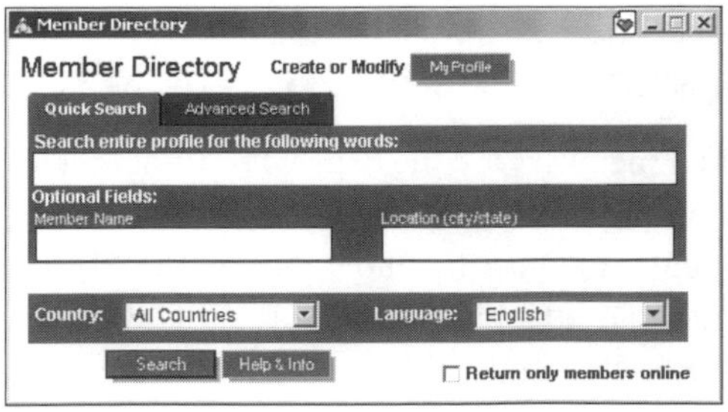

FIGURE 12.25

Searching AOL's Member Directory can help you find another AOL member.

- **White Pages**—Allows you to search for people through AOL. This is similar to a search over the Web. To access this feature, select White Pages from the People menu.

- **Get Directory Listing**—If you know a person's screen name and want to read their member profile, select Get Directory Listing from the People menu. Then, enter the screen name, click OK (see Figure 12.26), and you'll see the person's directory listing.

FIGURE 12.26

If you know a person's screen name, you can enter it to get their member profile.

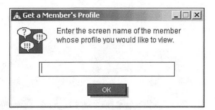

- **Locate Member Online**—By selecting this option from the People menu, you can find out whether a given member is online at the present time. If you know the person's screen name, you enter it, and AOL will tell you what they are doing on the service at the moment.

Other Folk-Finding Tips

The all-around easiest ways to find people online are those I've already described. But if those don't pay off for you, try the following methods.

Try an Advanced Search

People-finders are designed first and foremost to be easy to use. For that reason, many do not display their most advanced tools at first. They present an easy-to-use, quick form for general-purpose people-searching, but also supply an optional, advanced form for more sophisticated searches. The advanced form comes in handy when the basic form doesn't dig up the person you want.

For example, on Yahoo!'s people-finder page, you'll see a link labeled Advanced, which brings up the Advanced search page shown in Figure 12.27.

Besides providing you with more options for more narrowly identifying the person you're looking for, the Advanced search provides a check box for "SmartNames." When this check box is checked, Yahoo! searches not only for the exact name you supplied, but also for common variations of that name. If you entered "Edward," the search might match records for "Edward," "Ed," and "Eddy," too. This feature increases the chances of finding the right person when you're not sure which name form the person uses.

12

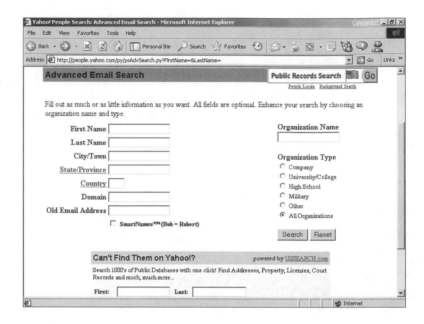

Use a Company or School Directory

Do you know the name of the company the person works for, or a school he or she
attends? Many companies, colleges, and universities have their own Web sites, and those
Web sites often contain employee and student directories you can browse or search (see
Figure 12.28). Just search for and go to the Web site, and then browse for a directory.

Try Name Variations

Might the person you're looking for sometimes use a different name than the one you've
been using as a search term? Try alternative spellings (Sandy, Sandi) or nicknames. Try
both the married name and birth name of people who may have married or divorced
recently. You may even want to try a compound name made out of both the birth name
and married name (for example, Jacqueline Bouvier Kennedy). I know both men and
women who use compound or hyphenated married names.

Use Old Communications to Start the New Ones

Do you know either the mailing address or phone number of the person, and just want
his or her email address? Don't be shy: Call or write, and just ask for the person's email
address so you can conduct future communication online. Life's too short.

FIGURE 12.28

Like many companies and schools, the University of Minnesota offers on its Web site a searchable directory of students and faculty.

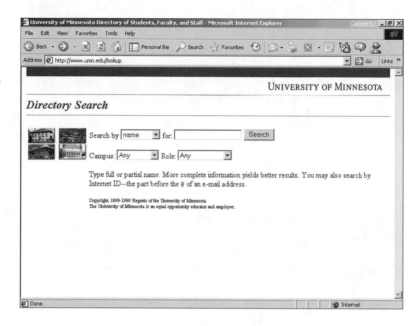

Summary

Most of the time, a search is a snap. Just type a likely sounding word in any search tool's text box, click the submit button, and wait for your hits. But the more you know about narrowing your searches by choosing just the right word, using multiple words, and using operators, the better your odds of always finding exactly what you're looking for.

12

CHAPTER 13

Downloading Programs and Files

The huge, diverse group of people who use the Internet have only one thing universally in common: They all use a computer. So it's no surprise that computer programs and files are the most common "things" you can acquire through the Internet. You can find online all kinds of Internet software, other kinds of programs (like games or word processors), documents (such as books or articles), and other useful files such as utilities and plug-ins.

To find a particular file or program you want, you can apply the search techniques you've already picked up in Chapter 12, "Searching." But in this chapter, you'll learn how to use search techniques that are better focused and faster so that you can find exactly the files you want. You'll also learn all about downloading the files you'll find, and about preparing those files for use on your computer.

What's Downloading, Anyhow?

Downloading is the act of copying a computer file from a server, through the Net, to your computer so you can use it there, just as if you had installed it from a disk or CD-ROM.

Click a Link, Get a File

Whether you've thought about it or not, when you're on the Web, you're really downloading all the time. For example, every time you open a Web page, the files that make up that page are temporarily copied from the server to your computer.

But here we're talking more deliberate downloading: You locate a link in a Web page that points to a file or program you want (see Figure 13.1). To download the file, click the link, and then follow any prompts that appear. It's really that simple.

FIGURE 13.1

You can download files from the Web simply by clicking links that lead to files, such as those shown here.

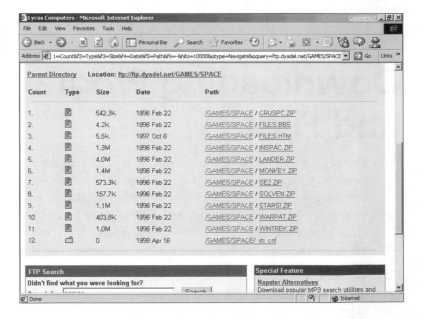

Observe that most of the file links in Figure 13.1 have the filename extension .zip. This extension indicates that these files are compressed archive files, also known as *Zip* files. You'll learn more about Zip files later in this chapter.

How Long Does Downloading Take?

The larger the file, the longer it will take to download. That's why the size of the file is usually shown somewhere in or near the link for downloading it (refer to Figure 13.1). The size is expressed in kilobytes (K or KB) for smaller files, or in megabytes (M or MB) for larger files. One M equals 1,024K.

How long does it take to download a file of a given size? That depends on many factors, including the speed of your Internet connection, and how busy the server is. But over a connection of 28.8Kbps, a 1MB file typically downloads in around 10 minutes, give or take.

> You might expect that downloading a file through a 56Kbps connection would take half as much time as doing so through a 28.8Kbps connection, but that's never the case.
>
> Even in the best case, current regulations limit the download speed over phone lines to 53Kbps, even if the modem handles 56Kbps. More importantly, a noisy phone or other factors can make a 56Kbps modem perform way below its top speed.
>
> Finally, other factors—pauses in the downloading caused by overly busy servers, the speed of your computer's hard disk, and so on—can affect download speed.
>
> In general, though, the faster your connection, the faster the download. A cable or DSL connection allows downloads to occur much more quickly than a dial-up connection.

You'll find lots of great stuff to download that's less than 1MB. However, many programs or multimedia files can be much, much larger. A download of the entire Internet Explorer program from Microsoft's Web site can take several hours, even through a 56Kbps connection.

With experience, you'll develop a sense of how long downloading a file of a given size takes on your system. After you have that sense, always carefully consider the size of the file and whether you want to wait that long for it, before starting the download.

Just for practice, and to understand what to do when you locate a file you want, download the Adobe Acrobat reader, a program that enables you to display documents in the Adobe Acrobat (.pdf) file format, which are common online. If you already have an Adobe Acrobat reader, or just don't want one, you can cancel the download before it finishes.

13

1. Go to Adobe's Web site at www.adobe.com, scroll to the bottom of the page, and click the button labeled Get Acrobat Reader (see Figure 13.2).

Button

FIGURE 13.2

Step 1: Click the Get Acrobat Reader icon.

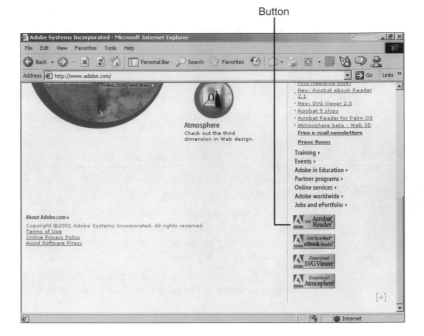

2. The first page you see (see Figure 13.3) will compare Acrobat Reader's functions with the full-featured Adobe Acrobat, which costs $249 retail. Because we just want to download a free program for now, click Get Acrobat Reader at the bottom of the page.

3. Complete the choices on the form, and then click the Download button (see Figure 13.4).

4. The exact dialog boxes you'll see differ by browser and computer type. Sometimes you may be asked whether you want to save it or run it from its current location. Usually it's smartest to choose the Save option, and then to open the file later. The next dialog box you might see prompts you to select the location (folder or desktop) and filename for the downloaded file (see Figure 13.5). Choosing a location is a good idea so that you can easily locate and use the file after downloading (you might even want to create a download folder to house all your downloaded files). Don't mess with the filename, though—if you don't supply a new filename, the file will be stored on your computer under its original name, which is usually best.

FIGURE **13.3**

*Step 2: Click the Get
Acrobat Reader button.*

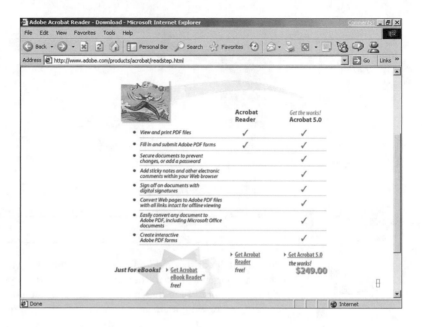

Download button

FIGURE **13.4**

*Step 3: Fill in the form,
and click Download.*

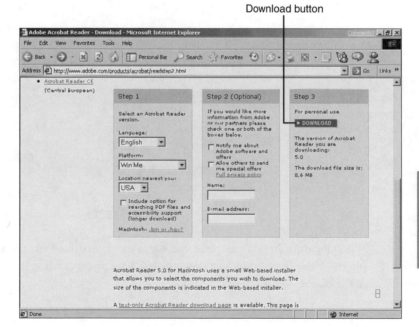

13

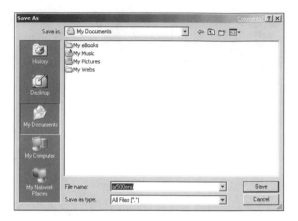

FIGURE 13.5

Step 4: Choose a location for the file and save it to disk.

When a link leads to a media file, such as a sound or video clip, you can choose the Open option (rather than Save to disk) when downloading. If you have the right plug-in program to play that type of file, as soon as the file has been downloaded, your browser can play the file automatically.

5. After you deal with any dialog boxes that appear, the download begins, and a status message appears. The status message usually features a Cancel button, so you can quit the download before it finishes if you want to (see Figure 13.6).

FIGURE 13.6

Step 5: The status message appears.

When the download is complete, the status message disappears. You can continue browsing or go use the file you just downloaded, which you can find in the folder you selected in the dialog box described in step 4.

In the download status message, some browsers also display an estimate of how much longer the download will take to finish. Although that estimate can be handy, it's just a guess, and should not be taken as an exact prediction of how long the download will take.

Choosing Files You Can Use

You can download any type of computer file, but not every file or program you find online works on every type of computer.

"Duh!" you might think. But you'd be surprised how often people forget this. Web browsing enables different kinds of computers to all look at the same online content, so after a while people tend to forget that on the Web, PCs, Macs, and other types of computers each use different kinds of files and programs.

When you search for files and programs, you must make sure that the ones you choose are compatible with your computer type, and often also with your operating system (Windows 95/98/Me/NT/2000/XP; DOS; Mac OS9 or OS X; UNIX flavor; and so on).

The Two File Types: Program and Data

Although there are dozens of different types of files, they all generally fall into either of two groups:

- **Program files**—A program file contains a program—a game, a word processor, a plug-in, a utility, and so on. Program files are almost always designed to run on only one type of computer and operating system. For example, a program file designed for a Mac typically will not run in Windows. However, many programs are available in similar but separate versions, one for each system type.

- **Data files**—A data file contains information that can be displayed, or used in some other way, by a program. For example, a word processing document is a data file, to be displayed by a word processing program. Like program files, some data files can be used only by a particular program running on a particular computer type. But most data file types can be used on a variety of systems.

13

Popular files are usually available from multiple servers, spread across the continent or globe. Often, a downloading page will refer to the servers as *mirror sites* because they all offer an identical copy of the file, a "mirror image."

Common Data File Types on the Net

When you encounter a link to a file, you'll usually have no trouble telling what system the file is made for.

Often, before arriving at the link, you will have navigated through a series of links or form selections in which you specified your system type, so when you finally see links to files, they all point to files that can run on your system. In other cases, the link itself—or text near the link—will tell you the system requirements for the file. *System requirements* are the computer type, operating system, and (for a data file) program required to use a particular file. Some files you'll encounter have special hardware requirements as well, such as a particular amount of memory.

Even when the link doesn't fill you in, you can often tell a file's system requirements by its filename extension, the final part of the filename that follows the period. (For example, in the filename MONTY.DOC, the extension is DOC.) Table 14.1 shows many of the most common file types online.

> Data files can often be converted and used by programs other than those in which they were created. For example, nearly all full-featured word processing programs can convert Microsoft Word (.doc) files so you can read or edit them. Most spreadsheet programs can handle an Excel or Lotus 1-2-3 file.
>
> If you lack the required program for using a particular kind of data file, check out any similar program you already own to see whether it can convert a file of that type.

TABLE 14.1 Common File Types You'll Find Online for Downloading

Extension	Type of File	Requirements
.exe, .com	Program file (a game, utility, application, and so on)	Runs on one (and only one) type of system. Always read any text near the link to be sure that a particular .exe or .com file will run on your computer.
.doc	Word document	Can be opened and edited in either the Windows or Mac version of Word, or Windows' WordPad program.
.pdf	Adobe Acrobat document	Can be opened in the Adobe Acrobat Reader program (available for a variety of systems) or in a browser equipped with an Adobe Acrobat plug-in. Can also be converted and displayed by some word processing programs.
.xls	Excel spreadsheet	Can be opened and edited in either the Windows or Mac version of Excel.

TABLE 14.1   continued

Extension	Type of File	Requirements
.txt, .asc	Plain text file	Can be opened in any word processor or text editor (such as Windows Notepad) on any system, and displayed by any browser.
.wri	Windows Write document	Can be displayed by Windows Write (in Windows 3.1) or WordPad (in Windows 95/98/NT/XP).
.avi, .mp3, .mov, .qt, .mpg, .au, .mid, .snd	Various types of media files	Can be run by various player programs, or by your browser if it is equipped for them.
.zip	Archive, containing one or more compressed files	Must be decompressed (unzipped) before the files it contains can be used; see "Working with Zip Files" later in this chapter.

Very few program files are designed to run on both Macs and PCs. However, if you use a PC, you should know that some programs work in multiple PC operating systems. For example, there are programs written to run in both Windows 3.1 and Windows 95/98/Me, and sometimes DOS, as well.

By and large, programs written just for DOS or Windows 3.1 will also run in Windows 95 or NT, although the reverse is never true. And most Windows 95 programs will run in Windows 98/Me or NT (or later versions of Windows), but some NT programs will not run in Windows 95. A very few specialized utility programs written for Windows 98/Me/2000/XP will not run in Windows 95.

If you use a PowerPC-based Mac, you know that you can run some Windows programs on your Mac using a Windows "emulator." You probably also know that those programs do not run as well there as native Mac programs do.

A program always runs best on the system for which it was written, so favor choices that match what you have. And even if you have a PowerPC-based Mac, always favor true Mac files over PC versions.

13

Finding Sites That Help You Find Files

Where you begin looking for a file depends on the manner in which that file is offered on the Web, or rather, in what way that file is licensed for use by those other than its creator. Most software falls into one of the following four groups:

- **Commercial**—The programs you can buy in a box at the software store. Many software companies have Web sites where you can learn about their products and often download them as well. Typically, you fill in an online form to pay for the software, and then download it.

- **Demo**—Demo software is commercial software that has some features disabled, or automatically stops working—*expires*—after you use it for a set number of days. Demo software is distributed free on commercial and shareware sites and provides a free preview of the real thing.

- **Shareware**—Shareware is software you're allowed to try out for free, but for which you are supposed to pay. After the trial period (usually 30 days), you either pay the programmer or stop using the program. Some shareware expires or has features disabled, like demo software, so you can't continue using it without paying.

- **Freeware**—Freeware is free software you can use all you want, as long as you want, for free.

All-Purpose Shareware Sites

Sites for downloading shareware appear all over the Web. Many popular shareware programs have their very own Web sites, and links to shareware products can be found on thousands of pages, such as Yahoo!'s shareware directory at

`www.yahoo.com/Computers_and_Internet/Software/Shareware/`

But when you're looking for a shareware, freeware, or demo program to do a particular job, you'll have better luck if you visit a Web site designed to provide access to a wide range of products, sites such as

- Shareware.com, whose easy-to-remember URL is `shareware.com` (see Figure 13.7)
- Download.com (can you guess the URL?)

These sites are much like the search tools you used in Chapter 12, providing search term boxes, directories, and other tools for finding files. But the hits they produce are always either links to files that match your search, or links to other Web pages from which those files can be downloaded.

> Shareware.com and Download.com are good places to find all sorts of software, including Internet client software, such as a new browser or FTP client.
>
> But a more efficient way to find and download Internet client software is to go to the Tucows directory at `www.tucows.com`, which is a special directory of Internet client software.

FIGURE 13.7

Shareware.com, a directory for finding shareware, freeware, and demo software.

The key to using Shareware.com, Download.com, and similar file-finders is to make sure that your search specifies both of the following:

- The kind of file or program you seek. Email, word processing, game, paint program—whatever you want.

- Your computer type and operating system. Windows 95/98/Me/XP, Mac OS8/OS9/OS X, and so on.

If you include this information in your search, the hit list will show only files and programs of the kind you want, and only those that run on your particular system.

Sites like Shareware.com don't actually store on their own servers the thousands of files to which they offer links. Rather, they find and show you links that lead to files stored on other servers and mirror sites for those other servers (see Figure 13.7).

13

If it's mainstream, commercial software you want to buy—you know, the stuff you buy in a box at the software store—check out one of the online software shops, such as Beyond.com (`beyond.com`) or MicroWarehouse (`warehouse.com`).

For practice, try finding a solitaire game for your system at Shareware.com, in the following example:

1. Go to Shareware.com at `www.shareware.com`, type `solitaire` in the box labeled Search For, choose your system type from the By Platform list, and then click the Search button (see Figure 13.8).

FIGURE **13.8**

Step 1: Type in solitaire *at Shareware.com and choose an operating system.*

2. Read the descriptions of the solitaire programs for your system type, choose a program that you'd like to have, and click its filename (see Figure 13.9).

3. A page appears with a description of the program. Click on the Download Now link, and a new list of links appears, each link pointing to the identical file stored on a different server. Click one to start the download (see Figure 13.10).

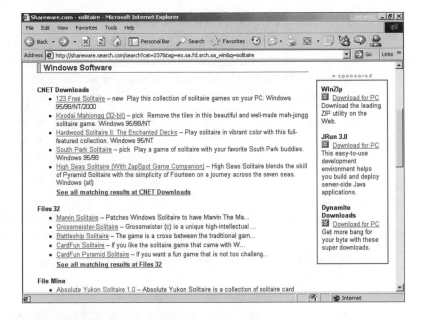

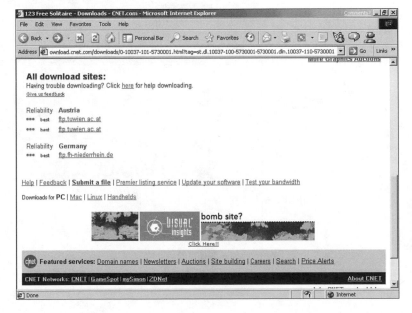

13

Commercial Software Sites

As a Web user, you have a lot to gain by frequenting the Web sites of any commercial software companies whose products you use regularly. There, you can not only learn about new and enhanced versions of products you use, but also pick up tips, free enhancements, product support, and fixes for common problems.

In particular, it's important to know about the Web site of the maker of the operating system you use on your computer: Microsoft's site (for Windows users) and Apple's (for Mac OS folks). On these sites, you can find all sorts of free updates and utilities for your operating system, fixes for problems, and news about upcoming new releases and enhancements.

Microsoft and Apple offer so many downloads that each provides its own search tools and directories for locating the file you need. The best places to start

- For Apple files is www.apple.com/support/ (see Figure 13.11).
- For Microsoft files is www.microsoft.com/downloads/ (see Figure 13.12).

FIGURE 13.11

Apple's support site offers a wealth of free files for Mac users.

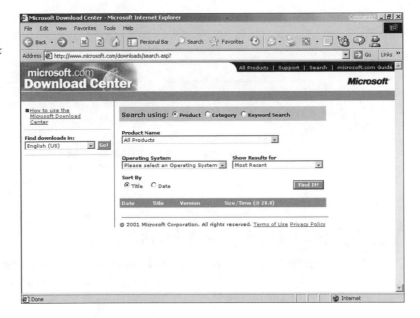

Working with Zip Files

The larger a file is, the longer it takes to download. So some files online are *compressed*—converted into smaller files—to cut the download time. After downloading, you must decompress a compressed file to restore it to its original size and use it.

Also, most application programs are made up not just of one fat file, but of a collection of program and data files. A single compressed file can pack together many separate files, so they can all be downloaded together in one step. When you decompress a compressed file containing multiple files—which is sometimes called an *archive*—the files are separated.

Several forms of compression are used online, but most compression programs create archive files that use a format called Zip. A Zip file uses the extension .zip, and it must be decompressed—*unzipped*—after downloading before you can use the file or files it contains.

You need a special program to unzip Zip files. If you don't already have one, the most popular shareware unzippers

- For Windows are WinZip, which you can download from www.winzip.com, or PKZip, which you can get from PKWare at www.pkware.com.
- For Macintosh is ZipIt, which you can download from http://www.maczipit.com/.

13

After installing an unzipping program, you can decompress any Zip file by opening the program, choosing the Zip file you want to decompress, and then choosing Extract from a toolbar or menu.

> One special type of `.exe` program file is called a *self-extracting archive*, which is a compressed file or files, just like a Zip file.
>
> Unlike a Zip file, however, a self-extracting archive file does not require an unzipping program. Instead, it decompresses itself automatically when you open it (usually by double-clicking). Most large applications offered online, such as Web browsers, download as self-extracting archives.

Watching Out for Viruses

A few years back, in the movie *Independence Day*, Jeff Goldblum stopped an intergalactic invasion by uploading a computer virus into the aliens' mothership and thereby scrambling the alien system.

A *computer virus* is program code secretly added to, or attached to, a file or email message that makes mischief when the file or message is opened. Often, the virus is designed to reproduce and spread itself from the file it travels in—its host file—to other files.

Computer viruses are created by immature, sick people, who get a thrill out of cheap little tricks—viruses that display silly messages on your screen—or major attacks—viruses that crash whole computer systems.

If you saw *Independence Day*, you might have wondered, "If Jeff Goldblum puts a virus on the Internet, and I happen to download a file containing that virus, what might happen to my computer? Would I still be able to conquer Earth? Can I get Jeff to come over and fix it?"

Viruses are a significant threat to anyone who spends time online, uses email, and downloads files. It's just plain silly to work on the Internet and not arm yourself with some protection.

> You can catch a virus from files you download, and from email messages (and files attached to email messages). The key rule when it comes to email is to never open any message or open any file from someone you don't know.

To play it , try to limit your downloading choices to commercial sites or reliable share-ware sources (such as Shareware.com). Big suppliers regularly scan files for viruses. In addition to exercising caution about where you download files from, you should also install and use a virus scanning program, such as Norton AntiVirus, which can find viruses in files and, in some cases, kill the virus while saving the file. And, make sure to keep your antivirus software current by regularly downloading the updates to it from the manufacturer.

> If you intend to scan for viruses, DO NOT open or run a file you have down-loaded until AFTER you have used your antivirus software to check it for viruses.

Remember: A virus in a file does no harm until you open the file (or run the program, if the file is a program). So you can download anything safely, and then scan it with the virus program before you ever open or run it. If the virus program detects a bug it cannot remove, just delete the file to delete the virus.

Downloading Files in AOL

Members of America Online have a special advantage in the area of downloads: AOL's Download Center. After signing on to AOL, you can access it by opening the AOL Services menu and selecting Download Center (see Figure 13.13).

FIGURE 13.13
AOL's Download Center offers links to all sorts of files and programs.

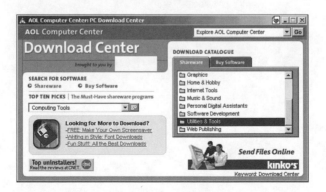

13

The right window offers two tabs: Shareware and Buy Software. The Buy Software tab connects you to commercial software, whereas the Shareware tab links to, well, share-ware.

Both tabs are organized into catalogues that are full of software you can download. After you've chosen the type of file that you want, you'll find a list of files that will fit your needs.

 America Online also offers a feature that's great for people who don't want to take the time to download a file during their online session. You can schedule a download for later by selecting the file(s) you want and clicking the Download Later button. Then, you can schedule the download for the middle of the night, when you're (perhaps) asleep.

Summary

Finding the files you need begins with starting at the right site: a commercial software site, a shareware search site, and so on. When you start in the right place, and understand the simple steps required to select, download, and (sometimes) unzip files, getting any files you want is a snap.

CHAPTER 14

Enjoying Safe Family Fun and Games

Is cyberspace a family place? If you have kids, you might be wondering. One day the media touts the Net as the greatest thing since Gutenberg, and the next it's the harbinger of the Apocalypse, an instrument of pornographers, pedophiles, and disgruntled loners.

Actually, it's neither. It's a tool, and like any tool, it can be put to good uses or bad. A hammer can build shelter or bash a finger. I think an adult has a right to use the Internet any way he or she wants to—within the law and without bothering anybody. But if you have kids who will use the Net (and they should!), you need to know how to insulate them from the Net's racier regions.

More importantly, there have been cases of pedophiles and other such creeps starting online relationships with kids (and gullible grownups!) that eventually lead to face-to-face meetings, and then to tragedy. In this chapter, you learn commonsense rules for creep-proofing your kids.

Choosing a Family Starting Point

A good first step for family Web surfing is to choose a good starting point, a "family home page" of sorts. A good general-purpose family page provides a jumping-off point in which all the links are family-friendly. Kids starting out should be taught to begin at that page, use only the links on that page, and use the Back button to return to that page after visiting any of its links. (If you make that page your home page, they can click the Home button to return to it anytime.) These habits corral a kid's surfing to a limited, appropriate range of sites.

One way to safeguard your Internet experience is to choose an Internet provider that censors content for you. These ISPs specialize in providing Internet service to families. Check out

- www.cleanfamily.com
- family.net
- ratedg.com

For most folks who want their Internet service controlled for the kids but free for the adults, these services are an extreme. But if the principal surfers in your home are the kids, you might want to see whether one of these services has a local access number for you.

You'll probably want to browse and search for a family page that best fits your family. Some good choices are

- Yahooligans! at www.yahooligans.com—A kid's offshoot of the Yahoo! search tool with links and a search engine that both lead only to good kid stuff (see Figure 14.1).
- 4Kids Treehouse at www.4kids.com—A colorful site with great links and activities for kids, plus resources for parents.
- Family.com at www.family.com—An online magazine.
- Ask Jeeves for Kids at www.ajkids.com.
- The American Library Association's Cool Sites for Kids page at www.ala.org/alsc/children_links.html.

After you've learned how to create Web pages (see Part II), you can create your own family home page and fill it with links you would like your kids to have easy access to.

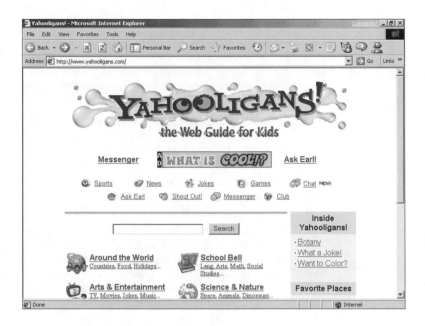

FIGURE 14.1

Yahooligans! makes a good starting point for family Web surfing.

Important Family Safety Steps

Everybody's different, and so is every family. It's not my place to say what's best for you or your kids, but if you want some guidance about keeping your kids safe online, permit me to offer a few suggestions here. Then follow your own judgment.

Supervise!

This one's so obvious, and yet so difficult. As a parent, I know that it simply isn't practical to supervise our kids every second of the day. And if you're a tired parent of a pre-teen, the idea of the kid going off to his room for an hour to surf the Net is appealing.

You must make your own choice about when to cut the cord, based not on what's convenient but on your kid. Some kids are mature enough to surf responsibly at seven, but others can't be trusted at 17. Only you know your kids well enough to decide.

If you're not sure whether your kid is ready to go solo but you don't have time to supervise, keep him offline until either you are sure that he's ready or you have the time. The Internet has lots to offer a kid, but your kid can live without it until the time is right for both of you.

14

I know some experts say it's not good to spy on your kids. But if your kid surfs unsupervised and you want to know what she's been up to, open the browser's history file to see exactly where she's been. It's the cyber-equivalent of searching your kid's room for drugs or weapons.

If your kid is visiting the Web sites of hate groups or providers of unsavory content, she might be picking up dangerous reinforcement of feelings or ideas that endanger both your kid and others around her. At the very least, your child's online habits might serve to tip you off that your kid is in trouble, in the same way that radical changes in appearance or mood might.

If you, as a diligent parent, notice signals that your kid might be at risk, it's important for you to find a way to supervise or control that kid's online activities, OR keep tabs on what she's been doing online, OR pull the plug.

Beyond that, though, it might be important to recognize that if your kid is in trouble online, that's probably a symptom of a larger problem that has nothing to do with the Internet. In such cases, controlling what your kid does online is only Step 1. After that, you need to identify and address the real problem, and maybe find some help for your child.

Don't Defeat Passwords

Your Internet connection, email account, and a few other activities require you to enter a username and password to prevent unauthorized access. Some software, particularly Internet connection software, enables you to enter the password in a dialog box once so that you never have to type it again. That's a convenient feature, but it enables anyone who can flip a switch to get online using your computer.

My advice is that you leave your computer configured so that a password is required for both connecting to the Internet and retrieving email. Never tell your kids the passwords, and never log on or retrieve email in their sight.

This will ensure that you always know when your kids are online, and that they cannot receive email from anyone without your knowledge.

Be Extra Careful with Broadband

If you use a broadband Internet connection, your connection can be always online, always ready to go. This condition makes it awfully easy for a child to sit down at your computer and go where he or she maybe shouldn't.

Be sure you do not check any "remember password" boxes when setting up and using your broadband connection. This will help ensure that no one uses the Internet without your permission and supervision.

In Windows, you can set up a password-protected screen saver, so that when you leave your computer, after a few minutes of inactivity, a nifty animated picture or other display covers your screen. No one can clear that picture and do anything on your computer without entering the password. This is a great way to keep your computer—and your kids—safe, particularly if you use a broadband connection.

To set up a screen saver, point to an empty area of your Windows desktop, right-click, choose Properties from the menu that appears, and then choose Screen Saver on the dialog box that appears. Be sure to check the check box marked "Password Protected."

Resist Chat

It's a shame to recommend resisting chat because there's plenty of good clean fun to be had in chat rooms. It must be said: Chat rooms are the most dangerous places on the Internet. This is not because of all the sex-related chat rooms, although it's related to those.

On the Web, the worst thing that can happen to a kid is that he or she will be exposed to ideas—words and pictures—that you don't approve of. In chat, your kids can easily meet up with people who may hurt them. People are much more dangerous than ideas.

It works like this: A pedophile or some other dangerous character—often posing as a kid—frequents chat rooms where kids hang out and establishes friendships, especially with lonely kids who are easy prey. As the friendship grows, the creep manipulates the kid into dropping the anonymous chat nicknames and exchanging email addresses for private correspondence. Eventually, a private, face-to-face meeting is arranged.

There already have been numerous cases of kids abused this way. And the initial contact is almost always made in a chat room.

Most chat clients (including Microsoft Chat) include a dialog box in which you can not only create your chat nickname, but also enter personal information such as your name or email address. (I pointed this out in Chapter 6, "Chatting and Instant Messenger," but it bears repeating.)

Because this information is accessible to others online with whom you chat, I strongly recommend entering nothing on such dialog boxes except your nickname.

It's also a good idea to change your nickname from time to time, to keep chat friendships from getting too close.

14

Obviously, I recommend never allowing a child to use chat unsupervised, even if that child is trusted to surf the Web unsupervised. Even supervised chatting is risky—by teaching a child how to chat, you increase the chances that the child might sneak into a chat session unsupervised.

In fact, if you don't use chat yourself, I would recommend simply not installing a chat client on your computer. Remember that many Web sites offer chat areas that anyone can access directly from his or her browser, without a chat client installed.

Online Rules for Kids

I know, I know, my kids hate rules, too. But these rules are pretty easy, and it's essential that you teach them to your kids even if you can't always be sure they will be followed. In particular, if you have older kids who you permit to use the Net unsupervised, it's important that they know the rules for safe surfing. (Some folks suggest writing these rules up, having the kids sign them as a contract, and then posting the contract on the wall behind the computer.)

Tell your kids the following:

- Never reveal to anyone online your real name, email address, phone number, mailing address, school name, or username/password without a parent's involvement and consent. Any other personal information, such as birthday or Social Security number, is also best kept secret. And never, ever, ever send anyone a picture of yourself.

- Never reveal anything about your parents, siblings, teachers, or friends. Any such information can help a creep find you, and it exposes family and friends to risks, too.

- Never arrange to meet in person any online friend unless a parent consents before the meeting is arranged, the parent will be present at that meeting, and that meeting will take place in a public setting, such as a restaurant or mall.

- Anytime you come across anything online that makes you uneasy, go elsewhere or get offline. There's too much good stuff online to waste time looking at the bad.

- Never download or upload a file, or install any software on the computer, without a parent's consent.

Resources for Parents

Want to know more about protecting your kids online, teaching them to use the Net smartly, finding great family sites, or just plain old parenting advice? You'll find all of this and more at the following sites:

- Parent Soup at www.parentsoup.com (see Figure 14.2).

- The Parents Place at www.parentsplace.com.

- Kids Health at www.kidshealth.org.

- All About Kids magazine at www.aak.com.

FIGURE 14.2

Parent Soup is one of the best online resources for moms and dads.

Censoring Web Content

You've probably heard that there are programs that can control what your kids see online. So why didn't I just mention them in the first place and save you all this "online rules" crud?

Well, it's debatable how effective these programs are. First, most are really focused on the Web and aren't much protection elsewhere, such as in chat or email. And most censoring programs—erring properly on the cautious side, I suppose—inevitably censor out totally benign stuff that you or your kids might find valuable. (You'll see an example of this later, with Content Advisor.)

Also, these programs might filter out sexual content, depictions of violence, and profanity, but what about ugly ideas? For example, these programs generally do not block out racist, sexist, or nationalist hate-mongering as long as those views are expressed without the use of profanity or epithets.

14

So even though these self-censoring tools are available, they're no replacement for adult supervision and safe-surfing practices. And if you really do supervise your kids, you probably don't need a censoring program. Still, you might find one or more of these programs useful, and they are getting better.

Getting a Safe-Surfing Program

Microsoft Internet Explorer has its own censoring program, which you'll learn about next. So does AOL, which you'll also learn about in a minute or two. But you might also want to check out the Web pages of other popular self-censoring utilities.

From these pages, you can learn more about each product and, in most cases, download a copy for your system:

- **Net Nanny**—www.netnanny.com
- **SurfWatch**—www.surfwatch.com
- **Cybersitter**—www.cybersitter.com
- **The Internet Filter**—turnercom.com/if
- **Cyber Patrol**—www.cyberpatrol.com

> If you use WebTV as your Internet window, note that it supplies its own censoring system that you can apply to restrict what your kids can see.

Using Internet Explorer's Built-In Content Advisor

Internet Explorer, versions 3 and newer, has its own built-in system called Content Advisor for controlling access to Web sites. Content Advisor works very much like the other safe-surfing programs, except it's a little harder to use than some, and it possesses many of the same strengths and drawbacks.

Understanding Content Advisor

Content Advisor relies on a rating system from the Recreational Software Advisory Council (RSAC), which also rates entertainment software and video games.

The RSAC ratings system assigns a score (0 to 4) to a Web site for each of four criteria: Language, Nudity, Sex, and Violence. The higher the score in each category, the more intense the content that page contains.

For example, if a site has a score of 0 in the Language category, it contains nothing worse than "inoffensive slang." A Language score of 4, however, indicates "explicit or crude language" on the site. After a Web site has been rated, the rating is built into the site so that Content Advisor can read the site's score before displaying anything.

Using the Content tab, you choose your own limit in each RSAC category. For example, suppose you are okay with violence up to level 3 but want to screen out all sexual content above a 2. After you set your limits and enable Content Advisor, Internet Explorer refuses to show you any page whose RSAC rating exceeds your limits in any category, unless you type in a password which you create. So, for example, if you screen out all nudity, and then try to go to Playboy's Web site, you'll be blocked (see Figure 14.3).

FIGURE 14.3

After you've enabled it, Content Advisor blocks Internet Explorer from displaying Web pages whose RSAC ratings exceed your limits.

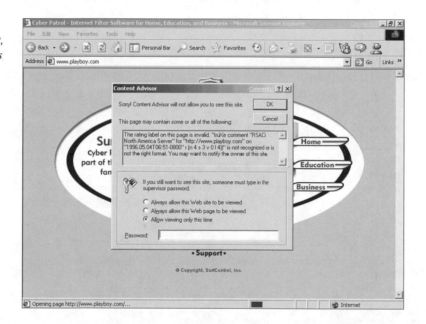

There's one problem: Only a tiny portion of sites online have been rated. Enabling Content Advisor therefore blocks not only rated pages you might find offensive, but also *all* pages—offensive or not—that have not been rated, which includes most of the Web.

As you might guess, blocking unrated pages severely cramps your surfing and has little to do with protecting you from offensive content. As you'll see in the upcoming example, you can choose an optional setting to allow unrated pages, but doing so defeats the purpose of Content Advisor because those pages will be permitted regardless of their content. You can also create a special list of pages that are always accessible (or never accessible) regardless of the Content Advisor's settings, but obviously that list would be pretty short relative to the wealth of sites available online.

14

Content Advisor works for both Web browsing and Microsoft's Chat program (see Chapter 6), blocking entrance to unsavory or unrated chat rooms.

To use Content Advisor for Chat, replace step 1 of the following example by opening Chat and choosing View, Options, and then choosing the Settings tab. Proceed with the remaining steps.

However, note that although Content Advisor might keep kids out of X-rated chats, it does nothing to protect them from the pervs who wander into G-rated chats. My advice, no matter what censorship tools you might deploy: Kids don't belong in chat. Period.

Here's how to enable and configure Content Advisor:

1. In Internet Explorer, open the Internet Options dialog box (choose Tools, Internet Options), and then choose the Content tab (see Figure 14.4).

FIGURE 14.4

Step 1: Open Internet Options and then choose the Content tab.

2. Click the Enable button to display the Content Advisor (see Figure 14.5).

3. The Rating scale appears, showing the current setting for Language.

   Point to the slider control, click and hold, and drag the slider along the scale (see Figure 14.6). As the slider reaches each marker on the scale, a description appears below the scale with the type of language that setting permits. The farther to the right you pull the slider, the more lenient the setting. (Think of 0 as a G rating, 1 as PG, 2 as PG-13, 3 as R, and 4 as X.) After you've found the rating level you want, release the slider.

FIGURE 14.5

Step 2: Click the Enable button to display Content Advisor.

FIGURE 14.6

Step 3: Adjust the slider.

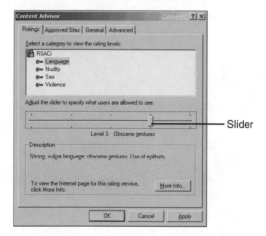

4. Click on Nudity and choose your rating for that category. Do Sex and Violence, too (see Figure 14.7).

5. When you have finished choosing ratings, click the General tab and check either (or neither, or both) of the following options (see Figure 14.8):

   Users Can See Sites That Have No Rating. Check this check box to allow the display of unrated pages. Content Advisor will continue to block rated pages that exceed your settings, but will permit unrated pages regardless of their content.

14

FIGURE 14.7

Step 4: Do the same for Nudity, Sex, and Violence.

FIGURE 14.8

Step 5: Click the General tab and then select User options.

Depending on whether this is the first time you've accessed Content Advisor and the exact order of steps you follow, you will be asked at some point to choose the supervisor password. Once it's entered, no one can change any Content Advisor settings without entering it.

Supervisor Can Type a Password to Allow Users to See Restricted Content. When this check box is checked, a dialog box pops up prompting for the Supervisor password whenever someone tries to open a page that Content Advisor would block. If the password is typed, the page appears. With this useful option, your kids can appeal to you for a temporary censorship waiver for a particular Web site.

6. Click the Approved Sites tab. Type the address of any Web site you want to be handled in a special way, and then click Always (to make this site always accessible, regardless of any other Content Advisor settings) or Never (to make this site inaccessible). Continue typing addresses and clicking Always or Never until the list shows all the sites for which you want special handling (see Figure 14.9). The approved sites show up with a green check mark next to them, while the disapproved sites have a red minus sign.

FIGURE 14.9

Step 6: At the Approved Sites tab, enter lists of approved and disapproved Web sites.

7. Click OK on any tab, and then click OK on the Internet Options dialog box. Your settings are now in effect, and they will stay in effect until you change them or click the Disable button on the Content tab. (The Supervisor password is required for disabling Content Advisor or changing the settings.)

Using AOL's Parental Controls

America Online has always touted itself as a family-friendly online service. As such, it's been at the forefront of developing technologies that allow parents to have control over what their children see and do online.

AOL's Parental Controls is a leader in this area, although it does suffer from some of the same drawbacks as some of the other Web-censoring programs. For example, if you choose the tightest security level ("Kids Only," which is designed for elementary-aged kids), it blocks such sites as the official sites of Britney Spears and the Backstreet Boys, which your kids may want to see.

14

At the core of Parental Controls are the screen names. You can have up to seven screen names per AOL account. This allows families to pay one monthly fee, yet allow all its members (unless it's a particularly large family) to have their own screen name.

Each screen name can also have its own settings, or level of access. Because of this, parents can let their teenagers see more content than their preschoolers are allowed access to. And, as long as you make sure each child only knows his or her own password, you can be relatively certain they're only seeing what you think is appropriate for them.

Parental Controls are available from the Settings tab within AOL. Click on Parental Controls, and then click the Set Parental Controls link. You'll then be viewing the Parental Controls screen at which you can change settings (see Figure 14.10).

FIGURE 14.10

AOL's Parental Controls allows different settings for different family members.

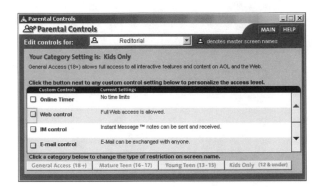

Each AOL account has a Master Screen Name; this is the only person who is allowed to change the Parental Controls settings for the others in the clan. You choose the screen name for which you would like to set Parental Controls in the box at the top of the window. Then, you're allowed to make the following choices for that person:

- **Online timer**—Allows you to set time limits for the user to be online.

- **Web control**—You can choose from four settings: Kids Only (12 and under), Young Teen (13–15), Mature Teen (16–17), and General Access (18 and older). Kids Only allows only access to AOL's Kids Only Channel, whereas General Access allows full, unrestricted movement on the Web.

- **IM control**—Allows you to set whether Instant Messages can be sent and retrieved.

- **E-mail control**—Allows you to customize whether email can be sent and retrieved, and from whom.

- **Chat control**—Allows you to block certain types of chat areas from access, or all chat within AOL.

- **Additional Master**—Allows you to make another screen name a Master, so you can have more than one person setting controls.

- **Download control**—You can determine what types of downloads (if any) you allow.

- **Newsgroup**—You can set the types of newsgroups you'll allow each screen name to access.

- **Premium Services**—Determine whether access to extra AOL services (for which you are charged extra) is allowed.

Summary

As you can see, there's no sure-fire way to protect unsupervised kids online. But there's no reason to worry, either. A few smart choices, along with your supervision and guidance, will enable your family to enjoy the Internet's benefits while steering clear of its troubles.

I know I mentioned a lot of scary stuff here, but I do want you to relax and enjoy the Net. Look at it this way: People get hit by cars every day. Now, does that mean you should never leave the house, or lay awake worrying? No. It just means that you should look both ways and hold your kid's hand when crossing.

14

CHAPTER 15

Buying and Selling on the Net

Only a few years ago, there was a huge hullabaloo about doing business online and the exploding interest in what we now call *e-commerce* (electronic commerce). But it was all talk—despite noises to the contrary, little real business was happening on the Web. Most business Web pages were mere e-advertising, not points of sale.

But today, you can buy or sell just about anything online. Companies are beginning to approach the Web not just as an intriguing place to experiment, but as a market they mustn't miss.

In this chapter, you'll get a taste of e-commerce from both sides of the e-counter. First, we'll learn how to shop and invest online safely. Next, you'll learn the ways you can do business online, and learn how to get started.

Shopping 'Til You Drop

Whattaya wanna buy? Whatever it is, you can probably buy it from a Web page that sells products, also known as a *virtual storefront* (see Figure 15.1).

"Virtual storefront" is just a fancy, highfalutin' buzzword for a Web page from which you can buy stuff. In coming years, you'll see the word "virtual" tacked onto all sorts of online activities to make them sound cooler: virtual jobs, virtual travel, virtual dentistry....

FIGURE 15.1

Virtual storefronts are the hip way to buy online, 24 hours a day, with no snotty clerks standing over you to make sure you're not shoplifting.

Using only the Web-surfing skills you already possess, you can enjoy the benefits of online shopping:

- **24-hour, 365-day shopping**—Except for rare moments when the server is down for maintenance and repair, online stores are always open.

- **Access to product photos and specifications**—While you're browsing an online catalog, you often can click links to display product photos, lists of options, and even detailed measurements or other specifications. Such stuff can help you make an informed buying decision.

- **Search tools**—Pages with extensive product listings often include a search tool for finding any product available from the merchant.

- **Web specials**—Some merchants offer discounts or other deals that are available only to those ordering online and not to phone, mail order, or in-person customers.

- **Custom ordering**—Some stores feature forms that let you specify exactly what you want (see Figure 15.2). For example, PC sellers that are online, such as Dell or Gateway, let you choose your PC's specifications—processor, hard disk size, CD-ROM speed, and so on—from lists in a form. When you finish, the price for your system appears, along with a link for placing the order. At an online clothing shop, you can specify exact measurements, color, monogramming, and other custom specifications.

FIGURE 15.2

Forms on virtual store-fronts can help you configure a custom order or get a price quote on one.

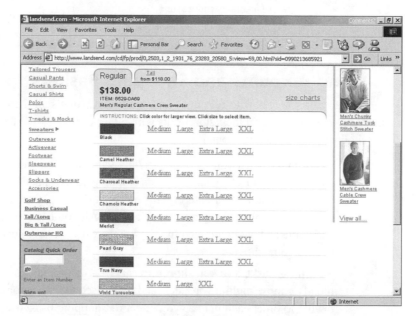

- **Mailing lists**—Many online merchants offer a form for subscribing to a mailing list with updates about new products and specials.

You know this already, but it bears repeating: Making an online purchase usually requires typing your credit card number and other sensitive information in a form. That's something you should never do on a site that's not secure.

Explore virtual storefronts to your heart's content, comparing prices and other terms to make the best buy. But when you arrive at the actual page where you fill in your order form or open an account with the merchant, confirm that the page is secure. In most browsers, a secure site is indicated by either a locked golden padlock or a solid (unbroken) gold key near the bottom of the window. If you see a broken key, an unlocked padlock, or no icon at all, buy elsewhere.

Caveat emptor—buyer beware—online as anywhere else. As an online consumer, it behooves you to be an informed one. You can find reviews of products and merchants all over the Web. One good way to find reviews is to use the product name along with the word "review" as a search term.

You might also want to check out the Web pages of consumer advocates who alert us to schemes, scams, and duds:

Consumer's Union (publishers of Consumer Reports magazine): www.ConsumerReports.org

Consumer World: www.consumerworld.org

Using Accounts and Shopping Baskets

You already know how to fill out a form, and usually that's all there is to shopping. But many merchants equip their storefronts with either or both of the following to make shopping there more convenient:

- **Accounts**—When you set up an account with an online merchant, you give that merchant a record of your name and shipping address, and often your credit card information, too. After entering this information once, you can shop and buy there at any time without having to enter it again. All you have to do is enter an account username and password, and the site knows who you are, how you pay, and where to ship your stuff.

- **Shopping baskets (a.k.a. shopping carts)**—A shopping basket lets you conveniently choose multiple products and then place the order for all of it, instead of having to order each item as you select it. Shopping baskets also provide you with a chance to look over your list of selections and the total price so you can change or delete items before committing to the order.

Often, accounts and shopping baskets require the use of *cookies* on your computer. If you have configured your browser to reject cookies and you try to set up an account or make a purchase, you might get a message from the site informing you that you must accept cookies in order to shop there.

In the following example, you can get a feel for accounts, shopping baskets, and virtual storefronts by finding and ordering music CDs from CD Universe, a popular source for CDs, tapes, and videos. Note that you don't actually have to make a purchase; I'll show you how to cancel before committing.

If music is what you want to buy, note that there's no need to buy a CD. Often, you can get exactly the tunes you want in near-CD quality MP3 files online, either free or for a fee that's lower than the cost of a CD. You can play your MP3 tunes on your PC, or on a handheld MP3 player. See Chapter 11, "Plug-In and Add-On Programs."

15

1. Go to CD Universe at www.cduniverse.com (see Figure 15.3).

FIGURE 15.3

Step 1: Go to CD Universe.

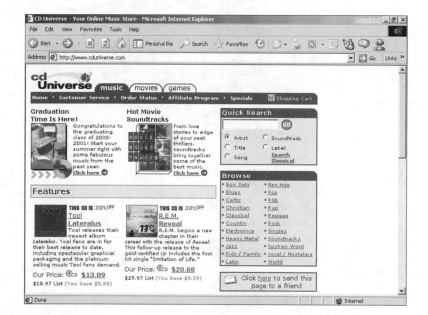

2. In the Quick Search form at the top of the page, type the name of a recording artist in the box to the right of the Artist box, and then click Go (see Figure 15.4).

3. After a few moments, a list appears with titles available from that artist (see Figure 15.5). If CD Universe isn't sure which artist you want, a list of artists matching your search term appears first. Choose one to display the list of titles.

FIGURE 15.4

Step 2: Enter the name of a recording artist and click Go.

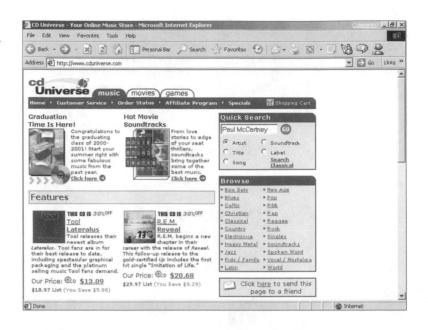

FIGURE 15.5

Step 3: Review the list of albums.

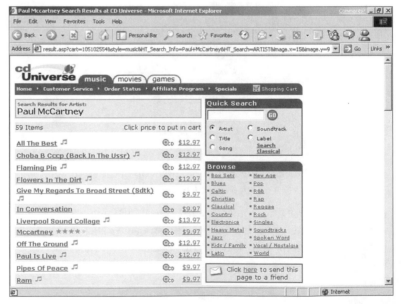

4. Choose a CD or tape by clicking its price (see Figure 15.6). If you're not sure which CD you want, click the title of the CD to learn more about it, including a list of songs.

FIGURE 15.6

Step 4: Choose a CD or tape by clicking its price.

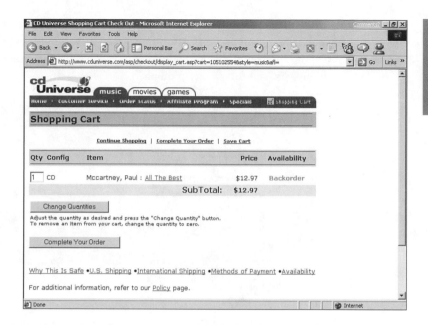

5. Review the info on the Shopping Cart screen, and then click Continue Shopping. Choose another title by clicking its price, and you will again see your Shopping Cart, now with two CDs listed (see Figure 15.7).

FIGURE 15.7

Step 5: Choose another title to be added to your cart.

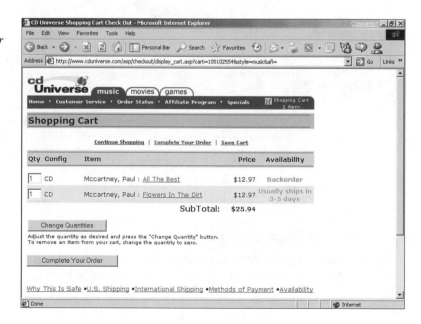

6. Click Complete Your Order to start the purchasing process. You will see the
   Account Entry screen (see Figure 15.8). To quit without purchasing anything, just
   leave the site now. To order your selections, click New Account, complete the form
   that appears, and follow any prompts.

FIGURE 15.8

*Step 6: Either cancel
your order now or fill
out the New Account
form to order your
selections.*

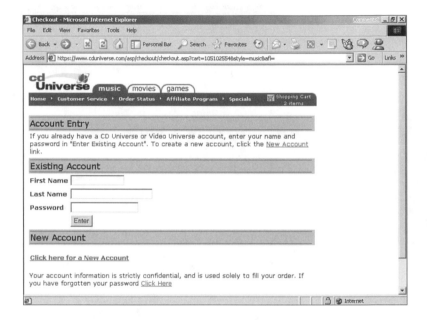

Immediately after you place an order from an online store, some sort of
confirmation of your order should appear in your Web browser. Many stores
also email you a confirmation of your order.

Make a note of any information that appears in the confirmation—
especially anything called an *order number*—and save any email message
you receive. You'll need this information to query the merchant if your merchandise doesn't arrive within the time promised, or if it isn't what you
ordered. If your order confirmation doesn't appear right away, find a shopping cart button to click to see your order.

Buying Stocks and Such

The Web is a great place to sell intangible goods, such as stocks or securities. After all, if
the product is intangible, why shouldn't the transaction be?

Obviously, such purchases carry the greatest risk of all online shopping activities. They generally involve moving around large amounts of money and putting it at risk in investments. But if that's your thing, you should know that trading online can be substantially cheaper than using a traditional broker, and in many cases your transactions are executed much more quickly—usually within minutes.

The steps for online investing are roughly the same as those for buying anything else online. Typically, you set up an account with an online brokerage, after which you may buy and sell at will.

However, note that opening an account with an online broker typically requires disclosing detailed information about yourself. You'll have to disclose your bank account numbers, Social Security number, and other private, sensitive information you don't have to reveal when making other kinds of purchases online.

Investment Starting Points

To learn more about investing online, or to take the plunge and buy those 1,000 shares of PepsiCo, consult the following sites.

For Financial Information and Advice

To learn more about online investing, read company profiles, and explore other money matters, check out the following sites:

- **Stockpoint**—www.stockpoint.com
- **CNN's Financial News Network**—cnnfn.com
- **Wall Street Journal**—www.wsj.com
- **Dow Jones Business Information Services**—bis.dowjones.com
- **MoneyAdvisor**—www.moneyadvisor.com
- **Success Magazine**—www.successmagazine.com
- **Yahoo! Finance**—quote.yahoo.com
- **The Motley Fool**—www.fool.com
- **NASDAQ**—www.nasdaq.com

For Making Investments

If you're ready to go ahead and put your money on the line (online!), visit these online brokers:

- **Mr. Stock**—www.mrstock.com
- **American Express Financial Services Direct**—www.americanexpress.com/direct

- **E*Trade**—www.etrade.com
- **Charles Schwab**—www.eschwab.com
- **Datek**—www.datek.com

Finding All the Sites Online That Sell What You Want

Instead of surfing blindly to various retailers and auction houses to find a particular item, you can call upon any of several services that search the shopping sites for a particular item and provide a list of links to sites that offer it. The price or current bid is included for each site (see Figure 15.9). These sites are sometimes called "shopping agents."

FIGURE 15.9

Sites like MySimon search multiple shopping/auction sites to help you find out who has the product you want for the best price.

 New shopping agents are coming online all the time. If you want to try one, it's a good idea to use a search engine to search for "shopping agents" and find the most recent sites.

Agents aren't foolproof—they can't find absolutely every site that might offer what you want. They'll only search the most popular shopping sites, or sites that have made a special business arrangement with them. But they might help you ensure that you get the best price (or best source) for that special item. And they often feature product information, reviews, and comparisons that can help you choose which product to buy. Check out:

- www.mysimon.com
- DealTime.com
- shop.Lycos.com
- ValueFind.com

Buying and Selling Through Online Auctions

Lately, auction houses have joined the ranks of the hottest places to pick up bargains or unusual items on the Net. Not only are online auction houses great places to pick up new and used merchandise—and especially hard-to-find collectibles—but the bidding process can be a lot of fun, too. eBay, at www.ebay.com (see Figure 15.10), might be the most popular online auction house now, but there others, including the following:

- Yahoo! Auctions: auctions.yahoo.com

FIGURE 15.10

eBay, a popular online auction house.

- **Amazon.com Auctions**—auctions.amazon.com
- **Auctions.com**—auctions.com
- **Butterfield & Butterfield**—www.butterfields.com

Also, you'll often see links to auctions on retail sites. You can bid on an item you might otherwise buy outright, and maybe save a bundle.

How Online Auction Houses Work

Although you can usually view the items up for auction without registering, you typically must register with the auction house—a quick process of filling in an online form—to bid on items or to sell an item. Once registered, you can use the search tools or categories on the auction house's page to browse for items to bid on. Note that most auctions go on for several days, and some go on for a week, so it's not necessary to sit in front of your computer for hours to join in the fun.

The auction house usually has no role in the actual financial transaction between seller and buyer, so a secure page is not really necessary. Typically, if you win an auction, the auction house emails both you and the seller to notify you about the win and to give you each other's contact info. After that, you and the seller have a set period of time in which to contact each other to arrange payment and shipping. Many sellers who use these auction houses are commercial merchants who can accept payment by credit card via email or telephone. Some individual sellers might require that you pay by money order or personal check.

eBay features a Feedback forum (see Figure 15.11) where buyers and sellers can post positive and negative comments about their experiences with each other. Before buying, you can always check out the comments others have made about the seller to determine whether that seller is a safe person to do business with.

FIGURE 15.11

Some auction houses have feedback forums so you can see what others have to say about a person before you do business with that person.

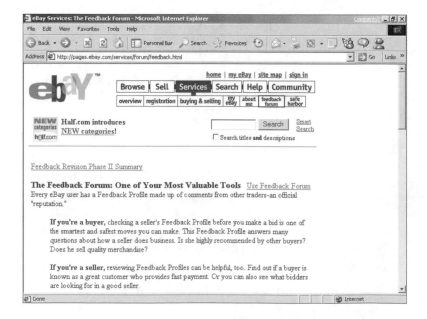

> To minimize the risk on bigger-ticket items, auction houses offer links to *escrow services* that make purchasing a little safer for buyer and seller (for a fee, of course).
>
> The buyer pays the escrow service, not the seller. The seller does not ship anything until he knows that the escrow service has the buyer's money. When the buyer informs the escrow service that the item has arrived, the escrow service pays the seller.

Bidding Tips

If you want to try, here are a few important tips:

- Always check out the feedback about a seller before bidding to make sure the seller is reliable.

- Before you bid on an item, always search the Web or other sources to see whether the same item is for sale elsewhere and for how much. That way you can be sure not to bid more than you would pay for the same item elsewhere. (Try a shopping agent for this.)

- Check out any payment terms in the listing. If no terms are listed, use the links provided to email the seller and ask what forms of payment the seller accepts (check, money order, and so on). You might want to think twice (or use an escrow service) before dealing with a seller who accepts only money orders, which is the second riskiest way to pay by mail after cash.

- Don't get carried away. In the heat of the auction, it's easy to get caught in a bidding war and wind up paying way too much for that Elvis candleholder you think you simply must have. Decide the most you're willing to pay and stick to it. If you lose, there will be other auctions.

Selling Tips

If you're interested in trying to sell something online, here are a few quick tips:

- **Be honest**—Don't overstate the importance or worth of the item you're trying to sell. Don't call it an antique unless it is one. Don't call it one-of-a-kind and then sell another one next week.

- **Be realistic**—Everyone thinks his or her own stuff is worth more than it is. If you have something that's worth more to you than it would be to anyone else, that's a keepsake. Why sell it? Keep your minimum pricing reasonable.

- **Provide a picture**—Descriptions are great, but most people want to see the real piece. A high-resolution photo will help drive your price up.

- **Send it quickly**—As soon as you receive payment, send the item you sold. It'll ease anxiety for the buyer, and help drive up your rating on the auction service.
- **Check other means of selling**—Sometimes, the newspaper or online classifieds are still the best way to sell an item.

Using a Payment Service

Online payment services like PayPal (`www.paypal.com`) and Billpoint (`www.billpoint.com`) offer secure transactions that can allow you to send or receive a payment instantly. All you have to do is set up an account at one of the services, and you can start using it to buy and sell.

The payments are processed rapidly, and the security of the transaction allows the merchandise to change hands more quickly.

Summary

By now you're ready to begin spending money online, making money online, or both. I hope you've seen that actually buying or selling on the Web is pretty easy, but doing either one *well*—taking into account all the risks and issues surrounding these activities—takes preparation, care, and practice.

CHAPTER 16

Going Wireless

This is a dangerous chapter to write, for couple of reasons. First, wireless technology is the fastest-evolving technology related to the Internet today. So, because things are changing so quickly, there's a very real chance that the stuff you read about in this chapter won't be the latest and greatest technologies any more.

Also, there are a lot of different options for how you access the Internet wirelessly. Web-ready cell phones, personal digital assistants (PDAs), laptops equipped with wireless technology, Pocket PCs, pagers, wireless email devices—the list goes on and on.

Within each of the above types, too, there is a wide variety of options from which to choose.

So, this chapter serves as an overview for how to benefit from the boom in wireless technology and gives you a few ideas of how it might fit into your life. If you're serious about investing in some wireless technology, you might want to look at a more detailed reference on the subject, such as a book devoted to it.

What Is Wireless Internet/Email?

Up to this point, we've covered Internet connections and gone through Web sites and newsgroups and email and so on. All of those possibilities involve your computer communicating with other computers in other parts of the world through the help of your Internet service provider.

Whether it's a dial-up or broadband connection, whether it's at work or at home, all that data we've been sending back and forth has been traveling through wires and cables.

You plug that phone line into your modem, and the data travels through that wire, out to a bunch of different wires. You hook up your Ethernet card to your DSL modem, and the data travels through those (albeit bigger) wires. At work, when you plug into your network, that network most likely connects to the Internet through—you guessed it—wires.

Now, imagine the world without wires. Imagine that as you're riding in the passenger seat on the way to the big sales presentation that you can use your laptop to receive an email with the latest PowerPoint sales presentation. Imagine that right after your broker calls you with a tip on a hot stock, you can end the call and check the stock's current price on the same cell phone you just used for the call. Imagine that you can synchronize your Palm handheld with your computer right before boarding a plane, and read your email and check out your favorite Web sites on the flight, without breaking the no-cell-phone rule.

It's all real. Wireless communication allows your piece of hardware—be it a PDA, cell phone, laptop, whatever—to receive information from the Internet over the air. Generally speaking, the data is transmitted from a service provider to some type of antenna that is connected to the hardware device you are using.

There's also another type of wireless Internet/email, like in the preceding airplane example, in which you synchronize your device with a computer that has a wire connection, download the Internet data, then view it later. We'll get more in-depth on both types of wireless in a minute.

Regardless of which type of wireless Internet you use, and regardless of which type of device you use, wireless Internet is what its name implies—access to the Internet, without wires.

Real-Time Versus Synched

With real-time wireless access, you are connected to the Internet wirelessly, live. That is, if you compose an email on the device you're using and send it, it goes, immediately. New emails pop into your Inbox all the time. When you check the baseball scores, they are up-to-date.

Synchronized connectivity is what many people do with their handheld PDAs. Palm devices, Handspring Visors, and Pocket PCs all allow this type of connecting. Using a provider such as AvantGo (a free service), you determine which sites you want to check in on when you connect. Then, when you synchronize your PDA with your computer, it will pull down the latest data from the Internet and load it into the PDA.

Then, you can check that data (including email) at a later time. If you reply to emails or compose new ones, they won't be sent until you synchronize again. Web sites aren't updated until you synchronize again.

It's a great way to use wireless without having to spend anything for a real-time connection. If your needs don't include having all-the-time access to the Internet, this might be the way for you to go. AvantGo (see Figure 16.1) has a directory of Web sites you can choose to have the service update. Depending on the type of device you have, you either get a scaled-down version of the site, or the full site.

16

FIGURE 16.1

AvantGo allows you to synchronize with the Internet.

 AvantGo also offers a paid service you can use if you choose live or real-time wireless Internet access.

Hardware to Get You Going

We've mentioned a few different types of hardware devices that you can use to access the Internet or email wirelessly. The varieties range widely; your choice should be made based on your personal situation.

For example, if you're constantly traveling for business within a specific region and use your laptop regularly during those travels, wireless connectivity for your laptop might be wise. If you don't need to have the whole laptop with you all the time but really need email availability and ease, a Web-enabled cell phone or wireless PDA might work for you.

Read through the following descriptions to help you decide what might be best for you.

> Cost is always going to be a factor, unless you're Bill Gates. (And if you are, Hi, Bill! Give me a call sometime!) Before investing in any of these technologies, examine not only the cost of the hardware, but also the cost of the service package you must buy to access the Internet wirelessly.

Wireless for Your Laptop

Lots of people who know only a little about wireless Internet might be surprised to find that wireless is the full-time connection choice for many people. That is, there are a lot of people who don't have a traditional "wired" connection at all; the only connection they use is wireless.

That's right, wireless technology is available for both laptops and desktop computers. It's not available all over the country yet, but like cellular phone service, it's only a matter of time. Like any other Internet service, you need the right kind of modem and a service plan. In this case, you'll need a wireless modem. For the desktop, the modem is external, with an antenna and a line that plugs into a special PC card. For a laptop, the modem either mounts to the back of the screen or plugs directly into a PC card slot in the side.

One company that provides this service is called Ricochet (www.ricochet.com; see Figure 16.2).

This type of service is great for the mobile professional. Individual packages start at around $80/month, and corporate discounts are typically available on multiple accounts. It allows your sales staff, for example, to keep in contact with the service department while on the road without ever having to plug in to a network connection or phone outlet.

FIGURE 16.2
Wireless access for your regular computer is available through companies like Ricochet.

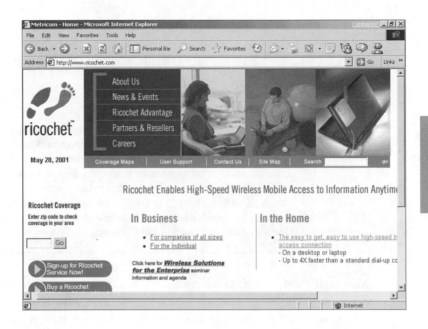

Another type of wireless service is satellite Internet. It uses a pizza-sized dish similar to the satellite television dishes (sometimes the same dish!), and gives you Internet access from satellite communications. Although this is wireless, of course, it's not really the type of wireless communications we're covering in this chapter. We're examining wireless connectivity that you can use on the go, and for satellite service, you need to stay close to the dish.

This is a radio-frequency-based transmission system. Depending on the provider you use, the service might have antennas mounted on local water towers or other tall structures, such as buildings or radio towers. Some providers rely on a line-of-sight method of transmission—that is, your antenna must be able to "see" the antenna it communicates with. Others use a broader transmission method more similar to those used by radio stations.

Regardless, you pay for the convenience of being mobile; there are typically much larger up-front and ongoing costs associated with this type of account than with a traditional dial-up plan.

Internet/Email into Your Cell Phone or Pager

Although it's only been around for a few years, this is actually one of the "oldest" of the wireless technologies. Cell phones and pagers have long been able to receive text messages, scores from stadiums around the country, stock quotes, and so on. It's been a pretty one-way service, however, and it's been costly.

Now, cell phones and pagers can receive longer messages than before, and you can even use them to respond, to a degree. It's a little clumsy, of course, to use a cell phone to type a message—to get an "o" for example, you press the "6" button three times. But it works.

Perhaps you've seen the commercial where the trendy Gen Xers are crowded into a loud dance bar, and they communicate back and forth to each other using this type of text messaging. Sometimes called "texting," it's a growing phenomenon in other parts of the world, and will soon be huge here in the U.S. It's a quick way to send very brief messages to a cell phone, and it can be done without having to talk, which makes it great for situations in which there is too much noise (such as in the aforementioned commercial) or where noise isn't appreciated (such as a library).

Many cell phone service providers allow you to use them for email if you want. Sometimes this carries a per-message fee, sometimes a flat monthly fee, and sometimes it's included free in a package deal. The way it works is this: To send you an email, the sender uses your phone number (including area code) as the name, followed by "@" and the domain of the service provider. An example of this might be 6125551212@verizon.com.

This is useful as an email forwarding tool. For example, if your ISP allows your email to be forwarded to another account for free, have them forwarded to your cell phone number (if that's free, too). Then, when you're on the road, you can check your emails. And they'll still be waiting for you on your regular computer, too.

Now, you can get the Web, or at least some of it, on your cell phone, too. The type of service varies greatly. Some providers create their own content (which they get from Web partners) and have it all ready for you at your fingertips when you want it. This can include stock quotes, news headlines, scores, weather, flight data, and so on (see Figure 16.3). Others use a "web clipping" feature that allows you to view scaled-down sites from other providers.

Newer Web frameworks allow sites to sense the type of device that is accessing it by detecting the type of browser being used. This allows the server to deliver the type of content that best suits that browser, and thus the device. In other words, down the road a bit you're likely to find more sites that "know" you are using a cell phone, and thus display the right kind of pages for you.

No industry standard has been developed for a cell phone–based browser, making it difficult for developers to accommodate them all. As the industry evolves, however, this technology will become more widespread.

FIGURE 16.3
Verizon Wireless offers a service that pushes info into your cell phone from the Web.

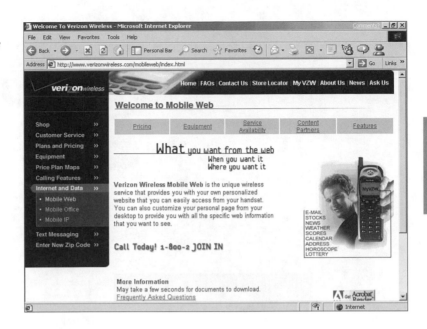

Handheld Computers

These are the fellas that force you to choose between synchronized and real-time Internet connectivity. There are lots of choices here, but they fall into two main categories: those that use the Palm operating system, and those that use Pocket PC technology, which is a Microsoft product.

On the Palm side, there are the Palm organizers themselves, some of which have built-in antennas for wireless access. Those that don't can add a wireless modem so you can access the Web and email. The primary competitor is the Handspring line of PDAs (see Figure 16.4).

On the Pocket PC side, there are several competitors for the hardware dollar. These include Compaq's iPaq line (see Figure 16.5) of handheld computers and Hewlett-Packard's Jornada.

This is not the book to discuss the relative merits of the different types of handheld computers. At this writing, the Palm/Pocket PC war is being fought tooth and nail. They both have great features and some limitations, all of which could easily make up another 400-page book.

FIGURE **16.4**

Handspring produces PDAs and modems that allow wireless access.

FIGURE **16.5**

Compaq produces a line of handheld computers through which you can access the Web wirelessly.

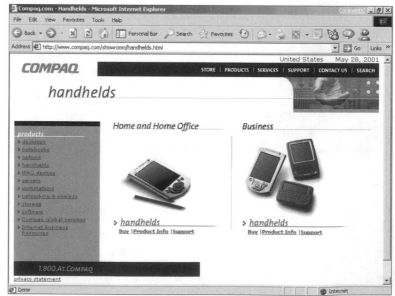

These are probably the most popular way to access the Internet wirelessly (be it real time or synched). They are big enough to allow you to compose an email without too much difficulty, yet small enough to be truly portable.

Service packages for wireless connections for these types of devices vary widely and depend on what features you expect to get (email, Web, or both). These offer a great middle ground between a cell phone, which is very limited in size and capabilities, and a laptop, which is bulky.

Wireless Email Devices

Wireless email devices fall somewhere between a PDA and a pager. A little like a pager on steroids, maybe.

The Blackberry models from RIM (see Figure 16.6) offer a small screen like a PDA, but with a tiny, built-in keyboard for composing messages. These are widely used in business (in part because of aggressive pricing for multiple-unit purchases). They allow you to stay connected to your email wherever you may be.

FIGURE 16.6

The Blackberry email unit includes a built-in, tiny keyboard.

In addition to sending and receiving email, you can keep an address book and calendar, use the built-in calculator, take notes, keep a task list, and more, all similar to what you can do on the Palm or Pocket PC. Two different models (the other is closer to pager-sized) are available.

Phone/PDA Combination

Ask any techie and he'll tell you: The future of wireless communication, and perhaps the Web in general, is in your cell phone. The cell phone has become such a staple of every-one's life—not just business people—that it only seems natural that its ability to communicate wirelessly would be used to the advantage of Web developers.

Although the cell phone is a staple, the PDA is the hottest form of technology. For business, for students—for anyone, really—PDAs are selling faster than any other device. It seemed only natural to try to combine the two technologies together in some way.

There are two ways to do this: Take the PDA and add a phone to it, or take a phone and add a PDA to it. Great news: They both work.

Kyocera (see Figure 16.7), among other cell phone manufacturers, is now building "smart phones" that include an internal screen and the Palm-based software. This eliminates the need to carry both types of devices, but the result is a somewhat clunky piece of machinery—all of the advances in size reduction over the years are lost.

FIGURE 16.7

Kyocera and other phone makers are now building phones with built-in PDAs.

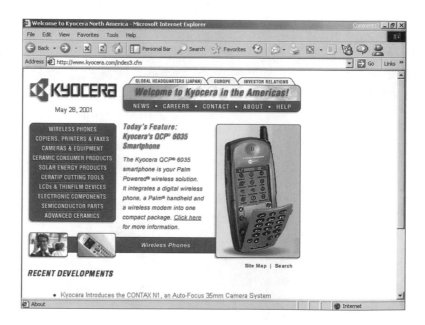

Still, it's better than carrying both pieces. The other obstacle is cost; these units are still in the $400–$500 range.

The other way involves adding a phone to your PDA. Handspring offers a product called the VisorPhone (see Figure 16.8) that allows you to literally insert a phone module into the PDA's expansion slot, and it allows the PDA to act as a phone. This option will also run $400–$500 by the time you add in the cost of the phone module.

FIGURE **16.8**

VisorPhone turns your Handspring PDA into a cell phone.

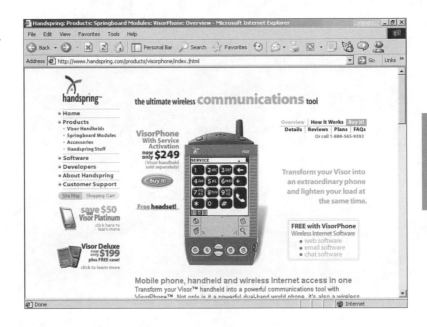

People might think you're a little strange if they see you talking into your PDA, but they'll get over it.

Summary

Wireless technology is evolving at a furious pace, and various technologies like PDAs and cell phones are being merged together for the good of all mankind. Well, okay, maybe not for the good of all mankind.

It's only a matter of time before the entirety of the Internet can be surfed from the palm of your hand for a price that is affordable to the common person.

PART II

Using a Free Web-Authoring Program

Chapter 17 Understanding Web Authoring

18 Getting Started with a Web Authoring Program

19 Choosing a Title, Text Colors, and Other Page Basics

20 Adding, Editing, and Formatting Text

21 Formatting Text

22 Organizing Text with Tables and Rules

23 Making Links

24 Using Links to Build a Web Site

25 Adding Pictures (and Picture Backgrounds)

26 Editing HTML

27 Dividing a Page into Frames

28 Designing Fill-in-the-Blanks Forms

29 Putting Multiple Links in One Picture

30 Publishing Your Page

31 Developing Your Authoring Skills

CHAPTER 17

Understanding Web Authoring

I can hear your motor running, so I know you're ready to dive in and start creating Web pages. But before building that first page, you need to acquire a rudimentary understanding of how Web pages are born and do some planning about what you want your page to be.

This chapter assumes that you have already installed Netscape Communicator 4.7 and its built-in Web-authoring program, Composer. If you have not, visit `http://wp.netscape.com/download/archive.html` and download Netscape Communicator version 4.7 for your system. (It's free.)

More recent versions of Netscape and Composer are available, as well. Although the exact steps for some features may differ slightly, you'll have little difficulty finding your way around a newer version of Composer using the material in this book.

Anatomy of a Web Page

Most Web pages contain, in addition to other optional parts, many of the elements described in this section. You should know what these parts are because the principal task in Web authoring is deciding what content to use for each standard part; a principal challenge is dealing with the different ways each browser treats the different parts. (More on that later in this chapter.)

Parts You See

The following Web page elements are typically visible to visitors through a browser (see Figure 17.1):

- A *title*, which graphical browsers (most Windows, Macintosh, and X Windows browsers) typically display in the title bar of the window in which the page appears.

FIGURE 17.1

Some common parts of a Web page.

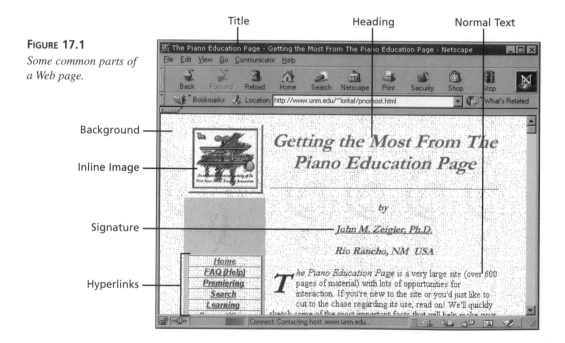

> The real title of a Web page does not appear within the page itself, but rather as the title of the browser window in which the page is displayed. However, most pages have another title of sorts—text or a graphic that is on the screen doing the job you typically associate with a title in books or magazines: sitting boldly and proudly near the top of the page to give it a name.

- *Headings*, which browsers typically display in large, bold, or otherwise emphasized type. A Web page can have many headings, and headings can be nested up to six levels deep; the page can have subheadings, sub-subheadings, and so on.

- *Normal text*, which makes up the basic, general-purpose text of the page. Traditionally, Web authors refer to lines or blocks of normal text as paragraphs. But in the parlance of the Netscape Editor, any discrete block of words on the page is a paragraph—whether the block is a heading, normal text, or something else determined by properties assigned to that paragraph.

- A *signature*, typically displayed at the bottom of the page. A signature usually identifies the page's author and often includes the author's (or Webmaster's) email address so that visitors can send comments or questions about the page. The email address is sometimes formatted as a mailto link so that visitors can click it to open their email program with a message preaddressed to the author.

- *Horizontal lines*, which dress up the page and separate it into logical sections.

- *Inline images*, which are pictures incorporated into the layout of the page to jazz it up or make it more informative.

- *Background color or pattern*, which is a solid color or an inline image that, unlike regular images, covers the entire background of the page so that text and other images can be seen on top of it.

- *Animations*, which can be text or pictures that appear within the layout of the Web page but move in some way. Pictures can flash on and off or cycle through simple animations, and text can flash or scroll across the screen.

- *Hyperlinks* (or simply *links*) to many different things: other Web pages, multimedia files (external images, animation, sound, or video), document files, email addresses, and files or programs on other types of servers (such as Telnet, FTP, and Gopher). Links can also lead to specific spots within the current page.

- *Imagemaps*, which are inline images in which different areas of the image have different links beneath them.

- *Lists*, which can be bulleted (like this one), numbered, and otherwise.
- *Forms*, which are areas in which visitors can fill in the blanks to respond to an online questionnaire, order goods and services, and more.

Parts You *Don't* See

In addition to the stuff you see in a Web page, the page—or, rather, the set of files making up the page—has a number of other elements that can be included. These elements aren't usually visible to the visitor, but here are their effects:

- **Identification**—Web page files can include a variety of identification information, including the name (or email address) of the author and special coding that helps search engines determine the topic and content of the page.
- **Comments**—Comments are text the author wants to be seen when the HTML code of the page is read directly, not when the page is displayed in a browser. Comments generally include notes about the structure or organization of the HTML file.
- **HTML**—Short for Hypertext Markup Language, it's the computer file format in which Web pages are stored. An HTML file is really just a text file with special codes in it that tells a browser how to display the file—the size to use for each block of text, where to put the pictures, and so on.
- **JavaScript code**—Within an HTML file, lines of JavaScript program code can add to the page special dynamic capabilities, like a time-sensitive message.
- **Java applets**—In separate files, Java program modules can enhance interaction between the visitor, the browser, and the server. Java is very popular for writing interactive games that can be played on the Web, for example.
- **Imagemap and forms processing code**—Program code used to process imagemaps and interactive forms.

Here's how you identify the parts of a Web page:

1. Open your Web browser, connect to the Internet, and go to any Web page you like, as shown in Figure 17.2. (You can use the copy of Netscape included with this book or use most any other browser you have.)
2. Look at the title bar of the window in which the browser appears (the bar along the top, where you usually see the name of a program you're using; see Figure 17.3). You probably see there the title of the Web page you're viewing and the name of the browser program you're using.

FIGURE 17.2

Step 1: Open your browser and view any page you like.

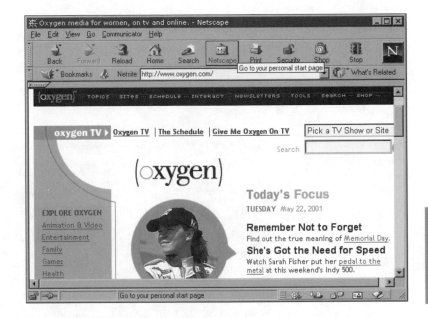

Title

FIGURE 17.3

Step 2: Find the Web page's title in the browser's title bar.

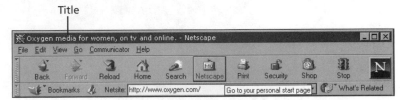

3. Explore the page (and others) and see whether you can identify any other parts described earlier in this chapter. (Refer to Figure 17.1 if you need to.)

In most browsers, a status bar appears at the bottom of the window. Whenever you point to a link (without clicking), you may see in the status bar the address to which that link leads.

Besides exploring where links lead, you can learn about the picture files you see in a Web page. Point to a picture, right-click, and then choose Properties from the menu that appears. A dialog box appears and tells you the filename, file size, and file type of the picture to which you pointed.

Using these techniques, you can develop your Web authoring skills by learning more about the design of the Web pages you visit.

How a Web Page Works

When you write a Web page, no matter how you go about it, what you really end up with is an HTML file that can be published on a Web server.

An HTML file (see Figure 17.4) contains all the text that appears on the page, plus HTML tags.

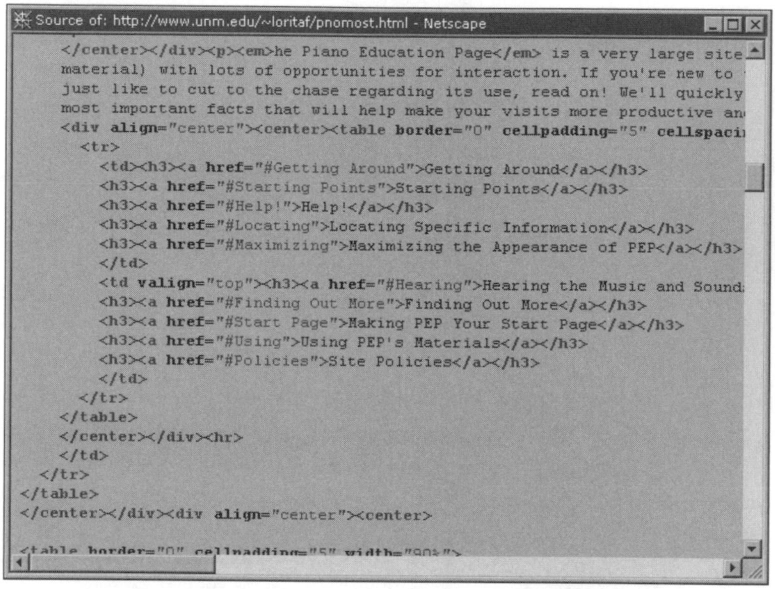

FIGURE **17.4**

*The HTML source file
of the page shown in
Figure 17.1.*

```
Source of: http://www.unm.edu/~loritaf/pnomost.html - Netscape
</center></div><p><em>he Piano Education Page</em> is a very large site
material) with lots of opportunities for interaction. If you're new to
just like to cut to the chase regarding its use, read on! We'll quickly
most important facts that will help make your visits more productive an
<div align="center"><center><table border="0" cellpadding="5" cellspacin
   <tr>
      <td><h3><a href="#Getting Around">Getting Around</a></h3>
      <h3><a href="#Starting Points">Starting Points</a></h3>
      <h3><a href="#Help!">Help!</a></h3>
      <h3><a href="#Locating">Locating Specific Information</a></h3>
      <h3><a href="#Maximizing">Maximizing the Appearance of PEP</a></h3>
      </td>
      <td valign="top"><h3><a href="#Hearing">Hearing the Music and Sound
      <h3><a href="#Finding Out More">Finding Out More</a></h3>
      <h3><a href="#Start Page">Making PEP Your Start Page</a></h3>
      <h3><a href="#Using">Using PEP's Materials</a></h3>
      <h3><a href="#Policies">Site Policies</a></h3>
      </td>
   </tr>
   </table>
   </center></div><hr>
   </td>
</tr>
</table>
</center></div><div align="center"><center>

<table border="0" cellpadding="5" width="90%">
```

Tags are codes in an HTML file that tell a browser what to do. For example, if the tag <b> appears before a word and the tag </b> appears after the word, those tags tell browsers to show that word in bold type when displaying the page.

Besides controlling the formatting of the page, the tags in an HTML file label each chunk of text as a particular element of the page. For example, HTML tags identify one line of text as the page's title, blocks of text as paragraphs, certain lines or words as links, and so on. Other HTML tags designate the filenames of inline images to be incorporated into the page by the browser when the page is displayed.

A Web *browser* is a program that knows how to do at least two things:

- Retrieve HTML documents from remote Web servers (by using a communications protocol named HTTP, about which you need to know nothing right now)
- Interpret the HTML tags in the document to display a heading as a heading, treat a link like a link, and so on

What's important to remember is that the HTML tags do not offer you the kind of control over the precise formatting of a page that you would have in a word processor. HTML mostly just identifies what's what. Each browser decides differently how to format those elements onscreen, though the two major browsers—Netscape and Internet Explorer—tend to show most Web pages almost identically.

Extensions are special additions to the standard HTML language, usually created by a browser maker to enable that browser to do tasks not included in HTML. See "Extensions: Love 'Em!, Hate 'Em!," later in this chapter.

At the time of this writing, the two most popular browsers—various versions of Netscape Navigator and Internet Explorer—comprise the overwhelming majority of the browser market. Although subtle differences exist in the HTML tags each one supports, the perpetual competition between these two has resulted in two browsers that display most Web pages identically. To most potential visitors on the Web, therefore, your Web page will look roughly the same as it does to you in Netscape as you work on it.

To folks using browsers other than the two big shots, your page will always show the same text content and general organization, but its graphical content and other aesthetics might vary dramatically from browser to browser. In fact, in some cases, pictures and any other graphical niceties might not even show up.

To illustrate this browser-to-browser variation, Figures 17.5 and 17.6 show exactly the same Web page as shown earlier, in Figure 17.1. That figure, however, displays the page through Netscape, and Figures 17.5 and 17.6 show it through two other browsers: Opera and DosLynx, respectively. Compare these two figures and observe how the presentation differs in each one.

DosLynx, the browser shown in Figure 17.6, is a *text-only* browser for DOS. (You remember DOS, don't you?) Disappearing rapidly from the Web (but still out there), these browsers cannot display inline graphics and display all text in the same-size typeface, although important elements, such as headings, can be made to stand out with bold type or underlining. Some people use text-only browsers out of choice, although most people do so because they lack the proper type of Internet account or the proper hardware for a graphical browser.

In addition to those using text-only browsers, others online can't see graphics because they have used the customization features in their browsers to switch off the display of graphics (which speeds up the display of pages).

FIGURE 17.5

*The same page as
shown in Figure 17.1 is
shown in Opera.*

FIGURE **17.5**

*The same page as
shown in Figure 17.1 is
shown in Opera.*

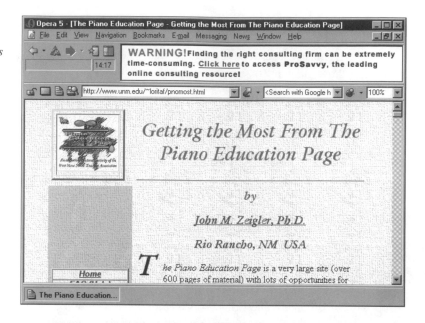

FIGURE **17.6**

*The same page, as
shown in Figures 17.1
and 17.5, shown in
DosLynx.*

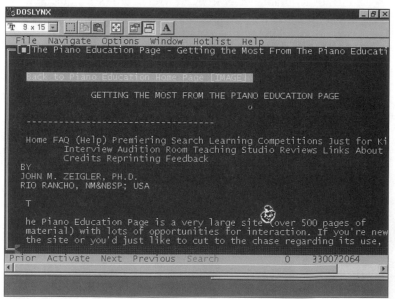

Although text-only browsers have all but disappeared, as a new Web author, you should
keep in mind the possibility that some folks can't see the pictures in your pages. For
them, you need to make sure that the text in the page gets the job done, whether the pictures appear or not.

Try it yourself....

1. View any Web page through your Web browser, as shown in Figure 17.7.

FIGURE **17.7**

Step 1: View any page.

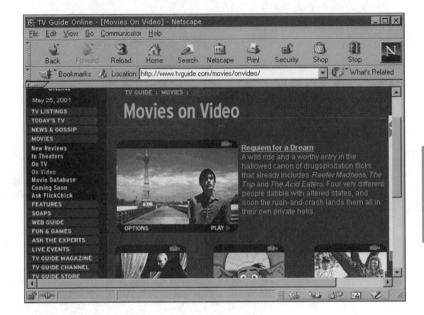

2. Change the view of your browser so that it shows the raw HTML source code of the page (see Figure 17.8):

In Netscape, choose View, Page Source.

In Internet Explorer, choose View, Source.

In another browser, look for a menu option that mentions Source or HTML.

FIGURE **17.8**

Step 2: Choose a menu item that displays the HTML source code of the page you're viewing.

3. Explore the HTML code (see Figure 17.9). Don't worry if lots of it look like gibberish—you don't really need to be able to "decode" an HTML file on sight. But if you look closely, you see the following within the various codes:

   • The actual text that appears on the page

   • Filenames of pictures in the page

   • Web addresses to which the links point

4. When finished examining the HTML source code, close the window in which the code appears so that the browser returns to its normal view.

FIGURE 17.9

Step 3: Explore the code, just to get a feel for what a Web page is really made of.

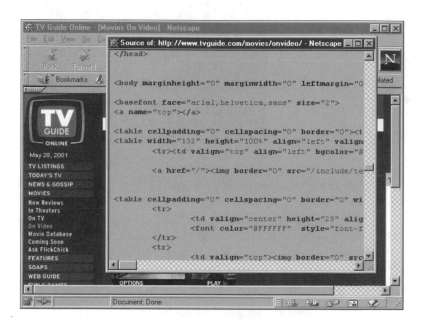

Pictures, Sound, and Other Media

Because an HTML file contains only text, the graphics you see in Web pages—and the multimedia you can access from Web pages—are not exactly a part of the HTML source file itself. Rather, graphics are linked to the page in either of two ways:

   • *Inline images* are graphics files whose filenames and locations are noted in the HTML file itself and identified as images by tags. Inline images are incorporated into the layout of the page—all the images you see through a browser when you access the page.

- *External media* are image, sound, or video files whose names and locations appear as links in the HTML file. These files do not appear or play automatically as part of the page. Instead, the page shows links that, when activated, download the file to play or display it.

Whether inline or external, the media files you use in your Web pages challenge the browsers that are used to view your page. The browser must be capable of displaying graphics to display inline graphics. External media files can be played by either the browser or, more commonly, helper applications (or plug-ins) opened by the browser.

When choosing to incorporate media into your page, you have to consider carefully the file types you use. The text-only rule of HTML files is what allows users of many different types of computers to access Web pages. Graphics files are less likely to be readable by a wide range of systems, and sound and video files, even less so. Even within the confines of PCs and Macintoshes, you need to consider whether your media will be supported by a broad spectrum of browsers or helper applications.

Extensions: Love 'Em!, Hate 'Em!

HTML is standardized so that any Web browser can read any Web documents—sort of.

Here's the deal: All modern browsers support all of HTML 4, a well-established set of tags set by the committees that oversee Internet standards. Standardization is good because it provides Web authors with a way to ensure that most browsers can read what they publish. Because any browser can understand and interpret all the HTML 4 tags, authors need only stick within the confines of those tags to ensure that their pages are accessible to the biggest possible online audience.

> HTML 5 won't be created. Instead, the next major change in Web page standards is named XHTML. Similar to HTML in many respects, XHTML will give Web authors the level of control over page formatting that one sees in word processing and desktop publishing. XHTML is also being developed to accommodate the growing range of noncomputer devices that will be using the Web: portable phones and automobile Internet devices, for example.

The problem with standards, though, is that they evolve slowly. On the Web, only downloads are permitted to be slow; evolution is required to be fast. Think about it: The first graphical browser emerged seven years ago, and now we're talking real-time video. The entire birth and maturation of the Web as a graphical, interactive environment took place within the equivalent of a single Presidential administration. Yikes!

When creating pages for a company intranet, where all users may have the same browser, you may not need to consider the extensions issue—you can apply all tags supported by the browser.

Leading browsers, including both Netscape and Internet Explorer, support all of HTML 4, the current standard. Still, the pace of Web page enhancement is so great that both Netscape and Microsoft continue to incorporate in their browsers extra tags and other capabilities that are not part of any approved HTML standard. These additional tags are extensions.

An *extension* is an HTML tag that makes possible some new capability in a Web page but is not yet part of the formal HTML standard.

The effects of these extensions, when used in a Web document, can usually be seen only through a browser that specifically supports them. Of course, Navigator supports many Netscape extensions, and Internet Explorer supports many Microsoft extensions. But subtle differences exist. For example, scrolling text banners that can appear in a box in the page layout in Internet Explorer appear instead in the status bar in some versions of Netscape. However, not all browsers support all extensions. That's why you need to be careful with 'em.

In general, whenever an incompatible browser accesses a page that uses these tags, nothing dire happens. The fancy extension-based formatting doesn't show up, but the meat of the page—its text and graphics—remain readable.

Authors who want to take advantage of extensions are concerned that some visitors are not seeing the page in its full glory. That's why, more and more, you see messages like "Best when viewed through Netscape Navigator" or "Enhanced for Internet Explorer" on Web pages. That's the author's way of telling you that he or she has used extensions—and if you want to enjoy all the features of the page, you had better pick up a compatible browser.

Ways to Organize a Web Site

Finally, before you dive into creating Web pages, you must give some thought to the following issues:

- How can my message be broken down into an organized series of topics?
- How long of a Web page, or how many Web pages (linked together into a Web site), are required in order to say what I have to say?

> After you've developed and refined the topic breakdown and outline of your message, you might find that you've already composed the headings for your Web pages.

Jot down a list of the topics or subtopics your document will cover. How many do you have, and how much material is required for each topic? After this simple exercise, you begin to get a good sense of the size and scope of your document.

Now look at the topics. Do they proceed in a logical order from beginning to end, with each new part depending on knowledge of the earlier parts? Or, does the material seem to branch naturally to subtopics (and sub-subtopics)? How might you reorder the topics to make the flow more logical or group related topics together?

As you work on your breakdown (not that kind of breakdown—your topic breakdown), a simple outline begins to emerge. The more you refine the outline before you begin composing your document, the more focused and efficient your authoring becomes. More important, the resulting Web document presents your message in a way that's clear and easy to follow.

> To plan a document with three or more pages, storyboard it by roughing out each page on a piece of paper to decide which information belongs on each page. Tape the papers to a wall and draw lines or tape strings to plan links among the pages.

While you're building your outline, consider the logical organization of your presentation and how its material might fit into any of the common organizational structures seen on the Web:

- **Billboard**—A single, simple page, usually describing a person, small business, or simple product. Most personal home pages are this type. They often contain links to related (or favorite) resources on the Web, but not to any further pages of the same document.

- **One-page linear**—One Web page, short or long, designed to be read more or less from top to bottom. Rules are often used to divide up this type of page into virtual "pages." Readers can scroll through the entire page, but a table of contents and targets can be used to help readers jump down quickly to any section. This type is best used for fairly short documents (fewer than 10 screens full) wherein all the information flows naturally from a beginning to an end.

- **Multipage linear**—The same general idea as the one-page linear type, but broken up into multiple pages that flow logically, one after the other, from beginning to end, like the pages of a story. You can lead the reader through the series by placing a link at the bottom of each page, leading to the next page.

- **Hierarchical**—The classic Web structure. A top page (sometimes confusingly called a *home page*) contains links to other pages, each covering a major subject area. Each of those pages can have multiple links to still more pages, breaking the subject down further and getting into even more specific information. The result is a tree structure, like the one shown in Figure 17.10.

FIGURE 17.10

A hierarchical structure.

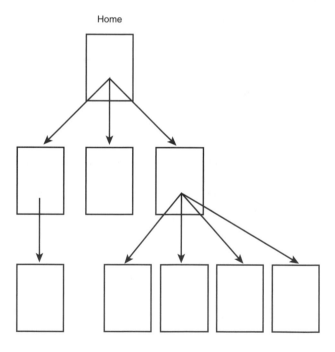

Home

- **Web**—As shown in Figure 17.11, a hierarchical structure without the hierarchy. In this multipage document, any page can have a link leading to any other page. It might be a "top" page, but from there, readers can wander around the Web in no particular path. Web structures are loose and free-flowing and are, therefore, best suited to fun, recreational subjects or to subjects that defy any kind of sequential or hierarchical breakdown. (Hint: Before you resort to using a Web structure, make sure that your message really calls for one—you might just be having trouble focusing.)

FIGURE 17.11

A Web structure.

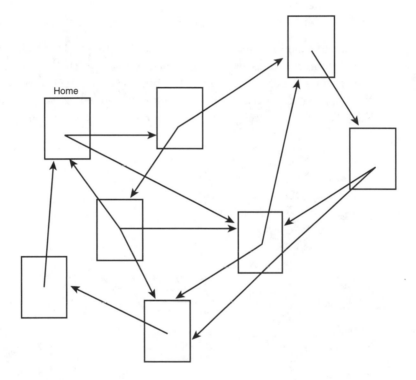

You can organize information in other ways; variations on each of the structures presented here. But one of these structures should resemble the general shape of your message, and thus your document. To put it another way, if you haven't yet decided which of these structures is best for the Web page you want to create, you need to play with your message some more and break it down in different ways until a structure reveals itself to you.

Summary

You can create your Web page by getting some good coffee, sitting down, and fiddling for a while with a template or any Web page editor. In the end, you have an HTML file suitable for publishing (if not for reading).

But is it a file that achieves your goals for wanting a Web page in the first place? If you're looking for cyberfriends, will your page appeal to them? If you're looking for clients or customers, does your page make you look better than your competitors look? If you're offering useful information, are you doing so in a way that visitors to your page will find intuitive and easy to navigate?

To create a page that hits its mark, you must first ground yourself in the basics of how a Web document works and what it can and cannot do. That's what you've picked up in this chapter. I didn't attempt to dictate how your document should look, feel, or operate—that has to be your inspiration. But I've tried to feed your thoughts so that you can make informed choices during whatever tasks you choose to take on next.

CHAPTER 18

Getting Started with a Web Authoring Program

When you work in a WYSIWYG Web page editor (like Netscape Composer, included with this book), your page looks (with minor exceptions) just the way it will look to most visitors on the Web.

That's a powerful convenience; without it, Web authors have had to guess about the appearance of their pages while fiddling with all the HTML code. To check their work, authors had to open the file in a browser and then go back to the HTML code to make adjustments. With a WYSIWYG editor, you can see and do it all in one window, live and in color.

This chapter examines the general operation of Composer so that you know your way around when you approach the specific authoring tasks coming up in later chapters.

This chapter assumes that you have already installed Netscape Communicator 4.7 and its built-in Web-authoring program, Composer. If you have not, visit `http://wp.netscape.com/download/archive.html` and download Netscape Communicator version 4.7 for your system. (It's free.)

More recent versions of Netscape and Composer are available, as well. Although the exact steps for some features might differ slightly, you'll have little difficulty finding your way around a newer version of Composer using the material in this book.

Opening Composer

When you install Composer, a shortcut for opening the program is automatically added to your Windows Start menu.

- To open Composer, click the Start button, and then choose Programs, Netscape Communicator, Netscape Composer (see Figure 18.1).

FIGURE 18.1

Opening Composer.

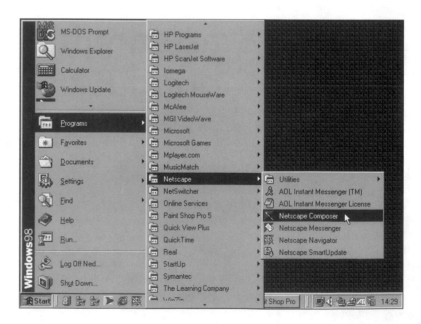

- To close Composer, choose File, Exit or click the X button in the upper-right corner of the Composer window (see Figure 18.2).

FIGURE 18.2
Closing Composer.

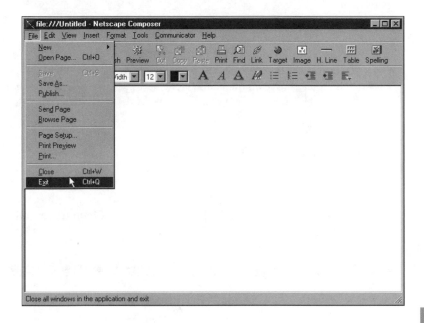

When Composer opens, it automatically opens a new, blank Web page file. You can start typing right away to begin creating your first Web page.

18

Exploring the Composer Toolbars

You perform many activities in Composer by clicking buttons on its two main toolbars: Composition and Formatting (see Figure 18.3). Composer actually has four toolbars. It also has the taskbar, which appears at the bottom of the Composer window, but which has no role in Web authoring, and the Edit Mode toolbar, which you won't use until Chapter 26, "Editing HTML," so ignore it for now. You learn much more about these toolbars over the next several chapters; for now, it's enough just to know where they are.

Composition Toolbar

FIGURE 18.3

You do most things in Composer by clicking buttons and picking from list boxes on the Composition and Formatting toolbars.

Formatting Toolbar

Most buttons are easy to identify by their icons (and names, on the Composition toolbar). But note that every button (or list box) on the toolbars has a *tooltip*, a name that appears to identify the button.

To learn the name of any button or list box, point to it (don't click) and pause a moment. The name of the button appears.

You can choose to display any toolbar (for ready use) or hide it (to free up more screen area for examining your creations). The following example shows how to hide and display toolbars:

1. Open Composer and look at the two rows of buttons beneath the menu bar (see Figure 18.4).

FIGURE 18.4

Step 1: Open Composer and check out the toolbars.

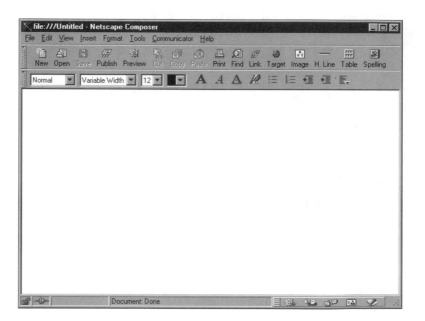

2. Click View, and then click Show (see Figure 18.5). In the menu, a check mark appears next to the name of each toolbar that's displayed.

3. To hide a toolbar, click its name.

4. To redisplay a toolbar you've hidden, repeat Steps 2 and 3.

Figure 18.5
Step 2: Open the View menu.

Starting a New Web Page

When you open Composer, it automatically opens to a new, blank page, so you can get right to work. As soon as Composer appears, you can begin applying the page-composition skills you learn later in this book.

> You can also start a new, blank Web page at any time from within Composer, by choosing File, New, Blank Page.
>
> The new page opens in a new Composer window, so the page you were editing previously remains open behind it. You can go back and close the previous page, or switch back and forth between the pages as needed.

Saving and Naming Web Page Files

Whether you create it with a template or from scratch, you need to save your new Web page file early and often.

When you save a file in Composer, you give it a name—presumably the name by which it will be stored on a Web server when published. And when it comes time to publish a Web page, names can be tricky. For example, Windows 98, Windows 2000, Windows Me, and even the Macintosh all allow you to use spaces and punctuation in filenames, but you should not do so when naming Web page files. Composer permits you to do it, but when you attempt to publish the files, you will find that browsers cannot open them.

In general, as long as you use a filename extension of .htm or .html and eliminate spaces and punctuation, you can give your page files any name you like. However, you can avoid certain kinds of compatibility problems by making sure that your filenames conform to the "8.3" filename rule: The filename must be no more than eight characters long with an extension of no more than three (.htm, not .html); for example:

```
nedsnell.htm
```

Also, when a page will be the "top" page of a multipage Web presentation, standard practice is to name it index.html (or index.htm). Most Web servers are configured to open the file index.html automatically when a visitor specifies a Web site address or directory but not a specific file. However, this system works only if you have your own directory on the server. Usually, you will. But if you share a directory with others, odds are that you won't be the first to post a file named index.html, so the server won't accept your document. For this reason, sometimes you should choose your server (see Chapter 30, "Publishing Your Page") and find out about its naming guidelines before settling on final names for your HTML files.

When creating a multipage Web site, saving all the page files in the same folder on your PC is important. Doing so not only makes publishing easier, but it also simplifies other tasks, such as creating links between pages.

The best approach is to create a new, empty folder on your PC and store in it all the files that make up the site—including not only the HTML files, but also other files that come into play, such as picture files.

1. Click the Save button on the Composition toolbar, as shown in Figure 18.6, or choose File, Save.

FIGURE 18.6

Step 1: Click the Save button or choose File, Save.

Save ——

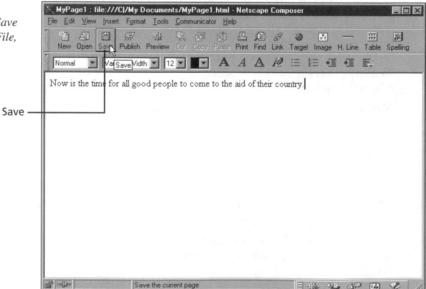

2. Choose a folder in which to save the page file (see Figure 18.7). (To create a new folder to save in, click the Create New Folder button.) Then name the file as you would when saving a file in any Windows program and click the Save button.

FIGURE **18.7**

Step 2: Pick a folder and type a filename.

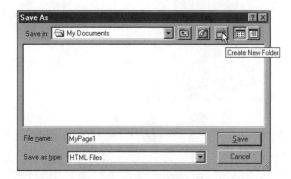

3. Enter a title for this page, as shown in Figure 18.8. (Don't feel pressured; you can always change the title later, as you learn to do in Chapter 19.)

FIGURE **18.8**

Step 3: Type a title.

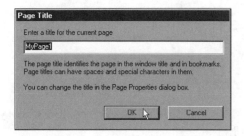

18

After the first time you save a file, you no longer need to perform Steps 2 and 3 when you save again. Simply performing Step 1 saves the file.

Editing Pages You've Saved

As you work on Web pages, you'll probably create them over a series of editing sessions. You need to open existing files and close them when you're done. The following example shows how to close files and to reopen them each time you want to work on them.

1. To close a page file (without closing Composer), choose File, Close, as shown in Figure 18.9.

FIGURE **18.9**
*Step 1: Choose File,
Close to close a file.*

FIGURE **18.9**
*Step 1: Choose File,
Close to close a file.*

2. To open a page file, choose File, Open Page (see Figure 18.10).

FIGURE **18.10**
*Step 2: Choose File,
Open Page.*

3. Click the Choose File button to navigate to the folder where you've stored the page file (see Figure 18.11).

FIGURE **18.11**
*Step 3: Use Choose
File to open the folder
where the file is stored.*

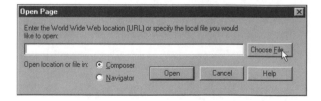

4. Choose the file's name from the Open HTML File dialog box and click Open (see Figure 18.12).

FIGURE 18.12

Step 4: Click the file's name and then click Open.

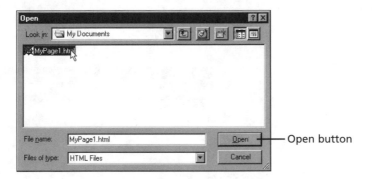

Open button

Checking Out Your New Page in a Web Browser

In Composer, your Web pages will appear pretty much the same as they will when viewed through a browser and the Internet. Still, you should preview your page through your Web browser from time to time to evaluate its true appearance.

Check out the page in a few different browsers, to make sure that it looks okay to everyone online, no matter what browser they use.

1. Save the file in Composer, as shown in Figure 18.13.

2. Click the Preview button on the Composition toolbar (see Figure 18.14).

The page opens in Navigator, as shown in Figure 18.15. To return to editing your page, switch to Composer by clicking its button on the Windows taskbar.

18

FIGURE **18.13**
Step 1: Save the file.

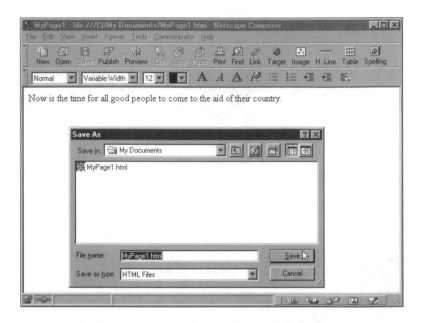

FIGURE **18.14**
Step 2: Click Preview.

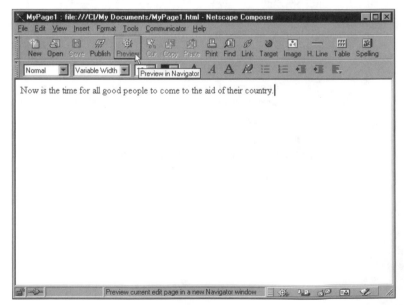

18

FIGURE 18.15

The page appears in Navigator.

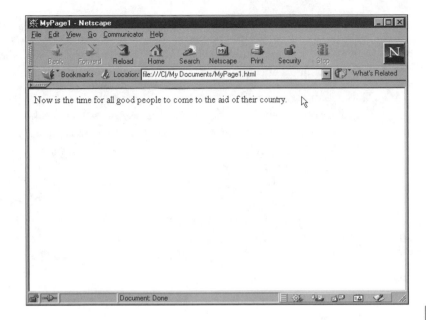

Printing Pages

When developing your pages, you might find that printing them from time to time is useful. Reviewing printouts of your pages may help you see typos or other errors you might miss when reading a page online (a trick of the eyes).

To print a page you're editing, click the Print button on the Composition toolbar or choose File, Print. The page is printed exactly as it would be from a Web browser—text formatting and pictures are included on the printout, but any background patterns you might have added are omitted to keep text legible. The page is broken up into appropriately sized chunks to fit on paper pages.

Although you might want to print your pages for reference, do not rely on printouts as accurate representations of your page's appearance online.

Summary

Composer does a great deal—too much, in fact, for this chapter to even scratch the surface. Still, in this chapter, you've wrapped your arms around the job and learned how to get into, out of, and around Composer. As mundane as those tasks are, they're the essential foundation to productive Web authoring. You're on your way.

But for all that Composer is, one thing it is not is smart. It can't tell you whether the content you've created is well organized, well presented, or well written. And although it applies HTML tags to your document dutifully, it cannot tell you whether you've selected the most effective tags for presenting the content at hand.

Thus, Composer is a replacement for only time and labor, not for judgment. To author an effective Web document, you must acquire a sense of Web aesthetics. You pick up much of this sense as you work through this book. But you must also study other pages you see online and mentally catalog the design aspects and content approaches that sing to you—and those that annoy, bore, or baffle you.

Chapter 19

Choosing a Title, Text Colors, and Other Page Basics

There's the forest, and then there are the trees.

In Web authoring, the trees are the content—the words, the pictures, the links. But before you start planting pines, you're smart to deal with a few quick, easy elements that affect your page at a higher level: the title, color scheme, and other stuff that defines the shape and function of the forest.

This chapter assumes that you have already installed Netscape Communicator 4.7 and its built-in Web-authoring program, Composer. If you have not, visit `http://wp.netscape.com/download/archive.html` and download Netscape Communicator version 4.7 for your system. (It's free.)

> More recent versions of Netscape and Composer are available, as well. Although the exact steps for some features may differ slightly, you'll have little difficulty finding your way around a newer version of Composer using the material in this book.

About Page Properties

Everything you learn in this chapter has to do with stuff that's generally described as page properties, settings that affect the overall look and function of your page.

Unlike with all other parts of your page, such as the page's text and pictures, you do not create the page properties within the work area in Composer. Instead, you use two special dialog boxes: Page Properties and Page Colors and Background.

You use these dialog boxes to change your page's title, choose a scheme of complementary text and background colors, and embed special identification information that does not actually appear on the page but rather helps search tools (such as Yahoo! or Google) properly catalog your pages.

Choosing an Effective Page Title

You must enter a carefully worded title for each page you publish, because the title describes your page to the Web in myriad ways.

For example, when a visitor to your page creates a bookmark or favorite for your page in his or her browser, the title typically becomes the name of the bookmark or favorite.

Also, Web directories (such as Yahoo!) and *spiders* (programs that build Web directories by searching the Web and cataloging its contents) use the title as a primary reference for what the page is about. Give your page a poorly worded title, and it might not come up in the hit list when folks search on the very topic your page covers.

> When people use Yahoo!, Excite, and other Web-searching tools, you want them to find your page when your page really matches what they want, and *not* to find your page when it's not a good match. Entering a good, descriptive title is one step in ensuring that match.

Don't confuse the page title with any big, bold heading that may top a Web page and serve as its apparent title. Remember: By the time a visitor sees that top-level heading, he or she has already arrived at your page and is presumably already interested in its subject, so that top heading can be more creative than the real page title—even subtle. But the true title must be descriptive, not clever.

 Remember: The title entered in the Page Properties dialog box does not appear on the page itself, but rather in the title bar of the browser window in which the page is displayed.

An effective title should accurately describe the contents or purpose of your page. The title should also be fairly short—no more than six to eight words—and its most descriptive words should appear first.

A bookmark list or Web directory often has room for only the first few words of a title, so your title needs to be short, and those first few words must be meaningful.

The following are some good titles:

Sammy's Racquetball Directory

The Video Store Online

All About Trout Fishing

Marvin C. Able's Awesome Home Page

Weehauken, NJ, Events for July

In these good examples, notice that the most specific, important descriptor appears within the first three words: Racquetball, Video, Trout, Marvin C. Able, and Weehauken, NJ, Events.

Notice also that the fewest possible words are used to nail down the page. In the first example, you learn in three words that this page is a directory of racquetball-related information and that it's Sammy's directory (to distinguish it from any other racquetball directories). What more do you need to know?

The following, for comparison, are some lousy titles:

My Home Page

Things to Do

Schedule of Events

A Catalog of Links and Documents Provided as a Public Service for Persons Researching Population Trends

19

In the first three crummy examples, the titles are nondescript; they contain nothing about the specific contents of the page. The last example, although containing some useful information at the end, would be trimmed to its first four or five words in a bookmark list, and those first few words say nothing useful.

Now that you know a little more about effective titles, you may want to change the titles of pages you've already started developing. The following example shows how.

1. In Composer, open (or create) the page file whose title you want to change.

2. Choose Format, Page Colors and Properties (see Figure 19.1).

FIGURE 19.1

Step 2: Choose Format, Page Colors and Properties.

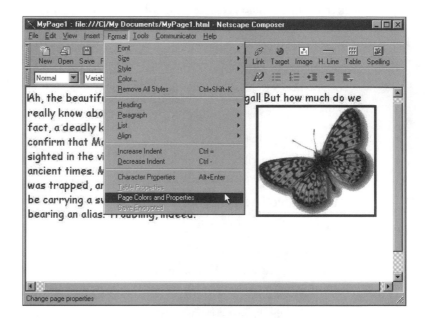

3. In the Title area, type (or edit to your liking) the title shown (see Figure 19.2).

When typing your new title, be careful to capitalize and spell it exactly as you want it to appear in a title bar or bookmark list.

Don't bother trying to use character formatting, such as bold or italics, in the title. No character formatting is possible within the text-entry areas in the Page Properties dialog box, and even if it were, it wouldn't show up anywhere titles typically appear.

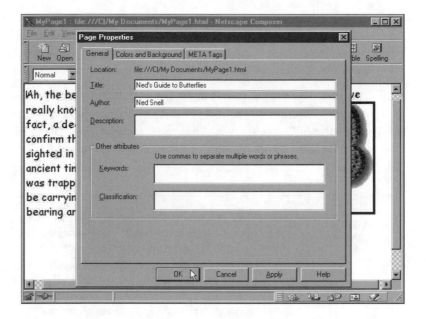

FIGURE 19.2

Step 3: Type your title.

4. You may optionally type your name in the Author area, although this information will not appear anywhere on the page. Instead, it will appear within the HTML code to identify the author to anyone examining the code, usually a fellow Web author who admires your handiwork.

5. Finally, you may type a description for your page. To learn more about the description, see the next section, "Helping Search Pages Catalog Your Page."

Helping Search Pages Catalog Your Page

Most folks who publish a Web page want it found by everybody online who may have a remote interest in the page's topic. (If you intend to keep the Web page you're creating a big, fat secret, you can skip this part.)

Obviously, the key to exposing yourself is to ensure that the page shows up in the major (and minor) search pages, such as Yahoo! (www.yahoo.com), Excite (www.excite.com), and AltaVista (www.altavista.com). If your page is about duck diseases, you want to be sure that whenever anyone enters the search term "sick duck," "duck illness," or "shaggy beak," a link to your page will appear high in the list of results.

In some cases, you must manually register your page with a search tool or use a Web promotion service to do it for you. But many search pages catalog the contents of the Web automatically. These search pages use programs, sometimes called crawlers or spiders, that roam around the Web, give Web pages a quick glance, and then attempt (with varying success) to automatically assign each page to one or more related categories. The more accurately your pages are categorized by these programs, the more likely they are to be found by exactly the folks you want to attract.

The most important step in ensuring that the spiders categorize a page correctly is giving it a good, descriptive title, as described earlier in this chapter (all spiders look at page titles). But in Composer, you can increase the accuracy with which you'll be categorized by typing a brief Description in the Page Properties dialog box (Format, Page Title and Properties).

Besides title and description, there are two other ways you can describe your page to search engines, helping those engines do a better job of leading visitors to your pages: Keywords and Classification.

- Keywords are any important terms with which your page might be associated. For example, the site for a reptile store might use the keywords pet, reptile, snake, herp, lizard, turtle, tortoise, etc. Think of words visitors might enter as search terms when seeking a site like yours; those are your keywords.

- Classification is a category or class in which your site belongs: Shopping, business, recreation, and so on.

To add keywords and/or a classification to your site, type them in the boxes provided on the General tab of the Page Properties dialog (refer to Figure 19.2). As directed on the dialog box, type a comma between each keyword in the Keywords box, or between multiple classifications in the Classification box. (In both boxes, insert dashes between multi-word terms; for example, `reptile-store` could be one keyword.)

Many spiders read the description and regard the words in it as clues to the page's proper category. If your page is about bicycles, including a description that contains words like *bicycle*, *bike*, *cycling*, *cycle*, *cyclist*, *Huffy*, and so on may increase the chances that those interested in cycling find your page through searches.

Also, when a search turns up your page, many search engines display the description along with the link to your site. A well-worded description helps ensure that folks who will be interested in your site get there.

Choosing Custom Colors for a Whole Page

In general, the visitor's browser—including Netscape and Internet Explorer—chooses the colors for the text and background of a page. Folks are then free to choose color schemes they find pleasing to their own eyes, and to have all Web pages show those colors, unless…

Unless the Web author (that's you) has applied custom colors. *Custom colors* are selected colors for the background and text that override the browser's color settings so that the Web author—not the browser—controls the color of text and the background.

> Note that custom colors affect only text and background colors. They have no effect on the colors in pictures or picture backgrounds [see Chapter 25, "Adding Pictures (and Picture Backgrounds)"]. Pictures are always displayed with whatever colors they were created with, regardless of any settings in the page properties or the browser.

You can assign custom colors separately for each of the following page elements:

- **Normal text**—All text in the page that is not a link.
- **Link text**—All links in the page except those that are active or visited (described next).
- **Active Link text**—Immediately after a link has been clicked by the visitor, it may remain visible for a few moments while the browser retrieves the file to which the link points. While the link remains visible, it changes color to indicate that it has been activated.
- **Followed link text**—Links that the visitor has previously used through his or her browser. In your own travels online, you may have noticed that when you return to pages you've visited before, links you've used appear in a different color from those you've never clicked.
- **Background**—The entire background area of the page can be a solid custom color. The background color always sits behind text or images in the page, never covering them, obscuring them, or affecting their color.

19

> The text colors you select in the Page Properties box automatically affect the page elements they're supposed to, freeing you to forget about text color when composing your page.
>
> But note that, as you work on your page, you can selectively choose the color of any block of text, to give it special emphasis. The color you choose need not be one of the colors you selected in the Page Properties box; it can be any color you want. To learn how to choose the color of a selected block of text, see Chapter 21, "Formatting Text."

1. Open the page whose colors you want to choose.

2. Choose Format, Page Colors and Properties.

3. In the Page Properties dialog box, select the Colors and Background tab (see Figure 19.3).

> Be careful that the text and link colors you choose stand out against the background color. For example, if you select a dark background color, all the text colors must be light so that the text will be legible atop the background.

FIGURE 19.3

Step 3: Select the Colors and Background tab.

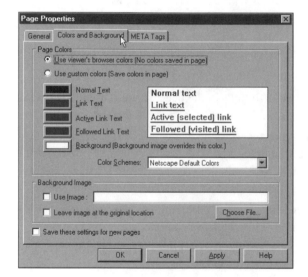

4. The default choice, Use Viewer's Browser Colors, lets your visitor's browser determine the color scheme. Override this setting by selecting Use Custom Colors (see Figure 19.4).

5. Click the button to the left of Normal Text (see Figure 19.5). A chart of colors appears.

6. Click the box showing the color you want to use, and then click OK.

7. Repeat Steps 4 and 5 for the other text types and background.

FIGURE **19.4**

*Step 4: Click a button
next to any page ele-
ment to display a list of
colors to choose from.*

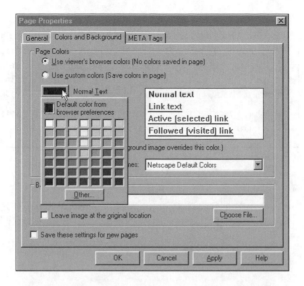

FIGURE **19.5**

Step 5: Click a color.

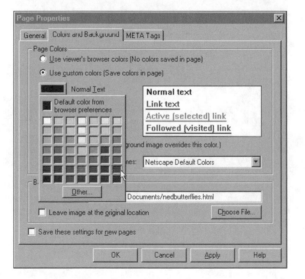

19

Do what you want, but bear in mind that it's sort of a waste of time to get
too esoteric when choosing colors. Visitors will be running monitors with
varying color capabilities and browsers with varying levels of support for colors, so it's unlikely that the colors will appear to others in the precise hue
you choose.

In other words, it's meaningful to fuss over whether to make text red or blue, but to click Custom so that you can choose that exact shade of Mediterranean sea blue (the one the bridesmaids wore at your wedding) because it's a half-shade brighter than the blue that's in the color list...well, that's probably splitting hairs.

If a very specific color is essential to your design, it's better to use that color in a picture (or picture background) you create.

Summary

Choosing your page properties is a snap, and it's also important. Doing it not only starts defining your page's appearance and purpose, but also forces you to begin thinking more clearly about those aspects. There's nothing like thinking up a title to help you focus your plans for your page.

CHAPTER 20

Adding, Editing, and Formatting Text

Somebody once said to me, "Writing isn't so tough: All you have to do is find a quiet spot and open a vein."

That's true, actually, but to the extent that writing a Web page can be made less immediately life threatening, a WYSIWYG editor does just that. The principal job in creating the text of a Web page involves two main tasks: getting the text into the file (by typing it, copying it, or importing it) and assigning paragraph properties to each block of text. The properties tell browsers how to present that text.

In this chapter, you learn how to get text into your Web page files, format it by assigning properties, and edit it. Dealing with the text first is usually the best way to build a Web page; it forces you to think about and resolve issues related to the organization and flow of content.

This chapter assumes that you have already installed Netscape Communicator 4.7 and its built-in Web-authoring program, Composer. If you have not, visit http://wp.netscape.com/download/archive.html and download Netscape Communicator version 4.7 for your system. (It's free.)

More recent versions of Netscape and Composer are available, as well. Although the exact steps for some features may differ slightly, you'll have little difficulty finding your way around a newer version of Composer using the material in this book.

Understanding Paragraphs and Their Properties

What makes a particular paragraph into a heading or something else is the properties you assign to the paragraph. Assigning properties to a paragraph is no different from assigning a style in a word processor, and usually it's just as easy. In a nutshell, you type a line or block of text and then assign properties to that paragraph to identify it as a heading, body text paragraph, or whatever. *Voilà*.

Composer calls each discrete chunk of text—all the text between paragraph marks (the character you type when you press Enter)—a *paragraph*, whether it's a heading, one line in a list, a multiline paragraph, or just a bunch of words.

Note that paragraph properties apply only to entire paragraphs. For example, you cannot format two words in the middle of a paragraph as an address and the rest of the paragraph as a heading. Either the whole paragraph is one thing, or the whole paragraph is something else.

Understanding What Each Paragraph Property Does

You assign paragraph properties through the Paragraph Format drop-down list on the Format toolbar (see Figure 20.1). The most important paragraph properties are described in the following sections and are shown in Netscape, Internet Explorer, and most other browsers as they appear in Figures 20.2 and 20.3.

Normal

Use the Normal property for general-purpose text—like what you're reading right now. Most browsers display Normal paragraphs in a plain font with no special emphasis (such as bold or special color). Normal is the meat and potatoes of your Web page.

FIGURE 20.1
*You assign paragraph
properties with the
paragraph format list
on the Format toolbar.*

Headings (1–6)

Use headings the way you see them used in this book: to divide and label the logical sections of the page or Web page. You can use as many as six levels of headings, ranging in relative importance from 1 (most important or prominent) to 6 (least important or prominent).

Because the level-1 heading is the most prominent, it is often reserved for the apparent title of your page—the one that appears within the page itself (not to be confused with the Web page title entered in the Page Properties dialog box).

In most browsers, a level-1 heading is displayed as the biggest, boldest text on the page. Level 2 headings are smaller and not bold, or they are de-emphasized in some other way. Level 3 gets less emphasis than 2 but more than 4, and so on. (Six levels require lots of variation, and the difference between headings only one level apart is barely distinguishable in some browsers, as you can see in Figure 20.2.)

Text-based browsers, which can't display varying font sizes, use bold, underline, or even numbers to show the varying heading levels.

You can use whatever heading levels you want, but, in general, obey the numbers. Subheadings within a section should have a higher-level number than the heading for the section. For example, a section that begins with a level-2 heading might have level-3 subheadings under it. The subsections under the level-3 heads might have sub-subsections with level-4 heads, and so on.

20

FIGURE 20.2

Paragraphs and their properties: headings, normal text, and address.

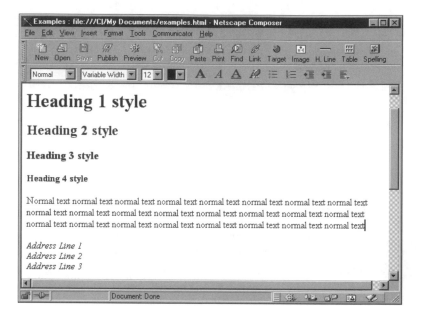

Address

Use the Address property for creating an *address block*, a line or many lines identifying someone, which usually lists an email address, a snail-mail address, or other contact information.

The Address property is used most often for the signature at the bottom of the page, but it can be used to give any address information on your page a unique style that sets it apart from other text. Most browsers display address blocks in italicized type.

Assigning the Address property to an email address on your page does not, by itself, make the address a mailto link that a visitor can click to send email. However, an email address with the Address property can be a mailto link—you just have to make it one.

To learn how to create a mailto link, see Chapter 23, "Making Links."

Formatted

"Formatted" might seem like a misnomer because text assigned the Preformatted property is in fact less formatted by the browser than any other kind. What *formatted* means in this context is *preformatted*—you have already lined up and spaced the text in a particular way, and you want browsers to leave that formatting alone.

Typically, browsers capable of displaying *proportionally spaced* fonts (such as the TrueType Arial or even the snappy font you're reading now) use those fonts for most text because they look better than typewriter-style *monospaced* fonts (such as Courier New). Also, browsers ignore tabs, extra spaces, and blank lines (extra paragraph marks) in HTML files.

Suppose that you want to show a text chart or table on your page, or words arranged in a certain way. Tabs are *verboten*, so you need to use spaces and a monospaced font to make the words line up right. But if browsers are permitted to do their regular thing with that text, they strip out the extra spaces, display the text in a proportional font, and generally screw up your lovely alignment job.

 You can use the Formatted property to create the effect of tables in your Web page, but you can also create real tables that look much better (see Chapter 22, "Organizing Text with Tables and Rules").

For example, observe the careful alignment of columns and the use of a monospaced font in the simple table shown in Figure 20.3. This table uses the Formatted property. Notice how the browser's display font and regularity of spacing differ in the formatted table from the other text in the figure.

FIGURE 20.3

Paragraphs and their properties: "formatted" text.

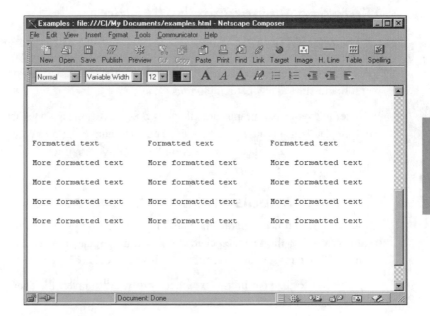

20

You can apply paragraph properties in whatever way suits you. (No HTML police will stop you—at least not yet.) But it's good practice to think of these properties as a way to determine the role a paragraph plays in your page, not the appearance of the paragraph.

For example, there's no technical reason that you can't write a lengthy paragraph and make it a heading, rather than body text, to make it stand out on the page. But different browsers use different methods to make a heading look like a heading; some make headings big and bold, others underline, and some even number headings according to their levels. Some Web search engines catalog pages according to heading content because headings generally contain subject information. Putting ordinary paragraph information into a heading might generate some screwy hits on your page from Web searches.

Use properties conservatively, according to their designated roles. Save your artistry for character formatting, images, backgrounds, and other ways you can spice up a page.

Entering Text and Assigning Properties

You can add text to a page and assign properties to that text in several different ways, all of which are described in the following sections.

Entering Paragraphs by Typing

When you create a new Web page, the edit cursor appears automatically at the top of the Web page. Type away. To correct mistakes and make changes as you go, use the Backspace, Delete, and Insert keys just as you would in any Web page. To end a paragraph and start a new paragraph, press Enter.

By default, your paragraphs are all set as body text (unless you select a different property before you begin typing a paragraph). You can change them to other paragraph properties at any time, as described in the section "Assigning Paragraph Properties to Existing Text," later in this chapter.

Typing Symbols and Special Characters

Sometimes, you need characters that don't appear on your keyboard, such as the copyright symbol or the accented characters used in languages other than English. For these types of occasions, Composer offers its Insert Special Characters menu.

1. Point to the spot in the text where you want to insert the character and click to position the edit cursor there.

2. Click Tools, and then choose Character Tools, Insert Special Character (see Figure 20.4).

FIGURE 20.4

Step 2: Choose Tools, Character Tools, Insert Special Character.

3. Click the character or symbol you want to insert. After you click it, it appears on your page where you pointed the edit cursor (see Figure 20.5).

FIGURE 20.5

Step 3: Choose the character you want.

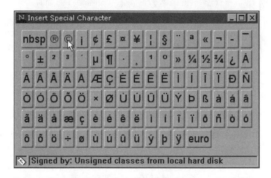

Copying Text from Another Document

The following To Do describes how to copy text from another document in Windows—such as a word-processing file or spreadsheet file—and place it in Composer so that it can be incorporated in your Web page. This method is a convenient way to use preexisting text, such as portions of your résumé or a description of your business, in your Web page without retyping it.

20

> If you want to use most or all of another document's contents in a new Web page, you may find that simply converting that document into a new Web page Is more convenient than using copy-and-paste, as described here.

1. Open the application normally used to edit or display the document from which you want to copy, and open the file (see Figure 20.6).

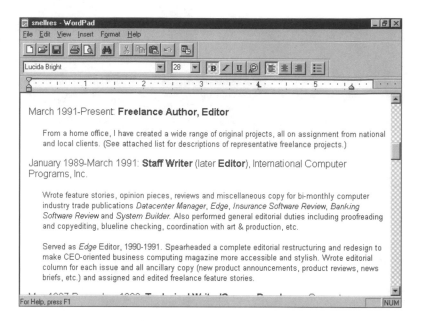

2. Use your mouse to highlight the desired text (see Figure 20.7). (To copy an entire
    document into your Web page, choose Edit, Select All in the application used to
    open the Web page.)

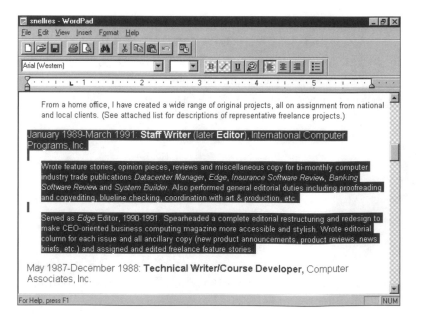

3. Press Ctrl+C to copy the selection to the Windows Clipboard. (Alternatively, you can click the Copy button on the toolbar or choose Edit, Copy.)

4. Open Composer and open (or create) the Web page into which you want to copy the text (see Figure 20.8).

FIGURE 20.8

Step 4: Open the Web page in Composer.

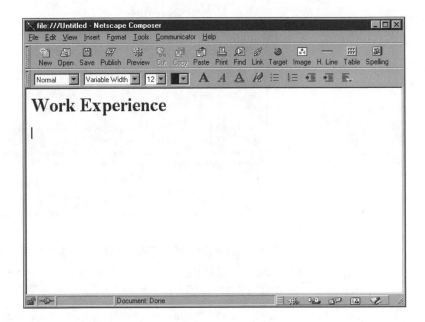

5. In the page, click the general spot where you want to copy the text. (If you've just created the Web page, the text must be copied to the top of the Web page where the edit cursor is already located. In a page that already has text, you can click at the beginning or end of any paragraph to add the selection to that paragraph, or press Enter between paragraphs to start a new paragraph for the selection.)

6. Press Ctrl+V to copy the selection into the page (see Figure 20.9). (Alternatively, you can click the Paste button on the Composer toolbar or choose Edit, Paste.)

20

> When pasted into a blank Web page, the text is automatically assigned the Body Text paragraph property. You can then change it to any other paragraph property.
>
> When pasted into a Web page with other paragraphs in it, the text is automatically assigned the same property as the paragraph it is inserted into or adjacent to.

FIGURE 20.9

Step 6: Insert the text.

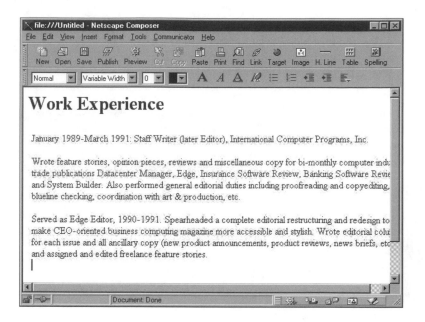

Assigning Paragraph Properties to Existing Text

The process of assigning properties involves two steps. First, you select the paragraph or paragraphs, and then you choose the properties:

- To select one paragraph, position the edit cursor anywhere within it (by either clicking within the paragraph or pressing the arrow keys until the cursor arrives within the paragraph). Note that positioning the cursor within the paragraph is sufficient; you don't need to highlight the whole paragraph.

> If working *sans mouse*, you can select multiple paragraphs by positioning the edit cursor anywhere in the first paragraph and holding down the Shift key while using the arrow keys to move to anywhere in the last paragraph in the selection.

- To select two or more paragraphs, click anywhere in the first paragraph, drag to anywhere in the last paragraph, and release, as shown in Figure 20.10.

After the paragraphs are selected, you assign a paragraph property by clicking the Choose a Paragraph Format drop-down list (at the left end of the Format toolbar).

FIGURE 20.10

Selecting multiple paragraphs to assign them all the same paragraph property.

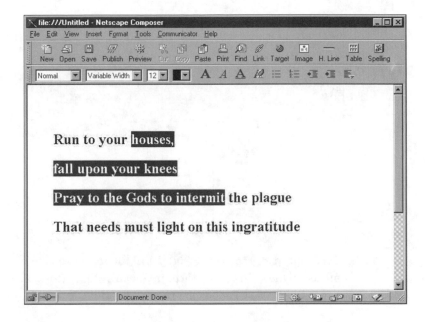

Although a certain logic can help you enter your paragraphs and then assign properties, you can do the opposite. To assign properties as you type a paragraph:

1. Click the spot where you want the paragraph to go (see Figure 20.11).

FIGURE 20.11

Step 1: Click where you'll type the new text.

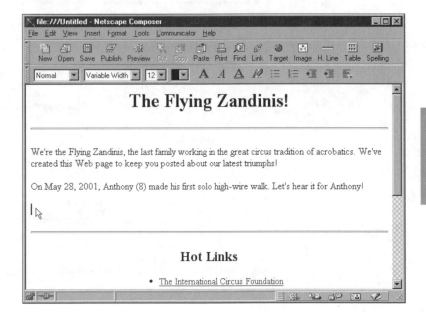

20

2. Click the Choose a Paragraph Format drop-down list on the Format toolbar and select a paragraph style (see Figure 20.12).

FIGURE 20.12

Step 2: Choose a style.

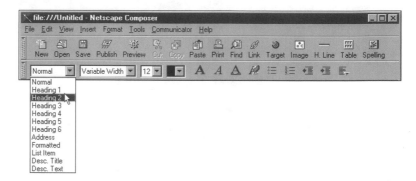

3. Type your paragraph (see Figure 20.13). It appears on the page as you type it, formatted in the style you selected. If you press Enter (to end the paragraph and start a new one), the new paragraph reverts to the Body Text style.

FIGURE 20.13

Step 3: Type away.

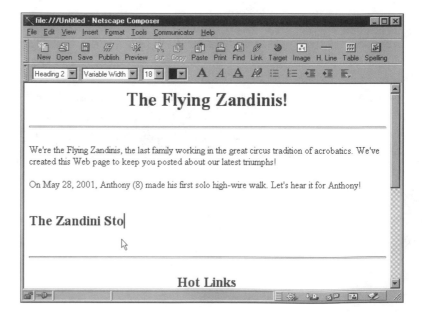

To learn the details of creating and formatting lists, see Chapter 21, "Formatting Text."

Aligning and Indenting Text

On the Format toolbar, you find five buttons that control the position of a paragraph on the page (see Figure 20.14).

FIGURE 20.14

The alignment buttons and indent buttons control the position of text within the width of the page.

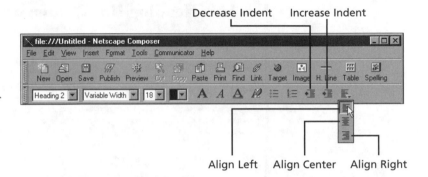

Decrease Indent   Increase Indent

Align Left   Align Center   Align Right

You can use these buttons (as described on the next few pages) on any paragraph, in any style. For example, you can use the Align Center button to center a paragraph whether the style of that paragraph is Body Text, List, Heading 2, or anything else.

Aligning Paragraphs

You can align any paragraph in any of three different ways (see Figure 20.15): tight against the left side of the page (the default choice), centered on the page (align center), and hard to the right side (align right). The following To Do shows how.

Most of the time, left alignment is best, especially for Body Text paragraphs. Center can be nice for large headings (such as Heading 1 or Heading 2 style), especially if it is not used too much. Save right alignment for special needs.

Our eyes are accustomed to left-aligned text, especially for body text. A big, centered heading looks good on some pages, and right alignment can create a nice effect when text is put to the right of a graphic [see Chapter 25, "Adding Pictures (and Picture Backgrounds)"]. However, centered Body Text paragraphs can appear a bit odd, and centered lists look downright strange.

20

Here's how you align paragraphs:

1. Select the paragraph or paragraphs you want to align (see Figure 20.16).

FIGURE 20.15
Left-aligned (the default), center-aligned, and right-aligned.

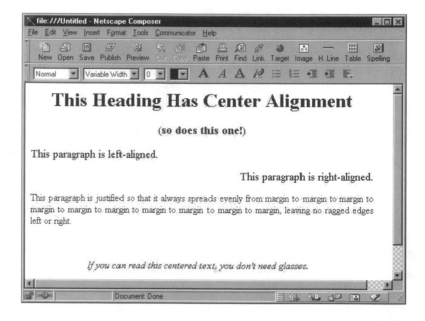

FIGURE 20.16
Step 1: Select the paragraphs to align.

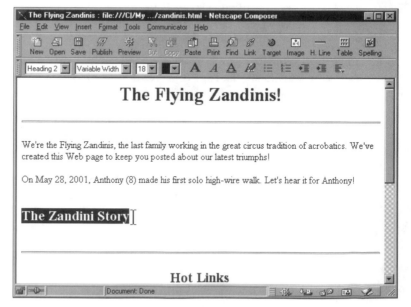

2. Click one of the alignment buttons on the Formatting toolbar: Align Left, Align Center, or Align Right (see Figure 20.17). (If the paragraph is already aligned in any way other than left, you also see an Align Left button when you point to the toolbar.)

Center

FIGURE 20.17

Step 2: Click an alignment button.

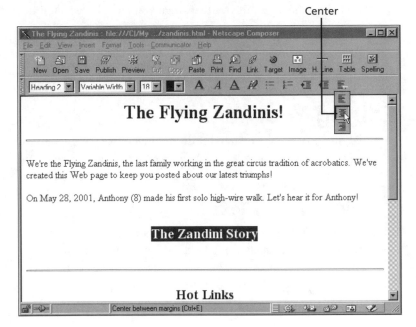

Indenting Paragraphs

Besides choosing the alignment of paragraphs, you can *indent* them, pushing them away from the left margin just as you would in a word processor.

Composer supports multiple indent levels; you can increase the indent several times to push the paragraph farther away from the left margin. Decreasing the indent pulls the text back toward the left margin.

- To indent a paragraph, select it and then click the Increase Indent button on the Format toolbar. To indent even farther to the right, click the Increase Indent button again.
- To decrease the indent (move the left edge of the paragraph back toward the left margin), click the Decrease Indent button.

Adding Blank Line Spaces in a Page

Except within the Formatted paragraph style, HTML does not recognize paragraph marks in the HTML file as blank lines or extra blank spaces as extra blank spaces. Thus, browsers generally ignore these characters when displaying a page. To create extra white space between paragraphs or extra spaces in a line, Web authors must use the HTML tags for line breaks and nonbreaking spaces, respectively.

20

Composer, however, figures that when you press Enter multiple times, you want to add white space—so it automatically inserts the appropriate tags.

So trust your word-processing instincts: To start a new paragraph, press Enter. To add a blank line, just press Enter again.

Editing Your Text

Editing a Web page is straightforward, much like editing any word-processing document. To do almost anything, highlight the text you want to change and then make the change. You can also search for a text string using the Composer Find in Page tool.

Highlighting Text

To highlight text with your mouse, position the cursor at the start of the area you want to highlight, and then click and hold the left mouse button. Drag to the end of the selection, and release the mouse button. Note that you can select as much text as you want in this way: a few characters, a word, a whole paragraph, or a group of paragraphs.

> When you drag through an area that includes both text and images, only the text is selected. Images must be selected separately.

You can also highlight a selection for editing in other ways:

- Double-click a word to select it.
- Double-click at the beginning of a line to select the first word.
- Double-click at the end of a line to select the last word.
- Position the pointer to the left of a paragraph, double-click to select the entire paragraph, or single-click to select just the line the cursor is next to.

Replacing Selected Text

When text is selected, begin typing. The selection is deleted immediately and replaced with whatever you type. Any surrounding text that was not highlighted remains unaffected.

You can also replace a highlighted selection with the contents of the Clipboard by choosing Edit, Paste. (Of course, you must previously have cut or copied something to the Clipboard; see the section "Copying or Moving Selected Text," later in this chapter.)

Deleting Selected Text

Press the Delete key to delete the selection.

> You can right-click selected text to display a context menu with choices for changing properties, for creating links, and for cutting, copying, and pasting (refer to Figure 20.5, shown earlier).

To delete the selection from its current location but copy it to the Windows Clipboard so that it can be pasted elsewhere in the page (or into another page or another Windows document), click the Cut button on the toolbar or choose Edit, Cut.

Copying or Moving Selected Text

To copy a highlighted selection, click the Copy button on the toolbar or choose Edit, Copy. Then click in the location where you want the copy to go, and click the Paste button or choose Edit, Paste.

To move a highlighted selection, click the Cut button on the toolbar or choose Edit, Cut. Then click in the location where you want the selection moved, and click the Paste button or choose Edit, Paste.

Undoing Edits ("Goofs")

If you goof on any edit and wish that you hadn't done it, you can undo it.

To undo the last edit you made, choose Edit, Undo.

Checking Your Spelling

Of course, some goofs go unnoticed too long for Undo to do much good—especially spelling errors. Fortunately, Composer has a spelling checker to rescue you.

To check spelling in a page, click the Spelling button on the Composition toolbar. Composer finds the first word it doesn't recognize (like all spelling checkers, it finds not so much misspelled words as words not in its dictionary), and displays the dialog box shown in Figure 20.18.

20

FIGURE 20.18

*Click the Spelling but-
ton to open this box for
fixxing yor speling.*

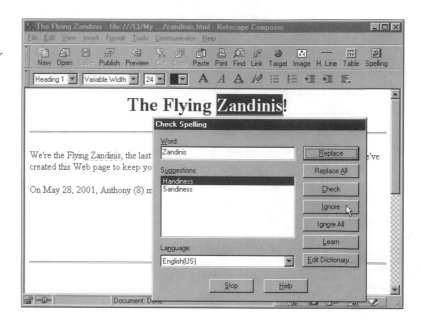

In the Check Spelling box, you can

- Click any correct word listed in the Suggestions box and then click either the Replace button to change the misspelled word to the suggestion or Replace All to change all words spelled this way to the suggestion you chose.

- Edit or retype the word in the Word box to correct it and then click either the Replace button to change the misspelled word to the new version or Replace All to change all words spelled this way to the new version.

- Click Ignore to skip a word that's spelled correctly and just not recognized (like *Snell*).

- Click Ignore All to ignore this word everywhere in the page.

- Click Learn to add to the dictionary a correctly spelled but unrecognized word (like *Snell*) so that Composer no longer regards it as misspelled, in this or any other page you spell-check.

After you do any of these actions, the spelling checker moves on to the next word it doesn't recognize.

Tips for Good Text Design

It's your page, and far be it from me to tell you what it should look like. However, if you are interested in some of the accumulated wisdom of the Web masters, here are a few things to keep in mind when working with text on your page:

- Write clearly and be brief. Web surfers are an immediate-gratification, fast-food–type lot. To hold them, you must dole out your message in quick, efficient bites.

- Break up your message into pages of reasonable length, and break up pages into at least two or three sections (three is best) delineated by headings, pictures, or horizontal lines (see Chapter 21, "Formatting Text"). This technique makes your page more attractive and inviting and also allows visitors to scan your page easily for items of interest.

- Don't overdo emphasis. Look through your page and watch for overuse of bold, italics, and custom font sizes and colors. Watch also for the use of headings or other properties used to pump up a paragraph that really belongs in body text. Let your page's organization (and pictures) create visual interest, and let your choice of words emphasize important ideas. Use bold to light up a word or two and use italics for things that belong in italics, such as book titles or foreign phrases.

- Proofread carefully on your own before publishing. In addition, have someone else check your spelling and critique your writing and layout.

- Always use a signature (see Chapter 23, "Making Links").

Summary

Composer provides simple toolbar buttons, dialog boxes, and menus for applying properties to paragraphs—the most important activity in building a Web page.

20

CHAPTER **21**

Formatting Text

It's easy—too easy, in fact—to begin thinking that a Web page is made up of three basic parts: text, images, and links. Although that's generally true, it tends to imply that text is for content, images are for show, and links are for action.

The facts are a little muddier than that. Text is first and foremost a vehicle for information, but when text is dressed up in a fancy font or cool color, it contributes both content and design—feeding two brain hemispheres for the price of one. Similarly, organizing text into a bulleted or numbered list affects both content and style.

This chapter assumes that you have already installed Netscape Communicator 4.7 and its built-in Web-authoring program, Composer. If you have not, visit `http://wp.netscape.com/download/archive.html` and download Netscape Communicator version 4.7 for your system. (It's free.)

More recent versions of Netscape and Composer are available, as well. Although the exact steps for some features may differ slightly, you'll have little difficulty finding your way around a newer version of Composer using the material in this book.

Working with Lists

You can use buttons on the Format toolbar to create two kinds of lists in Composer (see Figure 21.1):

- **Numbered list**—A list whose items are numbered from top to bottom.
- **Bulleted list**—An ordinary, indented bulleted list.

FIGURE 21.1

List styles you can create in Composer.

But the choices don't stop there! You can change the bullet style or numbering type of your plain-vanilla bulleted or numbered list (see Figure 21.2).

Which kind of list should you create for a given purpose: bulleted or numbered? I dunno. It's your Web site. Do what you feel like.

If you want a principle to guide you, try this technique: When the order of the items in the list is important, as in step-by-step instructions, use a numbered list. When the order doesn't matter, use a bulleted list.

FIGURE 21.2

Optional numbering and bullet styles.

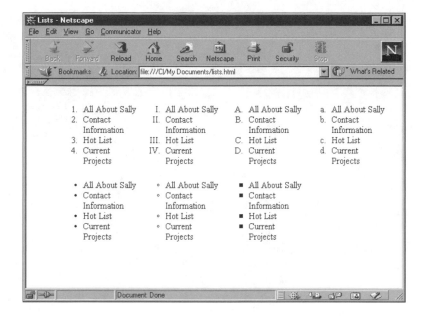

In some pages you see online, you see cool list bullets that are geometrical, multicolored, and even animated. These are not real bullets assigned by a bullet style attribute, but rather images inserted right before each line of text [see Chapter 25, "Adding Pictures (and Picture Backgrounds)"].

Creating Basic Lists

As with all other text formatting, you create a list by first typing the text of one or more list items; each item is a separate paragraph (press Enter after typing each item), and each item can be as long or as short as you choose. You then apply list formatting as described in the following example.

1. Type the list items and press Enter after each one so that each list item is on a separate line (see Figure 21.3).
2. Select the entire list (see Figure 21.4).

List formatting is paragraph formatting, so you can select a list by starting the selection anywhere in the first item and then dragging down to anywhere in the last item.

21

FIGURE 21.3

Step 1: Type the list items.

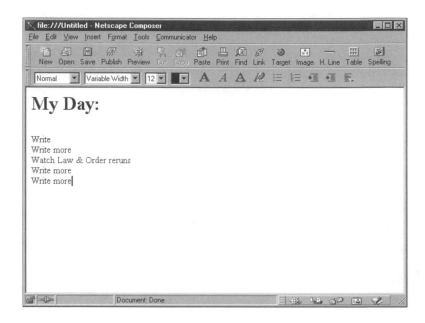

FIGURE 21.4

Step 2: Select the list.

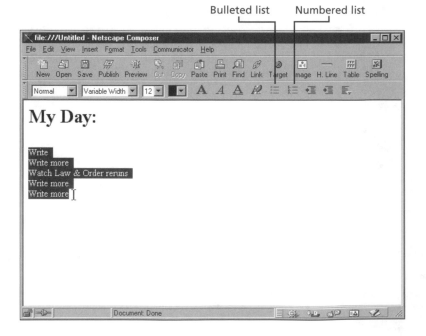

3. Click one of the two list buttons on the Format toolbar: Numbered List or Bulleted List (see Figure 21.5).

FIGURE 21.5

After Step 3, the list is formatted with the list style of your choice.

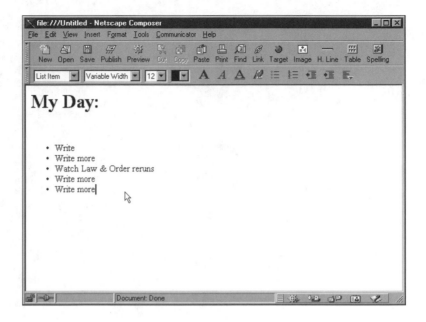

The items in a list can be formatted in any style. You can make a list of headings, for example. However, note that the bullets and numbers at the beginning of the list usually do not change size, regardless of the size of the text. For that reason, you should keep list text in the Normal style or as a high-level heading (such as Heading 3 or 4).

If you want really big, bold text for list items, forget about regular list formatting and instead add graphical bullets (as described in Chapter 25) that are big and bold enough to suit the power of the text.

Changing the Look of a List

You can make a pretty good-looking list just by clicking a button, as you did in the preceding example. But you don't have to settle for what you get. You can easily modify the appearance of a list, choosing the numbering style (A B C or I II III, for example) or bullet symbol.

1. Select the list (see Figure 21.6).

2. Choose Format, Character Properties (see Figure 21.7).

3. Select the Paragraph tab. The type of list you have assigned appears in the List Style box in the middle of the dialog box. You can leave it or change the list type using the drop-down list.

21

FIGURE 21.6
Step 1: Select the list.

FIGURE 21.7
Step 2: Choose Format, Character Properties.

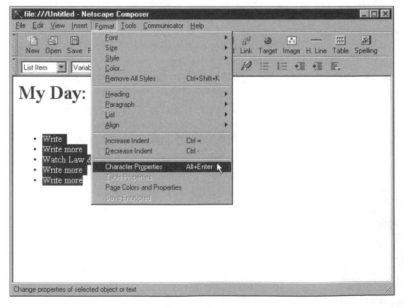

4. Depending on the selected list style, a list of options is available from a second drop-down list in the dialog box. If Bullet is the list style, you get a list of options for the Bullet style to use. If Numbered List is the list style, you get options for the Number style. Choose from the list the bullet or numbering style you want (see Figure 21.8).

FIGURE 21.8
Step 4: Choose your style options from the list.

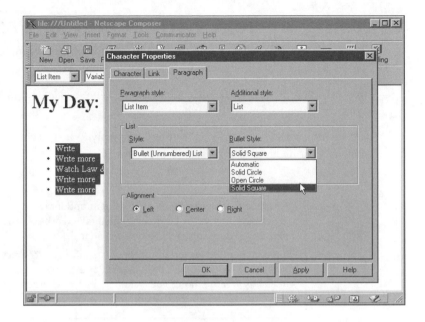

5. Click OK. The look of the list is changed (see Figure 21.9).

FIGURE 21.9
Old list, new look.

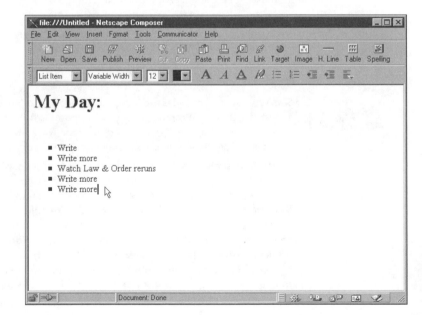

21

Dressing Up Text with Character Properties

Paragraph properties always apply to a whole paragraph; for example, you cannot make part of a paragraph a heading and another part normal text.

However, you can apply character properties to a single character in a paragraph, a few words, a whole paragraph, or a whole document.

Character properties are optional settings you apply to text to change its appearance, such as a particular font (typeface) or bold formatting.

Paragraph properties (such as alignment and indenting) and character properties (such as font or boldfacing) generally work together to define the look of a paragraph and the text within it.

Keep in mind, however, that browsers apply some character formatting to text based on paragraph style alone. For example, they automatically show headings in large, bold type. When you apply character formatting, you override any default formatting that the browser applies.

The most common use of character properties is to emphasize words by making them bold, italic, or underlined, just as you would when formatting a document in a word processor. But you can also change the color of characters, change the font (typeface) or size, and so on.

Some character properties are based on extensions to HTML. As you might expect, anything you can do to text in Composer is fully supported by your popular friends Internet Explorer and Netscape Navigator. Among other browsers, however, you find a slippery slope of support levels.

Nearly all graphical browsers support relative font sizes. Most support character styles such as bold, italic, and underline; however, some browsers interpret these styles as merely "emphasis" and decide on their own how to show that emphasis. For example, text you make italic might show up underlined (and not italic) in a browser that makes its own rules for emphasizing text. Unusual styles, such as superscript and blinking text, are not often supported outside the Netscape and Microsoft camps. Text color is an offshoot of custom colors and is supported in any browser that supports custom colors (as long as the visitor has not disabled that support).

Choosing Fonts

When you open Composer's font list, you'll see every Windows font installed on your PC, plus a few new choices. You can use any font in the list, but there are good reasons for self-limiting your font choices to a much narrower range than what Composer makes available.

Choosing a font instructs the browser to use the selected font (or, in a few cases, a font from the same family). The trick is that the font you choose, if it's not one of the very few built into Composer, must be installed on the visitor's computer (either PC or Macintosh), or the visitor's browser must have a special built-in font viewer.

For example, if you set text in Century Gothic, your visitors will see that font only if they happen to have Century Gothic installed on their computers. Otherwise, the text reverts to a font selected by the browser.

You'll have best luck with fonts if you keep the following guidelines in mind:

- The Variable Width and Fixed Width options each allow the visitor's browser to apply whatever variable or fixed-width font it happens to use by default.
- Helvetica/Arial are two proportionally spaced sans serif fonts. (*Sans serif* means that the font lacks the decorative lips or bars that appear at the points of characters in serif fonts.) A browser on a computer lacking Helvetica or Arial can substitute another sans serif proportional font.
- Times is a serif proportional font for which a similar font, such as Century Schoolbook, can be substituted.
- Courier is a monospaced font (like that used to display text in the fixed-width character property or Preformatted paragraph property). Another monospaced font, such as Letter Gothic, can be substituted by the browser.

Here's how to choose a font for text:

1. Select the exact characters to which you want to apply a new font (see Figure 21.10).
2. Choose Format, Font.

Fonts are a form of character formatting, not paragraph formatting, so they affect only the exact characters you select. To apply a font to a whole paragraph, you must select the whole paragraph.

21

3. Choose from the list of choices the font you want to apply (see Figure 21.11).

FIGURE 21.10
Step 1: Select the characters.

FIGURE 21.11
Step 3: Choose a font.

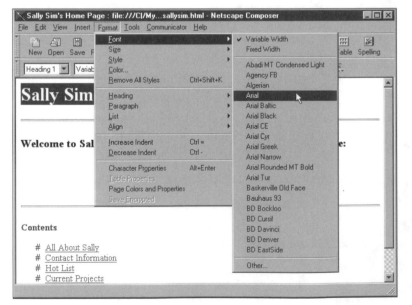

Choosing a Size for Text

The paragraph style determines size. For example, if text set in the Heading 3 style looks too small to you, the best solution is to change it to a bigger style, such as Heading 2 or

Heading 1. Still, you can fine-tune the size of selected text easily, when the size chosen by the style isn't exactly what you want.

> If you click Larger Text Size and the selected text does not get any bigger, the text is already set at the largest size allowed. Similarly, if the Smaller Text Size option does nothing, the text is already set at the minimum size allowed.

Here's how to choose the size of text:

1. Select the exact characters you want to make bigger or smaller (see Figure 21.12).

Figure 21.12

Step 1: Select the characters.

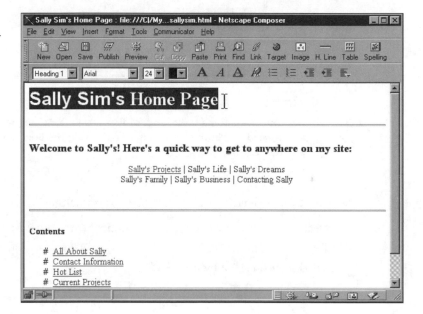

2. Locate the font size drop-down list on the Formatting toolbar.
3. To adjust the size of the selected text, select the font size (see Figure 21.13).

Making Text Bold, Italic, or Underlined

Just as in any letter or report you might create, bold, italic, and underlining are valuable tools in a Web page for making text stand out or for making it match editorial standards (such as setting book titles in italics). These styles are easy to use, but use them sparingly; too much of this stuff makes text busy and hard to read.

21

Figure **21.13**

*Step 3: Select a
smaller or larger font
size.*

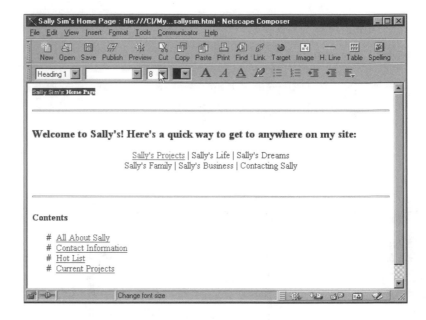

You can combine these kinds of formatting; for example, you can make the
selected text both bold and italic by clicking the Bold button and then the
Italic button.

Here's how to apply bold, italic, or underline text formatting:

1. Select the exact characters you want to format (see Figure 21.14).

2. Click a button to format the selected characters: the Bold button, Italic button, or
   Underline button (see Figure 21.15).

Rather than use the buttons, you can apply text styles by choosing Format,
Style from the menu. The menu offers not only the familiar bold, italic, and
underline choices, but also more esoteric character styles, such as
strikethrough and subscript. Use the esoteric stuff sparingly, though,
because it is not supported in all browsers.

To remove bold, italic, or underlining, select the text and click the button
again. For example, to make some bold text not bold, select it and click the
Bold button.

FIGURE 21.14

Step 1: Select the characters.

FIGURE 21.15

Step 2: Click Bold, Italic, or Underline (see Figure 21.16).

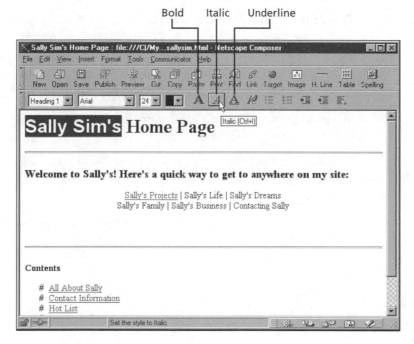

21

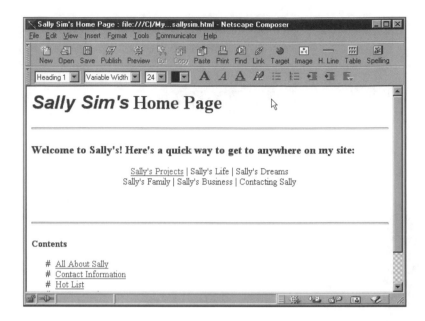

FIGURE **21.16**
Italics applied.

Choosing the Color of Text

In Chapter 19, "Choosing a Title, Text Colors, and Other Page Basics," you learned how to choose a coordinated color scheme for your Web page—a scheme for making sure that all the colors used for text, the background, and other objects all work together. If you do that, you probably won't be choosing colors selectively for blocks of text.

Still, you might want to give a heading or other selected text its own, unique color. The following example shows how.

1. Select the exact characters for which you want to choose a color (see Figure 21.17).

2. Choose Format, Color.

3. Click the colored square containing the color you want to apply, and then click OK (see Figure 21.18).

FIGURE 21.17

Step 1: Select the characters.

FIGURE 21.18

Step 3: Click the color you want.

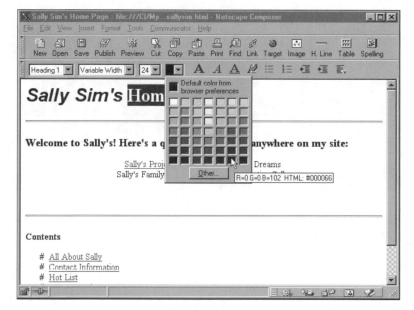

21

Summary

Still think that images are the meat of a page's looks? You haven't entered a single image, and yet you've discovered an easy arsenal of techniques for dressing up a page, including list formatting, custom colors, and fonts.

Sure, you still want to use images, but as your pages evolve, always remember that you have these simple but effective design tools available to you.

CHAPTER 22

Organizing Text with Tables and Rules

Between text and pictures is a gray area. The objects in this area affect the composition and organization of a Web page, but they aren't exactly text or pictures; they are tables and horizontal lines (sometimes also known as horizontal rules).

Tables are a great way to organize text in a meaningful, attractive way. And horizontal lines divide pages up visually into meaningful sections, making the page both more appealing and easier to read. In this chapter you'll learn how to apply these "gray area" techniques to make the most of text.

This chapter assumes that you have already installed Netscape Communicator 4.7 and its built-in Web-authoring program, Composer. If you have not, visit `http://wp.netscape.com/download/archive.html` and download Netscape Communicator version 4.7 for your system. (It's free.)

> More recent versions of Netscape and Composer are available, as well. Although the exact steps for some features may differ slightly, you'll have little difficulty finding your way around a newer version of Composer using the material in this book.

About Horizontal Lines

The simple, straight lines running horizontally across many Web pages (see Figure 22.1) have always been known in Web parlance as *horizontal rules* because they're created by the HTML tag <HR>—HR for *h*orizontal *r*ule.

FIGURE 22.1

Horizontal lines are easy to create in various widths and thicknesses and offer an easy, attractive way to organize a page.

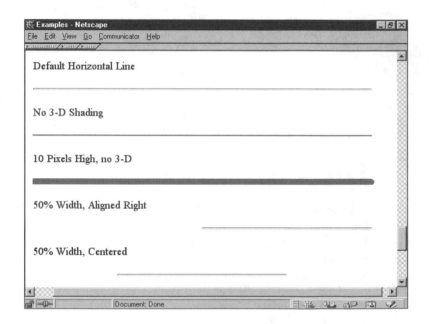

Netscape apparently thinks that the term *rule* is confusing, so in Composer it's a horizontal *line*. No matter. Rules are made to be broken, or lines, or something like that.

> In some pages, you see cool, graphical horizontal lines that zigzag, flash, or scroll. These are not real HTML "horizontal lines," but rather pictures inserted to achieve the same effect as a line (only cooler).
>
> You learn how to add these picture lines in Chapter 25, "Adding Pictures (and Picture Backgrounds).

Virtually any browser (even a text-only browser) can show a horizontal line because any computer system can draw one across the screen (even if the line is made up of only underscores or dashes). Lines are a universal way to add some visual interest to your page and break up logical sections of a page or document to communicate more effectively.

1. Click in your page at the spot where you want to insert the line (see Figure 22.2).

FIGURE 22.2

Step 1: Click where you want the line.

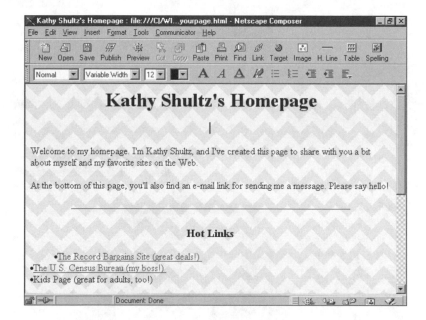

2. Click the H. Line button on the Composer toolbar (see Figure 22.3).

Here's how to change the look of a horizontal line:

1. Double-click a line you've inserted to open the Horizontal Line Properties dialog box (see Figure 22.4).

2. Type a number in the Height box to change the thickness of the line; a higher number makes a thicker line. A height of 2, 3, or 4 makes a good, everyday line. A height of 6 or 8 makes a fat, bold statement.

In the Horizontal Line Properties dialog box, in the list box next to Width, always leave the choice % of Window selected. This option ensures that the number you type in the Width box expresses the width as a percentage of the page's width. Choosing the other option may produce unpredictable results on visitors' screens.

FIGURE **22.3**

*Step 2: Click the H.
Line button.*

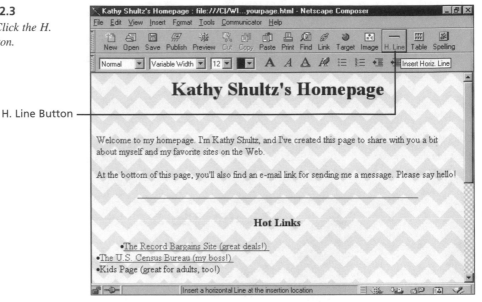

H. Line Button

FIGURE **22.4**

*Step 1: Double-click
any horizontal line to
adjust its properties.*

3. To make the line shorter than the full width of the page, type a Width value less than 100. For example, a width of 50 creates a line half the width of the page.

4. Choose an alignment (Left, Right, or Center) for your line. (Note that alignment is irrelevant if the width is 100.)

5. Check the 3-D shading box if you want the line enhanced with a nifty shadow. Note that the shadow makes the line look a little thicker; after adding 3-D shading, you may choose to reduce the Height value.

6. Click OK to see the results of your changes (see Figure 22.5).

FIGURE 22.5
A line transformed.

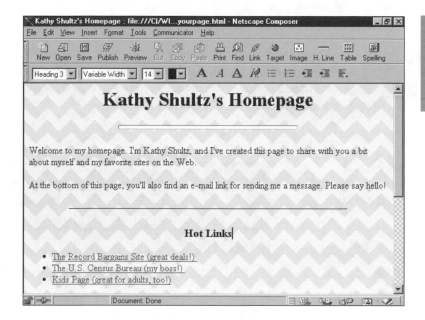

If you *really* like the look of the line you've created and want to use the same style of line often, return to the Horizontal Line Properties box by double-clicking the line and checking the check box labeled Save Settings as Default.

From then on, all new lines you create automatically take on that style you like so much. On those rare occasions when you want something different, you can simply change the properties for individual lines.

About Tables

A table—regardless of the medium in which it appears—is composed of chunks of information arranged in rows and columns. The grid of rows and columns forms the cells in which you can organize text.

In a table, the box made by the intersection of a column and a row is a *cell*; cells contain the table content, or *data*.

You can put text or pictures in a table cell. You learn how to put a picture in a table cell in Chapter 25.

Although rows, columns, and data are the minimum requirements for any table, a more elaborate table contains additional elements (see Figure 22.6). It might have column or row headings and a caption above or below it. It might have solid lines, or *borders*, appearing on all sides and between cells to form a grid. Note, however, that the borders might be omitted so that cell data is neatly organized in rows and columns, but not boxed up (see Figure 22.7).

FIGURE 22.6

Parts of a table (not all are required).

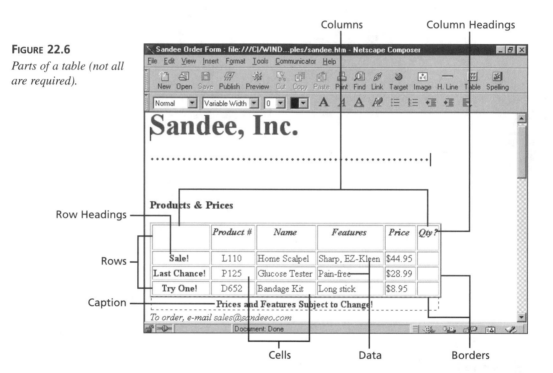

Tables are *transparent*—the page's background color or pattern shows through areas not covered by cell data or borders. However, a table can have its own background (see Figure 22.8), which does not cover the borders or cell data, but does cover the page's background.

You can do a great deal to format tables to your liking. But keep in mind that the precise formatting of your tables is greatly controlled by the browser displaying it.

The height and width of cells are calculated automatically based on the number of columns and the length of the cell content. The width of a column is determined by the width necessary to contain the longest cell data in the column. When the data in a cell is long or when a table has many columns, the cell content may be wrapped automatically to allow the table to fit within the window.

FIGURE 22.7

A table with no visible borders.

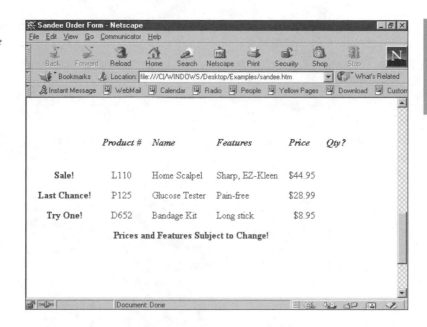

FIGURE 22.8

A table with its own background.

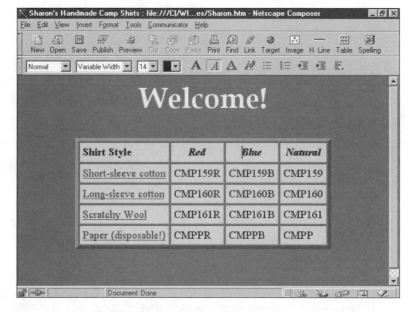

Table Basics

The difficulty of creating tables is directly proportional to how fancy you wanna make 'em. A simple, basic table is a snap, as the following example's show. Fancier tables are a little more trouble (as you learn later in this chapter), but then, shouldn't they be?

Keep your first tables simple and get more creative with tables only when you have the basics down pat. You'll do fine. Here's how you insert a new table:

1. Click at the spot in your page where you want to insert a table.
2. Click the Table button on the Composer toolbar or choose Table, Insert Table (see Figure 22.9).

FIGURE 22.9
Step 2: Click the Table button.

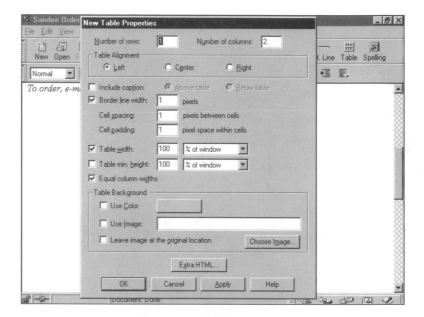

3. In the Number of Rows and Number of Columns boxes, choose the number of rows and columns for the table.
4. Adjust in the dialog box any of the other options you want to change; you'll learn what all these options mean during the remainder of this chapter. (Note that you can ignore these options for now and adjust them later in the Table Properties dialog box, as described later in this chapter.)
5. Click OK (see Figure 22.10).

The dashed lines that show the table borders (see Figure 22.10) and gridlines appear just to show you where your table is—they don't show up when the page is viewed through a browser. That's okay—a table without borders still organizes its contents into rows and columns and can look pretty cool. But if you really want visible borders, you'll learn how to add them later in this chapter.

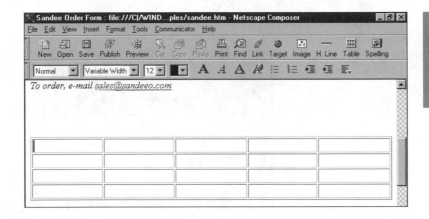

FIGURE 22.10
A new table, ready for content or formatting.

Filling in the Table

Filling in the cells of a table is simple: Just click in the cell and type away, as the following example shows.

When typing in a cell, you can press Enter to start a new paragraph within the cell. You can also apply virtually any type of text formatting you would apply anywhere else in a Web page using the same selection techniques and formatting tools. Specifically, you can apply the following:

- Paragraph styles (normal or heading, for example)
- Fonts and attributes (bold, italic, and color, for example)
- List formatting (bulleted or numbered)
- Alignment (left, right, or center)
- Indenting

The thing to keep in mind about alignment and indenting in table cells is that the formatting is relative to the *cell*, not to the whole page or even the table. For example, if you apply Center alignment to text in a cell, the text is positioned in the center of the cell, not in the center of the table or page.

In addition to being able to put ordinary text in table cells, you can also put pictures and links in them. To add a link, just type the text in the cell, highlight it, and then create the link as you would any other link (see Chapter 23, "Making Links").

To learn how to put pictures in table cells, see Chapter 25.

1. Click in the cell in which you want to type (see Figure 22.11).

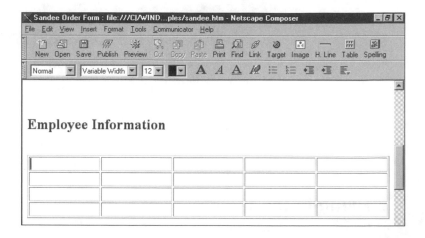

2. Type whatever you want (see Figure 22.12). Observe that the height of the cell expands as necessary to accommodate whatever you type.

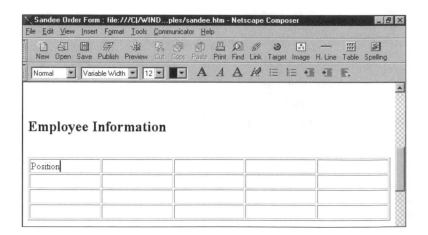

3. Press the Tab key to jump to the next cell (or click in the cell you want to fill next). See Figure 22.13.

Editing and Formatting Tables

So now you've got a table, and you've got formatted text in it. Happy now? If so, congratulations—you're easy to please. If not, note that you can add cool borders to your table, add and delete columns and rows, add a background color, add a table caption above or below the table, and so on.

FIGURE 22.13
Step 3: Press the Tab key to jump to the next cell, and keep typing.

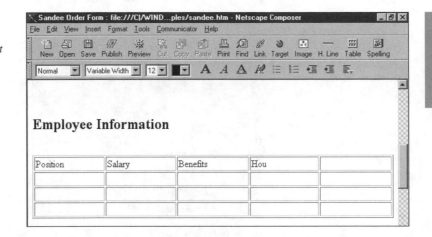

In short, creating the table is only the beginning. You can do so much more, mostly just by changing settings in the Table Properties dialog box (see Figure 22.14), as shown in the following examples.

To experiment with borders, captions, and anything else in the Table Properties dialog box, make any changes in the dialog box and then click the Apply button rather than OK.

The changes are made in the table, but the Table Properties dialog box remains open so that you can try different settings without having to reopen it.

Keep experimenting, clicking Apply each time, and then click OK when you see what you want to keep, or click Cancel to close the dialog box without making any changes to the table.

Because that box is where it all happens, though, first you need to know how to open it. To open the Table Properties dialog box:

1. Click anywhere in the table.
2. Choose Format, Table Properties from the menu bar.

You can also open the Table Properties box by right-clicking on the table and choosing Table Properties from the menu that appears.

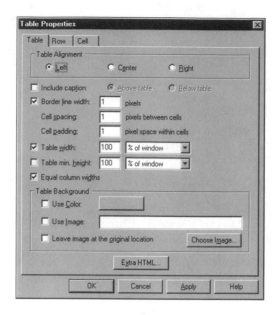

FIGURE 22.14

Use the three tabs of the Table Properties dialog box to change the look of your table.

1. In the Table tab of the Table Properties box, check the check box next to Border Line Width.

2. In the box to the right of Border Line Width, type a number for the width (line thickness). For example, type 4 to create a border that's four pixels wide. The higher the number, the thicker the border. A 1-pixel border is thin and delicate; a 6-pixel border is bold and sassy (see Figure 22.15).

3. Click OK.

Unless you add a background to a table, the page's background color (or background picture) shows through the table (but does not obscure the table's content or borders). But a table can have its own background, different from that of the page, to make the table—and more important, its contents—really stand out.

The following example shows how to give a table its own background color. To learn how to give a table its own background picture, see Chapter 25, "Adding Pictures (and Picture Backgrounds)."

1. In the Table tab of the Table Properties box, check the Use Color check box.

2. Click the button to the right of Use Color to display a list of basic colors to use for the table background (see Figure 22.16).

3. Click the box containing your color choice and then click OK in the Tables Properties dialog box.

FIGURE 22.15
A nice, fat, 6-pixel border.

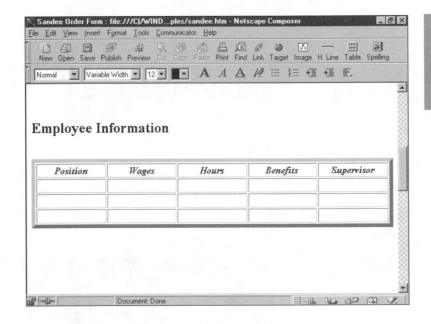

FIGURE 22.16
Step 2: Click the button to the right of Use Color to display a chart of colors to use for your table background.

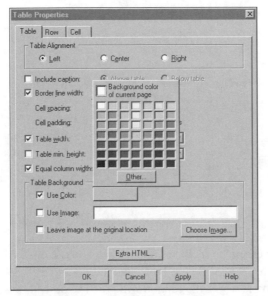

You can use a different background for a selected cell or row than for the rest of the table; for example, you can give the top row its own, unique background color to make column headings stand out.

To begin, click in a cell whose background you want to choose (or any cell in the row or column whose background you want to choose) and open the Table Properties dialog box. Choose the Row tab (to choose a background color for the row) or the Cell tab (to choose a color for a cell). On the tab you selected, check the Use Color check box and choose a color.

Adding a Caption

A *caption* is a title or other label for a table that appears directly above or below the table (see Figure 22.17). Although the text of the caption does not appear within a table cell, the caption is a part of the table—if you move or delete the table, the caption goes with it.

FIGURE 22.17

A caption titles a table.

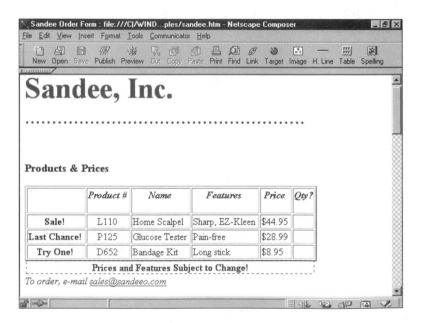

To add a caption, check the Include Caption check box in the Table Properties dialog box, choose Above Table or Below Table, and then click OK. A dashed line (refer to Figure 22.17) appears where the caption will go. (The dashed line shows up only in Composer; it doesn't appear when the page is browsed.) Click in the box and type your caption.

Creating Column and Row Headings

What's a *heading*, anyway? It's text that's formatted differently from the rest of the table data (and maybe also enclosed in cells that are formatted differently) so that it is clearly not meant as table data, but rather as a descriptive label for a row or column (see Figure 22.18).

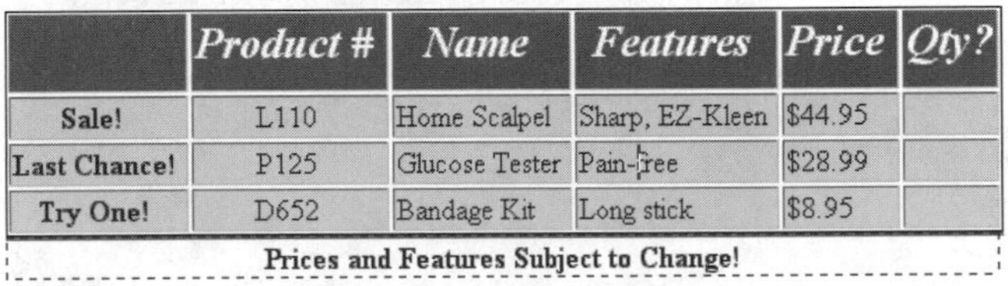

FIGURE 22.18

Apply unique text or cell formatting to a row or column to create headings.

	Product #	Name	Features	Price	Qty?
Sale!	L110	Home Scalpel	Sharp, EZ-Kleen	$44.95	
Last Chance!	P125	Glucose Tester	Pain-free	$28.99	
Try One!	D652	Bandage Kit	Long stick	$8.95	
Prices and Features Subject to Change!					

You can create column or row headings by simply applying unique formatting to the text in the top or bottom rows (column headings) or leftmost or rightmost columns (row headings).

Applying bold or italic, making the font different, increasing the text size, giving the row containing the headings their own background (as you learn to do in the next section), choosing a unique text color, or doing all of the above is an easy way to create headings.

Working with Rows, Columns, and Cells

When you first create a table, as described earlier in this chapter, you choose the number of rows and columns and you get a table that's a nice, regular grid. Often, that's just what you want. But, sometimes, after entering some of your data, you find that you need to add or delete rows or columns or change other aspects of the table's appearance.

In the next few sections, you learn how to manipulate rows, columns, and cells to create precisely the table you want.

Changing the Width or Alignment of a Table

By default, the tables you create fill the full width of the page. You can choose to make your tables narrower than that.

When a table is narrower than the full width of the page, you have another decision to make: alignment. Do you want the table to be positioned along the left side of the page (left alignment), on the right (right alignment), or in the center (center alignment)? The following example shows how to change table width and alignment.

1. Click anywhere in the table and choose Format, Table Properties.

2. To change the width, make sure that the Table Width check box is checked on the Table tab and that the % of Window option is selected in the box to the right of Table Width. Then enter the percentage of the window you want the table to fill (see Figure 22.19). For example, enter 50 to make the table half as wide—50 percent—as the full width of the page.

FIGURE 22.19
Step 2: Change the percentage width.

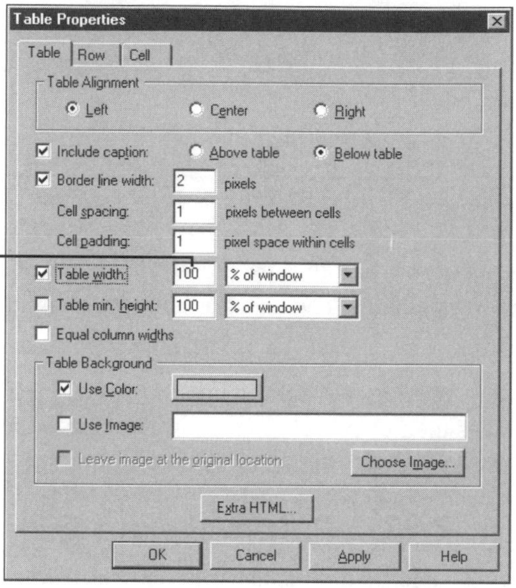

Specify Width Here ———

3. If the width is less than 100 percent, you might select an alignment for the table. By default, tables are left-aligned. To change that, choose an option from the top of the Table tab: Center or Right. Figure 22.20 shows a table with changed width and alignment.

FIGURE 22.20
A changed table: 75 percent wide, center alignment.

	Product	Name	Features	Price	Qty?
Sale!	L110	Home Scalpel	Sharp, EZ-Kleen	$44.95	
Last Chance!	P125	Glucose Tester	Pain-free	$28.99	
Try One!	D652	Bandage Kit	Long stick	$8.95	
Prices and Features Subject to Change!					

When choosing a width, avoid changing the % of Window option to its alternative, pixels. Choosing this option enables you to specify the table width as a number of pixels on a screen rather than as a percentage of the window.

Different monitors and computers running at differing resolutions handle that instruction in unpredictable ways. For example, a table 240 pixels wide appears as about half the width of the screen on a computer configured to use the Windows minimum standard resolution (640×480). But the same table, on a computer configured for higher resolutions, might fill only 30 percent, 25 percent, or even less of the screen. Stick with percentages.

Adding and Deleting Rows and Columns

When entering data, you can jump from cell to cell by pressing the Tab key. The Tab key moves among the cells like a reader's eyes, moving from left to right across a row, and at the end of a row it jumps to the leftmost cell in the row below.

But guess what? When you reach the end of the final row and press Tab, a new row appears with the edit cursor positioned in its leftmost cell, ready for a cell entry. This feature enables you to define your table without knowing exactly how many rows it will have. You can simply keep entering data and using Tab to move forward until all the data has been entered. As you go, Composer keeps adding rows as they are needed.

Of course, you might sometimes want to add columns or add new rows between existing rows rather than at the bottom of the table. The following example shows how.

1. Click in a row directly above or below where you want the new row to appear, or in a column directly to the left or right of where you want the new column.

2. Choose Insert, Table, as shown in Figure 22.21.

3. Choose Row (to add a new row) or Column (to add a column).

To delete a whole table, click anywhere in the table and choose Edit, Delete Table, Table.

To delete rows or columns, always begin by positioning the edit cursor anywhere in the row or column you want to delete. Choose Edit, Delete Table and then choose Row or Column from the menu that appears.

FIGURE 22.21

Step 2: Choose Insert, Table.

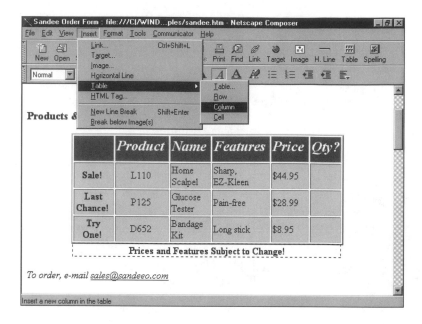

When you delete rows or columns, keep in mind the following:

- Any data in the deleted row or column is deleted too.
- When you delete a row, rows below it shift upward to fill the gap.
- When you delete a column, rows to the right shift to the left to fill the gap.

Turning Table-Type Text to a Table

Say that you've already got some text—for example, rows and columns of text you've cut and pasted into Composer from another document, such as a word processing document. Using the Composer Tabelize feature, you can transform that text into a table in a snap.

To use Tabelize, the text must already be arranged in rows and columns. Each "row" of the text must end in a carriage return, just as if you had pressed Enter at the end of each line, to break the line. The columns might be formed by spaces or commas between what would be the contents of each cell.

For example, the following text uses spaces to form its columns (this formatting works best when each cell contains only a single word):

Blue Orange Gray

Purple Red Yellow

Aqua Maroon Fuchsia

When cells can contain two or more words, commas are used to mark the columns:

Mark Antony, Cleopatra, Julius Caesar

Romeo, King Lear, Hamlet

The following example shows how to tabelize this type of text.

1. Create or copy-and-paste the text in Composer.

2. Select the text to be tabelized (see Figure 22.22).

FIGURE 22.22

Step 2: Select the text to be tabelized.

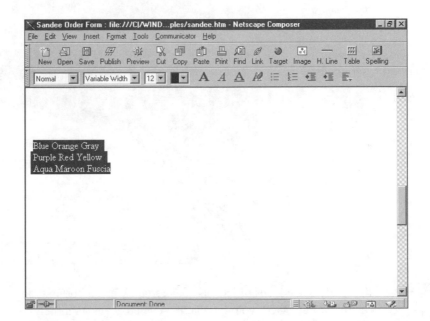

3. From the menu bar, choose Tools, Tabelize.

4. Choose By Commas (if commas separate the columns) or By Spaces (if spaces separate the columns). The result appears in Figure 22.23.

FIGURE 22.23

A table from text.

Blue	Orange	Gray
Purple	Red	Yellow
Aqua	Maroon	Fuscia

Using a Big Table to Control Page Layout

As you move along through this book, you find that it's very difficult to control the exact location of objects in a Web page, the way you would in a desktop publishing program.

Generally, you must settle for positioning pictures and paragraphs in rough association with another, leaving it up to the visitor's browser to arrange the page.

A popular way to get around this limitation is to create a table that fills the entire page and then put all the page's contents in table cells (see Figure 22.24). This approach gives you much better control of where objects appear in relation to one another.

FIGURE 22.24

The dashed lines displayed by Composer reveal that this whole page is a table, which keeps the page elements neatly organized.

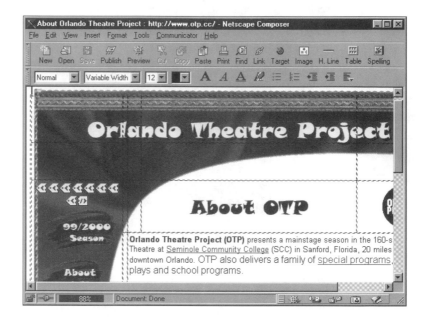

If you use some kinds of templates or certain Web authoring programs (such as Microsoft Publisher), you find that these approaches might rely heavily on tables for page layout. For example, if you create a layout in Publisher and then use the Publisher tools to convert the layout into a Web page, you will discover that the resulting page is a big table. Publisher does this to preserve the organization of the page as faithfully as possible.

You needn't do anything special to use a big table for page layout. Just start with a blank, empty page and then insert a table. Use the Table Properties dialog box to make the table's width 100 percent of the window. The new table takes up the full width of the page, and its height expands as you add the page's contents to the cells.

When pages are formatted with tables this way, borders typically are not used. But you can add the borders if you want to. It's your page.

Advanced Web authoring tools, such as Macromedia Dreamweaver and Microsoft FrontPage, do enable you to precisely position text and graphics in a Web page (without using a table), just as you would in a desktop publishing program. In FrontPage, this capability is called *absolute positioning*.

The downside of absolute positioning is that it relies on a less-than-well-standardized set of technologies, collectively called Dynamic HTML (DHTML), that are supported in Internet Explorer 5 and in Netscape Navigator 4–6, but barely supported anywhere else.

If you use absolute positioning or other DHTML tools, but still want your Web pages accessible to everybody, you must offer two versions of your pages online: One for those using browsers that support DHTML and another (without absolute positioning) for everybody else.

Summary

A simple table is a simple deal. And that's the best way to start—simple. Don't get wrapped up in long, complex tables too soon. Try sticking with simple tables of just a dozen cells or so, not just because it's a good way to learn, but also because big, hairy tables defeat their own purpose: They confuse visitors rather than inform them. Eventually, you move up the table growth curve to tougher, smarter table techniques.

CHAPTER 23

Making Links

Links are one of the great mysteries of Web authoring. Everything else is up front and visible; everything else just has to look right. A link, on the other hand, has to do something—it has to act right. Links are mysterious because what they do when they are activated is not immediately visible to the naked eye.

Fortunately, creating links is surprisingly simple. The only tricky part is correctly phrasing the underlying URL. With an eye toward the real linking pitfalls, this chapter shows what links are all about.

This chapter assumes that you have already installed Netscape Communicator 4.7 and its built-in Web-authoring program, Composer. If you have not, visit `http://wp.netscape.com/download/archive.html` and download Netscape Communicator version 4.7 for your system. (It's free.)

More recent versions of Netscape and Composer are available, as well. Although the exact steps for some features may differ slightly, you'll have little difficulty finding your way around a newer version of Composer using the material in this book.

What's in a Link?

Every link has two parts. Creating links is a simple matter of choosing a spot on the page for the link and then supplying both parts:

- **The link text**—the actual text (or graphic) that appears on the page to represent the link. When a visitor activates a link, he or she clicks the link text to activate the unseen URL underneath.

- **The link location**—the URL describing the page, file, or Internet service to be accessed when the link is activated.

You can create menus or directories of links, like those shown in Figure 23.1, by making each link a separate line in a list. But links don't have to be on separate lines, as Figure 23.1 shows. You can use any words or phrases in your page as links, including headings (or words in headings), words in body text paragraphs, list items, or even single characters in any paragraph property.

FIGURE 23.1

Links (underlined) in text and by themselves in a menu.

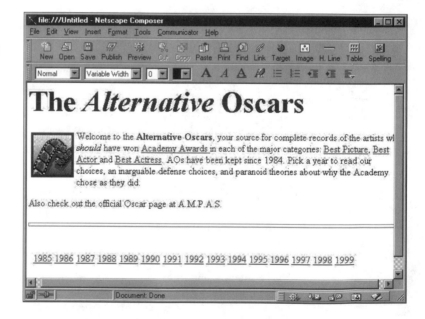

The link text takes on the paragraph properties of the text it is inserted into or closest to, but you can change the paragraph properties of the link text at any time, just as you would for any other text. The underlying link is undisturbed by such changes.

What's Linkable?

A link can point to any resource that can be expressed in a URL or to *local files* (files residing on the same server as the page containing the link). That includes not only remote Web pages and other pages and files residing on the same Web server as your document, but also newsgroups and articles within them, email messages, and FTP servers. In your travels on the Web, you've already encountered links pointing to all these types of resources.

A link can point to a specific location within a Web page—even to a specific location within the same page containing the link. For example, in a long Web page, each entry in a table of contents can be a link pointing to a specific section of the page (see Figure 23.2). This concept allows visitors to navigate quickly and easily within the page. The spots within pages to which a link can point are *anchors*.

FIGURE 23.2

A menu (table of contents) made up of links to pages within the same document or site.

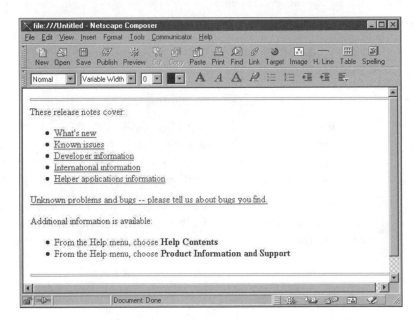

To create a link, you use the same procedure regardless of the type of resource to which the link points. However, for each type of resource, you must consider certain issues when composing the URL for the link. The next several sections describe in detail the special considerations for each type of URL.

Web Pages

Web pages are the most commonly linked resource, and for good reason: You can bet that anybody viewing your Web page can view any other Web page, so links to Web pages are a reliable way to provide information. Linking to Web pages also allows your visitors to apply a consistent set of navigation techniques.

URLs pointing to Web pages always begin with the protocol designator `http://`. The protocol is followed by the Web server hostname, the directory path to the page file, and the actual HTML file of the page:

```
http://hostname/pathname/file.HTM
```

In some cases, you can omit the filename. Some Web servers have default files they display automatically whenever someone accesses the server or a directory without specifying a filename. For example,

```
http://www.mcp.com/
```

accesses the default page for the server `www.mcp.com`, and

```
http://www.mcp.com/sams/
```

accesses the default page for the directory `sams` on the server `www.mcp.com`.

Note that the preceding directory examples end in a slash. You should always use a slash to end an HTTP URL that does not end with a filename; the slash instructs the server to access the default file (usually `INDEX.HTML`). Some servers can still access the default file if you leave off the slash, but some don't. In a link, use the slash, for safety's sake.

Finally, always be careful to follow the exact capitalization of the URL as it would appear in the Navigator Location box when you view the page. Many Web servers are case sensitive and don't recognize the directory or filename if it is not properly capitalized.

Anchors in Pages

Web pages can contain predefined locations to which links can point. These spots are called anchors in HTML (and are created with the `<a>` tag—*A* for anchor).

You can add anchors to your own Web pages and then link to those anchors from elsewhere in the same page or from other pages you create. In addition, you can create links to point to any existing anchors in other pages on the Web.

When you create an anchor, give the anchor a name. You create links to anchors as you do to a Web page, with one difference: You add the name of the anchor to the URL you enter for the link.

You can use a *relative pathname* to point to an anchor in another file stored on the same server (to link from one page of a multipage document to an anchor in another page in the document, for example). See the following section, "Local Files."

Local Files

Just as you can link to resources on any server, you can link to resources residing on the same server as your Web document. Obviously, you would do this when linking among the pages of a multipage presentation. But you might also choose to link to anything on your local Web server that relates to the topic of your page, such as another Web document or a text file containing related information.

 Technically, the pathnames you enter to create links to local files are not URLs. When you're creating a link, however, you enter these pathnames in the same place you would enter a URL for linking to a remote resource. That's why I refer to them generically as *URLs*.

When you phrase the URLs to create links to local resources, you have to consider the differences between *relative* pathnames and *absolute* pathnames.

Relative Pathnames

Relative pathnames include only the information necessary to find the linked resource from the document containing the link. In other words, the path given to the file is *relative* to the file containing the link; from outside that file, the information supplied as the URL for the link is insufficient to locate the file.

Suppose that all the pages of your multipage document share the same directory on the server and that one of those pages is named FLORIDA.HTM. To link from any page in your document to FLORIDA.HTM, you need to enter only the filename as the URL for the link; for example:

FLORIDA.HTM

Suppose that all pages except the top page reside in a folder or directory named STATES and that this folder is within the same folder containing the top page. To link from the top page to FLORIDA.HTM in the STATES directory, you would enter the directory and filename, separated by a slash; for example:

STATES/FLORIDA.HTM

This approach works as far into the folder hierarchy as you want. Just be sure to separate each step in the path with a slash. For a file several levels beneath the file containing the link, you might enter

`ENVIRO/US/STATES/FLORIDA.HTM`

Suppose that you're linking from a page lower in the directory hierarchy to a page that's higher. To do this, you must describe a path that moves up in the hierarchy. As in DOS (and in FTP servers), a double period (..) is used in a path to move up one level. For example, let's create a link from the FLORIDA page back to the top page (call it TOP.HTM), which you can assume is one level above FLORIDA. For the URL portions of the link, you would enter

`../TOP.HTM`

If TOP.HTM were three levels above FLORIDA, you would type

`../../../TOP.HTM`

Use relative pathnames to link together the pages of a multipage document on your PC. Because the paths are relative, when you publish that document to a server, the interpage links still work properly. See Chapter 24, "Using Links to Build a Web Site."

Finally, suppose that you want to link to a local file that resides in a folder that is not above or below the file containing the link but is elsewhere in the hierarchy. This link would require a path that moves up the hierarchy and then down a different branch to the file. In such a case, you use the double periods to move up and then specify the full directory path down to the file.

Suppose that you want to link from

`ENVIRO/US/STATES/FLORIDA.HTM`

to

`ENVIRO/CANADA/PROVINCE/QUEBEC.HTM`

The phrasing you need is

`../../../CANADA/PROVINCE/QUEBEC.HTM`

The three sets of double periods move up to the ENVIRO directory; then the path down from ENVIRO to QUEBEC.HTM follows.

On DOS and Windows systems, a relative or absolute path might include the letter of the hard drive, but it must be followed by a vertical bar (|) rather than the standard colon; for example:

`C|/STATS/ENVIRO/CANADA/PROVINCE/QUEBEC.HTM`

Absolute Pathnames

Absolute pathnames give the complete path to a file, beginning with the top level of the directory hierarchy of the system. Absolute pathnames are not portable from one system to another. In other words, while composing a multipage document on your PC, you can use absolute pathnames in links among the pages. However, after you publish that document, all the links become invalid because the server's directory hierarchy is not identical to your PC's.

In general, you use absolute pathnames only when linking to specific local resources (other than your own pages), such as FAQs, residing on the server where your page will be published.

Absolute pathnames are phrased just like relative pathnames, except that they always begin with a slash (/) and they always contain the full path from the top of the directory hierarchy to the file; for example:

`/STATS/ENVIRO/CANADA/PROVINCE/QUEBEC.HTM`

Other Internet Services

In addition to Web pages and their anchors, links can point to any other browser-accessible servers. But before linking to anything other than a Web page or an anchor, keep in mind that not all browsers—and, hence, not all visitors—can access all these other server types.

Nearly all browsers can handle FTP. Less common is mail access, and even less common is newsgroup access. Netscape Navigator has native support for both. Other browsers open helper applications for mail. For example, Internet Explorer opens Outlook Express when a mailto or news link is activated. Still, many browsers have no news or mail access.

FTP

Using a link to an FTP server, you can point to a directory or to a specific file. If the link points to a directory, clicking the link displays the list of files and subdirectories there (see Figure 23.3), and each listing is itself a link the visitor can click to navigate the

23

directories or download a file. If the link points to a file, the file is downloaded to the
visitor's PC when he or she activates the link.

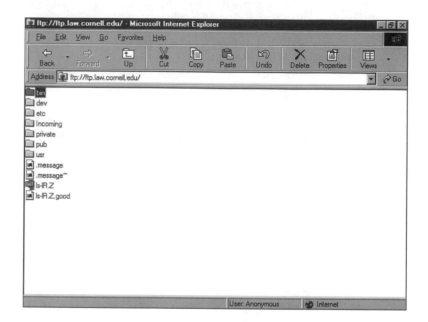

 If you create a link to an HTML file residing on an FTP server, clicking the
link downloads the file and displays it, just as though it were on a Web
server.

To link to an anonymous FTP server, use the protocol designator `ftp://`, followed by the
name of the FTP server, the path, and the filename (if you are linking to a file), as the
following examples show:

- `\ftp://ftp.zdnet.com`—Links to the ZDNet anonymous FTP server and displays the
  top-level directory

- `ftp://ftp.zdnet.com/pub`—Links to the ZDNet anonymous FTP server and displays
  the contents of the PUB directory

- `ftp://ftp.zdnet.com/pub/pcmag/support.txt`—Links to the ZDNet anonymous FTP
  server and downloads the file SUPPORT.DOC from the PCMAG directory

Observe that you do not end an FTP URL with a slash when linking to a directory. This technique differs from an HTTP URL, where a slash is always advisable except when accessing a specific HTML file.

You can link to non-anonymous, password-protected FTP servers. However, in most cases, these types of servers have been set up precisely to prevent public access. A URL to a non-anonymous FTP server includes a username and password for accessing that server, so anyone who accesses your page can access the FTP server—or read the URL activated by the link to learn the password.

Obviously, you should never create a link to a non-anonymous server unless you have express permission to do so from the server's administrators. Getting such permission is unlikely.

To link to a non-anonymous FTP server for which you have permission to publish a link, you phrase the URL exactly as you would for anonymous FTP, except that you insert the username and password (separated by a colon) and an @ sign between the protocol and the path, as shown in the following line:

```
ftp://username:password@ftp.mcp.com/pub/secrets.doc
```

This URL downloads the file secrets.doc from a password-protected server for which the username and password in the URL are valid.

23

News

A link can open a newsgroup article list or point to a specific article within that list. Although both newsgroups and the articles they carry come and go, a link to the article list might be valid for years. On the other hand, a link to a specific article might be valid for only a few days—until the article ages past the server's time limit for newsgroup messages, at which point the article is automatically deleted from the server.

Thus, the best use of news links is to point to the article list of a newsgroup whose topic relates to that of the Web document. If a newsgroup contains an article that you want to make a long-term part of the page, copy the article into a separate file and link to that file or simply copy it into a Web page.

Before copying a news article into a page, check for copyright notices in the article. Whether the article is copyrighted or not, email the author and request permission to use the article.

To link to a newsgroup to display the current article list, use the protocol designator `news:` followed by the name of the newsgroup. (Note that a `news:` URL omits the double slashes used in HTTP, and FTP.) For example, the following are valid news links:

```
news:alt.video.dvd
```

or

```
news:news.announce.newusers
```

To link to an article, find the message ID in the article's header; it's often enclosed between carats (< and >) or labeled *Message ID* by most newsreaders (see Figure 23.4). (Exactly how it appears depends on which newsreader program you use.)

FIGURE 23.4

A news article header in Outlook Express, showing the message ID (it's labeled "Message-ID" and appears about halfway down the list).

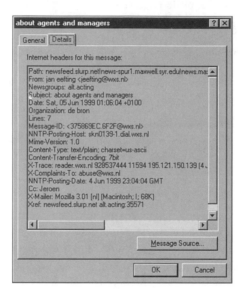

To phrase the URL, use the protocol designator `news:` followed by the message ID. Note that you do not include the carats, and you do not need to include the newsgroup name in the URL.

Mail

Mail URLs can be the most difficult to goof up. You enter `mailto:` followed by an email address. That's it. (Note that a `mailto:` URL omits the double slashes used in HTTP, FTP, and Gopher URLs.) For example,

```
mailto:nsnell@mailserver.com
```

Before putting an email address other than your own in a link, ask permission from the addressee.

The most common use of mailto: links is in a signature at the bottom of a page. But you can use a mailto: link anywhere it makes sense to offer your readers a way to contact you or someone else.

Follow these steps to explore the way the links you see online are phrased:

1. Connect to the Internet and open your Web browser. (Use either the Netscape Navigator browser included with this book or Internet Explorer. These steps may not work with other browsers.)

2. Go to any page you like and locate a link on it.

3. Point to the link (don't click) and then look in the status bar at the bottom of the browser window. The URL to which the link point appears there, shown exactly as it is phrased in the HTML file.

4. Explore other links this way. In Web pages you visit regularly, try to find links to

   - Other Web pages
   - Anchors
   - Files
   - FTP directories
   - Email addresses

Creating New Links

Creating a new hyperlink is a two-part job:

1. First, you create the link text, the text that a visitor would click to activate the link.

2. Next, you attach the URL to the link text.

The following example shows how easy it is to create a new link to a Web page:

1. Type and format the text that will serve as the link text (see Figure 23.5).

2. Select the text (see Figure 23.6).

23

FIGURE 23.5

Step 1: Type the link text.

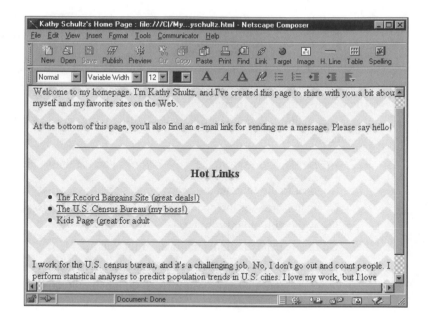

Although you can apply character formatting (such as fonts or italics) to the link text you create, don't do it. Just apply the paragraph style you want to use and leave it at that.

Browsers usually display link text with unique formatting (usually underlining and a blue color) to help visitors instantly identify links on a page. You don't want your character formatting to make finding links tricky for your visitors by changing the link text formatting they're accustomed to seeing.

3. Click the Link button on the Standard toolbar (see Figure 23.7).

4. In the box labeled Link To, type the complete URL (see Figure 23.8). Be sure to include the `http://` part at the beginning. Then click OK.

You can use a picture as link text so that clicking the picture activates the link (see Chapter 25).

You can even put multiple links in one picture so that clicking each part of the picture leads to a different place. You learn how to do this in Chapter 29, "Putting Multiple Links in One Picture."

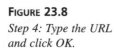

FIGURE 23.6
Step 2: Select the link text.

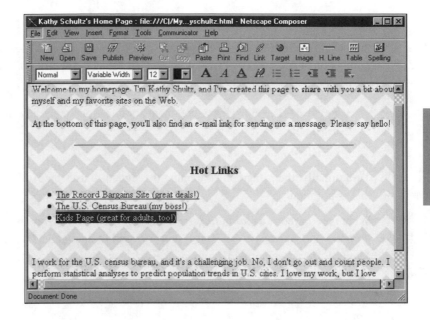

23

Link Button

FIGURE 23.7
Step 3: Click the Link button.

FIGURE 23.8
Step 4: Type the URL and click OK.

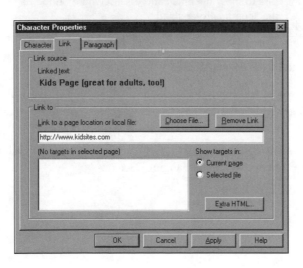

Creating a Signature (Linking to Email)

A *signature* is nothing more than some sort of generic sign-off message that has an email address embedded within it. A few stock wording choices—in popular flavors—are

- **Inviting**—Comments? Questions? Email me at `nsnell@mailserver.com`.
- **Formal**—If you have any comments or questions regarding this page, contact `nsnell@mailserver.com`.
- **Efficient**—Feedback: `nsnell@mailserver.com`.

Traditionally, the paragraph containing the signature uses the Address property, although that is not required.

What is required is a *mailto link*—a link that, when clicked, opens the visitor's email program and starts a new message, preaddressed to an email address specified in the link. Mailto links let you provide your visitors with an easy way to contact you (or anyone else you choose).

> When you create the link text of a mailto link, the text does not have to show the exact email address because most visitors' email programs use the right address automatically when they click the link. So you may choose text such as "Contact Me," rather than your email address.
>
> However, some visitors use Internet software that doesn't support mailto links; these visitors see the link text okay, but nothing happens when they click it. So when you choose not to use the email address as the link text, be sure to show the email address elsewhere on the page, for the benefit of the "non-mailto-enabled."

Here's how to create a signature:

1. Click where you want the signature to be located (usually at or near the end of the page) and type the signature message, including the email address (see Figure 23.9).

2. Select some text in the message—your name or an email address—to serve as link text for the mailto link (see Figure 23.10).

3. Click the Link button.

FIGURE 23.9

Step 1: Type the signature.

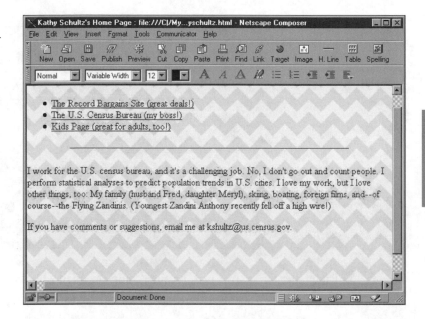

FIGURE 23.10

Step 2: Select the part of the signature that will be an email link.

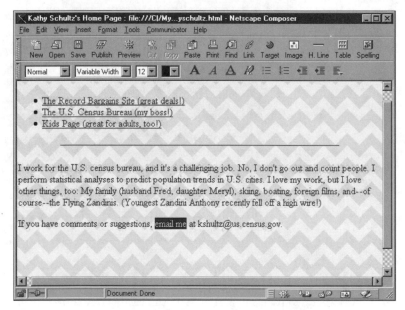

4. In the Link Location box, type `mailto:` (see Figure 23.11).

FIGURE 23.11
Step 4: Type mailto:
to start the URL.

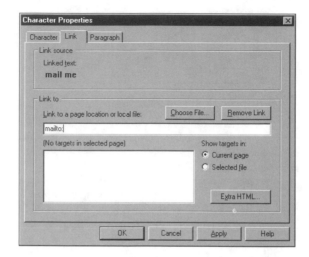

5. Right after the mailto: part, type the complete email address and click OK (see Figure 23.12).

FIGURE 23.12
Step 5: Type the email address.

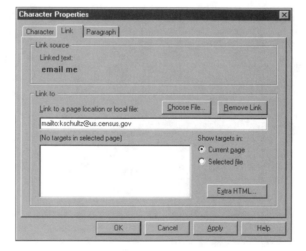

Copying Links from Other Pages

Anywhere you see a hyperlink, you can easily copy it from your Web browser right into a Composer page by using copy-and-paste techniques.

In fact, a page you've just accessed on the Web makes the most reliable source for a link. If you copy a file's URL while viewing it and paste it as a link into a page you're creating, you can trust that the link will probably work properly (until and unless the page or other resource is moved or removed).

Sources for copying links include

- The Address box in your browser (where the URL of the current page appears)
- The Bookmarks list (in Navigator) or the Favorites list (in Internet Explorer)
- The header of a news article in your Internet newsreader program
- The header of a mail message in your email program
- Any link appearing in a Web page

When copying a link into your page, keep in mind the following:

- The link text may or may not be copied, depending on what browser you use; instead, the link text that appears in Composer might sometimes be the URL itself. To give the link a name to appear instead of its URL, edit the link as described later in this chapter (see the section "Editing Links.")
- The link takes on the paragraph properties of the paragraph in which it is inserted or the one closest to it. Remember, though, that a link can accept any paragraph properties or character properties— although in most browsers, the character properties cannot override the default way that links are displayed. That's a good thing because you don't want your formatting to disguise the fact that a link is a link.

Copying and pasting, in case you've forgotten, is a two-part deal. First, you copy something to the Windows Clipboard, and then you paste it from the Clipboard into the place you want it to go. You can accomplish each half of the job in several ways. You have several ways to copy and several to paste, and you can combine any copy method with any paste method and get the same results.

To copy:

- **A link to the Web page appearing in your browser (Netscape or Internet Explorer)**—Right-click the URL in the Address box and then choose Copy from the menu that appears (see Figure 23.13).
- **A link shown in a Web page**—Right-click the link and choose Copy Link Location, if Navigator is your browser, or Copy Shortcut, if Internet Explorer is your browser (see Figure 23.14).

FIGURE 23.13

Copying a link to the current Web page.

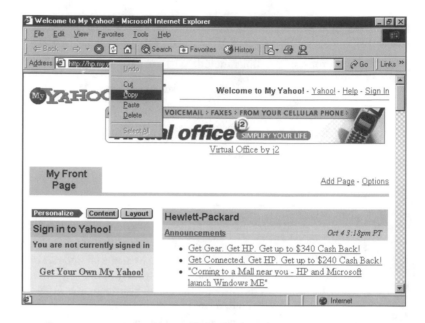

FIGURE 23.14

Copying a link from a link in a Web page.

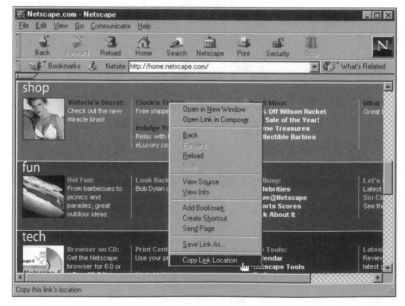

• **A link appearing in the Navigator Bookmarks list or the Internet Explorer Favorites list**—Right-click the desired bookmark and choose Copy Location from the menu.

- **A link appearing in the header of a news or mail message**—Open the message and locate the desired link in the message header. Right-click the link and choose Copy Link Location.

To paste a link from the Clipboard into your page, do the following:

1. Create and select the link text as usual, and then click the Link button.

2. Press Ctrl+V to copy the URL into the Link Location box.

Checking That Links Lead Where They're Supposed To

When you've created links that lead from your page to other pages online, the only way to make absolutely sure that links lead where they're supposed to is to test the links online, after you've published your page. Still, you can do a reliable prepublishing link check at any time, right from within Composer:

1. Connect to the Internet, open Composer, and open the page file whose links you want to test.

2. Click the Browse button to preview the current page in Navigator.

3. Click any links in the page to see whether they work.

> Even if your links work, be careful to test them again, online, after you have published your page.
>
> You learn more about testing your links in Chapter 30, "Publishing Your Page."

Editing Links

You can change anything about a link: the link text, the URL, the type of link, and more. That's handy if you decide to change the wording of the link text or if you need to update a link when the URL of the page it leads to changes:

- To change link text, just edit the text any way you want. Usually, the link behind the source is undisturbed by the editing. If, after editing the source, you see that the link is gone or that it is not connected any more to the exact words you want, just highlight the text and re-create the link.

23

- To change the URL or any other "behind the scenes" aspect of a link, right-click the link and choose Link Properties from the menu that appears (see Figure 23.15). On the dialog box that appears, change what needs changing, and click OK.

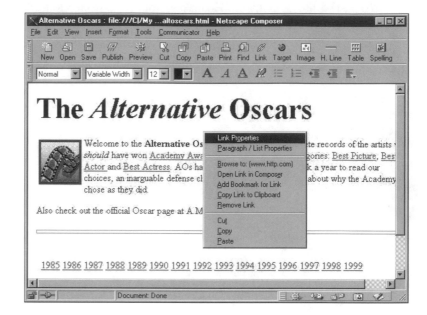

Delinking Text

Suppose that you want to remove a link from your page and keep its link text on the page. You could simply delete the link and retype the text. That's a solution for a link or two, but if you want to kill all the links in a large section or in an entire page, all the retyping would be tedious.

The following example shows how to revert a link into ordinary text on the page.

1. Select the link, or select an entire section of a page containing multiple links you want to remove (see Figure 23.16).

2. Right-click the selection and choose Remove Link or Remove All Links in Selection from the menu that appears (see Figure 23.17).

FIGURE 23.16
Step 1: Select the link or links.

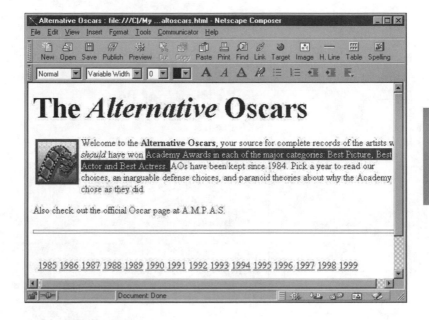

FIGURE 23.17
Step 2: Right-click and choose Remove Link.

Understanding Targets

A *target* is a hidden HTML tag—hidden in that it is not visible to the visitor, but is visible to you in Composer (see Figure 23.18) so that you can see where you put it. In Composer, a target in a file is indicated by a target icon, as shown in Figure 23.18).

The target icons used to indicate a target location are visible in Composer only when you are working in Normal Edit mode. In Preview mode, the targets are invisible, just as they would be to a visitor browsing your page.

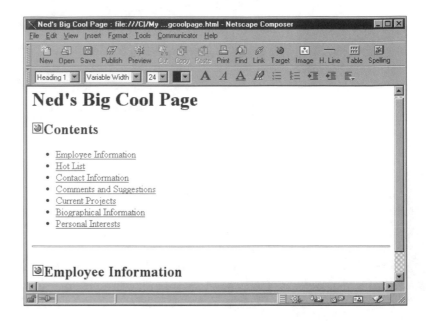

A target provides a location in a page that a link can point to; clicking the link takes a visitor to that exact spot rather than just to the top of the page. A single page can have many targets, each one with a unique name so that a link can point to one and only one particular target. The link that points to a target can be in either the same page the target is in or another page.

Why use targets? Several common scenarios involve long Web pages where, without targets, the visitor would have to do lots of scrolling to locate particular information on a page:

- At the top of a very long Web page (such as a Frequently Asked Questions, or FAQ, file), you can include a list of links, each of which points to a different part of the file. The links enable the visitor to jump easily to any part of the file rather than have to scroll through it to find a particular section.

- You might want to use targets when links on one page refer to particular parts of another page that happens to be a long one. The links can point to targets in the long page, to take the visitor directly there in one click.

- In a frames-based page (see Chapter 27, "Dividing a Page into Frames"), links in one frame can bring up particular parts of a file displayed in another frame. Like the other techniques, this one reduces the visitor's need to scroll, making a Web site easier to navigate.

Creating Targets in a Page

Before you can begin linking to targets, you must insert those targets in the page. The following example shows how to insert targets in a page in Composer. Note that you can choose from two basic methods: Create a target that marks a spot, and create a target that marks certain text.

Which method should you use and when? It doesn't make much difference.

Attaching targets to text makes the most sense when each section where you want to put a target begins with a unique heading, as in a FAQ. When that's the case, attaching targets to text saves you the extra step of having to name your targets.

However, the text must be different for each target in the page; no two targets in a file can share the same name.

1. Click at a spot where you want a link to lead, or select the text to which you want a target attached.

If you select text when performing step 1, make sure that your selection does not include a paragraph mark. If it does, you find that the Target Properties dialog box doesn't let you create the target.

To avoid selecting a paragraph character, don't run the selection all the way to the end of a line. (Make sure that the selection ends with a character.)

2. Click the Target button on the Composition toolbar (see Figure 23.19).

Target Button

FIGURE 23.19
Step 2: Click Target.

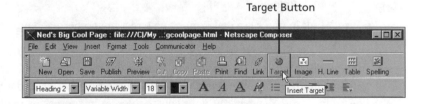

3. Type a name for this target and click OK (see Figure 23.20).

23

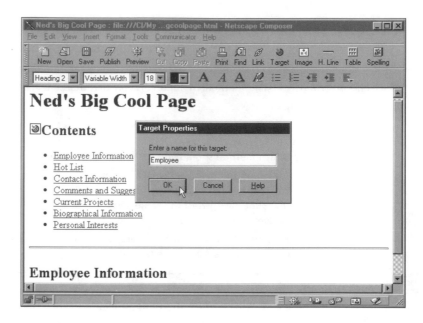

FIGURE 23.20

Step 3: Name the target and then click OK.

Deleting Targets

To delete a target, click the target icon to select it and press the Del key. If the target was attached to text, the text remains, but the target is gone.

Linking to Targets

You can create three kinds of links that point to targets:

- A link within the same page as the target to which it points.
- A link in one page that points to a target in another page in a multipage Web site you're creating in Composer.
- A link in one page that points to a target in another page online that's not one of yours.

In the following pages, you will learn how to link to targets in the same page and to targets in other pages online. See Chapter 24, "Using Links to Build a Web Site," to learn how to link from one page of your own to a target in another page of your own.

In Chapter 25, "Adding Pictures (and Picture Backgrounds)," you learn not only how to add pictures to your pages, but also how to use a picture as a link.

> I'm jumping ahead a little, therefore, getting into pictures here, but I should tell you now that links using any type of link source—text, pictures, or even multilink imagemaps (see Chapter 29, "Putting Multiple Links in One Picture")—can point to targets.

Linking to a Target in the Same Page

In Composer, creating links to targets in the same file is easier if you have only one file open, so that's where you begin, in the following example.

> As shown earlier in this chapter, putting a table of contents at the top of a long page is customary, with each entry in the TOC linking to a target in a section of the page.
>
> If you create a long page of this type, you should also put a link on every section that jumps back to the TOC so that visitors can easily jump back and forth from the TOC to different sections.
>
> Put a target right over the TOC, and insert a link at every section that points back to that target, to get visitors back to the top.

1. Create and select the link text, as you would when creating any kind of link, and then click the Link button.

2. A list of targets in the current page appears in the box labeled Select a named target. Click the name of the target you want the link to point to, and then click OK (see Figure 23.21).

> The list of targets is organized alphabetically, by target name, so find the target you want by name. Don't assume that the targets are listed in the same order in which they appear in the page—from top to bottom, unless you were careful when naming them to alphabetize them or number them consecutively, from top to bottom.

Linking to Targets in Other Pages Online

The easiest way to link to a target in someone else's page online is to find on that page a link that points to the target to which you want to link. For example, if you want to link to a particular part of a FAQ file online, find in the FAQ's table of contents a link that points to that part. Then copy that link from the Web page into your own page using copy and paste.

FIGURE 23.21

Step 2: Choose a target from the list.

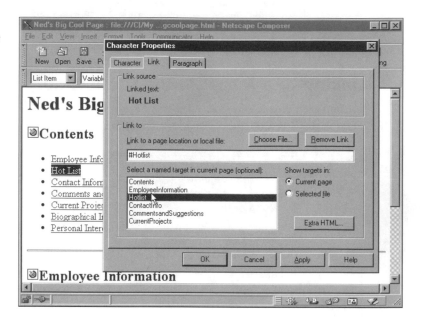

FIGURE 23.21

Step 2: Choose a target from the list.

As always, when linking to pages that are not your own, you should email the Webmaster of the page to which you want to link and ask whether it's okay.

Some Webmasters might say that it's okay to link to the page, but not to targets within the page. This situation might happen when the page contains advertising or other information that the Webmaster wants all visitors to see; linking to targets would allow them to bypass this type of material.

Another method is to learn the target's exact URL, which is made up of the page's URL, a pound sign (#), and the target name. For example, the following URL:

```
http://www.test.com/sample.htm#target1
```

points to a target named target1 in a page file named sample.htm on a server named www.test.com.

The easiest way to learn the URLs of targets in an online document is to browse to the document in your Web browser and find in that document the links that point to the targets. When you point to a link (don't click), the status bar at the bottom of the browser window (in Navigator or Internet Explorer) shows the full URL to which that link points—including the target name.

After you know the complete URL, you can create a link to it like any other link to a Web page, by typing it in the URL box in the Link tab of the Character Properties dialog box (see Figure 23.22).

23

FIGURE 23.22

You can enter a URL that includes a target name directly in the Link tab on the Character Properties dialog box.

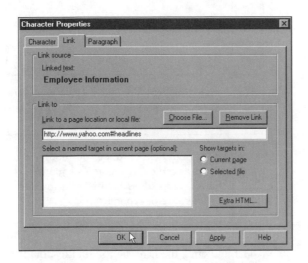

Creating Links that Download Files

You might have content that you want to offer your visitors, but don't want to turn into a Web page. For example, if you have a long story, report, or other document in a word processing file, you might want to offer that file for downloading rather than turn it into a Web page (or series of Web pages).

You can offer any kind of computer file for downloading—documents, sound clips, or pictures, for example. The steps for creating links to files are the same—no matter what type of file you want to offer—as the following example shows.

One caveat to keep in mind: To use a file you provide, the visitor must have the right program. For example, if you publish a Word file, the visitor must have a program that can display (or convert) Word files to view it. You cannot do much about this situation, except to try to offer only popular, widely used file types, such as Word (.doc) for documents, .avi for video clips, or .wav for sound clips.

1. Get the file to which you want to link, and move or copy it to the folder where your Web page files are stored.

Figure 23.23

Step 1: Put the file in the same folder as the Web page file.

2. In the Web page in Composer, type and format the link text as usual.

In the link text (or right next to it), be courteous and tell your visitors the file type (so that they can tell whether it's a file they're equipped to view) and size (so that they can "guesstimate" how long it will take to download at the speed of their Internet connection).

3. Select the link text and click the Link button on the Composition toolbar.

4. Click the Choose File button (see Figure 23.24).

Figure 23.24

Step 4: Click Choose File.

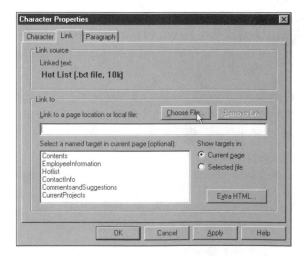

5. Use the dialog box to browse to the file you want this link to download, select that filename, and click Open (see Figure 23.25).

FIGURE 23.25

Step 5: Browse to the file.

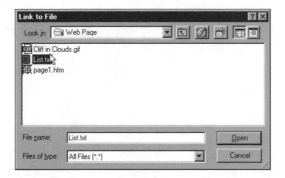

When you publish this Web page online, you must remember to also publish the file to which the link points and make sure that it's stored in the same directory online as the page containing the link; otherwise, the link doesn't work.

Summary

Just because you can link everywhere doesn't mean that you should, Pages with extraneous links are no more useful than linkless ones. Carefully check out each place to which you will link. Is it really useful to your readers? Does it provide something new or simply duplicate material your other links already lead to? Does it appear to be on a reliable server or on one that's often inaccessible or slow?

Your goal should not be to provide your readers with as many links as possible, but rather with a choice selection. And you know that you must check, update, and add to your links often. Do that, and your visitors will return often.

CHAPTER **24**

Using Links to Build a Web Site

There are pages, and then there are *sites*—groups of pages linked together. (The term *Web site* is also used to refer to the server on which those pages are published.)

Without carefully created links and targets, a set of Web pages is no site— it's just a bunch of individual, unrelated pages. Link those pages in just the right way, and they become a cohesive site your visitors can explore to enjoy all that's offered on every page.

In this chapter, you'll revisit the various ways a Web site can be structured (first introduced in Chapter 17, "Understanding Web Authoring") and learn how and when to deploy each method in your own projects.

This chapter assumes that you have already installed Netscape Communicator 4.7 and its built-in Web-authoring program, Composer. If you have not, visit `http://wp.netscape.com/download/archive.html` and download Netscape Communicator version 4.7 for your system. (It's free.)

More recent versions of Netscape and Composer are available, as well. Although the exact steps for some features may differ slightly, you'll have little difficulty finding your way around a newer version of Composer using the material in this book.

What separates basic Web authoring tools like Composer from big leaguers like Microsoft FrontPage or Macromedia Dreamweaver? Well, other than a few bells and whistles, the most important difference is that pro tools include *site-management* features.

With site management, you can display a diagram of all the interlinked pages in a Web site. You can add or delete pages or move pages around, and all the links among pages are automatically adjusted so that they still lead where they're supposed to. You can apply a *theme* to a Web site so that all its pages share a common style.

Starting out, creating single pages and basic Web sites of maybe five pages or so, you don't need site-management capabilities. But as you move up to bigger, more complex sites, you should start hinting that, for your next birthday, you want a Web authoring program with site management.

The Basic Act: Linking One Page to Another

Composer makes it easy to link pages you've created while they're still on your PC. The trick is to create the pages first and then build the links as described in the following example.

1. Create the Web pages that will make up your Web site, and save them all in the same folder (see Figure 24.1).

2. Type and format the text that will serve as the various links.

3. Select the text of one link source (see Figure 24.2).

FIGURE 24.1

Step 1: Create your pages and store them together in a folder.

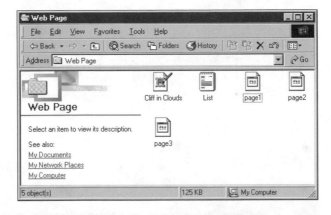

FIGURE 24.2

Step 3: Select a link source.

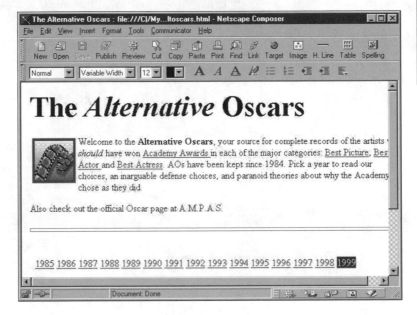

One good way to link pages is to create a block of links—containing a separate link for each page—and put it at the bottom of every page. That way, your visitors can jump from any page in your Web site to any other with just one click.

After you've created the block of links, you can use copy-and-paste to copy the block from one page to others (see Chapter 20, "Adding, Editing, and Formatting Text").

Besides (or in addition to) using a block of text links, you can use picture links (see Chapter 25, "Adding Pictures (and Picture Backgrounds)") or an imagemap (see Chapter 27, "Dividing a Page into Frames") to create a navigation bar, a graphical link block for each page in the site.

4. Click the Link button on the Composition toolbar.

5. In the box labeled URL, type the complete filename of the page file to which this link points (including the .htm or .html part—see Figure 24.3). Do not put http:// or anything else at the beginning. The filename alone does it. Then click OK.

FIGURE 24.3

Step 5: For the link URL, type the filename of the page to which to link.

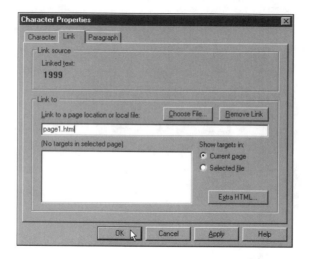

Linking from One Page to a Target in Another

In Chapter 23, "Making Links," you learned the fine art of linking to targets, a technique used most often to link from one part of a long page to another. But you can also jump from one of your pages to a particular target point in another of your pages. The procedure is essentially similar to linking from one page to another.

1. Open the page containing the target and double-click the target icon of the target you want to link to, to display the Target Properties box. Jot down the target's name.

2. Open the page where the link will live, create and select the link text as you would when creating any kind of link, and then click the Link button.

3. In the Link to box, type the filename of the page containing the target (see Figure 24.4). Don't put `http://` or anything else in front of the filename.

FIGURE 24.4

Step 3: Type the file-name of the page con-taining the target.

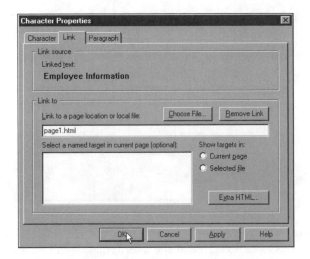

4. Immediately following the filename, type # followed by the name of the target and then click OK (see Figure 24.5).

FIGURE 24.5

Step 4: Add a pound sign (#) and the target name to the filename.

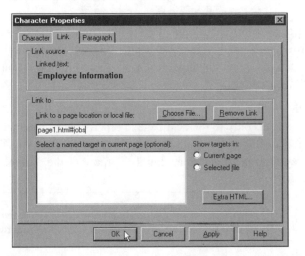

Site-Design Tips

The skills outlined in the preceding examples are all you need to stitch multiple pages into a coordinated site. All you need now is a little guidance about ways you can organize information into a Web site. The remainder of this chapter offers tips for choosing a site design.

Building a Multipage Linear Site

In a multipage linear site, the pages and links are set up in a way that encourages the reader to read a group of pages in a particular order, from start to finish (see Figure 24.6).

FIGURE 24.6

The structure of a multipage linear site.

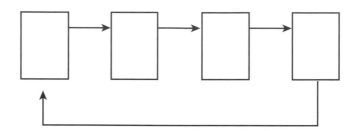

This design makes sense when the content your site delivers is made up mostly of medium-size blocks of text (around one screen) that should be read in a particular sequential order, from beginning to end. (Some people call it a *slide show* structure because the visitor steps through the pages in order, as in a slide show.)

Suppose that this book were converted into a Web site. Its chapters serve the reader best when they're read in order, because each chapter builds on material from the ones before it. To encourage readers to proceed in order, the site would be designed so that the natural flow from page to page (or from chapter to chapter) follows the proper order. Other content that fits this design includes a story that's too long to fit on one page or lengthy step-by-step instructions.

Each page in a multipage linear site features a prominent link, often labeled Next or Continue, that leads only to the next page in order. Other links can be offered as well, but be careful about offering too many links in these types of pages—the links enable the reader to stray from the order, defeating the purpose of the design.

The Microsoft PowerPoint program (included in most versions of Microsoft Office) is designed to help you quickly build an attractive slide-show presentation.

Recent versions of PowerPoint can convert their slide presentations into multipage linear Web sites. They convert each slide into a separate Web page and then automatically insert the navigation buttons (Back and Next, for example). It's a fast and easy way to make a Web site from content you might already have on hand.

Tips for Multipage Linear Site Design

When developing a multipage linear Web site, keep in mind the following tips for good design:

- Try to divide the material into pages that have just enough content (text and images) to fill the screen. Because the visitor is moving sequentially through the pages, he or she should not have to scroll, too. Putting just the right amount of text on each page enables visitors to conveniently explore the whole site just by clicking the Next link that you provide.

- A Next link on each page is the only link that's required and, often, the only one you want. However, if you can offer a Back link (pointing to the preceding page) without cluttering up the design, try to offer that link on each page after the first one so that the reader can review content, if necessary. Also handy is a Back to Start link that points to the first page, so that the reader can conveniently jump from any page to the beginning.

- The last page in the order should always contain a link back to the first page, even if you choose not to provide this type of link elsewhere.

Working with One-Page Linear Pages

When the following conditions are true, a one-page linear design is a terrific (and often overlooked) approach (see Figure 24.7):

- You have lots of text to deliver.
- That text is naturally divided into many small sections.
- You want to deliver the text in an efficient way.

This structure is often applied to lengthy reference material provided as one part of a larger, multipage site, but a well-designed one-pager can actually serve as your whole site.

Although readers can always scroll through the entire page, the top of the page typically shows a list of links—a table of contents or index of sorts. Each link points to a target (see Chapter 23) somewhere down in the page. The links help readers quickly find particular information without having to scroll for it.

The longer the page and the more separate sections it has, the more important the table of links at the top is.

If a page is only three or four screens long, the visitor can pretty easily explore it by scrolling. Five screens or longer, and you owe your visitors the assistance of some links.

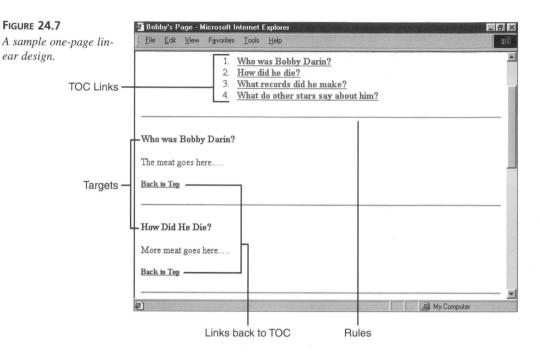

FIGURE 24.7

*A sample one-page lin-
ear design.*

Tips for One-Page Linear Design

When developing a one-page linear design, keep in mind the following tips for good design:

- At the top of the page, or adjacent to the table of contents, insert a target. Between each logical section of the page, insert a Back to Top link that points to the target at the top. This link enables the reader to conveniently return to the TOC after reading any section.

- Limit pictures (see Chapter 25). The danger of this design is that the long page will contain so much data that it will take a long time to download to the visitor's browser. But text—even lots of text—moves through the Internet pretty quickly. If you limit yourself to an image or two, usually at the top of the page, you can lend some visual interest while still enabling the page to download quickly.

- Scroll through the page. If the total page exceeds 15 screens, consider breaking it up into a hierarchical or multipage sequential design.

- Use horizontal rules (see Chapter 22, "Organizing Text with Tables and Rules") to divide sections of the text visually.

Making a Web-Style Site

In a Web structure, anything goes (see Figure 24.8). Any page can link to any other page, or to all other pages. This structure makes sense when the various pages contain information that is related to information on other pages, but there's no logical order or sequence to that information.

FIGURE 24.8

A Web-style structure.

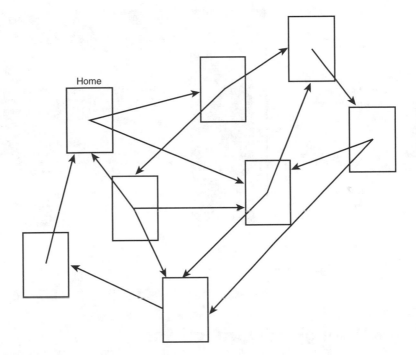

In a Web-style site, a "top" page might be provided as a starting point (as in a hierarchical site, as described later in this chapter), but from there, readers can wander around the site in no particular path. Web structures are best suited to fun, recreational subjects or to subjects that defy any kind of sequential or hierarchical breakdown.

Typically, each page of a Web-style site contains a block of links—often in a column along one side of the page or in a block at the bottom—that lead to every other page in the site (see Figure 24.9).

Tips for Web-Style Design

When developing a Web-style site, keep in mind the following tips for good design:

- Before you resort to a Web structure, make sure that your message really calls for one—you might just be having trouble recognizing the logical organization of your content.

- Visitors can easily get lost in a Web-style site. I recommend always including a "top" page that serves as an all-purpose starting point and then making sure that every page in the site contains an easily identifiable link back to the top page. That way, lost visitors can easily get back to a landmark from which to set off down a new path.

FIGURE 24.9

Each page in a Web-style site typically contains a block of text links (or a navigation bar) to all other pages in the site, if there aren't too many.

Navigation Bar —

Text Links —

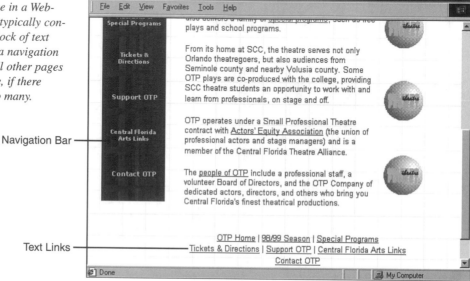

Making a Hierarchical Site

The most well-organized design (see Figure 24.10), a hierarchical Web site starts out with a general, "top" page that leads to several second-level pages containing more specific information. Each of these second-level pages leads to third-level pages containing more specific info about the second-level page to which they are linked, and so on.

The careful organization of a hierarchical site is not for the mere sake of neatness. The structure of the page actually helps the visitor find what he or she wants, especially when the site carries lots of detailed information.

Suppose that the site sells clothes, and I want a dress shirt. The top page might show links to women's clothes and men's clothes. I choose the Men's link and arrive at a second-level page offering links to shirts, pants, and shoes. I choose Shirts, and I see a third-level page offering Dress and Casual. I choose Dress, and I'm there. The structure of the page makes my search easy, even though the site offers hundreds of items.

FIGURE 24.10
A hierarchical structure.

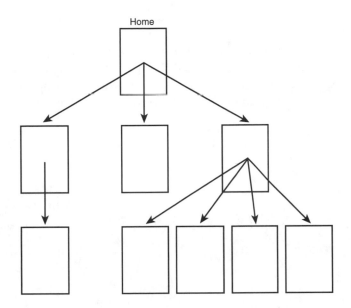

Tips for Hierarchical Design

When developing a hierarchical site, keep in mind the following tips for good design:

- As in a Web-style design, be sure that every page in the site contains an easily identifiable link back to the top page so that visitors can easily get back to the top without having to struggle up the hierarchy a level at a time.

- More than with any other design, a hierarchical structure demands that you think and plan carefully the content of each page and the organization of the pages so that the site flows logically. As with my shirt example, visitors should be able to drill intuitively down through the hierarchy to find specific information.

- Keep in mind that many levels are available to you. Don't try to link the top page to a dozen second-level pages—doing so suggests that you have not really figured out the organization. Ideally, each page should lead to no fewer than two pages and no more than seven or eight, in the level below it. Then again, don't follow arbitrary rules. Just be sure that the page organization and the natural organization of the content match.

24

Summary

The organization of pages in a site is not really a Web authoring challenge: It's a content-management issue. Understand exactly what you're trying to say and how to say it best, and the correct site structure will become immediately apparent to you. All that's left is adding some links (and maybe targets), and you know how to do that already, don't you?

CHAPTER **25**

Adding Pictures (and Picture Backgrounds)

Pictures are like salt: Add the right amount in the right way, and your Web page becomes tastier—but add too much, and your visitors will wind up logging off the Internet to go get a soda.

In this chapter, you'll learn not only how to add images (and image backgrounds) to your pages and to control the appearance of those images, but also how to use images wisely, for the best effects.

This chapter assumes that you have already installed Netscape Communicator 4.7 and its built-in Web-authoring program, Composer. If you have not, visit http://wp.netscape.com/download/archive.html and download Netscape Communicator version 4.7 for your system. (It's free.)

More recent versions of Netscape and Composer are available, as well. Although the exact steps for some features may differ slightly, you'll have little difficulty finding your way around a newer version of Composer using the material in this book.

Inserting a GIF or JPEG Image in Composer

Before beginning the steps to insert an image in a Web page, first prepare your image file or files as discussed in Part III. Be sure that the image file is stored in the same folder as the Web page file in which you will insert it. (If it isn't, move or copy it there before beginning the example.)

1. Click in your page at the spot where you want to insert the image.
2. Click the Image button on the Composition toolbar (see Figure 25.1).

Image Button

FIGURE 25.1

Step 2: Click Image.

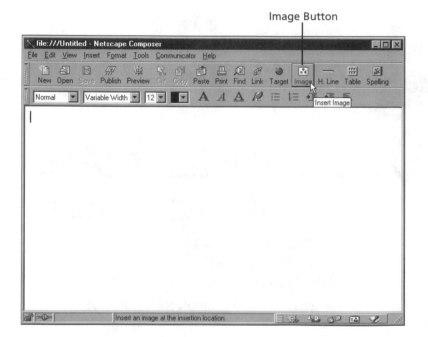

3. Click the Choose File button (see Figure 25.2).
4. Navigate to the folder containing the image file, click its name, and click Open (see Figure 25.3).
5. The Image Properties box shows the filename in the Image Location window. If it's the image you want, click OK (see Figure 25.4). If not, click Choose File and find the right image.

Choose File Button

FIGURE 25.2
Step 3: Click Choose File.

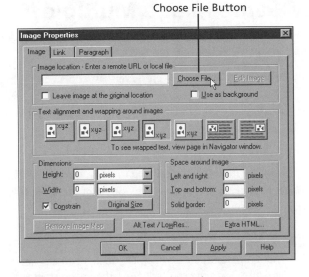

FIGURE 25.3
Step 4: Choose the file.

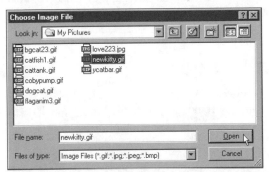

25

FIGURE 25.4
Step 5: Click OK.

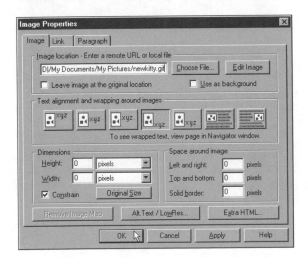

Using the Same Image Multiple Times

If you want to use the same image multiple times in a page, you don't need multiple copies of the image with different filenames.

A single copy of an image file on a Web server can appear in the same page—or in several pages—as many times as you like. Just choose the same filename when inserting each copy of the image, or use copy-and-paste to insert multiple copies of the same image. This technique is especially useful when you use graphical bullets in a list (see "Inserting Fancy Bullets and Rules," later in this chapter).

To use copy-and-paste, insert the image one time, right-click, and choose Copy from the menu that appears. Click in the page where you want the copy to go and then choose Edit, Paste from the menu bar.

> You can paste as many copies as you like without having to click Copy again. Until the next time you click Copy, the image stays in the Windows Clipboard, ready to be pasted anywhere you want it.

Deleting an Image

To delete an image, click it once to select it and then press the Delete key. Note that deleting an image merely removes it from the Web page. The file itself is not deleted; it remains on your hard drive to be used another time.

Choosing an Image's Size and Other Properties

After you've inserted an image (or while inserting it for the first time), you can change its appearance in a variety of ways, all by choosing options in the Image Properties dialog box (see Figure 25.5).

The Image Properties dialog box opens while you are inserting an image, as shown earlier in this chapter. You can open the dialog box later for an image you have already inserted by double-clicking the image.

The next several pages describe ways you can use the Image Properties dialog box to change a picture's appearance.

FIGURE 25.5

Use the Image Properties dialog box to change an image's role in the layout of a page.

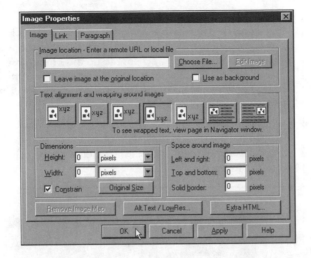

Changing the Dimensions (Size and Shape) of an Image

From right within Composer, you can change the size of an image, and you can change its shape, stretching or squeezing (and distorting) it, as you learn to do shortly. But first…

As a rule, you get better results if you choose the size and shape of the image in the application used to create it or in a good image-editing program (such as Paint Shop Pro) rather than in Composer or most other Web authoring programs.

Why? Well, Composer can't really change the dimensions of an image. Instead, it applies tags to the HTML file that browsers use to resize the image when displaying it. A browser is not as sophisticated a graphics scaler as a real image-editing program, and the likelihood of unattractive "artifacts" in the scaled image (such as streaks through the image) or a loss of the transparency of a transparent GIF file is high.

With that caveat, the following example shows how to change the size and shape of an image in Composer, when doing so seems prudent to you.

1. Double-click the image to open the Image Properties dialog box.

2. Observe the Height and Width boxes shown in the Dimensions area (the numbers show the number of screen pixels) and "guesstimate" how much to change those numbers (see Figure 25.6). For example, if Width is 200 and you want to make the image half as large, you enter 100 for the width. (After you change the width, the height changes automatically.) Click OK to close the dialog box and see how your picture looks at its new size.

25

If you don't change both the width and height of the image by exactly the same proportion, the image winds up stretched out of shape, in one dimension or the other. You may choose to do this on purpose, to achieve a particular effect. But if you want to change just the size of the image without changing its shape, make sure that the Constrain box is checked in the Image Properties dialog box.

When Constrain is checked, you need to change only one dimension. Change the width, and the height changes automatically to maintain the picture's original shape at its new size. Change the height, and the width changes automatically.

FIGURE 25.6

Step 2: Change the width (or height) to change an image's size.

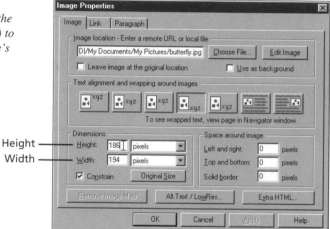

Height ——————

Width ——————

3. To change the shape of the image, click to clear the Constrain box (see Figure 25.7). Then change the width or height as desired and click OK to see the results.

Controlling Alignment

A picture's *alignment* describes its position on the page and how it relates to any text adjacent to it.

By default, a picture aligns to the left side of the page (just like left-aligned text). The first line of any text immediately following the picture appears to the right of the picture, near its bottom. If the text runs for more than one line without an intervening paragraph break, all lines after the first line appear underneath the image. This default alignment is called *bottom alignment* (see Figure 25.8).

FIGURE 25.7

Step 3: To change an image's shape, clear the Constrain box and change the width or height.

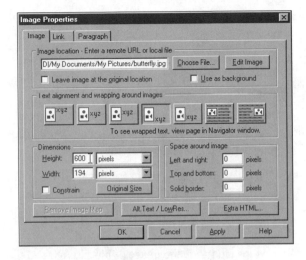

To understand alignment options, you need to understand what the baseline of text is. The *baseline* is the line the letters sit on when you write them. Most letters appear entirely above that line, but a few—such as lowercase *j* and *y*—have descenders that drop down below the baseline.

The default, bottom alignment, aligns the baseline with the bottom of the image so that any descenders drop lower than the bottom of the image.

25

FIGURE 25.8

The default alignment for images, known as "bottom" alignment.

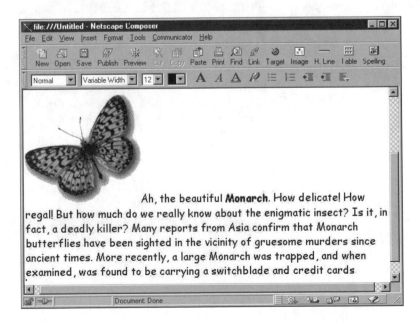

To change a picture's alignment, choose from the options in the Align Text to Image box in the Image Properties dialog box. The other choices (besides At the Bottom) are

- **At the Top**—The first line of text appears to the right of the top of the image, with the top of the text aligned to the top of the image. Any lines after the first line appear underneath the image.
- **In the Center**—The first line of text appears to the right of the image, with the baseline of the text aligned to the vertical center of the image. Any lines after the first line appear underneath the image.

The bottom two alignment options, Wrap to the Left and Wrap to the Right, are special "wrapping" options. Unlike all the other options, which can put only the first line of text alongside the image, right and left allow multiple lines of text to appear alongside a picture:

- **Left**—Text wraps alongside the image, with the image to the left of the text (text on the right).
- **Right**—Text wraps alongside the image, with the image to the right of the text (text on the left); see Figure 25.9.

FIGURE 25.9

Left alignment and right alignment (shown here) allow multiple lines of text to wrap alongside an image.

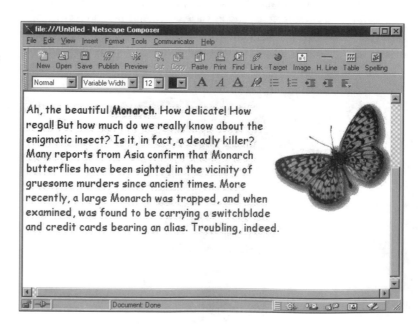

All the alignment options are represented reasonably accurately when you view a page in Composer, but sometimes the representation is not 100 percent accurate. Always evaluate your alignment formatting by viewing the page in a Web browser.

Controlling Spacing and Borders

To add a border around a picture, or to change the amount of space between the image and what's around it, use the spacing options in the Image Properties dialog box:

- To increase the space between the sides of the image and adjacent text, tables, or other objects, enter a number of pixels in the Left and Right boxes.

- To increase the space between the top and bottom of the image and adjacent text, tables, or other objects, enter a number of pixels in the Top and Bottom boxes.

- To add a black border all around the image (see Figure 25.10), enter in the Solid Border box a number of pixels for the thickness of the border.

Typing 4 in the Solid Border box makes a nice, bold border like the one shown in Figure 25.10. A lower number makes a finer border; a higher number, a thicker one. A border thicker than about 8 pixels is probably overkill.

25

FIGURE 25.10

The same page shown in Figure 25.9 but with additional space around the image (30 pixels left and right) and a 4-pixel border indicated in the Image Properties dialog box.

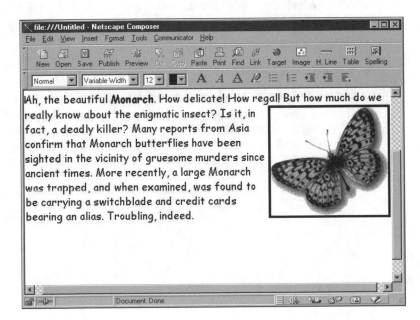

Entering Alternate Text

You can help some visitors cope with your images by entering alternate text in the Image Properties dialog box (see Figure 25.11).

FIGURE 25.11

You can use alternate text to help some visitors with slow connections or nongraphical browsers.

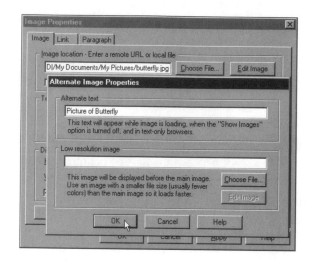

Alternate text is any block of words you want to appear in place of the graphic in browsers that do not support graphics. Try to supply informative text to replace the idea that was originally communicated by the image. Also, many browsers that support text alternates display an image placeholder, something like <image>, if you don't supply a text alternative representation. The text alternate is not only more informative in such browsers, but also better looking.

Entering Images in Table Cells

You put an image in a table cell (see Chapter 22, "Organizing Text with Tables and Rules") exactly as you put one in a page. The only difference is that you must first click in the cell to position the edit cursor there. You can then click the Insert Image button and insert the picture exactly as you would anywhere else in a Web page (see Figure 25.12).

FIGURE 25.12

To insert a picture in a table cell, click in the cell just before clicking Insert Image.

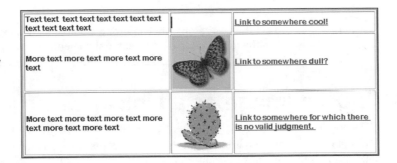

Inserting Fancy Bullets and Rules

No doubt you've seen some highfalutin' pages that feature cool, multicolored graphical bullets and horizontal lines. These objects are not actual bullets and lines of the kind you create with the list buttons and the H. Line button. Instead, they're just inline images that *look* like bullets and lines (see Figure 25.13).

FIGURE 25.13

Fancy bullets and rules are just image files used in place of horizontal lines and list bullets.

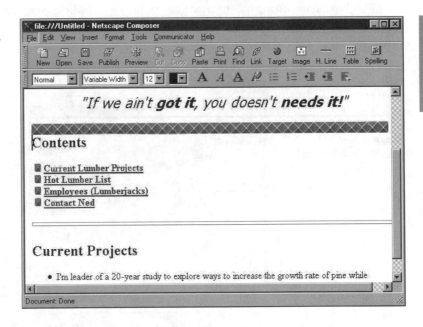

25

Line-type images, sometimes called *bars*, are simply inserted between paragraphs. The bullets are inserted before individual lines of text, using any paragraph style other than List. (If you use List, you get your cool bullets *plus* the list's bullets or numbers. Icky.)

To get the best results when inserting a bullet image next to a line of text, align the image using At the Center alignment.

Using an Image as a Link

As you learned in Chapter 23, "Making Links," every link has two parts: the *link text* (the thing a visitor sees and clicks) and the *link location*, the URL (or local path and file-name) to which the browser goes when the link is clicked.

Making an image into a link is just a matter of attaching the link location to an image. In fact, it's exactly like creating a text link; the only difference is that you select an image rather than a block of text before clicking the Link button.

1. Click to select the image you want to make into a link.
2. Click the Link button on the Composition toolbar.
3. Use the dialog box to create any of the types of links you learned to create in Chapter 23—a link to a Web page, an email address, or an anchor, for example (see Figure 25.14).

FIGURE 25.14

Step 3: Fill in the Link tab of the Image Properties dialog box for an image link exactly as you would for a text link.

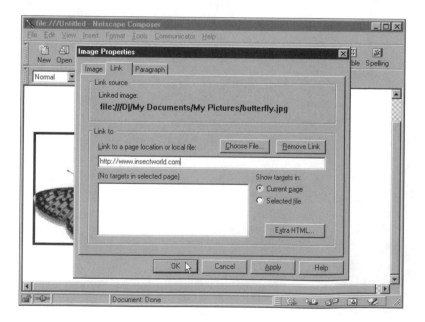

Adding a Picture Background

As an alternative to a background color (which you learned to add in Chapter 19, "Choosing a Title, Text Colors, and Other Page Basics"), you can apply as a background a *tiled image*, an image file (GIF or JPEG) repeated across the entire background.

> An image background automatically supercedes a background color. If you create an image background, any selection you may have made for the background color is irrelevant.

When this image has been designed carefully to match up perfectly with its mates at all four corners, the tiling creates a seamless "texture" effect, as if one enormous image covered the background (see Figure 25.15). Fortunately, the effect is created from only one small image; accessing an image file large enough to cover a page would choke most Internet connections.

FIGURE 25.15

A tiled background texture.

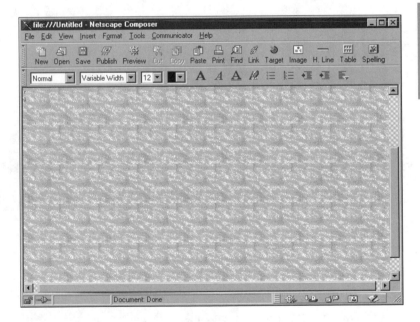

You can choose, as an alternative to a background texture, to tile an image that doesn't match up perfectly with its copies at the edges. Using this technique, you can create some fun background effects, as shown in Figure 25.16.

Be careful with backgrounds. If you don't choose carefully, you can wind up making your text illegible, or at least hard on the eyes.

Use custom text colors (see Chapter 19) to contrast the text with the background. Use light colors to stand out against dark backgrounds, and dark colors to stand out against light backgrounds.

Even with those precautions, a tiled-image background is usually too much when seen behind a page with lots of text on it. A way around this problem is to use a snazzy tile background behind your logo or brief text on a top page and then switch to a solid color or no background on text-heavy pages to which the top page links.

FIGURE 25.16

A fun background made of a tiled image.

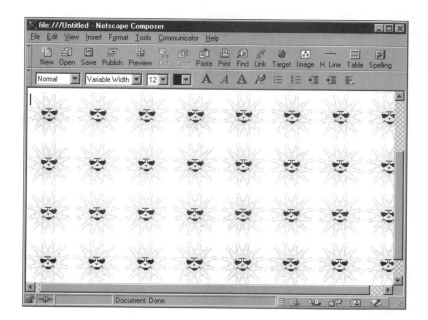

Finally, you can use as a background a single, large image file that covers the entire page background (and thus requires no tiling). Be careful when using this technique to use an image with a low resolution and few colors to keep the image size small and the page's appearance fast.

Many "full page" background images do not actually cover the full background; rather, they often take the form over very tall, narrow bars. Because the bar is so tall, the browser does not tile it and left-aligns it on the page. The file itself is reasonably small, yet it lends a graphical flair to the whole page without obscuring text.

> Tiled background images automatically supercede a background color because they cover the whole background.
>
> But if you use a nontiled image and the image does not happen to fill the background, you might use a background color along with it. The background color affects only the portion of the background not covered by the image.

Here's how to add a picture background:

1. Store the GIF or JPEG image you want for a background in the same folder as the page in which you want to use it.

2. In Composer, open the page to which you want to add a background and click Format, Page Colors and Properties.

3. In the Background Image box on the Colors and Background tab, type the filename of the image you want to use (or click Choose File to navigate to it) and click OK (see Figure 25.17).

FIGURE 25.17

Step 3: Type the filename of the background image.

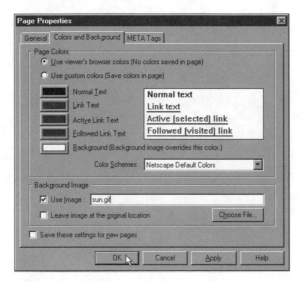

25

Summary

In the cookie that is a Web page, images are the chocolate chips. And as we all know, the best cookie strikes just the right chip-to-cookie ratio—too many chips is as bad as none at all. (Replace with your favorite ratio-balancing analogy: pizza crust:cheese, peanut butter:jelly, RAM:processor speed, or longevity:fun, for example.)

The issue is not just whether you use graphics or how many you use, but *why* you use them. Do the images add something useful to your page—like photos of people the page is by or about or images of products and places described—or are they mere decoration? An image or two added for the sake of style is worthwhile, but only if the image succeeds in actually enhancing style. If the image seems like a generic one dropped there merely for the sake of having an image, dump it. Dress your page with careful text formatting, the natural beauty of solid organization, and strong writing.

CHAPTER **26**

Editing HTML

The easiest and most reliable way to create a Web page is to use a WYSI-WYG editor. But no matter which editor Web authors use, they often reach a point where they want to do something that's perfectly possible in an HTML Web page but for which their WYSIWYG authoring program offers no buttons or menu items. If you reach that point, you might want to move beyond Composer into the realm of the HTML source file itself.

This chapter introduces you to HTML source files and how new tags and attributes are applied.

This chapter assumes that you have already installed Netscape Communicator 4.7 and its built-in Web-authoring program, Composer. If you have not, visit http://wp.netscape.com/download/archive.html and download Netscape Communicator version 4.7 for your system. (It's free.)

This chapter also assumes that you have downloaded a free trial of the HTML editor HTML Assistant Pro. You can download it from http://www.exit0.

Reading an HTML File

Recall from Chapter 17, "Understanding Web Authoring," that an HTML source file consists of four basic elements:

- The text to be displayed on the page
- The filenames of inline images
- The URLs or filenames for links (and the text or image filenames for the link source)
- HTML tags and attributes, which tell browsers which lines are images, links, headings, or normal paragraphs, for example

The best way to learn about HTML is to study HTML files and compare them with the output in a browser. Figure 26.1 shows a basic Web page displayed in Netscape, and Figure 26.2 shows the HTML source file for the same page.

FIGURE 26.1

A basic Web page, as interpreted by a browser.

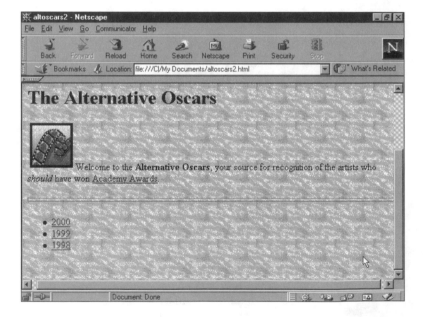

In Figure 26.2, notice that HTML tags are always enclosed within angle brackets (< >) and that each content element of the page—a paragraph or image filename—is surrounded by a pair of tags. Compare Figures 26.1 and 26.2 carefully, and you quickly see how HTML tags tell a browser what to do with the text and files that make up a Web page.

Most Web pages contain more elaborate coding than what you see in the example illustrated by Figures 26.1 and 26.2. However, this example contains all the basics and shows how HTML tags are applied. When you understand this example, you'll know enough to apply virtually any other HTML tag.

FIGURE 26.2

The HTML source code for the Web page shown in Figure 26.1.

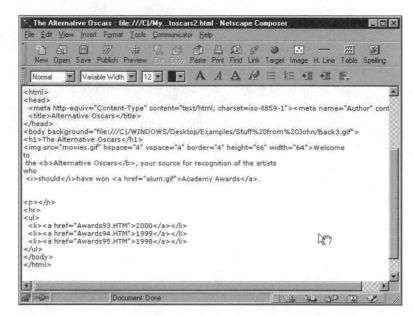

While examining Figure 26.2, observe that you typically (but not always) need two HTML tags to identify a page element: one tag that has no slash (/) inside the first angle bracket and another that has a slash there. The no-slash version is used to mark the beginning of a page element, and the slash version (sometimes called the *close tag*) marks the end. For example, the tag <HTML> at the top of the file marks the beginning of the entire HTML document, and the close tag </HTML> marks the end.

Now take a look at how the tags, text, and filenames work together to build a page. Every HTML document begins with the following command:

<HTML>

This command tells the browser that it's reading an HTML document and should interpret it as such. Typically (but not always), the next tag is the following:

<HEAD>

26

This line informs the browser that what follows <HEAD> is header information. Information entered in the header is not displayed as part of the page but is important because it describes your document to the browser and to Web search engines and directories. The header portion of an HTML file created in Composer contains all the information you entered in the Composer Page Properties dialog box. This includes not only such standard elements as the document title, but also header elements created by Composer automatically. These are indicated with two types of tags:

```
<META NAME=...>
<HTTP-EQUIV>
```

The next two tags, <TITLE> and </TITLE>, surround the text of the Web page title. After the title and any other header lines, the tag </HEAD> informs the browser that the header is over. Next comes the body of the page, kicked off by the <BODY> tag. The body contains everything that's displayed on the page itself.

The first element of the body in Figure 26.2 is a heading. The heading tags are easy to remember: <H1> is a level 1 heading, <H2> is a level 2 heading, and so on. The first heading in the example is a level 1 heading:

```
<H1>The Alternative Oscars</H1>
```

Notice that the end of the heading is marked with </H1>.

The inline image (GIF file movies.gif) is indicated with the <IMG SRC...> tag, like the following:

```
<IMG SRC="movies.gif"...>
```

Note that the image filename must be enclosed in quotes. In Figure 26.2, optional attributes for spacing, image dimensions, and a border around the image appear between the beginning of the <IMG SRC...> tag and the close angle bracket (>) that ends it. Attributes are always optional and go inside the tag itself (between the angle brackets).

 The <IMG SRC...> tag requires no close tag.

Immediately following the end of the <IMG SRC...> tag comes a normal text paragraph (beginning with Welcome). Note that no tag is required in order to identify it; any text in an HTML document is assumed to be a normal paragraph unless tags indicate otherwise. However, keep in mind that while entering normal text, you cannot simply type a carriage return to start a new paragraph. To break a paragraph and begin a new one, you must enter the new-paragraph tag (<P>). Ending a paragraph with a close-paragraph tag (</P>) is proper, but doing so is not required.

Embedded within the normal paragraph are a few more tags:

- The set <B> and </B> surrounding Alternative Oscars applies bold character formatting.

- The set <I> and </I> surrounding should applies italic character formatting.

- The tag beginning with <A HREF... creates a link to another page, using the text Academy Awards as the link source. In the link, the <A HREF= portion indicates that, when activated by a reader, the link should open the file or URL named in quotes. The text between the close angle bracket following the filename and the close tag </A> is the text that is displayed in the page as the link source.

Following the normal paragraph is a new-paragraph tag that inserts a blank line before the horizontal line (<HR>) that follows. All by itself, the <HR> tag inserts a line; width=100% is an attribute, one of the optional properties you can apply to a horizontal line's properties extensions (see Chapter 22, "Organizing Text with Tables and Rules").

The <UL> tag starts an unnumbered list. (Look for the </UL> tag that closes the list.) Each list item is surrounded by <LI> and </LI> and contains a link (<A HREF) to another page in the document.

At the bottom of the file, the </BODY> tag closes off the body and the </HTML> tag indicates the end of the HTML document.

That's it. To learn more about the HTML source code of pages you've created in Composer or any page you see on the Web, follow the steps in the next section.

Viewing the HTML Source Code of a Document

26

A great way to learn more about HTML is to study the source code for Web pages. You can study the source code for pages you view on the Web or look at the underlying source code for pages you create in Composer. You can even view the source code for a page you're editing, make a small change with the Composer menus or toolbar buttons, and then view the source code again to see how the HTML code has been changed. Give it a try!

To view the HTML source for a page you're looking at:

- In Internet Explorer, choose View, Source.
- In Netscape, choose View, Page Source.

Using Composer to Insert an HTML Tag

When you've built a document in Composer but need to add a tag here or there for which Composer offers no button or menu, the Composer Insert HTML Tag function allows you to do so conveniently, without having to fuss with the whole HTML source file.

1. Click in the page at the spot where you want the object or formatting applied by the tag to go.

2. Choose Insert, HTML Tag (see Figure 26.3).

FIGURE 26.3

Step 2: Choose Insert, HTML Tag.

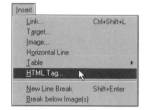

3. Type your entry, and then click OK (see Figure 26.4).

FIGURE 26.4

Step 3: Type the tag.

Adding Attributes with the Composer Advanced Edit Buttons

When performing many kinds of activities in dialog boxes in Composer—inserting or formatting an image, for example—you see an Extra HTML button somewhere in the dialog box, like the one shown in Figure 26.5. The button enables you to code attributes or other options manually into the HTML tag controlled by the dialog box.

However, the Extra HTML button has little immediate value when you're writing HTML. For the most part, all optional attributes you might want to use are already available in the dialog box. Also, the button enables you to insert any attributes or other code between the tag and its closing tag—for example, anywhere between <TABLE> and </TABLE> when you click the button in the Insert Table dialog box. However, this method does not give you control of the position of the added attributes among other attributes within the tags, and position is sometimes important.

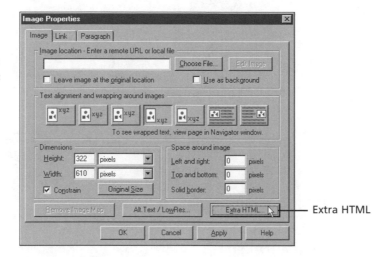

Extra HTML

I've told you about the Extra HTML button 'cause it's there and 'cause, for all I know, you might find it useful. But if you really want to apply attributes not featured on the Composer menus and toolbar buttons, I recommend steering clear of the Extra HTML button and editing the HTML source file, as described in the next section. Doing so, you develop greater skill and confidence working with HTML, and you avoid niggling little problems that the button can bring about.

Editing an HTML Source File Directly

The Composer Insert HTML Tag function is terrific for inserting a tag or two in a file, but for more serious HTML work, simply editing the HTML source file itself is easier.

Many Web authoring programs include an HTML source editor (but not Composer). But for basic changes, any text editor will do. Windows has a built-in text editor, Notepad (see Figure 26.6). To open Notepad, click the Windows Start button and choose Programs, Accessories, Notepad.

To open one of your Composer pages in Notepad to edit its HTML, open Notepad and then choose File, Open. In the Open dialog box, open the Files of Type list (see Figure 26.7) and choose All files (doing so makes HTML files, and all other file types, appear in the lists of files the Open dialog shows). Then browse to your file and click the Open button.

26

FIGURE 26.6

You can use Windows notepad to edit HTML source code directly.

FIGURE 26.7

Choose All Files from the File of type list to choose an HTML file to edit.

About HTML Assistant Pro

Some WYSIWYG editors do all the HTML work for you (behind the scenes), and some flat HTML editors and text editors let you edit the source code, but give you little or no help with it. Somewhere between those two extremes lie professional HTML editing tools like HTML Assistant Pro, which you can download in a free trial version from http://www.exit0.com (see Figure 26.8).

FIGURE **26.8**

*HTML code being
edited in HTML
Assistant.*

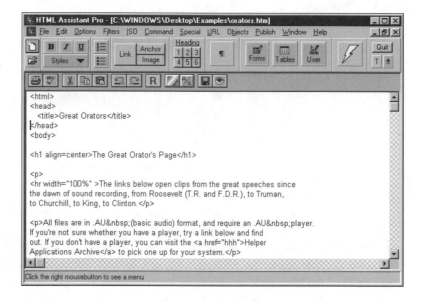

To open HTML Assistant Pro, choose Programs, HTML Assistant Pro 2000,
Pro 2000 from the Windows Start menu. (If the Welcome screen appears,
click the Continue with Mission button.)

For readers of this book, HTML Assistant Pro provides another important
benefit—one that requires no HTML coding.

Composer includes no facility for creating Web pages with *frames*—pages
divided into two or three separate panels that each show a different file.
Using a tool built into HTML Assistant Pro, you can easily produce a frames
page, with no HTML coding.

In Chapter 27, "Dividing a Page into Frames," you'll learn how to create
frames in HTML Assistant Pro.

26

Although an HTML editor produces and edits simple text files, it also offers menus and
toolbar buttons to make entering tags more convenient and accurate.

For example, in HTML Assistant Pro, you apply the tags for bold character formatting by
simply highlighting text and then clicking the B button on the toolbar (see Figure 26.9).
Rather than see the text turn bold (as you do in a WYSIWYG editor), you see the bold
tags (<B>, </B>) appear around the text. These editors don't show you the effects of your
coding (you need to view the file in a browser to check its appearance), but they do make
working with raw HTML easier, and they help ensure that you enter the codes correctly.

FIGURE 26.9
HTML Assistant Pro toolbars offer most of the tools you need for applying tags without typing.

Bold   Heading Levels   Preview

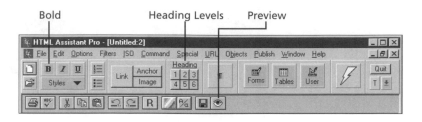

When working in HTML Assistant Pro, you can click the Preview button on the toolbar (the creepy eye; refer to Figure 26.9) to view the page in the default browser on your PC.

Typically, you compose in HTML Assistant Pro by typing only the text you want to display (or entering filenames for images or URLs for links), highlighting the text with your mouse, and then clicking a toolbar button to apply a set of tags to the selected text. The tags are displayed instantly in the document. For example, you could type a line of text and then click a number (1–6) under Heading on the top toolbar to assign heading tags to the text.

Note too that you needn't manually code such structure tags as <HTML>, <HEAD>, or <BODY>; HTML Assistant Pro adds these automatically when you create the file.

In Chapter 31, "Developing Your Authoring Skills," you'll learn about other Web authoring environments, such as Microsoft FrontPage, which you can add to your arsenal as your skills advance.

If you need to do lots of HTML coding to do stuff Composer doesn't do, consider moving up to one of these professional-level Web authoring tools so that you can perform the same tasks more conveniently and in true WYSIWYG fashion.

Editing Composer Pages in HTML Assistant Pro

Before you can begin using HTML Assistant Pro to edit pages you've created in Composer, you need to know how to open a Composer page in HTML Assistant Pro.

Begin by opening HTML Assistant Pro. Choose File, Open to display the Open dialog box (see Figure 26.10); then browse to and open your Composer file.

FIGURE 26.10
Choose File, Open to browse for and open a Composer page in HTML Assistant Pro.

When finished editing the HTML of your page, save the file by choosing File, Save. Then re-open the page in Composer (to continue editing) or Navigator (to view the results).

Many of the HTML features you can add in HTML Assistant Pro cannot be previewed in Composer. You can view the proper effects of your HTML work in Navigator, but in Composer, some tags added by HTML Assistant Pro will show up not as they would appear online, but instead indicated by little yellow tag icons. These tags simply mean that you've used tags a browser would understand, but Composer doesn't.

26

Using HTML Assistant Pro to Add Sound and Video to Your Web Pages

Composer's ability to add media files to your pages is pretty much limited to pictures. But by using HTML Assistant Pro in concert with Composer, you can easily insert inline video files, background sounds, and scrolling marquees to your pages. The following example's show how.

Before you can add a video clip or background sound, you need to have a video (.AVI) file (for video) or a Windows Wave (.WAV) sound file (for sound).

Composer can't play background sounds. View the page in Internet Explorer to hear the sound. (Make sure your speakers are switched on!)

1. Store your Wave file in the same folder where the Web page is stored.

2. Open the Web page file in HTML Assistant Pro.

3. Click at the end of a line anywhere in the BODY section of the file and press Enter to start a new line.

4. Choose Special, Sound Attributes.

5. In the Loop section of the Sound Attributes dialog box, select the number of times you want the sound to play, or choose Infinite to make the sound play repeatedly for as long as the visitor displays the page (see Figure 26.11).

FIGURE 26.11

Step 5: Choose Loop options to control how many times the sound plays.

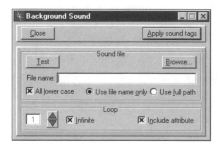

6. Click the Apply sound tags button.

Creating a Times Square-Style Animated Marquee

A *marquee* is a short slice of animated text that scrolls through a Web page. The effect is like the scrolling marquee on the New York Times building in Manhattan, the one people in movies are always watching for bulletins during a crisis. Marquees are a fast way to add a little action to a page, and are usually used for text you really want the visitor to notice.

> At this writing, scrolling marquees are enabled by a Microsoft extension, and are supported in Internet Explorer but not in Netscape Navigator or in other browsers. Navigator users will see your marquee text as regular, static text on the page.

1. Open the Web page file in HTML Assistant Pro.

2. Study the BODY section of the HTML code to locate the place in the page layout where you want the marquee to appear.

3. Click at the end of a line and press Enter to start a new line.

4. Choose Special, Apply Marquee Attributes.

5. Choose options for how you want your marquee to behave (see Figure 26.12). For example, choose Scroll to make the text scroll across the page, Slide to make it slide back and forth, or Alternate to alternate between sliding and scrolling. In the Loop box, choose the number of times you want the marquee to do its thing before stopping, or choose Infinite to make the marquee scroll (or slide) repeatedly for as long as the visitor displays the page.

FIGURE 26.12

Step 5: Choose options for how you want your marquee to behave.

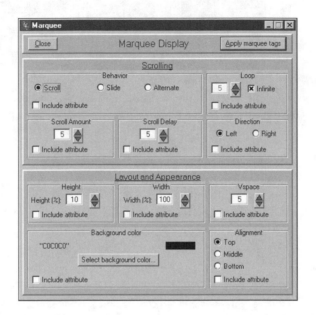

6. Click Apply Marquee Tags. You'll see a fresh set of tags with the cursor positioned between them.

7. Right where the cursor is, type the text for the marquee (see Figure 26.13).

Inserting an Inline Video Clip

OK, I'll tell you how to add an inline video clip (a video clip that appears within the page layout, like an image), because HTML Assistant Pro provides such a handy way to do it. But that doesn't mean I recommend it....

Here are the problems, in no particular order: 1) The clips work only when the page is viewed through Internet Explorer, not in Navigator or in any other browser; 2) An inline clip may dramatically slow down the performance of your page, annoying visitors (unless they have a really fast Internet connection, such as cable Internet or DSL); and

26

3) A nice inline picture or animation really makes more sense. Save video for external presentation.

That said, I know you.… There's just no holding you back, is there? The following example shows how to add an inline video clip.

FIGURE 26.13

Step 7: Type the text for the marquee between the tags.

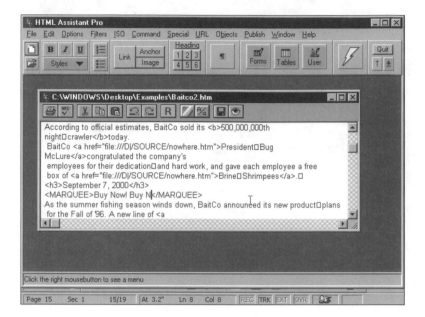

Before you insert a video clip, you must have one on-hand, in AVI format (using the filename extension .avi). You can find such clips online in clip art libraries, or you can create your own AVI files if you have a video capture card in your PC. You can plug a camcorder or VCR into a port on the capture card, play a tape in the VCR or camcorder, and use the card's software to save the incoming video in an AVI file.

Keep in mind that video files are very large. A mere minute can take up several megabytes, which takes up a big chunk of your allotted space on the Web server and also forces long waits for those with slower Internet connections. The video capture software usually offers options for keeping the file size down, at the cost of making the video clip smaller (in onscreen area) and fuzzier.

If you want a quick way to find an AVI file to use for practice (without downloading one from the Web), use the Windows Find facility and search for *.avi. Odds are the search will turn up a few AVI files you didn't even know you had, deposited on your PC by various programs or Web sites.

1. Store the AVI file in the same folder as the Web page (or copy it there).

2. Open the Web page file in HTML Assistant Pro.

3. Study the BODY section of the HTML code to locate the place in the page layout where you want the video clip to appear.

4. Click at the end of a line and press Enter to start a new line.

5. Choose Special, Video Clip.

6. In the Video Clip URL section of the dialog box, choose Use File Name Only (see Figure 26.14).

FIGURE 26.14

Steps 6: Choose Use File Name Only.

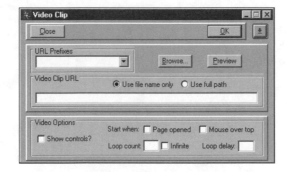

7. Click the Browse button, navigate to the video clip, and click the Open button.

8. Click OK on the Video Clip dialog box.

Summary

26

Coding HTML is no great challenge. In fact, the beauty of HTML is that coding simple stuff—such as text paragraphs, links, and inline images—is actually simple, and coding more complex elements builds naturally on the skills required for the easy stuff.

As a Composer author, you won't spend much time coding the simple stuff because Composer offers buttons and menus for all of it. Instead, you can lay out most of your document in Composer and then use Insert HTML Tag or an HTML editor to code the rest.

CHAPTER 27

Dividing a Page into Frames

If you've hit frame-based pages in your browsing, you know that they're cool. They make your display look like the control panel of a jet fighter—so many different, independent chunks of information stimulating your brain at one time. (If you're not sure what I mean, peek ahead to Figure 27.1.)

It's like the picture-in-picture feature on a new television, for people with eyes so info-hungry that just one program—or one page—at a time provides inadequate sensory input. Of course, frames also greatly expand the author's ability to offer a variety of page-navigation scenarios to visitors.

 This chapter assumes that you have already installed Netscape Communicator 4.7 and its built-in Web-authoring program, Composer. If you have not, visit http://wp.netscape.com/ download/archive.html and download Netscape Communicator version 4.7 for your system. (It's free.)

This chapter also assumes that you have downloaded a free trial of the HTML editor HTML Assistant Pro. You can download it from http://www.exit0.com.

What Does It Take to Make a Frames Page?

In a frame-based page, the content of each frame is contained in a separate HTML page (see Figure 27.1). If the page features three frames, it has at least three separate HTML files, one to appear in each frame.

FIGURE 27.1

A frame-based page.

Frame Definition Page

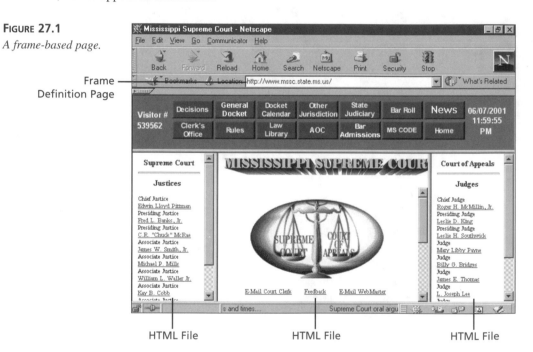

HTML File   HTML File   HTML File

In addition to those "content" HTML files, another HTML file ties all the others together—the frame definition page.

The *frame definition page* is a special HTML file that creates and controls a frame-based Web page. The file contains the filename of the HTML file that's to be displayed in each frame, plus tags dictating the number and size of the frames.

Creating a frame-based page requires three basic steps:

1. Create the various individual HTML pages to be displayed within the frames.

2. Create the frame definition page to define the number, size, and other aspects of the frames.

3. Tie one HTML file to each frame.

When publishing and publicizing your frame-based page, you direct visitors to the frame definition page, not to any of the content files displayed within the frames.

The Frame Definition Page

The frame definition page supplies no content to the page; it merely specifies how the page will be split up and which HTML page will be displayed in each frame.

In Figure 27.1, the URL shown in the address box is that of the frame definition page; that's the URL a visitor accesses to open the page. The frame definition page then takes care of displaying the pages within the frames.

In the frame definition page, you can insert a message to be displayed only to visitors who can't see links. (See the section "Accommodating the Frame-Intolerant," later in this chapter.)

The Frame Content

A separate HTML file, which you compose like any other Web page, supplies the content of each frame. You create and format these pages like any other Web page file; however, when composing files to be displayed in frames, you must try to account for the size and shape of the frame in which you plan to display it.)

Browsers help adjust content for frames: They automatically shorten horizontal lines and wrap text to fit within a frame. Alignment properties are also preserved in a frame; for example, if your text is centered in the page when you compose it, the browser centers the text within the frame when displaying it. However, browsers cannot adjust the positions or spacing of images (or images used as rules or bullets); images often make framing difficult.

27

Note that each page in a frame can have its own, unique background image or color, defined in the content file.

Frames are not created in Composer, but you can create your content files in Composer and tie them together under a frame definition page you create with HTML or another tool (as you do in the next example) and then check your work by previewing the page in Netscape or another browser.

Browsers automatically add scrollbars to a frame when the contents exceed the frame size. But a frames page showing a collection of fragmentary files and scrollbars is unappealing, and visitors tire quickly of excessive scrolling—especially horizontal scrolling to read wide text. Whenever practical, make the content fit the frame—or vice versa.

Using HTML Assistant Pro to Create a Frames Page

Because Composer contains no built-in tools for making frames, you need to code the frames directly in HTML or bring in another tool to help. The easier method is to bring in another tool, and—lucky you—you have one: HTML Assistant Pro.

1. In Composer, compose the content pages to be displayed in the frames. Try to organize and format them, if possible, in a way that minimizes the need for visitors to scroll them in their frames. (Keep in mind that you can always fine-tune them later, after seeing how they look in their frames.)

2. Open HTML Assistant Pro by choosing Programs, HTML Assistant Pro 2000, Pro 2000 from the Windows Start menu. (If the Welcome screen appears, click the Continue with Mission button.)

3. Choose Special, QuickFrames from the menu bar (see Figure 27.2).

4. Click the picture that matches the style of frames page you want to create (see Figure 27.3).

5. In the picture of the frame, click in any frame (see Figure 27.4).

FIGURE 27.2

Step 3: Choose Special, QuickFrames in HTML Assistant Pro.

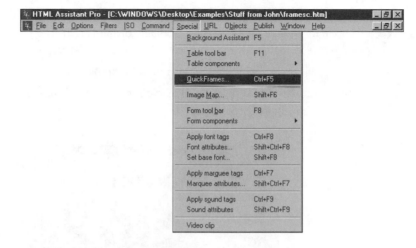

FIGURE 27.3

Step 4: Click the type of frames page you want.

FIGURE 27.4

Steps 5–7: Click a frame in the picture, choose a few options, and enter the filename of the HTML file to appear in that frame.

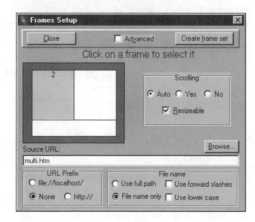

27

6. Under URL Prefix, click None; under File Name, click File Name Only.

7. Under Source URL, type the filename of the HTML file you want displayed in the frame you clicked in Step 5. (Or click Browse to browse for it.)

8. Repeat Steps 5–7 for all other frames in the picture.

9. When you have supplied a filename for all frames, click the Create Frame Set button (see Figure 27.5).

FIGURE 27.5

Step 9: Click Create Frame Set.

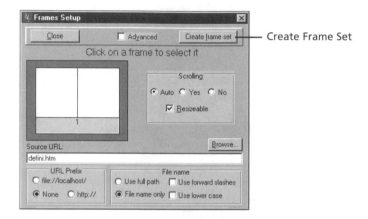

Create Frame Set

10. Choose File, Save, and save the new frame definition page. Be sure to save it in the same folder as its content files (the ones created in step 1).

> If you want to change the number or organization of the frames after creating the frame definition page in HTML Assistant Pro, you must edit the HTML directly; no easy dialog box appears for revising the frames.
>
> An easier technique, however, is to simply create a new frame definition page (choosing new options along the way) and incorporate the same content files as in the preceding version. Doing so takes only a minute or two and is quicker than fussing with the code.

11. Still in HTML Assistant, click the Preview button to see the page displayed in your default browser (see Figure 27.6).

12. Leave your browser open, and open Composer.

13. Make any changes you want to the content files to improve their appearance in their frames. After changing a file, save it in Composer and open the frame definition page in Composer or in your browser to check your work.

FIGURE 27.6

*Step 11: Click the
Preview button to view
the frames page in
your browser.*

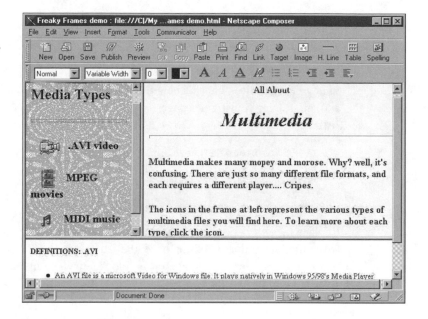

FIGURE 27.6

*Step 11: Click the
Preview button to view
the frames page in
your browser.*

When you publish a frames page to the Web (see Chapter 30, "Publishing Your Page"), you must be certain to publish the frame definition page and each of the separate content pages.

Even though you can't view the frames in Composer, you can open the frame definition page in Composer and use the Composer publishing tools to publish the frame definition page. You can finish up by publishing each of the content pages separately.

You can also publish your frames page simply by uploading all its files via FTP or using the publishing tools in HTML Assistant Pro.

Creating Frames in HTML

27

Most folks' frames needs are more than satisfied by HTML Assistant Pro, as shown in the preceding example. But if you want greater control over your frames, you want to edit the HTML source directly, in either HTML Assistant Pro or in another tool.

If you don't know how to edit HTML, see Chapter 26, "Editing HTML."

1. In Composer, compose the content pages to be displayed in the frames. Try to organize and format them, if possible, in a way that minimizes the need for visitors to scroll them in their frames. (Keep in mind that you can always fine-tune them later, after seeing how they look in their frames.)

2. In any HTML editor, create a new HTML file, including the required structure tags and the title for your frames page:

```
<HTML>
<HEAD>
<TITLE>Frames Demo</TITLE>
</HEAD>
    <BODY>
    </BODY>
</HTML>
```

3. Replace the <BODY> tags with <FRAMESET> tags, as shown in the following code. (Note that in a frame definition page, the <FRAMESET> block replaces the <BODY> block, and you cannot include a <BODY> block anywhere in the file.)

```
<HTML>
<HEAD>
<TITLE>Frames Demo</TITLE>
</HEAD>
    <FRAMESET>
    </FRAMESET>
</HTML>
```

The <FRAMESET> tags enclose the entire definition of the frames. All further coding is inserted between these tags.

4. The frames page is split into two columns without any rows. Therefore, in the <FRAMESET> tag, you add the COLS attribute. Suppose that you want the first column to be narrow (30 percent of the window) and the second column to take up the remainder of the window.

```
</FRAMESET>
```

> In the <FRAMESET> tag in the example, COLS="*,70%" or COLS="30%,70%"
> would have the same effect as the entry shown.

5. Having defined the frames, you define their content by adding the <FRAME SRC> tag and the filenames of the content files (in quotes). In the columns on the page, the files are displayed in the same order (from left to right) in which they appear in the <FRAMESET> block (from top to bottom). In the following example, the page file MULTI.HTM is displayed in the first (left) column:

```
<FRAMESET COLS="30%,*">
    <FRAME SRC="MULTI.HTM">
    <FRAME SRC="DESCRIP.HTM">
</FRAMESET>
```

6. Review the completed code of the frame definition page:

```
<HTML>
<HEAD>
    <TITLE>Frames Demo</TITLE>
</HEAD>
    <FRAMESET COLS="30%,*">
        <FRAME SRC="MULTI.HTM">
        <FRAME SRC="DESCRIP.HTM">
    </FRAMESET>
</HTML>
```

7. Choose File, Save, and save the new frame definition page. Be sure to save it in the same folder as its content files (the ones created in step 1).

8. Test your new page by opening the frame definition page in your browser (see Figure 27.7).

FIGURE 27.7

Step 8: Test the page in a browser.

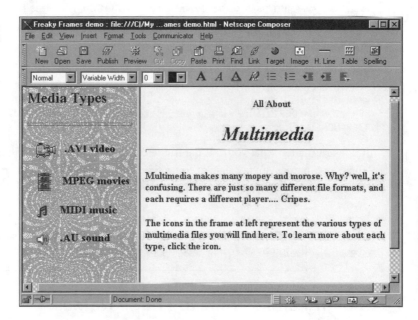

27

Specifying the Frame in Which a Linked Page Opens

If you code your frame definition pages as shown up to this point in the chapter, a link that appears in any of the pages opens its corresponding file in the same frame that holds the link. In other words, if I click a link that's shown in the upper-left frame, the page opened by that link also appears in the upper-left frame, replacing the file that was there.

If you want a link in one frame to open a new page in another frame, you must do two things:

- In the <FRAME SRC> lines of the frameset, give each frame a name.
- In the links within the content files, indicate the name of the frame in which the linked file should open.

Naming the Frames

Using the page created in the preceding example as a starting point, name the frames. Add the NAME= attribute to the <FRAME SRC> tag after the filename (and a blank space), as shown in the following code:

```
<FRAMESET ROWS="75%,*")
<FRAMESET COLS"30%,*")
<FRAME SRC="MULTI.HTM" NAME="Icons">
<FRAME SRC="DESCRIP.HTM" NAME="Text">
</FRAMESET>
<FRAME SRC="DEFINI.HTM" NAME="Definitions">
</FRAMESET>
```

It doesn't matter what you call the frames, as long as you give each one a unique name. The frame names are not displayed on the page, just in the source code.

To name frames while creating them in the Frames Setup dialog box in HTML Assistant Pro, click the Advanced check box. Doing so expands the dialog box to reveal a box in which you can type a name for each frame.

Making Links Point to Frame Names

After naming the frames, you must edit the links within the content files to add the *target*: the name of the frame in which the linked files should open.

To code your targets in HTML, you must add the TARGET= attribute and the frame name (in quotes) to the link, following the filename, as in the following example:

```
<A HREF="avidef.htm" TARGET="Definitions"></a>
```

When the link shown is executed, the file AVIDEF.HTM opens in the frame named Definitions (the bottom frame), replacing DEFINI.HTM.

Suppose that you want every link in the MULTI.HTM file to open its file in the Text frame. When all links are to open in the same frame, you can save time by using the <BASE TARGET> tag in the content file's header. All links in a file containing a <BASE TARGET> tag open their files in the frame named by <BASE TARGET>; you do not need to add any TARGET attributes to the link tags, as in the following example:

```
<HTML>
<HEAD>
<TITLE>
<BASE TARGET="Text">
</HEAD>
<BODY>
page definition goes here
</BODY>
</HTML>
```

All links in the sample content file open their files in the Text frame.

Accommodating the Frame-Intolerant

For all that frames can deliver, they can also make you pay.

Frames generally slow down initial access to a page (because the browser must download multiple files) and, when poorly designed, force visitors to do lots of scrolling simply to read the contents of a single page. Frames are supported in all versions of Internet Explorer and Netscape Navigator released since about 1997 and in some—but not all— other browsers.

Besides all that, many folks online (especially relative newcomers to the Web) simply don't like navigating frames pages; they find them confusing.

For all these reasons, many authors who create frames pages also create a non-frames version, with identical content, and give visitors a choice of which version to view. The easiest way to do this task is to create a non-frames page that contains links to each of exactly the same, separate content pages also opened by the frame definition page.

Another useful touch is to add a "noframes" message to the frame definition page. When a visitor using a non-frames–capable browser opens the frame definition page, the message appears in place of the frames. The message can include a link to the non-frames version; for example:

27

```
Sorry, your browser does not support frames. To view the non-frames version of
the Web site, click here.
```

Two easy ways to create the noframes message are

- Open the frame definition page in HTML Assistant Pro and look for the <NOFRAMES> tag near the bottom of the file. Replace the sample text there (This is where to put text that browsers without frames support will display) with your message and URL.

- Open the frame definition page in Composer. Because Composer does not support frames, it shows the sample noframes message created by HTML Assistant Pro—it acts, in effect, like a non-frames–capable browser. You can edit the message right there in Composer, add your URL pointing to the non-frames version, and then save the file.

Summary

Frames are an exercise in careful choices and organization. Most important among the choices is deciding whether to even use frames. When you're committed to using frames, always try to supply a useful <NOFRAME> message and an alternative version for the frame-less.

CHAPTER 28

Designing Fill-in-the-Blanks Forms

You know forms. They're those fill-in-the-blanks parts of Web pages you use to enter search terms, register with a Web site, make e-purchases, and much more. In fact, Web forms are really the only way a Web visitor can send information to a Web site through the Web (email doesn't count).

A signature containing your email address (see Chapter 23, "Making Links") is sufficient for providing visitors with a way to send you comments and questions. But if your site is visited hundreds or thousands of times a day or you want to collect orders or mailing list signups online, you need a more efficient method—a way to collect all the information sent by visitors, store it in a database, and then work with it in a meaningful way. That's what forms make possible.

The material in this chapter requires a basic understanding of HTML and basic familiarity with HTML Assistant Pro. If you lack this knowledge, you skipped Chapter 26, "Editing HTML." Tsk, tsk. Go take a quick tour of Chapter 26, and then come back. I'll wait.

Understanding Forms

A *form* is a Web page (or a part of a Web page) that collects information from your visitors by prompting them to select options from lists, check boxes, and other such form fields (see Figure 28.1). When done supplying information, the visitor clicks a Submit button to send the data to the server to be processed. (An optional *Reset* button also is often provided; this button clears all the forms entries a visitor has made so that he or she can start over, if necessary.)

FIGURE 28.1

Forms use fields to collect information from visitors.

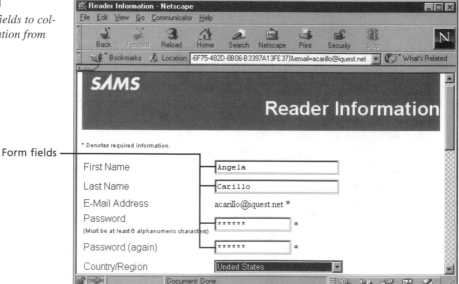

Creating the part of a form you see is easy—in fact, HTML Assistant Pro 2000 can even create one for you, in several different ways. But the part you see is only half the form; the other half consists of various behind-the-scenes programming for collecting and processing the data visitors enter and storing it in a form that's useful to you.

That processing can happen in several different ways; for example, if you use Microsoft FrontPage as your authoring tool and if the Web server on which you publish the page containing the form is equipped with the Microsoft software FrontPage Extensions, you can configure nearly all aspects of processing from within FrontPage, and you will need no other programming to process your form.

But if you do not use FrontPage and the extensions, a short program called a *script* must be custom-written to process your form, and that script must be properly set up on the Web server. The script can be programmed in any of several different programming languages (CGI scripts, created in the Perl programming language, are the most common). Such programming generally exceeds the capabilities and ambitions of beginning Web authors—although, if you're so inclined, plenty of good books can teach you.

For beginners, I think that the best approach is this: You worry about what appears onscreen, and you let someone else worry about the scripting.

If you will publish on your Internet provider's Web server, you can simply define the form's onscreen appearance (as you learn to do in this chapter) and then talk with your Internet provider about how you want the data handled. In all likelihood, the Internet provider will have a script already written that can be modified to suit your particular needs.

Creating the Visible Form

Alas, Composer includes no tools for making forms. But HTML Assistant Pro 2000 provides easy-to-use tools for creating the form.

Although the data processing aspects of forms can be tricky, creating the form itself in HTML Assistant Pro is a snap. The next several pages show several different ways you can quickly produce any type of form you desire.

Building a Fast, Easy Form with a Template

HTML Assistant Pro includes a form template you can use to create a new form in a snap. Based on your selections in a simple dialog box, HTML Assistant Pro builds a basic form for you. You can start your page in HTML Assistant Pro, create the form, and then finish the page in Composer, or you can switch from Composer to HTML Assistant Pro to add the form and then jump back to Composer when your form has been added.

Composer cannot give you a WYSIWYG view of your form. To preview your form, you must view the page in a browser. In Composer, the form fields are indicated with yellow tag icons, like all HTML tags that Composer does not recognize.

28

1. Open HTML Assistant Pro by clicking the Windows Start button and choosing Programs, HTML Assistant Pro 2000, Pro 2000 (see Figure 28.2).

FIGURE 28.2

Step 1: Open HTML Assistant Pro 2000.

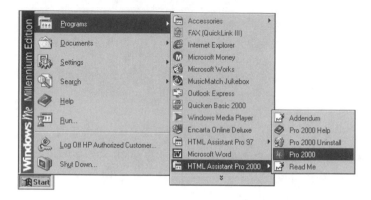

2. Choose File, Open to open a page.
3. Browse to and select a page you've been working on in Composer (see Figure 28.3).

FIGURE 28.3

Step 3: Choose a file to add a form to.

4. Look carefully at the Body section of the HTML, and locate the spot in the page where you'll want to insert the form (see Figure 28.4).
5. Click at that spot and choose Special, Form Components, Form from the menu bar (see Figure 28.5).
6. Click the Create a Form Template button (see Figure 28.6).

FIGURE 28.4

Step 4: Find the area within the page where you want to add a form.

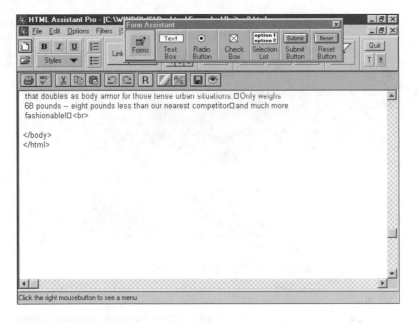

FIGURE 28.5

Step 5: Choose Special, Form Components, Form.

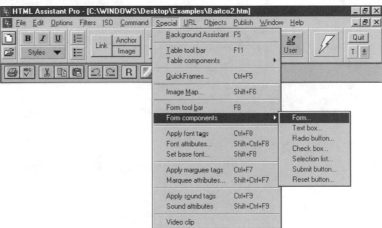

FIGURE 28.6

Step 6: Click Create a Form Template.

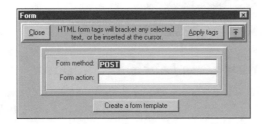

28

7. Check the check boxes next to any form "data input" types you want to include (see Figure 28.7). (If you don't quite recognize what these items are yet, just don't worry about it. They're covered later in this chapter, in the section "Adding Form Fields.") When finished, click OK.

8. To view the results, click the Preview button (the button with an eye icon on the far right side—see Figure 28.8).

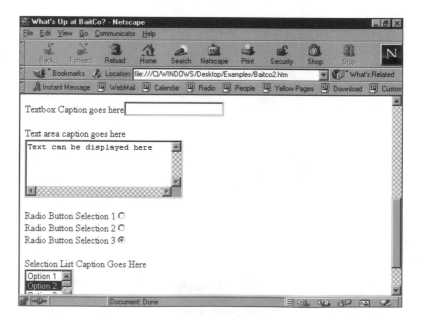

Example: Edit Your Form Labels in Composer

The form added by HTML Assistant Pro has boilerplate text all over it, stuff like "Option 1" and "Text Goes Here." Obviously, you want to change these labels, or *captions*, to text that means something to you and your visitors.

You can do this right in HTML Assistant, if you're comfortable rooting around in HTML. But because you'll do most of your other authoring in Composer, you might as well switch over and do the work there:

1. Open Composer, and open in Composer the file you added a form to.

2. Composer displays its tag icons where the form fields are; the other text, before and after each tag, is the boilerplate text you can replace (see Figure 28.9).

The labels that begin with the word Option are the individual options on a drop-down list.

FIGURE 28.9

Composer displays your form's labels, plus tag icons representing the form fields.

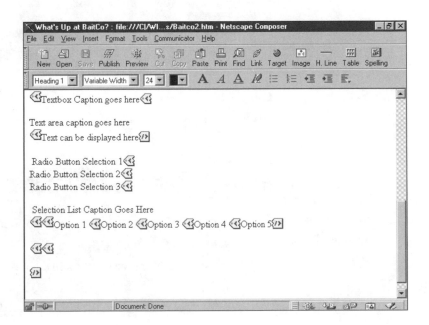

3. Highlight any block of text.

4. Type its replacement.

In the boilerplate form field labels on your HTML Assistant-built form, watch for the word *can*, as in "Text can be displayed here." That word tips you off that the label in that case is not required. You can replace the text containing *can*, but you might also erase it altogether.

28

Adding Form Fields

Besides providing a template for making forms, HTML Assistant offers the Form Assistant toolbar (see Figure 28.10), from which you can quickly create forms containing precisely the fields you require.

FIGURE 28.10

Use the Form Assistant toolbar to add individual fields to a form.

Form Assistant Toolbar

To display the Form Assistant toolbar, choose Special, Form Tool Bar from the HTML Assistant Pro menu bar.

To add fields, you click buttons on the Form Assistant toolbar:

 Text Box

Radio Button

Check Box

Selection List

Submit Button

Reset Button

1. Open the page file in HTML Assistant Pro.

2. Choose Special, Form Tool Bar to display the Form Assistant toolbar.

3. Examine the HTML code carefully, to locate the section where your form is located. The form code begins with the tag <FORM...> and ends with the tag </FORM>.

4. Examining the form field tags already in place, locate and click in the spot where you want to add a new field (see Figure 28.11).

FIGURE 28.11

Step 4: Choose the spot in the code where you will add a new form field.

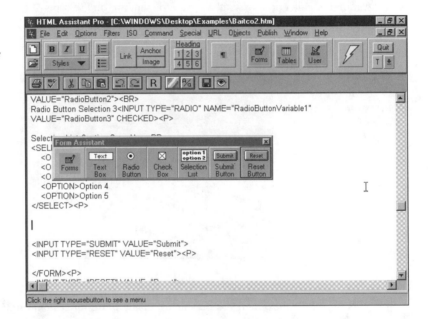

5. Press Enter to start a new line on which to add the field.

6. On the Form Assistant toolbar, click the button for the form field you want to add.

Customizing Fields

When adding form fields, you can customize their appearance or action. For example, when adding a text box, you can choose to make it a multiline text box rather than the default single-line text box, to give your visitors room to type longer input.

To choose options for a form field while creating it, don't click the button for the field on the Form Assistant toolbar. Instead, right-click the button. An options dialog box (different for each form field) appears (see Figure 28.12). Choose your options and then click the Apply Tags button in the dialog box.

28

FIGURE 28.12

*Right-click a button on
the Form Assistant
toolbar to see options
for customizing that
field.*

Again, the exact options you see vary, depending on the type of field you double-clicked.
Most options are self-explanatory. You can expand these dialog boxes by clicking the
Advanced check box you see in each dialog box (see Figure 28.13).

FIGURE 28.13

*Click the Advanced
check box to see
advanced options for a
form field.*

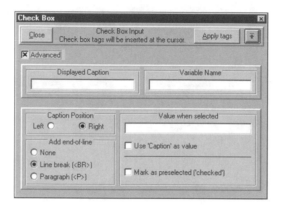

One option you see in most dialog boxes for customizing form fields is
Variable Name. This name, which does not appear in your page, is used by
the CGI programmer to determine what happens to the data the visitor will
type there.

For example, the variable name for a text box intended to collect the visitor's first name could be FIRSTNAME. Choosing these variables enables you
to communicate more effectively with your CGI programmer, giving you the
ability to tell him or her exactly what you want done with each piece of
input collected.

However, you'll see two important options, especially when you've clicked the
Advanced check box that might not be so self-explanatory:

- **Value**—In one-line and scrolling text boxes, this is an optional, default form entry
  you offer your visitors to save them time. For example, if you predict that most
  visitors will probably make a particular entry in a text box, you can make that

entry appear to be pre-entered on the form. The visitor can always change that entry, but if the initial value is what he would have chosen or typed anyway, he can skip that field. Some Web authors also use the Initial Value field to display within the form an instruction for using the form ("Type your address here").

- **Mark as Preselected**—In lists, check boxes, and radio buttons, you can specify that a particular field or list item is automatically selected so that visitors who would have made the same selection can skip the field.

Summary

As you can see, building a form is easy—even fun. And building the data-handling can be fun, too—but you must be willing to commit yourself to moving a notch higher in your technical expertise.

28

CHAPTER **29**

Putting Multiple Links in One Picture

You've seen 'em—those cool-looking pictures and button bars in Web pages that contain multiple links. Click one button or one part of the picture and you go one place; click another part, you go somewhere else. It's a pro touch.

But it's not out of your league, now that you have 19 chapters of Web authoring training already under your belt. In this chapter, you learn how to apply some of the HTML skills from Chapter 26, "Editing HTML," and scripting skills from Chapter 28, "Designing Fill-in-the-Blanks Forms," to make these multilink pictures happen.

This chapter assumes that you have already installed Netscape Communicator 4.7 and its built-in Web-authoring program, Composer. If you have not, visit `http://wp.netscape.com/download/archive.html` and download Netscape Communicator version 4.7 for your system. (It's free.)

This chapter also assumes that you have downloaded a free trial of the HTML editor HTML Assistant Pro. You can download it from `http://www.exit0.com`.

This chapter also assumes that you have downloaded the image map program MapEdit. You can download it from `http://www.boutell.com/mapedit/`.

About Imagemaps

You know that an image file can serve as a link source; clicking the image activates the link. By creating an imagemap, you can make different areas within one image activate different links. Figure 29.1 shows an imagemap.

FIGURE 29.1

Clicking on different parts of this imagemap activates different links.

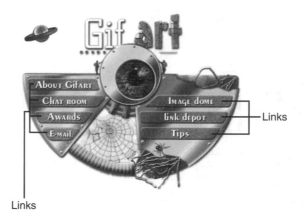

An *imagemap* is an inline image containing multiple links, each of which is activated when the visitor clicks a different area of the image.

Imagemaps are used for fancy jobs, such as maps—click a country or state and a link opens a document about it. But imagemaps have more mundane uses as well; for example, most button bars you see online are imagemaps. The whole bar is one big GIF file, but the imagemap assigns a separate URL to each button.

The links in an imagemap can point anywhere that any other link can point: to another Web page, to an email address, to a bookmark (*target*), or to a file for download or display, for example.

Server-Side Versus Client-Side

29

An imagemap can be written as a server-based, imagemapping script, or it can be coded into the HTML file itself to be run by the browser, or *client*. When the imagemap code is inserted directly into the HTML file, it's a *client-side* imagemap. When a script on the server is required, the code is a *server-side* imagemap.

 To learn more about scripts, see Chapter 28, "Designing Fill-in-the-Blanks Forms."

Which should you create? Here's the full poop: Client-side imagemaps are much easier to create than server-side imagemaps. Client-side imagemaps work only when the page is viewed through an imagemap-compatible browser, but, fortunately, the overwhelming majority of folks online today use browsers that can handle client-side imagemaps. Client-side imagemaps are supported by

- Every version of Internet Explorer since its debut
- Netscape Navigator versions 2 and later

These browsers (which together represent about 90 percent of the browsers used on the Web) support not only client-side imagemaps, but also server-side imagemaps.

A very small proportion of folks online—those using graphical browsers other than the ones I listed—cannot use client-side imagemaps, but *can* use server-side imagemaps. Of course, those using text-only browsers cannot use any kind of picture links, including any sort of imagemap, whether client or server.

As you know from Chapter 28, writing scripts requires more technical expertise than most beginning Web authors care to develop. On top of that, publishing your scripts on a server requires close collaboration with the administrator of the Web server where your pages will be published to ensure that you write your script in a language the server supports and follow other rules that vary from server to server. Server-side imagemaps require much more work than client-side imagemaps and expand the reach of your page by only a tiny proportion.

Given that, I recommend doing what most Web authors do these days:

- Stick to client-side imagemaps.
- Make sure that a block of text links on the page repeats all links that are in any imagemap (or other picture link) on the same page (see Figure 29.2).

FIGURE 29.2

Always repeat any links in an imagemap (or any other picture link) in text links on the same page, to serve those whose browsers don't support imagemaps or pictures.

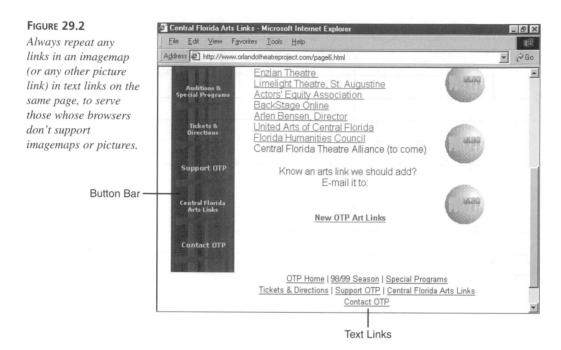

Button Bar ─────

Text Links

Your client-side imagemaps will work great for nearly all visitors. And the text links will serve not only visitors whose browsers don't support client-side imagemaps, but also those with text-only browsers and those who have turned off the display of images in their browsers to speed up surfing.

Choosing (or Creating) Images Suited for Imagemapping

You can use any GIF or JPEG image for an imagemap, whether it's one you created or a copyright-free piece of clip art. The best image for an imagemap is one that's clearly and obviously divided into distinct regions.

After seeing the image, a visitor *must* instinctively expect different regions to lead to different places. If the image's regions are not clearly defined, a visitor might assume that the image is a picture link leading only one place and click it without carefully choosing a region. Or the visitor might not even realize that the picture contains any links and fail to exploit the useful tool you have so thoughtfully provided.

For example, consider the image shown in Figure 29.3. This image is a poor choice for an imagemap because it does not appear to have distinct segments or regions. The image shown in Figure 29.4 is a better choice because it is divided naturally into identifiable shapes that visitors will naturally assume contain different links.

FIGURE 29.3

This image would make a poor imagemap. How could you tell which parts to click?

FIGURE 29.4

This image, clearly divided into distinct regions, is a better choice.

Creating an Imagemap

To use MapEdit to create a client-side imagemap, you first create your page (in Composer or another tool) and insert in the page the image you will use for the imagemap. You then open the page in MapEdit to turn the image into an imagemap, as described in the following example.

In general, you should finish all other aspects of the page (in Composer or in another Web authoring program) before using MapEdit to make one or more images in the page into imagemaps.

Why? Well, if you change the size or shape or any other aspects of an image in the page after you create the imagemap, the imagemap might not work properly anymore. In practice, you can probably do some manipulation of the page safely after adding the imagemap, but it's hard to predict which kinds of changes will create problems later and which won't. You should leave MapEdit for the final step.

> If, after creating an imagemap, you decide that you must make major changes to the page (or if you've already made such changes and discover that your imagemap no longer works properly), the best solution is to reopen the page and image in MapEdit (as described in steps 2 through 5 of the example) and adjust the regions as needed.

1. Using Composer or another tool, create the page and insert in it the image that will become the imagemap.

2. Open MapEdit from the Windows Start menu by choosing Programs, MapEdit, MapEdit.

3. Choose File, Open HTML Document.

4. Navigate to and select the file of the Web page you created in Step 1 and then click Open.

5. The list shows all the image files in the page. Click the one that will serve as the imagemap and then click OK.

FIGURE 29.5

Step 5: From the images shown in the page you opened in step 4, choose the one for the imagemap.

6. Consider the general shape of the first region to which you want to attach a link: Is it more or less circular or rectangular, or is it a more irregular polygon? Decide what the closest shape is and then click that shape in the toolbar.

7. Click and drag to draw a shape that generally covers the region:

- For a circle, click in the center of the region and drag outward. When the shape generally covers the region, click once.

- For a rectangle, click in the upper-right corner of the region and drag diagonally toward the lower-right corner. When the shape generally covers the region, click once.

- For a polygon, click one corner of the region and drag to another corner to draw a line. Click the corner you've arrived at to stop that line and then drag to the next corner. Continue until you have drawn a shape completely around the region and then right-click.

FIGURE 29.6

Step 7: Click a shape tool and draw a shape to define the region.

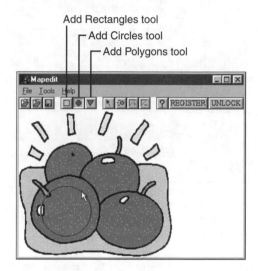

Add Rectangles tool
Add Circles tool
Add Polygons tool

If you don't like the point where you started a shape, press Esc to clear the shape and start over.

In steps 6 and 7, don't fuss too much over trying to perfectly match a shape to a region. As long as the shape you draw roughly covers the region and does not overlap with other shapes you draw for other regions, it's no big deal if some gaps occur between the shapes covering regions or if the shape covers a little bit of space outside the region.

Understanding this, you find that in most cases you can use the Circle or Rectangle tools to draw your rough shapes, resorting to the more laborious Polygon tool for only special circumstances.

8. Fill in the URL to which a visitor should be taken when clicking this region and click OK (see Figure 29.7).

FIGURE 29.7

Step 8: Fill in the URL to which this region points.

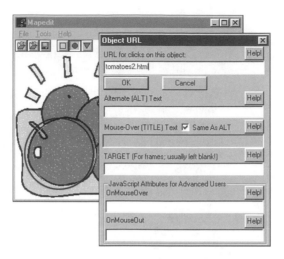

The TARGET field in the dialog box shown in Figure 29.7 is not for entering the name of a bookmark (see Chapter 23, "Making Links") as you might expect, but rather for choosing the *target frame*.

If the HTML file you opened in step 2 will be part of a frames-based Web page, you can enter in the TARGET field the name of the frame in which you want the file or page opened by this link to appear. See Chapter 27, "Dividing a Page into Frames."

9. Repeat Steps 6, 7, and 8 for each region in the image (see Figure 29.8). (You can use different kinds of shapes and different kinds of URLs for different regions.)

FIGURE 29.8

Step 9: Complete the regions.

29

10. Choose File, Save HTML Document to save the Web page file with its new imagemap added to it.
11. Preview the file in a Web browser to test the links.

In Step 8 of the example, you can enter any type of URL: one pointing to a Web site or Web page (for example, http://www.samspublishing.com), the filename of another Web page in your Web site, stored in the same folder (page2.html), a link to an email address (mailto:me@server.com), or the name of a file for downloading (resume.doc).

To make the link point to a particular bookmark (*target*), add a hash mark and the bookmark name (#hours3) to the URL as described in Chapter 23.

Summary

Imagemaps are pretty cool and not too hard to make. Just be sure that you choose an image in which the regions to which you attach links are easy for visitors to recognize.

CHAPTER **30**

Publishing Your Page

You didn't become a Web author just to share your accomplishments with your canary. Of course, you want to get your work on a Web server so that it can be visited, loved, and lauded by those burgeoning Web masses.

Composer is a big help with publishing. By setting up a few defaults and properly organizing your files, you wind up with the ability to publish your pages (and then update them later) with a few quick clicks.

About Web Servers

As you've known for a number of chapters, you need space on the hard disk of a Web server to publish your page on the Web.

By now, you probably already know where you intend to publish your page. Nearly all Internet accounts—whether with a regular Internet service provider or with an online service, like AOL—now include a few megabytes of Web server space in the deal (see Figure 30.1). Most folks publish their first Web pages in the space supplied by their Internet providers.

FIGURE 30.1

Most folks just starting out with Web publishing should use any Web server space that comes free with their Internet or online service account.

Free Web Space Deal ——

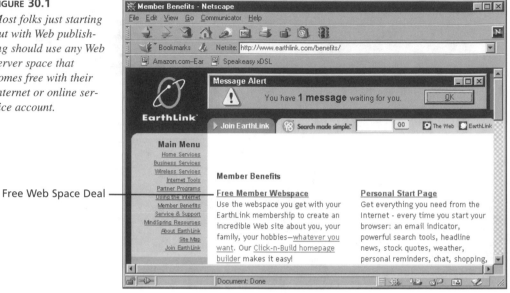

Note that Web space suppliers usually make a distinction between personal home pages and commercial pages (those used to promote a business). On the assumption that a commercial page generally gets more traffic than a personal one, suppliers might charge a higher rate for space used by a commercial page.

If your Internet provider gives you free space, the provider might require that the space be used for only a personal page and might charge an additional monthly fee if you use the space for commercial purposes. (Exceptions may be made for not-for-profits; talk to your provider.)

In case your Internet provider offers no server space to you, here are some other ways to pick up Web server space:

Before choosing a provider for Web space, visit that company's Web page a few times at different hours. If the server sends pages slowly at certain hours or seems to be unavailable from time to time, look for a better-equipped provider.

- **At work or school**—Your employer or school might have a Web server on which you are permitted to store your page. Certainly, if your page is strictly work related (or school related), you're most likely to gain permission to publish it on the server for free.

  However, note that free access to corporate and university servers is diminishing rapidly as demand grows and as organizations look for ways to earn money from their Internet connections. Also, many university systems, as well as some corporate systems, are overtaxed and might have outdated server hardware or inadequate connection speeds. Using a slow or unreliable system provides poor service to your visitors; forking over a few dollars a month for space on a fast commercial server might be a better choice in the long run than using free space on a poor server.

- **From a Web hosting service**—A growing number of companies online offer Web space "hosting services." Many such services are just Internet providers making a few bucks on the side by leasing server space, often for just a few dollars a month.

  You can also find "free" server space offered by a variety of companies sometimes called *online communities*. In exchange for your free space, you agree to include required advertising on your pages (see Figure 30.2).

> Finding Web hosting services by surfing is easy. You can enter the search term *Web hosting* in any search engine or visit the HostSearch site (www.hostsearch.com), a search tool specifically for finding server space (see Figure 30.3).
>
> Some hosting services are set up to offer free or low-cost space for pages with particular worthy topics: the arts or nonprofit organizations, for example.

- **The build-your-own method**—If your Web page requires extra-tight security (for online sales) or makes extensive use of CGI scripts (especially for forms), an in-house Web server might be your answer. Building your own Web server is a more practical solution than ever (even for relatively small companies), thanks to lower-priced server computers (especially Pentium-based PCs); cheaper, simpler server software (primarily from Microsoft, although free, open-source alternatives are also available); and the wide availability of high-speed data lines (such as ISDN or T1).

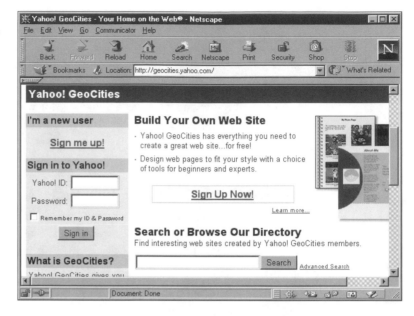

Setting up a Web server is not cheap. The hardware and software for a decent server is coming down rapidly, to a reasonable cost for a small business (less than $5,000). But the 24-hour, high-speed dedicated Internet connection that a Web server demands might cost more than four times that much—every month. Although effectively administering a Web server is getting easier all the time, the job essentially demands one or more full-time experts.

The combined cost of server, connection, and staff now falls within the means of most companies with more than 100 employees, or smaller companies whose line of business makes Web service a high priority. For other small companies and for individuals, however, leasing space on someone else's server is a far more sensible option.

Increasingly, commercial hosting services not only provide space, but can also supply (for a higher fee) e-commerce services. The hosting company can take care of processing orders and credit card transactions for you, so you can set up an online store without having to worry about all the e-details.

30

How Much Space Do I Need?

Good question. Odds are that you need very little, starting out.

As I've reminded you in past chapters, the more a page contains, the bigger its file. Pictures (and picture backgrounds) dramatically increase the amount of space a page requires (and the time it takes to appear to a visitor). Sound, video, and large file downloads also might dramatically increase the amount of space you need.

If you have followed the tips I've offered for keeping the performance of your page sprightly, you'll find that each page occupies very little space. A basic page—a screenful or two of text graced with two or three small picture files and maybe a picture background—typically requires less than 100KB of server space (often much less). You can store at least a dozen such basic Web pages in 1MB of server space. (There are 1024 kilobytes in a megabyte).

Most Internet providers and online services supply at least 3MB of free space to each customer; many supply as much as 10MB. That's enough to store 100 basic pages and have a few megs left over for a short video clip or two.

The following example shows how to determine the minimum amount of disk space required by your page files.

> The following example assumes that you have stored all the files for the page—the HTML file or files and picture files, for example—in the same folder on your hard disk.

1. In Windows, open the folder in which your Web page files are stored.

2. Press and hold the Ctrl key and click one by one all the files that are a part of the page. (The folder shouldn't have any files that aren't part of the page, but if it does, don't click those.)

3. When all the files are highlighted, you see the amount of space they occupy reported at the bottom of the folder window (see Figure 30.4). The Web page in this example (which includes two screenfuls of text, two pictures, and a picture background) requires only 5.16KB of space!

FIGURE 30.4

Step 3: Read the size of the combined files.

Amount of space required

Preparing to Publish

Before publishing, you want to have acquired your server space and given your page a final once-over. Even if you miss a mistake, you can easily fix it later and publish the correction.

The last thing you need to do before publishing is to get some important information from whomever is supplying your Web server space. Specifically, you need to know:

- **The name of the communications protocol required for uploading your files**—Many servers allow you to use the Web protocol (HTTP) for uploading files, whereas some require that files be uploaded via FTP. (Composer supports both methods.)

- **The complete address and path where your files will be stored**—You need to know the complete URL of the directory in which your files will be stored, including the server name, the path to your directory, and the name of your directory.

Ideally, you have your own separate directory for all your files. Having your own directory prevents conflicts that might arise if any other file on the system (a page, image, or other file) uses the same filename as one of your files.

It's standard practice to name the top page of a multipage Web site index.htm (or index.html).

Unless you have your own directory on the server, though, do not name any page index.htm (or index.html). Although this name is often used for the top page in a multipage Web page, if the directory already contains a file named index.htm, the server rejects yours—or overwrites the other!

30

- **The rules or restrictions for filenames on the server**—Different server platforms have different rules for filenames. For example, DOS-based servers and some UNIX servers do not permit filenames longer than eight characters or file extensions of more than three characters. Ideally, you find out about these types of restrictions before you create and name your files. But, if you composed your page without first finding out about the server, you should check for naming restrictions and change any filenames as needed.

If you find that you must alter any filenames, be sure to check and adjust any links between pages before and after publishing.

- **Your unique username and password for gaining upload access to the server**—Your server supplier should give you a username and password for uploading your files.

If you get server space from your Internet provider, the username and password you use to publish will probably be the same ones you always use to connect to the Internet.

Publishing from Composer

Most server providers prefer that you *upload*—copy your Web files from your PC to the Web server—using an Internet tool named FTP.

If you're familiar with FTP, you can always do it that way. But the publishing facilities built in to Composer can be much easier to use. More important, when you make changes to your pages online.

Even if you do know FTP, I recommend giving the Composer publishing tools a shot anyway. (If you don't already know FTP, you have no need to learn now—at least for publishing purposes.)

1. Connect to the Internet.

2. In Composer, open the HTML file you want to publish.

3. Click the Publish button on the Composer toolbar to open the Publish dialog box.

4. The page's title and HTML filename already appear in the box. Fill in the rest of the Publish dialog box with the address to which you will publish and the user-name and password your server provider gave you (see Figure 30.5).

FIGURE 30.5

Step 4: Complete the dialog box by filling in the address to publish to, your server user-name, and your pass-word.

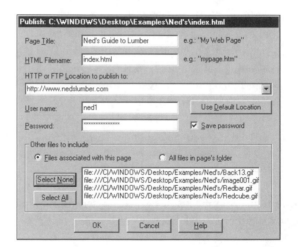

5. In the area at the bottom of the Publish dialog box, make sure that all the files required for your Web site have been included. If you've followed the advice given throughout this book—store all HTML files, pictures, and whatever in the same folder—this job is easy; simply select the All Files in Page's Folder option to send all files to the server (see Figure 30.6).

If you do not want to send all the files in the folder to the server, leave the All Files in Folder option unselected. Press and hold the Ctrl key and select one by one all the files in the folder you want to upload.

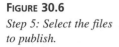

FIGURE 30.6

Step 5: Select the files to publish.

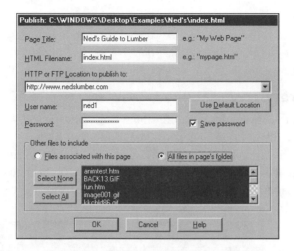

30

6. Click OK. In a few moments, a message appears and reports that the files have been uploaded. They are now on the Web, available to all.

Viewing Your Page Through the Internet

After you publish, you must test your page through the Web, viewing it exactly as your visitors will. Besides, it's fun to see the page online.

To view your page online, just open your browser, connect to the Internet, and go to the same address you typed in step 4 of the example for publishing. Explore your page, evaluating its appearance and testing all your links.

Testing and Maintaining Your Page Online

You haven't simply published a Web page. You've established a Web presence—hopefully one that will expand and evolve with time (most do). After your page is online, you should know how to update it—so that you can improve and enlarge it over time—and how to test it so that you can keep it performing reliably for your visitors.

Testing Your Pages

Okay, as you've worked on your page, you've evaluated its appearance by previewing it in Netscape, and by now you've checked out the page online through Netscape. So that means it's perfect, right?

Not necessarily. You might not be aware of all sorts of little glitches until you go looking for them. The next few sections show you how to thoroughly test your page after it's online so that you can make sure that your visitors have precisely the experience you want them to have.

Testing Browser Variability

You know that your page looks and functions fine when viewed through Netscape. But what about the rest of the Web population—those using earlier versions of Netscape or those using various versions of Internet Explorer or any of a dozen other browsers? How will your page look to them? Figures 30.7 through 30.10 illustrate how exactly the same page can appear dramatically different in different browsers.

FIGURE **30.7**

Ned's Lumber, as seen through Internet Explorer 5.

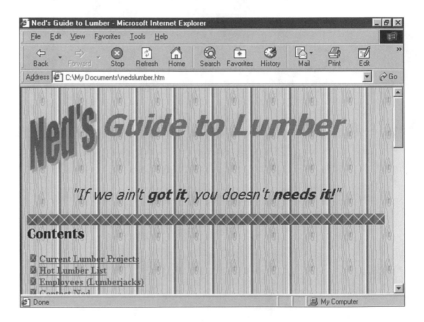

To make sure that your page's appearance is acceptable to all, you should view your page online through a variety of different browsers, just to see if any serious problems arise when using browsers other than Netscape 4. If you discover any problems in a particular browser environment, you must decide whether to adjust your page to eliminate the problem (which may involve compromising some of your formatting or other fancy features) or to sacrifice the performance of your page for one segment of the audience to preserve its performance for another.

FIGURE 30.8

Ned's Lumber, as seen through Netscape Navigator 4.

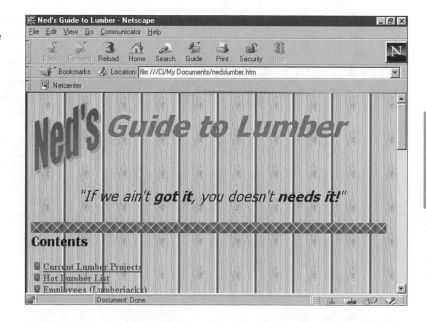

30

FIGURE 30.9

Ned's Lumber, as seen through Cello.

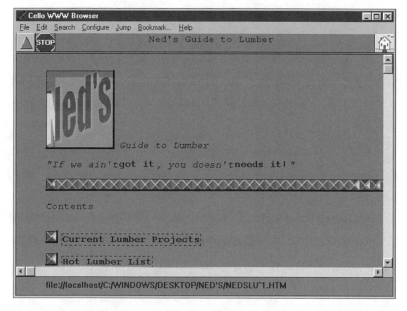

FIGURE 30.10

Ned's Lumber, as seen through DOSLynx.

Don't worry about whether the page looks identical through all sorts of browsers. It won't, and it doesn't have to. The question is "Does the page look okay in every browser?" Is all the text legible? Do the links work? If a picture or other element does not appear, does something else on the page fulfill the same function?

For example, if a bunch of links in an imagemap do not appear (or don't work) when displayed through a particular browser, are duplicate text links available? If your company logo doesn't show up, is the company name presented in a heading? If the background doesn't show up, is all the text legible without it?

You should keep some other browsers around to see how the other half sees you. You can download many different browsers from the Web for free. A good place to start is the Tucows Internet software directory (www.tucows.com), from which you can download many different browsers (see Figure 30.11).

Which browsers should you test in? Well, the overwhelming majority of the folks online browse the Web through Internet Explorer or Netscape Navigator, so you need to test in the latest version of each of those "Big Two" browsers, at least.

Keep in mind that not everybody keeps up with the latest browser versions, so a page that looks fine in the current version of Internet Explorer or Netscape might show some trouble when viewed through a browser from just a year or two ago.

FIGURE 30.11

The Tucows directory at www.tucows.com is a good place to pick up various browsers for testing.

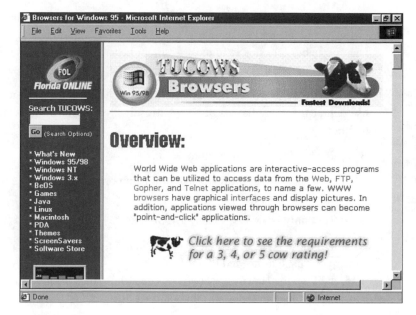

30

If you rummage through the CD-ROMs you have lying around (especially any that were bundled with computer books), you might find some that have older versions of Internet Explorer or Navigator you can use for testing your pages.

You often see outdated computer books for sale, sometimes for as little as $2, in big bins at bookstores. (It breaks my heart.)

Often, those books include CD-ROMs that have obsolete versions of various Web browsers. For a few bucks, you can pick up some old browser versions for testing and also pick up a lovely artifact of computer history. Check the book's copyright date before buying; a browser from any year before 1997 is probably too old to bother with.

Also, each of these browsers is available in different versions for different types of computers. For PCs alone, you can get Internet Explorer in three different "current" versions: a 16-bit version, the regular 64-bit version, and a 128-bit version for top-of-the-line PCs, like those with Pentium III and IV processors. Add to these the various Internet Explorer versions for other system types (such as Macintosh), and you must realize that you really have more than one Internet Explorer to consider. (Several different Netscape versions are available too.)

If your page looks okay in the most recent versions of Netscape and Internet Explorer (all versions released within about the past two years), you can rest assured that your page probably looks okay to most—but not necessarily all—folks on the Web.

After you've tested for the Netscape and Microsoft worlds, about 10 to 20 percent of Web users remain whose view of your page you don't know. Of those, many probably use one of the many flavors of NCSA Mosaic, the original Web browser, now largely defunct.

Beyond Mosaic, you may want to test in

- Older, graphical browsers that don't support recent Netscape or Microsoft extensions, such as Cello.
- Text-only browsers, such as DOSLynx.

Although these types of browsers are on their way out, you need to test in them and adjust your page as needed if you really want it to behave properly for absolutely all potential visitors. However, you must accept that doing so inevitably forces you to restrict your page to the most minimal formatting.

If you're really concerned about reaching everyone, supply your page in two versions: a fancy, extension-rich version and a very plain HTML 2–based version—and offer either from a universally visible top page. This is also a great way to accommodate differing connection speeds and patience levels. The version provided for older browsers usually also includes little or no multimedia, so those with slow Internet connections can enjoy your pages without waiting an eternity for them to appear (see Figure 30.12).

Testing at Different Resolutions

Within the past year or so, it has become standard practice to design Web pages to look their best when displayed on a computer screen running at 800×600 resolution, the most common setting now used by most folks on PCs and Macintoshes.

The compromise is effective: Users of computers running at the minimum Windows resolution of 640×480 need only do a little scrolling to see all of an 800×600 Web page, and the page appears acceptably large to those using higher resolutions.

Figures 30.13 through 30.15 show how the same Web page (one designed for 800×600) appears to visitors at three different resolutions.

FIGURE 30.12

To take advantage of advanced formatting while still supporting older browsers, you can create two versions of your pages—one simple, the other fancy—and give your visitors a choice between the two, from the top page.

30

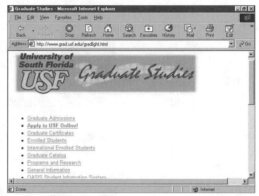

FIGURE 30.13

A page designed for 800×600 resolution on a display running at 640×480. The visitor must scroll to see the whole page.

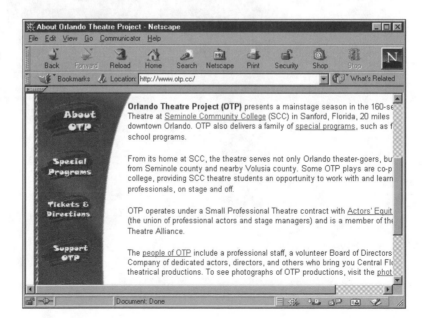

FIGURE 30.14

A page designed for 800×600 resolution on a display running at 800×600. The page image neatly fills the window.

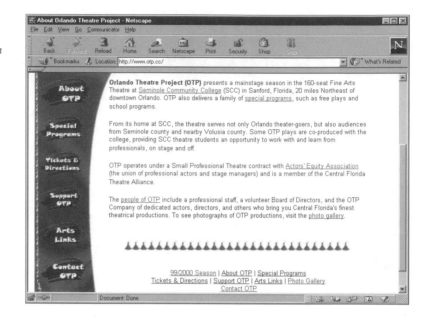

FIGURE 30.14

A page designed for 800×600 resolution on a display running at 800×600. The page image neatly fills the window.

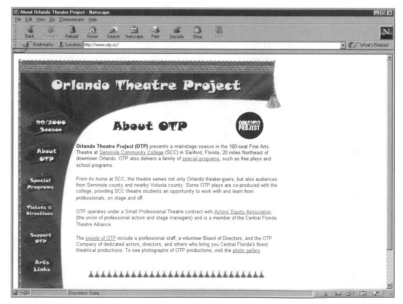

FIGURE 30.15

A page designed for 800×600 resolution on a display running at 1024×768.

You may recall that I recommend running your PC at 800×600 when using Netscape Composer. If you do and you design pages to look good on your own screen, you're designing for 800×600 without even having to think about it!

Display resolution is a factor only when pages contain pictures, tables, forms, or frames. The layout of a page containing only text is automatically fit to the size of the window in which it is displayed.

Tables and horizontal lines automatically refit themselves to varying resolutions when you have specified their width as a percentage of the window, not as a number of pixels (see Chapter 22, "Organizing Text with Tables and Rules"). However, when a table contains pictures, the results of that refit may not be appealing. Always test such pages at varying resolutions.

30

When evaluating your page, you're smart to check out how it looks at varying resolutions. To do that, you must change your display resolution in Windows and then view the page:

- To change your display resolution, open Windows Control Panel and double-click the Display icon. Choose the Settings tab and drag the slider control labeled Screen Area (in Windows 98) or Desktop Area (in Windows 95) to the resolution you want (see Figure 30.16).

FIGURE 30.16

Drag the slider control under Screen Area to change the display resolution in Windows.

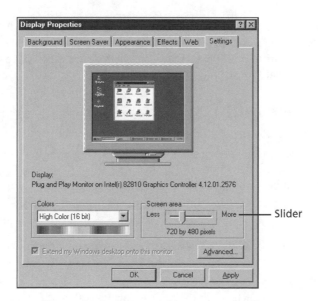

Slider

- After changing the resolution, when you open your browser you might find that the browser window is no longer fit perfectly to maximized full-screen size. To make the browser fill the screen, double-click the title bar at the top of the browser window.

> If you think that changing resolutions this way is a pain, you can download a free program named BrowserSizer from ApplyThis Software, at www.vasile.com/racecar/stampware/browsersizer/.
>
> BrowserSizer provides a simple menu from which you can easily change the size of the browser window (either Internet Explorer or Netscape Navigator) to a size that mimics the way the browser would appear at a particular resolution. This program gives you a fast and simple way to check your page's appearance in varying resolutions.

Testing Link Validity

Finally, you *must* test all the links in your page.

After you've verified the links among your own files—between your pages and to images and external media—you needn't recheck them unless you change a file. Retesting all such links whenever you make *any* changes to your Web site is a good practice. Even seemingly small changes to a single page can sometimes inadvertently scramble links.

When your page contains *external* links—links to other people's Web pages or to any file other than those you control on the server—you need to check these links often because the files they point to might have moved or their names might have changed. I recommend checking all external links at least once a month.

Evaluating Your Page's Ergonomics

The preceding sections in this chapter have explained only how to check your page's technical integrity. What about its fuzzy qualities—its look, its feel, its *mise-en-scéne*? And what about its interaction with visitors? Can they find what they came for? Do they see the parts of your message you want them to see? Do they naturally follow paths through your page to certain items, or are they frustrated by lots of blind alleys and backtracking?

The best way to answer these questions is to gather some friends (ideally friends who don't already know too much about your page or its subject) and cooperative strangers and watch them browse your page (no coaching!). Watch what they choose to click and what they skip. Note whenever they move down a path and fail to find what they expected or hoped to find. And, of course, listen to their comments.

Finally, remember always to use a signature with your email address. That way, people can send you comments and constructive criticisms.

Here's one final way to check out your pages: Any time, any place that you have an opportunity to visit your pages away from home, do it. In particular, look for opportunities to test your pages through other types of computers (such as Macintoshes) and varying connection speeds. You may find such opportunities

- When visiting friends who use the Internet
- At a local library that has a public Internet terminal
- At work

30

Updating Your Page

Okay, you've found some stuff you want to fix or updates to make. What's the procedure?

Begin by editing the original files on your PC in Composer. (You cannot edit the copies of the files that are on the Web server; you must work with what's on your PC.)

After making all your changes and testing the results offline in one or more browsers on your PC, start the publishing steps exactly as you did earlier in this chapter. Click the Publish button on the Composer toolbar to open the Publish dialog box (see Figure 30.17).

Here's the cool part: Composer remembers the server name and all the other stuff you entered when you originally published the page. As long as you change nothing in the Publish dialog box (see Figure 30.17) and simply click its OK button, that's all you have to do. The changed files are uploaded to the server, replacing the old pages and using the same settings you entered when you first published this page. (Depending on how your server and Internet account are set up, you might be prompted to sign on to the Internet or to supply your authentication information, but that's the most you have to do.)

Of course, you must retest your page after uploading changes. But you knew that, right?

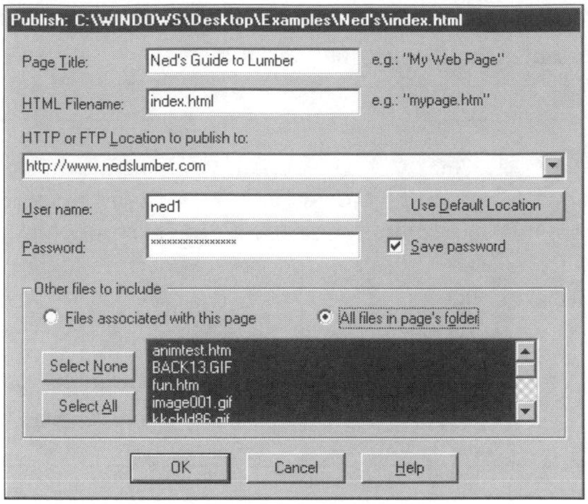

FIGURE 30.17

Click OK in the
Publish dialog box
(without changing any-
thing) to publish
changes to a Web page.

Publish: C:\WINDOWS\Desktop\Examples\Ned's\index.html

Page Title:	Ned's Guide to Lumber	e.g.: "My Web Page"
HTML Filename:	index.html	e.g.: "mypage.htm"

HTTP or FTP Location to publish to:

http://www.nedslumber.com

User name: ned1   Use Default Location

Password: xxxxxxxxxxxxxxx   ☑ Save password

Other files to include

○ Files associated with this page   ● All files in page's folder

Select None   animtest.htm
                BACK13.GIF
Select All   fun.htm
                image001.gif
                kkcbld86.gif

OK   Cancel   Help

Summary

Publishing is a simple activity (and relatively foolproof) as long as you've taken care in the preparation of your page. Simple mistakes, like putting files for the same page in different directories, are the kinds of things that most often cause publishing problems.

If you are careful with your filenames and locations, obey your server's rules, and follow the publishing steps, you'll find publishing one of the more satisfying aspects of authoring—the reward for a job well done.

CHAPTER **31**

Developing Your Authoring Skills

I tell you nothing here that immediately adds to your authoring skill set. (I know—it's a cheap trick. It's like when they forced you to show up for the last day of high school and then let you goof off all day anyway.)

What you do get in this chapter is a graduation speech from Part II of this book, or, rather, a send-off with a purpose. If you've hit most or all of this Part, you've built a solid foundation as an author. But there's always more to learn, always that one new trick that can make a good Web page into a great one. You now possess all the prerequisites needed to understand more advanced authoring information that you might find in other books or on the Web. So in this last hurrah, you find tips for developing your new skills.

Getting Your Own Domain (Your Own Dot-Com)

If you simply take some space on someone else's server, your page is accessible through the Web but it doesn't have the sort of catchy Web address that gives you a Web identity, such as `www.buick.com`. Instead, your page's address is expressed as a directory on the server; for example, `www.serviceco.com/neddyboy/fredo/`.

If you want to have your own Internet name, you must register your own Internet domain and then have that domain set up on the server on which you will publish your pages.

When you check to see whether the domain you want to use is available (as you will in the next example), you might receive a message that the name is available for purchase or lease, for a particular sum.

Because a domain costs only $70, a number of companies have snapped up every domain name they can think of that anyone might want to use. But they have no intention of using the names; they intend to sell them, often for much more than $70.

Because the technical details of setting up your domain on the server must be taken care of by whomever controls your server, I recommend having your Internet provider (or whoever else controls the server you use) take care of both registering and setting up your domain for you. Most providers will register a domain for a small fee, or even for free.

Whether you set up your domain yourself or have someone else do it, you still must pay some fees to Network Solutions (or one of the other domain registration services; see Tip on next page), the organization that manages domains for the Internet. At the time of this writing, Network Solutions charges $70 to establish the domain, which includes two years of keeping the domain. After that, you must pay $35 per year to maintain it. Typically, if your provider sets up your domain, it can also collect the fees and forward them to Network Solutions for you.

FYI, Network Solutions is no longer the only source for registering a domain name, although it remains the largest. There are others you may use, including `register.com`, `siteleader.com`, and `worldwidedomains.com`. The process for registering on all such sites is similar, but prices may vary, so check 'em out.

Although you might need help setting up the domain, you can choose the name all by yourself. The trick is that the domain must be absolutely unique—it can't be the same as any other domain already in use. You can use the Network Solutions Web site to find out whether the domain you want is available, as described in the following example.

The final part of the domain name can be .com or .cc (both for commercial sites, the most common), .org (organization, like a foundation or other not-for-profit), .edu (educational institution), or .net (network). If you're not sure what to use, you're probably a .com.

Being a .com, as opposed to an .org or other domain type, has an advantage. The .com suffix is so common that many Web users—particularly newcomers—have a habit of assuming that all addresses end in .com. Tell people that your page is at www.nedco.org, and a surprising number of them will try to reach you at www.nedco.com and never understand why you're not there.

1. Think about what you want your Internet domain to be; for example, `www.cathycorp.com`. Have a few options ready, in case one or more are already taken.

2. Visit the Network Solutions Web site at `www.networksolutions.com` (see Figure 31.1).

31

FIGURE 31.1

Step 2: Visit Network Solutions at `www.networksolutions.com`.

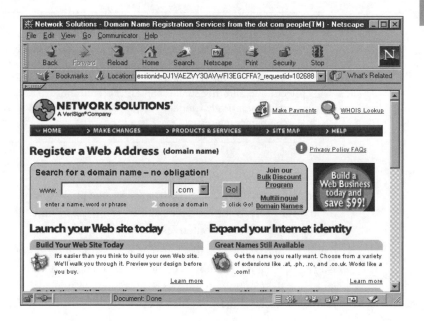

3. In the Search for a Domain Name box at the top of the page, type the domain you chose in step 1 and click the Go! button to the right of the box (see Figure 31.2).

When typing your proposed domain in step 3, don't precede it with the `http://` or the www part. These elements are part of a typical Web site address, but not really part of the domain. For example, if you want your Web site address to be `http://www.wild.com`, just type `wild` in step 3 and use the list box provided to choose the `.com` suffix.

FIGURE 31.2

Step 3: Type your chosen domain in the Search box.

4. A report appears, telling you that your chosen name is or is not available (see Figure 31.3). It also shows alternative domain names you might want to consider registering, either instead of or in addition to your favorite.

Why register one or more of the alternative names? Well, businesses protective of their name recognition who don't want to take any chances that potential customers will wind up at the site of a shrewd competitor with a too-close domain name often buy up not only the most likely domain name, but also all other similar names. Those businesses then use a Redirect option to automatically funnel all visitors from the alternative domain names to the company's main site.

If the name is available, proceed to step 5.

If the name *is not* available, you can scroll the page to reveal the box labeled Search for More Web Addresses and try a different name there or choose from among any available alternatives displayed on the report.

5. Contact your server provider as soon as possible and fill out the paperwork to register the domain. (If you're feeling brave, you can scroll to the bottom of the page and click the Continue button to buy the domain yourself. Your server provider can still set up your domain on his server.)

After you set up your domain, you have all new settings to use when you publish pages: a new server address and new username and password, for example. The person who sets up your domain on the server gives you this information; don't forget to use it when you start publishing to your new domain.

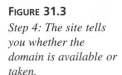

FIGURE 31.3

Step 4: The site tells you whether the domain is available or taken.

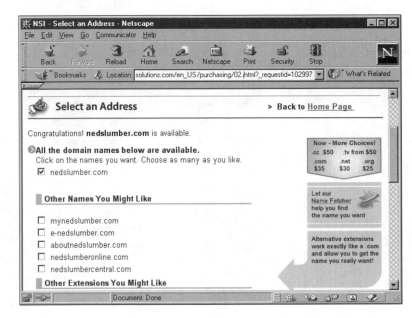

Advancing to New Authoring Tools and Techniques

Sculptors start with Play-Doh and work their way up to marble. Like a sculptor, if you continue authoring, your needs will one day advance beyond Composer's capabilities.

The next few pages describe two of the leading Web authoring environments and related tools. Any of them would make a fitting next step for an experienced Composer author.

Microsoft FrontPage

If you've cut your authoring teeth in Composer, a logical step up is to FrontPage, the Microsoft Web authoring environment for Microsoft Windows. Figure 31.4 shows FrontPage in action.

You can get FrontPage in some editions of Microsoft Office (bundled with Word, Excel, and so on) or by itself.

Why FrontPage? Well, performing many of the basic tasks you already know about is similar in both Composer and FrontPage. You don't have to relearn how to do many things you already know how to do. That frees you up to move ahead to the things FrontPage does that Composer doesn't do.

FIGURE 31.4
*FrontPage, the
Microsoft commercial
Web authoring soft-
ware.*

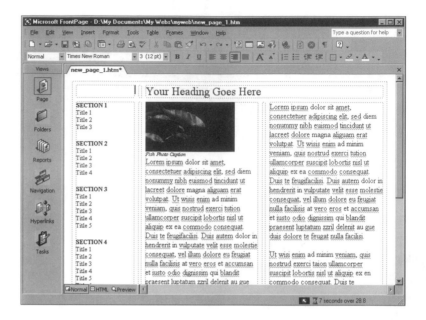

For example, you insert a picture in FrontPage almost exactly as you do in Composer.
But after you insert that picture, a Picture toolbar appears automatically whenever a picture is selected. The toolbar offers buttons for all sorts of advanced stuff, like adjusting
the contrast and brightness of the picture or positioning the picture *absolutely*—locking it
into an exact spot on the page, as you would in a desktop publishing program.

FrontPage also adds a site-management facility that's especially valuable when you begin
to manage Web sites with many interlinked pages. The facility can show you a diagram
of a whole Web site and of the interrelationships among the pages (see Figure 31.5).
From this view, you can add and delete pages to and from the site and move pages
around. FrontPage automatically updates the links and navigation bars on other pages in
the site so that everything still works together properly.

You can learn more about FrontPage at www.microsoft.com/frontpage/.

If you have ambitions to become a professional Web author in a company,
you have another good reason to learn how to use FrontPage.

Most companies want the Web authors they hire to be able to use a range
of Web authoring tools and to possess other skills (such as Java or CGI programming). But FrontPage is now the most widely used Web authoring
application, so knowing how to use it is essential for any job-hunting
author.

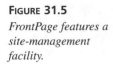

Figure 31.5

FrontPage features a site-management facility.

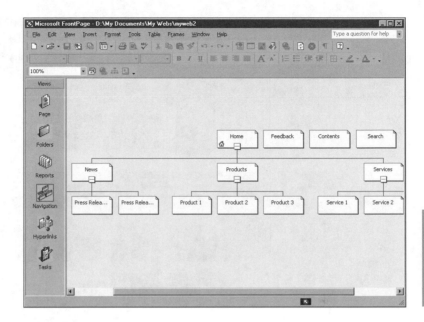

31

Macromedia Dreamweaver

Dreamweaver (see Figure 31.6) "…is the solution for professional Web site design and production," according to its maker, Macromedia. What that really means is that it's an all-around Web authoring tool that includes advanced graphics creation, editing facilities, site management, and more.

Dreamweaver is similar to FrontPage in most respects, but a little more powerful, a little more difficult to learn and use, and more expensive. Although FrontPage suits both beginners and pros, Dreamweaver is really for ambitious Web authoring professionals who want every bell and whistle at their command.

The Future of Web Authoring: XHTML

Every time the HTML standard changes, new formatting tricks and other capabilities are available to apply in Web pages and everybody runs out to get new tools (or learn new tags) to apply those features. To some extent, your "moving up" as a Web author depends a great deal on how and when HTML "moves up."

FIGURE 31.6
*Macromedia
Dreamweaver.*

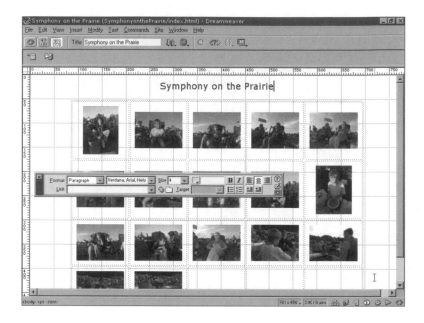

The current HTML standard is HTML 4.01, and an HTML 5 won't be created. Instead, HTML is merging with another document-formatting standard, XML (eXtensible Markup Language), to create a new standard for the Web pages of the future: XHTML (eXtensible Hypertext Markup Language). In fact, you can already see some XHTML-based Web pages online.

For general Web authoring, XHTML will be very similar to HTML. But the new language will be applied much more broadly than the old and will be used to enable browser-like features in such devices as digital TVs, portable phones, and even auto PCs (computers you use in your car). Estimates were that by 2002, 75 percent of the viewing of Internet documents would take place on these types of alternative platforms. To accommodate this change, XHTML is being designed to be highly *portable* (able to work on lots of different kinds of devices) while also being *extensible* (easily upgradable with new capabilities).

As a Web author, you will see a few years pass before you have to think much about XHTML, and by that time WYSIWYG tools will crank out XHTML the same way that tools like Composer crank out HTML today. (Very simple tools already are available for converting existing HTML files to XHTML format.) If you plan to do Web authoring in the long term, keep your eye on XHTML. It is the future.

How to Grow as a Web Author

What can you do next? How will you advance to the next level? More important, how can you keep a keen edge on the skills you've already mastered? Here are a few important habits you can adopt to prosper and grow.

Observe

When on the Web, don't just browse. Think about the pages you visit. Study them carefully, not at a technical level but rather at an aesthetic one. If a page impresses you, ask yourself why. Is it the images, the layout, the writing, the colors, or some combination of these factors? Bookmark sites that impress you and visit them often. Make a mental catalog of what grabs (or loses) your interest as a browser. Odds are that many other people respond the same way.

Dissect

When a page really impresses you, save it on your PC (in Internet Explorer, choose File, Save As) and then study it offline. Consider such questions as:

- What types of image files were used, and what properties are applied to them?
- What is the flow of text elements and properties on the page?
- What special techniques show up in the HTML code if you view the source file?
- In a multipage Web site, how much information is on a page?
- How many pages are there, and in what ways are they interlinked?

Summary

You've picked up a great start, and now you know as much about Web authoring as you might ever need. But there's always more to learn, always room to grow.

31

PART III

Creating Your Own Web Graphics with Paint Shop Pro

Chapter 32   Paint Shop Pro Basics, Tools, and Preferences

33   Opening, Saving, and Printing Files

34   Creating Your First Image

35   Creating and Working with Selections

36   Working with Deformations

37   Drawing Tools and Techniques

38   Painting Tools and Techniques

39   Creating Cool Text Effects

40   Applying Filters

41   Retouching Your Images

42   Preparing Your Graphics for the Web

43   Buttons and Seamless Tiles

44   Animation

45   Advanced Animation

CHAPTER **32**

Paint Shop Pro Basics, Tools, and Preferences

Even as a digital artist and author on the subject of image manipulation programs, I never cease to be amazed when a new version of one of my favorite programs hits the store shelves. Just when I think the software couldn't possibly get any better, the engineers and programmers still come up with ideas and features that make me say "WOW!"

 This chapter assumes that you have already installed Paint Shop Pro. You can get a free demo version at `http://www.jasc.com`.

That truly was the first comment out of my mouth when I ran the first beta copy of Paint Shop Pro 5, and it is still true for version 7. I can't believe the new features that have been packed into this already amazing piece of software.

With the success of Paint Shop Pro, and with the ever-growing popularity of the World Wide Web (and the need, therefore, for users to create their own Web-ready images), there is an increasing number of new users. Along with the increase in new users comes a need for material aimed at helping them get the most from the increasingly complex (yet still remarkably easy-to-use) Paint Shop Pro.

Now that version 7 has appeared, I believe that there is an even bigger need for more help and that a good Paint Shop Pro book is a must.

Version 7 of Paint Shop Pro truly moves this already fine product to a much higher level. With this version come many new features and options that represent new concepts. To use this latest version effectively, you—the reader and digital artist—must learn to use these new higher-level features.

Why do you and others like you use Paint Shop Pro? I believe that there are several reasons. Paint Shop Pro, even with its new list of high-end features, is relatively easy to use and carries a modest price tag. Many competing products can easily cost 8 to 10 times more.

Another attractive feature of Paint Shop Pro is its speed. Some users say that opening Paint Shop Pro and making a correction to an image is faster than working in some other imaging programs. Personally, I like some of the features in Paint Shop Pro that you just don't find in other software (one of my favorites is the Hot Wax filter).

As you read this book and become more familiar with Paint Shop Pro, I'm sure you'll find reasons of your own that make your experience with this fun-to-use, powerful paint program a great one.

Overview of New Features

Version 7 of Paint Shop Pro is amazing in its depth. Some of the new features were previously available only on programs costing hundreds of dollars more. Other new features are not available at any price, except in Paint Shop Pro.

The following paragraphs outline some of these new features; I go into more detail on how to access and use these features in later chapters.

- **Automatic Correction**—With a single command, you can now correct some of the most common image flaws, such as red-eye, color balance, saturation, brightness, fading, and small scratches. You can also reduce damage to images caused by excessive JPEG compression, missing scan lines from a video capture, and blobs and banding caused by scanning copies of an image.

- **Easier Manual Correction**—Using Manual Color Correction, you can now adjust selected colors within an image, preventing other colors (such as official company colors) from being unnecessarily changed.

- **Adjustable Zoom Area**—If you've zoomed into a small area of a larger graphic, you can use the Overview window to quickly view a smaller version of the graphic in its entirety. You can also use the Overview window to change the zoomed-in area of the graphic in which you're currently working.

- **More Complex Objects**—When you create bitmap or vector objects, you can now add gradient, pattern, or texture to the object's outline or fill.

> Vector objects are objects that still can be manipulated after they have been created. Unlike normal bitmapped objects, vector objects can be updated at any time. Paint Shop Pro now allows you to create fully editable text and shapes. This includes creating text that flows along a path.

- **Improved Color Palette**—The new Color Palette allows you to change not only the foreground and background colors used with the drawing tools, but to quickly select gradient, pattern, and texture effects as well.

- **Numerous Special Effects**—Of course, there are many new special effects you can add to your images, including lighting, fur, brush strokes, sunburst, soft plastic, aged newspaper, sepia, colored foil, sandstone, fine or rough leather, and enamel. And with the help of the new Effects browser, you can try out various special effects before you apply them.

- **Easy Alignment of Objects**—The objects you create (such as text, circles, or lines) are now easier to place exactly where you want them by using the new Snap to Grid and Snap to Guides commands. In addition, vector objects can now be grouped when needed for easier manipulation. Vector objects can also be arranged in relation to *other* vector objects (such as behind or in front of them), making it much easier for you to place the objects you create exactly where you want them.

- **Data Loss Prevention**—Prevent your changes from being lost accidentally by having Paint Shop Pro automatically save them for you at whatever intervals you desire. This can be done by using the new Autosave option.

- **Workspace Setup**—You can now save the position and settings related to your toolbars, palettes, gridlines, ruler, and zoom level, along with a list of open images in a workspace. Later, when you open that workspace, Paint Shop Pro automatically will be set up exactly the way it was before, so you can get back to work without a lot of fuss.

32

- **Web Preview**—Get an accurate estimate of how an image will look out on the Web by previewing it in up to three different Web browsers. In your Web browser, you can also preview your selection of format, such as BMP, JPEG, PNG, or GIF.
- **Create New Shapes**—Export any object (or group of objects) you create to the Preset Shapes tool, and recreate it anytime.

In addition, you'll find that many new features have been added to Animation Pro as well:

- **PSP Browser integration**—Now you can use the Paint Shop Pro browser to locate and open your animations.
- **MPEG compatibility**—You now can open MPEG files in Animation Pro!
- **Web browser preview**—Similar to the new feature in Paint Shop Pro, this allows you to preview your animation as it will appear on the Web, using up to three different Web browsers.
- **Move the contents of a frame**—You now can use the Mover tool to adjust the contents of a frame.
- **Export back to PSP**—Now you can export an entire animation (or selected frames) back to Paint Shop Pro, creating a multilayered, single image that you can edit.
- **Onionskin View**—Use this view to temporarily overlay the contents of adjoining frames on top of the current frame, enabling you to make even fine adjustments with ease.
- **VCR controls**—The new VCR-like controls enable you to fast forward, pause, and even reverse your animation when previewing it.

Using Online Help

As with many other Windows programs, Paint Shop Pro offers extensive online help. You can access the online help feature from the menu bar. Choose Help, Help Topics to open the Paint Shop Pro Help panel (see Figure 32.1).

Paint Shop Pro's Help works in a manner similar to Windows 98 Help: Select a topic from the list on the left and it appears in the pane on the right. You might need to expand the listing (by clicking the plus sign in front of a book icon to "open" it) to locate the topic you want to display. Using the Index tab, you can search for a topic based on its presence in a heading; with the Search tab, you can search for a phrase located anywhere within a topic—in a heading, or within the body text itself.

Click a minus sign
to collapse the listing

FIGURE 32.1

*The Paint Shop Pro
Help panel.*

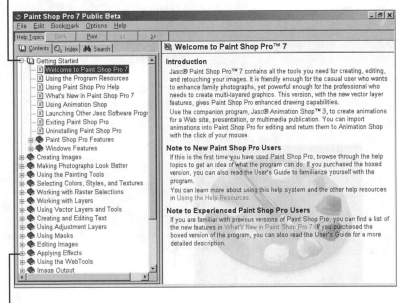

Click a plus sign
to expand the listing

Overview of the Paint Shop Pro Interface

To run Paint Shop Pro for the first time, click the Windows Start button and then choose Programs, Jasc Software, Paint Shop Pro 7 to open the main Paint Shop Pro window (see Figure 32.2). You also can double-click the PSP icon on the desktop (assuming you elected to place one there during installation) to start the program.

If you're a first time user, you'll notice how clean the interface is. If, on the other hand, you've used previous versions of Paint Shop Pro, you'll notice a few additions to the interface. If you've used or seen other graphics programs, you might also find yourself saying "Wow!" The Paint Shop Pro interface is clean and easy to use; it's even customizable.

When you run Paint Shop Pro initially, and at the beginning of each subsequent use (unless you turn off the feature), you'll see a Tip of the Day dialog box (see Figure 32.2).

Although you can turn off this feature, it's a useful way to pick up tips from the Paint Shop Pro team. To turn off the tips, remove the check mark from the Show Tips on Startup check box. To restore this feature, simply run the Tip of the Day from the Help menu and place a check mark in the Show Tips on Startup option.

FIGURE 32.2

*The Paint Shop Pro
main window.*

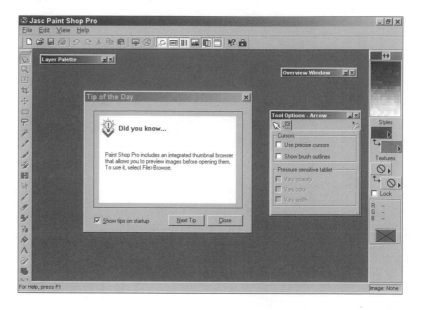

The title bar, the menu bar, and the Standard toolbar appear along the top of the main window.

The title bar is similar to any other Windows program's title bar in that it contains a control icon and the standard Windows window control buttons that enable you to minimize, maximize, and restore the program's main window, as well as close the program.

The menu bar should be somewhat familiar. It contains a list of commands that, when clicked, displays a pull-down menu of further commands. The various toolbars (of which the Standard toolbar is the only one initially displayed) contain icons that are basically shortcuts to some of the common menu choices. You'll learn more about the Standard toolbar buttons in a moment.

If you're familiar with other Windows programs, you might notice something that looks like another toolbar, but it isn't—at least, not according to Paint Shop Pro. The "toolbar" that you see initially displayed along the left side of the screen is called the Tool palette (or simply, "toolbox") and is described later this chapter.

You'll also notice a few floating title bars. Behind these title bars are *palettes* (special windows in which you can make color selections, select a paint or draw tool, change tool options, adjust the view, and so on). To display a palette, simply move the mouse pointer over its title bar. Initially, the following palettes are displayed:

- Along the left side of the screen is the Tool palette. It contains all the tools you need to create and manipulate your images. I'll explain each tool in more detail later in this chapter.

- Down the right side, you'll see the Color palette. The Color palette enables you to set the foreground and background colors, along with other color options (see the second half of this chapter for a demonstration).

- Floating somewhere in the main window, you'll see the Tool Options palette, the Layer palette, and the Overview window.

  The Tool Options palette enables you to set the various options for a particular tool (see the second half of this chapter for a demonstration).

  The Layer palette enables you to work with layers, a powerful feature introduced in Paint Shop Pro 5. I'll briefly cover the Layer palette later in this chapter.

  The Overview window allows you to adjust the area of a zoomed-in image that you want to view (see the second half of this chapter for a demonstration.)

Along the bottom of the main window is the status bar. It displays constantly updated information about the current image file and gives you information about the different tools available. When you move the cursor over a tool, the status bar displays a short description of the tool's function. With the cursor over the current image, you'll see the cursor's x and y coordinates. This information is extremely helpful under certain circumstances, as you'll see later. You'll also see the current image's size in pixels, its color depth, and its size in kilobytes.

32

The Standard Toolbar

The Standard toolbar holds some of the most frequently accessed menu choices (see Figure 32.3).

Having these popular menu choices available as icons means that often-used menu choices are one click away. For example, the first icon in the toolbar enables you to open a new image. Clicking the New icon (it looks like a small sheet of paper with one corner folded over) saves you from choosing File, New. The other icons in that grouping represent Open (File, Open); Save (File, Save); and Print (File, Print).

The next five icons on the toolbar represent the most common Edit menu choices: Undo (Edit, Undo); Redo (Edit, Redo); Cut (Edit, Cut); Copy (Edit, Copy); and Paste As New Image (Edit, Paste, As New Image).

Sequentially, the next two icons on the toolbar are the Full Screen Preview and the Normal Viewing (1:1) icons. Clicking the Full Screen Preview icon displays the active image against a black full-screen background. You can choose this option from the tool-bar or from the View menu. To return to normal viewing, click anywhere on the Full Screen Preview screen. The Normal Viewing (1:1) icon returns an enlarged or reduced image to normal (1:1) magnification.

FIGURE 32.3
The Standard toolbar.

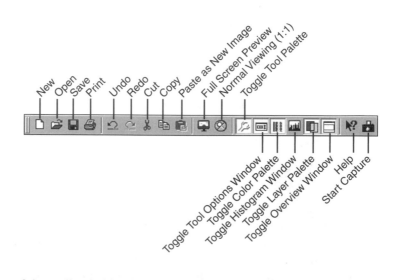

The next portion of the toolbar holds six icons that toggle the various palettes on and off. When the button is "pushed in," the associated palette appears. Click the button again (it will appear "pushed out") to remove that palette temporarily. Being able to toggle palettes on and off is helpful, especially if you run Paint Shop Pro on a lower-resolution screen or in a smaller window. Also, if you don't need immediate access to a certain palette, toggle it off. If you suddenly find that you're in need of something within that palette, though, you can simply toggle it back on.

On the far right of the toolbar are the last two icons—Help and Start Capture. Selecting the Help icon won't bring up online help, as you might expect. Rather, selecting this icon adds a question mark to the regular mouse cursor. That's when the magic starts. When you move this new cursor over virtually any part of the Paint Shop Pro window and click the mouse, you bring up the Help window with the help text set to whatever you clicked. For example, if you click the Help icon and then click the Color palette, the Help window opens with help specific to the Color palette. This feature is called *context-sensitive* help. Point-and-click help is great if you suddenly need help but can't remember the name of the tool or palette.

The Start Capture button is used to save the current screen view as a digital image file. You'll learn how to capture screen images in Chapter 33, "Opening, Saving, and Printing Files."

Other Toolbars

Paint Shop Pro provides other toolbars, each containing buttons related to accomplishing some specific task. The other toolbars (besides the Standard toolbar) include

- **Web Toolbar**—Contains buttons that enable you to prepare your image for display on the Internet.
- **Photo Toolbar**—Provides buttons you can use to import digital images from a camera, and to apply common corrections to those images, such as automatic scratch removal.
- **Effects Toolbar**—Allows you to quickly apply the most common image effects, or to preview various effects through the Effects Browser.
- **Browser Toolbar**—Contains buttons for copying, moving, deleting, renaming, locating, browsing, and sorting your images with the Paint Shop Pro Browser.

To display any of these additional toolbars, select them from the Toolbars dialog box (View, Toolbars).

The Toolbox

32

The toolbox, or Tool palette, quite naturally contains the Paint Shop Pro tools (see Figure 32.4).

You have tools to make selections, draw and paint, create lines and shapes, and more. As you pause the mouse over any tool in the toolbox, Paint Shop Pro displays a small tag (tooltip) telling you what the tool is.

Even better than just seeing the tool's name, though, when you point at a tool, you also see a description of what the tool does. This brief information appears in the lower left of the status bar. To see how this feature works, hold the mouse over one of the tool buttons and look for the tool description on the bottom-left side of the Paint Shop Pro window.

The following sections describe the tools that are available in Paint Shop Pro.

The Arrow Tool

The Arrow tool enables you to quickly bring an image to the front. This technique is helpful when you have several images open at one time. Simply select this tool and click the image you want to bring to the front.

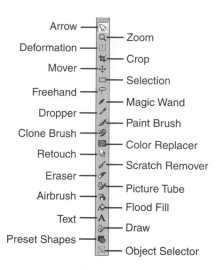

Figure 32.4

Paint Shop Pro's Tool palette.

Arrow — Zoom
Deformation — Crop
Mover — Selection
Freehand — Magic Wand
Dropper — Paint Brush
Clone Brush — Color Replacer
Retouch — Scratch Remover
Eraser — Picture Tube
Airbrush — Flood Fill
Text — Draw
Preset Shapes — Object Selector

The Arrow tool does double duty. It also enables you to scroll around images that are too big to be completely displayed in the window. To scroll around an image, simply click and drag with the Arrow tool (the cursor icon becomes a hand icon during this procedure) to move the image around within its window.

The Zoom Tool

The Zoom tool enables you to zoom in on an image for close-up, detailed work, and it also enables you to zoom out to see the entire image at once. Left-clicking the current image with this tool zooms in; right-clicking the current image zooms out. (Hold the Zoom tool and click the image area that you want centered while increasing or decreasing the zoom factor.) The Zoom factor appears in the title bar of the image window. A Zoom factor of 1:1 is normal; 1:5, and the image is displayed at 1/5th its normal size; at 5:1, it is five times as large as normal. After zooming in on an image, use the Overview window to see the complete image without returning to 1:1 view. To retain the same zoom factor but change the area being viewed, just drag the rectangle that appears in the Overview window.

The Deformation Tool

The Deformation tool enables you to rotate, resize, skew, or distort the current layer. (This tool is inactive on the Background layer.) With a multilayered image, you can use this tool to quickly rotate, resize, skew, or distort the contents on any layer other than the Background.

When you select the Deformation tool, a bounding box surrounds the object(s) on the current layer. This bounding box has several control handles: one at each corner; one in the middle of each side, the top, and the bottom; and one in the center. The control handles enable you to "deform" the object surrounded by the bounding box. For example, you can resize and rotate the object(s). I'll describe this process in more depth in Chapter 36, "Working with Deformations."

The Crop Tool

The Crop tool enables you to quickly crop an image. To do so, select the Crop tool and simply click a corner *handle* (one of the square boxes that surround an image) and drag to define the area of the image you want to keep.

If you're not satisfied with the sizing or placement of the cropped area, don't worry. You can easily resize the cropping area by clicking and dragging the edges of the area to adjust its size, and you can drag the cropped area until it fits exactly over the portion of the image you want to crop. Once the cropping area is suitably placed and sized, double-click anywhere within the image to finalize the cropping.

If you've taken a step that you're not happy with, you can always undo it by clicking the Undo button, or choosing Edit, Undo. In fact, you can undo several steps. Knowing that nothing's really permanent frees you to put a little playfulness into your explorations. Much can be learned by clicking away with some abandon. However, the best way to experiment is to work on backup copies. If you have only one copy of an image and you do make some irreversible change, you're out of luck. However, if you work on a backup copy, nothing you do in Paint Shop Pro can damage the original.

32

The Mover Tool

The Mover tool performs a little magic. It moves whatever you place the cursor over, no matter which layer is currently active. That is, the Mover tool knows which layer an object is on. If you have a green square on layer 1 and a red circle on layer 2, you can move either by simply selecting the Mover tool and clicking and dragging the object you want to move.

For this tool to perform its magic, though, each object must be on its own layer, because the Mover tool can't differentiate between objects on the same layer. It will move the entire layer that's associated with the object you click and drag. Still, this tool is useful for accurately placing multiple objects over several layers.

You can also use the Mover tool to reposition the selection marquee, the dashed outline that defines the current selection. Simply right-click with the Mover tool over the selected area, and then drag the marquee to a new location. Moving the selection marquee is especially helpful in several exercises in this book, where you need to manipulate the same size area of an image multiple times.

The Selection Tool

The Selection tool enables you to make selections. You can select rectangular, square, elliptical, and circular areas of an image for easier manipulation. Before you can cut, copy, and paste portions of an image, you must select those portions of the image. Selections also enable you to work on the selected area of an image without affecting the rest of the image.

To select a portion of the current image, simply click the Selection tool. Hold the Selection tool cursor over the active image and click and drag to define an area of the image. You can set the various selection shapes in the Tool Options window, which I'll describe later in this chapter, in the section on palettes.

The Freehand Tool

The Freehand tool enables you to draw freehand selections anywhere on the current image.

You can make three types of selections with the Freehand tool. You can simply draw a freehand selection, you can draw a point-to-point (or *polygonal*) selection, and you can draw a Smart Edge selection.

- The *Freehand* option enables you to draw selections of any shape. All you need do is click and drag the mouse to define the area you want to select.

- The *Point-to-Point* option enables you to make polygonal selections. Here, you click at each corner of the polygon as you move the mouse. When you're done, simply double-click to finish the polygonal selection.

- The *Smart Edge* option attempts to define your selection based on brightness and contrast between adjacent pixels. Draw loosely around the area you want to select, and let Smart Edge define the precise area for you.

The Magic Wand Tool

The Magic Wand tool enables you to select an area of your image based on its color. You simply select this tool and click within an area. All pixels of the same color and adjacent to the pixel under the cursor are selected, as if by magic. You can set rules and a tolerance level that will help this tool perform its magic. These options can be set in the Tool Options palette. You'll learn the ins and outs of making selections with the Selection, Smart Edge, and Magic Wand tools in Chapter 35, "Creating and Working with Selections."

The Dropper Tool

The Dropper tool enables you to pick up a color from the current image and use it to set the foreground and background color.

To set the foreground color, simply select the Dropper tool and click over a color in the current image. To set the background color, do the same but right-click instead.

The Paint Brush

The Paint Brush tool enables you to paint on your images. You can use the Tool Options palette to select different brushes and to set the opacity, hardness, size, and shape of the brushes. From the Tool Options palette, you also can select a texture that enables you to imitate painting over various surfaces. To learn how to paint with the Paint Brush tool, see Chapter 38, "Painting Tools and Techniques."

The Clone Brush

The Clone Brush tool enables you to copy portions of an image over another area of the same image or any other open image. This tool can selectively remove or edit parts of an image. For example, you can remove electrical lines from an otherwise pristine scenic photograph.

The Color Replacer

The Color Replacer tool you to selectively change one particular color to another throughout the entire image. The process for swapping color seems mysterious, but it is fairly simple.

To swap an existing color with a new color throughout an image, set the foreground to the old color and set the background to the new color. To do so, use the Dropper tool or click the foreground/background color swatches to display the Color dialog box.

With the colors set, select the Color Replacer tool and drag over the image to replace pixels matching the background color with the foreground color. You can swap all pixels of the background color in the image with the current foreground color by double-clicking anywhere in the image.

To replace pixels matching the foreground color with the background color, drag with the right mouse button, or double-right-click anywhere in the image to swap all instances of the foreground color with the current background color.

I'll describe this process again with some examples you can work through in Chapter 34, "Creating Your First Image."

32

The Retouch Tool

With the Retouch tool, you can selectively retouch areas of your images. The Retouch tool uses the same brush tips as the other painting and drawing tools, but the controls enable you to lighten, darken, soften, change the saturation, and more. Select this tool to make minor retouches to a photograph. I'll describe the process of retouching photographs in Chapter 41, "Retouching Your Images."

Scratch Remover

You can remove scratches from a photograph with the Scratch Remover tool. Basically, you select the area containing the scratch, and Paint Shop Pro analyzes the colors in the selection to arrive at the best mix with which to color the scratch.

The Eraser Tool

The Eraser tool enables you to erase portions of your image. You can erase an area of the image and replace it with the current background color or, on higher layers, make it transparent. The Eraser tool uses the same brush tips as the drawing and painting tools. You'll use the Eraser tool in various exercises throughout this book.

The Picture Tube

The Picture Tube tool, added in version 5, enables you to use tubes to paint on an image. Tubes are built from images arranged in a grid. These images, which usually share a common theme, display at random as you paint with the Tube brush. For example, one tube option is raindrops, which contains a number of different sized water drops that appear in order as you drag or click with the tool.

The Airbrush Tool

The Airbrush tool simulates an airbrush. Changing the Opacity and Density settings changes the amount of digital paint that is sprayed onto your image.

The Flood Fill Tool

The Flood Fill tool fills an image or a selected area of your image with either the current foreground color or the current background color. Clicking fills with the foreground color, and right-clicking fills with the background color.

You also can choose to fill with a pattern or with a gradient. In addition, you can use any image as a pattern for the fill.

Gradients can be multicolored (blending a yellow into a red, for example), and you can choose from several patterns. You can use gradients to give depth to an image, build complex masks, and create special effects. Examples appear throughout the book.

The Text Tool

The Text tool creates and enters text onto your images. The text can be in any font. The Text tool is quite easy to use. Simply select it and click somewhere within your image to bring up the Text Tool dialog box. You can select the font, the size, and several other options. This dialog box is also where you enter the text you want to appear in your image. You'll have many opportunities to use the Text tool as you work through this book.

The Draw Tool

The Draw tool enables you to draw lines on your images. You can set the width, choose whether or not the line will be anti-aliased, and select from Single Line, Bézier Curve, Freehand Line, and Point-to-Point Line. You can also decide if the lines should be drawn as vectors and if the path created by the line should be closed.

Anti-aliasing is a process that softens the hard edges in digital graphics. The process uses mathematics and involves applying varying shades of colors between the contrasting edges. This process produces a smoother, softer-looking image. You'll see how anti-aliasing affects different images throughout the rest of the book.

Bézier curves are named after the mathematician who developed the algorithm, or set of computer steps, that enables graphic artists to draw and manipulate smooth curves on the computer.

The Point-to-Point Line tool is similar to the Bézier Curve tool. The Bézier Curve tool allows you to make only two changes, though, and the Point-to-Point Line tool allows you to make unlimited changes.

The Preset Shapes Tool

The Preset Shapes tool enables you to draw stroked (outlined) or filled shapes such as rectangles, squares, ellipses, and circles. The shapes created with the Preset Shapes tool can be either bitmap or vector in nature. In Chapter 37, "Drawing Tools and Techniques," you'll learn to use the Preset Shapes and Draw tools.

The Object Selector Tool

Last but certainly not least, the Object Selector tool (also known as the Vector Object Selection tool) enables you to select and modify vector shapes that you created previously with the Text, Draw, or Preset Shapes tool. This assumes, of course, that you created these objects as vectors rather than bitmaps.

32

The Menus

The various menu choices are available from the main menu bar. Several of the choices will be familiar to you as a Windows user. The File, Edit, View, Window, and Help choices are similar to those choices in most Windows programs. However, they might include some new, unfamiliar choices.

Also, many main menu choices in Paint Shop Pro might be unfamiliar. You may not recognize choices, such as Image, Effects, Layers, Objects, Selections, and Masks, if you are new to digital imaging. These menu choices will rapidly become second nature, though, as you work your way through this book.

The following sections briefly outline the menu choices. You'll get some hands-on experience with the various choices as you work through the book.

The File Menu

The File menu enables you to open, close, create, save, import, export, browse, revert, print, and batch convert image files. A new option allows you to save and reload workspaces. As you work through the rest of the book, you'll become quite proficient at using the File menu options.

 The Revert choice under the File menu enables you to revert the file to the state it was in when you first opened it. This is analogous to closing the file, choosing not to apply the changes, and then re-opening the file. Be aware that Revert cannot be undone and will discard ALL of the changes you have made since you first opened the file.

One other choice under the File menu is Preferences, which I'll explain later in this chapter.

The Edit Menu

The Edit menu enables you to undo the most recent change, redo the last Undo, repeat a command, and access the Command History (multiple undo). The Cut, Copy, Copy Merged, Paste, Clear, Update Back to Animation Shop, and Empty Clipboard or Command History options also are available on the Edit menu.

Most of these choices should be familiar to you if you've used other Windows-based programs. A couple that might be unfamiliar are the Clear and Empty choices:

- Clear deletes anything in a selected area of your image. The selected area will delete to transparent if on a higher layer and will delete to the current background color if on the background layer. Although similar to cutting, the Clear option does not copy the selected area to the Clipboard. You'll have an opportunity to use the Clear option later in the book.

- Empty enables you to free up some computer memory. You can choose to empty either the Clipboard or the Undo (Command) history. If you have many files open and find that the system is running out of memory, you can get a little back by applying this feature.

The View Menu

The View menu gives you access to different viewing modes. You can view the image and the workspace in Full Screen Edit mode. This mode is toggled, meaning that you choose it from the View menu to select it and choose it again to deselect it. The Full Screen Edit mode opens the Paint Shop Pro window to completely cover any other open windows. In addition, this mode hides the menu bar, which you still can access by pressing and releasing the Alt key.

The next view is Full Screen Preview mode. In this mode, all that you see on the screen is your image. To return to Normal viewing mode, press the Esc key or click anywhere on the screen.

You can use other menu choices in the View menu drop-down box to zoom in and zoom out, or preview the image using your Web browser.

Finally, you can use the View menu to display the grids, rulers, and guides, and to access the Toolbars dialog box. I'll demonstrate the grids, guides, and rulers in several exercises throughout the book.

The Image Menu

The Image menu enables you to manipulate your images by flipping, mirroring, rotating, and resizing them. Here, you can access information about the current image, and enter creator information. In addition, you can combine images mathematically, add borders and frames, and protect your images with a digital watermark.

You can purchase many third-party filter programs, and access them through the Image, Plug-in Filters menu choice. I'll demonstrate how to install and set up filters in Chapter 40, "Applying Filters." (Paint Shop Pro comes with a number of its own filters, available through the Effects menu.)

32

Filters alter a pixel's color based on its current color, and the colors of the pixels near it.

The Effects Menu

The new Effects menu is the resting place for all the commands that allow you to add special effects to your images, such as 3D, Artistic, Illumination and Texture effects. You also can repair common problems with images such as underexposure, red eye, and scratches using the commands on this menu.

New on this menu is the Effects Browser that you can use to preview various effects on an image before applying them.

The Colors Menu

The Colors menu is where you can access all of the color options pertaining to your images. You can adjust the color, colorize, change the brightness and contrast, select a palette, set a color for transparency, and set the number of colors in your image.

As you work through the rest of this book, you'll use the choices under the Colors menu quite often—often enough that many of the choices and their options will become second nature.

The Layers Menu

From the Layers menu you can add, duplicate, delete, reorder, and change the properties of the various layers that make up your image.

The Objects Menu

With this new menu, you can control your objects completely, by arranging, resizing, grouping, and ungrouping them as needed.

The Selections Menu

The Selections menu enables you to manipulate selections. For example, you can create selections, modify the current selection, save and load selections, and create masks from your selections.

I'll demonstrate selections throughout the book, especially in Chapter 35.

The Masks Menu

The Masks menu gives you access to the masking functions. You can create, edit, save, and load masks.

The Window Menu

The options on the Window menu should be familiar to you if you've used Microsoft Windows for any length of time. This menu is pretty much standard across all Windows programs, with a few surprises: Use Fit to Image to resize a window to the exact size of an image, and use Duplicate to copy an entire image (all layers) to the Clipboard.

The Help Menu

The Help menu enables you to use online help, which was discussed earlier in this chapter. You can search for keywords and get context-sensitive help from the Help menu choices. You can even access the Jasc Web site for additional help, if needed.

Using the Palettes

Palettes are common in graphics programs. They operate like visual menus and let you set options for various tools. They are as follows:

- The Color palette
- The Tool Options palette
- The Layer palette
- The Tool palette
- The Overview window

You can turn the palettes on and off via the View, Toolbars command. Choose View, Toolbars to open the Toolbars dialog box (see Figure 32.5).

32

FIGURE 32.5

The Toolbars dialog.

To turn off a palette, simply remove the check mark next to its entry in the dialog box. To restore a palette place a check mark next to its entry.

The five palettes I mentioned (actually four palettes and one window) enable you to use the various settings and options associated with the palette.

The Color Palette

The Color palette enables you to set the foreground and background colors for the drawing and painting tools (see Figure 32.6).

FIGURE 32.6
The Color palette.

Set a color by moving the mouse over the Available Colors Panel in the Color palette. Clicking the left mouse button sets the foreground color, and clicking the right mouse button sets the background color. You can set stroke (line) and fill styles and textures in a similar manner.

To set colors more precisely, you can open the Color dialog box by clicking on either the foreground or background color box (see Figure 32.7).

The Tool Options Palette

The Tool Options palette enables you to set the options associated with a particular tool. Figure 32.8 shows the options you can set for the Paint Brushes tool Brush Tip.

FIGURE 32.7

The Color dialog box.

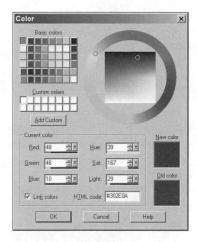

FIGURE 32.8

The Tool Options palette, showing the Brush Tip options for the Paint Brushes tool.

32

Like most of the palettes, the Tools Options palette does not display until you point to its title bar. It then remains open until you move the mouse pointer outside the palette's boundaries. While the palette is open, you can make as many selections as you like. To keep the palette open even while the mouse is elsewhere, click the Roll-up Mode/Always Open Mode button.

You'll notice at least two tabs in the Tools Option palette: The first tab presents options related to that tool (note that the icon for the current tool is displayed on this tab), and the second tab presents options for mouse/sensitive tablet operation. Additional tabs might appear depending on the current tool selected.

On the right, click the Tool Selection button to change to a different tool, rather than selecting the tool from the Tool palette.

The Layer Palette

The Layer palette enables you to set the options and blending modes for the layers that make up your images (see Figure 32.9).

FIGURE 32.9

The Layer palette.

You also can create and delete layers from within the Layer palette through the two small icons at the top left of the palette. The first enables you to create a new layer, and the second enables you to delete a layer.

You also can drag and drop layers onto either icon. Dragging and dropping a layer onto the New Layer icon duplicates the layer, and dragging and dropping a layer onto the small trash can icon deletes the layer.

The Tool Palette

The Tool palette contains the various tools that you can use to paint, draw, make selections, and so on. The tools in this palette were discussed previously in this chapter.

The Overview Window

The Overview window allows you to view an image in its entirety, even if that image is zoomed out, as shown in Figure 32.10. Simply move the mouse pointer over its title bar to display the window, or click the Roll-up Mode/Always Open Mode button to keep the window open.

FIGURE 32.10

The new Overview window.

As mentioned earlier, when you've zoomed an image, you can drag the rectangle that appears in the Overview window to change the part of the image being viewed in the main window.

Setting Preferences

Like many of today's advanced programs, Paint Shop Pro enables you to set various preferences. To set Paint Shop Pro's preferences, choose File, Preferences. Another pulldown menu opens with the choices you see in Figure 32.11.

FIGURE 32.11

The Preferences sub-menu.

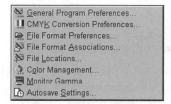

Each of the menu choices in this pull-down menu opens a dialog box in which you can set preferences to make using Paint Shop Pro easier.

General Program Preferences

You can tab through the Paint Shop Pro Preferences dialog box to set up levels of Undo (keeping in mind that higher levels take more memory), the size and color of the rulers, how cursors are displayed (precise or tool shape), and more (see Figure 32.12).

FIGURE 32.12

The Paint Shop Pro Preferences dialog box.

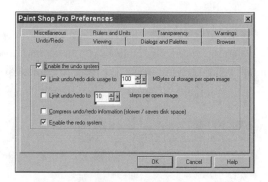

32

CMYK Conversion Preferences

The CMYK Conversion Preferences dialog box enables you to tell Paint Shop Pro how to handle conversions between CMYK, a standard file mode for high-end printing, and RGB files, the standard mode for onscreen computer images (see Figure 32.13).

FIGURE 32.13

The CMYK Conversion Preferences dialog box.

Unless you plan to send your images to a prepress shop (something you might want to do to print 5,000 full-color brochures), you really don't need to bother with this setting.

File Format Preferences

The File Format Preferences dialog box enables you to set the file format preferences for the PCD, PostScript, raw data (RAW), Windows Meta-File (WMF), and import file formats (see Figure 32.14). Most of these file types normally are not used, with one exception: PostScript files. PostScript files are vector based and are usually created by drawing programs, such as Adobe Illustrator and CorelDRAW.

FIGURE 32.14
The File Format Preferences dialog box.

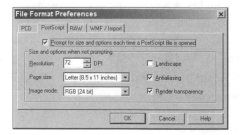

File Format Associations

The File Format Associations dialog box enables you to set and unset the file formats to associate with Paint Shop Pro (see Figure 32.15). Any file whose format is associated with Paint Shop Pro opens in Paint Shop Pro when you double-click on its icon.

FIGURE 32.15
The File Format Associations dialog box.

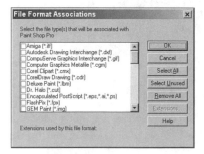

This feature is handy if, for example, you always want to edit JPG or GIF files with Paint Shop Pro. With their respective file formats set in the File Format Associations dialog box, you can open JPG and GIF files in Paint Shop Pro by double-clicking their icons in Windows Explorer.

File Locations Preferences

The File Locations dialog box enables you to select where various files are located, such as your Web browser, and the locations of temporary files Paint Shop Pro creates you're working on an image (see Figure 32.16).

Color Management Preferences

If you own Windows 98, Me, or NT, you can take advantage of the built-in color management of these operating systems through this command.

FIGURE 32.16

The File Locations dialog box.

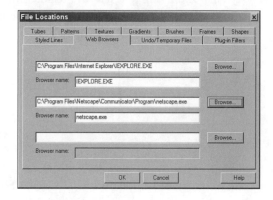

Monitor Gamma Adjustments

The Monitor Gamma Adjustment dialog box enables you to set the Gamma (the overall color cast and brightness/contrast) of your monitor (see Figure 32.17).

FIGURE 32.17

The Monitor Gamma Adjustment dialog box.

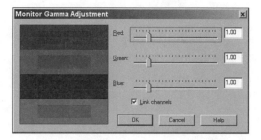

To brighten the display, move the sliders to the right. To darken it, move them to the left. If your monitor gives a color cast (that is, the neutral gray seems to contain a little red, green, or blue), you can adjust each color separately. To do so, unlink the channels and move the sliders separately until the color cast disappears.

If you're not sure how your display is set, you should ignore the settings in this dialog box and leave the defaults. You can't harm your monitor by playing with these settings, but they are best left alone if you think your monitor is functioning correctly.

32

Autosave Settings

New to version 7 are the Autosave Settings preferences, shown in Figure 32.18. Through these settings, you can turn on the Autosave feature and control how often Paint Shop Pro automatically saves your work. Using the Autosave feature might prevent accidental data loss, should your computer or power go out while working on an image.

FIGURE 32.18

The Autosave Settings dialog box.

Summary

You have covered a lot of ground already. You explored the Paint Shop Pro interface (maybe for the first time) and learned how to find your way around. You also glanced at the new features available in version 7.0. You should spend a little extra time now exploring the interface and familiarizing yourself with the different tools and menus.

CHAPTER **33**

Opening, Saving, and Printing Files

This chapter assumes that you have already installed Paint Shop Pro. You can get a free demo version at
http://www.jasc.com.

Opening a File

To get an image into Paint Shop Pro, you can create a new image (File, New), open an existing image (File, Open), or import an image from a digital camera, scanner (TWAIN), or screen capture (File, Import).

Opening a New File

To open a new file, choose File, New. Doing so opens the New Image dialog box (see Figure 33.1).

FIGURE 33.1
The New Image dialog box.

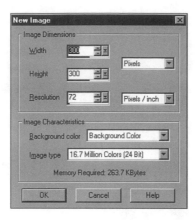

Within the New Image dialog box, you can set the width, height, and resolution of the new image. You also can set the background color and the image type (the number of colors used). You'll be accessing this dialog box many, many times as you work through the rest of this book.

Throughout this book, you will usually be given information regarding the dimensions, resolution, background color, and image type. Later, as you create your own images, you can decide on the settings that are appropriate for each one.

Opening an Existing File

You can open an existing file by choosing File, Open. This action opens the standard Windows Open dialog box (see Figure 33.2).

FIGURE 33.2
The Open dialog box.

You can open several files at one time if, for example, you want to work on more than one image. To do so, hold down the Shift or Ctrl key while selecting the image names from within the dialog box. Holding down the Shift key selects the filenames that are together in the list, and holding down the Ctrl key enables you to select out-of-sequence files.

The first time you run Paint Shop Pro after installing it, you're offered the opportunity to choose files that will be associated with the program. Any file that you associate can be opened by double-clicking its icon.

Starting with Paint Shop Pro 6 (and now with version 7), you can open EPS (Enhanced PostScript) files. These files are generally images created with drawing programs such as Adobe Illustrator or CorelDRAW. Many logos, for example, are created with this type of software. Previously, you would have had to save an illustration created in a drawing program in a bitmap format before opening it in Paint Shop Pro. This wasn't a problem if you owned the program with which the file was created. However, if you wanted to work on an existing illustration and you didn't own the drawing program, you were out of luck. Now, though, you can open the file easily and also set some of the options, such as anti-aliasing.

Browsing for an Existing File

You can use Paint Shop Pro's file browser to browse through files or folders, or you can enter a specific file or folder name (see Figure 33.3). You also can see previews of the files, if Paint Shop Pro recognizes them.

FIGURE 33.3
The Browse dialog box.

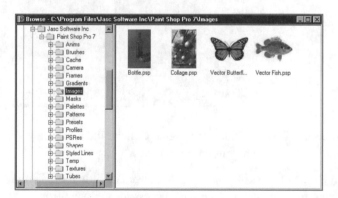

The file browser enables you to see all the images in a folder at a glance. A small button, or thumbnail, represents each image in the currently selected folder.

33

To open an image after identifying it from its thumbnail, simply double-click the thumbnail. After you open an image, you can manipulate it in many different ways. You'll learn about the amazing things that you can do with new and existing images as you progress through this book.

Importing Files

You can import images into Paint Shop Pro from any digitizing hardware, such as a scanner or a digital camera.

Paint Shop Pro offers an interface to your TWAIN hardware. When you buy a scanner or a digital camera, you must install it. Part of the installation process involves installing the drivers and the device's software. Figure 33.4 shows Paint Shop Pro importing a photo by running Hewlett-Packard's DeskScan II 2.7.

FIGURE 33.4

Paint Shop Pro running the TWAIN scanner driver for a Hewlett-Packard 4c desktop scanner.

If you have a TWAIN scanner or digital camera, the interface you see will depend on the software included with your specific device.

Although the process of importing an image is a little more complicated than simply opening a file, this step is much like accessing an image from your hard drive.

Saving Files

After you acquire your image, correct it, or manipulate it to your satisfaction, you need to save it to your hard drive.

Starting with version 5 and continuing with the present version, Paint Shop Pro has its own file format. If you created new layers or used any of the vector tools during the processing of your image, you should use Paint Shop Pro's native format, .psp, to save the file. This format preserves the layers and their associated blending modes and the vector object information. Saving under any other format, with the exception of the .psd file format (Photoshop's native format), discards any separate layer information and flattens the image into one layer.

Flattening the image is not a bad thing and is actually necessary for formats such as and GIF. However, if you've done extensive work with layers or with vector objects (such as vector text), you may want to save at least two copies of your image. One copy should be in .psp format and the other can be in some other format—GIF or JPG for a Web-based file, for example. Another factor to consider is saving the image as you work. You might want to create a temporary working directory and save incremental backups of your work. Even with the advanced state of today's technology, computers crash. They most often do so right after you've put in several hours of uninterrupted work and just before you finally decide that you should save the changes you've labored over.

You can save every 5 to 10 minutes or so and use names such as Image001, Image002, and so on. When you are finished, you can save the final image (most likely as a .psp file) and delete the Image00x files from your temporary folder.

Besides the Save option, you can use Save As or Save a Copy. These two options are essentially the same, except that Save a Copy doesn't affect the current image in any way.

For example, using Save As to save your image to the GIF format flattens the image and reduces the color palette to only 256 colors or fewer. Using Save a Copy saves a copy of the image with the layers flattened and the color palette reduced but leaves the current image in its unaltered state.

Exporting Files

In addition to saving your images, you can export them. Exporting your images requires the use of export filters. Exporting a file is similar to saving a file. The main difference is that exporting a file enables you to use certain export filters or plug-ins. Export filters or plug-ins allow third-party programmers to extend the built-in capabilities of a program such as Paint Shop Pro.

33

Paint Shop Pro comes with several built-in export filters. In fact, exporting is how you create tubes (at least in part).

In addition to the built-in export filters, many third-party filters are available. For example, you can get filters that hide a copyright number in your image to help you keep track of your digital artwork. One of my favorite export filters is SmartSaver from Ulead (see Figure 33.5).

FIGURE 33.5

Ulead's SmartSaver image export filter.

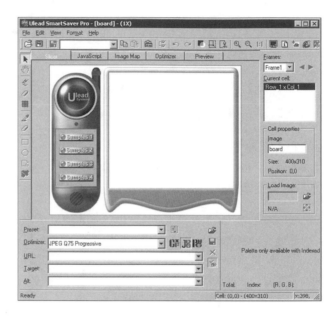

SmartSaver saves images in JPG, GIF, and PNG and is a Web-based image export filter. If you have to save Web-ready images on a regular basis, I highly recommend this filter. In addition to being a timesaver, SmartSaver offers real-time color resolution changes and transparency blends for GIF files. It offers 100 levels of JPG compression and more. You can get a free demo version of this wonderful plug-in from at http://www.ulead.com.

Printing Basics

After all the work you've put into your masterpiece, you might want to print it. Paint Shop Pro makes printing relatively easy. The first thing you should do is choose File, Page Setup to open the Page Setup dialog box (see Figure 33.6).

Within this dialog box, you can set the size and source of the paper. For most printers, the default settings, Letter and Automatically Select, should be fine.

FIGURE 33.6

The Page Setup dialog box.

You can set the Orientation option to either Portrait (vertical) or Landscape (horizontal). You also can choose whether to center the image on the page, and set the left and top margins. Using the Scale option, you can set the size of the image.

You also can specify the Print Output setting. If you own a color printer, you can select the Color option, or you can select Greyscale if you own a black-and-white printer (for example, a laser printer). Note that setting Greyscale will print a black and white image even on a color printer. You can even print a CMYK separation.

To preview the job before sending it to the printer, select File, Print to open the Print Preview screen (see Figure 33.7).

FIGURE 33.7

You can preview an image before you print.

33

This screen gives you an idea of what your printed image will look like. It is a good idea to preview your image if only to make sure the margins are set where they should be.

If you're satisfied with the preview, you can click the Print button. This step opens the Print dialog box specific to your printer and prints the image. It's as simple as that!

Multi-Image Printing

Introduced in version 6 and continuing in version 7, Paint Shop Pro offers the capability to print multiple images on one page. The images must currently be open in Paint Shop Pro for this tool to do its magic.

With the images you would like to print open in Paint Shop Pro, choose File, Print Multiple Images. Doing so will open a new window, showing you the open images on the left and a blank canvas on the right.

To add the images you want to print, simply drag and drop them onto the canvas where you want them (see Figure 33.8). You can resize the images when they are on the canvas.

FIGURE 33.8

The multi-image printing.

You can save and open layouts that you've created. This can be a real timesaver if you are creating several layouts with the same number of images placed in the same way.

This new feature also can save you money as well as time if you find yourself printing photo-quality images on expensive photo paper. You simply can print photo paper.

Summary

In this chapter, you learned how to open, save, import, export, and print your images. You might want to practice opening some images (you can find a few nice images on the Paint Shop Pro CD-ROM) and saving them as different file types. You might even open a file and print it to see how images look from your printer.

In the next chapter, I'll show you how to create your first image. I'll discuss some of the concepts with which you should be familiar before starting an image, and take you on a brief tour of the various tools available in Paint Shop Pro.

33

CHAPTER 34

Creating Your First Image

This chapter introduces the following topics regarding images:

- Issues to consider before constructing your first image
- Creating your first image
- Editing your first image
- Fixing mistakes in an image

Issues to Consider Before Constructing an Image

It's often quite tempting to just jump right in and start painting and drawing when creating a new image. However, if you stop for a moment and think about the image before you actually begin, you can save yourself time and possibly money.

Some things to consider include the overall size of the image (including its dimensions), the number of colors needed (which can affect the resulting file size), and the file size, especially if the image is intended for the Web.

Choosing an Image Size

Whether the image is intended for the Web, general onscreen viewing, or print media, the dimensions are among the first things to consider.

If your image is intended for onscreen presentation, you'll usually want it to fit within the limits of a computer screen.

More and more people are using 800×600 settings for their computer monitors. Some are even using much higher resolutions. Nevertheless, many people still run their screens at 640×480. If you know your audience well or are designing for a particular screen resolution, you're all set. If not, choose the resolution of your own screen or smaller.

With that decision out of the way, it's time to decide on the resolution in terms of dots per inch (dpi) or pixels per inch (ppi). If you're designing for onscreen or Web use, set the resolution to 72dpi, which is the norm for most computer screens. The differences you encounter won't be significant and, for onscreen use, the most important aspect to consider is width and height anyway.

If you'll be printing your image or having it printed, the dpi you choose will become a more important issue. If your final output is destined for print, you'll want to use a much higher resolution than that for onscreen presentations.

Most of today's printers are capable of 300×300, 600×600, or higher resolution, and sending a 72dpi image to one of those printers will result in either a much smaller image than you want or final print quality that's just not acceptable.

Be aware, though, that images with a higher resolution will be much larger. An image at 72dpi that's 4"×6" (which is about the standard size for prints you get back from most one-hour photo stores) is about 385KB uncompressed, whereas the same image at 300dpi takes up a whopping 6MB of hard drive space.

Keep in mind, too, that downsizing an image results in better quality than upsizing an image. If you take a small image and make it larger, you'll be disappointed with the results. If you take a larger image and make it smaller, though, the results, although not perfect, will be much better.

Choosing an Image Type

Another issue to consider is the image type, or number of colors (color resolution). If you're scanning an image into Paint Shop Pro, you should normally use the highest setting available—especially for real-world images such as photographs. You should use a lower color setting when scanning in black-and-white art, though. If you're opening and working on an existing image, plan to stay with the existing color resolution.

Normally, your scanning software will adjust the number of colors based on the type of image it's scanning. You can still use a higher number of colors, especially if you apply effects to the image.

When you're finished working on the image, you can lower the number of colors if necessary. This change decreases the final file size and may even be necessary if you are saving to a file type such as GIF.

When you're starting a new image, you are faced with many color resolution options. This is when you have to decide on the image type. The image type you choose depends on the image you are creating and its intended purpose (such as the final output method).

Generally, you should start out with high color resolution, especially if you intend to use any of the special effects in Paint Shop Pro. Most of the effects are grayed out or otherwise not available when you work on lower color resolution images.

You can always change the image type after you complete the image. In fact, this step is necessary if you're working on an image with thousands or millions of colors that needs to be converted to a GIF file for the Web.

I recommend keeping a copy of the original image in the higher color resolution in case you need to make changes later. This approach means that you won't have to change the color resolution over and over, which ultimately degrades an image's quality.

34

The choice for image type or number of colors is set when you open a new image. The New Image dialog box pops up when you choose File, New. You can set the width, height, and resolution. You also can set the background color and the image type. For image type, you can choose from the following options:

- 2 Colors (1 Bit)
- 16 Colors (4 Bit)
- Grayscale (8 Bit)
- 256 Colors (8 Bit)
- 16.7 Million Colors (24 Bit)

You can also reset the color resolution by choosing Colors, Decrease Color Depth or Colors, Increase Color Depth. The Decrease Color Depth menu gives you more control than you get from the New File dialog box and the Increase Color Depth menu choice. From the Decrease Color Depth menu, you can also choose 32,000 colors, 64,000 colors, or an arbitrary number of colors for any image.

Normally, I start an image with 16.7 million colors so that I can effectively apply all the tools at my disposal. The image can always be downgraded to a lower color resolution when I'm done. That said, let's open a new image and explore a few of the available tools.

Creating a Simple Image

The best way to learn is to roll up your sleeves and get right to it. The following exercise introduces the Paint Shop Pro tools used for drawing, painting, and creating lines and shapes.

Using the Preset Shapes Tool

To get started, open a new image at 500×500 pixels with the resolution set to 72ppi, the background color set to White, and the image type set to 16.7 Million Colors. Then follow these steps:

1. Select the Preset Shapes tool from the Tool palette.
2. Set the stroke and fill colors by moving the mouse over the color swatches. Left-click to set the stroke and right-click to set the fill color.
3. In the Tool Options window, click the button to the right of the shape in the Shape Type option. Choose the Rectangle shape from the flyout menu (see Figure 34.1). Set the Line Width to 2. Leave the Antialias option checked or place a check mark in the option if none is present, but remove the check mark from the Create as Vector option. Leave Retain Shape unchecked, as well.
4. Click and drag the mouse within the image window. As you drag the mouse, a rectangle forms, grows, and changes shape. When you release the mouse, a perfect rectangle will be drawn where the outline was.

Try another!

1. Reset the foreground color by choosing a color from the color swatch in the Color palette.
2. Under the Color Swatches, click and hold the Fill Style to set the style. You can choose, for example, No Fill to create an outlined shape (see Figure 34.2).

FIGURE 34.1

Choosing a preset shape type.

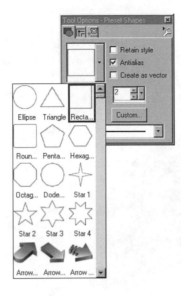

FIGURE 34.2

Choosing a Fill Style.

34

3. Choose another color and, in the Tool Options window, set the Shape Type to Circle.

4. Click and drag the mouse in the image window again. This time you'll draw a circle. You might notice that, unlike the rectangular shape, the circle is drawn from the center out. This piece of information will come in handy when you want to draw more complex shapes by combining various lower-level shapes.

Avoiding Aliased Images

If you haven't placed a check mark in the Antialias check box of the Tool Options window, and if your circle is large enough and it contrasts enough in color with the background, you may notice that it's a bit jagged (see Figure 34.3).

FIGURE 34.3

An aliased circle.

This jaggedness is called *aliasing*, and it's the result of taking an analog shape, such as a circle, and digitizing it. A shape such as a circle is *analog* by nature in that it has an infinite number of points that make up its circumference.

When you draw a circle on a computer screen, it must be represented by pixels. All these pixels together make up a grid of 640×480 pixels, 800×600 pixels, 1,024×768 pixels, and so on. Because the circle is being drawn on a grid, it is digitized. That is, only a certain number of points are available, and each point on the circumference of the circle that is being drawn must be represented by one of the pixels that make up the grid on your computer screen.

What all this really means to you, the digital artist, is that many of your shapes and lines will be aliased. This, of course, means that your images will have jagged edges. Or does it? Actually, it does and it doesn't. How can that be, you ask? Simple! You can use a process known as antialiasing to give jagged edges the appearance of being smooth.

Antialiasing uses mathematics and shades of colors that range between the colors along the edge to fool your eye into believing that the edge is smooth.

Figure 34.4 shows another filled circle drawn in Paint Shop Pro. This time, when I drew the circle, I placed a check mark in the Antialias check box in the Tool Options window.

FIGURE 34.4
An antialiased circle.

To show you the difference, I zoomed in on both Figure 34.3 (the aliased circle) and Figure 34.4 (the antialiased circle). Seeing the two images side by side will give you a better idea of what aliasing and antialiasing are all about (see Figure 34.5).

FIGURE 34.5
Aliased and antialiased circles side by side.

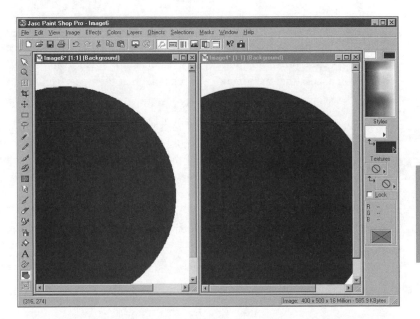

34

The image containing the aliased circle is obviously made up solely of black and white pixels, whereas the image containing the antialiased circle shows pixels of varying shades of gray along the circle's edge. It's those pixels that give the second circle its appearance of smoothness.

Using Brush Tips

Close the image on which you've been doodling and open a new image with the same settings as before. (You can save the first one if it is the beginning of a masterpiece you want to get back to later.) Then follow these steps:

1. Select the Paint Brush tool. In the Tool Options window, click the Paint Brush Options tab to open the Brush Tip palette (see Figure 34.6).

FIGURE 34.6

The Brush Tip palette.

2. Use the controls in the Brush Tip palette to set the various options for the Paint Brush tool. You can set the size, the opacity, the hardness, the density, and the step of the brush. In addition, you can select a brush from the pull-down menu. To access that menu, click the brush icon at the upper-right of the tabbed palette.

   You can choose from a variety of brushes. I'll talk more about brushes in Chapter 38, "Painting Tools and Techniques."

3. After you are finished selecting a brush and playing with the settings, draw on the new image to get the feel of the various brushes and their settings. Change the color, the brush type, and the opacity to see what happens.

One nice option here is the brush preview in the upper-left corner of the Brush Tip tabbed palette. This small window shows you what the brush looks like and gives you a good idea of the effect you'll get when you use any given brush.

4. Try lowering the opacity. If you lower the opacity enough, you'll be able to see previous lines you've made through the new lines you're drawing. This powerful feature enables you to mimic real-world drawing tools.

A new option in the Tool Options window, first introduced in version 6, is the addition of a control button next to the spin controls (the spin controls are the small arrows that enable you to change a numeric setting by clicking either the up arrow or the down arrow). The new control buttons can be recognized by the small icon with a small underlined, black, downward-pointing arrow. Clicking one of these, where available, will open a small sliding control. The sliding control, although not as accurate as the spin control, is much quicker to use when precision is not as important.

Figure 34.7 shows how I mimicked an orange highlighter marker drawn over some black text.

FIGURE 34.7
Orange highlighter over black text.

To create this quick highlighter fakery, I simply added black text to a new image and then drew over the text with an orange brush. I set the brush to Normal with the shape set to Round, and I set the size to 104 (just enough to cover the height of the text).

I set the Opacity to 52 (I played around with this setting a couple of times and used Edit, Undo until I got just the opacity effect I wanted). I set the Hardness to 0 (I wanted a very soft edge so that it would blend into the white background, as an older marker might do). I left the Density set to 100 and the Step set to 25. All of these settings combined to give the effect I wanted, that of a marker highlighting some text.

Try playing around with the brushes and their settings to see how they work. Don't worry if some of the options seem confusing for now.

Editing a Simple Image

Paint Shop Pro also enables you to edit existing images. You can use the drawing and painting tools as well as the Text, Line, and Shape tools to change an image.

34

Two other tools that enable you to edit an existing image are the Color Replacer tool and the Retouch tool. The Retouch tool acts much the same as the Paint Brush tool and, in fact, you can set the options for this tool as if it were a brush.

The difference is that you can use the Retouch tool to apply various retouching effects such as Lighten, Darken, Soften, Emboss, and more. I'll cover these options in more depth in Chapter 41, "Retouching Your Images."

The Color Replacer tool, although powerful, can be somewhat confusing. I think, though, that if you follow along with the next example, the workings of this tool will become clear.

To see how the Color Replacer tool works, open a new 500×500 image with a white background and the image type set to 16.7 million colors. Then follow these steps:

1. Set the stroke style to none and set the fill color to black. Make sure that it's black; it must have the value 0 for each of the colors Red, Green, and Blue. You can see these numbers scroll as you move over the color swatch in the Color palette.

2. You should be able to move the mouse far enough to the left of the color swatch to get the color to perfect black. If you can't quite get it, just complete the following two steps:

    a. Click the fill style swatch to bring up the Color dialog box (see Figure 34.8).

FIGURE 34.8
The Color dialog box.

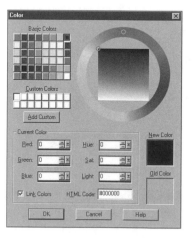

    b. With the Color dialog box open, you can easily enter the RGB values. After you enter zeros for each entry, click OK and the foreground color will be perfectly black.

Within the Color dialog box, you will see a swatch in the upper-left corner. This swatch contains some common colors, including pure red, yellow, green, cyan, blue, magenta, black, and white. Clicking one of these small squares is a great way to quickly select one of these commonly used colors.

3. Draw two circles that don't touch. You can place them in opposite corners, as I've done in Figure 34.9.

FIGURE 34.9

Two circles filled with black.

4. Change the fill color to a really dark blue. You don't have to be too fussy, just make sure that the color is almost black. The values for the color I'm using are R: 4, G: 4, and B: 8.

5. With the new fill color set, draw a Filled rectangle so that it partly covers each circle, as shown in Figure 34.10.

6. Set the stroke color to a bright yellow and click the Lock option in the Color palette.

7. Select the Color Replacer tool.

8. Click the Color Replacer Options tab (the second tab) in the Tool Options window and set Tolerance to 0.

34

FIGURE 34.10

Two circles filled with black and a nearly black rectangle.

9. Set the stroke color to a nice bright yellow. You don't need to be fussy; just select a color that's different from the two circles and the rectangle. You can set the stroke color by left-clicking a color in the main color swatch in the Color palette.

10. With the new stroke color set and the fill color still set to the color you chose for the rectangle, double left-click anywhere in the image.

    The rectangle should turn yellow. What happened? It turned yellow because that's the current stroke color. The Color Replacer tool replaced all the pixels in the image containing the current fill color with pixels using the current stroke color.

11. You can reverse the process by double-clicking. Try it. Double right-clicking replaces pixels containing the current stroke color with pixels using the current fill color.

12. With the image back to its original state, bump Tolerance up to around 80.

    Double left-clicking replaces the color of all three objects with the current stroke color.

The Tolerance setting controls how close a color needs to be to the color being changed before it gets replaced with the new color. Almost like magic, right? And now you know how it works.

I encourage you to play with this awesome tool until you feel comfortable with it.

Fixing Errors

To help you keep your creativity alive, Paint Shop Pro has an Undo feature (a multiple Undo feature, actually). If you make a change (or several changes) to an image and find that you don't like the change or that it isn't quite what you expected, you can undo it.

To undo the most recent change, choose Edit, Undo. This backs up to just before the most recent change you made. To see Undo in action, open a new file and draw a shape. Then follow these steps:

1. Select another tool, such as the Draw tool or the Paint Brush tool, and draw over the shape you created.

2. Choose Edit, Undo, and the line or the mark you made will disappear.

3. Choose Edit, Undo again, and the shape disappears, too.

4. Oops! What if you intended to keep the first shape? No problem! Choose Edit, Redo to make the shape reappear.

There's even an Undo History. If you choose Edit, Command History, you'll get the Command History dialog box (see Figure 34.11).

FIGURE 34.11

The Command History dialog.

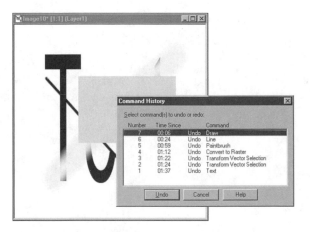

34

In Figure 34.11, the Command History dialog box contains a list of the most recent changes made to the image. These changes are visible in the image, of course. To restore the image to an earlier state, simply click the corresponding point in the Command History dialog box and select Undo.

Unfortunately, the history is linear, so you can't pick and choose which Undos you want. Anything else that is highlighted in the list is also undone. This feature is a great way to return to a specific point in your work, though.

Summary

In this chapter, you learned a little about how to create an image, draw shapes, and use the Paint Brush tools. You also learned how to edit an image and how to change any color in the image to another color. Also, you saw how to undo an error and redo the Undo, and you took a quick look at the Undo History feature.

CHAPTER 35

Creating and Working with Selections

A *selection* masks off an area of an image so that you can make changes to that area without affecting the rest of the image. You can fill selections, run effects on them, and more. You can save selections and load them later. You also can copy and paste selections within an image or from one image to another, and you can add to and subtract from selections.

 This chapter assumes that you have already installed Paint Shop Pro. You can get a free demo version at http://www.jasc.com.

Using the Selection Tools

Selections are essential for creating and manipulating digital images, and Paint Shop Pro provides a number of tools for making selections. From the Tool palette, you can select one of three selection tools:

- The Selection tool
- The Freehand tool
- The Magic Wand tool

Each of these tools is discussed in the following sections.

The Selection Tool

The Selection tool enables you to make selections using different shapes. After choosing the Selection tool, you can set the desired shape in the Tool Options window. You can choose from a rectangle, a square, an ellipse, a circle, and many other shapes. Using the Selection tool is similar to using the Preset Shapes tool.

To try out the Selection tool, open a new 500×500 image at 72dpi with the background set to white, and then follow these steps:

1. Select the Selection tool.

2. In the Tool Options window, set the shape to Rectangle. For the moment, ignore the Feather value and the Antialias check box.

3. Place the mouse cursor in the upper-left corner of the image, and click and drag toward the lower-right corner of the image.

   As you drag the mouse, you'll see an outline of a rectangle. When you release the mouse, however, the rectangle becomes a marquee (see Figure 35.1). Some people refer to this marquee as "marching ants" because of the movement.

4. To clear the selection, either choose Selections, Select None or click anywhere outside the marquee area.

Try making a couple of selections using the other shapes. If you forget to remove one selection before making another, the first selection disappears. Later in this chapter you'll see how you can keep any current selection and either add to it or subtract from it. You'll also learn how to modify the selection.

The Freehand Tool

The second selection tool is the Freehand tool. You can use the Freehand tool to draw freehand selections. Doing so enables you to isolate irregular-shaped areas of an image.

To see how this tool works, clear any other selections you still have active by choosing Selections, Select None. Select the Freehand tool and click and drag it around the image as if you were drawing a doodle.

FIGURE 35.1

A rectangular selection.

As you draw, you'll see a line being drawn by the tool. When you release the mouse button, the line turns into a marquee, and a straight line may join the starting and ending points if they are far enough apart (see Figure 35.2).

FIGURE 35.2

A Freehand tool selection.

35

The Freehand tool has several settings available from the Tool Options window, as well. You can draw freehand as you did in the previous example. You can also make point to point or Smart Edge selections.

Point to point enables you to draw polygonal selections. To do so, select the Freehand tool and set the Selection Type option to Point to Point in the Tool Options window.

Move the mouse cursor into the image and click. Move the mouse again and click once more. As you continue to move and click, you'll see lines being drawn between the points you click. To finish the selection, simply double-click. You should end up with a polygonal selection (see Figure 35.3).

FIGURE 35.3

A polygonal selection.

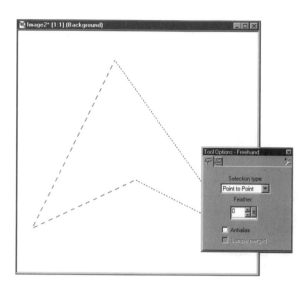

The third option for the Freehand tool is the Smart Edge. With the Smart Edge option, Paint Shop Pro can help you make difficult selections along the edges of contrasting areas. To see how this option works, clear any current selections you have by choosing Selections, Select None. Then follow these steps:

1. Select the Preset Shapes tool and set the Style to Filled in the Tool Options window. Draw a circle in the upper-right corner of the image. Change the shape to a rectangle and draw a rectangle below and to the right of the circle (see Figure 35.4).

   If you're not sure how to complete these steps, refer to Chapter 34, "Creating Your First Image."

2. With the shapes drawn, select the Freehand tool and set the Selection Type option to Smart Edge in the Tool Options window.

3. Move the mouse cursor to a point along the bottom-left of the circle.

FIGURE 35.4

A circle and a rectangle drawn with the Preset Shapes tool.

4. Click and drag the mouse toward the rectangle. As you drag, you'll see a bounding box (see Figure 35.5). When you get to the point where you're just overlapping the rectangle, as shown in Figure 35.5, release the mouse button.

FIGURE 35.5

A bounding box highlights the edge that the Smart Edge is selecting.

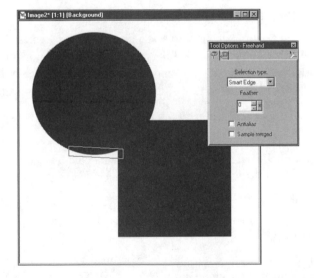

5. Click the mouse again without moving it and then move the mouse to the lower-left corner of the rectangle.

6. Double-click the mouse; you should end up with a selection like the one in Figure 35.6.

35

Figure 35.6

A completed selection along the lower left of the circle and the rec-tangle drawn with the Smart Edge Freehand tool.

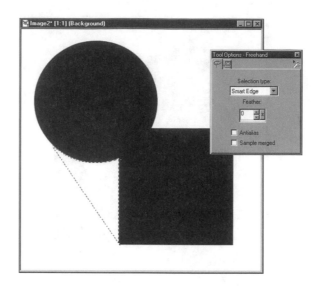

Although this powerful tool is a bit difficult to work with at first, it is worth learning. The Smart Edge option of the Freehand tool enables you to make selections around areas that might otherwise be impossible.

The Magic Wand Tool

You can use the Magic Wand tool to select areas of an image based on the RGB value, hue, or brightness. You can set the Tolerance level to select more or fewer pixels, based on the relative values. The Magic Wand tool is quite easy to use. You simply select it, set the options, and click on a portion of the image that you want selected.

To try this tool, open a new 500×500 image at 72dpi with the background set to white and follow these steps:

1. Draw a filled rectangle in one color (I used a pale blue) and a filled circle in a very different color (I used red). Make the shapes overlap, as shown in Figure 35.7.

2. Select the Magic Wand tool.

3. In the Tool Options window, set the Match Mode option to RGB and the Tolerance option to 10.

4. Click the circle. The circle should be outlined by a selection marquee. The marquee means that the circle has been selected. Nothing else has been selected, though, only the circle.

Only the circle is selected because it is red, the rectangle is blue, and the background is white. If the overlapping rectangle were a shade of red that closely matched the red of the circle and the Tolerance was high enough, the rectangle would be selected also.

FIGURE 35.7

A circle and a rectangle drawn with the Shapes tool.

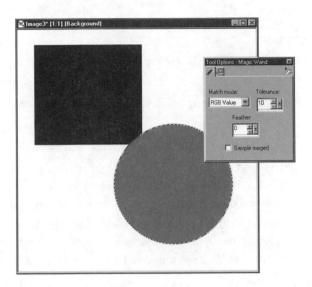

The Magic Wand tool doesn't care about the shapes of the areas it's selecting; it bases its selections on the Match Mode and Tolerance settings.

You might have noticed a Sample Merged check box in the Controls palette for some of the selection tools. When checked, this option allows selections to be made throughout all the layers of an image.

You can also make and adjust selections using the Selections menu. From the Selections menu you can choose

- Select All (Ctrl+A), which selects the entire image.
- Select None (Ctrl+D), which deselects the current selection.
- From Mask (Shift+Ctrl+S), which makes a selection based on the current mask.
- Invert (Shift+Ctrl+I), which inverts the selection. If you still have the circle selected from the previous section and you choose Selections, Invert, everything but the circle is selected. If you choose Selections, Invert again, the circle is reselected. Try it!
- Matting, which can remove fringes that sometimes appear around a selected area.
- Modify, which can modify a selection. (I'll cover this in more depth in the next section.)
- Hide Marquee (Shift+Ctrl+M), which hides the marquee while leaving the selection active.

35

- Convert to Seamless Pattern, which creates seamless tiles for repeating patterns and backgrounds.
- Promote to Layer (Shift+Ctrl+P), which turns a selection into a new layer.
- Load from Disk, which loads a saved selection from your disk drive.
- Load from Alpha Channel, which loads a selection that you saved as a channel.
- Save to Disk, which saves a selection to your hard drive.
- Save to Alpha Channel, which saves a selection in an Alpha channel.
- Float (Ctrl+F), which floats the selection and enables you to move it around the image while leaving the area below untouched. In other words, you create a duplicate of the selected area, which you can freely move around within the image.
- Defloat (Shift+Ctrl+F), which drops the selected area. When you defloat a selection, you can still move the selected area around, but it will be the actual area that moves and not a duplicate of the area. Of course, you can float the selection again.

I'll explore some of these options in the next section and use most of these tools extensively throughout the remainder of the book.

Although you could move selections in previous versions of Paint Shop Pro using the Mover tool (and you may have noticed that the Selection tool changes into the Mover tool when you move the cursor inside of a selection), the movement wasn't very precise. Starting with version 7, though, you can now move a selection using the cursor keys. To do so, hold down the Shift key and use one of the cursor keys to move the selection. Doing so moves the selection in precise one-pixel increments. If you feel the need for a little more speed, hold down the Ctrl key at the same time. Doing so will move the selection by 10 pixels at a time.

Editing Selections

Making a selection is not necessarily the end of your work. You can add to the selection, subtract from the selection, expand and contract the selection, and more.

Adding to a Selection

After making an initial selection, you can add to it. To see how this option works, open a new 500×500, 72dpi image with the background set to white. Then follow these steps:

1. Choose the Selection tool and, in the Tool Options window, set the Selection Type to Rectangle.
2. Draw a rectangular selection in the upper-left corner of the image.

3. Place the mouse in the lower-right corner of your selection (not too near the corner, though) and, while holding down the Shift key, draw another rectangular selection.

   You should now have an area selected that resembles two overlapping rectangles (see Figure 35.8). Interesting.

FIGURE 35.8

Adding to a selection.

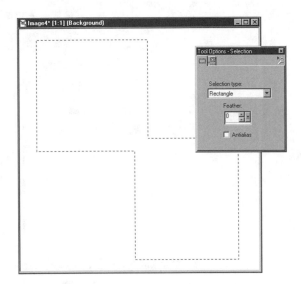

4. Try that again, but this time change the Selection Type to Circle and start somewhere near where the two rectangles overlap.

Hmmm… you should now have a fairly complex shape building up, consisting of a couple of rectangles and a circle (see Figure 35.9).

You might be getting the idea that you can actually create some fairly complex shapes using just the selection tools, and you are right. In addition to adding to a selection, you also can subtract from it, as discussed in the next section.

Subtracting from a Selection

To subtract from a selection, choose a selection tool and, while holding down the Ctrl key, make a selection that overlaps the currently selected area. To give it a try, follow these steps:

1. Choose the Selection tool and, in the Tool Options window, set the Selection Type to Circle.

2. On the selection made in the previous section, move the mouse to the middle of the first circular area you created.

35

3. Hold down the Ctrl key and draw a circular selection. When you release the mouse button, the new circle will be cut from the selected area (see Figure 35.10).

FIGURE 35.9

Adding more to a selection.

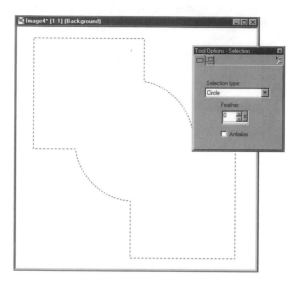

FIGURE 35.10

Subtracting from a selection.

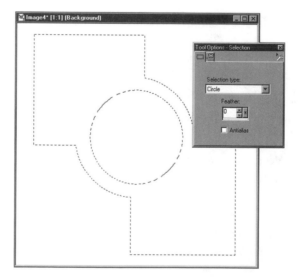

Wow! Can you see some of the possibilities? You can use any of the selection tools to add to and subtract from a selection. Using these tools together, you can make very sophisticated selections. These selections can be around existing portions of an image or, as you've just done, on new images.

To see how these techniques can be used, I created a Star shape, added a rounded rectangle and subtracted another rounded rectangle. If you fill the image with blue and add an Inner Bevel effect, the result could easily become a button for a Web page (see Figure 35.11).

FIGURE 35.11

Creating a button image from selections.

All these techniques are covered throughout this book. In fact, by the end of this book, you'll be able to create interfaces, or buttons, like the one pictured in Figure 35.11.

Expanding and Contracting a Selection

Sometimes a selection is almost right, but not quite the way you want it. You might need to expand or contract the selection. To do so, choose Selections, Modify, Expand or Contract and then enter a value in the dialog box. This step expands or contracts the selection by the number of pixels you enter in the dialog box.

Growing a Selection

At other times, you might need to include a little more of an area that has similarly colored pixels. You can do so by choosing Selections, Modify, Grow Selection. This option is useful if you made a selection with the Magic Wand tool and, with the setting you chose for Tolerance, selected most of the area you needed. Instead of resetting Tolerance and trying again, Selections, Modify, Grow Selection is often enough to get those extra pixels.

35

Selecting Similar Areas

Growing a selection grabs adjoining pixels, but what if the area you want isn't contiguous to the area you've already selected? Simple. You can select areas in the image based on whether or not they are *similar* to the area already selected.

For example, say you have some black text on a white background, and you select the background area by clicking the background with the Magic Wand tool. Doing so selects the background area around the text, but it doesn't select the white area inside letters such as O and P.

No problem. Choose Selections, Modify, Select Similar. This selects the rest of the white areas (because the background that you selected is white), including those pesky areas inside certain letters.

Loading and Saving Selections

What should you do if you've made a really complex selection and you'd like to save it? You should do just that. Save it!

With an area selected, you can save the selection in two ways. You can save the selection to disk, where it will remain until you need it later, or you can save it to an Alpha channel. *Alpha channels* are special areas that keep selections. These channels are saved along with the file and can be reloaded later.

To save a selection as a file, choose Selections, Save to Disk. A standard Windows Save dialog box enables you to name and save the selection.

To save a selection as an Alpha channel, choose Selections, Save to Alpha Channel. This option opens the Save to Alpha dialog box, in which you can choose the document with which to save the channel and see the available channels (see Figure 35.12).

FIGURE 35.12

Save to Alpha dialog box.

After you select the document and click OK, you can name the selection. This option is handy if you'll be saving multiple selections with a document. After you save a selection, you can reload it into the current image. The nice thing about saving a selection to disk is that you can also load the selection into other images, as well.

To load a selection that you saved as a file, choose Selections, Load from Disk. This step brings up a standard Windows Open dialog box, where you can browse for and open any selection you previously saved.

To load a selection that has been saved as an Alpha channel, choose Selections, Load from Alpha Channel. Doing so opens the Load From Alpha dialog box, which enables you to choose the document and the channel you want to load (see Figure 35.13).

FIGURE 35.13

Load from Alpha dialog box.

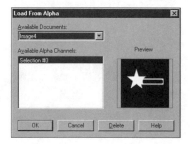

Note that the Load from Alpha dialog box shows a thumbnail preview of the selection, which comes in handy if you have saved several selections. Being able to choose the selection visually is a big plus if, like me, you're too lazy to name your selections as you save them.

Summary

Now that you've learned the basics of creating and editing selections, it's time to move on to Chapter 36, "Working with Deformations."

Don't worry if you think that you haven't had much practice with selections. You'll be using selections throughout the remainder of the book, and you'll soon have made enough of them to be considered an expert.

35

CHAPTER **36**

Working with Deformations

You can use menu choices to resize, rotate, add perspective to, and skew your images. Even better, though, you can apply these deformations to your images interactively. In this chapter, you'll learn how to apply these effects simply by clicking and dragging the mouse.

This chapter assumes that you have already installed Paint Shop Pro. You can get a free demo version at `http://www.jasc.com`.

Using the Deformation Tool

If you can believe it, all these cool deformations described above can be applied with one single tool! To see this tool in action, open a new 500×500, 72dpi image with a white background. Then follow these steps:

1. In the Layer palette, click the Create Layer icon to add a new layer over the background layer. I know we haven't covered layers yet, but you don't really need to know how they work at this point. If the Layer palette is not visible choose View, Toolbars and, in the Toolbars dialog box that appears, place a check mark in the Layer Palette option.

2. In the Layer Properties dialog box, click OK.

3. Set the background color to black. This is the color with which your text will be filled. Also, set the Stroke Style to none.

4. Select the Text tool and click in the middle of the image to open the Text Entry dialog box.

5. In the Text Entry dialog box, enter some text. The text you enter doesn't really matter; it could be your name, for example. Be sure the size is large (you'll see the text appear within your image so you can change the size as needed). Also, be sure you place a checkmark in the Antialias option and that you choose Floating for the Create As type so that you can move the text around within the image (see Figure 36.1).

FIGURE 36.1

The Text Entry dialog box.

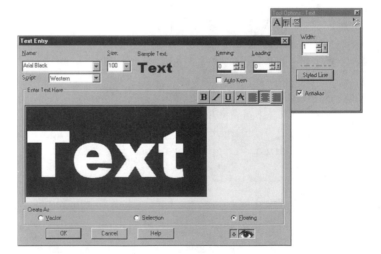

6. Click OK to place the text as a new floating selection over the new layer (see Figure 36.2).

7. With the text still "floating," you should be able to click and drag it into place. To do so, simply move the mouse over the text until the cursor changes to a four-headed arrow, and then drag the text into place.

8. Select the Deformation tool. When you do, you'll notice a change in your image. A bounding box is added with several control handles (see Figure 36.3).

FIGURE 36.2

Text as a floating selection over a new layer.

FIGURE 36.3

The Deformation tool's bounding box and control handles with the Layer palette shown.

36

9. As you move the mouse over the bounding box and the different control handles, the mouse pointer changes, too.

If you move the mouse inside the bounding box away from any of the control handles, the pointer changes to a cross with an arrowhead at each end. This pointer enables you to move the selection along with the bounding box. Try it; move the text around the image.

As you move the pointer, the bounding box follows; when you release the mouse button, the text snaps back inside the bounding box.

10. Move the pointer over one of the corner or side handles.

As you move over a side handle, the mouse pointer becomes a two-headed arrow with a small rectangle above it. As you move the pointer over a corner handle, the mouse becomes a four-headed arrow (different from the four-headed arrow described previously) with a small rectangle over it.

Each type of control handle enables you to resize the bounding box, and the selection contained within it, interactively:

- With the side handles, you can adjust the width and height separately.
- With the corner handles, you can adjust the width and height of the selection simultaneously.

Try it. Move the mouse pointer over one of the handles and click and drag it. As you do, release the mouse button, the text resizes so that it fits into the box again.

If the resizing moves the text from the center of the image, just grab the text (or the bounding box, actually) and move it back into position (see Figure 36.4).

FIGURE 36.4

Text enlarged with the Deformation tool.

Rotating Text

With the text resized, try rotating it. Simply grab the right side of the center control handle and give it a spin. When you move the pointer over the control handle box, the mouse becomes a crosshair in the box and two circular arrows appear.

When you get it into position, double-click the mouse. You should see the selection marquee appear around the text again and should have something similar to Figure 36.5.

FIGURE 36.5

Text rotated with the Deformation tool.

Using the Perspective, Shear, and Distort Options

In this section, I'll use a practical application of the Deformation tool to demonstrate the Perspective, Shear, and Distort options. Follow these steps:

1. Open a new 500×500, 72dpi image with the background set to white.

2. Create a new layer by clicking the New Layer icon located in the top left corner of the Layer palette.

3. Select the Text tool.

4. Set the background color to a mid-to-dark gray and add some text as you did in the preceding example.

5. Choose Image, Flip to flip the text (see Figure 36.6).

6. Select the Deformation tool and move the text a little to the right.

7. Grab the middle control handle along the bottom of the bounding box and drag down to resize the text vertically (see Figure 36.7).

FIGURE 36.6

*Text flipped with
Image, Flip.*

FIGURE 36.7

*Text resized with the
Deformation tool.*

8. Hold down the Ctrl key and drag the bottom-left corner to the left so that the bottom of the text gets larger while the top remains the same (see Figure 36.8). This is how you can add perspective to an image. If the text seems to be running off the right side of the image, just drag the text toward the center with the mouse.

9. Add a little shear to the text by holding down the Shift key while you drag any of the corners. I've sheared both bottom corners to the right a little (see Figure 36.9).

FIGURE 36.8

Perspective added with the Deformation tool.

FIGURE 36.9

Shear added with the Deformation tool.

36

10. With the deformations complete, double-click within the bounding box to apply the deformations. Choose Selections, Select None to deselect the text.

11. Select the Text tool and enter the same text with the same size and font settings that you used for the deformed text. Make sure that you choose a color other than white or the color you used for the deformed text.

12. Position the text directly over the deformed text, as shown in Figure 36.10.

Figure 36.10

Text with a perspective shadow.

Amazing! You've just created a much sought-after effect. You've created text with a per-spective shadow.

Adding a Shadow Effect

If you're daring enough, you can finish up this chapter by making the shadow seem a lit-tle more realistic. To do so, you'll have to employ a technique from Chapter 34, "Creating Your First Image," and use a new technique as well. Follow these steps:

1. Access the Command History command and up to the point just before you added the new text. You should be at the point where you just finished deforming the text.

2. Click the foreground color swatch and set the color to white. Click the background color swatch and set the color to a medium gray.

3. Set the Stroke style to Foreground Gradient.

4. Select the Flood Fill tool.

5. Click the Stroke Style to open the Gradient dialog box.

6. Set Fill Style to Linear Gradient and set the gradient to Foreground-Background. You can do so by clicking the flyout menu next to the gradient thumbnail and choosing the gradient from the list (see Figure 36.11).

7. Click anywhere in the selected text to fill it with the gradient. The letters should get more faded as hey get closer to the bottom of the image.

8. Use the Text tool to add the same text as before.

9. Maneuver the text into place over the perspective shadow (see Figure 36.12).

FIGURE 36.11

The Tool Options window, showing the Gradient Fill options.

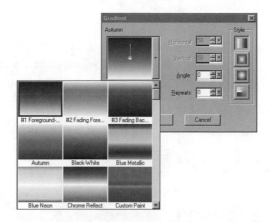

FIGURE 36.12

Text with fading perspective shadow.

Wow! Now that is amazing! I consider this to be a fairly advanced technique, and here you've done it after only a few hours with the program.

Some other deformations are available under the Image, Deformations menu. I'll cover these later, though, in Chapter 40, "Applying Filters."

Summary

Although this chapter may have seemed long, it wasn't really. It's just that you covered quite a bit, even if it was with only one tool. You've just created a really cool image and some text. Not bad for an chapter's work.

I'd say that you're ready to head on to the next chapter, where you'll learn how to use the drawing tools.

CHAPTER **37**

Drawing Tools and Techniques

Paint Shop Pro provides a number of drawing tools. For example, you can use the Draw tool to draw lines of varying thicknesses, and you can use the various Preset Shapes tools to draw different shapes, such as rectangles and circles.

Starting with version 6, the drawing tools have vector capabilities; and now in version 7, you can create your own shapes. I'll introduce some of these capabilities in this chapter.

The Drawing Tools and Their Options

Like other tools, the Draw and Preset Shapes tools have options that you can set to change their behavior. All line styles and shapes can be created as either vectors or bitmaps. In this chapter I'll describe the bitmap behavior.

The Draw tool has four styles. You can draw Single lines that are straight and go from one point on your image to another; Bézier curves, which can be manipulated as vectors, even with the Create as Vector box unchecked;

Freehand curves, which cannot be changed after you've drawn them (unless you create them as vectors); and Drawing lines, which are the most flexible and behave like Bézier curves on steroids. In this chapter I'll cover Single lines and Freehand curves and touch on Bézier curves.

> Even if you're not totally new to digital graphics, you might not recognize terms such as Bézier and vector. *Bézier* refers to a type of curve that is drawn on your computer screen using a mathematical formula developed by a French mathematician named Bézier (hence the term Bézier curve). *Vectors* refer to lines and curves saved in computer memory as mathematical formulas rather than as bitmaps. A bitmap is simply an array (much like a spreadsheet, except that all the cells are the same size) of pixels, each containing its own color information.

The Preset Shapes tool is near the very bottom of the Tool palette, and the Draw tool is directly above the Preset Shapes tool. The Preset Shapes Tool icon has a small blue rectangle and a red ellipse on it, and the Draw Tool icon has a curve and a small pencil on it.

If you haven't yet opened an image in Paint Shop Pro, all of the icons in the Tool palette will be displayed in shades of gray. With an image open, most of the icons will be displayed in color. Any icons displayed in shades of gray are not available for use. For example, the Object Selector will not be available unless there's an active layer with vector objects on it.

Besides having four styles of line tools to choose from, you also can set the width of the lines and choose aliased or antialiased. You also have the option of setting the tracking for Freehand curves, which determines how closely a curve follows the mouse as you draw it. For all lines you can set the Cap, which determines how the end of the line will be drawn; the Miter, which determines how lines are joined; and the Miter Limit, which determines the length of miter joins.

Starting with version 6 and continuing in version 7, you also can choose whether lines will be Stroked (outlined), Filled, or both. These options can be set in the Color palette.

The Preset Shapes tool has a couple more options than the Draw tool. You can choose from the following shapes:

- Rectangles
- Squares
- Rounded-rectangles

- Rounded-squares
- Ellipses
- Circles
- Triangles
- Pentagons
- Hexagons
- Octagons
- Two different star shapes
- Three different arrow shapes

37

The shape can be filled in the current background color or simply stroked (outlined). You can choose the thickness of the stroke, and you can choose to have the shapes antialiased or aliased by adding or removing a check mark from the antialias option. In addition, all shapes can be drawn as bitmaps or vectors.

The best way to see how these options work is to roll up your sleeves and do a little drawing. So let's get started.

Drawing Shapes

To get a feeling for the Preset Shapes tool, open a new 500×500 image with the resolution set to 72 pixels per inch, the background color set to white, and the image type set to 16.7 million colors. Then follow these steps:

1. Set the background color to anything but white and select the Preset Shapes tool.

2. If the Tool Options window is not visible, turn it on by clicking the Toggle Tool Options Window icon in the toolbar or by choosing View, Toolbars and placing a check mark next to the Tool Options Window option in the Toolbars dialog box.

   The Tool Options window is where you can set the options that are available for the Preset Shapes tool (see Figure 37.1). This assumes that you've selected the Preset Shapes tool.

FIGURE 37.1

The Tool Options window.

3. Set Shape to Ellipse, Style to Filled (this is set in the Color palette), ignore Line Width for the moment, and place a check mark in the Antialias check box. Be sure that the Create as Vector option is unchecked, for now.

4. While holding down the Shift key, click and drag the mouse anywhere in your image, and you'll notice a circular outline being drawn.

5. Move the mouse until you get a good-size circle and then release the mouse. When you release the mouse, a filled circle appears where the outline was (see Figure 37.2).

You'll notice that the circular shape is drawn outward from the point where you first began to click and drag. Knowing this trick makes it easy to place your circles. How? You can place your cursor anywhere on the image by viewing the current mouse coordinates. In the bottom-left corner of the main Paint Shop Pro window is a set of numbers. These numbers are the current x and y coordinates of the mouse pointer.

To see how these coordinates work, move the mouse pointer onto the image and watch the numbers as you move the mouse around the image window. The numbers constantly change as you move the mouse. You can use these numbers as a guide for placing the mouse pointer anywhere on your image.

To see how this technique works, follow these steps to draw a bull's-eye:

1. Choose Edit, Undo to undo the last circle that you drew.

2. Set the background color to black by moving the mouse pointer over the black area of the main color swatch and clicking or, if you have trouble setting the color this

way, click the background color swatch to bring up the Color dialog box and set the color to black.

3. In the Color dialog box, you can choose the color directly from the color grid if the color you want is there (see Figure 37.3). You also can choose the color from the color wheel (and fine-tune it with the square inside the wheel), or you can enter the exact RGB values for the color. The RGB values for black are 0, 0, 0.

37

FIGURE 37.3

The Color dialog box.

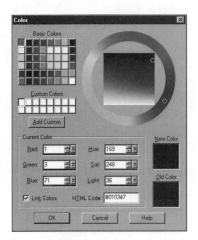

4. With the background color set to black, set the foreground color to red by clicking the foreground color swatch and choosing red from the Color dialog box. The reason to set the two colors is that you can easily switch between them by clicking the small two-headed arrow between the foreground and background color swatches. This technique makes it easy to use two colors without going back to the Color dialog box or guesstimating the colors with the main color swatch.

5. If you're not comfortable moving the mouse into position using the coordinates, you can turn on the grid. To do so, choose View, Grid. This action places a grid over the entire image (see Figure 37.4).

6. The default setting for the grid has a line every 10 pixels. You can change this setting to suit your needs for a particular image. To change the spacing of the grid, choose File, Preferences, General Program Preferences.

7. In the Paint Shop Pro Preferences dialog box, click the Rulers and Units tab to open the dialog box that enables you to set the grid preferences (see Figure 37.5).

8. Change both the Horizontal and Vertical Spacing to 50 and click OK. This gives you a more workable setting for drawing the bull's-eye.

FIGURE **37.4**

*The image window
with the grid visible.*

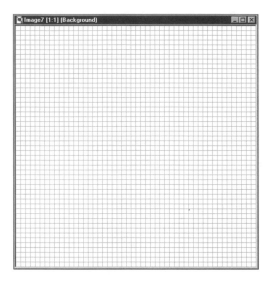

FIGURE **37.5**

*The Paint Shop Pro
Preferences dialog box.*

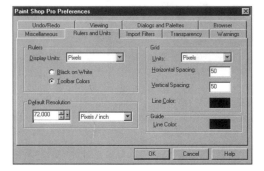

9. If you've chosen to go with the coordinates method, place the mouse pointer at the coordinate 100,100.

   If you're using the grid, move the mouse pointer to where the fourth set of grid lines intersect in the upper right corner.

10. Click and drag the mouse until you get a circle that's about 300 pixels in diameter. You can see the diameter of the circle in the lower-left corner of the main window as you drag the mouse.

> You can hold down the Shift key after clicking the shape to draw a perfect circle.

Along with the current coordinates, you get additional information in this portion of the main window. This information is very helpful when drawing or painting.

The additional information depends on the particular tool you're using. For example, if you're using the Preset Shapes tool to draw a rectangle, you will see the coordinates of the upper-left corner and the lower-left corner as well as the width and height of the rectangle. If you're using the Draw tool to draw a line, you'll see the starting and ending coordinates as well as the angle of the line.

11. Swap the foreground and background colors by clicking the small two-headed arrow between the foreground and background color swatches.

12. Place the mouse at coordinates 125 for both the x and y and draw another circle. Make this circle about 250 pixels in diameter. You should now have two concentric circles (see Figure 37.6). If you're using the grid, you should start your circle where the fifth line intersects.

> You can save a few mouse clicks when drawing your circles for the bull's-eye. To do so, simply draw the circles in the background color by clicking and dragging with the right mouse button. This great shortcut works in other situations as well. Click and drag with the left (primary) mouse button to draw with the foreground color; do so with the right (secondary) mouse button to draw with the background color.

13. Swap the foreground and background colors again, and then draw a third circle.

14. Continue swapping the foreground and background colors and drawing smaller and smaller circles until the image contains five concentric circles (see Figure 37.7).

FIGURE 37.6

Partially completed bull's-eye.

37

FIGURE 37.7
The completed bull's-eye, created with the Preset Shapes tool.

15. Save this image so that you can load it later. To save the image, choose File, Save. Give the image a name (`bullseye.psp` will do nicely) and choose a folder in which to store it. I often save files in a temporary folder if I think I'll need them to complete a drawing at a later sitting.

You might want to open a new file at this point and explore the other shapes that you can create with the Preset Shapes tool. Try using different colors and drawing stroked (outlined) shapes as well as filled shapes. Use the grid to help you place various shapes, and try to draw something by combining the different shapes, colors, fills, and strokes (outlines).

Drawing Lines

You can use the Draw tool to draw straight lines and curved lines. You can set the width of the line and whether the line is antialiased in the Tool Options window.

The Single Line Tool

As an exercise, and to get some hands-on experience with the Draw tool, you can add an arrow to the bull's-eye from the previous exercise.

Open the bull's-eye file that you saved, and then follow these steps:

1. Set the foreground color to a shade of blue or some color other than the black and red you used for the rings of the bull's-eye.

2. Select the Draw tool and, in the Tool Options window, set the Line Type to Single Line and the Width to 12, and place a check mark in the Antialias check box. Make sure the Create as Vector option is unchecked. For now, you can ignore the settings for Curve Tracking, Cap, Join, and Miter Limit. These options are accessible under the Draw Options (second) tab of the Tool Options window with the Draw tool selected.

3. Place the mouse pointer near the center of the bull's-eye. Click and drag toward the upper-right corner of the image until the line goes past the outer circle of the bull's-eye (see Figure 37.8).

FIGURE 37.8

Adding an arrow to the bull's-eye with the Draw tool.

4. Set the Line tool's width to 2 and draw a smaller line perpendicular to the first line and across the first line about a third of the way up from the center of the bull's-eye (see Figure 37.9).

FIGURE 37.9

Creating an arrowhead at the end of the line.

5. Draw two more lines that extend toward the center of the bull's-eye, starting at the ends of the cross line (see Figure 37.10).

FIGURE 37.10

Completing the arrow-head lines.

6. You might want to zoom in to help with the placement of the lines. To do so, select the Zoom tool and click near the area on which you're working, in this case the center of the image. When you've zoomed in enough, reselect the Line tool and draw the lines.

7. To fill in the arrowhead, select the Flood Fill tool. In the Controls palette, set Fill Style to Solid Color, Match Mode to RGB, Tolerance to about 10, and Opacity to 100.

8. Click inside the areas of the arrowhead where the circles are showing through.

9. If the color leaks out to fill other parts of the drawing, choose Edit, Undo and set Tolerance to a lower value.

10. The fill doesn't fill in the areas completely because of the antialiased lines that make up both the circles and the arrowhead (see Figure 37.11).

FIGURE 37.11

The nearly completed arrowhead, needing some touchups.

To fix this small problem, you can fill in the areas by hand. Select the Paint Brushes tool and, in the Tool Options window, select the Paint Brush tab.

11. Set Shape to Round, Size to 1 or 2, Opacity to 100, Hardness to 0, and Density to 100; ignore the Step setting for now.

12. Zoom in as much as you need to and fill in the areas that didn't get color from the Flood Fill tool.

Your final image should resemble Figure 37.12.

A while back, I created a banner to advertise a marketing group's Web site, starting with an image very similar to the bull's-eye. With the addition of a little text and a couple of special effects, you can use this image as a banner for your Web site.

FIGURE 37.12
The final bull's-eye image, complete with arrow.

The Bézier Curve Line Tool

The Bézier Curve Line tool is a little harder to understand and control than the Single Line tool. However, the Bézier Curve tool is a powerful addition to Paint Shop Pro and enables you to draw smooth curves that you couldn't draw with the older versions (previous to version 5) of this product. Getting used to this tool will also give you a head start on understanding the vector tools discussed later.

Again, the best way to learn how to use this tool is to jump right in and draw some curves. Follow these steps:

1. Open a new 500×500 image with the resolution set to 72 pixels per inch, the background color set to white, and the image type set to 16.7 million colors.

2. Select the Draw tool and, in the Tool Options window, set Line Type to Bézier Curve and Width to 10. Place a check mark in the Antialias check box and make sure that the Create as Vector and Close Path options are unchecked. You can turn the grid on or off for this exercise. Make sure that the Stroke Style in the Color palette is set to a solid color, and that the Fill Style is set to none.

   In Figure 37.13, I've placed several crosses with numbers to help you follow along as I show you how to draw your first Bézier curve.

FIGURE 37.13
Several crosses help with your first Bézier curve.

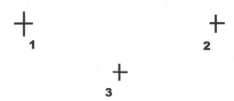

3. The Bézier Curve Line tool requires a few mouse clicks (and a little magic) to draw your curve. Place your mouse pointer on your image at approximately the position of the first cross in Figure 37.13.

   Click and drag the mouse to a point that's about where I've placed the second cross in Figure 37.13 and release the mouse button.

4. Move the mouse pointer to where I've drawn the third cross and click the mouse button. A control handle should appear. Ignore it for the moment, move the mouse a little to the right (near where I've placed the second cross), and click once more. Don't release the mouse yet. A second control handle should appear (see Figure 37.14).

FIGURE 37.14

Drawing a smooth Bézier curve with the Line tool.

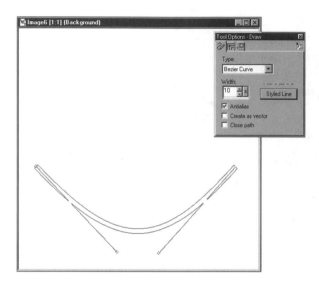

The control handles, although a little difficult to see on the printed page and with my crosses in the way, should be readily visible as straight red lines with circular ends.

5. Now move the mouse around without releasing the button. You should see the curve bend and twist as you move the mouse around.

   After you release the mouse, the curve will be drawn in the width you specified in the Tool Options window (see Figure 37.15). Be sure to click near the second and third crosses so that your curve resembles the one in Figure 37.15.

FIGURE 37.15

A smooth Bézier curve drawn with the Line tool.

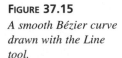

FIGURE 37.15

A smooth Bézier curve drawn with the Line tool.

37

Points 1 and 2 are the endpoints of the curve, and points 3 and 4 are where the control handles will appear. You can use this method to create semicircular curves. In fact, you can manipulate the first control handle as well as the second. Give it a try!

To create S curves, click once in the third position and then click again above and to the right or left of the middle of the first two points.

You should spend some time learning how this tool works. It is a powerful addition to Paint Shop Pro, and learning how to use it will give you an edge over other Paint Shop Pro artists. Figure 37.16 shows some curves drawn with the Bézier Line tool.

FIGURE 37.16

Some S-shape and semicircular curves drawn with the Bézier Curve.

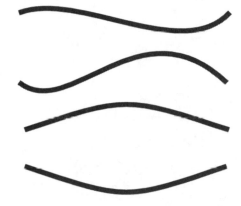

Summary

In this chapter, you learned how to draw shapes, lines, and curves. You also learned how to use the coordinates and other information displayed at the lower-left corner of the main window. Finally, you learned how to use the grid feature and how to set its options.

You're ready to move on to the next chapter, where you'll learn how to use the painting tools.

CHAPTER **38**

Painting Tools and Techniques

Paint Shop Pro provides a number of painting tools: the Paint Brush, the Airbrush, the Flood Fill, and the Clone Brush tools. In this chapter, you'll learn how to use these tools effectively.

Some readers may consider the Picture Tube a painting tool, and rightly so. However, the Picture Tube is complex enough to deserve its own chapter.

Painting and Drawing with the Paint Brush Tool

The Paint Brush tool (the tenth tool from the top in the Tool palette; it looks like a small paint brush) enables you to draw and paint freehand lines with a variety of brushes and textures. After selecting the Paint Brush tool, you can set the various options in the Tool Options window (see Figure 38.1).

FIGURE 38.1

The Tool Options window, showing the controls for the Paint Brush tool.

Using the Tool Controls

From within the Tool Options window, under the Paint Brush Options tab (the leftmost tab), you can set the shape and the brush type (this option is accessible under a small icon containing a brush and a small black triangle placed in the upper-right corner of the Tool Options window). You can also set the size, opacity, hardness, density, and step. Clicking the Brush Types icon opens a pull-down menu from which you can select the brush type.

To see how these settings work, open a new 500×500 image with the resolution set to 72 pixels per inch, the background color set to white, and the image type set to 16.7 million colors. Then follow these steps:

1. Select the Paint Brush tool.

2. Set the foreground color to a pale blue.

3. In the Tool Options window, set Shape to Round, the brush type to Normal, Size to 13, Opacity to 100, Hardness to 50, Density to 100, and Step to 25. Some of these settings are the defaults and may not need to be set.

4. Click and drag in the image to draw a line (see Figure 38.2).

5. Increase the Size setting to 45 and decrease the Hardness setting to 20. If you have trouble getting these exact numbers by moving the slider, don't worry about it. Either get as close as you can or click in the small window to the right of the slider and enter the value.

6. Draw another line. Compared to the first line, the new line is larger and its edges are softer (see Figure 38.3).

7. Set the foreground color to a bright yellow and change the brush option so that the brush is a pencil. To do so, click the Brush Types icon and choose Pencil from the drop-down menu.

8. Set Opacity to about 30 and then draw another line that passes over the first two.

FIGURE 38.2

Drawing a line with the Paint Brush tool.

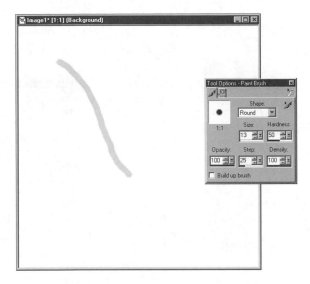

FIGURE 38.3

Drawing a larger, softer line with the Paint Brush tool.

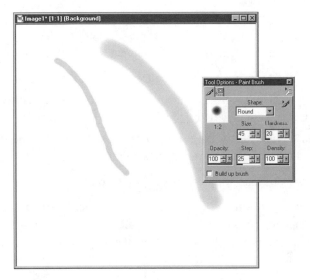

38

The mark made by the pencil is different from the mark made by the brush. In addition, you can see the first two lines through the third line (see Figure 38.4).

Try drawing some lines with the other options. Each is a different brush shape.

Try varying the opacity and the color that you're using. If you'd like to draw with the background color, you can do so by clicking and dragging with the right mouse button.

FIGURE 38.4

Drawing a third line with the Paint Brush.

When you've drawn a few lines, you can try the Density control. Density controls how much paint the brush lays down. The higher the density, the more paint is laid down. To see how the Density setting controls the output, follow these steps:

1. Select the Paintbrush option; the Density setting should move to 100.

2. Drag the Density slider to about 50, and you'll notice that the brush preview starts to resemble the Pencil brush.

3. Draw a line at this setting and compare it to one of the lines you drew with the Pencil option. The lines are quite similar.

Changing the various settings gives you quite a bit of control over the Paint Brush tool.

The Step setting is a bit more mysterious than the other settings. It works in combination with a brush's diameter. The "step" is a percentage of the diameter of the brush. For example, with the brush Size set to 30 and the Step set to 30, the brush operates at 100 percent and draws a definite line (because 30 is 100 percent of 30).

With Size set to 30 and Step set to 60, the brush paints only 50 percent of the time (because 30 is 50 percent of 60; see Figure 38.5).

As you increase Step relative to the brush size, less paint is used.

Play around with the Size and Step settings until you're comfortable with them.

FIGURE 38.5

The left line shows the Step option at 100 percent (both Size and Step set to 30), and the right line shows the Step option at 50 percent (Size set to 30 and Step set to 60).

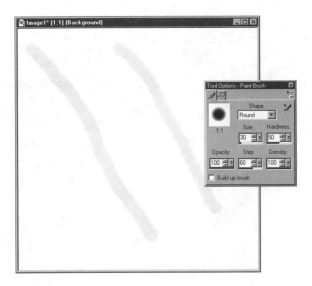

38

Custom Brush Tips

You've seen how the various controls work, and you've used several brush tips. You can also use custom brushes to create new effects.

Click the Brush Options icon and, from the pull-down menu, choose Custom. Use the Custom Brush dialog box to select a custom brush (see Figure 38.6).

FIGURE 38.6

The Custom Brush dialog box.

Choose one of the brushes and click and drag within the image. The pattern you've chosen is used as a brush for the lines you're drawing.

Figure 38.7 shows some paint strokes drawn with the leaf brush in various colors.

You might notice that some of the settings for the Paint Brush tool are grayed out in the Controls palette. These tools are not available for use with this particular brush.

Practice using some of the brushes. When you're done, you can set the Paint Brush tool back to Normal or to one of the other options.

FIGURE 38.7

The Custom Brush, used to draw some leaves in different colors.

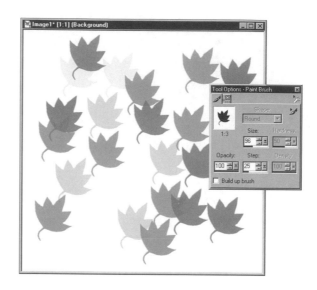

Using Patterns and Textures

Along with the different tips and other settings, you can choose from several patterns and textures.

You can choose a pattern from the Color palette by clicking the Foreground Style icon and choosing from the pull-down menu in the open Pattern dialog box. Choices include Blue String, Cement, Fabric, Finished Wood, and more.

To see how the patterns work, click the Foreground Style icon and choose a pattern. When you draw or paint, the pattern appears under your brush strokes. In Figure 38.8, the Finished Wood pattern has been applied with a very wide Normal brush.

Applying a texture is similar to applying a pattern. To try out a texture, click Edit, Undo (if you just finished trying out the pattern brush) to clear the image and click the Foreground Texture icon in the Color palette. From the flyout menu select Texture and release the mouse button. Click the Foreground Texture icon again to bring up the Texture dialog box and choose a texture. With the texture chosen, simply apply it using the Paint Brush tool. Figure 38.9 shows a Woodgrain texture applied with a large brush.

There are many textures that you can try, including Clouds, Course Canvas, and Crumpled Paper.

FIGURE 38.8
Finished Wood pattern applied with a wide brush set to Normal.

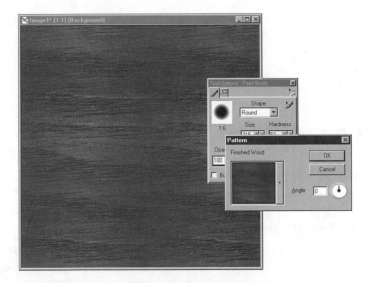

FIGURE 38.9
Woodgrain texture applied with a wide brush set to Normal.

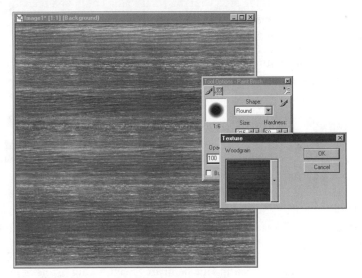

Using the Airbrush Tool

The Airbrush tool allows paint to build up if you stay in one place for a moment. Note that the paint buildup isn't a selectable option; rather, it is the behavior of the Airbrush tool. In other aspects, the Airbrush tool acts much like the other Paint Brush tools. You can still change the various options and settings in the Tool Options window, and you can still use patterns and textures.

To see how the airbrush effect works, select the Airbrush tool (the sixth icon from the bottom in the Tool palette; it looks like a spray can) and draw a few lines, stopping every so often. When you stop, keep the mouse button down; you'll notice that the paint builds up. This effect is more noticeable with Opacity set fairly low. Even then, the brush will build up paint until it completely covers whatever is beneath it.

Using the Flood Fill Tool

You can use the Flood Fill tool (the fifth icon from the bottom of the Tool palette; it looks like a tilted paint can) to fill areas of an image with either a color, gradient, pattern, or texture.

Filling an Area with a Solid Color

To fill an area with a solid color, simply set the foreground or background color to the color you want to use and click within the area you want to fill. Clicking with the left mouse button fills the area with the foreground color, and clicking with the right mouse button fills the area with the background color.

Several factors determine how the Flood Fill tool fills an area. If you've made a selection and you click within the selected area, the Flood Fill tool fills that area. If you've made a selection and you click outside the selection, even if you've chosen to hide the selection marquee, the Flood Fill tool has no effect.

You can also click in an area that already contains a certain color. The Flood Fill tool will then fill the area that contains that color. It may also fill surrounding areas, depending on the settings that you've chosen. Changing the Tolerance option, for example, determines how much of an area is filled. Higher Tolerance allows more of an area to be filled, whereas a lower Tolerance setting constrains the fill to areas that are similar in color or exactly the same color as where you initially click. You can change the Tolerance setting in the Tool Options window under the Flood Fill Options (first) tab.

Match Mode also affects how an area is filled. Selecting RGB compares neighboring pixels' RGB values, selecting Hue compares neighboring pixels' hues, selecting Brightness compares neighboring pixels' brightness values, and selecting None fills the entire area, regardless of any settings. You can change the Match Mode setting in the Tool Options window under the Flood Fill Options (first) tab. Once a comparison has been made according to Match Mode, a pixel will be filled according to the Tolerance setting.

You can also choose the Flood Fill tool's Opacity. A higher value makes the fill more opaque, and a lower value makes the fill more transparent.

Finally, you can set the patterns and textures options for each Fill style by clicking the Style or Texture icons in the Color palette. Each Fill style has different options associated with it. For example, you can set the direction of a Linear Gradient fill.

Filling with a Gradient

In addition to filling an area with a solid color, you can fill it with a gradient. A *gradient* is a blend from one color to another or several colors blended together, as in a multicolored gradient, which I will discuss in the next section.

Figure 38.10 shows the gradient styles that are available in Paint Shop Pro.

FIGURE 38.10

Paint Shop Pro has several gradient fill styles.

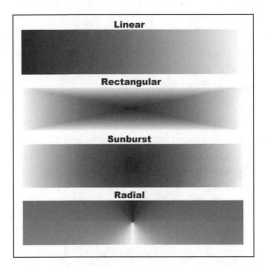

You can set the angle for the Linear gradient, and you can set the horizontal and vertical starting points for the Rectangular, Sunburst, and Radial gradients. To access these options, click and hold the mouse over the Style icon in the Color palette. When the fly-out menu appears, choose the gradient icon. Release the mouse button and click the icon again to open the Gradient dialog box. The next section will explain how to use the settings in the Gradient dialog box and how to create your own multicolored gradients.

Creating and Editing Multicolored Gradients

Starting with version 6, and continuing with version 7, Paint Shop Pro enables you to edit, create, save, and load multicolored gradients. This is a very powerful tool that can give you amazing effects with a couple of mouse clicks.

The button bar in Figure 38.11 was created using the built-in Metallic 2 gradient, which is a grayscale gradient that uses various shades of gray and white to achieve a metallic effect.

FIGURE 38.11

A metallic button bar created using a multi-colored Gradient fill.

To create the button bar, I filled a rectangular selection with the gradient set to Linear at an angle of 0 degrees. I then filled three more selections with the same gradient at an angle of 180 degrees. Finally, I added some shadows, highlights (done using black and white lines drawn with the Draw tool), and the text. All of these techniques will be explored throughout the remainder of the book. The following steps illustrate how to create an image like the one shown in Figure 38.11:

1. Select the Flood Fill tool.

2. Set Fill Style to gradient by clicking and holding the mouse over the Foreground Style icon in the Color palette.

3. Click the Foreground Style icon to bring up the Gradient window (see Figure 38.12).

FIGURE 38.12

The Gradient window in the Tool Options window.

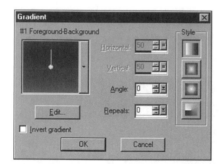

4. Choose one of the gradients that shipped with Paint Shop Pro 6 by clicking the downward-facing arrow to the right of the Gradient space to activate the drop-down menu.

If you'd like to create your own gradient, follow these steps:

1. From the Gradient Editor dialog box, you can create new gradients, rename or copy existing ones, and import/export gradients that you create (see Figure 38.13). You can access the Gradient Editor dialog box by clicking the Edit button on the Gradient dialog box (refer to Figure 38.12).

FIGURE 38.13

The Gradient dialog box.

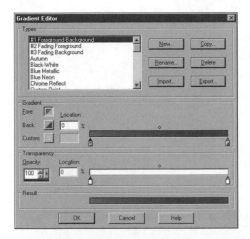

FIGURE 38.13

The Gradient dialog box.

38

In the Types window, you'll notice a list of existing gradients. These are the gradient styles that shipped with Paint Shop Pro. Any gradients that you create or import will also be in this list.

Near the middle of the dialog box you'll see a representation of the current gradient. This area is where you'll edit existing gradients or create your own.

2. Click the New button.

3. In the New Gradient window, enter a name for your gradient. I entered "MyGradient". The editing area will fill with one color, and there will be only two sliders, one at each end.

4. Click the leftmost slider and click the color swatch to the left of the filled area to bring up the Color dialog box (see Figure 38.14—its small arrow will turn black).

FIGURE 38.14

Select the leftmost slider to change one of the colors in your new gradient.

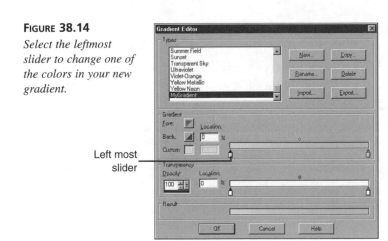

Left most slider

5. Select a light blue color.

6. Click the rightmost slider and then click the small color swatch again to bring up the Color dialog box.

7. Select a medium brown.

8. Click between the two sliders at the bottom of the filled area (see the marked area in Figure 38.15) and a new slider will appear.

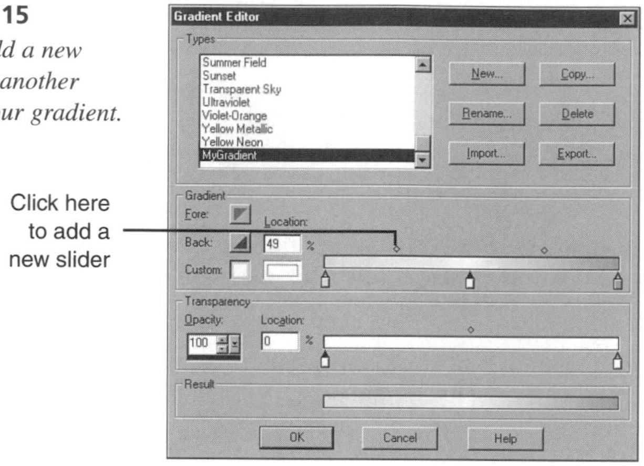

FIGURE 38.15

Click to add a new slider and another color in your gradient.

Click here to add a new slider

9. Click the color swatch and, this time, choose white for the color.

You've just created a multicolored gradient in the pattern that many artists use for chrome.

Here are some tips you can use to manipulate the appearance of your custom gradients:

- You can move the sliders around and add more, changing the color of each as you go. Also, you can move the small diamond slider at the top of the fill area to change the way that colors interact with each other in your gradient.

- To remove any of the sliders you added, simply click and drag them off the dialog box. Doing so will cause them to disappear.

- You can change the transparency of your gradient, as well. This is accomplished using the fill area at the bottom of the Gradient dialog box.

  The principles are the same as when you add sliders and colors to a gradient, except that you don't choose a color. Instead, you can set the amount of transparency at any point in the gradient.

The sliders will change shades from white to gray and finally to black as you make an area more transparent.

- Take a look at some of the included gradients to see how they were created.

I encourage you to play with the various settings to see what cool gradients you can create.

10. When you're done creating your new gradient, click OK. The new gradient will be added to the list and ready for you to use.

To share your gradient with others, click Export. Doing so will bring up the Export dialog box, which will enable you to name and save the file. This file can then be sent to others for them to use in their own artwork.

If someone sends you a gradient file, you can add it to your collection by opening the Gradient dialog box and clicking the Import button.

As you'll soon discover, multicolored gradients are a very powerful addition to Paint Shop Pro's collection of tools.

38

Filling with a Pattern

Along with solid colors and gradients, you can also use the Flood Fill tool to fill an area with a pattern. To set the pattern, select the Flood Fill tool. In the Color palette, click and hold the mouse over the Foreground Style icon, release the mouse button, and then click the Foreground Style icon again to open the Pattern dialog box. Click the pattern swatch to bring up the menu of patterns (see Figure 38.16).

FIGURE 38.16

The Pattern dialog box.

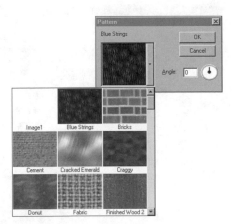

You can select any open image from the Pattern Source pull-down menu, as well as any built-in patterns. If some part of the current image is selected when you choose the pull-down menu, the selected area will be chosen as the pattern.

This option enables you to quickly fill an area or an entire image with a predefined pattern. If the area you're filling is larger than the pattern you've selected, the pattern will tile over the selected area.

> Because the pattern fill repeats in the same manner as a Web page background, you can get a good idea of how your tiles will look. Simply create a new image that's larger than the pattern and use the Flood Fill tool to fill the image with the pattern.

Learning the Mysteries of the Clone Brush Tool

The Clone Brush (the eleventh tool from the top of the Tool palette; it resembles two paint brushes) is a mysterious and powerful tool. You can use the Clone Brush tool to paint over an area of an image with another area of the same image or an area from another open image or from one layer to another.

In Figure 38.17, I've started cloning the image in the foreground into the image in the background. The image in the background was opened as a new file with a white background. I then opened the file I wanted to clone and set the texture of the Clone Brush tool to Woodgrain.

FIGURE 38.17

Using the Clone Brush tool to "paint" one image onto another.

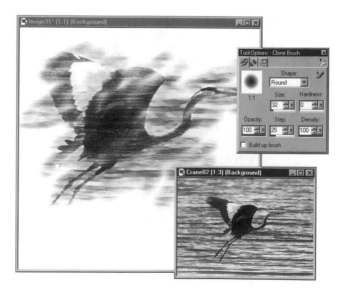

> The Clone Brush tool can be used only on 16 million color and grayscale images. If you need to apply this tool to a 256 (or less) color image, change the color depth (choose Colors, Increase Color Depth, 16 Million Colors), apply the tool and change the depth back (choose Colors, Decrease Color Depth—and choose the color depth you need).

I activated the Clone Brush tool by right-clicking the image at the position I wanted to clone.

All I needed to do to draw a clone of the bird was to draw in the new image by clicking and dragging. Because of the Texture feature, I got a nice artsy-looking clone of the bird in the new image.

The Clone Brush can also remove blemishes from portraits, remove telephone wires from photographs, and retouch images. I will demonstrate this tool in more depth in Chapter 41, "Retouching Your Images."

The options available for the Clone Brush tool, under the Clone Brush Options (second) tab in the Tool Options window, are Aligned and Non-aligned. You can also set a texture for the brush, sample merged layers, and use the Build-up Brush.

The Aligned option moves the source area relative to the original area even if you release the mouse and start to clone again. The Non-aligned option restarts the source area from the original area if you release the mouse and start again. If you're cloning a layered image, the Sample Merged option draws from all layers, and the Build-up Brush functions the same as was described in Chapter 32, "Paint Shop Pro Basics, Tools, and Preferences."

Summary

In this chapter, you've learned how to use Paint Shop Pro's many painting tools. I've just hinted at the real power of some of these tools. As you work through the rest of this book, you'll learn to apply this power.

CHAPTER 39

Creating Cool Text Effects

Paint Shop Pro enables you to enter text into your images via the Text tool. No explicit special effects are built into the Text tool. However, with a little ingenuity and the application of some of the other Paint Shop Pro tools and effects, you can create some amazing effects with text.

This chapter assumes that you have already installed Paint Shop Pro. You can get a free demo version at
http://www.jasc.com.

Using the Text Tool

The Text tool itself is straightforward and easy to use. To add text to your images, simply select the Text tool (the button with the big "A" on it) and click where you want the text to be in your image. Doing so opens the Add Text dialog box (see Figure 39.1).

FIGURE 39.1
The Text Entry dialog.

In the Text Entry dialog box, you can select the name, size, and script of a font. You can choose whether or not to add bold, italic, underline, or strikethrough. You also can adjust the *kerning* and *leading* (pronounced "ledding") or use auto kerning. Adjustable kerning and leading are new features that were added in version 6 and continue to be available in version 7. You also can choose to enter your text as Vector, Selection, or Floating. (We'll examine these options in more detail as we progress through this, and other, chapters.)

Kerning refers to the spacing between letters, and *leading* refers to the spacing between lines of text.

Figure 39.2 shows four lines of text with carriage returns between the lines. The first and last lines have the leading set to 0, and the second line has the leading set to 10 (notice the difference in the spacing between the first and second lines and the second and third lines).

FIGURE 39.2
Several lines of text showing different leading values.

Leading 0
Leading 10
Leading 20
Leading 0

The difference between the third and fourth lines is even greater with the leading set to 20.

Kerning works similarly, except that the spacing affected is that between each letter. Kerning can make text more readable. Figure 39.3 shows two lines of text; the first has no kerning, and the second has auto kerning enabled.

FIGURE 39.3

Two lines of text, showing no kerning and auto kerning.

No Kerning
Auto Kerning

Note, in the second line, how the *e* in *Kerning* snugs in closer to the *K* and that there is a little less space on either side of the *i*.

To activate the Kerning option, click between two letters in the text entry area and enter a value in the Kerning option box. Negative numbers move the letters together and positive numbers move the letters apart.

You also can choose the alignment of your text and decide whether it should be created as a vector or a selection or whether it should float. Last, but not least, you can enter the text itself. The Add Text dialog box shows a preview of the text as you enter it. You can see the font and style, and you can get an idea of the size of the text, as well.

You might notice that the predefined sizes in the Add Text dialog box are limited. However, you can simply enter whatever value you want in the window above the Size box. This method helps if, for example, you want to use a font size that's bigger than the largest predefined size of 72 points.

After you've chosen your font, its size, style, and script, and have entered the actual text, what then? Now, you get to play around with it and see what kind of weird and wonderful things you can do to it.

The next few techniques will illustrate the different "Create As" types. Again, these are Vector, Selection, and Floating.

Creating Wooden Textured Text

This first technique uses the Selection type of text.

You can use some of the built-in textures along with a filter or two and selection manipulation to create some pretty cool text effects. This next exercise shows you how to create a textured wood effect. Follow these steps:

1. Open a new 500×200–pixel image with the resolution set to 72 pixels per inch. Set the background color to white and the image type to 16.7 million colors.

2. Set the foreground color to a medium brown. I chose R: 172, G: 114, B: 68 RGB values and a white background color.

Select the Text tool and, in the Text Entry dialog box, set the options as follows:

3. Name: Arial Black

    Size: 72

    Script: Western

    Create As Selection (this will give you a selection in the outline of your text rather than text in a specific color)

    Alignment: Left (although this setting really matters only when you're entering more than one line of text)

    Under Styles, set the Fill to Paint (it's the icon with a small paintbrush) and the Stroke to None (the icon is a circle with a stroke through it)

    Under Textures set both the Fill and the Stroke to none

4. Type in the text that you want to use and click OK. With a little thought, I came up with the word *Wooden*.

    In Figure 39.4, you can see that the text comes into the image surrounded by the selection marquee.

FIGURE 39.4

Text surrounded by the selection marquee.

This effect is perfect for your immediate purposes because you will be painting over the text. With the selection marquee around the text, you won't be able to paint outside the lines. This feature would have been great back in the days of the coloring book.

If you need to move the text around, you can do so by moving the mouse pointer over the text until the pointer turns into a four-headed arrow. All you need to do then is click and drag the text into position. If doing so leaves behind text in a visible color, you don't have the background color set to white. Choose Edit, Undo, reset the background color, and move the text again.

It's time to add some texture and color to the text. Follow these steps to do so:

1. Select the Paint Brush tool.

2. Click the Foreground texture icon in the Color palette and set the option to texture. Click the texture icon and select Woodgrain from the pull-down menu in the Texture dialog box.

3. Click the Paint Brush Options tab in the Tool Options palette and set the options as follows:

   Shape: Round

   Brush Options: Normal

   Size: 200

   Opacity: 100

   Hardness: 50

   Density: 100

   Step: 25

4. Move the mouse pointer to the left of the text and, while holding down the left mouse button, sweep the mouse over the text and back again.

   You should get a good covering of paint, but not to the point where the grain disappears (see Figure 39.5).

FIGURE 39.5

Brown woodgrain texture painted onto the text.

This text already looks good, but the job isn't finished yet.

5. Choose Selections, Modify, Feather, and then enter a value of 5 for the number of pixels. This setting expands the selection a little and changes the overall effect. Click OK to apply the Feather setting.

39

> *Feathering* a selection not only expands the selection but also softens the edges. This option can be useful for creating certain effects and for softening the edges of shapes and other objects that you select with the selection tools. I sometimes use this option. To see the difference feathering makes, try following along with an exercise where I use feathering and, at the same time, create the same effect without the Feathering option. You also can try different values for the Feathering option to see the changing overall effect. In fact, this type of experimenting has resulted in many of the techniques that I use when creating digital images.
>
> A higher Feathering value gives you more softness, and a lower value gives you less softness. Play around to see exactly what the effect will be when you change the value.

6. Swap the foreground and background colors by clicking the small, two-headed arrow between the foreground and background color swatches. Choose Effects, Artistic Effects, Hot Wax Coating. Adding Hot Wax Coating brings out the grain, makes the wood texture look a little aged and a bit more realistic and, because of the feathering, adds some definition to the edges of the text.

Your final result should resemble Figure 39.6. Not a bad effect for the amount of work involved.

FIGURE 39.6

Final wooden-textured text created with Paint Shop Pro.

Creating Chrome Text

Chrome text is one of the most popular text effects. I've received many emails asking how to accomplish a chrome effect with different software. The next exercise shows one way to create this effect in Paint Shop Pro.

Have you ever looked at something that's chrome plated? Not just seen something in chrome, but really looked at it? Take a moment now to step into your kitchen and take a really good look at the faucet fixtures. Go ahead, I'll wait.

What did you see? I'll bet you saw that the fixtures were mostly shades of pale gray (almost but not quite white), with some darker shades (heading into shades that were almost black) that defined the shape of the fixtures, right?

I discovered a Paint Shop Pro technique that mimics true chrome quite closely. To see how this technique works, follow these steps:

1. Open a new 500×200–pixel image with the resolution set to 72 pixels per inch.

2. Set the background color to white and the image type to 16.7 million colors.

3. Set both the foreground and background colors to white.

4. Select the Text tool and click somewhere in the image to bring up the Text Entry dialog box. Enter the following options in the Add Text dialog box:

   Name: Arial Black

   Script: Western

   Size: 72

   Create As: Floating

   Alignment: Left

   Under Styles, set the Fill to Paint (it's the icon with a small paintbrush) and the Stroke to None (the icon is a circle with a stroke through it).

   Under Textures set both the Fill and the Stroke to none.

5. Enter some text and click OK. I, quite naturally, entered the word *Chrome*.

   If the text from the previous exercise or some other session is still visible, just highlight the existing text with the mouse before you enter the new text to replace the old text.

   The text should be white on white, and it should be visible only because it's surrounded by the selection marquee (see Figure 39.7).

   Choose Selections, Modify, Feather, and enter a value of 1.

FIGURE 39.7

White-on-white text surrounded by the selection marquee.

6. Choose Effects, Artistic Effects, Hot Wax Coating.

7. Repeat the process to add another coat of Hot Wax. You should see your text starting to appear in a light shade of gray (see Figure 39.8).

39

FIGURE 39.8

A coat of Hot Wax added to the white-on-white text.

The next step is part of the trick to getting the text to appear as if it is chrome plated.

8. Choose Selections, Modify, Feather, and then enter 8 for the value in the Number of Pixels spin box.

9. Click OK to feather the selection around your text.

10. Apply another coat of Hot Wax by choosing Effects, Artistic Effects, Hot Wax Coating. Apply a few more coats until your text looks like that in Figure 39.9.

FIGURE 39.9

Final chrome text, created by manipulating the selection and applying multiple coats of the Hot Wax filter.

I applied six coats of Hot Wax to arrive at the final image you see in Figure 39.9. Two were applied before feathering and four more after feathering.

 You can easily repeat the application of a filter or effect by choosing Edit, Repeat [filter], where [filter] will be the name of the last filter you applied. This can save you a couple of mouse clicks.

If you look at the text and remember your recent trip to the kitchen, I'm sure you'll agree that the effect does a pretty good job of mimicking true chrome plating.

Adding a Drop Shadow

Adding a drop shadow to text used to be a cumbersome process requiring several steps. However, Paint Shop Pro and many other imaging software companies have added drop shadows to their standard repertoire.

To effectively use the Drop Shadow filter to create interesting effects with your text, follow these steps:

1. Open a new 500×200–pixel image with the resolution set to 72 pixels per inch. Set the background color to white and the image type to 16.7 million colors.

2. Choose a background color (this will be the color that the Text tool will use for your text) and set the Foreground Style to none. Select the Text tool and then click your image to bring up the Text Entry dialog box.

3. Leave most of the settings from the last two exercises, but choose a different font if you'd like. I chose Staccato BT and set the size to 96 points (see Figure 39.10).

FIGURE 39.10

Text added to a new image and still surrounded by the selection marquee.

You can enter values for the text size that are different from the ones you see in the pull-down menu. To do so, simply click in the Size window and enter a new value.

The selection marquee surrounds the text. Don't deselect the text. (You might not have this font on your system but the results you get will be similar regardless of the font you choose.)

4. Choose Effects, 3D Effects, Drop Shadow to open the Drop Shadow dialog box (see Figure 39.11).

5. Click the Color button to open the Color dialog box and choose a color for your drop shadow. I'll stick with black.

6. To arrive at the image in Figure 39.12, set the options in the Drop Shadow dialog box as follows: Color is Black, Opacity is 50, Blur is 5, Vertical Offset is 11, and Horizontal Offset is 8.

You can use drop shadows to give the appearance of depth to your text. A closer, darker, sharper-edged shadow (as shown in Figure 39.13) gives the appearance of the text being just slightly above the screen (or printed page).

39

FIGURE 39.11

The Drop Shadow dialog box.

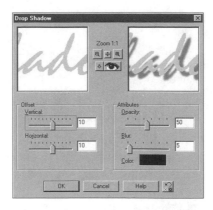

FIGURE 39.12

Drop Shadow added to text.

FIGURE 39.13

Sharp-edged, dark drop shadow added to text.

To achieve the hard-edged, close shadow, I used the following values:

Opacity: 80

Blur: 3

Vertical Offset: 7

Horizontal Offset: 5

The following values produced the drop shadow effect in Figure 39.14:

Opacity: 60

Blur: 15

Vertical Offset: 15

Horizontal Offset: 11

FIGURE 39.14
*Softer-edged, lighter
drop shadow added to
text.*

Note how the text appears to hover higher in Figure 39.14 than it does in Figure 39.13. This effect is due to the softness and different offsets of the shadow in Figure 39.14.

You should experiment with the various settings in the Drop Shadow dialog box to see how they affect the appearance of your text.

Adding a Glow to Your Text

With the popularity of the television show *X-Files*, people have been asking how to create the glowing text effect seen in the opening credits.

The following exercise shows you how to create the glow. Follow these steps:

1. Open a new 500×200–pixel image with the resolution set to 72 pixels per inch. Set the background color to black and the image type to 16.7 million colors.

2. Set the background color to a bright green (I used R:30, G:255, and B:45) and set the Foreground Style to none. Select the Text tool and click in the image to bring up the Text Entry dialog box.

3. Use the settings from the previous exercise and choose a font that resembles a typewriter font. I chose Times New Roman (see Figure 39.15).

FIGURE 39.15
*Bright green text on
black.*

4. Choose Selections, Select None to deselect the text (or you can right-click the image when the Selection tool is selected).

5. Choose Effects, Blur, Gaussian Blur, and then set Radius to 5.00. Click OK.

6. Apply the Gaussian Blur one more time with the same settings. The text should now have very soft edges and be blurry (see Figure 39.16).

39

FIGURE 39.16

Bright green text on black applications of the Gaussian Blur filter.

7. Change the background color to black and click in the image again to open the Text Entry dialog box. Click OK to add the same text to the image.

8. The text comes into the image in black this time. All that you need to do is position it over the blurry green text from the preceding steps.

   Move the mouse pointer over the text until the four-headed cursor appears and click and drag the black text into place over the green text.

9. Choose Selections, Select None to remove the marquee, and you should end up with text that resembles Figure 39.17.

FIGURE 39.17

Final glowing, X-Files–type text.

Creating Text on a Path

New to version 6, and continuing with version 7, is the capability to produce vector shapes and, using that option, create text on a path such as a circle. The following exercise will show you how that's done.

1. Open a new 500×500–pixel image with the resolution set to 72 pixels per inch. Set the background color to white and the image type to 16.7 million colors.

2. Set the foreground color to black. Set the Foreground Style to Paint and the Background Style to None.

3. Select the Preset Shapes tool and, in the Tool Options palette, select the Ellipse from the Shape Type drop-down menu and set the Line Width to 2. Place a check mark in both the Anti-alias and Create as Vector check boxes.

4. Place the cursor near the upper-left corner of the image and, while holding down the left mouse button and the shift key, drag the mouse toward the bottom-right corner of the image to draw a circle (see Figure 39.18).

5. Set the background color to the color you want your text to be, set the Foreground Style to None, and set the Background Style to Paint. Select the Text tool and move the mouse pointer over the circle until the cursor changes to a plus sign with an *A* and a small semi-circle (see Figure 39.19).

FIGURE 39.18
Vector circle.

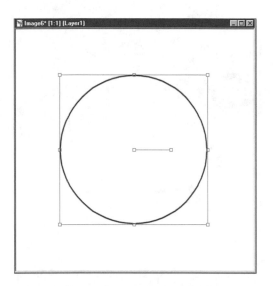

FIGURE 39.19
Text on a path cursor.

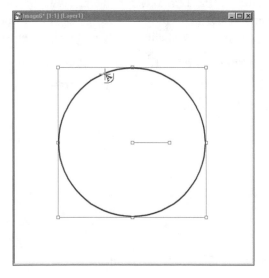

6. Click the left mouse button to open the Text Entry dialog box.

7. In the dialog box, enter your text. Make sure that Floating is checked in the Create As option.

8. Your text should come in around the circle that you drew in step 4 (see Figure 39.20).

FIGURE 39.20

Text in a circle.

After some experimentation, you might notice that the text always comes in at the same orientation. At first, this might seem to be a problem. However, it's a simple matter to rotate the text. Simply select the Deformation tool, move the cursor over the selected text and rotate it, move it into place, and click Apply in the Tool Options window.

All that's left is to remove the circle. To do so, right-click the Ellipse layer in the Layer palette and choose Clear from the menu.

Choosing Selections, Select None will leave you with perfect text along a circular path (see Figure 39.21).

FIGURE 39.21
Completed text in a circle.

Vector Text

Although vector text is not in and of itself an effect, I thought I'd illustrate one of the properties of creating text as a vector.

To demonstrate the difference between vector text and regular bitmap text (Selection and Floating), I'll have you enter some text as a vector and enlarge it. I'll then have you do the same using bitmap (Floating text).

When you compare the two at the end of the exercise, you'll have a good idea of how they differ.

1. To see the differences, open two new 500×500–pixel images at 72dpi with the background set to white and Image Type set to 16.7 million colors.

2. Set the background color to black, set the foreground style to none, and set the background style to paint. Select the Text tool and left-click in one of the images to bring up the Text Entry dialog box.

3. In the Text Entry dialog box, change the size to 96, place a check mark next to Floating, and then enter the word Bitmap.

    The text should almost fill the horizontal space of the image.

39

4. Move the text into the center of the image and select the Deformation tool. Click and drag down on the control handle at the center of the bottom of the bounding box until you've reached nearly the bottom of the image window.

    Repeat the process by dragging upward on the top center control handle. The text should almost fill the image at this point.

5. Choose Selections, Select None, and you should have something that resembles Figure 39.22.

Notice the poor quality of the enlarged text? This is what happens when you enlarge a bitmap.

Repeat the whole process on the second image but this time set Create As to Vector in the Text Entry dialog box.

You'll notice that this time the text comes in with a bounding box already around it. Drag the bottom handle down and the top handle up again to enlarge the vector text.

To finish (and this is an option you'll need to do often before applying any kind of effect to vector text), you'll need to convert the text to bitmap.

I know, it seems kind of funny to do so, but this will enable you to compare the two images and see the true difference between them.

FIGURE 39.22

Deforming (especially enlarging) bitmapped text changes the quality.

To convert the text, choose Layers, Convert to Raster.

See how smooth the (formerly) vector text is (see Figure 39.23). Compare that to the text you entered and deformed as bitmap. Quite a difference.

FIGURE 39.23
Deforming vector text makes no noticeable change to the quality of the text.

There will be times when you'll want to create the text as bitmap, other times when you'll want to create it as vector, and still others when you'll create it as vector and convert it to raster (raster is another word that describes bitmapped images).

Using combinations of the types of text and the different filters available, Paint Shop Pro can produce a nearly unlimited number of text effects. All you need to do is play around, try new things, apply filters, and have some fun.

There are probably enough text effects to be the subject of a whole book. We've still got plenty of other topics to cover, however.

To learn a few more text effects, visit my Web site at `http://www.grafx-design.com`. You'll find some other text effects, along with some more advanced Paint Shop Pro techniques.

Summary

In this chapter, you learned how to enter text with the Text tool and how to create some cool effects, including wooden textures, chrome, and drop shadows, using Paint Shop Pro options.

39

CHAPTER 40

Applying Filters

Filters, a type of built-in or third-party plug-in, are extensions to a program. Filters add functionality to a program by allowing you to create an effect that you otherwise could not create. Some filters come with Paint Shop Pro, and other filters (often referred to as plug-ins) are available from third-party software companies.

In this chapter, I'll show you some of the built-in filters and some of my favorite third-party plug-ins. I will also show you some of the cool effects you can accomplish with these filters. The following issues are covered:

- Understanding filters
- Using Paint Shop Pro's built-in filters
- Finding cool plug-ins
- Installing plug-ins
- Using third-party plug-ins

 This chapter assumes that you have already installed Paint Shop Pro. You can get a free demo version at http://www.jasc.com.

Why Filters?

As I mentioned, filters and plug-ins extend the capabilities of a program such as Paint Shop Pro.

Many of today's imaging programs are written to be *extensible*, which means that they can have their functionality extended through the use of add-on software. This technology enables other programmers to write software that literally can be plugged into the main program.

If you've purchased and installed a plug-in program, it should be available under the Effects, Plug-in Filters menu in Paint Shop Pro.

Where You Can Get Plug-ins

As I said earlier, some filters are included with Paint Shop Pro, and others are available from third parties. Most, if not all, of the companies that write plug-ins are on the Web, and some offer free demos of their plug-ins.

Plug-ins range from free (or nearly free) to shareware (priced from $15 to $25) to commercial products (priced from $50 to $200 or more).

The Web addresses of several companies mentioned in this chapter follow:

- Alien Skin at http://www.alienskin.com. Alien Skin makes the very popular Eye Candy plug-in.
- Auto F/X at http://www.autofx.com. Auto F/X makes plug-ins such as Page Edges, Photo/Graphic Edges, Typo/Graphic Edges, The Ultimate Texture Collection, and more.
- Flaming Pear at http://www.flamingpear.com/. Flaming Pear is the creator of BladePro, a relatively new but increasingly popular plug-in that enables you to add textures and bevels to objects.
- MetaCreations at http:www.metacreations.com. MetaCreations, widely known for its 2D and 3D imaging products, also produces Kai's Power Tools (KPT). KPT is a collection of awesome filters that enable you to create gradients and textures and manipulate images.
- Wacom at http://www.wacom.com. If you're lucky enough to own a Wacom graphics tablet, you should also have a copy of PenTools. This product, which ships with every tablet from Wacom, offers a collection of cool effects that work with your pen and tablet.

I won't cover all the filters available on the market (there are just too many, with more coming to market weekly, it seems). Whole books could be written on the subject. I won't even cover each separate filter in any given package (again, there are just too many). However, I will show you some of my favorites, give you an idea of how to use them, and suggest what you can accomplish with them.

Using Built-In Filters

You've already seen examples of at least one of the built-in filters. I've used the Hot Wax Coating filter in a couple of examples to add even more texture to the woodgrain texture and to create a chrome effect. Paint Shop Pro has a few more built-in filters, though, and the nicest are the Effects filters, many of which were new as of version 6 with even more added to version 7. In fact, there are so many built-in filters available now, that I won't even list them all here. To see what's available, choose Effects from the menu and then choose a submenu, such as 3D Effects or Artistic. That should give you an idea of just how many filters come with Paint Shop Pro 7.

Buttonize Filter

The Buttonize filter (choose Effects, 3D Effects, Buttonize enables you to instantly create rectangular buttons from any image. Figure 40.1 shows the Buttonize dialog box.

FIGURE 40.1

A button being created with the Buttonize filter and the Buttonize dialog box.

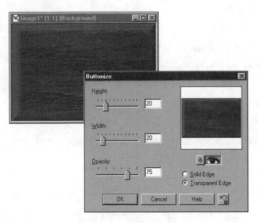

40

You can see the settings I've chosen for the button and the result of applying those settings in Figure 40.1.

You can change the height, width, and opacity of the bevel. You also can choose a solid or transparent edge. You can use the Auto Proof feature so that the changes you're applying can be viewed in real time.

Both the Solid Edge and Transparent Edge options use the current background color for the bevel. The difference is that the solid edge is a solid color, using only shades of the background color, whereas the transparent edge allows the image to show through, as seen in Figure 40.1.

Chisel Filter

The Chisel, Chisel) adds an outer bevel around the current selection. This bevel can be transparent or in the background color. You can also adjust the size of the bevel.

You can see the effect of the bevel in the preview window of the dialog box and, as a result of my clicking the Preview icon, in the image behind the dialog box in Figure 40.2.

FIGURE **40.2**
The Chisel effect to some text.

In this dialog box, you can set the size of the bevel and whether it should be transparent or created with the current background color.

Cutout Filter

The Cutout filter (choose Effects, 3D Effects, Cutout) makes selections appear to be cut out of the background. Essentially, this filter adds a shadow to the inside of the object (see Figure 40.3).

You can fill in the area with white, if you like. You also can set the interior and shadow colors, the opacity and blur of the shadow, and the vertical and horizontal offsets of the shadow.

FIGURE **40.3**

The Cutout effect being
applied to some text.

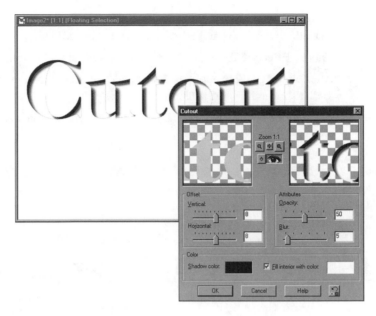

The vertical and horizontal offsets enable you to move the shadow around to get different effects.

The Blur setting also affects this feature. A softer blur makes the cutout appear higher than the same effect done with less blurring.

The Opacity setting affects how opaque or transparent the resulting shadow will be.

Drop Shadow Filter

The Drop Shadow effect adds a drop shadow to selected objects. This effect is often used on text.

You can set the color, the opacity, and the blur of the shadow. You also can set the vertical and horizontal offsets of the shadow (see Figure 40.4).

One effect that I like is to apply the drop shadow to white text on a white background (see Figure 40.5).

To create this effect, open a new image with a white background and follow these steps:

1. Select the Text tool.
2. Add some text to your image, making sure that you set the color to White in the Text Entry dialog box or, as an alternative, set the Create As option to Selection to have the text come in as a selection.

40

3. Instead of seeing filled text, you'll see just a selection. (The text is still filled; it's just filled with white and is against a white background.)

4. Choose Effects, 3D Effects, Drop Shadow and set the options to your liking.

5. After clicking OK to apply the drop shadow, you will end up with a result similar to that shown in Figure 40.5.

   I've seen this effect used recently on television and in magazine ads. It is hard to believe that it's so simple.

FIGURE 40.4

The Drop Shadow effect being applied to text.

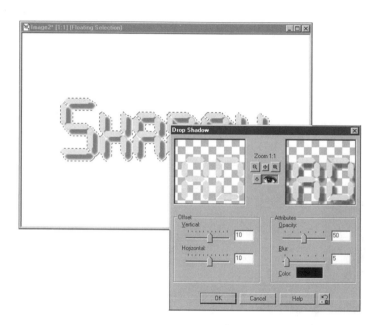

FIGURE 40.5

The Drop Shadow effect applied to white text on a white back-ground.

Recall also that many of the filters discussed in this chapter are used throughout various parts of the book. In Chapter 39, "Creating Cool Text Effects," for example, I used the Gaussian Blur filter for the *X-Files* text.

Filter Effects with Layer Blending Mode Variations

Sometimes you can filter to a layer and, with the help of a layer blending mode change, get a truly awesome effect.

To see an example of this technique, open a scan of a photo and follow along with the next example:

1. Choose Selections, Select All and Edit, Copy to copy the photograph.
2. Choose Edit, Paste as New Layer.
3. Choose Image, Effects, Black Pencil (this is a new filter that first shipped with version 6). This filter will give your photograph the effect of being drawn with a black pencil. But wait, the best is yet to come!
4. Change the layer blend mode in the Layer palette to Softlight.

Your photograph should resemble a softly colored, hand-drawn sketch (see Figure 40.6).

Figure 40.6 shows all three stages of the photograph. You can see the original photo, the layer with the Black Pencil filter applied, and the final image with the layer blending mode changed to allow the two layers to interact.

Examples of how some of the other built-in filters can be applied are shown throughout this book.

40

FIGURE 40.6

Applying the new Black Pencil the look of a hand-drawn sketch.

Using Third-Party Filters

Along with the filters that ship with Paint Shop Pro, numerous third-party filters (often referred to as plug-ins) are available.

Installing Plug-ins

Installing a plug-in package that can be used with Paint Shop Pro is a multistep process:

1. The first step is to install the software according to the manufacturer's instructions. These days, that usually involves inserting a CD-ROM into the drive and following a couple of short instructions.

   The most important point to note is where on your hard drive the plug-ins are installed.

   Normally, you'll want to keep all your plug-ins in separate folders under one main folder. For example, you might create a Plug-ins folder under the Paint Shop Pro folder and store all your plug-ins in separate folders there.

2. The second step to installing your plug-ins is to tell Paint Shop Pro where they are on your hard drive, which is the reason behind making a Plug-ins folder. After you've installed your plug-ins, choose File, Preferences, File Locations.

3. Choose the Plug-in Filters tab to bring up the Plug-in Filters options (see Figure 40.7).

FIGURE 40.7

The Plug-in Filters options.

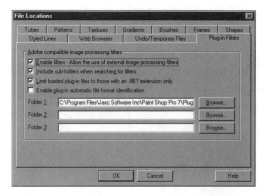

4. Enter the folder(s) where the filters are stored in the text box(es) at the bottom of the dialog box. For example, in Figure 40.7, I have entered c:\Program Files\ Jasc Software Inc\Paint Shop Pro 7\Plugins in the first folder area. You also can click the Browse button to find the appropriate folder instead of typing in the name.

The options you can set in the Plug-in Filters tab are as follows:

- **Enable Filters**—This option allows the use of external image processing filters. You should, of course, place a check mark next to this option if you want to use the filters you've installed.

- **Include Subfolders when Searching for Filters**—This option should be checked if you did as I recommended, and stored each plug-in package in its own subfolder.

- **Limit Loaded Plug-In Files to Those with an .8B? Extension Only**—This option should be checked if all the filters are 100 percent Photoshop compatible (which most of those available are). Paint Shop Pro enables you to use external plug-ins that are compatible with the industry standard. That standard is set by Adobe, the maker of Photoshop. Photoshop-compatible filters have a file extension that starts with 8B and ends with one other character. Normally, using only this type of filter results in fewer compatibility problems.

- **Enable Plug-In Automatic File Format Identification**—You can leave this option unchecked as I have done, or you can let Paint Shop Pro try to identify the file format of your filters.

- **Folder Names**—As mentioned previously, the next three entries in the dialog box are the most important. They tell Paint Shop Pro where to find your plug-ins.

With your plug-ins installed and with Paint Shop Pro aware of where they are, you should be able to find them under Effects, Plug-in Filters.

If you've installed Export filters, such as Ulead's SmartSaver, they will also be available under File, Export, Plug-in Export. Note that if you install filters while Paint Shop Pro is running, you might have to restart the program before the filters are available.

Alien Skin's Eye Candy

Eye Candy has long been one of my favorite plug-ins. It has some cool filters, such as Inner Bevel, Chrome, Fire, and Smoke. Figure 40.8 shows the Eye Candy dialog box for the Fire filter.

The Eye Candy dialog boxes are pretty much the same for all filters. The only changes are the particular options you can set.

One nice touch with the Eye Candy filters is the real-time preview window, which you can see in the lower-right corner of Figure 40.8. Figure 40.9 shows the result of applying both the Fire and Smoke filters.

I've seen many tips on applying a fire effect to text, but none comes close to the Eye Candy filter. You can get a demo of the Eye Candy filters at Alien Skin's Web site (http://www.alienskin.com).

FIGURE **40.8**
*Alien Skin's Eye Candy
dialog box Fire filter.*

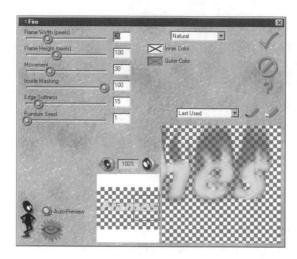

FIGURE **40.9**
*Alien Skin's Fire and
applied to some text in
Paint Shop Pro.*

Auto F/X's Photo/Graphic Edges

Auto F/X is the creator of several amazing filter packages. One of my favorites is
Photo/Graphic Edges.

Starting with the latest version, Photo/Graphic Edges operates as a standalone as well as
a plug-in. That is, you can run it separately as well as from within Paint Shop Pro.

The Photo/Graphic Edges filter enables you to add complex edges to your photographs.
You can also add certain effects, such as Sepia Tones, Grain, and Burns. Figure 40.10
shows the Photo/Graphic Edges dialog box.

Figure 40.11 is the result of adding both an edge and a burn effect to a photograph of
some fall leaves.

Along with the various effects that can be applied to an image with the Photo/Graphic
Edges filter, you can select from a large gallery of edges that come with the plug-in.

FIGURE 40.10

Auto F/X's Photo/Graphic Edges dialog box.

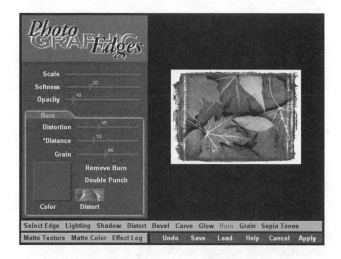

Visit Auto F/X's Web site at `http://www.autofx.com` for more information and to download a demo of this cool plug-in.

FIGURE 40.11

Auto F/X's Photo/Graphic Edges filter applied to a photograph of some fall leaves.

40

Flaming Pear's BladePro

There is a lot of fuss over this "new kid on the block" on the Paint Shop Pro Internet newsgroup (`comp.graphics.apps.paint-shop-pro`), and rightly so. This really cool plug-in enables you to add textures, lighting, and bevels to your images. All you need to do is select an object and call up the filter (Effects, Plug-in Filters, Flaming Pear, BladePro).

Figure 40.12 shows a template I created for my Web site, GrafX Design (`http://www.grafx-design.com`).

FIGURE 40.12

Radioactive symbol template created for the GrafX Design Web site.

After selecting it with the Magic Wand tool, I used BladePro (see Figure 40.13) to add a texture called Lizard to the symbol.

FIGURE 40.13

Flaming Pear's BladePro dialog box.

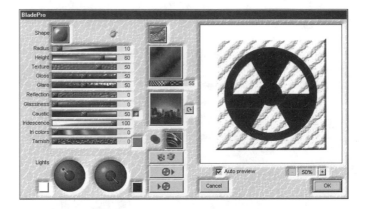

The result of applying the texture can be seen in Figure 40.14.

FIGURE 40.14

The Lizard texture from Flaming Pear's BladePro plug-in, applied to the radioactive symbol.

In addition to the extra textures and environments supplied with BladePro, many more are available from the Flaming Pear Web site (`http://www.flamingpear.com/`) and from other sites springing up all over the Web.

Typing `BladePro` into your favorite Internet search engine will undoubtedly turn up hundreds of sites where you can find more textures and environments for BladePro.

Of course, you can play around with the settings of the various options to create your own effects. These can be saved and passed on to friends or placed on your own Web site to be shared with the rest of the world.

To save a setting, click the bottom button at the middle of the interface. Clicking this button will bring up a dialog box where you can name and save your settings file.

Other Plug-ins

You can start finding cool plug-ins by checking out the demos of the ones I've mentioned here and the others listed at the beginning of this chapter. You're sure to find a product that meets your needs, whether it's to enhance your photographs or to help in the creation of Web graphics.

Summary

I hope you enjoyed this chapter. It was more of a reading and visual adventure than a hands-on experience. I wanted to use this time to give you an idea of what's available out there in the way of plug-ins, rather than just walk you through one or two examples.

I hope that you got an idea of why the topic of filters, both built-in and third-party, is one of my favorites. Filters really are fun to play with and, more than that, they really can add to your images in many ways.

40

CHAPTER 41

Retouching Your Images

We all have collections of snapshots that we cherish, right? Or we have a collection of old family photos, a few of which we'd like to frame and put up on a wall. Some of them are in good shape but, more often than not, some of them need at least some retouching. Paint Shop Pro has the tools you need to fix all but the worst of your images.

 This chapter assumes that you have already installed Paint Shop Pro. You can get a free demo version at http://www.jasc.com.

Using the Retouching Tools

Several kinds problems usually need correcting. Old snapshots often have scratches, dust spots, and bad brightness or contrast. Sometimes they have a less-than-sharp image because of the quality of the older camera lenses.

You can fix the dust spots and scratches by using a combination of the Dropper, Paint Brush, Retouch, and Clone Brush tools. In addition, you can fix most brightness and contrast problems by using the Brightness/Contrast feature, and you can fix the sharpness by using the Unsharp Mask filter.

Starting with version 7, you also can remove all but the worst dust marks and scratches using the new Scratch Remover tool.

I'll show you how to use each of these tools as we walk through the process of fixing the image you see in Figure 41.1.

FIGURE 41.1

An old family photograph in need of repair.

You can see that all the problems mentioned earlier exist in this particular photo. There are dust spots and a couple of scratches, the brightness and contrast are off, and the photo is not as sharp as it could be. I'll fix each of these problems in this chapter, starting with the brightness and contrast.

Fixing the Brightness and Contrast

To adjust the brightness and contrast of an image, choose Colors, Adjust, Brightness/Contrast.

Using the preview window, I bumped up the contrast of this image to +12, and I left the brightness alone. You can see the result, along with the Brightness/Contrast dialog box, in Figure 41.2.

You can see the original image to the left in the dialog box, and you can see the effect of the changes in the preview window to the right. You can click and drag the preview window, so that you can see different areas of the image.

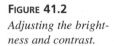

FIGURE 41.2

*Adjusting the bright-
ness and contrast.*

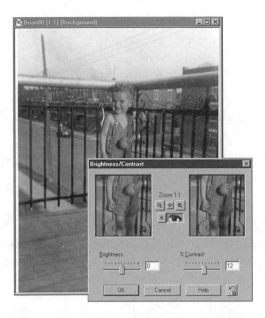

You also can zoom in and out on the preview by clicking either of the zoom icons (they both resemble magnifying glasses; one has a small plus sign and the other has a small minus sign). Also, you can move around the image quickly by clicking the icon between the zoom icons. Doing so will bring up a thumbnail of the image, with a small rectangle cursor that you can use to quickly hone in on an area of the image.

If zooming doesn't show you as much of the image as you'd like, you can place a check mark in the Auto Proof check box as I've done, so that the changes will be visible in the image itself. Doing so might slow down your system if you have limited memory or if you are working on a large image. If you'd rather be a little selective about viewing a preview, you can leave the Auto-preview turned off and click the Preview icon (it looks like an eye) when you want to see the effects of the changes you're making.

With the brightness and contrast adjusted, the next step is to remove the dust spots and scratches.

Removing Dust Marks and Scratches

You'll want to remove as many of the dust marks and scratches as you can before using the Unsharp Mask filter, because this filter can actually accentuate the bad spots of a photograph.

Removing the spots is tedious but fairly easy, and there are a couple of options available. You can use the new Scratch Remover tool, which is fairly easy to do, but may not give you the best results; or you can use the manual method that I'll outline a little further on.

41

To use the Scratch Remover tool, select the tool and simply draw the tool over the scratches or dust marks. You can set the width of the tool and the shape of the box that gets drawn around the marks you're removing. This is a great new tool and it's perfect for light duty on newer scans that only need a light touch-up.

For images that have bigger problems, though, I have a tried-and-true method that requires some time and attention, but that will leave you with great results.

The manual method requires a combination of the Dropper and Paint Brush tools. (This process involves switching between the two tools, picking up nearby colors with the Dropper, and applying them with the Paint Brush tool.)

Before you get down to the hard work of removing spots by hand, you might want to try). The Despeckle filter can remove some of the smaller spots and reduce the work you have to do manually.

Follow these steps to remove dust and scratches manually:

1. Zoom in on the image so that you can easily spot the dust marks you need to fix.

2. Select the Dropper (its icon resembles a small eyedropper) and use it to select a color near a spot that needs to be repaired. Switch to the Paint Brush tool to paint over the dust mark. First make sure that the brush is set to a small size, that the hardness is low (even setting it to 0), and that the opacity is about 50%.

   You constantly will be switching between the Dropper to pick up a new color and the Paint Brush tool to paint over a dust mark. Like I said, tedious…. It's worth the effort, though.

To help relieve the tedium, you can switch to the Dropper tool rapidly by holding down the Ctrl key with the Paint Brush tool selected.

Figure 41.3 is the result of running the Despeckle filter on the image.

Figure 41.4 is the result of removing all but the worst (the largest) of the remaining spots with the Paint Brush and Dropper tools.

Any remaining marks, such as the scratches, will have to be removed with the Clone As you might recall from Chapter 38, "Painting Tools and Techniques," the Clone Brush tool (which resembles two brushes together) copies one portion of an image over another.

FIGURE 41.3
The Despeckle filter removes most of the dust spots.

FIGURE 41.4
The rest of the spots have been removed manually with the Dropper and Paint Brush tools.

41

Select the portion you want to copy by right-clicking and then clicking and dragging to copy the area you've selected onto another area. As you draw with the Clone Brush tool, you'll see two cursors: One cursor shows you from where you're copying, and one shows you to where you're copying.

As with the Dropper/Paint Brush combination, you should constantly change from where you're copying by right-clicking in a new area.

As with the Dropper/Paint Brush combination, you'll want to zoom in to get a clear view of the areas that need work. You'll also want to adjust the Clone Brush settings in the same manner as you adjusted the Paint Brush tool. That is, you'll want a fairly small, soft, slightly transparent brush. Remember, you're correcting an existing image, not painting a new one.

You'll also want to keep changing the area from which you're cloning, depending on the area you want to cover. Just right-click when you want to select a new area and keep working.

Figure 41.5 is the result after using the Clone Brush tool on some of the worst marks.

FIGURE 41.5

The worst marks were removed manually with the Clone Brush tool.

Compare Figure 41.5 to the original image in Figure 41.1. Quite an improvement already, but there's more. The final touch-up is to sharpen the image with the Unsharp Mask filter.

Using the Unsharp Mask Filter

To fix the sharpness, or lack thereof, I'll use the Unsharp Mask filter. The Unsharp Mask filter mimics a traditional film compositing technique used to sharpen the edges of an image.

The Unsharp Mask works by increasing the contrast between adjacent pixels. The edges on which it works are based on the difference of the pixels in the image, using the values you enter for the different options. All of this sounds complex, and it is. Using the filter is not as complex, though.

To apply the Unsharp Mask, choose Effects, Sharpen, Unsharp Mask. This brings up the Unsharp Mask dialog box (see Figure 41.6).

FIGURE 41.6

The Unsharp Mask dialog box and the image to which the filter is being applied.

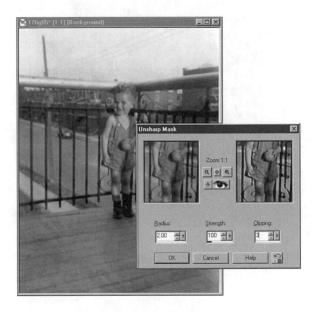

Aside from the usual Zoom, Auto Proof, and Preview options, you'll see three options that you can set: Radius, Strength, and Clipping.

- The Radius setting determines how many pixels in an area will be affected by the filter. As this number increases, so does the apparent sharpness of the image. Setting too high a number, though, simply increases the overall contrast of the image, especially if you also increase the Strength setting.

- The Strength setting affects how much the contrast will change over the areas affected by the filter. Setting this number too high simply makes the image appear to have too much contrast.

- The Clipping setting is important. This option determines how much contrast must exist between the pixels before the filter will be applied to an area. If "dust marks" (that is, white specks and small scratches) show up as you lower this value, you'll want to adjust it a little higher.

Basically, the values you enter depend on a particular image and the results you're after. I used 2.00 for the Radius setting, 100% for the Strength setting, and 3 for the Clipping value to arrive at the final retouched image shown in Figure 41.7.

41

FIGURE 41.7

The final retouched image with the contrast improved, all of the dust marks and scratches removed, and the sharpness corrected.

Compare this image to the original in Figure 41.1, and I'm sure you'll agree that it's a big improvement. This image could now be printed and hung.

Retouching to Remove Portions of an Image

Besides retouching older images, you might simply need to work on an area of a photograph to change some portion of the image. For example, you might want to remove someone's braces or make minor corrections to a person's complexion.

Retouching tricks such as these are certainly possible with Paint Shop Pro. Figure 41.8 shows a close-up of a portrait in which the model is wearing braces.

FIGURE 41.8

A portrait with the braces showing.

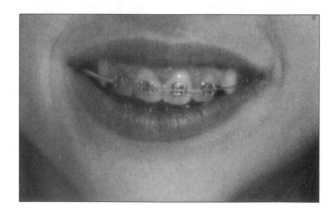

You can correct this lovely smile by using some of the same techniques you used to retouch the old photo in the previous exercise.

To remove some of the smaller offending areas, you can use the Dropper/Paint Brush technique.

Remember to lower the opacity of the Paint Brush tool so that you gradually cover an area as you work, rather than trying to speed things up by painting quickly over an area. It is better to work an area over several times than to make too large an adjustment that glaringly shows that the image has been retouched.

The whole idea is to do the retouching in a way that fools the viewer into believing that the image is in its pristine original condition. Use a "light hand," in the form of smaller, softer, more transparent brushes.

Figure 41.9 shows the result of using the Dropper/Paint Brush technique to remove the braces on the bottom teeth and at the sides of the mouth.

FIGURE 41.9

Initial retouching with the Dropper/Paint Brush technique removes some of the braces.

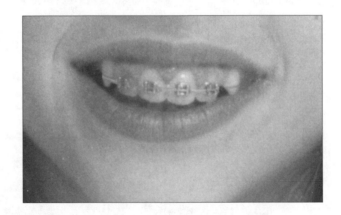

I think that's about as far as the Dropper/Paint Brush technique will carry me, though. It's time for the Clone Brush tool.

Using the Clone Brush tool, I can copy portions of the teeth where there are no braces over areas where the braces exist. Again, working with the Clone Brush tool, it's wise to make frequent backups.

You'll also want to constantly change the area from which you're cloning, so that you don't just copy large areas over existing areas. Doing so would be a dead giveaway that the image had been retouched.

Sometimes you'll unavoidably make a bit of a mess of an area with the Clone Brush tool. Don't panic, though. Here's a trick you can use to help fix some of those problem areas.

41

Figure 41.10 shows one such area caused by overworking the Clone Brush tool. You can see how the front tooth that I've been working on is slightly speckled.

FIGURE 41.10

A problem area caused by overworking the Clone Brush tool.

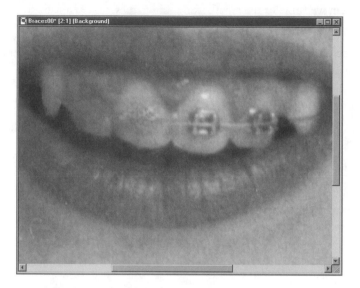

To fix this area, select the Freehand tool and set the feathering value to 2 or so. Use the Freehand tool to select the offending area (see Figure 41.11).

FIGURE 41.11

The problem area, selected with the Freehand tool.

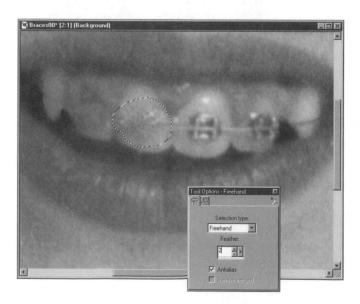

With the area selected, choose the Gaussian Blur filter (Image, Blur, Gaussian Blur) and turn on the Auto Proof option. Adjust the Radius setting until the area is corrected.

What you're going for is the removal of the marks made with the Clone Brush tool while maintaining the same graininess and appearance as the surrounding image.

Figure 41.12 shows the Gaussian Blur dialog box with the settings I used and the result of applying a Blur to the image.

FIGURE 41.12

The problem area, corrected with the application of the Gaussian Blur filter.

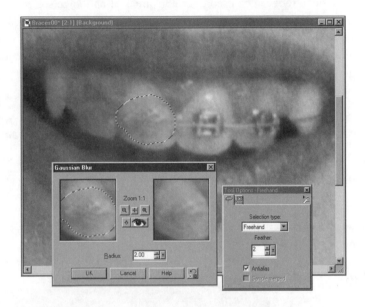

Figure 41.13 shows the image with the braces totally removed from the portrait.

FIGURE 41.13

Braces totally removed from the portrait.

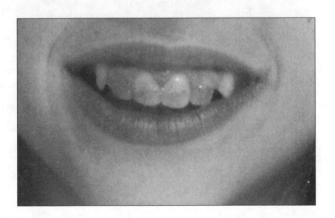

41

A few problem areas remain. The retouching has left some of the areas of the teeth a little darker than they should be. Fortunately, this defect is easy to correct.

To lighten up the areas that were darkened with the Clone Brush tool, I selected the Retouch tool (it resembles a small hand with one finger pointing downwards). Again, I set a soft brush with a low Opacity setting (these are in the Tool Options palette). I set the Tool controls to Lighten RGB and moved the brush around the offending area.

The Retouch tool can be used to change areas of an image selectively. You can choose Lighten RGB, Darken RGB, Soften, Sharpen, Emboss, Smudge, Push, Dodge and Burn (*dodge* and *burn* are photographic darkroom terms meaning lighten and darken), Saturation Up, Saturation Down, Lightness Up, Lightness Down, Hue Up, Hue Down, Saturation to Target, Lightness to Target, Hue to Target, and Color to Target. That's a lot of options!

Once you've selected the Retouch tool and set the Retouch mode, you can adjust the Brush Tip, as I've done in this exercise, to retouch small areas of the image.

As I worked, I changed the brush size and worked lightly over the areas I wanted to lighten. Figure 41.14 shows the final brace-less smile.

Perfect!

Work like this takes time and practice. Done properly, though, it's certainly worth the effort.

FIGURE 41.14
Final retouched smile.

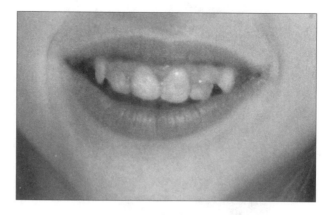

Summary

This chapter was a bit tough. Don't stop here, though. Retouching photographs is an art form that requires a lot of time and practice to get right. As you can see from the results, it's worth the time and effort.

As with any other art form, you'll get better with practice. I've shown you a couple of tricks and a shortcut or two. The rest is up to you. If you have images that need work, get them out and start playing around with the techniques I've described. You'll be amazed at the results.

Before getting back into more of the fun stuff, I'll tackle one more difficult subject in the next chapter: coloring and color correction.

41

CHAPTER 42

Preparing Your Graphics for the Web

Many digital artists today are creating graphics for the World Wide Web. Creating images for the Web, though, means working within certain limitations. You must be aware of things such as color palettes, dithering, anti-aliasing, and Web file formats.

You must also be aware of file compression. You don't need to know about it at the same level as programmers do, but you must be aware of the difference it can make with your images.

This chapter assumes that you have already installed Paint Shop Pro. You can get a free demo version at http://www.jasc.com.

Working with File Formats

One of the main concerns for any Web page designer is download time. The simple fact is, if your Web page takes too long to download to a user's computer, that user might get bored and simply jump to some other place on the Web. One way in which you can ensure that your page takes a reasonable amount of time to download is to compress your images. *Compression* is a process that shrinks a file down to essential data only. As you might suspect, compression also takes a bit of the clarity and detail away from the graphic image—although some images are affected very little by compression. As we continue through this chapter, you'll learn to identify the compression method you should use for each image (yes, there is more than one method).

So how do you compress a graphic image? Well, basically, you just save the file in a file format that uses compression. During the saving process, however, you can make some small changes to the way in which the file's compressed. This allows you to retain some additional clarity (while in turn, making the file bigger than it might normally be when fully compressed in that particular format.) Due to the current limitations of Web browsers, only two formats are available for Web graphics: GIF and JPG. Each of these two formats goes about compressing an image in its own way, and as you'll see in this chapter, each format is is a viable choice given a particular type of image.

Okay, okay, there is another format available for Web graphics, called "ping" or PNG. However, although the two most popular Web browsers display PNG files, only the latest version of Netscape (version 6.0) fully supports the file format. Internet Explorer (versions 4.0 to 5.5) fully supports the PNG Gamma feature, but only semi-supports the Transparency feature (Internet Explorer supports simple transparency only in paletted images). In non-paletted images, Internet Explorer displays the transparent areas as opaque. Because you can't depend on any given user having the current version of Netscape or Internet Explorer, you might not want to use PNG graphics on your Web pages.

In case you're interested, however, Paint Shop Pro 7 allows you to save images in PNG format, preserving even the gamma and transparency settings (which were not saved when PNG format was used in earlier versions of Paint Shop Pro). And PNG format does preserve a lot of the detail of photographic images while also providing a certain amount of compression. Given the current level of support for PNG on the Web, though, it is not the best choice for your Web graphics.

GIFs

GIF, or *Graphical Interchange Format*, is an image compression format originally developed by CompuServe. This format is one of the most popular formats for computer images. It also has a couple of features that make it appealing for Web graphics. Like any other format, though, it also has some shortcomings. In addition to lacking some desirable features, GIF has recently been surrounded by copyright infringement problems. The mathematical algorithm used to compress the image information, called LZW (for Lempel-Ziv & Welch, the mathematicians who developed it), is patented by Unisys. (An *algorithm* is a mathematical formula that can be programmed in computer language to perform a set of steps.)

GIFs: The Good, the Bad, and the Ugly

Although somewhat limited, GIF has some really good properties. For example, it can compress cartoons, illustrations, and images with large areas of similar color very well. Even with these types of images, though, GIF yields different results because of the way that the GIF compression algorithm works. You can see what I mean by looking at Figures 42.1 and 42.2.

FIGURE 42.1
Thick horizontal stripes: 1,292 bytes.

FIGURE 42.2
Thick vertical stripes: 1,540 bytes.

The figures are similar except that Figure 42.1 has horizontal bars and Figure 42.2 has vertical bars. Aside from that, both are the same size and have the same number of colors. Note the file sizes, though. Figure 42.2 is 248 bytes bigger than Figure 42.1. That's almost 20 percent bigger. Take a look at a few more images (Figures 42.3 and 42.4), and then you can examine why this size difference occurs.

42

FIGURE 42.3
Thin horizontal stripes: 1,299 bytes.

FIGURE 42.4
Thin vertical stripes: 2,679 bytes.

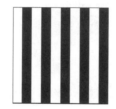

Wow! There's an even bigger difference between the file size of Figure 42.3 and that of Figure 42.4. The difference is 1,380 bytes—a whopping 106 percent. What's interesting, as well, is that there is only a very small difference in file size between Figure 42.1 and Figure 42.3—only seven bytes.

The way that the GIF algorithm compresses information explains the difference in file size. Large blocks of identical information that read from the top left and go across toward the right are well compressed. On the other hand, when information changes (for example, a color change), the GIF compression method starts to lose its power.

A GIF image in one solid color the same size as Figures 42.1 through 42.4 is 1,146 bytes—not much smaller than Figures 42.1 and 42.3. You can see the losses that happen, though, when you start breaking up the horizontal runs of a single color. Imagine how much room a vertical gradient would take up!

What all this means to you as a Web graphic designer is that there are no hard-and-fast rules when it comes to image compression. Sometimes GIF will be the method of choice and sometimes it won't. You'll really have to examine each image independently. For the most part, though, GIF works well with images that have a limited color palette.

There also are some cases when the only choice is to use GIF. One of these is when you want some of the image's information to be transparent.

Transparent GIFs

Transparent GIFs are handy when you have a background pattern on your Web pages. Without the Transparency option, you're limited to having a rectangle around your images, as in Figure 42.5.

FIGURE 42.5

Example of a nontransparent GIF.

FIGURE 42.5

Example of a nontransparent GIF.

Figure 42.5 shows a Web page with a GIF at the top. The GIF wasn't saved with the Transparency option activated. As a result, a dark rectangle appears around the word *Nontransparent.* Figure 42.6 shows the same Web page; in this example, however, the GIF was saved with the transparency option turned on.

FIGURE 42.6

An example of a transparent.

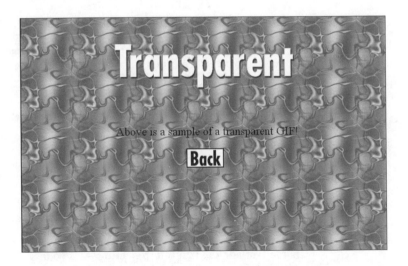

Notice how the background pattern is visible around and even through the letters. This Transparency option is available in most of today's graphics programs, including Paint Shop Pro 7.

42

Saving Transparent GIFs with Paint Shop Pro

Paint Shop Pro provides a wizard that makes it easy to save a transparent GIF. Follow these steps:

1. Open the image whose background you want to make transparent. I'm using the Giant Frog Supermarkets logo (a fictitious supermarket chain) shown in Figure 42.7.

FIGURE 42.7

You don't see giant amphibians these days.

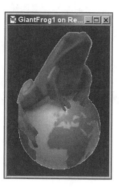

You might want to make sure that you've saved a copy of your file in the native Paint Shop Pro format before you reduce the colors and save the file as a GIF. That way, you'll have the original file with its layers and channels intact, should you need to make changes in the future.

2. Choose File, Export, GIF Optimizer. The GIF Optimizer dialog box is displayed (see Figure 42.8).

3. Select the option you want from the Transparency tab:

   - **None**—Use this option to remove transparency from a GIF.

   - **Existing Image or Layer Transparency**—Use this option if your image already contains a transparent layer or background, and you want to use it when converting the image to GIF.

   - **Inside/Outside the Current Selection**—Use either of these options if you've made a selection on the image, and you want either the selected or non-selected area made transparent.

   - **Areas That Match This Color**—If you choose this option, click the button to select a color. All pixels matching the color you select will be made transparent. You can select a color from the image directly by simply clicking on the image. After choosing the color, set the *Tolerance* level as well—this level determines how closely a color must match the color you select before it is made transparent.

FIGURE 42.8

The logo being transformed into a transparent GIF.

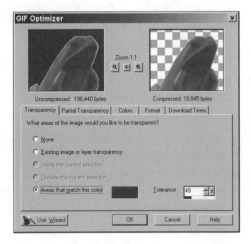

4. If your image contains partially transparent pixels (you reduced the opacity of a layer, inserted a mask, feathered a selection, or brushed or erased parts of the image using a reduced opacity level), click the Partial Transparency tab and tell Paint Shop Pro how you want the partially transparent pixels handled:

   - **Use Full Transparency for Pixels Below X% Opacity**—Use this option to change partially transparent pixels into fully transparent ones. The lower the value you enter however, the lower the number of partially transparent pixels that will be converted.

   - **Use a 50% Dither Pattern**—Use this option to blend the partially transparent pixels with a color you select. This is perhaps the best dithering method for a small color palette (256k colors).

   - **Use Error Diffusion Dither**—Use this option to blend the partially transparent pixels with a color you select. This is perhaps the most effective dithering method, especially for larger color palettes.

   If you choose anything other than the first option, select how to blend the partially transparent pixels:

   - **Yes**—Select this option to blend the pixels with the selected color.

   - **No**—Select this option to keep the partially transparent pixels their original color, but to make them opaque.

42

5. Reduce the size of the file with the options on the Colors tab:

- **Colors**—Select the maximum number of colors you want to use. You can reduce the file's size by selecting a smaller number of colors.

- **Dithering**—Select the amount of dithering (blending) you want used.

- **Palette**—Choose whether to use an existing color palette, or to reduce the size of the file by optimizing your colors. You might want to choose the middle ground and go with a standard set of Web colors (which will ensure that the graphic will appear the same on most Web browsers) instead of selecting one of the two optimizing methods. To do that, choose Standard/Web-safe.

  You can increase the intensity of selected colors by boosting them. To do that, prior to opening the Optimize GIF dialog box, select an area of the image that contains the colors you want to boost (make more intense), and then use the Boost Selected Colors By option to increase those colors by the factor you select. You can also include the standard palette of Windows colors, which is a good option to use if the graphic will not be posted on the Web, but will be used in some Windows application.

6. With the Format tab, you can select how you want your Web graphic downloaded to the user's system:

- **Interlaced**—The file is downloaded to the user's machine in a quick format, with details filled in a little at a time. This option allows the user to see the image quicker, but fuzzier (at least, initially).

- **Non-interlaced**—With this option, the image is downloaded to the user's system one line at a time.

7. To see how long it will take for the user to download your file from the Web, click the Download tab. When you're through selecting options, click OK to save the file.

You might have noticed the Use Wizard button on the Transparency tab. Clicking this button displays a wizard that can help you use some of the more esoteric options of creating a transparent GIF. These include choosing a background color that will closely match the background you intend to display your GIF image against. This can be important if there is a lot of anti-aliasing in your image. I encourage you to explore the wizard to see what it has to offer.

JPGs

JPGs or, more properly, *JPEGs* (pronounced "jay-pegs;" it stands for *Joint Photographic Experts Group*), is a somewhat misunderstood compression method. Images compressed using the JPG algorithm often get a bad rap from users who view the resulting images with 256-color systems (otherwise known as 8-bit systems, for the amount of memory used to store individual colors). Because JPGs are 24-bit images, they often dither badly on 8-bit systems. On a 16- or 24-bit system, however, a JPG saved with a high-quality setting can be a fairly high-quality image. In addition, the JPG image can often be much smaller than the same image saved with another compression method.

In Windows, you can change from an 8-bit to a 16- or 24-bit "system" by simply changing the color depth you use. To do that, click the monitor icon that appears on the Taskbar, or open the Control Panel and double-click the Display icon. Then make the change in depth on the Settings tab, from the Colors list. To change from a lower color depth (8-bit) to something higher (such as 24-bit), the graphics card in your computer must support it. (A higher depth displays graphics with more detail, since there is a bigger array of colors from which to choose.) In addition, your monitor must be capable of displaying this larger palette of colors. Luckily, in Windows, you'll only see color depth settings that are supported on your system. I'll discuss the factors surrounding color depth in more detail later in this chapter.

Did You Lose Something?

Another misunderstood aspect of JPG files is that the compression algorithm used is known as a *lossy compression method*. In other words, some information is discarded during compression. Losing information might seem like a problem but, in fact, it saves a lot of space while changing the quality very little. With an appropriate compression setting, the lost information is not readily visible to the human eye. The savings derived from compressing an image might work against you, though, as you can see from Figures 42.9 through 42.11. (You'll learn how to change the compression factor you use when saving JPG images in a moment.)

Figure 42.9 was saved at 1 percent compression and is 243,712 bytes. It closely resembles the original file, which is 252,576 bytes.

Figure 42.10 was saved in the same manner except that the compression setting was changed to 55 percent. I'm not sure what the final print will look like in the book, but on my screen it was very difficult to see any difference. This version, though, takes up only 43,008 bytes. Quite a large savings.

The final JPG (Figure 42.11) was saved with a setting of 90 percent compression. Although this image will take the least amount of time to download from the Web, I think you'll agree that the last little saving in disk space (and download time) wasn't

42

worth it. (Look at how chunky the clouds appear.) This file, which now takes up 13,312 bytes, isn't the best quality.

FIGURE 42.9
Cliff in Clouds wallpaper saved with 1 percent compression.

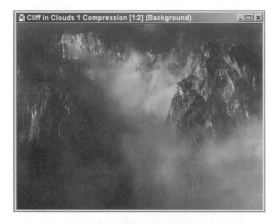

FIGURE 42.10
Cliff in Clouds saved with 55 percent compression.

FIGURE 42.11
Cliff in Clouds saved with 90 percent compression.

You can see, though, that the JPG format typically enables you to save a lot of space and bandwidth without compromising the quality of your Web graphics. Even so, you should be aware of a problem that can occur because of what the lossy compression method does to images that are edited and resaved in the JPG format. Figure 42.12 is a 300 percent blowup of the GrafX Design logo. Figure 42.13 shows the same logo edited and resaved as a JPG five times.

FIGURE 42.12
GrafX Design logo saved as a JPG.

FIGURE 42.13
GrafX Design logo edited and resaved as a JPG five times.

Notice the marks around the image in Figure 42.13. They're in Figure 42.12, as well, but they're not as noticeable. These marks are called *artifacts* and are a result of the way that the JPG compression algorithm works. Artifacts can appear in JPG images as a result of several things:

- A high compression factor used in saving a JPG image.
- Saving and resaving a JPG image.
- Any JPG image that contains sharp edges, such as a border, line, or large text. In such a case, the artifacts (square blocks of the wrong color, or color bleeding) will appear along the sharp edges.

42

Along with the added artifacts, resaving a JPG many times can actually add to the size of the final image. Luckily, in Paint Shop Pro 7, you can remove these artifacts from an image easily, restoring its quality. You'll learn this technique later in this chapter.

> Lossless compression formats use a method of compression that assures that no information is lost. An image can be compressed and uncompressed many times with no changes to the image. Compared to lossless compression formats, lossy compression methods achieve much higher compression ratios, but they do so by discarding some of the information that makes up the image. Normally, the fact that these methods discard information is not a problem. The compression algorithms discard information in such a way that the changes are too subtle to be picked up by the human eye. The changes can become apparent, though, at very high compression rates or after successive compressions.

Why Use JPG?

After reading the last bit about JPGs and how this method discards some information, you may be wondering why you should use this format for your Web graphics. Take another look at Figures 42.9 and 42.10. Figure 42.9 is more than 243,000 bytes, and Figure 42.10 is just over 42,000 bytes! I doubt that you can really tell the difference between the two. I normally save with a much lower compression setting and was rather surprised at the quality of Figure 42.10.

Remember, too, that Figure 42.9 is a JPG that is already much smaller than the original 24-bit image. The bottom line is that if you have an image with a subtle blend of color, such as a portrait or a gradient, JPG is a good format.

Adjusting the Compression Factor on a JPG Image

When saving (or resaving) an image in JPG format, you can select the amount of compression you want to use. Compressing an image will reduce its size and, therefore, the time needed to download that file from the Web and to view it—however, with higher compression levels, you might lose some of the image's definition. So play around with the compression factor until you find something with which you can live. Paint Shop Pro 7 contains a JPG optimizer that will let you easily play with your compression settings until you achieve the results you're looking for. Follow these steps:

1. Choose File, Export, JPEG Optimizer. The JPEG Optimizer dialog box appears, as shown in Figure 42.14.

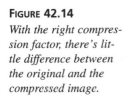

FIGURE 42.14

With the right compression factor, there's little difference between the original and the compressed image.

2. Select the compression factor you want from the Set compression value to box. You can use the before and after views at the top of the dialog box to gauge the best compression factor to use.

3. To quickly review download times for the current compression factor, click the Download Times tab.

4. Normally, JPG files are displayed over the Web in Standard format, one line at a time. To display them using the Progressive format (as a complete, but fuzzy image that's gradually updated), click the Format tab and select the Progressive option.

5. When you're through selecting options, click OK to save the file.

You might have noticed a button called Use Wizard in the JPEG Optimizer dialog box. Clicking this button displays the JPEG Wizard that walks you through the steps of optimizing your graphic. However, unlike the same wizard that is accessible through the GIF Optimizer dialog box, this wizard seems to muck up the options and actually make it more difficult for you to select the compression factor you want. Heed my advice, and this time, skip the wizard.

Removing Artifacts from a JPG Image

As you learned earlier in this chapter, if you save and resave a compressed JPG image, you'll eventually end up with artifacts. Artifacts can also appear if you compress an image too severely, or if you try to save an image with sharp edges in JPG format. Artifacts appear as a blocks or color bleeding on the image. Before you follow these steps, you need to remove any selections in the image. In addition, the image must be grayscale, or 24-bit, for this command to be available. So change the color depth if needed, and then follow these steps to remove the artifacts:

42

1. Choose Effects, Enhance Photo, JPEG Artifact Removal. The JPEG Artifact Removal dialog box appears, as shown in Figure 42.15.

FIGURE **42.15**

*Restoring some quality
to a JPG image.*

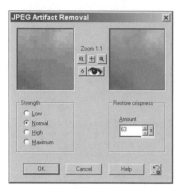

2. Select the strength you want to use. The strength level determines how aggressively Paint Shop Pro removes artifacts from the image. Here, a higher strength value might give you a lesser number of artifacts, but it might also reduce a certain amount of crispness (contrast) in the image.

3. Select the amount of crispness you want to restore to the image. The crispness factor tells Paint Shop Pro to restore contrast to the image, where there might have been contrast in the uncompressed image. It does this while maintaining the small file size. The downside here is that adding crispness back to an image can generate anomalies that have the same adverse effect as artifacts. Use the before and after pictures at the top of the dialog box as your guide. Keep in mind that the better you make the image, the larger the resulting file will be.

4. Choose OK to apply your changes.

GIF or JPG?

The debate over which format is better still rages every so often on Usenet. My opinion is that each format has its place, just as the native formats of the various image programs do. Under some circumstances, a JPG beats out a GIF file in terms of quality and size; at other times the best choice is GIF. Personally, I take the time to view my images in both formats. I also take the time to play around with the number of colors when previewing my images as GIFs, as well as to try out the different palettes.

When I'm previewing a JPG, I try different compression settings. There really is no hard-and-fast answer. Even after creating more computer graphics than I can count, I still play around with each new image to get the best quality/size ratio that I can.

Adjusting Color Depth

Color depth is a way of describing how many colors your hardware and software are capable of displaying. The buzzwords most often used are 8-bit, 16-bit, and 24-bit. Of course, color depth is sometimes described by the actual number of colors being displayed, such as 256 colors or 16.7 million colors.

Hardware is the real determining factor. Your Web browser, for example, will display as many colors as your system can use. The next limiting factor is the type of image being displayed. GIFs are capable of displaying only 256 separate colors. However, these colors can be chosen from all 16.7 million available colors. JPGs can display up to 16.7 million colors, which makes the JPG format a popular choice for photographs and other real-world images.

8-Bit Color

Eight-bit or 256 colors is what some systems use, although they are often capable of displaying more. Sometimes referred to as Video Gate Array (VGA), 8-bit is somewhat limited. With your system set to 8-bit, you're at the mercy of your browser software, as you'll see later, in the section on palettes.

16-Bit Color

Sixteen-bit color, often referred to as "hi color," is a good choice if your system's video memory is limited. Using 16-bit color is a great compromise between speed and color. With 16-bit color, up to 64,000 colors are possible (65,536 actually). With 64,000 colors, your Webviewing experience will be much more enriched. Using this color depth reduces the need for dithering.

Dithering, a process used to fool the eye into seeing more colors than are actually available, is discussed in depth a little later in this chapter.

24-Bit Color

Twenty-four–bit is the best color depth to use when creating and viewing computer images. To use this color depth, though, your video card must have at least 1MB of memory. The reason is that for each pixel you must have 24 bits (or 3 bytes) of memory available. With a little simple arithmetic, you can see that a 640×480 screen, which has 307,200 pixels (640×480), requires 307,200×3 bytes per pixel, which equals 921,600 bytes. Now that you have a basic understanding of color depth, it's time to look at palettes.

42

Using Palettes

Traditionally, a palette was a surface where an artist mixed colors before applying them to the canvas. In computer graphics, a palette is somewhat similar. Most graphics programs have a window where you can pick your colors. In certain circumstances, your color choices are limited. Those limited sets of colors also are referred to as *palettes*.

Palettes are more important when working with GIF images. Because of their limited color depth, GIF images can use only a select palette. This palette, though, can contain a different selection of colors. Sometimes you have control over the selection of the colors and, unfortunately, sometimes you don't.

Problems with Limited Palettes

One problem associated with limited palettes is that, if you choose to work with a limited palette while creating your images, many of the features of your graphics programs will not be available to you. Options such as drop shadows and blurring need to have access to the full range of colors to do their magic. The alternative here is to create your image using higher color depth and then reduce the depth.

You should always keep a copy of the image with the greatest color depth and highest resolution. This extra copy makes applying subsequent changes much easier. Saving your image as a BMP, an uncompressed TIF, or a PCX, for example, is something you should always consider doing. These formats, which are "lossless" because they store all the information about the image rather than trying to condense it, tend to take up a little more room, though, so you also might want to consider having some sort of backup system if you're going to be creating lots of images.

How to Build or Select a Palette

When you open an image that uses 4- or 8-bit color, such as a GIF, a limited palette containing the colors in that image is created, and displayed on the Color Palette. A limited palette is also created whenever you reduce the color depth of an image to something below 24-bit. This palette, called the Image Palette, lists the colors available to you for that image. You can open up the Image palette and add, edit, or remove colors from it. Figure 42.16 shows the Edit Palette dialog box from Paint Shop Pro. (You can display this dialog box by choosing Colors, Edit Palette from the menu.)

Double-clicking one of the colors in the Edit Palette dialog box brings up the Color dialog box (see Figure 42.17).

FIGURE 42.16

The Edit Palette dialog box.

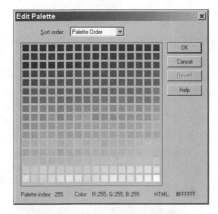

FIGURE 42.17

The Color dialog box.

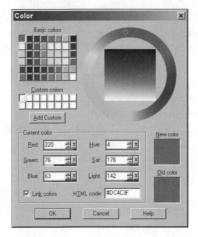

You can change the color you double-clicked to any one of 16.7 million other colors. In Paint Shop Pro, just enter the RGB values in the boxes in the lower-right corner of the dialog box. This new color is then available in the palette. Note that the HSL model is available in the Color dialog box, as well.

Exact Palette

The *exact palette* is built from the colors currently being used in an image. If the number of colors exceeds that for the palette you're building, you can change some of the colors to others that are similar or you can allow the program to dither the colors for you. Normally, this becomes an issue only when you need to convert the image to a lower color resolution mode before saving the image.

42

Adaptive Palette

Most Web browsers use an *adaptive palette* when loading an image that doesn't fit their own color palettes. There are a few gotchas involved here, though. You'll be okay if all the images share the same palette. If, on the other hand, you have a couple of images that use different palettes, you might find that your images have dithered terribly.

The problem is that while you're working on your images, you're probably working on them one at a time, right? So you create one image, save it, and go on to create the next one. You get this great idea for a different set of colors and create the second image with a completely new color scheme from the first. You then save the image after adjusting the mode appropriately. Still no problem.

> To avoid the problem described here, you can create one image for a Web page, save the colors used in an image (the Image Palette) to a file, and then load that palette of colors for your next image. To save the Image Palette, choose Colors, Save Palette.

You then sign on to the Internet and load your Web page. Oh-oh! The colors on both images look really bad. What happened? Well, what happened is that if the browser is running on an 8-bit setup, it can't show you 256 colors from one image and another 256 from the next. It can display only 256 different colors at one time. This limitation brings us to the dreaded Netscape or Web palette.

Web Palette

The Web palette is the scourge of Web graphics artists the world over. This palette consists of 216 colors that, if used when constructing your images, display your images the same way on every platform.

I say *scourge* because 216 colors is not very many, and the color choices are abysmal. For example, there are only 6 shades of gray.

Why 216 colors and not 256? Because the operating system—Windows, for example—and the browser—Netscape, let's say—use 40 colors between them, which leaves 216 colors. This palette is sometimes called *the cube*, which refers to its being a 6×6×6 cube: six colors wide, six colors high, and six sides (6 times 6 times 6 equals 216).

Because of the popularity of Web graphics, many graphics programs now include a version of the Web palette, Paint Shop Pro included. Although this feature makes the process of creating images that use this set of colors easier, it doesn't change the fact that you are limited to this particular color set.

So, what can you do? One answer is to use your own set of colors, being careful that all your images use the same restricted palette. The other option is to hope that many readers of your pages will be using machines capable of displaying more than 256 colors. This may be a pretty safe bet, considering that most people are using computers that contain graphics cards capable of displaying colors in *at least* 24-bits.

Of course, you could build your graphics with these limitations in mind and take them into account when the images are really important for navigation around your site.

Loading a Palette

Paint Shop Pro comes with several palettes you can use to create your images, including its Safety (Web) palette. To load one of these pre-made palettes (or an image palette you've saved on your own), follow these steps:

1. Choose Colors, Load Palette.

2. Change to the folder that contains the palette you want to use. Paint Shop Pro keeps its pre-made palettes in the \Program Files\Jasc Software Inc\Paint Shop Pro 7\Palettes folder.

3. Select the folder you want to use and click OK. The colors in the image and on the Color Palette are changed to the limited colors in the palette.

Previewing Your Images in SmartSaver

One product that can help if you're using a high-color, high-resolution system and are worried about what your readers will see when viewing your graphics on the Web is Ulead's SmartSaver Pro software (see Figure 42.18).

Although this book shows the preview in black and white, you can probably tell that there's not much difference between the original on the left and the image on the right. The image on the right is what a family photo would look like when displayed using a 256 color GIF file. The download time posted at the top left is minimal, so you can see that I struck a good bargain between quality and download time. Using SmartSaver, you can play around with your images, as I did, until you find the exact format and color depth that you can live with.

SmartSaver Pro valuable for more than its preview screen, though. This software also enables you to choose from a wider range of colors than would normally be available. Notice the Colors spin control near the bottom left of Figure 42.18. You can set any value between 2 and 256. Playing with the numbers means that you can shave some extra weight off your images while keeping the colors and quality at an acceptable level.

42

FIGURE 42.18

*Ulead's
SmartSaver Pro.*

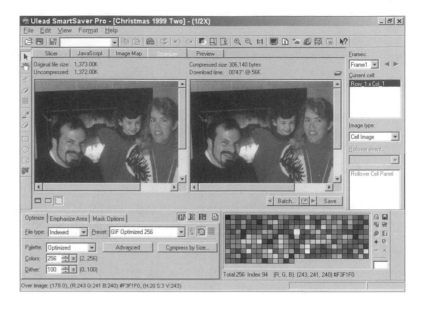

SmartSaver Pro works with GIF, JPG, and PNG images and lets you set a variable quality for all images, as well. SmartSaver Pro acts as a "File, Export" extension to Paint Shop Pro. You can also use SmartSaver Pro on a standalone basis. Either way, SmartSaver Pro is something to consider if you create a lot of Web graphics.

SmartSaver Pro is a shareware product available from Ulead. Registration is about $60. You can download a trial version from Ulead's Web site at `http://www.ulead.com`. Although SmartSaver Pro doesn't overcome the Web palette limitations, it reduces the frustration level.

Understanding Dithering

Dithering, which applies only to GIF images, is one of those big bugaboos that is constantly argued about on Usenet. *Dithering*, put simply, is a process of constructing the color for a single pixel from a combination of the colors in surrounding pixels. You may remember from school how blue and yellow, when mixed together, give you green. Color mixing is the principle behind dithering.

In practice, dithering is quite complex. There are several mathematical functions available when dithering images. One of these is known as *diffusion* (see Figure 42.21). Which dithering processes are available with your software depends on which program you're using. Just as you must decide in which format to save your files, you must also select which dithering process to use. I suggest experimenting with several settings to see which method best suits a particular image. In Paint Shop Pro, the dithering choice (diffusion vs. no dither-nearest color) is made when you decrease the color depth of an image.

Image software, be it your graphics program or your browser, resorts to dithering when it cannot display the entire color palette of an image. The results can vary. Figure 42.19 is an image that hasn't had its reduced.

FIGURE 42.19

Twenty-four–bit image.

Figure 42.20 is the same image reduced to 16 colors (or 16 levels of gray, if you will). No dithering has been applied.

FIGURE 42.20

Sixteen-color image with no dithering.

Notice the distinct banding within the sky and its reflection in Figure 42.20. Without the help of dithering, the process to reduce the number of colors must choose a nearest match (what Paint Shop Pro calls "nearest color"). On the other hand, the diffusion

42

method of dithering was applied to Figure 42.21 during color reduction, with perhaps better results.

FIGURE 42.21

Sixteen-color image reduced with diffusion dithering.

Some people may regard the speckling, which is a result of the dithering, as unacceptable. You'll have to decide how to handle this problem when it comes to designing your own Web graphics. If you're going to display 256-color images that were created as 24-bit images, you'll have to decide whether to dither. One option is to choose colors that closely match those available in the palette with which the images will ultimately be displayed.

Understanding Anti-aliasing

Before I explain what anti-aliasing is, I'll cover aliasing. Of course, these two subjects are closely related. People almost never discuss aliasing, though.

Aliasing

Aliasing is what happens when analog data is represented on a digital system. A curved line drawn on a grid is a good example of analog data on a digital system (see Figure 42.22).

When the analog data is converted to digital, some problems arise. The digital system in this example is the grid. To convert the analog line to a digital line, each point in the grid might represent either a point in the line, by being filled in, or an area where the line does not exist, by remaining white. A square cannot be partly filled; it must be either filled in or not. That's all part of its being digital.

FIGURE 42.22

A line of grid representing analog data on a digital system.

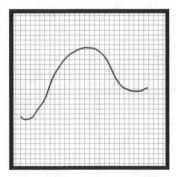

Okay, no problem, right? The line goes through the different squares, so you fill in each square that the line goes through. This requirement isn't a problem with some of the portions of the line, such as the portion circled in Figure 42.23.

FIGURE 42.23

A portion of the line that is easily converted to digital.

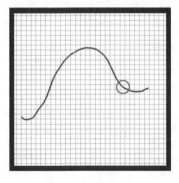

But what about sections like the one circled in Figure 42.24?

FIGURE 42.24

A portion of the line that is not easily converted to digital.

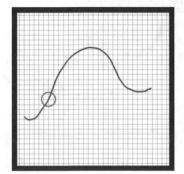

42

That portion cuts right across the intersection of four points. That's where aliasing comes in. An algorithm decides where all the portions fit in the digital system.

Figure 42.25 demonstrates what the resulting digital line might look like.

FIGURE 42.25

A digital version of the line.

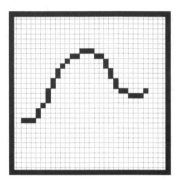

See how it looks choppy? The same thing will happen to any aliased text you display on your Web pages.

Anti-aliasing

Is there a solution? Yep! It comes in the form of—ta-da—*anti-aliasing*. What anti-aliasing attempts to do, using mathematics again, is to fill in some of the digital system with colors that are between the two adjoining colors. In this case, a medium gray would be between the black and the white. Some gray squares placed in the grid might help soften up the *jaggies* (see Figure 42.26).

FIGURE 42.26

Anti-aliased line.

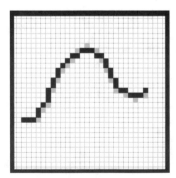

Keep in mind that this example was drawn by hand, and the resolution of the final printing in the book might not show an improvement. To give you a better idea of aliased versus anti-aliased, here are a couple of lines drawn with Paint Shop Pro. The first, seen in Figure 42.27, is aliased.

FIGURE 42.27
An aliased line.

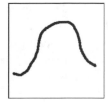

Figure 42.28 shows an anti-aliased line drawn in Paint Shop Pro.

FIGURE 42.28
Anti-aliased line.

So there'll be no mistaking the difference, Figures 42.29 and 42.30 are the aliased and the anti-aliased lines, respectively, blown up 500 percent.

FIGURE 42.29
The aliased line at 500 percent.

FIGURE 42.30
The anti-aliased line at 500 percent.

42

Notice the jagged appearance of the line in Figure 42.29, whereas the line in Figure 42.30 is smooth. Of course, at this resolution, the line in Figure 42.30 seems a little blurry. This factor is something else to consider when using the anti-aliasing option for your graphics. The fuzziness can be especially problematic with text. Text, as well as the rest of an image, is generally anti-aliased whenever it is resized, so you might want to add text only after you have decided on the final size of your image. This technique helps keep your text more readable.

Summary

This was another fun chapter. There was a lot of information here, though, and I covered a lot of theory. You are now well armed when it comes to creating Web graphics. Chapter 43, "Buttons and Seamless Tiles," covers the creation of buttons, GIFs, and other images that you can use on your Web pages.

CHAPTER 43

Buttons and Seamless Tiles

When it comes to creating or maintaining Web sites, you'll need to create several types of graphics. The most common types are buttons and seamless tiles. Fortunately, Paint Shop Pro excels at helping you create these types of graphics.

 This chapter assumes that you have already installed Paint Shop Pro. You can get a free demo version at http://www.jasc.com.

Creating Buttons

Buttons are an important part of any Web page. They help your visitors navigate through your site and can even tell people a little about your style and the style of your site.

Buttons can range from the plain and ordinary, such as regular filled rectangles, to the more elaborate, such as 3D buttons, to the outrageous, such as wildly textured and weirdly shaped buttons. With one, simple command, you can even create buttons from an image of your choice!

Ordinary Buttons

You can create simple buttons with ease in Paint Shop Pro. Simply select the Preset Shapes tool (it resembles a blue rectangle with a red ellipse over it), set the foreground color to the color you want your buttons to be, and draw some shapes.

You'll want to add text, of course, or some type of icon (see Figure 43.1).

FIGURE 43.1

Some simple buttons created in Paint Shop Pro.

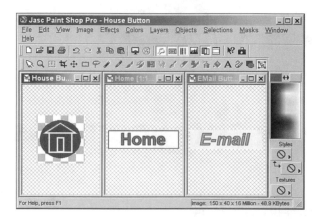

The buttons shown in Figure 43.1 were created with techniques from the early chapters in this book. To create these images, I used tools such as the Preset Shapes tool, the Text tool, and the Draw tool.

Simple buttons are okay and, in some cases, even better than something more elaborate. If you're selling a product, for example, which has nothing to do with graphics or imaging, you might not want the navigational elements on your site to get in the way of the product you're actually selling.

If, however, you want something a little flashier, you're in luck. Paint Shop Pro does that, too, with a little help from you, the digital artist.

More Elaborate Buttons

You can get more elaborate by simply adding shadows or some dimensionality to your buttons. To get the effect of depth, you'll need to make a few selections and use some gradients. Here's how you can add depth to a rectangular button that would ordinarily be, well…ordinary:

43

1. Open a new image at the size you want your button to be (or a little larger).

2. Select the Selection tool (it resembles a dashed-line rectangle) and, in the Tool Options window, set Selection Type to Rectangle.

3. Draw a rectangular selection that mostly fills the image.

4. Select the Flood Fill tool (it resembles a tipped-over paint bucket) and set the foreground color to a light shade of the color you want the button to be and set the background color to a dark shade of the color you want the button to be. I choose light blue and dark blue.

5. Set Fill Style to Linear Gradient.

6. Select Foreground-Background as the Gradient and set the Angle to 135 degrees.

7. Click within the selection to fill the area with the gradient (see Figure 43.2).

FIGURE 43.2

The beginning of a 3D rectangular button.

8. Choose Selections, Modify, Contract and enter a number that will give you the size of border you want. Try 10 or so, depending on the size of your button.

9. Swap the foreground and background colors by clicking the small two-headed arrow between the foreground and background color swatches.

10. In the Tool Options window (click the first tab), set the match mode to None. This setting ensures that the complete selection is filled, even though it is currently filled with a gradient. Normally, you'll want the fill to stop when it "sees" a color change. Choosing None for the match mode makes the fill cover everything, regardless of what's currently occupying the space.

11. Click within the selected area to fill the inner rectangle with the opposite linear gradient (see Figure 43.3).

FIGURE 43.3

A completed 3D rectangular button.

These buttons are easy to make, can be virtually any shape (try using circles or ellipses), and look great on a Web page. They are also easy to modify for any color scheme.

Complex 3D Textured Buttons

Paint Shop Pro also enables you to create textured 3D buttons. The next exercise shows you how to use layers and blending modes, along with selections, to create buttons that are more complex.

Open a new image and give it 200 as the width and 100 as the height. Also, make sure you use 16.7 million as the color depth. Set the background color of the image to white for now. Then follow these steps:

1. Create a new layer by clicking the Create Layer icon in the upper-left corner of the Layer palette.

2. Select the Selection tool and, under the Selection tab in the Tool Options window, set the selection type to Rectangle and set Feather to 0.

3. Draw a rectangular selection, as shown in Figure 43.4.

FIGURE 43.4

A rectangular selection.

4. Select the Flood Fill tool and fill the selection with black. You can do so by setting the foreground color to black, selecting the Flood Fill tool, setting the fill style to Solid Color, and clicking within the rectangular selected area. You'll now have a black rectangle.

5. Deselect the rectangle, then select the Selection tool and set the style to Ellipse, set Feather to 0, and turn off the Antialias option.

6. Place the cursor's crosshairs in the middle of the left side of the black rectangle and draw down and the left until you have an ellipse that covers part of the left side of the rectangle (see Figure 43.5).

FIGURE 43.5

An elliptical selection drawn on the left side of the rectangle.

7. Set the Lock Transparency toggle to on (it's the last icon to the right in the Layer palette, and it resembles a small lock). The small lock next to the layer's name should be visible (it normally has a red X across it).

8. Select the Flood Fill tool, set the foreground color to a shade of gray, set Fill Style to Solid Color, and click in the selected area. Only that part of the area taken up by the button should turn gray (see Figure 43.6).

43

FIGURE 43.6

An elliptical selection partially filled with gray.

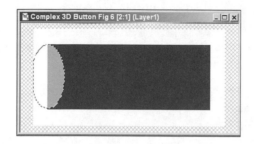

9. Select the Mover tool, right-click the elliptical selection, and drag it to the right side of the black rectangle. Select the Flood Fill tool and fill the right ellipse with the same gray color (see Figure 43.7).

FIGURE 43.7

Both ellipses filled with gray.

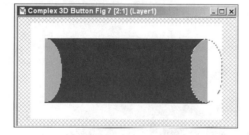

10. Choose Selections, Select None.

11. Select the Magic Wand tool and click the black area of the button to select it.

12. Select the Flood Fill tool and set Fill Style to Linear Gradient.

13. Set Gradient to Metallic, and set Angle to 180.

14. Click anywhere in the black area within the selection.

You should have something that resembles Figure 43.8.

FIGURE 43.8

A Metallic gradient fills the middle of the button.

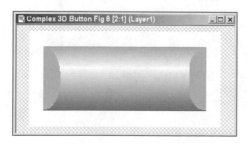

15. Choose Selections, Select None.

16. Select the Magic Wand tool. In the Tool Options window, set Match mode to RGB, and Tolerance to zero. Click the left side of the button to select it.

17. Select the Dropper tool and pick up a light color from the gradient. Get close to the highlight, but don't take the actual highlight color.

18. Select the Flood Fill tool, set the fill style to Solid Color, and click the left side of the button to fill it with a much lighter gray.

19. With the Magic Wand tool, click the right side of the button to select it.

20. Select the Dropper tool and pick up a color from the shadowed area of the button. Use the Flood Fill tool to fill the right side of the button with the darker gray color.

21. Select the Magic Wand tool (it resembles a small magic wand) and click outside of the button. Choose Selections, Invert to invert the selection. This technique is a great way to select an area that has several colors.

22. Choose Effects, Blur, Gaussian Blur and set the value to about 2.00.

You'll now have a great 3D button, as shown in Figure 43.9.

FIGURE 43.9

3D button created with selections, fills, and a Gaussian Blur.

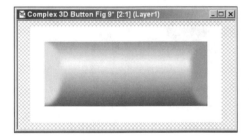

Let's see what else you can do using the Layers feature. Try these steps:

1. Create a new layer and call it "Texture." (You can name the other non-Background layer "Button" to help you keep them straight.)

2. Change back to the Button layer.

3. Choose the Magic Wand tool and click somewhere outside the button. Choose Selections, Invert. Make the texture layer current.

4. Choose the Flood tool. Set the Foreground color to a medium gray. Select the Wrap texture for the Foreground, and then fill the selection.

5. Set the texture layer's mode to Overlay.

FIGURE 43.10

Texture overlaid on a 3D button.

If you find, like I do, that the button is a little too bright or that there should be more texture showing, no problem. Obviously, you can't add to the opacity of the texture—it's at the max. However, you can reduce the opacity of the button layer. Try setting it to about 85 percent. Hmmm… that doesn't seem to have much effect. Try turning off the Background layer. Voilá!!! A more professional button would be hard to find (see Figure 43.11).

FIGURE 43.11

Final 3D, textured button.

Using the Buttonize Effect

You can create a button quickly from any existing image or selection by using the Buttonize Effect. The result is similar to the complex 3D textured button described in the previous section, but much simpler to create. However, using the manual method described earlier provides you with more control over the end result (allowing you to create rounded edges, for example), so choose the method that gives you the look you want.

Follow these steps to create another button:

1. Open a new image and give it 200 as the width and 100 as the height. Also, make sure you use 16.7 million as the color depth. Set the background color of the image to white for now.

2. Choose the Flood tool. Set the Foreground color to a medium dark gray. Set the Foreground Texture to Lands, and then fill the background.

3. Set the Background color to a light gray, and then choose Effects, 3D Effects, Buttonize. The Buttonize dialog box appears, as shown in Figure 43.12.

4. Set the Height and Width to 11. Set the Opacity to 43, and then click OK.

There! Add some text, and you have a pretty neat button in just a few minutes, as seen in Figure 43.13.

Adding the Buttonize effect.

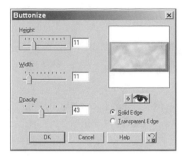

FIGURE 43.13

A quick and easy textured button.

Of course, you can use the Buttonize effect on any image, including a photograph, as shown here in Figure 43.14.

FIGURE 43.14

Buttonize any you want, so let your imagination be your guide.

Creating Seamless Tiles

A seamless tile is an image that, when tiled or repeated, forms a seamless pattern. Therefore, you can use a relatively small image file that will tile itself on your Web page. Creating seamless tiles is something that is discussed constantly on Usenet.

Of course, the object is to get the sides to match up so that the smaller tile appears to be one large image when it's placed on your pages. Before showing you how to create a seamless tile, I'll explain the basic principles.

The Basics of Seamless Tiles

The object of a seamless tile, once again, is to get the edges of your image to match up so that when the image is tiled, it appears to be one big image. Demonstrating this is easier than trying to explain it.

Suppose you have an image that you want to tile, and suppose the image is square. (This technique works just as well if the image is a rectangle.) The goal is to swap the diagonal quarters of the image. (I *told* you this concept was hard to explain.) To get a better idea of what I'm talking about, take a look at the diagram in Figure 43.15.

FIGURE 43.15

Quartered image, showing the original placement of the quarters.

1	2
3	4

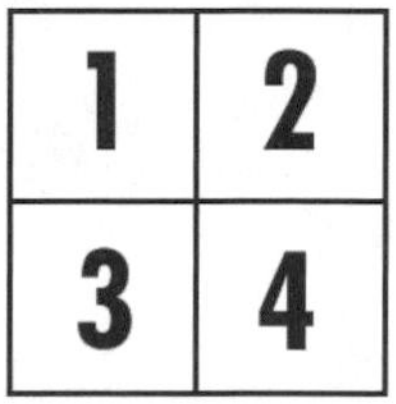

What you need to do is cut the image into quarters and swap the diagonal corners. This step allows your image to tile seamlessly. When you move the pieces, the image should resemble Figure 43.16.

FIGURE 43.16

Quartered image with the final placement of the quarters.

4	3
2	1

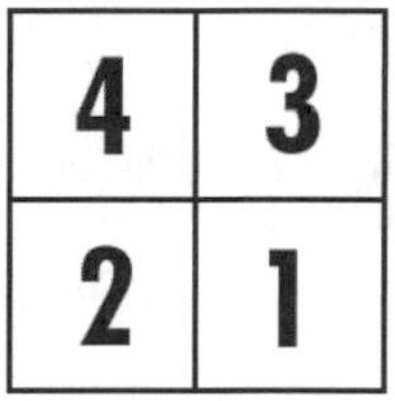

The reason this technique works is hard to see, but essentially you're cutting the image and rearranging it so that the edges formed by the cutting process are on the outside of the new image. Because the new edges were joined before you cut them, they match up when the image is tiled. Although this process is hard to visualize, it does work.

Figure 43.17 shows a textured image.

FIGURE 43.17

A textured image.

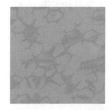

Figure 43.18 shows the same image with the corners numbered as in Figure 43.15.

FIGURE 43.18

The textured image showing the numbered quarters.

Of course, you don't have to draw the numbers on the image. I've done so here to demonstrate the process more clearly. Figure 43.19 is the image after the quarters have been swapped. Note that the numbers are still in place.

FIGURE 43.19

The textured image showing the numbered quarters with corners swapped for tiling.

Figure 43.20 is the image with the quarters swapped and the numbers removed. This image will now tile seamlessly.

FIGURE 43.20

The textured image with quarters swapped for tiling.

You might notice, however, that although the edges now match up, the center of the image has a vertical seam and a horizontal seam running through it.

If you get rid of the vertical and horizontal seams, this image will be ready to tile. The way to get rid of the seam is to use the Clone tool. Although it's a little difficult to master, the tool is very effective, as you'll see in the next section.

Creating Seamless Tiles with Paint Shop Pro

Creating seamless tiles with Paint Shop Pro requires a little work; you must cut and paste the four quarters yourself. Follow these steps to create your own tiles:

1. Open a textured image and note its dimensions. This information is visible on the status bar at the bottom right of the screen. For this exercise, I created a 200×200 image, and then added "texture" by using the Paint Brush and Fill tools.

2. Create a new file with the same dimensions as the textured image (see Figure 43.21).

43

FIGURE 43.21

The textured image and a new image in Paint Shop Pro.

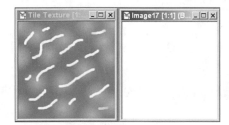

As described earlier in this chapter, you must swap the diagonally opposed quarters.

3. Select the Selection tool and set its selection type to Rectangle and Feather to 0.

4. Place the cursor in the middle of the textured image. Remember that computers start counting at zero, not one. Therefore, the middle of the sample 200×200 textured file will be 99,99—not 100,100. You can see where you are on the image by looking at the mouse coordinates displayed at the bottom-left of the Paint Shop Pro screen.

5. With the cursor in the middle of the image, click and drag the mouse to the upper-left corner of the image. Release the mouse and choose Edit, Copy.

6. Click somewhere in the new image to make it current and choose Edit, Paste, As New Selection.

7. Move the selection into the opposite corner of the new image from where it was in the textured image (see Figure 43.22).

FIGURE 43.22

The first corner moved to the new image.

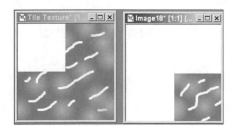

8. Continue cutting and pasting until all quarters have been moved to the new file (see Figure 43.23). You can move the selection marquee on the original image by right-dragging it using the Mover tool. Moving the marquee may prove easier for you, rather than reselecting each corner.

FIGURE 43.23

All quarters moved to the new image.

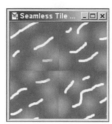

9. Select the Clone Brush tool (it resembles two small brushes) and right-click to select a source area. Move the mouse around the seamed center area, drawing over the seams until you can no longer distinguish the seams.

You can also use the Paint Brush tool to fine-tune the image. After using the Clone Brush and working with it a bit, I ended up with the image in Figure 43.24.

FIGURE 43.24

Final seamless tile in Paint Shop Pro.

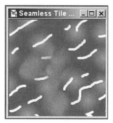

To see what the final seamless background would look like, I created a new 600×600 image in Paint Shop Pro and, using the Paint Bucket tool, filled the new image with the seamless tile (see Figure 43.25).

Using the Convert to Seamless Pattern Option

Paint Shop Pro offers a quicker way to change a pattern into a seamless image, suitable to use as a Web page background. The results, although good, may not be as nice as a seamless image you can create yourself by using the procedure described in the previous section. The result, as it were, is in the eyes of the beholder. You may want to perform both procedures on a potential image, and choose the one you like the best.

FIGURE 43.25

A tiled example of the final seamless tile.

43

Follow these steps to create a seamless pattern from an existing image:

1. Open a textured image. For this exercise, I reused my original texture file from the last procedure.

2. Using the Selection tool, select an area in the center of the image. Unfortunately, the way Paint Shop Pro creates the image, you won't be able to keep all of your texture—so you won't be able to make the selection area as big as the entire image. I simply selected a square in the center of my image, leaving an "edge" of about 30 pixels.

3. Choose Selections, Convert to Seamless Pattern. Paint Shop Pro creates a seamless pattern from the selection and places it in a new window. If you get an error message telling you that the selection area is too close to the edge of the image, use the Selections, Modify, Contract command to make the selection smaller.

4. Save your new image.

To test the seamless tile that Paint Shop Pro created, I once again created a new 600×600 image in Paint Shop Pro and, using the Paint Bucket tool, filled the new image with the seamless tile (see Figure 43.26). You can see there is some difference between this result and the one shown in Figure 43.25. Which is better? Hard to say. Again, the choice will depend on the texture file with which you begin.

FIGURE 43.26

A tiled example of the final seamless tile.

Summary

You can find tutorials and techniques for creating more types of Web graphics all over the Web. You might want to start at GrafX Design (`http://www.grafx-design.com/`) or at Jasc Software, Inc. (`http://www.jasc.com`).

That's pretty much it for the part of the book that covers Paint Shop Pro. The next two chapters show you how to use Animation Shop to create animation.

Chapter **44**

Animation

Animation is one of the hottest topics on the Web today. You can use Animation Shop alone or with Paint Shop Pro to create cool animations for your Web pages. Jasc's Animation Shop 3, which ships with Paint Shop Pro 7, is powerful yet easy to use.

> This chapter assumes that you have already installed Paint Shop Pro. You can get a free demo version at http://www.jasc.com.

Animation Concepts

Whether it's an animated GIF for your Web page or the latest box office blockbuster, all animations are basically the same. The concept involves rapidly displaying a series of images, or frames, so that the human eye is fooled into seeing one long, continuously moving picture.

In movies, for example, each frame is captured on film and is then displayed on a screen, using a movie projector. Each frame is displayed for a very short time, followed by the next frame, and so on.

In animated GIFs, a digital artist uses computer software to create each frame. The frames are then displayed, using other software such as a Web browser. Because each frame is rapidly displayed in succession, the person viewing the animation sees one continuous movie.

Why Use Animation?

I have to tell you, I was one of the last people to jump on the animated GIF bandwagon. At first, I found the animations cheesy and poorly done. As the animations got better and the software to create them more powerful, I changed my tune.

In the world of the Web, many different elements are competing for your reader's attention. Even a single Web page can offer dozens of images for your reader's eyes to wade through. This situation is the same on virtually every Web page. If you want to run a banner ad, how do you attract a reader's attention? How do you get his or her eyes to see through all the other flashy, attractive graphics on the same Web page?

One answer is animation. By animating an image, you make it stand out. You make it attract the reader's attention. Many of the ad banners you see at the top of Web pages these days are animated.

Animation Shop enables you to animate your ads and buttons, and other graphical elements, too.

Building an Animation

Recall that an animation is a series of images or frames. You can create these frames in Paint Shop Pro or, to some extent, in Animation Shop.

You can start Animation Shop by clicking Start and choosing Programs, Jasc Software, Animation Shop 3. Alternatively, if you're running Paint Shop Pro, you can choose File, Jasc Software Products, Launch Animation Shop.

Animation Shop's interface is simple and quite similar to Paint Shop Pro's (see Figure 44.1).

The tools are quite basic and are more useful for touching up an animation than creating one. Creating an animation with both Paint Shop Pro and Animation Shop is quite easy, though, as the following exercise shows.

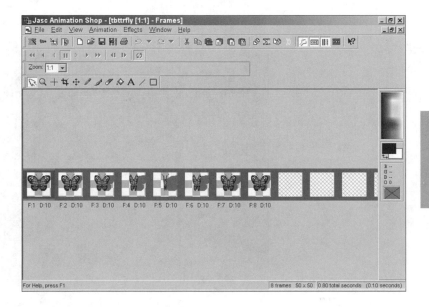

FIGURE 44.1
Animation Shop's interface.

Creating Your First Animation

The best way to how to use Paint Shop Pro to create an animation is to dive right in. Try this exercise:

1. Start Paint Shop Pro.

2. Create a new 400×100, 72-pixel-per-inch image with the background color set to black and the image type set to 16.7 million colors.

3. Create a second image with the same settings.

4. Turn on the grid (View, Grid).

5. Select the Preset Shapes tool (it resembles a small blue rectangle with a red ellipse in front of it).

6. In the Tool Options window, set the shape to Ellipse.

7. Set the foreground color to blue, the background color to green and, in the first image, draw a circle near the left side. I used the grid, placed the mouse pointer at the center of the second vertical line (with the grid set to 50 pixels), and drew a 50-pixel circle.

   I repeated this process with red as the background color and drew a circle in the second image at the center of the second-to-last vertical line (see Figure 44.2).

8. Use the Layers, Merge, Merge All (Flatten) command to merge the two layers in each file into a single layer.

FIGURE 44.2

Two images containing colorful circles.

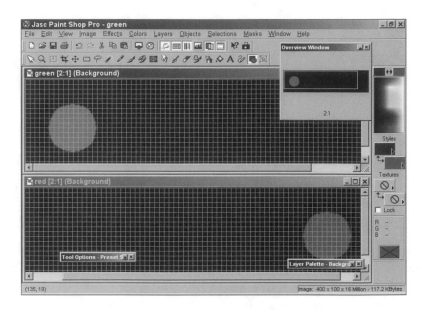

9. Save each image. I saved them both as PSP files in a temporary folder and called the first one green and the second one red (inventive, eh?).

10. With the images safely saved on your hard drive, run Animation Shop.

11. Choose File, Open and open the Green.psp image. You should see the image appear on the screen.

12. Choose Animation, Insert Frames, From File.

13. Browse to the folder where you stored the PSP files and choose the Red.psp file. You'll now have one image with two frames.

    You might see only one frame, but you can use the slider bar at the bottom of the image to scroll between both images (see Figure 44.3).

Now you have all that's necessary for an animation. It might be a simple one, granted, but it is indeed an animation. To see your new movie, click the View Animation button.

When the flashing circles start to drive you crazy, turn off the animation by clicking the small X in the upper-right corner of the window or View Animation button again. That's it! You've created an animated GIF!

When you play an animation, the new VCR Controls toolbar becomes active (see Figure 44.3). With its buttons, you can step through an animation frame by frame, fast forward (or fast reverse) the animation, and even pause the animation when you get too dizzy! Play the green-red animation again and try out each of these nifty buttons.

FIGURE 44.3

Two-frame animation in Animation Shop.

VCR Controls

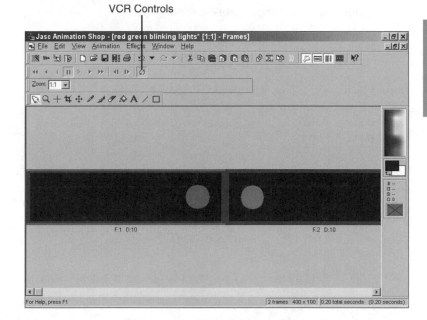

Of course, it was small, and it didn't do much. However, with a little tweaking, it could be pretty cool, as simple as it is. In fact, I have a similar animation running in the middle of an image on my Web page. You can view the animation by entering the following URL into your Web browser: `http://www.grafx-design.com/HireUs.html`.

On that page, you'll see a rocket ship, and below it, two small blinking lights. The concept behind those lights is the same as the ones you've just created.

The lights I used are smaller (and a little less annoying). I also played around with adding frames with the lights turned off and turned on, and I played with the inter-frame timing, as well.

Even as small as those lights are, they grab your attention. They're almost hypnotic (and that's the intent).

Saving and Previewing an Animation in Your Web Browser

Now in Animation Shop 3, you can preview how your animation will look when it appears in a Web browser. This will help you work out any flaws prior to posting the animation to your Web site. Follow these steps:

1. Select View, Preview in Web Browser. The Preview in Web Browser dialog box, shown in Figure 44.4, appears.

FIGURE 44.4

Select the options you want to use to preview animation.

2. Select the format(s) you want to use, such as animated GIF.
3. Adjust the size dimensions if needed, and select the Web page Background color.
4. Choose the Web browser(s) you want to use for the test, and click Preview. Since you have not yet saved the animation, the Animation Quality Versus Output Size dialog box appears. After you have saved the animation, you'll be able to skip the remaining steps; the animation simply appears in your Web browser(s).
5. You can create a smaller file if you're willing to sacrifice some quality. Adjust the Quality vs. Size slider as desired, and click Next.

    You can further adjust the size of your file by clicking Customize. Here, you can remove non-visible elements from the file, save only the parts of each frame that changes, save only unique frames, make unchanged pixels transparent, and enable browser-specific optimizations.

6. Animation Pro optimizes the file based on your selections. Click Next.
7. A comparison between the original and optimized files is shown. Click Next.
8. Final file statistics are displayed. Click Finish to view the animation in your selected Web browser(s). Figure 44.5 shows our animation in Internet Explorer.

FIGURE **44.5**

*A preview of our ani-
mation.*

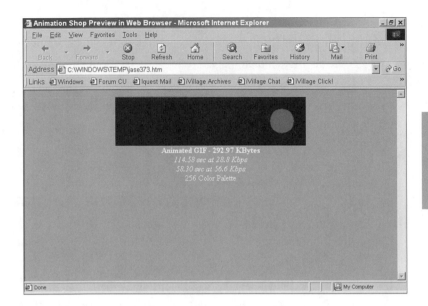

Editing Your First Animation

If you'd like to tweak the animation you just created, you can do so in Animation Shop.
The first step is to create a blank, black rectangle to serve as a frame in which both lights
are off. To do so, follow these steps:

1. From Animation Shop, choose Animation, Insert Frames, Empty.

2. For the moment, leave the defaults set in the Insert Empty Frames dialog box and
   click OK. You'll now have a new frame in your animation.

3. The frame appears in front of the other two frames. You can use the scrollbar at the
   bottom of the window to scroll to the frame. You'll see that it's empty—transparent, in fact.

4. You can fill it with black by setting the foreground color to black and using the
   Flood Fill tool to fill the entire frame with black.

5. Click the View Animation button to view the new version of your animation.
   Because of the speed with which your frames are being displayed, the extra frame
   is hard to see.

Now try this:

1. Stop the animation if it's still running.

2. Select the Arrow tool and use it to choose the all-black frame. (A red border
   appears at the top and bottom of the selected frame.)

3. Choose Animation, Frame Properties.

4. Under the Display Time tab, enter 100 for the display time and click OK.

5. Run your animation again (click the View Animation button). Be sure to save this animation, as you will use it in the following sections.

Notice the difference? The lights flash, then there's a pause, followed by the lights flashing, another pause, and so on.

You can edit this animation further by adding other black frames (adding blank frames) or changing the amount of time that a frame is displayed.

Using the Mover Tool to Edit the Animation

You can use the new Mover tool in Animation Pro 3 to move the contents of a single animation within its frame. We'll use this tool to add a falling effect to our animation. Follow these steps:

1. Use the Pointer tool to select the frame with the red ball.

2. Click Copy, and then click Paste Before Current. A copy of the red ball frame is pasted in front of it.

3. Click the Mover tool, and then move the frame contents up, so that the red ball appears near the top of the frame, as shown in Figure 44.6.

FIGURE 44.6

Move the red ball to the top of its frame.

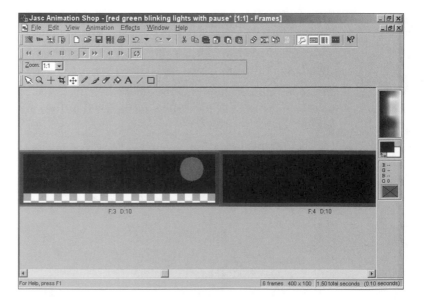

4. Use the Fill tool to add black to the blank area that was created at the bottom of the frame.

5. Click the frame that shows the red ball in the middle of the frame (F:3), and then click Paste After Current.

6. Use the Mover tool to move the contents of F:4 (the fourth frame) so that its red ball appears near the bottom. Use the Fill tool to fill the blank area that's created with black. The sequence of red ball frames looks something like the one shown in Figure 44.7.

44

FIGURE **44.7**

Down goes the red ball.

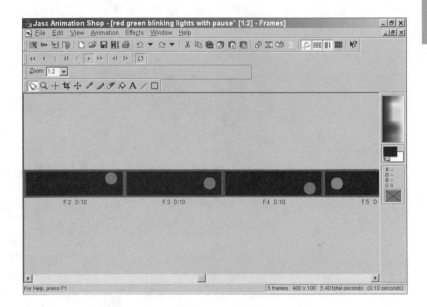

7. Repeat steps 1 to 6 to add similar frames for the green ball.

8. Save, and then view the animation by clicking the View Animation button. Neat, eh?

You could get a ball to "bounce" by simply adding additional frames with the ball in the middle of a frame, and then at the top again.

Using Transitions

Animation Shop has some built-in effects—called *transitions*—that can be used with your animations. A transition is a way to move from one image to another. Transitions include effects such as fading from one image to another.

To see how transitions work, follow these steps in Animation Shop:

1. Select the black frame with the Arrow tool and press Delete, or click Delete Frames to delete that frame. You'll be left with six frames: three green lights and three red lights.

2. To run a transition effect on the animation, click F:3 (the red ball at the bottom of the third frame) and choose Effects, Insert Image Transition. Doing so brings up the Insert Image Transition dialog box (see Figure 44.8).

FIGURE 44.8

The Insert Image Transition dialog box.

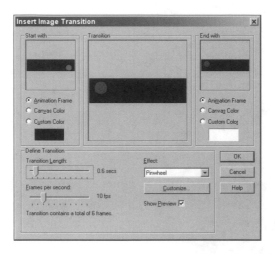

3. Transition effects add an effect between frames or from one frame to an effect. Play with the various transitions to see what they do. I selected Pinwheel, which will wipe between the two frames like a rotating pinwheel. I also set the Transition Length to six-tenths of a second to speed up the transition.

4. To see this effect, simply click OK to close the Insert Image Transition dialog box, and then click View Animation. Note how the image goes through a transition from one frame to the other. You'll also notice that additional frames creating the transition were automatically added to your animation.

You can add different effects, as well. You can apply a long list of built-in effects to your animation. I think, for example, that the Spin effect would be a good way to treat some text.

Speaking of text, Animation Shop also enables you to create some text effects; they're discussed next.

Creating Text Effects

To create an animation using the built-in text effects, open a new animation in Animation Shop (choose File, New) and choose Effects, Insert Text Effects. *Text effects*, or *text transitions*, are transformations involving text. For example, you can cause text to appear to wave in the wind. In the Insert Text Effect dialog box, you can add text and choose an effect (see Figure 44.9).

FIGURE 44.9

The Insert Text Effect dialog box.

Of course, you can create your own text animations, using Paint Shop Pro to create the text frames and then importing the frames into Animation Shop. You might want to play around with some of the built-in effects to see what's possible, though.

Certainly, if you want truly spectacular results, you'll want to create your frames in Paint Shop Pro. You can actually create a multilayered image in Paint Shop Pro and use the layers as frames for an animation. This technique enables you to create the best animations for your Web pages, you'll see in the next chapter.

Summary

This chapter introduced GIF animation and Animation Shop 3. I showed you how to create a simple two-frame animation, how to insert frames, and how to change the timing of the frames. I also showed you how to apply some of the built-in effects that come with Animation Shop.

In the next chapter, I'll walk you through the process of using Paint Shop Pro and Animation Shop 3 to create a more complex animation.

CHAPTER **45**

Advanced Animation

The best way to create an animation is to create a layered image in Paint Shop Pro and open the PSP file as a multiframed animation in Animation Shop. With the file saved as a PSP file, you can go back and make any changes, add new layers, rearrange the layers, and so on.

These two programs form a powerful combination for creating animated GIFs for your Web pages.

Using Layers and Masks in Animation

Using Paint Shop Pro and Animation Shop together enables you to create amazingly complex animations.

You can create an image in Paint Shop Pro, using layers, masks, and any of the effects you'd like. Then you can import the resulting file into Animation Shop as a multiframed animation.

The following section shows you how to build a spinning globe animation.

Putting Your Own Spin on the World

You'll need to find an image of the world that has been flattened. Many clip art sites and CD-ROMs have maps of the world and globes, so you should be able to find one similar to the one I'm using.

If you're handy with the Paint Brush tools, you might even create your own. Figure 45.1 shows the image I'm using.

FIGURE 45.1

The (pre-Columbus) world.

This map shows the world flattened out. Actually, the map shows two copies of the world so that you can wrap the entire image around a sphere and not miss any parts or have any unruly seams.

The world image I'm using is 524×150. To leave some space around the edges of the new image that I'll be creating, I'll open a new 200×200 image. What I'll be doing is cutting and pasting 150×150 portions of the flattened globe into different layers of the new image. Here are the general steps:

1. Open a new 200×200 image. Name the image "Globe."

2. In the Background layer, create a centered, blue circle that's 150 pixels in diameter (see Figure 45.2).

FIGURE 45.2

This circle will become the oceans.

3. Make copies of the blue circle for each layer onto which you will be pasting a portion of the globe.

    You can make the copy by clicking and dragging the Background layer onto the Create Layer icon each time you want to create a new layer.

4. Then copy and paste a portion of the globe to a new image, resize the canvas to 150×150, and apply the Circle Deformation filter (choose Image, Deformations, Circle) to the new image. This deformed portion of the globe will be copied again and pasted onto the new blue circle layer.

5. Repeat this process until you've copied the entire globe into new layers of the new file.

I'll walk through creating the first few layers:

1. I've opened the World image and created the blue ball (Globe) 200×200 image (see Figure 45.3).

FIGURE 45.3

The World and Globe files in Paint Shop Pro.

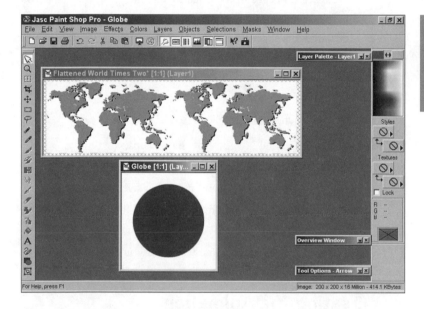

45

2. To start, select the Selection tool, set the selection type to Square and the Feather value to 0, and turn off anti-aliasing.

3. Place the mouse pointer at 0,0 in the World image and make a 150×150–pixel selection.

4. Choose Edit, Copy, or click the Copy button to copy the selection to the Clipboard.

5. Then choose Edit, Paste, As New Image.

6. Expand the image size with Image, Resize because only the portion of the image that has information gets pasted.

   Therefore, because of the transparent background, the image comes in smaller than 150×150.

7. To resize the new image, choose Image, Canvas Size and enter 150 for both New Width and New Height.

8. To make a sphere of the new area that you've copied from the flattened world, apply the Circle effect with Effects, Geometric Effects, Circle.

   Doing so wraps the image around a sphere, giving it back its shape (remember that you are using a flattened image of Earth).

9. Choose Selections, Select All and Edit, Copy to copy this portion of the world to the Clipboard.

10. Add a layer to the Globe image (the one that you created and added a blue ball…er, oceans to) by clicking and dragging the Background layer onto the Add New Layer icon.

11. Name this layer World01 by double-clicking the layer in the Layer palette and giving the layer a name in the dialog box that appears.

12. Paste the portion of the world you just created directly onto this layer by choosing Edit, Paste, As New Selection.

That's how each layer is created.

To create the second layer, follow these steps:

1. Start the selection on the World image at 20,0 (for each new layer, move 20 pixels to the right) and copy and paste this selection.

2. Resize it and add the circle effect, and then select it and paste it onto a new blue circle.

Create each new layer the same way until you have 15 World layers. You'll need all 15 to get the entire globe into the animation.

Creating the Animation

To save the image so that it can be opened in Animation Shop, I turned on all the layers except the Background layer. (I turned off most of them as I created each layer to avoid confusion.)

Animation Shop adds each visible layer as a frame when it opens a PSP file.

With the file saved, it's time to open it in Animation Shop. Before doing so, though, you must change the preferences in Animation Shop. In Animation Shop, choose File, Preferences, General Program Preferences and click the Layered Files tab (see Figure 45.4).

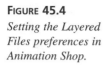

FIGURE 45.4

Setting the Layered Files preferences in Animation Shop.

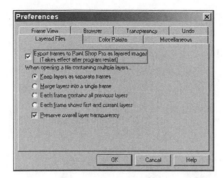

Select the Keep Layers as Separate Frames option and click OK. This feature causes Animation Shop to open a multilayered file and keep each layer as a separate frame. It's a very powerful feature.

With the preferences set up properly, it's time to open the image. Choose File, Open and browse to the file you saved in Paint Shop Pro. In my case, it's the Globe file (the final image I saved in Paint Shop Pro).

To view the animation, click the View Animation button. If the image checks out, you can save it as a Web-ready animated GIF.

Spreading Your Wings

If you'd like to practice some of the techniques I've described in this chapter, you can open the `bttrfly.psp` file that comes with Paint Shop Pro.

Open it in Paint Shop Pro and examine each layer; you can open the file in Animation Shop as well to see how the final animation turned out.

I suggest you create a few animations using images created in Paint Shop Pro. Start with a few layers and see how the process works; then attack a more ambitious project. Remember to have some fun and try different things as you work with both of these amazing programs.

Summary

In this chapter, I showed you how to create a multiframe animation from a multilayered Paint Shop Pro file. I also introduced you to the optimization process. I encourage you to build a few animations and experiment with both Animation Shop and Paint Shop Pro.

45

INDEX

Symbols

3D buttons, 720-721
3D textured buttons, 722-725
4Kids Treehouse Web site, 264
8-bit color, 707
16-bit color, 707
24-bit color, 707
56K modems, 21
256 color, 707
< >(angle brackets), HTML tags, 462
@ (at symbol), 80
( ) (parentheses), search terms, 233
+ (plus sign), search terms, 231

A

<A HREF> tag, 465
abbreviations (shorthand), 141-142
absolute pathnames, 409
absolute positioning, 401

access
Internet, 29-30
news servers, 122
newsgroups, 49
real-time wireless, 294-295
restrictions, 8
accounts
access numbers, 48
billing, 48
broadband, 37
availability, 37
Cable Internet, 36-39
child proofing, 266
DSL, 36-39
Cable Internet, 36-39
dial-up
online service accounts, compared, 36
PPP, 36
selecting, 47-49
DSL, 36-39
email-only, 40
free, 45-46
ISPs, 44
local access numbers, 40, 49-50

local ISPs, 46
logging in/out, 50
newsgroup access, 49
online services, 36, 41-43
online shopping, 282
passwords, 49-50
pricing plans, 48
signup programs, 50-52
sources, 40
switching, 48
toll-free access, 40
usernames, 49-50
Web server space, 49
Active X controls, 201
adaptive palettes, 710
Add Text dialog box, 647-649
adding
Address Book entries, 96-97
audio/video, 471
blank lines, 359
bookmarks, 182
drop shadows, 654-657
Explorer bars, 162
fields to forms, 496-499
HTML tags, 466-467
images, 446
rows/columns, 397
selections, 600-601
address blocks, 348
address books (email), 95-97
Address property, 348
addresses
Collected Addresses (Navigator), 181
email, 15, 59, 81
@ (at symbol), 80
changing to avoid spam, 148
LDAP directories, 238-239
email servers, 53
IP, 53
mailing lists, 133
spoofing, 145-146
subscription, 132

Web, 60-61, 348
components, 61-63
editing, 64-66
entering, 63-66
http/https, 62
incorrect, 65
Adobe Acrobat, 247-250
Adobe Web site, 247
Advanced Research Projects Agency (ARPA), 7
Advanced Search feature (Navigator), 175
Airbrush tool, 556, 637-638
AKC (American Kennel Club) Web sites, 74-75
algorithms, 695
aliasing, 714-718
Alien Skin Web site, 666, 673
alignment
images, 450-452
paragraphs, 357-358
tables, 395-397
All About Kids magazine Web sites, 269
alpha channels, 604
alt (alternative) newsgroups, 126
AltaVista, 217
alternative text, 454
Amazon.com Auctions, 289
Amazon.com Web site, 61
America Online. *See* AOL
American Express Financial Services Direct Web site, 287
American Library Association Cool Sites for Kids Web site, 264
Anchorage, Alaska, Daily News Web site, 61
anchors, 405-406
and operator, 231
angle brackets (< >), HTML tags, 462
Animation Pro, 546
Animation Shop, 734
text effects, 743
transitions, 741-742

animations, 733
  advantages, 734
  Animation Shop, 734
  creating, 735-737
  editing, 739-740
  frames, 739
  moving, 740-741
  previewing, 738
  saving, 748-749
  spinning globe, 746-748
  text effects, 743
  transitions, 741-742
  turning off, 736
  VCR Controls toolbar, 736
  viewing, 736
  Web pages, 309
anti-aliasing, 557, 714
  aliasing, 714-718
  images, 584-586
anti-virus software, 93, 261
AOL (America Online), 32, 42
  advantages, 186-187
  Channels, 189-190
    Computing Center, 192-193
    Entertainment, 190
    Kids Only, 190-191
    News, 193
    Personal Finance, 191
  chat rooms, 109-110
    lobbies, 110
    moving between, 111
    People Connection, 109
    Town Square, 109
  directory listings, 241
  disadvantages, 187-188
  downloading, 194-197
  email, 101
  emergence, 185
  files, downloading, 261-262
  installing, 194-197
  Instant Messenger, 118-119
  keywords, 193

  Locate Member Online option, 241
  navigating, 193-194
  newbies, 192
  newsreaders, 124
  obtaining, 194
  overview, 186-188
  Parental Controls, 187, 275-277
  People Directory, 240
  people searches, 239-241
  software, 194
  Welcome screen, 188-189
  White Pages, 241
Apple downloads Web site, 258
applets, 201, 310
archive files, 259
**ARPA (Advanced Research Projects Agency),
  7**
Arrow tool, 551-552
arrows, 624-626
artifacts, 705-706
.asc files, 253
Ask Jeeves, 217
Ask Jeeves for Kids, 264
at symbol (@), 80
attachments (email), 97
.au files, 253
auctions online, 289-290
  bidding, 291
  feedback, 290
  payment services, 292
  security, 291
  selling, 291-292
  transactions, 290
Auctions.com, 289
audio
  adding, 471
  downloading, 203
  MP3s, 210-211
  playing, 204-206
  streaming, 206-209
Auto F/X filters, 674-677
Auto F/X Web site, 666, 675

AutoSave (Paint Shop Pro), 568
AutoSave Settings dialog box, 568
AutoSearch (Internet Explorer), 159
availability
    broadband accounts, 37
    domains, 532
AvantGo, 295
.avi files, 253

B

<B> tag, 465
B4 (before), 142
Back button, 70
backgrounds, 309
    images as, 457-459
    seamless tiles, 726-728
        converting to seamless patterns, 730-731
        creating, 728-730
    tiled images as, 459
BadMail from Spam List Web site, 147
balloons (Chat), 112
<BASE TARGET> tag, 487
baselines, 451
before (B4), 142
Beyond.com, 255
Bézier, 618
Bézier Curve Line tool, 627-629
Bézier curves, 557
bidding (auctions), 291
Bigfoot Web site, 236
billboards, 319
billing
    Internet accounts, 48
    ISPs/online services, 51
Billpoint Web site, 292
bits per second (bps), 20
biz (business) newsgroups, 126
Blackberry wireless email, 301
Blacklist of Internet Advertisers Web site, 147

BladePro filters, 675
body (email), 87
<BODY> tag, 464
bold HTML tag, 465
bold text, 375-376
bookmarks (Navigator), 182-184
books online Web sites, 13
Boolean logic, 231
borderless frames, 77
borders
    images, 453
    tables, 386
bps (bits per second), 20
brightness
    image retouching, 680-681
    preferences, 567
Brightness/Contrast dialog box, 680
broadband accounts, 36-37
    availability, 37
    Cable Internet, 36-38
        cost, 38
        disadvantages, 39
        Road Runner, 37
    child proofing, 266
    DSL, 36-39
brokers online, 287
Browse dialog box, 571
Browser toolbar, 551
browsers. *See also* AOL
    Advanced Search, 175
    animations, 738
    chat rooms, 105
    extensible, 200
    HTML variations, 313
    Internet Explorer
        AutoSearch, 159
        basic features, 158
        Content Advisor, 166
        content options, 166
        downloading, 153-156
        Explorer bar, 160-162
        Favorite Places, 163-164

general options, 165-166
installing, 157
IntelliSense, 158
launching, 157
obtaining, 152
one-click buttons, 159
Related Links, 159
selecting, 151-152
versions, 152
native support, 200
Navigator, 6, 169
basic features, 175-176
bookmarks, 182-184
Collected Addresses, 181
downloading, 170-172
installing, 172-174
instant messaging, 181
launching, 174-175
My Netscape, 176
My Sidebar, 176-179
Netscape pages, accessing, 175
obtaining, 170
Preferences, 180-181
screen names, 175
selecting, 170
searches, 181
Task toolbar, 175
Themes, 179-180
plug-ins, 201
text-only, 313, 316
Web
frames support, 77
home pages, 58-59
Web page appearances, 520-524
BrowserSizer, 528
browsing (Web), 10-11
Brush Tip palette, 586-587
brush tips, 635
bttrfly.psp file, 749
BTW (by the way), 142
Buddy List (AOL), 118

built-in filters, 667
Buttonize, 667-668
Chisel, 668
Cutout, 668-669
Drop Shadow, 669-671
layer blend mode, 671
bulleted lists, 366
bulletin boards, 16
bullets, 455
burning, 690
business Web sites, 11
Butterfield & Butterfield Web site, 289
Buttonize dialog box, 667, 725
Buttonize Effect, 725-726
Buttonize filter, 667-668
buttons
3D, 720-721
3D textured, 722-725
Back, 70
Buttonize Effect, 725-726
creating, 719-720
Forward, 70
Home, 70
navigation, 69-70
Stop, 70
by the way (BTW), 142

C

Cable Internet accounts, 36-38
cost, 38
disadvantages, 39
hardware requirements, 38
Road Runner, 37
captions (tables), 394
Car Prices Web site, 60
categories
search sites, 218-219
Yahoo!, 219, 223
cc (carbon copy), 90

CD Universe Web site, 283-286
CD-ROM drives
    Mac requirements, 25
    PC requirements, 24
cell phones
    Kyocera, 302
    PDA combinations, 301-303
    wireless Internet access, 297-298
cells (tables), 385
    images, adding, 454
    moving between, 397
    text, entering, 389-390
censoring programs, 269-271, 274-275
    Content Advisor, 270-271
    rating Web site content, 270
Channels (AOL), 189-190
    Computing Center, 192-193
    Entertainment, 190
    Kids Only, 190-191
    News, 193
    Personal Finance, 191
character properties, 372
    bold/italic/underline, 375-376
    color, 378
    fonts, 373
    size, 374-375
characters (Chat), 116
Charles Schwab Web site, 288
chat rooms, 17, 104. *See also* **instant messaging**
    AOL, 109-110
        lobbies, 110
        moving between, 111
        People Connection, 109
        Town Square, 109
    browsers, 105
    chat windows, 107-108
    child proofing, 267-268
    finding, 105
    ignoring members, 110
    members, 105
    Microsoft Chat, 112-113

    balloons, 112
    characters, 116
    Compose pane, 117
    conversations, viewing, 112
    entering rooms, 116-117
    identities, 114-116
    joining, 113-114
    launching, 113
    nicknames, 114
    personal information, 115
    statements, typing, 117
    netiquette, 137-139
        flames, 139
        grammar, 139
        keeping current, 138
        personal discussions, 139
        quoting, 139
        sarcasm, 139
        shouting, 138
        staying on topic, 138
    nicknames, 105
    sex-oriented, 104
    shorthand, 141-142
    smileys, 140-141
    usernames, 106
    Yahoo!, 105-108
chat windows (Yahoo!), 107-108
children (online safety)
    AOL, 275-277
    broadband connections, 266
    censoring programs, 269-271, 274-275
    chat rooms, 104, 267-268
    Content Advisor, 166, 270-271
    Parental Controls (AOL), 187
    parental supervision, 265-266
    passwords, 266
    resources, 268
    rules for, 268
    safe Web sites, 264
Chisel dialog box, 668
Chisel filter, 668
chrome text, 652-654

Cinemapop.com Web site, 209

circles, 620-624

circular text, 658-660

Classic Theme (Navigator), 180

Clean Family Web site, 264

Clear command (Edit menu), 559

Cleveland Rock & Roll Hall of Fame Museum
Web site, 60

client-side imagemaps, 503-504

clients

Internet software, 30-31

server relationships, 9

Clone Brush tool, 555, 644-645, 687

closing HTML tags, 463

CMYK Conversion Preferences dialog box,
565

CNN Web site, 12, 60

Collected Addresses, 181

College Solutions Web site, 61

color depth, 707, 582

Color dialog box, 562, 588-589, 621

Color Management Preferences dialog box,
567

Color palette, 562

Color Replacer tool, 555, 588-590

colors

dithering, 707, 712-714

images, 581-582

replacing, 588-590

text, 378

Web pages, 340-343

Colors menu, 560

Colors tab (GIF Optimizer dialog box), 700

columns (tables), 397

.com domain, 533

.com files, 252

Command History dialog box, 591

comments, 310

commercial domains, 533

commercial software, 254, 258

commercial Web pages, 512

communications media, 8

communications software, 30

Communicator suite, 171

comp (computer-related) newsgroups, 126

companies

Internet access, 29

people searches, 242

Compaq iPaqs, 26-27

complaint reports (spam), 145

Compose pane, 117

Composer, 324

alignment, 396

blank lines, adding, 359

character properties, 372

custom colors, 340-343

designing Web pages, 363

editing, 329-331, 470-472

fonts, 373

headings, 395

horizontal lines, 382-384

HTML tags, adding, 466-467

images

adding, 446

size/shape, 449-450

indenting paragraphs, 359

launching, 324

lists, 366-371

paragraphs

aligning, 357-358

properties, 346-350

publishing Web pages, 517-519

printing, 333

saving, 327-329

search pages, registering, 339-340

spell checking, 361-362

starting, 327

symbols/special characters, 350

Tabelize feature, 398-399

tables. *See* tables

text

bold/italic/underline, 375-376

color, 341, 378

copying/pasting, 351-353, 361

deleting, 361
entering, 350
highlighting, 360
properties, 354-356
replacing, 360
size, 374-375
titles, 336-337, 339
toolbars, 325
tooltips, 326
undoing edits, 361
viewing, 331
composing
email messages, 87-90
newsgroup messages, 130-131
compression, 694
adjusting, 704
files, downloading, 694
lossless, 704
lossy, 701-705
CompuServe (CSi), 43
computers
CD-ROM drives, 24-25
costs, 23
handheld, 299-301
hard disks, 24-25
iMacs, 25
Internet requirements, 24-25
memory, 24-25
monitors, 24-25
offline, 8
online, 8
operating systems, 24-25
PCs, 24
processors, 24-25
selecting, 22-23
Computing Center Channel, 192-193
configuring
Content Advisor, 272-275
domains, 533-534
Internet connections without signup programs, 52-55
Messenger, 83-84

newsreadres, 123-124
Outlook Express, 83-84
Connection Wizard, 52-55
connections
broadband, 36-39, 266
Internet, without signup programs, 52-55
local access numbers, 49-50
modems, 19
56K, 21
speed, 20-21
telephone line interference, 21
passwords, 49-50
usernames, 49-50
wireless, 294
cell phones, 297-298
cell phones/PDA combination, 301-303
email devices, 301
handheld computers, 299-301
hardware, 296
laptops, 296-297
pagers, 297-298
radio-frequency-based system, 297
real-time, 294-295
consumer advocates, 282
Consumer Reports Web site, 282
Consumer World Web site, 282
Contacts (Internet Explorer), 161
**Content Advisor (Internet Explorer), 166,
270-275**
Content Options (Internet Explorer), 166
context-sensitive help, 550
contracting selections, 603
contrast
image retouching, 680-681
preferences, 567
**Convert to Seamless Pattern command
(Selections menu), 600**
cookies
online shopping, 282
spam generation, 144
copy shops, 30

copying
  images, 448
  links, 418-421
  text, 351-353, 361
costs
  Cable Internet, 38
  computers, 23
  domains, 532
  DSL, 39
  Internet accounts, 48
  MailStation, 27
  Net appliances, 26
  online services, 42
  Web servers, 515
Crop tool, 553
CSi (CompuServe), 43
CSPAN Web site, 210
the cube, 710-711
curved lines, 627-629
Custom Brush dialog box, 635
customizing
  brush tips, 635
  My Sidebar, 178-179
  My Sidebar tabs, 178
  Personal bar, 162
Cutout filter, 668-669
cyber cafés, 29
Cyber Patrol Web site, 270
Cybersitter Web site, 270

D

data files, 251-253
databases (search sites), 215-216
Datek Web site, 288
DealTime Web site, 289
decompressing files, 259
Defloat command (Selections menu), 600

Deformation tool, 552
  perspective, 612-613
  shadows, 614
  text, 607-608
    flipping, 611
    resizing, 610
    rotating, 610
    shearing, 612
    vector, 662
Deleted folder (email), 85
deleting
  artifacts, 705-706
  bookmarks, 184
  Explorer bars, 162
  image portions, 686-690
  images, 448
  rows/columns, 397
  tables, 397
  targets, 426
  text, 361
demo software, 254
density controls, 634
design
  hierarchical sites, 443
  multipage linear sites, 439
  one-page linear pages, 440
  text, 363
  Web-style sites, 441
Despeckle filter, 682
DHTML (Dynamic HTML), 401
dial-up accounts, 36, 47-49
dialog boxes
  Add Text, 647-649
  AutoSave Settings, 568
  Brightness/Contrast, 680
  Browse, 571
  Buttonize, 667, 725
  Chisel, 668
  CMYK Conversion Preferences, 565
  Color, 562, 588-589, 621
  Color Management Preferences, 567

Command History, 591
Custom Brush, 635
Drop Shadow, 655
Edit Palette, 708
Eye Candy, 673-674
File Format Associations, 566
File Format Preferences, 566
File Locations Preferences, 566
Find a Chat, 111
Gaussian Blur, 689
GIF Optimizer, 698-700
Gradient, 614, 639
Gradient Editor, 640
Horizontal Lines Properties, 383
Insert Image Transition, 742
Insert Text Effect, 743
JPEG Optimizer, 704
Load From Alpha, 605
Monitor Gamma Adjustments, 567
New Image, 569, 581
Open, 570
Open HTML File, 331
Page Properties, 336
Page Setup, 574
Paint Shop Pro, 565, 621
Pattern, 636, 643
Photo/Graphic Edges, 674
Publish, 518
Save to Alpha, 604
Sound Attributes, 472
Table Properties, 388
Target Properties, 425
Text Entry, 608, 648
Tip of the Day, 547
Toolbars, 551, 561
Unsharp Mask, 685
Video Clip, 475
diffusion, 712
Digital Subscriber Line (DSL), 36-39
directories
LDAP, 238-239
listings (AOL), 241

People (AOL), 240
search sites, 219, 223
Discover **magazine Web site, 233**
discussion groups. *See* **mailing lists**
disk space, 171
dithering colors, 707, 712-714
.doc files, 252
dodging, 690
domains
availability, 532
.com, 533
configuring, 533-534
costs, 532
.edu, 533
names, 532
.org, 533
registering, 532
URLs, 531
DosLynx, 313
Dow Jones Business Information Services
  Web site, 287
Download.com, 254
downloading
AOL, 194-197
audio/video files, 203
disk space considerations, 171
files, 30, 246
  AOL, 261-262
  compressed, 259
  connection speeds, 247
  considerations, 255
  decompressing, 259
  download status message, 251
  links, 246, 429-431
  mirror sites, 251
  operating system compatibility, 251
  .pdf files, 247-250
  times, 247
  viruses, 260-261
Internet Explorer, 153-156
MP3s, 210
Navigator, 170-172

newsgroup lists, 124-125
software, 13, 253
    commercial, 258
    shareware, 254-257
Draw tool (lines), 557, 617, 624
curved, 627-629
single, 624-626
drawing
Airbrush tool, 637-638
arrows, 624-626
Clone Brush tool, 644-645
Flood Fill tool, 638
    gradient fills, 639
    multicolored gradient fills, 639-643
    opacity, 638
    pattern fills, 643-644
    solid color fills, 638-639
lines, 624
    curved, 627-629
    Paint Brush tool, 632
    single, 624-626
Paint Brush tool, 631
    brush shapes/types, 632-634
    brush tips, 635
    density controls, 634
    patterns/textures, 636
    Step settings, 634
S curves, 629
shapes, 619-624
Dreamweaver, 537
drives (CD-ROM), 24-25
Drop Shadow dialog box, 655
Drop Shadow filter, 654-657, 669-671
drop shadows, 654-657
Dropper tool, 555
dust/scratches, 682-683
image portions, 687
DSL (Digital Subscriber Line), 36-39
DSL Marketplace Web site, 40
dust, removing, 681-684
Dynamic HTML (DHTML), 401

E

E*Trade Web site, 288
e-commerce (electronic commerce), 279
accounts, 282
advantages, 280
auctions, 289-290
    bidding, 291
    feedback, 290
    payment services, 292
    security, 291
    selling, 291-292
    transactions, 290
CD Universe example, 283-286
consumer advocates, 282
cookies, 282
investing, 286-287
order confirmations, 286
security, 281
shopping agents, 288-289
shopping baskets, 282
virtual storefronts, 279-281
Earthlink Web site, 45
eBay Web site, 60, 289
Edit menu, 558-559
Edit Palette dialog box, 708
editing
animations, 739-740
form labels, 494-495
HTML source code, 467
images
    color replacements, 587-590
    undoing, 591
links, 421
palettes, 708-709
selections
    adding to, 600-601
    expanding/contracting, 603
    growing, 603
    loading, 605
    saving, 604
    selecting similar areas, 604

similar areas, 604
subtracting from, 601-603
tables, 390-392
text
  copying/pasting, 361
  deleting, 361
  highlighting, 360
  replacing selected, 360
  undoing, 361
URLs, 64-66
Web pages, 329-331
.edu (educational) domains, 533
Effects menu, 560
Effects toolbar, 551
electronic commerce. *See* **e-commerce**
email, 15
address books, 95-97
addresses, 15, 59, 81
  @ (at symbol), 80
  changing to avoid spam, 148
  LDAP directories, 238-239
AOL, 101
attachments, 97
folders, 85
free, 101
incoming mail server, 84
mailing lists, 132
media, 16
messages
  addressing, 97
  body, 87
  carbon copying, 90
  composing, 87-90
  forwarding, 93-95
  headers, 87
  quotes, 94
  receiving, 92-93
  replying, 93-95
  sending, 90-92
  viewing, 85
  viruses, 93

netiquette, 137-139
  flames, 139
  grammar, 139
  keeping current, 138
  personal discussions, 139
  quoting, 139
  sarcasm, 139
  shouting, 138
  staying on topic, 138
outgoing mail server, 84
passwords, 53
programs, 80
  Eudora, 82
  Messenger, 81-84
  navigating, 84
  online service limitations, 83
  Outlook, 82
  Outlook Express, 81-84
server addresses, 53
shorthand, 141-142
signatures, 416-418
smileys, 140-141
spam, 142
  addresses, changing, 148
  complaint reports, 145
  email filters, 148
  filtering, 147
  online services, 144
  replying, 146-147
  spoofing, 145-146
  user identifications, 143-144
usernames, 53
Web-based, 100-101
wireless, 294
  cell phones, 297-298
  cell phones/PDA combination, 301-303
  handheld computers, 299-301
  hardware, 296, 301
  laptops, 296-297
  pagers, 297-298
  radio-frequency-based system, 297
  real-time, 294-295

email-only accounts, 40

emoticons, 140-141

Empty command (Edit menu), 559

Emusic Web site, 210

Entertainment Channel, 190

Epicurious Web site, 60

EPS (Enhanced PostScript) files, 571

Eraser tool, 556

ergonomics, 528

ESPN Web sites, 71, 74

Eudora, 82

exact palettes, 709

exact phrase matches, 232

Excite, 217

Excite Email Lookup, 236

.exe files, 252, 260

existing files
    finding, 571-572
    opening, 570-571

expanding selections, 603

Explorer bar, 160
    adding/deleting, 162
    Contacts, 161
    Favorites, 161
    History, 161
    Personal Bar, 160-162
    Search Companion, 161

export filters, 574

exporting files, 573

extensible browsers, 200

extensions
    files
        .asc, 253
        .au, 253
        .avi, 253
        .com, 252
        .doc, 252
        .exe, 252
        .gif, 573
        .mid, 253
        .mov, 253
        .mp3, 253

.mpg, 253
.pdf, 252
.psd, 573
.psp, 573
.qt, 253
.snd, 253
.txt, 253
.wri, 253
.xls, 252
.zip, 253
HTML, 313

external links, 528

external media, 317

Eye Candy dialog box, 673

Eye Candy filters, 673

F

family Web surfing, 264

Family.com, 264

Family.net, 264

FAQs (Frequently Asked Questions), 138

Favorite Places, 163-164

Favorites (Internet Explorer), 161-164, 182

feathering selections, 652

fields (forms)
    adding, 496-497
    customizing, 497-499

File Format Associations dialog box, 566

File Format Preferences dialog box, 566

File Locations Preferences dialog box, 566

File menu, 574, 558-559

files
    archive, 259
    audio
        downloading, 203
        MP3s, 210-211
        playing, 204-206
        streaming, 206-209
    bttrfly.psp, 749

compressing, 694
data, 251-253
downloading, 30, 246
 AOL, 261-262
 compressed, 259
 connection speeds, 247
 considerations, 255
 decompressing, 259
 links, 246, 429-431
 mirror sites, 251
 operating system compatibility, 251
 .pdf files, 247-250
 status message, 251
 times, 247
 viruses, 260-261
email attachments, 97
EPS, 571
exporting, 573
extensions
 .asc, 253
 .au, 253
 .avi, 253
 .com, 252
 .doc, 252
 .exe, 252
 .gif, 573
 .mid, 253
 .mov, 253
 .mp3, 253
 .mpg, 253
 .pdf, 252
 .psd, 573
 .psp, 573
 .qt, 253
 .snd, 253
 .txt, 253
 .wri, 253
 .xls, 252
 .zip, 253
finding, 571-572

GIFs, 695
 advantages/disadvantages, 695-696
 JPEGs, compared, 706
 transparent, 696-700
HTML, 312-313
 browser variations, 313
 extensions, 313
 tags, 312
 text-only browsers, 313-316
importing, 572
JPEGs, 700-702
 advantages, 704
 artifacts, 703-706
 compression adjustments, 704
 GIFs, compared, 706
 lossy compression, 701-705
local, 405-407
opening
 existing, 570-571
 multiple, 571
 Paint Shop Pro, 569-570
PNG, 694
printing, 574-575
program, 251-253
reverting, 558
saving, 573
self-extracting archive, 260
unzipping, 259
video
 downloaded, playing, 204-206
 downloading, 203
 streaming, 206-209
fills
 gradient, 614, 639-643
 opacity, 638
 pattern, 643-644
 solid color, 638-639
Film.com Web site, 209
filtering
 messages, 137
 spam, 147-148

filters, 665
  BladePro, 675
  built-in, 667
    Buttonize, 667-668
    Chisel, 668
    Cutout, 668-669
    Drop Shadow, 669, 671
    layer blend modes, 671
  Despeckle, 682
  Drop Shadow, 654-657
  export, 573-574
  Gaussian Blur, 689
  Paint Shop Pro, 560
  Photo/Graphic Edges, 674-677
  plug-ins, 666-667
  repeating, 654
  third party plug-ins, 677
    Auto F/X Photo/Graphic Edges, 674-677
    BladePro, 675
    Eye Candy, 673
    installing, 672-673
  third-party, 574
  Unsharp Mask, 684-686
financial advice Web sites, 287
Find a Chat dialog box, 111
finding
  chat rooms, 105
  files, 571-572
  Internet software, 31-32
  local ISPs, 46
  mailing lists, 132
  MP3s, 210
  newsgroups, 125-127
  people, 234
    advanced searches, 241
    AOL, 239-241
    company directories, 242
    LDAP directories, 238-239
    name variations, 242
    people-finders, 234-237
    school directories, 242
  plug-ins, 201-202

  search sites, 217-218
  streaming audio/video files, 209
  Web space, 512-513
flames, 139
Flaming Pear BladePro filters, 675
Flaming Pear Web site, 666
Flash, 203
flattening images, 573
flipping text, 611
Float command (Selections menu), 600
floating selections, 600
Flood Fill tool, 556, 638
  gradient fills, 639-643
  opacity, 638
  pattern fills, 643-644
  solid color fills, 638-639
folders (email), 85
fonts, 349, 373
for what it's worth (FWIW), 142
Form Assistant toolbar, 496-497
Format tab (GIF Optimizer dialog box), 700
Formatted property, 348-349
formatting tables, 390-392
forms, 490-491
  fields
    adding, 496-497
    customizing, 497-499
  labels, editing, 494-495
  processing codes, 310
  spam generation, 143
  templates, 491-494
  Web pages, 310
Forte, Inc., Web site, 123
Forward button, 70
forwarding email messages, 93-95
frames, 76-77, 478-479
  animations, 739
  borderless, 77
  content, 479-480
  creating
    HTML, 483-485
    HTML Assistant Pro, 480-482

definition page, 478-479
names, 486
noframes messages, 487-488
panes, 76
publishing, 479
targets, adding, 486-487
Web browser support, 77
<FRAMESET> tag, 484
Free Agent, 123
free email, 101
free Internet accounts, 45-46
free Internet software, 32
Freehand tool, 554, 594-598
freeware, 254
Frequently Asked Questions (FAQs), 138
From Mask command (Selections menu), 599
FrontPage, 535-536
FTP links, 409-411
FWIW (for what it's worth), 142

G

games, 14
Gaussian Blur dialog box, 689
Gaussian Blur filter, 689
General Options (Internet Explorer), 165-166
.gif file extension, 573
GIF Optimizer dialog box, 698-700
GIFs (Graphic Interchange Format)
adding, 446
advantages/disadvantages, 695-696
JPEGs, compared, 706
dithering, 712-714
transparent, 696-700
glowing text, 657-658
Google, 217
GoTo Web site, 217
government Web sites, 11
Gradient dialog box, 614, 639
Gradient Editor dialog box, 640

gradients, 639
custom, 640
shadows, 614
GrafX Design Web site, 675
grids, 621
growing selections, 603

H

<H1> tag, 464
handheld computers, 299-301
Handspring, 299
hard disks, 24-25
hardware
CD-ROM drive requirements, 24-25
costs, 23
hard disks, 24-25
iMacs, 25
Internet options, 8
Internet requirements, 24-25
memory, 24-25
modems, 19-21
Net appliances, 26-28
monitors, 24-25
operating systems, 24-25
processors, 24-25
selecting, 22-23
wireless Internet, 296
cell phones, 297
cell phones/PDA combinations, 301-303
email devices, 301
handheld computers, 299-301
laptops, 296-297
pagers, 297
<HEAD> tag, 464
headers
email messages, 87
HTML, 464

headings
  tables, 395
  Web pages, 309, 347
help
  context-sensitive, 550
  Paint Shop Pro, 546-547
Help menu, 561
helper programs, 201
  audio/video, 203
    downloaded, playing, 204-206
    streaming, playing, 206-209
  finding, 201-202
  installing, 202
Hide Marquee command (Selections menu), 599
hiding
  Composer toolbars, 326
  marquees, 599
  palettes, 561-562
hierarchical Web pages, 320, 442-443
highlighting text, 360
history
  Internet, 7
  Internet Explorer, 161
hit lists, 224-225
Home button, 70
home pages, 58-59, 512
Horizontal Line Properties dialog box, 383
horizontal lines
  HTML tag, 465
  images as, 455
  Web pages, 309, 382-384
hosting services, 513
HostSearch Web site, 513
hot wax coating, 653
<HR> tag, 382, 465
HTML (Hypertext Markup Language), 312-313, 462-464
  browser variations, 313
  extensions, 313, 317-318
  frames pages, creating, 483-485
  headers, 464

horizontal lines, 465
inline images, 464
links, 465
paragraphs, 464
source code, 465-467
tags, 312
  < >(angle brackets), 462
  <A HREF>, 465
  <B>, 465
  <BASE TARGET>, 487
  <BODY>, 464
  Composer, 466-467
  <FRAMESET>, 484
  <H1>, 464
  <HEAD>, 464
  <HR>, 382, 465
  <HTML>, 463
  <I>, 465
  <IMG SRC>, 464
  <NOFRAMES>, 488
  opening/closing, 463
  <P>, 464
  <TITLE>, 464
  <UL>, 465
text-only browsers, 313-316
titles, 464
unnumbered lists, 465
Web pages, 310
HTML Assistant Pro, 468-470
  audio/video, 471
  Composer pages, editing, 470-472
  forms
    fields, 496-499
    labels, 494-495
    template, 491-494
  frames pages, creating, 480-482
  inline video clips, adding, 473-475
  launching, 469
  marquees, creating, 472-473
<HTML> tag, 463
http/https, 62
Hypertext Markup Language. *See* HTML

I

<I> tag, 465
i-opener, 26
IBTD (I beg to differ), 142
identification information, 310
identities (Chat), 114-116
iMacs, 25
Image menu, 559
Image Palette, 708
imagemaps, 502
    client-side, 503-504
    creating, 505-509
    images, selecting, 504
    links, 69
    processing codes, 310
    server-side, 503-504
    Web pages, 309
images
    adding, 446
    aliasing, 584
    alignment, 450-452
    alternative text, 454
    anti-aliasing, 557, 584-586
    backgrounds, 457-459
    borders, 453
    bullets/rules, 455
    burning, 690
    color, 588-590
    color depth, 582
    copying/pasting, 448
    creating
        brush tips, 586-587
        Preset Shapes tool, 582-583
    deleting, 448
    dodging, 690
    editing
        color replacements, 587-590
        undoing, 591
    exporting, 573
    extensible programs, 666
    finding, 571-572

    flattening, 573
    importing, 572
    inline
        HTML, 464
        Web pages, 309, 316
    links, 69, 456
    multiple, 576
    opening
        existing, 570-571
        multiple, 571
        Paint Shop Pro, 569-570
    previewing, 711
    printing, 574-575
    .psd, 573
    .psp, 573
    retouching, 679
        brightness/contrast, 680-681
        dust/scratches, 681-684
        portions, deleting, 686-690
        sharpening, 684-686
        tools, 679-680
    saving, 573
    scanning, 581
    selecting, 504
    shapes, 449-450, 582-583
    size, 449-450, 580
    spacing, 453
    table cells, 454
    tiled backgrounds, 459
    types
        colors, 581-582
        selecting, 580-582
<IMG SRC> tag, 464
importing files, 572
in other words (IOW), 142
Inbox (email), 85
incoming mail servers, 84
indenting paragraphs, 359
InfoSpace Web site, 236
inline images
    HTML, 464
    Web pages, 309, 316

inline video clips, 473-475
Insert Image Transition dialog box, 742
Insert Text Effect dialog box, 743
installing
    AOL, 194-197
    disk space considerations, 171
    Internet Explorer, 157
    Navigator, 172-174
    plug-ins, 202
    third-party filters, 672-673
instant messaging. *See also* **chat rooms**
    messages, 118-119
    Navigator, 181
Instant Messenger, 118-119
IntelliSense, 158
interfaces, 547-549
Internet Explorer
    Active X controls, 201
    applets/scripts, 201
    AutoSearch, 159
    basic features, 158
    Content Advisor, 166, 270-275
    content options, 166
    downloading, 153-156
    Explorer bar, 160-162
    Favorite Places, 163-164
    frames support, 77
    general options, 165-166
    helper programs, 201
    home page, 58
    HTML extensions, 318
    installing, 157
    IntelliSense, 158
    launching, 157
    Media pane, 209
    obtaining, 152
    one-click buttons, 159
    plug-ins, 201
        audio/video, 203
        downloaded audio/video, playing, 204-206
        finding, 201-202
        installing, 202
        MP3s, 210-211
        streaming audio/video, 206-209
    Related Links, 159
    selecting, 151-152
    toolbars, 70
    URLs, 64-66
    versions, 152
Internet Explorer 6.0
    Content advisor, 271
    media options, 209
Internet Filter, The Web site, 270
Internet Movie Database Web site, 61
Internet Relay Chat (IRC), 17, 112
Internet Service Providers. *See* **ISPs**
internetworks, 6
Invert command (Selections menu), 599
investing online, 286-287
IOW (in other words), 142
IP addresses, 53
iPaqs, 26-27
IRC (Internet Relay Chat), 17, 112. *See also*
    Microsoft Chat
ISPs (Internet Service Providers), 44
    billing, 51
    families, 264
    local, 40, 46
    national, 44
    newsgroups, 122
    password for mail reception, 92
    setup software, 44
    signup software, 50-52
    toll-free access, 40
italic HTML tag, 465
italic text, 375-376

J

jaggies, 716
Java, 22, 201, 310

JavaScript
    scripts, 201
    Web pages, 310
JPEG Optimizer dialog box, 704
JPEG Wizard, 705
JPEGs (Joint Photograph Expert Group), 700-702
    adding, 446
    advantages, 704
    artifacts, 703-706
    compression adjustments, 704
    GIFs, compared, 706
    lossy compression, 701-705
junk email. *See* **spam**

K

k12 (education-related) newsgroups, 126
Kai's Power Tools (KPT), 666
kbps (kilobytes per second), 20
kerning text, 648
keyboard shortcuts, 599-600
keywords (AOL), 193
kids online. *See* **children**
Kids Only Channel, 190-191
kilobytes per second (kbps), 20
KPT (Kai's Power Tools), 666
Kyocera cell phones, 302

L

labels (forms), 494-495
laptops
    Internet use, 22
    wireless Internet access, 296-297
laughing out loud (LOL), 142
launching
    Composer, 324
    HTML Assistant Pro, 469

    Internet Explorer, 157
    Messenger, 81
    Microsoft Chat, 113
    Navigator, 174-175
    Outlook Express, 81
    Paint Shop Pro, 547
layer blend modes, 671
Layer palette, 563-564
layers (animations)
    saving, 748-749
    spinning globe, 746-748
Layers menu, 560
layout, 400
LDAP (Lightweight Directory Access Protocol), 238-239
leading text, 648
libraries, 13
lines, drawing, 624
    curved, 627-629
    Paint Brush tool, 632
    single, 624-626
links, 59, 404
    absolute pathnames, 409
    anchors, 405-406
    converting to ordinary text, 422
    copying/pasting, 418-421
    creating, 413-414
    download files, 246, 429-431
    editing, 421
    external, 528
    FTP, 409-411
    home pages, 59
    HTML tags, 465
    imagemaps, 69
    images, 69, 456
    Internet navigation, 68-69
    local files, 405-407
    locations, 404
    mailto, 412-413, 416
    newsgroups, 411-412
    relative pathnames, 407-408
    resources, 405

signatures, 416-418
targets
  between pages, 436
  creating, 426
  other pages, 427-429
  same files, 427
testing, 421, 528
text, 68, 404, 414
Web pages, 309, 406, 434-436

List of Lists Web site, 132

List Web site, 46

lists
bulleted, 366
newsgroups
  downloading, 124-125
  finding, 125-127
  subscribing to, 126-128
numbered, 366
Web pages, 310, 366
  appearances, 369-371
  creating, 367-368

listserv (mailing lists), 132
address differences, 133
finding, 132
manual, 132
messages, 137
subscribing, 133-135
subscription addresses, 132
welcome message, 135-136

Liszt Web site, 132

Load from Alpha Channel command (Selections menu), 600

Load From Alpha dialog box, 605

Load from Disk command (Selections menu), 600

loading
palettes, 711
selections, 605

lobbies (AOL chats), 110

local access numbers, 40, 48-50

local files, 405-407

local ISPs, 40, 46

Locate Member Online option (AOL), 241

logging in/out, 50

LOL (laughing out loud), 142

lossless compression, 704

lossy compression, 701-705

lurking (newsgroups), 131

Lycos, 217

Lycos shopping Web site, 289

M

Mac OS8/OS9/OS X, 31

Macamp Web site, 211

Macromedia Dreamweaver, 537

Macromedia Web site, 203

Macs
computer requirements, 25
program files, 253

Magic Wand tool, 554, 598-600

mailing lists, 16, 132
address differences, 133
finding, 132
manual, 132
messages, 137
netiquette, 137-139
  flames, 139
  grammar, 139
  keeping current, 138
  personal discussions, 139
  quoting, 139
  sarcasm, 139
  shouting, 138
  staying on topic, 138
shorthand, 141-142
smileys, 140-141
spam generation, 144
subscribing, 133-135
subscription addresses, 132
welcome message, 135-136

MailStation, 27

How can we make this index more useful? Email us at indexes@samspublishing.com

mailto links, 412-413, 416
Major League Baseball Web site, 101
Manage Bookmarks window, 183
manual database searches, 215
manual mailing lists, 132
MapEdit, 505-509
marquees
    creating, 472-473
    hiding, 599
masks (animations)
    saving, 748-749
    spinning globe, 746-748
Masks menu, 560
mathematical algorithms, 695
Matting command (Selections menu), 599
McAfee Web site, 93
Media pane (Internet Explorer), 209
Media Player
    MP3s, 211
    streaming audio/video, 207
members (chat rooms), 105, 110
memory, 24-25
menu bar, 548
messages
    download status, 251
    email
        addressing, 97
        body, 87
        carbon copying, 90
        composing, 87-90
        forwarding, 93-95
        headers, 87
        quotes, 94
        receiving, 92-93
        replying, 93-95
        sending, 90-92
        viewing, 85
        viruses, 93
        Web-based, 100-101
    instant, 118-119
    mailing lists, 137

newsgroups
    composing/replying, 130-131
    lifespan, 122
    posting, 122
    reading, 129-130
    sorting, 129
    submessages, 130
    threads, 130
noframes, 487-488
texting, 298
welcome, 135-136
Messenger
    Address Book, 96-97
    configuring, 83-84
    file attachments, 97
    folders, 85
    launching, 81
    messages
        composing, 87-90
        forwarding, 93-95
        receiving, 92-93
        replying, 93-95
        sending, 90-92
        viewing, 85
        viruses, 93
    navigating, 84
    newsgroups, 85
        finding, 125-127
        lists, downloading, 124-125
        subscribing to, 126-128
    newsreaders, 123-124
    spam, filtering, 148
MetaCreations Web site, 666
Microsoft Chat, 112-113
    balloons, 112
    characters, 116
    Compose pane, 117
    Content Advisor, 272
    conversations, viewing, 112
    identities, 114-116
    joining, 113-114
    launching, 113

nicknames, 114
personal information, 115
room entry, 116-117
statements, typing, 117
Microsoft downloads Web site, 258
Microsoft FrontPage, 535-536
Microsoft Internet Explorer. *See* **Internet Explorer**
Microsoft Network (MSN), 43, 217
MicroWarehouse Web site, 255
.mid files, 253
mirror sites, 251
misc (miscellaneous) newsgroups, 126
modems, 19
56K, 21
speed, 20-21
telephone line interference, 21
Modern Theme (Navigator), 180
Modify command (Selections menu), 599
MoneyAdvisor Web site, 287
Monitor Gamma Adjustments dialog box, 567
monitors
gamma preferences, 567
Mac requirements, 25
PC requirements, 24
monospaced fonts, 349
Motley Fool Web site, 287
.mov files, 253
Mover tool, 553-554, 740-741
moving
animations, 740-741
selections, 600
table cells, 397
text, 650
MP3s, 210-211, 253
.mpg files, 253
Mr. Stock Web site, 287
MSN (Microsoft Network), 43, 217
MSN Messenger, 119
multi-word search terms, 230
multicolored gradient fills, 639-643

multimedia, 22
Active X controls, 201
applets/scripts, 201
external, 317
Flash, 203
helper programs, 201
Media Player. *See* Media Player
MP3s, 210-211
plug-ins, 201
audio/video, 203-206
finding, 201-202
installing, 202
streaming audio/video, 206-209
QuickTime player, 204
RealPlayer, 207-208
Shockwave, 203
multipage linear sites, 320, 438
design, 439
one-page linear pages, 439-440
multiple files, 571
multiple images, 576
munging spam, 145-146
museums, 11
music
MP3s, 210-211
Web sites, 14
My Netscape, 176
My Sidebar, 176-179
My Simon Web site, 289

N

NAME= attribute, 486
names
domains, 532
frames, 486
NASA Web site, 61
NASDAQ Web site, 287
national ISPs, 40, 44
native browser support, 200

How can we make this index more useful? Email us at indexes@samspublishing.com

natural language queries, 230
navigating
    AOL, 193-194
    email programs, 84
    Internet, 67
        AKC exercise, 74-75
        ESPN exercise, 71-74
        links, 68-69
        navigation buttons, 69-70
navigation buttons, 69-70
Navigator
    Active X controls, 201
    Advanced Search, 175
    applets/scripts, 201
    basic features, 175-176
    bookmarks, 182-184
    Collected Addresses, 181
    downloading, 170-172
    helper programs, 201
    HTML extensions, 318
    installing, 172-174
    instant messaging, 181
    launching, 174-175
    My Netscape, 176
    My Sidebar, 176-179
    Netscape pages, accessing, 175
    obtaining, 170
    plug-ins, 201
        audio/video, 203-206
        finding, 201-202
        installing, 202
        MP3s, 210-211
        streaming audio/video, 206-209
    Preferences, 180-181
    screen names, 175
    searches, 181
    selecting, 170
    Task toolbar, 175
    Themes, 179-180
Navigator 6, 169

Net appliances, 26
    cost, 26
    i-opener, 26
    iPaqs, 26-27
    limitations, 27-28
    MailStation, 27
Net Nanny Web site, 270
netiquette, 137-139
    flames, 139
    grammar, 139
    keeping current, 138
    personal discussions, 139
    quoting, 139
    sarcasm, 139
    shorthand, 141-142
    shouting, 138
    smileys, 140-141
    spam, 142
        addresses, changing, 148
        complaint reports, 145
        email filters, 148
        filtering, 147
        online services, 144
        replying, 146-147
        spoofing, 145-146
        user identifications, 143-144
    staying on topic, 138
Netscape Communicator, 118, 171
Netscape Composer. See Composer
Netscape Messenger. See Messenger
Netscape Navigator. See Navigator
Netscape Web site, 217
Network Abuse Clearinghouse Web site, 147
Network Solutions, 532-533
NetZero, 45
New Image dialog box, 569, 581
New York Stock Exchange Web site, 60
newbies, 192
News Channel, 193
news servers, 122
news Web sites, 12

newsgroups, 16, 121
accessing, 49
alt (alternative), 126
biz (business), 126
comp (computer-related), 126
finding, 125-127
folders, 85
ISPs, 122
k12 (education-related), 126
links, 411-412
lists, downloading, 124-125
lurking, 131
messages
    composing/replying, 130-131
    lifespan, 122
    posting, 122
    reading, 129-130
    sorting, 129
    submessages, 130
    threads, 130
misc (miscellaneous), 126
netiquette, 137-139
    flames, 139
    grammar, 139
    keeping current, 138
    personal discussions, 139
    quoting, 139
    sarcasm, 139
    shouting, 138
    staying on topic, 138
news servers, 122
newsreaders
    configuring, 123-124
    offline news reading, 129
    online services, 124
    software, 123
Paint Shop Pro, 675
rec (recreational), 126
reliability, 16
sci (science-related), 126
searching, 125

shorthand, 141-142
smileys, 140-141
spam
    generation, 143
    spoofing, 145-146
subscribing, 125-128
newsreaders
configuring, 123-124
offline news reading, 129
online services, 124
software, 123
NHL (National Hockey League) Web site, 61
nicknames
chat rooms, 105
Microsoft Chat, 114
NNTP servers, 122
noframes messages, 487-488
<NOFRAMES> tag, 488
Normal property, 346
normal text, 309
Norton Web site, 93
not operator, 231
not-for-profit domains, 533
notebook computers, 22
numbered lists, 366

O

Objects menu, 560
obtaining
AOL, 194
Internet Explorer, 152
Navigator, 170
offline, 8
offline news reading, 129
on the other hand (OTOH), 142
one-click buttons (IE), 159
one-page linear pages, 320, 439-440
online, 8

online auctions, 289-290
bidding, 291
feedback, 290
payment services, 292
security, 291
selling, 291-292
transactions, 290
online communities, 513
online help, 546
online investing, 286-287
online services, 41-42
advertising, 42
AOL, 42
billing, 51
CompuServe, 43
cost, 42
dial-up, compared, 36
flexibility, 41
local access numbers, 40
MSN, 43
newbies, 192
newsreaders, 124
performance, 42
setup software, 44
signup software, 50-52
software, 48, 83
spam, 144
toll-free numbers, 40
unique content, 41
online shopping, 279
accounts, 282
advantages, 280
auctions, 289-290
bidding, 291
feedback, 290
payment services, 292
security, 291
selling, 291-292
transactions, 290
CD Universe example, 283-286
consumer advocates, 282
cookies, 282

order confirmations, 286
security, 281
shopping agents, 288-289
shopping baskets, 282
virtual storefronts, 279-281
opacity (fills), 638
Open dialog box, 570
Open HTML File dialog box, 331
opening files
existing, 570-571
multiple, 571
Paint Shop Pro, 569-570
opening HTML tags, 463
operating systems
file download compatibility, 251
Mac requirements, 25
PC requirements, 24
operators (search terms), 229-232
or operator, 231
order confirmations, 286
.org (organization) domain, 533
organizing Web pages, 318-321
OTOH (on the other hand), 142
Outbox (email), 85
outgoing mail servers, 84
Outlook, 82
Outlook Express
Address Book, 96-97
configuring, 83-84
file attachments, 97
folders, 85
launching, 81
messages
composing, 87-90
forwarding, 93-95
receiving, 92-93
replying, 93-95
sending, 90, 92
viewing, 85
viruses, 93
navigating, 84
newsreaders, 123-124

newsgroups, 85
    finding, 125-127
    lists, downloading, 124-125
    subscribing to, 126-128
spam, filtering, 148
Overview window, 564

P

<P> tag, 464
Page Properties dialog box, 336
Page Setup dialog box, 574
pagers, 297-298
Paint Brush tool, 555, 631
    brush shapes/types, 632-634
    brush tips, 586-587, 635
    density controls, 634
    dust/scratches, deleting, 682-683
    image portions, deleting, 687
    lines, drawing, 632
    patterns/textures, 636
    Step settings, 634
Paint Shop Pro, 544
    Animation Pro, 546
    antialiasing images, 584-586
    brush tips, 586-587
    context-sensitive help, 550
    demo download, 543
    files
        exporting, 573
        finding, 571-572
        importing, 572
        multiple, opening, 571
        opening, 569-571
        printing, 574-575
        saving, 573
    filters, 560
    images, 587-590
    interface, 547-549
    launching, 547

menu bar, 548
menus, 558-560
multi-image printing, 576
newsgroups, 675
online help, 546
Overview window, 564
palettes, 548-549, 561
    Color, 562
    Layer, 563-564
    Tool, 564
    Tool Options, 562-563
    viewing/hiding, 561-562
preferences, 564-565
    AutoSave, 568
    CMYK Conversion, 565
    color management, 567
    File Format, 566
    File Format Associations, 566
    File Locations, 566
    general, 565
    monitor gamma, 567
Preferences dialog box, 621
Preset Shapes tool, 582-583
selection tools, 593
    Freehand tool, 594-598
    Magic Wand tool, 598-600
    Selection tool, 594
Standard toolbar, 549-550
status bar, 549
Tip of the Day, 547
title bar, 548
Tool palette, 548
toolbars, 551
toolbox, 551
    Airbrush tool, 556
    Arrow tool, 551-552
    Clone Brush tool, 555
    Color Replacer tool, 555
    Crop tool, 553
    Deformation tool, 552
    Draw tool, 557
    Dropper tool, 555

Eraser tool, 556
Flood Fill tool, 556
Freehand tool, 554
Magic Wand tool, 554
Mover tool, 553-554
Object Selector tool, 557
Paint Brush tool, 555
Picture Tube tool, 556
Preset Shapes tool, 557
Retouch tool, 556
Scratch Remover tool, 556
Selection tool, 554
Text tool, 557
tooltips, 551
Zoom tool, 552
Undo feature, 591
undoing edits, 553
version 7, 544-546
Paint Shop Pro Preferences dialog box, 565
painting
Airbrush tool, 637-638
Clone Brush tool, 644-645
Flood Fill tool, 638
gradient fills, 639-643
opacity, 638
pattern fills, 643-644
solid color fills, 638-639
Paint Brush tool, 631
brush shapes/types, 632-634
brush tips, 635
density controls, 634
patterns/textures, 636
Step settings, 634
palettes, 708
adaptive, 710
Brush Tip, 586-587
editing, 708-709
exact, 709
Image, 708
limitations, 708
loading, 711

Paint Shop Pro, 548-549, 561
Color, 562
Layer, 563-564
Tool, 548, 564
Tool Options, 562-563
viewing/hiding, 561-562
Web, 710-711
Palm, 299
panes (frames), 76
paragraphs, 346-350
Address, 348
aligning, 357-358
blank lines, adding, 359
copying text from documents, 351-353
Formatted, 348-349
headings, 347
HTML, 464
indenting, 359
Normal, 346
symbols/special characters, 350
text
entering, 350
properties, 354-356
Parent Soup Web site, 269
Parental Controls (AOL), 187, 275-277
parental supervision, 265-266, 271
Parents Place Web site, 269
passwords
child proofing, 266
email, 53
Internet accounts, 49-50
screen savers, 267
pasting
images, 448
links, 418-421
text, 361
Pattern dialog box, 636, 643
patterns
fills, 643-644
Paint Brush tool, 636
payment services, 292

PayPal Web site, 292
PCs
    computer requirements, 24-25
    program files, 253
PDAs (Personal Digital Assistants), 293
    cell phone combinations, 301-303
    Handspring, 299
    Palm, 299
.pdf files, 247-248, 250-252
people, finding, 234
    advanced searches, 241
    AOL, 239-241
    company directories, 242
    LDAP directories, 238-239
    name variations, 242
    people-finders, 234-237
    school directories, 242
People Connection, 109
People Directory, 240
People Search, 236-237
Pepsi Web site, 10
Personal Bar (Internet Explorer), 160-162
Personal Digital Assistants. *See* PDAs
Personal Finance Channel, 191
Personal Toolbar, 182-184
Photo toolbar, 551
Photo/Graphic Edges dialog box, 674
Photo/Graphic Edges filter, 674-677
photographs, retouching
    brightness/contrast, 680-681
    dust/scratches, 681-684
    portions, deleting, 686-690
    sharpening, 684-686
    tools, 679-680
phrasing search terms
    exact phrase matches, 232
    multi-word, 230
    natural language, 230
    operators, 229-232
    parentheses, 233
    simple, 225-229
Picture Tube tool, 556

PKZip, 259
playing
    audio/video files
        downloaded, 204-206
        streaming, 206-208
    MP3s, 211
plug-ins, 200-201
    audio/video, 203
        downloaded, playing, 204-206
        streaming, 206-209
    export filters, 573
    filters, 666-667
    finding, 201-202
    installing, 202
    MP3s, 210-211
    third-party, 677
        Auto F/X Photo Graphic Edges, 674-677
        BladePro, 675
        Eye Candy, 673
        installing, 672-673
plus signs (+), search terms, 231
PNG files, 694
point to point selections, 596
Point-to-Point tool, 554
portals (Web), 59
posting newsgroup messages, 122
PowerPoint, 438
PPP accounts, 36
preferences
    grids, 621
    Navigator, 180-181
    Paint Shop Pro, 564-565
        AutoSave, 568
        CMYK Conversion, 565
        color management, 567
        File Format, 566
        File Format Associations, 566
        File Locations, 566
        general, 565
        monitor gamma, 567
presentations, converting to Web sites, 438

Preset Shapes tool, 557, 618-619
buttons, 720
images, creating, 582-583
shapes, 619-624
previewing
animations, 738
images, 711
printing
files, 574-575
multiple images, 576
Web pages, 333
processors, 24-25
Prodigy Web site, 45
program files, 251-253
Promote to Layer command (Selections menu), 600
properties
Address, 348
Formatted, 348-349
Normal, 346
text, 354-356
proportionally spaced fonts, 349
.psd file extension, 573
.psp file extension, 573
public libraries, 29
Publicly Accessible Mailing Lists Web site, 132
Publish dialog box, 518
publishing Web pages, 15
Composer, 517-519
preparations, 516-517
viewing, 519

Q

.qt files, 253
queries, 230
QuickTime player, 204
quotes (email), 94

R

radio broadcasts, 14
radio-frequency-based transmission systems, 297
Rated G Web site, 264
rating Web site content, 270
reading newsgroup messages, 129-130
real-time wireless access, 294-295
RealGuide Web site, 209
RealPlayer, 207-208
rec (recreational) newsgroups, 126
receiving email messages, 92-93
Register.com Web site, 532
registering
domains, 532
Web pages, 339-340
Related Links (Internet Explorer), 159
relative pathnames, 407-408
repeating filters, 654
replacing
colors, 588-590
text, 360
replying
email messages, 93-95
mailing lists messages, 137
newsgroup messages, 130-131
spam, 146-147
reporting spam, 145
resizing text, 610
resolutions, 524, 527-528
resources
links, 405
online child protection, 268
Retouch tool, 556-557, 588, 690
retouching images, 679
brightness/contrast, 680-681
dust/scratches, 681-684
portions, deleting, 686-690
sharpening, 684-686
tools, 679-680
Revert command (File menu), 558

reverting files, 558
Ricochet Web site, 296
Road Runner Cable Internet, 37
Rock & Roll Hall of Fame Museum Web site, 60
rotating text, 610
ROTFL (rolling on the floor laughing), 142
rows (tables), 397
Rulers and Units tab (Paint Shop Pro Preferences dialog box), 621

S

S curves, 629
Sams Publishing Web site, 66
satellite Internet, 297
Save to Alpha Channel command (Selections menu), 600
Save to Alpha dialog box, 604
Save to Disk command (Selections menu), 600
saving
    animations, 748-749
    files, 573
    media files, 205
    selections, 604
    transparent GIFs, 698
    Web pages, 327-329
scanning images, 581
schools
    directories, 242
    Internet access, 29
    Web sites, 11
sci (science-related) newsgroups, 126
SciFi Channel Web site, 60
Scratch Remover tool, 556, 682
scratches, removing, 681-684
screen savers, 267
scripts, 201, 491
scrolling marquees, 472-473

seamless tiles, 726-728
    converting to seamless patterns, 730-731
    creating, 728-730
Search Companion (Internet Explorer), 161
search engines, 214
search pages, 339-340
search sites, 213-214
    categories, 218-219
    databases, 215-216
    directories, 219, 223
    finding, 217-218
    misleading advertisements, 217
    search terms, 216, 223-225
        boxes, 229
        exact phrase matches, 232
        hit lists, 224-225
        multi-word, 230
        natural language, 230
        operators, 229-232
        parentheses, 233
        simple phrasing, 225-229
        submitting, 223
    site-only searches, 233
search terms
    boxes, 229
    categories, compared, 219
    exact phrase matches, 232
    hit lists, 224-225
    multi-word, 230
    natural language, 230
    operators, 229-232
    parentheses, 233
    phrasing, 225-229
    search sites, 223-225
    submitting, 223
search terms (search sites), 216
searching
    Navigator, 181
    newsgroups, 125
security
    access restrictions, 8
    auctions, 291

chat rooms, 104
child proofing, 271
children
    AOL, 275-277
    broadband connections, 266
    censoring programs, 269-275
    chat rooms, 267-268
    Content Advisor, 166, 270
    parental supervision, 265-266
    passwords, 266
    resources, 268
    rules for, 268
family-friendly ISPs, 264
online shopping, 281
Parental Controls (AOL), 187
screen savers, 267
viruses
    email attachments, 98
    file downloads, 260-261
Select All command (Selections menu), 599
Select None command (Selections menu), 599
selecting
AOL, 186-188
computers, 22-23
dial-up accounts, 47, 49
email folders, 85
fonts, 373
identities, 114-116
images
    colors, 581-582
    imagemaps, 504
    size, 580
    types, 580-582
Internet accounts, 48-49
Internet Explorer, 151-152
Navigator, 170
usernames/passwords, 49-50
Selection tool, 554, 594
selections, 593
adding to, 600-601
alpha channels, 604
editing, 604

expanding/contracting, 603
feathering, 652
floating, 600
growing, 603
loading, 605
moving, 600
point to point, 596
saving, 604
similar areas, 604
Smart Edge, 596
subtracting from, 601-603
tools, 593
    Freehand, 594-598
    Magic Wand, 598-600
    Selection, 594
Selections menu, 560, 599
self-extracting archive files, 260
selling (online auctions), 291-292
sending
email messages, 90, 92
instant messages, 118-119
mailing list messages, 137
Sent folder (email), 85
server-side imagemaps, 503-504
servers
client relationships, 9
email addresses, 53
incoming mail, 84
list. *See* listserv
news, 122
outgoing mail, 84
Web, 511, 515
shadows, 614
shapes
drawing, 582-583, 619-624
images, 449-450
Preset Shapes tool, 618
shareware, 254-257
Shareware.com, 254
sharpening images, 684-686
shearing text, 612

Shockwave, 203
shopping agents, 288-289
shopping baskets, 282
shopping online, 279
  accounts, 282
  advantages, 280
  auctions, 289-290
    bidding, 291
    feedback, 290
    payment services, 292
    security, 291
    selling, 291-292
    transactions, 290
  CD Universe example, 283-286
  consumer advocates, 282
  cookies, 282
  order confirmations, 286
  security, 281
  shopping agents, 288-289
  shopping baskets, 282
  virtual storefronts, 279-281
  Web sites, 13
shorthand, 141-142
signatures
  email, 416-418
  Web pages, 309
signup programs, 50
  alternatives, 52-55
  function, 51
  running, 51-52
simple searches, 225-229
Single Line tool, 624, 626
single lines, 624-626
site management, 434
SiteLeader Web site, 532
size
  images, 449-450, 580
  text, 374-375, 649
Sleenet Web site, 61
Smart Edge selections, 596
Smart Edge tool, 554

SmartSaver
  export filter, 574
  images, 711
SmartSaver Pro, 711
.snd files, 253
software. *See also* utilities
  anti-virus, 93, 261
  AOL, 194
  BrowserSizer, 528
  censoring, 269-271, 274-275
  commercial, 254, 258
  demo, 254
  downloading, 13, 253
  email, 80
    Eudora, 82
    Messenger. *See* Messenger
    navigating, 84
    online service limitations, 83
    Outlook, 82
    Outlook Express. *See* Outlook Express
  extensible imaging, 666
  Flash, 203
  freeware, 254
  HTML Assistant Pro, 468-470
    audio/video, 471
    Composer pages, editing, 470-472
    form fields, 496-499
    form labels, 494-495
    forms template, 491-494
    frames pages, creating, 480-482
    inline video clips, adding, 473-475
    launching, 469
    marquees, creating, 472-473
  included in popular operating systems, 31
  Internet, 30
    clients, 30-31
    communications, 30
    downloading, 30
    finding, 31-32
    free, 32
    suites, 32-33
    Windows 95, 31
    Windows 98/NT/20000, 31

newsreaders, 123
online services, 44, 48
Paint Shop Pro. *See* Paint Shop Pro
QuickTime player, 204
RealPlayer, 207-208
shareware, 254-257
Shockwave, 203
signup programs, 50-52
trial, 32
Web sites, 13
solid color fills, 638-639
Sonique Web site, 211
Sound Attributes dialog box, 472
source code (HTML)
editing, 467
viewing, 465
spam, 142
addresses, changing, 148
complaint reports, 145
email filters, 148
filtering, 147
online services, 144
replying, 146-147
spoofing, 145-146
user identifications, 143-144
Spambuster utility, 148
Spameater Pro utility, 148
special characters, 350
speed
DSL, 39
file downloads, 247
modems, 20-21
Web pages, loading, 67
spell checking, 361-362
spiders, 216
spinning globe animation, 746-748
spoofing spam, 145-146
Sputnik, 7
Standard toolbar, 549-550
starting. *See* **launching**
startup pages, 58-59, 512
status bar, 549

Step settings, 634
Stockpoint Web site, 287
stocks, 286-287
Stop button, 70
streaming audio/video, 204
finding, 209
playing, 206-208
submessages (newsgroups), 130
submitting search terms, 223
subscribing
mailing lists, 133-135
newsgroups, 125
subscription addresses, 132
subtracting selections, 601-603
Success Magazine Web site, 287
suites
Internet software, 32-33
Netscape Communicator, 171
SurfWatch Web site, 270
symbols, 350
syntax diagrams, 134
sysadmins (system administrators), 145

T

Table Properties dialog box, 388
tables, 385-386
alignment, 395-397
borders, 386
captions, 394
cells, 385
creating, 387-388
deleting, 397
editing, 390-392
formatting, 390-392
headings, 395
images, adding, 454
moving between cells, 397
page layout control, 400
rows/columns, 397

tabelizing text, 398-399
text, entering, 389-390
transparency, 386
width, 395-397

tags (HTML), 312
  < > (angle brackets), 462
  <A HREF>, 465
  <B>, 465
  <BASE TARGET>, 487
  <BODY>, 464
  Composer, 466-467
  <FRAMESET>, 484
  <H1>, 464
  <HEAD>, 464
  <HR>, 382, 465
  <HTML>, 463
  <I>, 465
  <IMG SRC>, 464
  <NOFRAMES>, 488
  opening/closing, 463
  <P>, 464
  <TITLE>, 464
  <UL>, 465

Target Properties dialog box, 425
TARGET= attribute, 486
targets, 423-424
  creating, 425
  deleting, 426
  frames, 486-487
  linking, 426, 436
  order, 427
  other pages links, 427-429
  same file links, 427

Task toolbar, 175
TCP/IP (Transmission Control Protocol/Internet Protocol), 7-8
telephone lines, 21
testing
  links, 421
  Web pages, 519
    browser variability, 520-524
    links, 528
    resolutions, 524, 527-528

text
  addresses, 348
  animation effects, 743
  baselines, 451
  bold/italic/underline, 375-376
  character properties, 372
  chrome, 652-654
  circular, 658-660
  colors, 341, 378
  copying, 351-353, 361
  deforming, 607-610
  deleting, 361
  designing, 363
  drop shadows, 654-657
  entering, 350, 647-649
  fonts, 373
  formatting, 348-349
  feathering, 652
  fire effect, 673
  flipping, 611
  glowing, 657-658
  headings, 347
  highlighting, 360
  hot wax coatings, 653
  image alternatives, 454
  kerning, 648
  leading, 648
  links, 68, 404
    converting to ordinary text, 422
    formatting, 414
  lists, 366-371
  moving, 650
  normal, 309, 346
  perspective, 612-613
  properties, assigning, 354-356
  replacing selected, 360
  resizing, 610
  rotating, 610
  shadows, 614
  shearing, 612
  size, 374-375, 649
  spell checking, 361-362

How can we make this index more useful? Email us at indexes@samspublishing.com

symbols/special characters, 350

tabelizing, 398-399

tables, 389-390

undoing edits, 361

vector, 661-663

wood-textured, 649-652

Text Entry dialog box, 608, 648

text messaging, 298

Text tool, 557, 647-649

chrome text, 652-654

wooden-textured text, 649-652

text-only browsers, 313, 316

texting, 298

textures, 636

Themes (Navigator), 179-180

third-party filters, 574, 677

Auto F/X Photo Graphic Edges, 674-677

BladePro, 675

Eye Candy, 673

filters, 666-667

installing, 672-673

threads (newsgroups), 130

tiles (seamless), 726-728

converting to seamless patterns, 730-731

creating, 728-730

Time Warner Road Runner Cable Internet, 37

Tip of the Day, 547

title bar, 548

<TITLE> tag, 464

titles

HTML, 464

Web pages, 308, 336-339

tolerance levels (GIFs), 699

toll-free access, 40

Tool Options palette, 562-563

Tool Options window, 619

Tool palette. *See* **toolbox**

toolbars

Browser, 551

Composer, 325

Effects, 551

Form Assistant, 496-497

Internet Explorer, 70

Paint Shop Pro, 551

Personal, 182-184

Photo, 551

Standard, 549-550

Task, 175

VCR Controls, 736

Web, 551

Toolbars dialog box, 551, 561

toolbox, 551, 564

Airbrush, 556

Arrow, 551-552

Clone Brush, 555

Color Replacer, 555

Crop, 553

Deformation, 552

Draw, 557

Dropper, 555

Eraser, 556

Flood Fill, 556

Freehand, 554

Magic Wand, 554

Mover, 553-554

Object Selector, 557

Paint Brush, 555

Picture Tube, 556

Preset Shapes, 557

Retouch, 556

Scratch Remover, 556

Selection, 554

Text, 557

tooltips, 551

Zoom, 552

tools

Airbrush, 637-638

Bézier Curve Line, 627-629

Clone Brush, 644-645, 687

Color Replacer, 588, 590

Deformation

flipping text, 611

perspective, 612-613

resizing text, 610

rotating text, 610

shadows, 614

shearing text, 612

text, 607-608

vector text, 662

Draw (lines), 624

curved lines, 627-629

single lines, 624-626

drawing, 617-619

Dropper

dust/scratches, 682-683

image portions, deleting, 687

Flood Fill, 638

gradient fills, 639-643

opacity, 638

pattern fills, 643-644

solid color fills, 638-639

Mover, 740-741

Paint Brush, 631

brush shapes/types, 632-634

brush tips, 586-587, 635

density controls, 634

dust/scratches, deleting, 682-683

image portions, deleting, 687

lines, drawing, 632

patterns/textures, 636

Step settings, 634

Preset Shapes

buttons, creating, 720

images, creating, 582-583

shapes, drawing, 619-624

Retouch, 588-690

retouching, 679-680

Scratch Remover, 682

selection, 593

Freehand, 594-598

Magic Wand, 598-600

Selection, 594

Single Line, 624-626

Text, 647-649

chrome text, 652-654

wooden-textured text, 649-652

tooltips

Composer, 326

Paint Shop Pro, 551

Town Square, 109

Toyota Web site, 58

transitions (animations), 741-742

Transmission Control Protocol/Internet Protocol (TCP/IP), 7-8

transparency

GIFs, 696-700

tables, 386

Transparency tab (GIF Optimizer dialog box), 698

Trash folder (email), 85

trial software, 32

TrueType fonts, 349

Tucows software directory Web site, 112, 254

turning off animations, 736

TV broadcasts, 14

Twins Magazine Web site, 61

.txt files, 253

U

<UL> tag, 465

Ulead SmartSaver. *See* **SmartSaver**

Ulead Web site, 574, 712

underlined text, 375-376

Undo feature (Paint Shop Pro), 553, 591

undoing text, 361

Uniform Resource Locators. *See* **URLs**

United Nations Web site, 60

United Negro College Fund Web site, 60

unnumbered lists, 465

Unsent Messages folder (email), 85

Unsharp Mask dialog box, 685

Unsharp Mask filter, 684-686

unzipping files, 259

updating Web pages, 529

URLs (Uniform Resource Locators), 60-61
  components, 61-63
  domains, 531
  editing, 64-66
  entering, 63-66
  http/https, 62
  incorrect, 65
US Internet Web site, 45
Usenet, 122
usernames
  chat rooms, 106
  email, 53
  Internet accounts, 49-50
  Navigator, 175
utilities. *See also* **software**
  PKZip, 259
  Spambuster, 148
  Spameater Pro, 148
  WinZip, 259
  ZipIt, 259

V

ValueFind Web site, 289
VCR Controls toolbar, 736
Vector Object Selection, 557
vector text, 661-663
vectors, 618
video
  adding, 471
  downloading, 203
  inline clips, 473-475
  playing, 204-206
  streaming, 206-209
Video Clip dialog box, 475
video conferences, 17
View menu, 559
viewing
  animations, 736-738
  Composer toolbars, 326

  email messages, 85
  HTML source code, 465
  images, 711
  Microsoft Chat conversations, 112
  palettes, 561-562
  Web pages, 10, 331, 519
virtual storefronts, 279-281
viruses
  email, 93, 98
  file downloads, 260-261
VisorPhone, 302
voice conferences, 17

W

Wacom Web site, 666
Wall Street Journal Web site, 287
Weather Channel Web site, 105
Web
  addresses, 60-61
    components, 61-63
    editing, 64-66
    entering, 63-66
    http/https, 62
    incorrect, 65
  browsers. *See* browsers
  browsing, 10-11
  clipping, 298
Web authoring. *See also* **HTML; Web pages**
  Composer. *See* Composer
  tools
    Dreamweaver, 537
    FrontPage, 535-536
    XHTML, 537-538
Web pages. *See also* **Web sites**
  absolute positioning, 401
  advanced features, 22
  animations, 309
  applets, 310
  backgrounds, 309, 457-459

billboards, 319
buttons
    3D, 720-721
    3D textured, 722-725
    Buttonize Effect, 725-726
    creating, 719-720
character properties, 372
comments, 310
Composer. *See* Composer
custom colors, 340-343
dissecting, 539
downloads, 247-250
elements, identifying, 310-311
ergonomics, 528
external media, 317
file formats, 694, 697
fonts, 373
forms, 310, 490-491
    fields, 496-499
    labels, 494-495
    processing codes, 310
    templates, 491-494
frames, 76-77, 478-479
    borderless, 77
    content, 479-480
    creating, 480-485
    definition page, 478-479
    naming, 486
    noframes messages, 487-488
    panes, 76
    publishing, 479
    targets, adding, 486-487
    Web browser support, 77
GIFs, 695
    advantages/disadvantages, 695-696
    JPEGs, compared, 706
    transparent, 696-700
headings, 309
hierarchical, 320
horizontal lines, 309, 382-384
HTML. *See* HTML
identification information, 310

imagemaps, 309, 502
    client-side versus server-side, 503-504
    creating, 505-509
    images, selecting, 504
    processing codes, 310
images
    adding, 446
    alignment, 450-452
    alternative text, 454
    borders, 453
    bullets/rules, 455
    copying/pasting, 448
    deleting, 448
    links, 456
    size/shape, 449-450
    spacing, 453
    table cells, 454
inline images, 309, 316
inline video clips, 473-475
Java, 22
JavaScript, 310
JPEGs, 700-702
    advantages, 704
    artifacts, 703-706
    compression adjustments, 704
    GIFs, compared, 706
    lossy compression, 701-705
layout, 400
linking together, 434-436
links, 59, 309, 404
    absolute pathnames, 409
    anchors, 405-406
    converting to ordinary text, 422
    copying/pasting, 418-421
    creating, 413-414
    download files, 429-431
    editing, 421
    file downloads, 246
    FTP, 409-411
    local files, 405, 407
    locations, 404
    mail, 412-413

mailto, 416
newsgroups, 411-412
relative pathnames, 407-408
resources, pointing to, 405
signatures, 416, 418
testing, 421
text, 404
text formatting, 414
Web pages as, 406
lists, 310, 366
appearances, 369-371
creating, 367-368
loading time, 67
marquees, 472-473
multipage linear, 320
navigating, 67
AKC exercise, 74-75
ESPN exercise, 71-74
links, 68-69
navigation buttons, 69-70
normal text, 309
observing, 539
one-page linear, 320, 439-440
organizing, 318-321
paragraphs
aligning, 357-358
blank lines, adding, 359
indenting, 359
properties, 346-350
publishing, 15
Composer, 517-519
preparations, 516-517
viewing, 519
scripts, 491
search pages, registering, 339-340
search sites, 213-214
categories, 218
categories versus search terms, 219
databases, 215-216
directories, 219, 223
finding, 217-218

misleading advertisements, 217
search term, 216
search terms, 223-225
site-only searches, 233
signatures, 309
space
amount required, 515-516
finding, 512-513
home/commercial, 512
hosting services, 513
spell checking, 361-362
tables, 385-386
alignment, 395-397
borders, 386
captions, 394
cells, 385
creating, 387-388
deleting, 397
editing, 390-392
formatting, 390-392
headings, 395
moving between cells, 397
page layout control, 400
rows/columns, 397
tabelizing text, 398-399
text, entering, 389-390
transparency, 386
width, 395-397
targets, 423-424
creating, 425
deleting, 426
linking, 426, 436
order, 427
other pages links, 427-429
same file links, 427
testing, 519
browser variability, 520-524
links, 528
resolutions, 524, 527-528
text
bold/italic/underline, 375-376
color, 341, 378

copying from documents, 351-353, 361
deleting, 361
designing, 363
entering, 350
highlighting, 360
properties, assigning, 354-356
replacing selected, 360
size, 374-375
symbols/special characters, 350
undoing edits, 361
titles, 308, 336-339
updating, 529
URLs, 60-61
    components, 61-63
    editing, 64-66
    entering, 63-66
    http/https, 62
    incorrect, 65
viewing, 10
Web sites, compared, 11
Web structure, 321
Web palette, 710-711
Web portals, 59
Web servers, 511
costs, 515
space, 49
Web sites. *See also* **Web pages**
4Kids Treehouse, 264
Adobe, 247
AKC (American Kennel Club), 74-75
Alien Skin, 666, 673
All About Kids magazine, 269
AltaVista, 217
Amazon.com, 61
Amazon.com Auctions, 289
American Express Financial Services Direct, 287
American Library Association cool Sites for Kids, 264
Anchorage, Alaska, Daily News, 61
Apple downloads, 258

Ask Jeeves, 217
Ask Jeeves for Kids, 264
Auctions.com, 289
Auto F/X, 666, 675
BadMail from Spam List, 147
Beyond.com, 255
Bigfoot, 236
Billpoint, 292
Blacklist of Internet Advertisers, 147
books online, 13
brokers, 287
businesses, 11
Butterfield & Butterfield, 289
Car Prices, 60
CD Universe, 283, 286
censoring programs, 270-271
Charles Schwab, 288
child protection
    AOL, 275-277
    broadband connections, 266
    censoring programs, 269-271, 274-275
    chat rooms, 267-268
    Content Advisor, 270
    parental supervision, 265-266
    passwords, 266
    resources, 268
    rules for, 268
Cineapop.com, 209
Clean Family, 264
CNN, 12, 60
College Solutions, 61
commercial software downloads, 258
Consumer Reports, 282
Consumer World, 282
CSPAN, 210
Cyber Patrol, 270
Cybersitter, 270
Datek, 288
DealTime, 289
Discover magazine, 233
Dow Jones Business Information Services, 287

Download.com, 254
DSL Marketplace, 40
E*Trade, 288
Earthlink, 45
eBay, 60, 289
Emusic, 210
Epicurious, 60
ESPN, 71, 74
Eudora, 82
Excite, 217
Excite Email Lookup, 236
family-friendly starting points, 264
Family.com, 264
Family.net, 264
Film.com, 209
financial advice, 287
Flaming Pear, 666
Forte, Inc., 123
games, 14
Google, 217
GoTo, 217
governments, 11
GrafX Design, 675
hierarchical, 442-443
HostSearch, 513
HTML Assistant Pro download, 468
InfoSpace, 236
The Internet Filter, 270
Internet Movie Database, 61
kid-safe, 264
libraries, 13
List of Lists, 132
The List, 46
Liszt, 132
Lycos, 217
Lycos shopping, 289
Macamp, 211
Macromedia, 203
Major League Baseball, 101
McAfee, 93

MetaCreations, 666
Microsoft downloads, 258
MicroWarehous, 255
MoneyAdvisor, 287
Motley Fool, 287
Mr. Stock, 287
MSN, 217
multipage linear, 438-440
museums, 11
music, 14
My Simon, 289
NASA, 61
NASDAQ, 287
Net Nanny, 270
Netscape, 217
Network Abuse Clearinghouse, 147
Network Solutions, 533
New York Stock Exchange, 60
news, 12
NHL (National Hockey League), 61
Norton, 93
Paint Shop Pro download, 543
Parent Soup, 269
Parents Place, 269
PayPal, 292
Pepsi, 10
PKZip, 259
PowerPoint presentation conversions, 438
Prodigy, 45
Publicly Accessible Mailing Lists, 132
QuickTime Player, 204
radio broadcasts, 14
Rated G, 264
rating content, 270
RealGuide, 209
RealPlayer, 207
Register.com, 532
Ricochet, 296
Rock & Roll Hall of Fame Museum, 60
Sams Publishing, 66

schools, 11
SciFi Channel, 60
shareware downloads, 254-257
Shareware.com, 254
shopping, 13
SiteLeader, 532
Sleepnet, 61
software, 13
Sonique, 211
Spambuster, 148
Spameater Pro, 148
Stockpoint, 287
Success Magazine, 287
SurfWatch, 270
Toyota, 58
Tucows software directory, 112, 254
TV broadcasts, 14
Twins Magazine, 61
Ulead, 574, 712
United Nations, 60
United Negro College Fund, 60
US Internet, 45
ValueFind, 289
Wall Street Journal, 287
Wamcom, 666
Weather Channel, 105
Web pages, 11, 434-436
Web-Style, 441
WebCrawlwer, 217
White House, 166
Winamp, 211
WinZip, 259
World Wide Domains, 532
Yahoo!, 217
    Auctions, 289
    directory, 132
    People Search, 236
    shareware directory, 254
Yahooligans!, 264
ZipIt, 259

Web space
    amount required, 515-516
    finding, 512-513
    home/commercial pages, 512
    hosting services, 513
Web structure (Web pages), 321
Web toolbar, 551
Web-based email, 100-101
Web-style sites, 441
WebCrawler, 217
welcome messages, 135-136
Welcome screen (AOL), 188-189
White House Web site, 166
White Pages (AOL), 241
Winamp Web site, 211
Window menu, 561
windows
    Manage Bookmarks, 183
    Overview, 564
    Tool Options, 619
    Yahoo! chat, 107-108
Windows 95/98/NT/2000/ME, 31
Windows Media Player. *See* **Media Player**
WinZip, 259
wireless Internet, 294
    cell phones, 297-298
    cell phones/PDA combination, 301-303
    email devices, 301
    handheld computers, 299-301
    hardware, 296
    laptops, 296-297
    pagers, 297-298
    radio-frequency-based system, 297
    real-time, 294-295
wizards
    Connection, 52-55
    JPEG, 705
wooden-textured text, 649-652
World Wide Domains Web site, 532
World Wide Web. *See* **Web**
.wri files, 253
WWW. *See* **Web**

X – Y – Z

XHTML, 317, 537-538

.xls files, 252

Yahoo!, 217
    Auctions, 289
    categories, 219, 223
    chat rooms, 105-108
        chat window, 107-108
        options, 108
        signing up, 106
    directory Web site, 132
    Messenger, 119
    People Search, 236-237
    shareware directory, 254

Yahooligans!, 264

.zip files, 253, 259

ZipIt, 259

Zoom tool, 552